FORTY ONE YEARS IN INDIA

FORTY ONE YEARS IN INDIA

FROM

Subaltern to Commander=in=Chief

BY

FIELD - MARSHAL

LORD ROBERTS OF KANDAHAR

V.C. K.P., G.C.R., G.C.S.I., G.C.I.E.

NEW EDITION IN ONE VOLUME

WITH FORTY FOUR ILLUSTRATIONS

GYAN

Published by

Gyan Publishing House
5, Ansari Road
Daryaganj, New Delhi-110002
Phone: 011-47034999, 9811692060
E-mail: books@gyanbooks.com

Distribution Network
gyanbooks.com
India, USA, Canada, UK, Australia, France

ISBN : 978-81-212-3399-6 (PB)
First Published, 1900

2nd Impression 2020

Printed at: Gyan Press, Delhi.

Forty One Years in India
Author: Lord Roberts of Kandahar

FORTY-ONE YEARS IN INDIA

FROM

Subaltern to Commander-in-Chief

BY

FIELD-MARSHAL

LORD ROBERTS OF KANDAHAR

V.C. K.P., G.C.B., G.C.S.I., G C.I.E.

NEW EDITION IN ONE VOLUME

WITH FORTY FOUR ILLUSTRATIONS

London

MACMILLAN AND CO., LIMITED

NEW YORK: THE MACMILLAN COMPANY

1900

FIELD-MARSHAL LORD ROBERTS, V.C.

From
a photograph by Messrs. Bourne and Shepherd.

PUBLISHED JANUARY 4, 1897.

First Edition (before publication). January 2, 1897.
Second Edition (before publication). January 2, 1897.
United States Edition. January 4, 1897.
Indian Edition. January 4, 1897.
Third Edition. January 4, 1897.
Fourth Edition. January 4, 1897.
Fifth Edition. January 14, 1897.
Sixth Edition. January 16, 1897.
Seventh Edition. January 21, 1897.
Eighth Edition. January 27, 1897.
Ninth Edition. February 3, 1897.
Tenth Edition. February 8, 1897.
Eleventh Edition. February 12, 1897.
Twelfth Edition. February 17, 1897.
Thirteenth Edition. February 23, 1897.
Fourteenth Edition. February 26, 1897.
Fifteenth Edition. March 8, 1897.
Sixteenth Edition. March 18, 1897.
Seventeenth Edition. April 6, 1897.
Eighteenth Edition. April 28, 1897.
Nineteenth Edition. May 31, 1897.
Twentieth Edition. July 7, 1897.
Twenty-first Edition. July 31, 1897.
Twenty-second Edition. August 28, 1897.
Twenty-third Edition. September 21, 1897.
Twenty-fourth Edition. October 21, 1897.
Twenty-fifth Edition. November 18, 1897.
Twenty-sixth Edition. December 14, 1897.
Twenty-seventh Edition. January 4, 1898.
Twenty-eighth Edition. May 11, 1898.
Twenty-ninth Edition, one volume (for Colonies). May 24, 1898.
Thirtieth Edition, one volume. September, 1898.
Thirty-first Edition, one volume. January, 1900. *Reprinted July*, 1900.
Thirty-second Edition, two volumes. January, 1900.

TO THE COUNTRY TO WHICH I AM SO PROUD OF BELONGING,

TO THE ARMY TO WHICH I AM SO DEEPLY INDEBTED,

AND TO MY WIFE,

WITHOUT WHOSE LOVING HELP

MY 'FORTY-ONE YEARS IN INDIA'

COULD NOT BE THE HAPPY RETROSPECT IT IS,

I DEDICATE THIS BOOK.

PREFACE TO THE FIRST EDITION.

I WOULD never have ventured to intrude upon the public with my personal reminiscences had I not been urged to do so by friends who, being interested themselves in what I was able to tell them of India as my father knew it, and as I found it and left it, persuaded me that my experiences of the many and various aspects under which I have known the wonderful land of my adoption and its interesting peoples would be useful to my countrymen. It was thought that I might thus contribute towards a more intimate knowledge of the glorious heritage our forefathers have bequeathed to us, than the greater number of them possess, and towards helping them to understand the characteristics and requirements of the numerous and widely different races by whom India is inhabited.

It is difficult for people who know nothing of Natives to understand and appreciate the value they set on cherished customs, peculiar idiosyncrasies, and fixed prejudices, all of which must be carefully studied by those who are placed in the position of their Rulers, if the suzerain Power is to keep their respect and gain their gratitude and affection.

The Natives of India are particularly observant of character, and intelligent in gauging the capabilities of those who govern them; and it is because the English Government is trusted that a mere handful of Englishmen are able to direct the administration of a country with nearly three hundred millions of inhabitants, differing in race, religion, and manners of life. Throughout all the changes which India has undergone, political and social, during the present century, this feeling has been maintained, and it will last so long as the services are filled by honourable men who sympathize with the Natives, respect their prejudices, and do not interfere unnecessarily with their habits and customs.

My father and I spent between us nearly ninety years in India. The most wonderful of the many changes that took place during that time may be said to date from the Mutiny. I have endeavoured in the following pages to explain the causes which, I believe, brought about that terrible event—an event which for a while produced a much-to-be-regretted feeling of racial antagonism. Happily, this feeling did not last long; even when things looked blackest for us, it was softened by acts of kindness shown to Europeans in distress, and by the knowledge that, but for the assistance afforded by the Natives themselves, the restoration of order, and the suppression of a fierce military insurrection, would have been a far more arduous task. Delhi could not have been taken without Sikhs and Gurkhas; Lucknow could not have been defended without the Hindustani soldiers who so nobly responded to Sir Henry Lawrence's call; and nothing that Sir John Lawrence might have done could have prevented our losing, for a time, the whole of the country north of Calcutta, had not the men of the Punjab and the Derajat* remained true to our cause.

It has been suggested that all outward signs of the Mutiny should be obliterated, that the monument on the Ridge at Delhi should be levelled, and the picturesque Residency at Lucknow allowed to fall into decay. This view does not commend itself to me. These relics of that tremendous struggle are memorials of heroic services performed by Her Majesty's soldiers, Native as well as British; and by the civilians who shared the duties and dangers of the army. They are valuable as reminders that we must never again allow ourselves to be lulled into fancied security; and above all, they stand as warnings

* Tracts beyond the Indus.

that we should never do anything that can possibly be interpreted by the Natives into disregard for their various forms of religion.

The Mutiny was not an unmitigated evil, for to it we owe the consolidation of our power in India, as it hastened on the construction of the roads, railways, and telegraphs, so wisely and thoughtfully planned by the Marquis of Dalhousie, and which have done more than anything to increase the prosperity of the people and preserve order throughout the country. It was the Mutiny which brought Lord Canning into closer communication with the Princes of India, and paved the way for Lord Lytton's brilliant conception of the Imperial Assemblage — a great political success which laid the foundation of that feeling of confidence which now, happily, exists between the Ruling Chiefs and the Queen-Empress. And it was the Mutiny which compelled us to reorganize our Indian Army and make it the admirable fighting machine it now is.

In the account I have given of our relations with Afghanistan and the border tribes, I have endeavoured to bring before my readers the change of our position in India that has been the inevitable consequence of the propinquity upon our North-West Frontier of a first-class European Power. The change has come about so gradually, and has been so repeatedly pronounced to be chimerical by authorities in whom the people of Great Britain had every reason to feel confidence, that until recently it had attracted little public attention, and even now a great majority of my countrymen may scarcely have realized the probability of England and Russia ever being near enough to each other in Asia to come into actual conflict. I impute no blame to the Russians for their advance towards India. The force of circumstances—the inevitable result of the contact of civilization with barbarism — impelled them to cross the Jaxartes and extend their territories to the Khanates of Turkestan and the banks of the Oxus, just as the same uncontrollable force carried us across the Sutlej and extended our territories to the valley of the Indus. The object I have at heart is to make my fellow-subjects recognize that, under these altered conditions, Great Britain now occupies in Asia the position of a Continental Power, and that her interests in that part of the globe must be protected by Continental means of defence.

The few who have carefully and steadily watched the course of events, entertained no doubt from the first as to the soundness of these views; and their aim has always been, as mine is now, not to sound an alarm, but to give a warning, and to show the danger of shutting our eyes to plain facts and their probable consequences.

Whatever may be the future course of events, I have no fear of the result if we are only true to ourselves and to India. Thinking Natives thoroughly understand the situation; they believe that the time must come when the territories of Great Britain and Russia in their part of Asia will be separated only by a common boundary line, and they would consider that we were wanting in the most essential attributes of Rulers if we did not take all possible precautions, and make every possible preparation to meet such an eventuality.

I send out this book in the earnest hope that the friendly anticipations of those who advised me to write it may not be seriously disappointed; and that those who care to read a plain, unvarnished tale of Indian life and adventure, will bear in mind that the writer is a soldier, not a man of letters, and will therefore forgive all faults of style or language.

ROBERTS.

30th September, 1896.

KASHMIR GATE AT DELHI.

CONTENTS.

CHAPTER I.

CHAPTER II.

CHAPTER III.

CHAPTER IV.

CHAPTER V.

CHAPTER VI.

CHAPTER XVI.

CHAPTER XVII.

CHAPTER XVIII.

CHAPTER XIX.

CHAPTER XX.

CHAPTER XXI.

CHAPTER XXII.

CHAPTER XXIII.

CHAPTER XXIV.

CHAPTER XXXIV.

CHAPTER XXXV.

CHAPTER XXXVI.

CHAPTER XXXVII.

CHAPTER XXXVIII.

CHAPTER XXXIX.

CHAPTER XL.

CHAPTER XLI.

CHAPTER XLII.

CHAPTER XLIII.

CHAPTER XLIV.

CHAPTER XLV.

CHAPTER XLVI.

CHAPTER XLVII.

CHAPTER XLVIII.

CHAPTER XLIX.

CHAPTER L.

CHAPTER LI.

CHAPTER LII.

CHAPTER LIII.

CHAPTER LIV.

CHAPTER LV.

CHAPTER LVI.

CHAPTER LVII.

CHAPTER LVIII.

CHAPTER LIX.

CHAPTER LX.

CHAPTER LXI.

PEIWAR KOTAL.

LIST OF ILLUSTRATIONS

FORTY-ONE YEARS IN INDIA

FORTY-ONE YEARS IN INDIA.

CHAPTER I.

FORTY years ago the departure of a cadet for India was a much more serious affair than it is at present. Under the regulations then in force, leave, except on medical certificate, could only be obtained once during the whole of an officer's service, and ten years had to be spent in India before that leave could be taken. Small wonder, then, that I felt as if I were bidding England farewell for ever when, on the 20th February, 1852, I set sail from Southampton with Calcutta for my destination. Steamers in those days ran to and from India but once a month, and the fleet employed was only capable of transporting some 2,400 passengers in the course of a year. This does not include the Cape route; but even taking that into consideration, I should doubt whether there were then as many travellers to India in a year as there are now in a fortnight at the busy season.

My ship was the Peninsular and Oriental Company's steamer *Ripon*, commanded by Captain Moresby, an ex-officer of the Indian Navy, in which he had earned distinction by his survey of the Red Sea. A few Addiscombe friends were on board, leaving England under the same depressing circumstances as myself, and what with wind and weather, and the thought that at the best we were bidding farewell to home and relations for ten long years, we were anything but a cheerful party for the first few days of the voyage. Youth and high spirits had, however, re-asserted themselves long before Alexandria, which place we reached without incident beyond the customary halts for coaling at Gibraltar and Malta. At Alexandria we bade adieu to Captain Moresby, who had been most kind and attentive, and whose graphic accounts of the difficulties he had had to overcome whilst mastering the navigation of the Red Sea served to while away many a tedious hour.

On landing at Alexandria we were hurried on board a large mastless canal boat, shaped like a Nile dahabeah. In this we were towed up the Mahmoudieh canal for ten hours, until we arrived at Atfieh, on the Nile; thence we proceeded by steamer, reaching Cairo in about sixteen hours. Here we put up at Shepherd's Hotel for a couple of days, which were most enjoyable, especially to those of the party who, like myself, saw an eastern city and its picturesque and curious bazaars for the first time. From Cairo the route lay across the desert for ninety miles, the road being merely a cutting in the sand, quite undistinguishable at night. The journey was performed in a conveyance closely resembling a bathing-machine, which accommodated six people, and was drawn by four mules. My five fellow-travellers were all cadets, only one of whom (Colonel John Stewart, of Ardvorlich, Perthshire) is now alive. The transit took some eighteen hours, with an occasional halt for refreshments. Our baggage was carried on camels, as were the mails, cargo, and even the coal for the Red Sea steamers.

On arrival at Suez we found awaiting us the *Oriental*, commanded by Captain Powell. A number of people met us there who had left England a month before we did; but their steamer having broken down, they had now to be accommodated on board ours. We were thus very inconveniently crowded until we arrived at Aden, where several of the passengers left us for Bombay. We were not, however, much inclined to complain, as some of our new associates proved themselves decided acquisitions. Amongst them was Mr. (afterwards Sir Barnes) Peacock, an immense favourite with all on board, and more particularly with us lads. He was full of fun, and although then forty-seven years old, and on his way to Calcutta to join the Governor-General's Council, he took part in our amusements as if he were of the same age as ourselves. His career in India was brilliant, and on the expiration of his term of office as member of Council he was made Chief Justice of Bengal. Another of the passengers was Colonel (afterwards Sir John Bloomfield) Gough, who died not long ago in Ireland, and was then on his way to take up his appointment as Quartermaster-General of Queen's troops. He had served in the 3rd Light Dragoons and on the staff of his cousin, Lord Gough, during the Sutlej and Punjab campaigns, and was naturally an object of the deepest veneration to all the youngsters on board.

At Madras we stopped to land passengers, and I took this opportunity of going on shore to see some old Addiscombe friends, most of whom were greatly excited at the prospect of a war in Burma. The transports were then actually lying in the Madras roads, and a few days later this portion of the expedition started for Rangoon.

At last, on the 1st April, we reached Calcutta, and I had to say good-bye to the friends I had made during the six weeks' voyage, most of whom I was never to meet again.

On landing, I received a letter from my father, who commanded the

Lahore division, informing me that the proprietor of Spence's Hotel had been instructed to receive me, and that I had better put up there until I reported myself at the Head-Quarters of the Bengal Artillery at Dum-Dum. This was chilling news, for I was the only one of our party who had to go to a hotel on landing. The Infantry cadets had either been taken charge of by the Town Major, who provided them with quarters in Fort William, or had gone to stay with friends, and the only other Artilleryman (Stewart) went direct to Dum-Dum, where he had a brother, also a gunner, who, poor fellow, was murdered with his young wife five years later by the mutineers at Gwalior. I was still more depressed later on by finding myself at dinner *tête-à-tête* with a first-class specimen of the results of an Indian climate. He belonged to my own regiment, and was going home on medical certificate, but did not look as if he could ever reach England. He gave me the not too pleasing news that by staying in that dreary hotel, instead of proceeding direct to Dum-Dum, I had lost a day's service and pay, so I took care to join early the following morning.

A few years before, Dum-Dum had been a large military station, but the annexation of the Punjab, and the necessity for maintaining a considerable force in northern India, had greatly reduced the garrison. Even the small force that remained had embarked for Burma before my arrival, so that, instead of a large, cheery mess party, to which I had been looking forward, I sat down to dinner with only one other subaltern.

No time was lost in appointing me to a Native Field Battery, and I was put through the usual laboratory course as a commencement to my duties. The life was dull in the extreme, the only variety being an occasional week in Fort William, where my sole duty was to superintend the firing of salutes. Nor was there much in my surroundings to compensate for the prosaic nature of my work. Fort William was not then what it has since become—one of the healthiest stations in India. Quite the contrary. The men were crowded into small badly-ventilated buildings, and the sanitary arrangements were as deplorable as the state of the water supply. The only efficient scavengers were the huge birds of prey called adjutants, and so great was the dependence placed upon the exertions of these unclean creatures, that the young cadets were warned that any injury done to them would be treated as gross misconduct. The inevitable result of this state of affairs was endemic sickness, and a death-rate of over ten per cent. per annum.*

* In the fifty-seven years preceding the Mutiny the annual rate of mortality amongst the European troops in India was sixty-nine per thousand, and in some stations it was even more appalling. The Royal Commission appointed in 1864 to inquire into the sanitary condition of the army in India expressed the hope that, by taking proper precautions, the mortality might be

Calcutta outside the Fort was but a dreary place to fall back upon. It was wretchedly lighted by smoky oil-lamps set at very rare intervals. The slow and cumbrous palankin was the ordinary means of conveyance, and, as far as I was concerned, the vaunted hospitality of the Anglo-Indian was conspicuous by its absence.

I must confess I was disappointed at being left so completely to myself, especially by the senior military officers, many of whom were personally known to my father, who had, I was aware, written to some of them on my behalf. Under these circumstances, I think it is hardly to be wondered at that I became terribly home-sick, and convinced that I could never be happy in India. Worst of all, the prospects of promotion seemed absolutely hopeless; I was a supernumerary Second Lieutenant, and nearly every officer in the list of the Bengal Artillery had served over fifteen years as a subaltern. This stagnation extended to every branch of the Indian Army.

There were singularly few incidents to enliven this unpromising stage of my career. I do, however, remember one rather notable experience which came to me at that time, in the form of a bad cyclone. I was dining out on the night in question. Gradually the wind grew higher and higher, and it became evident that we were in for a storm of no ordinary kind. Consequently, I left my friend's house early. A Native servant, carrying a lantern, accompanied me to light me on my way. At an angle of the road a sudden gust of wind extinguished the light. The servant, who, like most Natives, was quite at home in the dark, walked on, believing that I was following in his wake. I shouted to him as loudly as I could, but the uproar was so terrific that he could not hear a word, and there was nothing for it but to try and make my own way home. The darkness was profound. As I was walking carefully along, I suddenly came in contact with an object, which a timely flash of lightning showed me was a column, standing in exactly the opposite direction from my own house. I could now locate myself correctly, and the lightning becoming every moment more vivid, I was enabled to grope my way by slow degrees to the mess, where I expected to find someone to show me my way home, but the servants, who knew from experience the probable effects of a cyclone, had already closed the outside Venetian shutters and barred all the doors. I could just see them through the cracks engaged in making everything fast. In vain I banged at the door and called at the top of my voice—they heard nothing. Reluctantly I became convinced that there was no alternative but to leave my shelter and face the rapidly increasing storm once more. My bungalow was not more than half a mile away, but it took me an age to accomplish this short

reduced to the rate of twenty per thousand per annum. I am glad to say that this hope has been more than realized, the annual death-rate since 1882 having never risen to seventeen per thousand.

distance, as I was only able to move a few steps at a time whenever the lightning showed me the way. It was necessary to be careful, as the road was raised, with a deep ditch on either side; several trees had already been blown down, and lay across it, and huge branches were being driven through the air like thistle-down. I found extreme difficulty in keeping my feet, especially at the cross-roads, where I was more than once all but blown over. At last I reached my house, but even then my struggles were not quite at an end. It was a very long time before I could gain admittance. The servant who had been carrying the lantern had arrived, and, missing me, imagined that I must have returned to the house at which I had dined. The men with whom I chummed, thinking it unlikely that I should make a second attempt to return home, had carefully fastened all the doors, momentarily expecting the roof of the house to be blown off. I had to continue hammering and shouting for a long time before they heard and admitted me, thankful to be comparatively safe inside a house.

By morning the worst of the storm was over, but not before great damage had been done. The Native bazaar was completely wrecked, looking as if it had suffered a furious bombardment, and great havoc had been made amongst the European houses, not a single verandah or outside shutter being left in the station. As I walked to the mess, I found the road almost impassable from fallen trees; and dead birds, chiefly crows and kites, were so numerous that they had to be carried off in cartloads. How I had made my way to my bungalow without accident the night before was difficult to imagine. Even the column against which I had stumbled was levelled by the fury of the blast. This column had been raised a few years before to the memory of the officers and men of the 1st Troop, 1st Brigade, Bengal Horse Artillery, who were killed in the disastrous retreat from Kabul in 1841. It was afterwards rebuilt.

Dum-Dum in ruins was even more dreary than before the cyclone, and I felt as if I could not possibly continue to live there much longer. Accordingly I wrote to my father, begging him to try and get me sent to Burma; but he replied that he hoped soon to get command of the Peshawar division, and that he would then like me to join him. Thus, though my desire to quit Dum-Dum was not to be immediately gratified, I was buoyed up by the hope that a definite limit had now been placed to my service in that, to me, uninteresting part of India, and my restlessness and discontent disappeared as if by magic.

In time of peace, as in war, or during a cholera epidemic, a soldier's moral condition is infinitely more important than his physical surroundings, and it is in this respect, I think, that the subaltern of the present day has an advantage over the youngster of forty years ago. The life of a young officer during his first few months of exile, before he has fallen into the ways of his new life and made friends for himself, can never be very happy; but in these days he is encouraged by the feeling that, however distasteful, it need not necessarily last very long; and he can look forward to a rapid and easy return to England and friends at no very distant period. At the time I am writing of he could not but feel completely cut off from all that had hitherto formed his chief interests in life—his family and his friends—for ten years is an eternity to the young, and the feeling of loneliness and home-sickness was apt to become almost insupportable.

The climate added its depressing influence; there was no going to the hills then, and as the weary months dragged on, the young stranger became more and more dispirited and hopeless. Such was my case. I had only been four months in India, but it seemed like four years. My joy, therefore, was unbounded when at last my marching orders arrived. Indeed, the idea that I was about to proceed to that grand field of soldierly activity, the North West Frontier, and there join my father, almost reconciled me to the disappointment of losing my chance of field service in Burma. My arrangements were soon made, and early in August I bade a glad good-bye to Dum-Dum.

CHAPTER II.

When I went to India the mode of travelling was almost as primitive as it had been a hundred, and probably five hundred, years before. Private individuals for the most part used palankins, while officers, regiments, and drafts were usually sent up country by the river route as far as Cawnpore. It was necessarily a slow mode of progression—how slow may be imagined from the fact that it took me nearly three months to get from Dum-Dum to Peshawar, a distance now traversed with the greatest ease and comfort in as many days. As far as Benares I travelled in a barge towed by a steamer—a performance which took the best part of a month to accomplish. From Benares to Allahabad it was a pleasant change to get upon wheels, a horse-dâk having been recently established between these two places. At Allahabad I was most kindly received by Mr. Lowther, the Commissioner, an old friend of my father's, in whose house I experienced for the first time that profuse hospitality for which Anglo-Indians are proverbial. I was much surprised and amused by the circumstance of my host smoking a *hookah* even at meals, for he was one of the few Englishmen who still indulged in that luxury, as it was then considered. The sole duty of one servant, called the *hookah-bardar*, was to prepare the pipe for his master, and to have it ready at all times.

My next resting-place was Cawnpore, my birthplace, where I remained a few days. The Cawnpore division was at that time commanded by an officer of the name of Palmer, who had only recently attained the rank of Brigadier-General, though he could not have been less than sixty-eight years of age, being of the same standing as my father.

From Cawnpore I went to Meerut, and there came across, for the first time, the far-famed Bengal Horse Artillery, and made the acquaintance of a set of officers who more than realized my expectations regarding the wearers of the much-coveted jacket, association with whom created in me a fixed resolve to leave no stone unturned in the endeavour to become a horse gunner. Like the Cavalry and Infantry of the East India Company's service, the Artillery suffered somewhat from the employment of many of its best officers on the staff and in civil appointments; the officers selected were not seconded or replaced in their regiments. This was the case in a less degree, no doubt, in the Horse Artillery than in the other branches, for its *esprit* was great, and officers were proud to belong to this *corps d'élite.* It certainly was a splendid service; the men were the pick of those recruited by the East India Company, they were of magnificent physique, and their uniform was singularly handsome. The jacket was much the same as that now worn by the Royal Horse Artillery, but instead of the busby they had a brass helmet covered in front with leopard skin, surmounted by a long red plume which drooped over the back like that of a French Cuirassier. This, with white buckskin breeches and long boots, completed a uniform which was one of the most picturesque and effective I have ever seen on a parade-ground.

The metalled highway ended at Meerut, and I had to perform the remainder of my journey to Peshawar, a distance of 600 miles, in a palankin, or doolie.

This manner of travelling was tedious in the extreme. Starting after dinner, the victim was carried throughout the night by eight men, divided into reliefs of four. The whole of the eight were changed at stages averaging from ten to twelve miles apart. The baggage was also conveyed by coolies, who kept up an incessant chatter, and the procession was lighted on its way by a torch-bearer, whose torch consisted of bits of rag tied round the end of a stick, upon which he continually poured the most malodorous of oils. If the palankin-bearers were very good, they shuffled along at the rate of about three miles an hour, and if there were no delays, forty or forty-five miles could be accomplished before it became necessary to seek shelter from the sun in one of the dâk-bungalows, or rest-houses, erected by Government at convenient intervals along all the principal routes. In these bungalows a bath could be obtained, and sorely it was needed after a journey of thirteen or fourteen hours at a level of only a few inches above an exceedingly dusty road. As to food, the *khansamah*, like 'mine host' in the old country, declared himself at the outset prepared to provide everything the heart of man could desire; when, however, the traveller was safely cornered for the rest of the day, the *menu* invariably dwindled down to the elementary and universal 'sudden death,' which meant a wretchedly thin chicken, caught, decapitated, grilled, and served up within twenty minutes of the meal being ordered. At dinner a variety was made by the chicken being curried, accompanied by an unlimited supply of rice and chutney.

I was glad to be able to break the monotony of this long journey by a visit to a half-sister of mine, who was then living at the hill-station of Mussoorie. The change to the delightful freshness of a Himalayan climate after the Turkish-bath-like atmosphere of the plains in September was most grateful, and I thoroughly enjoyed the few days I spent in the midst of the lovely mountain scenery.

My next station was Umballa. There I fell in with two other troops of Horse Artillery, and became more than ever enamoured with the idea of belonging to so splendid a service. From Umballa it was a two nights' journey to Ludhiana, where I rested for the day, and there met a cousin in the Survey Department, who had been suddenly ordered to Lahore, so we agreed to travel together.

The next halting place was Jullundur. To make a change, we hired a buggy at this place, in which to drive the first stage, sending our palankins on ahead; when we overtook them, we found, to our surprise, that their number had increased to six. We were preparing for a start, when it struck us that we ought to make some inquiries about the additional four, which, from the luggage lying about, we assumed to be occupied, but which appeared to be stranded for want of bearers to carry them on. The doors were carefully closed, and it was some time before we could get an answer to our offers of assistance. Eventually a lady looked out, and told us that she and a friend, each accompanied by two children and an *ayah*,* were on their way to Lahore; that the bearers who had brought them so far had run away, and that they were absolutely in despair as to how they were to proceed. It turned out that the bearers, who had been engaged to carry the ladies on the second stage towards Lahore, found it more amusing to attend the ceremony of the installation of the Raja of Kaparthala, then going on, than to fulfil their engagement. After discussing the situation, the ladies were persuaded to get out of their palankins and into our buggy. We divided the baggage and six doolies between our sixteen bearers, and started off, my cousin, the *ayahs*, and I on foot. It was then 10 p.m. We hoped relays of bearers for the whole party would be forthcoming at the next stage, but we were doomed to disappointment. Our reliefs were present, but none for the ladies. We succeeded, however, in inducing our original bearers to come on a further stage, thus arranging for the carriage of the *ayahs*, while we

* A Native woman-servant.

two men trudged on beside the buggy for another ten or twelve miles. It was a heavy, sandy road, and three stages were about as much as the horse could manage.

Soon after daybreak next morning we reached the Bias river. Crossing by a bridge of boats, we found on the other side a small one-roomed house with a verandah running round it, built for the use of the European overseer in charge of the road. On matters being explained, this man agreed to turn out. The ladies and children were put inside, and my cousin and I spent the day in the verandah; in the evening, with the assistance of the overseer, we were able to get a sufficient number of bearers to carry us all on to Mian Mir without further adventure. In the course of conversation we found that one of the ladies was the wife of Lieutenant Donald Stewart,* of the 9th Bengal Infantry, and that she and her friend were returning to join their respective husbands after spending the summer months at Simla. This meeting was the beginning of a close friendship with Sir Donald and Lady Stewart, which has lasted to the present day.

At Mian Mir (the military cantonment of Lahore) I stayed a few days with another half-sister, and from there, as the weather was beginning to get cooler, I travelled day and night. One evening about eight o'clock I was disappointed at not having come across the usual rest-house; lights could be seen, however, at no great distance, and I proceeded towards them; they turned out to be the camp fires of a Cavalry regiment which was halting there for the night. Being half famished, and fearing that my craving for food was not likely to be gratified unless someone in the camp would take pity upon my forlorn condition, I boldly presented myself at the first tent I came across. The occupant came out, and, on hearing the strait I was in, he with kindly courtesy invited me to enter the tent, saying, 'You are just in time to share our dinner.' My host turned out to be Major Crawford Chamberlain,† commanding the 1st Irregular Cavalry, the famous Skinner's Horse, then on its way to Peshawar. A lady was sitting at the table—Mrs. Chamberlain—to whom I was introduced; I spent a very pleasant evening, and in this way commenced another equally agreeable and lasting friendship.

CHAPTER III.

EVEN the longest journey must come to an end at last, and early in November I reached Peshawar. My father, who was then in his sixty-ninth year, had just been appointed to command the division with the

* Now Field Marshal Sir Donald Stewart, Bart., G.C.B., G.C.S.I.

† Now General Crawford Chamberlain, C.S.I., a brother of General Sir Neville Chamberlain.

temporary rank of Major-General. Old as this may appear at a period when Colonels are superannuated at fifty-seven, and Major-Generals must retire at sixty-two, my father did not consider himself particularly unlucky. As for the authorities, they evidently thought they were to be congratulated on having so young and active an officer to place in a position of responsibility upon the North-West Frontier, for amongst my father's papers I found letters from the Adjutant-General and Quartermaster-General expressing high satisfaction at his appointment to this difficult command.

It was a great advantage as well as a great pleasure to me to be with my father at this time. I had left India an infant, and I had no recollection of him until I was twelve years old, at which time he came home on leave. Even then I saw very little of him, as I was at school during the greater part of his sojourn in England, thus we met at Peshawar almost as strangers. We did not, however, long remain so; his affectionate greeting soon put an end to any feeling of shyness on my part, and the genial and kindly spirit which enabled him to enter into and sympathize with the feelings and aspirations of men younger than himself, rendered the year I spent with him at Peshawar one of the brightest and happiest of my early life. In one respect particularly I benefited by the intercourse and confidence of the year in question. My father spoke to me freely of his experiences in Afghanistan, where he commanded during the Afghan war first a brigade, and then Shah Shuja's contingent. The information I in this way gathered regarding the characteristics of that peculiar country, and the best means of dealing with its still more peculiar people, was invaluable to me when I, in my turn, twenty-five years later, found myself in command of an army in Afghanistan.

Eleven years only had elapsed since the first Afghan war, when my father went to Peshawar and found himself again associated with several Afghan friends; some had altogether settled in the Peshawar district, for nearly all of those who had assisted us, or shown any friendly feeling towards us, had been forced by Dost Mahomed Khan, on his return as Amir to Kabul, to seek refuge in India. One of the chief of these unfortunate refugees was Mahomed Usman Khan, Shah Shuja's Wazir, or Prime Minister. He had been very intimate with my father, so it was pleasant for them to meet again and talk over events in which they had both played such prominent parts. Usman Khan died some years ago; but visitors to India who travel as far as Peshawar may still meet his sons, one of whom is the Commandant of the Khyber Rifles, Lieutenant-Colonel Aslam Khan, C.I.E., a fine specimen of a Native soldier and gentleman, who has proved his loyalty and done excellent service to the State on many trying occasions.

My father had also been on terms of intimacy with Dost Mahomed himself and many other men of influence in Kabul, from whom, while

GENERAL SIR ABRAHAM ROBERTS, G.C.B.

From a photograph.

at Peshawar, he received most interesting letters, in which anxiety was often expressed as to whether the English were amicably disposed towards the Amir. To these communications my father was always careful to send courteous and conciliatory replies. The correspondence which took place confirmed him in his frequently expressed opinion that it would be greatly to the advantage of the Government, and obviate the necessity for keeping such large garrisons on the frontier, if friendly relations could be established with the Amir, and with the neighbouring tribes, who more or less looked to the Ruler of Kabul as their Chief. My father accordingly addressed the Secretary to the Government of India, and pointed out how successfully some of the most experienced Anglo-Indian officials had managed barbarous tribes by kindness and conciliation.

My father was prevented by ill-health from remaining long enough at Peshawar to see the result of his proposals, but it was a source of great satisfaction to him to learn before he left India* that they were approved by Lord Dalhousie (the Governor-General), and that they were already bearing fruit. That the Amir was himself ready to respond to any overtures made to him was evident from a letter written by a brother of the Dost's, which was discovered amongst the papers of Colonel Mackeson (the Commissioner of Peshawar) after his death. It was still more gratifying to my father to find that the views of Mackeson's successor, Lieutenant-Colonel Herbert Edwardes, on this subject entirely coincided with his own. This distinguished officer and brilliant administrator zealously maintained this policy, and succeeded in establishing such a good understanding with the Ruler of Kabul that, when the Mutiny broke out, Afghanistan stood aloof, instead of, as might have been the case, turning the scale against us.

The Peshawar division in 1852 was not only the most important, but the largest, in India. It included besides Attock, Rawal Pindi, and Jhelum, the hill-station of Murree, which had only been recently occupied. The cantonment of Peshawar had been laid out by Sir Colin Campbell (afterwards Lord Clyde), who commanded there when we first occupied that place in 1849. He crowded the troops, European

* Shortly before my father left Peshawar he received the following letter from Colonel Outram, dated Calcutta, the 23rd October, 1853: 'As I know that your views as to the policy that should be pursued towards Dost Mahomed must be in accordance with those of the Governor-General, I accordingly showed your letter to Grant, Courtney, and Colonel Low, all of whom were glad to learn that you entertained such sound views, opposed though they be with the general clamour for war with the Kabulese which appears to be the cry of the army. This, together with the wise forethought you displayed before the Kabul insurrection (which, though at the time it found no favour at Head-Quarters, was subsequently so mournfully established by the Kabul massacre, which would have been prevented had your warnings been attended to), shows how well you would combine the military and political control of the country beyond the Indus.'

and Native, into as small a space as possible in order that the station might be the more easily protected from the raids of the Afridis and other robber tribes, who had their homes in the neighbouring mountains, and constantly descended into the valley for the sake of plunder. To resist these marauders it was necessary to place guards all round the cantonment. The smaller the enclosure, the fewer guards would be required. From this point of view alone was Sir Colin's action excusable; but the result of this overcrowding was what it always is, especially in a tropical climate like that of India, and for long years Peshawar was a name of terror to the English soldier from its proverbial unhealthiness. The water-supply for the first five-and-twenty years of our occupation was extremely bad, and sanitary arrangements, particularly as regards Natives, were apparently considered unnecessary.

In addition to the cordon of sentries round the cantonment, strong piquets were posted on all the principal roads leading towards the hills; and every house had to be guarded by a *chokidar*, or watchman, belonging to one of the robber tribes. The maintaining this watchman was a sort of blackmail, without consenting to which no one's horses or other property were safe. The watchmen were armed with all sorts of quaint old firearms, which, on an alarm being given, they discharged in the most reckless manner, making it quite a work of danger to pass along a Peshawar road after dark. No one was allowed to venture beyond the line of sentries when the sun had set, and even in broad daylight it was not safe to go any distance from the station.

In the autumn of 1851 an officer—Captain Frank Grantham, of the 98th Foot—was riding with a young lady on the Michni road, not far from the Artillery quarter-guard, when he was attacked by five hillmen. Grantham was wounded so severely that he died in a few days, the horses were carried off, but the girl was allowed to escape. She ran as fast as she could to the nearest guard, and told her story; the alarm was given, and the wounded man was brought in. The young lady was called upon shortly afterwards to identify one of the supposed murderers, but she could not recognize the man as being of the party who made the attack; nevertheless, the murderer's friends were afraid of what she might remember, and made an attempt one night to carry her off. Fortunately, it was frustrated, but from that time, until she left Peshawar, it was considered necessary to keep a guard over the house in which she lived.

From all this my readers may probably think that Peshawar, as I first knew it, was not a desirable place of residence; but I was very happy there. There was a good deal of excitement and adventure; I made many friends; and, above all, I had, to me, the novel pleasure of being with my father.

It was the custom in those days for the General commanding one of the larger divisions to have under him, and in charge of the Head-Quarter station, a senior officer styled Brigadier. Soon after I went to Peshawar, Sydney Cotton* held this appointment, and remained in it for many years, making a great reputation for himself during the Mutiny, and being eventually appointed to the command of the division. The two senior officers on my father's staff were Lieutenant Norman† and Lieutenant Lumsden,‡ the former Deputy Assistant-Adjutant-General and the latter Deputy Assistant-Quartermaster-General. The high opinion of them which my father had formed was subsequently justified by their distinguished careers. Norman, with sixteen years' service, and at the age of thirty-four, became Adjutant-General of the Army in India, and a year or two later Secretary to Government in the Military Department. He finished his Indian service as Military Member of Council. Lumsden became Quartermaster-General, and afterwards Adjutant-General, the two highest positions on the Indian staff.

There was a separate mess for all the staff officers, and I remember a curious circumstance in connexion with that mess which, unless the exception proves the rule, is strong evidence against the superstition that thirteen is an unlucky number to sit down to dinner. On the 1st January, 1853, thirteen of us dined together; eleven years after we were all alive, nearly the whole of the party having taken part in the suppression of the Mutiny, and five or six having been wounded.

From the time of my arrival until the autumn of 1853, nothing of much importance occurred. I lived with my father, and acted as his Aide-de-camp, while, at the same time, I did duty with the Artillery. The 2nd Company, 2nd Battalion, to which I belonged, was composed of a fine body of men, who had a grand reputation in the field, but, being somewhat troublesome in quarters, had acquired the nickname of 'The Devil's Own.' Because of the unusually good physique of the men, this company was selected for conversion into a Mountain Battery, which it was thought advisable to raise at that time. I was the only subaltern with this battery for several months, and though my commanding officer had no objection to my acting as A.D.C. to my father, he took good care that I did my regimental duty strictly and regularly.

One very painful circumstance stamped itself on my memory. I was obliged to be present at a flogging parade—the only one, I am glad to say, I have ever had to attend, although the barbarous and degrading custom of flogging in the army was not done away with until nearly thirty years later.§ A few years before I joined the

* The late General Sir Sydney Cotton, G.C.B.

† Now General Sir Henry Norman, G.C.B., G.C.M.G., lately Governor of Queensland.

‡ Now General Sir Peter Lumsden, G.C.B.

§ 1881.

service, the number of lashes which might be given was limited to fifty, but even under this restriction the sight was a horrible one to witness. The parade to which I refer was ordered for the punishment of two men who had been sentenced to fifty lashes each for selling their kits, and to a certain term of imprisonment in addition. They were fine, handsome young Horse Artillerymen, and it was hateful to see them thus treated. Besides, one felt it was productive of harm rather than good, for it tended to destroy the men's self-respect, and to make them completely reckless. In this instance, no sooner had the two men been released from prison than they committed the same offence again. They were a second time tried by Court-Martial, and sentenced as before. How I longed to have the power to remit the fifty lashes, for I felt that selling their kits on this occasion was their way of showing their resentment at the ignominious treatment they had been subjected to, and of proving that flogging was powerless to prevent their repeating the offence. A parade was ordered, as on the previous occasion. One man was stripped to the waist, and tied to the wheel of a gun. The finding and sentence of the Court-Martial were read out—a trumpeter standing ready the while to inflict the punishment—when the commanding officer, Major Robert Waller, instead of ordering him to begin, to the intense relief of, I believe, every officer present, addressed the prisoners, telling them of his distress at finding two soldiers belonging to his troop brought up for corporal punishment twice in a little more than six weeks, and adding that, however little they deserved such leniency, if they would promise not to commit the same offence again, and to behave better for the future, he would remit the flogging part of the sentence. If the prisoners were not happy, I was; but the clemency was evidently appreciated by them, for they promised, and kept their words. I did not lose sight of these two men for some years, and was always gratified to learn that their conduct was uniformly satisfactory, and that they had become good, steady soldiers.

The Commissioner, or chief civil authority, when I arrived at Peshawar, was Colonel Mackeson, a well-known frontier officer who had greatly distinguished himself during the first Afghan war by his work among the Afridis and other border tribes, by whom he was liked and respected as much as he was feared. During Shah Shuja's brief reign at Kabul, Mackeson was continually employed on political duty in the Khyber Pass and at Peshawar. On the breaking out of the insurrection at Kabul, he was indefatigable in forwarding supplies and money to Sir Robert Sale at Jalalabad, hastening up the reinforcements, and maintaining British influence in the Khyber, a task of no small magnitude when we remember that a religious war had been proclaimed, and all true believers had been called upon to exterminate the Feringhis. While at Peshawar, as Commissioner, his duties were arduous and his responsibilities heavy—the more so as at that time the Afghan inhabitants of the city were in a dangerous and excited state.

On the 10th September, 1853, we were horrified to learn that Mackeson had been murdered by a religious fanatic. He was sitting in the verandah of his house listening to appeals from the decisions of his subordinates, when, towards evening, a man—who had been remarked by many during the day earnestly engaged in his devotions, his prayer-carpet being spread within sight of the house—came up and, making a low salaam to Mackeson, presented him with a paper. The Commissioner, supposing it to be a petition, stretched out his hand to take it when the man instantly plunged a dagger into his breast. The noise consequent on the struggle attracted the attention of some of the domestic servants and one of the Native officials. The latter threw himself between Mackeson and the fanatic, and was himself slightly wounded in his efforts to rescue his Chief.

Mackeson lingered until the 14th September. His death caused considerable excitement in the city and along the border, increasing to an alarming extent when it became known that the murderer had been hanged and his body burnt. This mode of disposing of one of their dead is considered by Mahomedans as the greatest insult that can be offered to their religion, for in thus treating the corpse, as if it were that of (by them) a hated and despised Hindu, the dead man is supposed to be deprived of every chance of paradise. It was not without careful and deliberate consideration that this course was decided upon, and it was only adopted on account of the deterrent effect it would have upon fanatical Mahomedans, who count it all gain to sacrifice their lives by the murder of a heretic, and thereby secure, as they firmly believe, eternal happiness, but loathe the idea of being burned, which effectually prevents the murderer being raised to the dignity of a martyr, and revered as a saint ever after.

It being rumoured that the Pathans intended to retaliate by desecrating the late Commissioner's grave, it was arranged that he should be buried within cantonment limits. A monument was raised to his memory by public subscription, and his epitaph* was written by the Governor-General himself.

* 'HERE LIES THE BODY

OF

FREDERICK MACKESON,

LIEUTENANT-COLONEL IN THE BENGAL ARMY, COMPANION OF THE BATH, AND COMMISSIONER OF PESHAWAR,

WHO WAS BORN SEPTEMBER 2ND, 1807,

AND DIED SEPTEMBER 14TH, 1853,

OF A WOUND INFLICTED BY A RELIGIOUS FANATIC.

He was the beau-ideal of a soldier—cool to conceive, brave to dare, and

Shortly before Mackeson's murder my father had found it necessary to go to the hill-station of Murree; the hot weather had tried him very much, and he required a change. He had scarcely arrived there, when he was startled by the news of the tragedy which had occurred, and at once determined to return, notwithstanding its being the most sickly season of the year at Peshawar, for he felt that at a time of such dangerous excitement it was his duty to be present. As a precautionary measure, he ordered the 22nd Foot from Rawal Pindi to Peshawar. This and other steps which he deemed prudent to take soon put an end to the disturbances.

No sooner had matters quieted down at Peshawar than the Jowaki Afridis, who inhabit the country immediately to the east of the Kohat Pass, began to give trouble, and we went out into camp to select a site for a post which would serve to cover the northern entrance to the pass and keep the tribesmen under surveillance. The great change of temperature, from the intense heat he had undergone in the summer to the bitter cold of November nights in tents, was too severe a trial for my father. He was then close on seventy, and though apparently active as ever, he was far from well, consequently the doctors strongly urged him not to risk another hot weather in India. It was accordingly settled that he should return to England without delay.

Shortly before his departure, an incident occurred which I will relate for the benefit of psychological students; they may, perhaps, be able to explain it, I never could. My father had some time before issued invitations for a dance which was to take place in two days' time—on Monday, the 17th October, 1853. On the Saturday morning he appeared disturbed and unhappy, and during breakfast he was silent and despondent—very different from his usual bright and cheery self. On my questioning him as to the cause, he told me he had had an unpleasant dream—one which he had dreamt several times before, and

---

strong to do. The Indian Army was proud of his noble presence in its ranks —not without cause. On the dark page of the Afghan war the name of "Mackeson" shines brightly out; the frontier was his post, and the future his field. The defiles of the Khyber and the peaks of the Black Mountain alike witness his exploits. Death still found him in front. Unconquered enemies felt safer when he fell. His own Government thus mourn the fall.

'The reputation of Lieutenant-Colonel Mackeson as a soldier is known to and honoured by all. His value as a political servant of the State is known to none better than to the Governor-General himself, who in a difficult and eventful time had cause to mark his great ability, and the admirable prudence, discretion, and temper, which added tenfold value to the high soldierly qualities of his public character.

'The loss of Colonel Mackeson's life would have dimmed a victory; to lose him thus, by the hand of a foul assassin, is a misfortune of the heaviest gloom for the Government, which counted him amongst its bravest and best.

'General orders of the Marquis Dalhousie, Governor-General of India, 3rd October, 1853.

'This monument was erected by his friends.'

which had always been followed by the death of a near relation. As the day advanced, in spite of my efforts to cheer him, he became more and more depressed, and even said he should like to put off the dance. I dissuaded him from taking this step for the time being; but that night he had the same dream again, and the next morning he insisted on the dance being postponed. It seemed to me rather absurd to have to disappoint our friends because of a dream; there was, however, nothing for it but to carry out my father's wishes, and intimation was accordingly sent to the invited guests. The following morning the post brought news of the sudden death of the half-sister at Lahore with whom I had stayed on my way to Peshawar.

As my father was really very unwell, it was not thought advisable for him to travel alone, so it was arranged that I should accompany him to Rawal Pindi. We started from Peshawar on the 27th November; and drove as far as Nowshera. The next day we went on to Attock. I found the invalid had benefited so much by the change that it was quite safe for him to continue the journey alone, and I consented the more readily to leave him, as I was anxious to get back to my battery, which had been ordered on service, and was then with the force assembled at Bazidkhel for an expedition against the Bori villages of the Jowaki Afridis.

Having said farewell to my father, I started for Bazidkhel early on the 29th November. At that time there was no direct road to that place from Nowshera, nor was it considered safe to travel alone along the slopes of the lower Afridi hills. I had, therefore, to go all the way back to Peshawar to get to my destination. I rode as fast as relays of horses could carry me, in the hope that I should reach Bazidkhel in time for the fun; but soon after passing Nowshera I heard guns in the direction of the Kohat Pass, and realized that I should be too late. I was very disappointed at missing this, my first chance of active service, and not accompanying the newly raised Mountain Train (as it was then called) on the first occasion of its being employed in the field.

The object of this expedition was to punish the Jowaki section of the Afridis for their many delinquencies during the three previous years. Numerous murders and raids on the Kohat and Peshawar districts, the plunder of boats on the Indus, and the murder of a European apothecary, were all traced to this tribe. They had been blockaded, and their resort to the salt-mines near Bahadurkhel and to the markets of Kohat and Peshawar had been interdicted, but these measures produced no effect on the recalcitrant tribesmen. John (afterwards Lord) Lawrence, who had come to Peshawar for the purpose of taking over frontier affairs with Edwardes, the new Commissioner, held a conference with the *maliks** of the villages connected with the Jowaki Pass, and being anxious to avoid hostilities, offered to

* Head men.

condone all past offences if the tribes would agree to certain conditions, which, briefly, were that no further crimes should be committed in British territory; that such criminals as had taken refuge in their villages should be given up; and that for the future criminals and outlaws flying from justice should not be afforded an asylum in Jowaki lands. To the second condition the whole tribe absolutely refused to agree. They stated, with truth, that from time immemorial it was their custom to afford an asylum to anyone demanding it, and that to surrender a man who had sought and found shelter with them would be a disgrace which they could not endure.

Afridis have curious ideas as to the laws of hospitality; it is no uncommon thing for them to murder their guests in cold blood, but it is contrary to their code of honour to surrender a fugitive who has claimed an asylum with them.

The sections of the tribe living nearest our territory agreed to the first and third of our conditions, no doubt because they felt they were in our power, and had suffered considerably from the blockade. But the Bori Afridis would make no atonement for the past and give no security for the future, although they admitted having robbed and murdered our subjects. There was nothing for it, therefore, but to send a force against them. This force consisted of rather more than 1,500 men, British and Native. The Afridis made no stand until we reached their main position, when they offered a stout resistance, which, however, proved of no avail against the gallantry of the Guides and 66th (now 1st) Gurkhas. The Bori villages were then destroyed, with a loss to us of eight men killed and thirty-one wounded.

Sufficient punishment having been inflicted, our force retired. The rear-guard was hotly pressed, and it was late in the evening before the troops got clear of the hills.

The tribesmen with whom we had just made friends sat in hundreds on the ridges watching the progress of the fight. It was no doubt a great temptation to them to attack the 'infidels' while they were at their mercy, and considerable anxiety was felt by Lawrence and Edwardes as to the part which our new allies would play; their relief was proportionate when it was found they intended to maintain a neutral attitude.

I shall not further describe the events of that day, more especially as I was not fortunate enough to be in time to take part in the proceedings. I have only referred to this expedition as being typical of many little frontier fights, and because I remember being much impressed at the time with the danger of trusting our communications in a difficult mountainous country to people closely allied to those against whom we were fighting. This over-confidence in the good faith of our frontier neighbours caused us serious embarrassments a few years later during the Umbeyla campaign.

The force remained in camp for some time for the protection of the men employed in building the post, which was called Fort Mackeson, after the murdered Commissioner. When it was completed we returned to Peshawar.

CHAPTER IV.

I HAD had a great deal of fever during my eighteen months' residence at Peshawar, and in April, 1854, I obtained six months' leave to Kashmir. I travelled *viâ* Murree to Abbottabad, along the route now well known as the 'Gullies.' Here I was joined by Lieutenant George Rodney Brown,* a subaltern of Horse Artillery, with whom I chummed at Peshawar.

Abbottabad was a very small place in those days. It was named after its first Deputy-Commissioner, James Abbott,† famous for his journey *viâ* Bokhara and Khiva to Russia in 1839, undertaken for the release of Russian prisoners who were kept as slaves by the Turkomans. He had just left, and had been succeeded as Deputy-Commissioner by a Captain Becher, who, fortunately for us, was away in the district. I say fortunately, because we were bent on visiting Khagan, and had obtained permission from the Commissioner of Peshawar to do so. He had told us to apply to Becher for assistance, but from what we heard of that officer, it did not seem likely he would help us. Khagan was beyond our border, and the inhabitants were said to be even more fanatical than the rest of the frontier tribes. The Commissioner, however, had given us leave, and as his Deputy appeared to be the kind of man to create obstacles, we made up our minds to slip away before he returned.

We started on the 21st May, and marched to Habibula-Ki-Ghari. Here the road bifurcates, one branch leading to Kashmir, the other to Khagan. We took the latter, and proceeded to Balakot, twelve miles further on, which was then our frontier post. There we found a small guard of Frontier Police, two of whom we induced to accompany us on our onward journey for the purpose of assisting to look after the baggage and collecting coolies. Three days' more marching brought us to Khagan. The road almost the whole way from Balakot ran along a precipice overhanging the Nainsukh river, at that time of year a rushing torrent, owing to the melting of the snows on the higher ranges. The track was rough, steep, and in some places very narrow. We crossed and recrossed the river several times by means of snow-bridges, which, spanning the limpid, jade-coloured water, had a very pretty effect. At one point our *shikarris*‡ stopped, and proudly told

* Now a retired Major-General.

† Now General Sir James Abbott, K.C.B.

‡ Men who carry the guns, and point out the most likely places for game, etc.

us that on that very spot their tribe had destroyed a Sikh army sent against them in the time of Runjit Sing. It certainly was a place well chosen for a stand, not more than fifty yards wide, with a perpendicular cliff on one side and a roaring torrent on the other.

The people apparently did not object to our being in their country, and treated us with much civility throughout our journey. We were enjoying ourselves immensely, so when an official cover reached us with the signature of the dreaded Deputy-Commissioner in the corner, we agreed that it would be unwise to open it just then.

Khagan was almost buried in snow. The scenery was magnificent, and became every moment more wonderful as we slowly climbed the steep ascent in front of us; range after range of snow-capped mountains disclosed themselves to our view, rising higher and higher into the air, until at last, towering above all, Nanga Parbat* in all her spotless beauty was revealed to our astonished and delighted gaze.

We could not get beyond Khagan. Our coolies refused to go further, alleging as their reason the danger to be dreaded from avalanches in that month; but I suspect that fear of hostility from the tribes further north had more to do with their reluctance to proceed than dread of falling avalanches. We remained at Khagan for two or three days in the hope of being able to shoot an ibex, but we were disappointed; we never even saw one.

We retraced our steps with considerable regret, and reached Habibula-Ki-Ghari on the 31st May. Here we received a second official document from Abbottabad. It contained, like the previous letter, which we now looked at for the first time, orders for our immediate return, and warnings that we were on no account to go to Khagan. Since then Khagan has been more than once visited by British officers, and now a road is in course of construction along the route we travelled, as being a more direct line of communication with Gilghit than that *viâ* Kashmir.

We made no delay at Habibula-Ki-Ghari, but started at once for the lovely Vale of Kashmir, where we spent the summer, amusing ourselves by making excursions to all the places of interest and beauty we had so often heard of, and occasionally shooting a bear. The place which impressed me most was Martund,† where stand the picturesque ruins of a once renowned Hindu temple. These noble ruins are the most striking in size and position of all the existing remains of the past glories of Kashmir.

From Martund we made our way to Vernag, the celebrated spring which is supposed to be the source of the Jhelum river. The Moghul Emperor Akbar built there a summer palace, and the arches, on which it is said rested the private apartments of the lovely Nur Jehan, are still visible.

* 26,000 feet above the sea-level. † Three miles east of Islamabad.

We wandered over the beautiful and fertile Lolab valley, and pitched our little camp in the midst of groves of chunar, walnut, apple, cherry, and peach trees; and we marched up the Sind valley, and crossed the Zojji La Pass leading into Thibet. The scenery all along this route is extremely grand. On either side are lofty mountains, their peaks wrapped in snow, their sides clothed with pine, and their feet covered with forests, in which is to be found almost every kind of deciduous tree. From time to time we returned for a few days to Srinagar, the capital of Kashmir, to enjoy the pleasures of more civilized society. Srinagar is so well known nowadays, and has been so often described in poetry and prose, that it is needless for me to dwell at length upon its delights, which, I am inclined to think, are greater in imagination than in reality. It has been called the Venice of the East, and in some respects it certainly does remind one of the 'Bride of the Sea,' both in its picturesqueness and (when one gets into the small and tortuous canals) its unsavouriness. Even at the time of which I am writing it was dilapidated, and the houses looked exactly like those made by children out of a pack of cards, which a puff of wind might be expected to destroy. Of late years the greater part of the city has been injured by earthquakes, and Srinagar looks more than ever like a card city. The great beauty of the place in those days was the wooden bridges covered with creepers, and gay with booths and shops of all descriptions, which spanned the Jhelum at intervals for the three miles the river runs through the town—now, alas! for the artistic traveller, no more. Booths and shops have been swept away, and the creepers have disappeared—decidedly an advantage from a sanitary point of view, but destructive of the quaint picturesqueness of the town.

The floating gardens are a unique and very pretty characteristic of Srinagar. The lake is nowhere deeper than ten or twelve feet, and in some places much less. These gardens are made by driving stakes into the bed of the lake, long enough to project three or four feet above the surface of the water. These stakes are placed at intervals in an oblong form, and are bound together by reeds and rushes twined in and out and across, until a kind of stationary raft is made, on which earth and turf are piled. In this soil seeds are sown, and the crops of melons and other fruits raised in these fertile beds are extremely fine and abundant.

The magnificent chunar-trees are another very beautiful feature of the country. They grow to a great height and girth, and so luxuriant and dense is their foliage that I have sat reading and writing for hours during heavy rain under one of these trees and kept perfectly dry.

The immediate vicinity of Srinagar is very pretty, and the whole valley of Kashmir is lovely beyond description: surrounded by beautifully-wooded mountains, intersected with streams and lakes, and gay with flowers of every description, for in Kashmir many of the gorgeous eastern plants and the more simple but sweeter ones of England meet on common ground. To it may appropriately be applied the Persian couplet:

> 'Agar fardos baru-i zamin ast, hamin ast, hamin ast'
> (If there be an Elysium on earth, it is this, it is this).

The soil is extremely productive; anything will grow in it. Put a stick into the ground, and in an extraordinary short space of time it becomes a tree and bears fruit. What were we about, to sell such a country for three quarters of a million sterling? It would have made the most perfect sanatorium for our troops, and furnished an admirable field for British enterprise and colonization, its climate being as near perfection as anything can be.

How sad it is that, in a country 'where every prospect pleases, only man' should be 'vile'! And man, as he existed in Kashmir, was vile—vile, because so miserable. The Mahomedan inhabitants were being ground down by Hindu rulers, who seized all their earnings, leaving them barely sufficient to keep body and soul together. What interest could such people have in cultivating their land, or doing any work beyond what was necessary to mere existence? However hard they might labour, their efforts would benefit neither themselves nor their children, and so their only thought was to get through life with as little exertion as possible—in the summer sitting in the sun absolutely idle the greater part of the day, and in the winter wrapped up in their blankets, under which were concealed curious little vessels called *kangris*, holding two or three bits of live charcoal. Every Kashmiri still carries one of these *kangris*, as the most economical way of keeping himself warm.

Early in September we said good-bye to the happy valley and returned to Peshawar, where I rejoined the Mountain Battery.

In November, to my great delight, I was given my jacket. At first my happiness was somewhat damped by the fact that the troop to which I was posted was stationed at Umballa. I did not want to leave Peshawar, and in the end I had not to do so, as a vacancy most opportunely occurred in one of the troops of Horse Artillery at that station, which was given to me.

Life on the frontier in those days had a great charm for most young men; there was always something of interest going on; military expeditions were constantly taking place, or being speculated upon, and one lived in hope of being amongst those chosen for active service. Peshawar, too, notwithstanding its unhealthiness, was a favourite station with officers. To me it was particularly pleasant, for it had the largest force of Artillery of any station in India except Meerut; the mess was a good one, and was composed of as nice a set of fellows as were to be found in the army. In addition to the officers of the regiment, there were a certain number of honorary members; all the staff and civilians belonged to the Artillery mess, and on guest-nights we sat down as many as sixty to dinner. Another attraction was the 'coffee shop,' an institution which has now almost ceased to exist, at which we all congregated after morning parade and freely discussed the home and local news.

The troop to which I was posted was composed of a magnificent body of men, nearly all Irishmen, most of whom could have lifted me up with one hand. They were fine riders, and needed to be so, for the stud-horses used for Artillery purposes at that time were not the quiet, well-broken animals of the present day. I used to try my hand at riding them all in turn, and thus learnt to understand and appreciate the amount of nerve, patience, and skill necessary to the making of a good Horse Artillery 'driver,' with the additional advantage that I was brought into constant contact with the men. It also qualified me to ride in the officers' team for the regimental brake. The brake, it must be understood, was drawn by six horses, each ridden postilion fashion by an officer.

My troop was commanded by Captain Barr, a dear old fellow who had seen a good deal of service and was much liked by officers and men, but hardly the figure for a Horse Artilleryman, as he weighed about seventeen stone. On a troop parade Barr took up his position well in advance and made his own pace, but on brigade parades he had to conform to the movements of the other arms, and on these occasions he used to tell one of the subalterns as he galloped past him to come 'left about' at the right time without waiting for his order. This, of course, we were always careful to do, and by the time we had come into action Barr had caught us up and was at his post.

During the winter of 1854-55 I had several returns of Peshawar fever, and by the beginning of the spring I was so reduced that I was given eight months' leave on medical certificate, with orders to report myself at Mian Mir at its expiration, in view to my going through the riding course, there being no Riding-Master at Peshawar.

I decided to return to Kashmir in the first instance, and thence to march across the Himalayas to Simla.

On my way into Kashmir I was fortunate enough to fall in with a very agreeable travelling companion—Lieutenant John Watson.* He was then Adjutant of the 1st Punjab Cavalry, and was looked upon as one of the most promising officers of the Frontier Force. We spent a very enjoyable time in Kashmir, and early in August I started for Simla with two brother officers named Light and Mercer, whose acquaintance I had only recently made, but who turned out to be very pleasant fellow-travellers.

We marched *viâ* Kishtwar, Chamba, and Dharmsala, a distance of about 400 miles, through most beautiful scenery. At the last-named

* Now General Sir John Watson, V.C., K.C.B.

place I parted from my companions, who travelled onwards to Simla by the Kulu valley, while I took the shorter route *viâ* Bilaspur.

The Simla of those days was not the busy and important place it has since become. The Governor-General seldom visited it, and the Commander-in-Chief only spent a summer there occasionally. When I arrived, Sir William Gomm, the Commander-in-Chief of that day, who had been spending the hot weather months there, was about to give up his command, and Colonel Grant,* who had been his Adjutant-General, had left not long before.

The only thing of interest to myself which occurred during the month I remained at Simla was that I lunched with Colonel Arthur Becher, the Quartermaster-General.† I think I hear my reader say, 'Not a very remarkable event to chronicle.' But that lunch was a memorable one to me; indeed, it was the turning-point in my career, for my host was good enough to say he should like to have me in his department some day, and this meant a great deal to me. Joining a department at that time generally resulted in remaining in it for the greater part of one's service. There was then no limit to the tenure of staff appointments, and the object of every ambitious young officer was to get into one department or another—political, civil, or the army staff. My father had always impressed upon me that the political department was *the* one to aspire to, and failing that, the Quartermaster-General's, as in the latter there was the best chance of seeing service. I had cherished a sort of vague hope that I might some day be lucky enough to become a Deputy Assistant-Quartermaster-General, for although I fully recognized the advantages of a political career, I preferred being more closely associated with the army, and I had seen enough of staff work to satisfy myself that it would suit me; so the few words spoken to me by Colonel Becher made me supremely happy.

It never entered into my head that I should get an early appointment; the fact of the Quartermaster-General thinking of me as a possible recruit was quite enough for me. I was in no hurry to leave the Horse Artillery, to which I was proud of belonging, and in which I hoped to see service while still on the frontier. I left Simla very pleased with the result of my visit, and very grateful to Colonel Becher, who proved a good friend to me ever after, and I made my way to Mian Mir, where I went through the riding-school course, and then returned to Peshawar.

The winter of 1855-56 passed much as the cold weather generally does in the north of India. Our amusements consisted of an occasional race-meeting or cricket match. Polo was unknown in those days, and hunting the jackal, a sport which has been a source of so much recreation to the Peshawar garrison for thirty odd years, had not then been thought of. It was a pleasant change to visit the outposts, and when-

* The late Field-Marshal Sir Patrick Grant, G.C.B., G.C.S.I.

† The late Major-General Sir Arthur Becher, K.C.B.

ever I got the chance I rode over to Mardan, where the Corps of Guides were stationed, commanded by that gallant soldier, Harry Lumsden,* who had raised the corps in 1846 under the auspices of Henry Lawrence. Many were the good gallops I enjoyed with his hawks, hunting the *aubara.*† Of work there was plenty at Peshawar, for the Brigadier, Sydney Cotton,‡ kept us alive with field days, carefully instilling into us his idea that parade-grounds were simply useful for drill and preliminary instruction, and that as soon as the rudiments of a soldier's education had been learnt, the troops should leave their nursery, and try as far as possible to practise in peace what they would have to do in war. Sydney Cotton was never tired of explaining that the machinery of war, like all other machinery, should be kept, so to speak, oiled and ready for use.

My dream of a staff appointment was realized more quickly than I had expected. In the early part of 1856 the Surveyor-General applied for the services of two or three experienced officers to assist in the survey of Kashmir. Lumsden, the D.A.Q.M.G., was one of those selected for the duty, and I was appointed to officiate for him. So delighted was I to get my foot on the lowest rung of the staff ladder, that I cheerfully agreed to the condition my Captain insisted upon, that I should perform my regimental duties in addition to the staff work. Things went merrily with me for a short time, when most unexpectedly my hopes of some day becoming Quartermaster-General of the Army in India were dashed to the ground by the Governor-General refusing to confirm my appointment, because I had not passed the prescribed examination in Hindustani. A rule existed requiring a language test, but it had seldom been enforced, certainly not in the case of 'acting appointments,' so that this refusal came as a great blow to me. It had, however, excellent results, for it made me determined to pass in Hindustani. It was then May, and in July the half-yearly examination was to be held. I forthwith engaged the best *munshi*§ at Peshawar, shut myself up, and studied Indian literature from morning till night, until I felt pretty confident of success.

* The late General Sir Harry Lumsden, K.C.S.I., C.B.

† Bastard florican.

‡ This officer arrived in India as a Cornet in the 24th Light Dragoons in the year 1810, and although, when he reached Peshawar with his regiment—the 22nd Foot—in 1853, he had been forty-three years in the army, and was sixty-one years of age, he had not even succeeded to the command of a battalion. He was an officer of unusual energy and activity, a fine rider, a pattern drill, and a thorough soldier all round. He was not fortunate enough to see much active service, but it must have been a source of consolation to him to feel, when ending his days as Governor of the Royal Hospital at Chelsea, that it was in a great measure owing to his foresight and decision that there was no serious disturbance at Peshawar during the eventful summer of 1857.

§ Instructor in Oriental languages.

Just before the examination took place, the officer who had stepped into my shoes when I was turned out (Lieutenant Mordaunt Fitz-Gerald, of my own regiment) was offered an appointment in the Punjab Frontier Force. He consulted me as to the advisability of accepting it, and I told him I thought he ought not to do so. I considered this most disinterested advice, for I had good reason to believe that I should be re-appointed to the staff, should the appointment again become vacant. Fortunately for me, Fitz-Gerald followed the usual procedure of those who delight in consulting their friends. He listened to my advice, and then decided not to follow it. Accordingly, he joined the Punjab Frontier Force, whilst I, having passed the examination, went back to the coveted appointment, and continued in the department, with the exception of one or two short intervals, until 1878, when I left it as Quartermaster-General.

The autumn of 1856 was a very sickly one at Peshawar; fever was rife amongst the troops, and in the hope of shaking it off Brigadier Cotton got permission to take a certain number into camp. It was September, and the sun was still very hot, so that it was necessary to begin the daily march long before dawn in order to reach the new camping ground while it was still tolerably cool. We crossed the Kabul river at Nowshera, which place was then being made into a station for troops, and marched about the Yusafzai plain for three weeks. The chief difficulty was the absence of water, and I had to prospect the country every afternoon for a sufficient supply, and to determine, with regard to this *sine quâ non*, where the camp should be pitched the next day. On one occasion the best place I could discover was between two and three miles off the main road. There was no difficulty in reaching it by day, but I was afraid of some mistake being made when we had to leave it in the small hours of the morning, few things being more bewildering than to find one's way in the dark from a camp pitched in the open country when once the tents have been struck. It was my duty to lead the column and see that it marched off in the right direction; knowing how anxious the Brigadier was that the new ground should be reached while it was cool, and the men be thus saved from exposure to the sun, I was careful to note my position with regard to the stars, and to explain to the officer who was in orders to command the advance guard the direction he must take. When the time came to start, and the Brigadier was about to order the bugler to sound the march, I saw that the advance guard was drawn up at right angles to the way in which we had to proceed. The officer commanding it was positive he was right, and in this he was supported by Brigadier Cotton and some of the other officers; I was equally positive that he was wrong, and that if we marched as he proposed, we should find ourselves several miles out of our course. The Brigadier settled the question by saying I was responsible for the troops going in the right direction, and ordering me to show the way. The country was perfectly bare, there was not a tree or object of any kind to guide me. and the distance seemed interminable. I heard opinions freely expressed that I was on the wrong road, and at last, when the Brigadier himself came up to me and said he thought I must have lost the way, I really began to waver in my conviction that I was right. At that moment my horse stumbled into a ditch, which proved to be the boundary of the main road. I was immensely relieved, the Brigadier was delighted, and from that moment I think he was satisfied that I had, what is so essential to a Quartermaster-General in the field, the bump of locality.

In October the Artillery moved into the practice camp at Chamkanie, about five miles from Peshawar. It was intended that we should remain there for a couple of months, but before the end of that time I had to join the General at Rawal Pindi, where he had gone on a tour of inspection. Being anxious not to shirk my regimental duty, I did not leave Chamkanie until the last moment, and had but one day in which to reach Rawal Pindi, a distance of one hundred miles, which I accomplished on horseback between 7 a.m. and 6 p.m., only stopping at Attock a short time for refreshment.[1]

This tour with General Reed ended my staff duties for a time, as the survey in Kashmir had come to an end and Lumsden rejoined his appointment before Christmas.

CHAPTER V.

TOWARDS the close of the year 1856, a rumour reached us that the Amir, Dost Mahomed Khan, was shortly expected to arrive at Peshawar to meet the Chief Commissioner, Sir John Lawrence, who had recently been made a K.C.B.

Before describing the Amir's visit and its results, it seems desirable that I should briefly explain how and why the visit was brought about, and then endeavour to show what an important bearing its results had on the great crisis which occurred so unexpectedly a few months later.

It will be remembered that the murdered Mackeson was succeeded as Commissioner of Peshawar by Herbert Edwardes, one of the most remarkable men that the Indian army has ever produced, and who, as I have already mentioned, entirely concurred in my father's expressed opinion as to the great advantage it would be for the Government of India to enter into more friendly relations with the Ruler of Kabul. They both held that the constant troubles all along our frontier were in a great measure due to the Amir's hostility, and that such troubles would increase rather than diminish unless we could succeed in establishing an *entente cordiale* with Dost Mahomed.

In 1854 Edwardes had a correspondence with the Governor-General on the subject, and on one occasion expressed himself as follows: 'My own feeling is, that we have much injured Dost Mahomed, and may very well afford to let by-gones be by-gones. It would contribute much to the security of this frontier if open relations of goodwill were established at Kabul. There is a sullenness in our present relations, as if both parties were brooding over the past, and expecting an opportunity in the future. This keeps up excitement and unrest, and prevents our influence and institutions taking root. I should be very glad to see a new account opened on the basis of an open treaty of friendship and alliance.'

Lord Dalhousie was quite in accord with Edwardes. He thought it very desirable to be on better terms with Kabul, but believed this to be a result difficult to attain. 'I give you,' he said in a letter to Edwardes, '*carte blanche*, and if you can only bring about such a result as you propose, it will be a new feather in your cap.'

Lord Dalhousie was supported by the British Government in his opinion as to the desirability of coming to a better understanding with the Amir. War with Russia was then imminent, and the strained condition of European politics made it expedient that we should be on more amicable terms with Afghanistan.

The Governor-General thus wrote to Edwardes:

'Prospects of a war between Russia and Turkey are watched with interest by all. . . . In England they are fidgety regarding this border beyond all reason, and most anxious for that declared amity and that formal renewal of friendly relations which you advocate in your letter.'

The balance of Indian opinion, however, was against our making overtures to Dost Mahomed. John Lawrence, at that time the great power in the Punjab, was altogether opposed to Edwardes's policy in this matter. He admitted that it might be wise to renew intercourse with the Kabul ruler if he first expressed his regret for previous misunderstandings; but later he wrote to Edwardes:

'I dare say you are right; still, I cannot divest myself of the idea that it is *a mistake*, and will end in mixing us up in Afghan politics and affairs more than is desirable. The strength which a treaty can give us seems to be a delusion. It will be like the reed on which, if a man lean, it will break and pierce his hand.'

John Nicholson, Outram, and James Abbott agreed with Lawrence. They urged that any advance on our part would be looked upon as an indication of conscious weakness; and the probability was that an arrogant, irritated Mussulman ruler would regard an overture as a proof of our necessity, and would make our necessity his opportunity. But Lord Dalhousie, while anxious to avoid any communication being made which could be liable to misconstruction, saw neither objection nor risk in opening the door to reconciliation, provided no undue anxiety was displayed on our part. The Governor-General practically left the matter in the hands of Edwardes, who lost no time in trying to attain the desired object. The greatest forbearance and diplomatic skill were necessary to bring the negotiations to a satisfactory termination, but they were concluded at last, most successfully, and to Edwardes alone is due the credit. It is instructive to read the full record* of this tedious and difficult piece of diplomacy, for it serves as an interesting example of Oriental subtlety and circumlocution, contrasted with the straightforward dealing of a high-minded Englishman.

The Amir wrote a letter to the Governor-General couched in most satisfactory terms, which he forwarded to Peshawar by the hand of his confidential secretary, and which received, as it deserved, a very friendly reply. This resulted in Dost Mahomed sending his son and heir-apparent, Sardar Ghulam Haidar Khan, to Peshawar, and deputing him to act as his Plenipotentiary in the negotiations. Ghulam Haidar Khan reached Peshawar in March, 1855, where he was met by the Chief Commissioner, and on the 30th of that month the treaty was concluded. 'It guaranteed that we should respect the Amir's possessions in Afghanistan, and never interfere with them; while the Amir engaged similarly to respect British territory, and to be the friend of our friends and the enemy of our enemies.'

The Governor-General had at first resolved to entrust to Edwardes the duty of meeting the expected Envoy from Kabul, and orders to that effect were issued. But Edwardes, more anxious for the success of the negotiations than for his own honour and glory, wrote to Lord Dalhousie suggesting that the Government of India should be represented by the Chief Commissioner of the Punjab, and promising to afford Sir John Lawrence all the assistance in his power. Edwardes believed that the importance of the treaty would be enhanced in the eyes of the Afghans by the presence of the higher official; and in this opinion the Governor-General concurred. On the conclusion of the treaty, Lord Dalhousie wrote to Edwardes: 'I congratulate you and myself and all else concerned on this successful issue of the negotiations, which have now lasted just a year.'

This treaty of March, 1855, was only preliminary to that for the ratification of which the Amir came in person to Peshawar the following year.

Towards the end of 1855 Dost Mahomed found himself in considerable difficulties, and appealed to us for assistance. A revolt had occurred at Herat, and a Persian army was preparing to besiege that fortress; the chiefs and people of Kandahar were disaffected; and the province of Balkh was threatened with invasion both by the King of Bokhara and by Turkoman hordes. The Amir looked upon Herat as

* See 'Memorials of the Life and Letters of Major-General Sir Herbert Edwardes.'

an integral part of the Afghan dominions, and was very desirous of re-establishing his authority over that place and preventing its falling into the hands of the Persians; but he felt himself too weak to have any hope of success without help from us in men and money. It was, therefore, Dost Mahomed's interest to convince the British Government that the Shah had infringed the conditions of an engagement entered into with us in 1853, under which Persia abandoned all claim to Herat. The Amir thus hoped to establish a quarrel between England and Persia for his own benefit, and to secure our assistance against the latter power. To further this design, Dost Mahomed offered to come to Peshawar and consult with the British authorities. Edwardes was in favour of the proposed visit. John Lawrence was opposed to it, saying he did not think much good would result from such a meeting, because it could hardly be anticipated that the views of the Amir and the British Government would coincide, and if Dost Mahomed should fail to obtain what he wanted, his dissatisfaction would be a positive evil. The Governor-General admitted the force of these objections, but in the end considered that they should be set aside if the Amir was in earnest in desiring a consultation. 'A refusal or an evasion to comply with his wish,' Lord Dalhousie thought, 'might be misunderstood, and although a meeting might lead to disappointment and disagreement, it would, at any rate, put the relations of the British Government with the Amir, as regards Herat, upon a clear footing.'

While this discussion was going on, the advance of a Persian army for the purpose of besieging Herat, coupled with the insults offered to the British flag at Teheran, led to the declaration of war between England and Persia. The Chief Commissioner was therefore directed to tell the Amir that he would be paid a periodical subsidy to aid him in carrying on hostile operations against Persia, subject to certain conditions. On receiving these instructions, the Chief Commissioner directed Edwardes to invite the Amir to an interview. Dost Mahomed accepted the invitation, but before the auspicious meeting could take place Lord Dalhousie had left India, and Lord Canning reigned in his stead. Lord Dalhousie resigned on the 29th February, 1856, after having filled the arduous and responsible position of Governor-General for no less than eight years, adding year by year fresh lustre to his splendid reputation.

The first day of 1857 witnessed the meeting between the Amir of Kabul and the Chief Commissioner of the Punjab. The Amir's camp was pitched at the mouth of the Khyber Pass, and that of the Chief Commissioner on the plain near Jamrud. Barr's troop of Horse Artillery formed part of the escort, so I was in the midst of it all. On the occasion of the Amir's first visit to the English camp, there was a force present of upwards of 7,000 soldiers, including three regiments of British Infantry; the troops lined the road for more than a mile, and it was evident that their strength and soldierly appearance inspired the Amir and his followers with a very salutary feeling of awe and admiration.*

The result of the conferences between these two great personages was an agreement confirming the treaty of the year before. In addition, the Amir bound himself to keep up a certain number of regular troops for the defence of Afghanistan, so long as the war with Persia continued, in consideration of a monthly subsidy of Rs. 100,000 and a gift of 4,000 muskets. He also engaged to communicate to the Government of India any overtures he might receive from Persia, and he consented to allow British officers to visit certain parts of his dominions, either for the purpose of assisting his subjects against Persia, or to ascertain that the subsidy was properly applied.

I have dwelt at some length on this treaty with Afghanistan, first, because the policy of which this was the outcome was, as I have already shown, initiated by my father; and, secondly, because I do not think it is generally understood how important to us were its results. Not only did it heal the wounds left open from the first Afghan war, but it relieved England of a great anxiety at a time when throughout the length and breadth of India there was distress, revolt, bloodshed, and bitter distrust of our Native troops. Dost Mahomed loyally held to his engagements during the troublous days of the Mutiny which so quickly followed this alliance, when, had he turned against us, we should assuredly have lost the Punjab; Delhi could never have been taken; in fact, I do not see how any part of the country north of Bengal could have been saved. Dost Mahomed's own people could not understand his attitude. They frequently came to him during the Mutiny, throwing their turbans at his feet, and praying him as a Mahomedan to seize that opportunity for destroying the 'infidels.' 'Hear the news from Delhi,' they urged; 'see the difficulties the Feringhis are in. Why don't you lead us on to take advantage of their weakness, and win back Peshawar?'†

But I am anticipating, and must return to my narrative.

The clause of the treaty which interested me personally was that relating to British officers being allowed to visit Afghanistan, to give effect to which a Mission was despatched to Kandahar. It consisted of three officers, the brothers Harry and Peter Lumsden, and Dr. Bellew, together with two of Edwardes's trusted Native Chiefs. The selection of Peter Lumsden as a member of this Mission again left the Deputy Assistant-Quartermaster-Generalship vacant, and I was a second time appointed to officiate in his absence.

Shortly afterwards the General of the division (General Reed) started on his tour of inspection, taking me with him as his staff officer. Jhelum was the first place we visited. Whether the sepoys had then

* 'Memorials of Major-General Sir Herbert Edwardes.' † *Ibid.*

any knowledge of what was so soon to happen is doubtful. If they had, there was no evidence that such was the case. Nothing could have been more proper or respectful than their behaviour; no crimes were reported, no complaints were made. The British officers, certainly, had not the slightest idea of the storm that was brewing, for they spoke in the warmest terms of their men.

From Jhelum we went to Rawal Pindi. John Lawrence happened to be in camp there at the time, and looked on at the General's inspection. At the conclusion of the parade he sent his secretary to ask me if I would like to be appointed to the Public Works Department. I respectfully declined the offer, though very grateful for its having been made. Some of my friends doubted the wisdom of my refusing a permanent civil appointment; but it meant having to give up soldiering, which I could not make up my mind to do, and though only officiating, I was already in the department to which of all others I wished to belong.

Nowshera was the last station we visited. It was the beginning of April, and getting rather hot for parading troops. I there met for the first time the present Commander-in-Chief in India, General Sir George White, who was then a subaltern in the 27th (Inniskilling) Regiment.

I recollect the commanding officer of the 55th, the Native Infantry corps at this station, who had served all his life with clean-looking, closely-shaven Hindustanis, pointing with a look of contempt, not to say disgust, to some Sikhs (a certain proportion of whom had been under recent orders enlisted in regiments of Native Infantry), and expressing his regret that he could not get them to shave their beards and cut their hair. 'They quite spoil the look of my regiment,' he said. In less than two months' time the Hindustanis, of whom the Colonel was so proud, had broken into open mutiny; the despised Sikhs were the only men of the regiment who remained faithful; and the commanding officer, a devoted soldier who lived for his regiment, and who implored that his men might not have their arms taken away, as he had 'implicit confidence' in them, and would 'stake his life on their fidelity,' had blown his brains out because he found that confidence misplaced.

Towards the end of April I was ordered to report on the capabilities of Cherat (now well known to all who have been stationed at Peshawar) as a sanatorium for European soldiers. I spent two or three days surveying the hill and searching for water in the neighbourhood. It was not safe to remain on the top at night, so I used to return each evening to the plain below, where my tent was pitched. On one occasion I was surprised to find a camp had risen up during my absence quite close to my tent. I discovered that it belonged to Lieutenant-Colonel John Nicholson, the Deputy-Commissioner, who was on his

BRIGADIER-GENERAL JOHN NICHOLSON, C.B.

From
a painting by J. R. Dicksee,
in
the possession of the Reverend Canon Seymour.

tour of inspection, and very soon I received an invitation to dine with him, at which I was greatly pleased. John Nicholson was a name to conjure with in the Punjab. I had heard it mentioned with an amount of respect—indeed, awe—which no other name could excite, and I was all curiosity to see the man whose influence on the frontier was so great that his word was law to the refractory tribes amongst whom he lived. He had only lately arrived in Peshawar, having been transferred from Bannu, a difficult and troublesome district ruled by him as it had never been ruled before, and where he made such a reputation for himself that, while he was styled 'a pillar of strength on the frontier' by Lord Dalhousie, he was looked up to as a god by the Natives, who loved as much as they feared him. By some of them he was actually worshipped as a saint; they formed themselves into a sect, and called themselves 'Nicholseyns.' Nicholson impressed me more profoundly than any man I had ever met before, or have ever met since. I have never seen anyone like him. He was the beau-ideal of a soldier and a gentleman. His appearance was distinguished and commanding, with a sense of power about him which to my mind was the result of his having passed so much of his life amongst the wild and lawless tribesmen, with whom his authority was supreme. Intercourse with this man amongst men made me more eager than ever to remain on the frontier, and I was seized with ambition to follow in his footsteps. Had I never seen Nicholson again, I might have thought that the feelings with which he inspired me were to some extent the result of my imagination, excited by the astonishing stories I had heard of his power and influence; my admiration, however, for him was immeasurably strengthened when, a few weeks later, I served as his staff officer, and had opportunities of observing more closely his splendid soldierly qualities and the workings of his grand, simple mind.

It was the end of April when I returned to Peshawar from Cherat, and rapidly getting hot. On the strength of being a D.A.Q.M.G., I had moved into a better house than I had hitherto been able to afford, which I shared with Lieutenant Hovenden of the Engineers. We were just settling down and making ourselves comfortable for the long hot weather, when all our plans were upset by the breaking out of the Mutiny.

CHAPTER VI.

THE first threatenings of coming trouble were heard in the early part of 1857. During the months of February, March, and April, rumours reached us at Peshawar of mysterious *chupattis* (unleavened cakes) being sent about the country with the object, it was alleged, of preparing the Natives for some forthcoming event. There was also an evident feeling of unrest and dissatisfaction in the minds of the sepoys. We heard that the 19th Native Infantry at Berhampur, a military station about 100 miles from Calcutta, had broken open the bells-of-arms,* and forcibly taken possession of their muskets and ammunition; that a sepoy named Mangal Pandy,† belonging to the 34th Native Infantry at Barrackpore, had attacked and severely wounded the Adjutant and Sergeant-Major of his regiment; that it was found necessary to disband the 19th on the 30th March, and the 34th on the 6th May; that bungalows had been burnt in several stations; and that the sepoys at the Schools of Musketry had objected to use the cartridges served out with the new rifles, because, it was asserted, they were greased with a mixture of cow's fat and lard, the one being as obnoxious to the prejudices of the Hindu as the other is to those of the Mussulman.

It seems strange on looking back that these many warnings should have passed almost unheeded, and that there should have been no suspicion amongst the officers serving with Native regiments that discontent was universal amongst the sepoys, and that a mutiny of the whole Bengal Army was imminent. But at that time the reliance on the fidelity of the Native troops was unbounded, and officers believed implicitly in the contentment and loyalty of their men. Their faith in them was extraordinary. Even after half the Native army had mutinied and many officers had been murdered, those belonging to the remaining regiments could not believe that their own particular men could be guilty of treachery.

At Peshawar there was not the slightest suspicion of the extent to which the evil had spread, and we were quite thunderstruck when, on the evening of the 11th May, as we were sitting at mess, the telegraph signaller rushed in breathless with excitement, a telegram in his hand, which proved to be a message from Delhi 'to all stations in the Punjab,' conveying the startling intelligence that a very serious outbreak had occurred at Meerut the previous evening, that some of the troopers from there had already reached Delhi, that the Native soldiers at the

* Place where the arms and accoutrements of Native regiments were kept.

† This name was the origin of the sepoys generally being called Pandies.

latter place had joined the mutineers, and that many officers and residents at both stations had been killed.

Lieutenant-Colonel Davidson, commanding the 16th Irregular Cavalry, who happened to be dining at mess that evening, was the first to recover from the state of consternation into which we were thrown by the reading of this telegram. He told us it was of the utmost importance that the Commissioner and the General should at once be put in possession of this astounding news, and at the same time impressed upon us the imperative necessity for keeping it secret.

Davidson then hurried off to the Commissioner, who with his deputy, Nicholson, lived within a stone's-throw of the mess. Edwardes drove at once to the General's house, while Nicholson came to our mess. He too pointed out to us the importance of preventing the news from getting about and of keeping it as long as possible from the Native soldiers.

We had at Peshawar three regiments of Native Cavalry and five of Native Infantry, not less than 5,000 men, while the strength of the two British regiments and the Artillery did not exceed 2,000. This European force was more than sufficient to cope with the eight Native corps, but in the event of any general disturbance amongst the Native troops, we had to calculate on the probability of their being joined by the 50,000 inhabitants of the city, and, indeed, by the entire population of the Peshawar valley; not to speak of the tribes all along the border, who were sure to rise.

It was an occasion for the gravest anxiety, and the delay of even a few hours in the sepoys becoming aware of the disastrous occurrences at Meerut and Delhi meant a great deal to us.

Fortunately for India, there were good men and true at Peshawar in those days, when hesitation and irresolution would have been fatal, and it is worthy of note that they were comparatively young men—Edwardes was thirty-seven, Nicholson thirty-five; Neville Chamberlain, the distinguished Commandant of the Punjab Frontier Force (who was hastily summoned from Kohat, where he happened to be on his tour of inspection), was thirty-seven; and the Brigadier, Sydney Cotton, though much older, being sixty-five, was not only exceptionally young for his years and full of energy and intelligence, but actually much younger than the average of General officers commanding stations in India.

At once, on hearing of the Mutiny, Edwardes, acting in unison with Nicholson, sent to the post-office and laid hands on all Native correspondence; the letters they thus secured showed but too plainly how necessary was this precaution. The number of seditious papers seized was alarmingly great; they were for the most part couched in figurative and enigmatical language, but it was quite sufficiently clear from them that every Native regiment in the garrison was more or less implicated and prepared to join the rebel movement.

A strong interest attaches to these letters, for they brought to light the true feeling of the Natives towards us at the time, and it was evident from them that the sepoys had really been made to believe that we intended to destroy their caste by various unholy devices, of which the issue of contaminating cartridges was one. The seeds of disaffection had been sown by agitators, who thought they saw an opportunity for realizing their hope of overthrowing our rule, maintained as it was by a mere handful of Europeans in the midst of a vast population of Asiatics. This feeling of antagonism, only guessed at before, was plainly revealed in these letters, never intended to meet the European eye. Some corps did not appear to be quite so guilty as others, but there could now be no doubt that all were tainted with disloyalty, and that none of the Hindustani troops could any longer be trusted.

In the afternoon of Tuesday, the 12th May, I received a note from the General commanding the division directing me to present myself at his house the following morning, which I accordingly did. Besides General Reed I found there the Brigadier, Sydney Cotton; the Commissioner, Herbert Edwardes; the Deputy Commissioner, John Nicholson; Brigadier Neville Chamberlain, and Captain Wright, Deputy Assistant-Adjutant-General, who, like myself, had been summoned to record the decisions that might be arrived at.

This meeting was a most momentous one, and I remember being greatly impressed with the calm and comprehensive view of the situation taken by Edwardes and Nicholson. They had already been in communication with the Chief Commissioner, and had, previous to the meeting, received a telegram from him approving generally of the several proposals they contemplated. John Lawrence also informed them that the authorities at Lahore had decided on disarming the Native troops at Mian Mir that very morning.

The problem to be solved was how the Punjab could best be made secure with the small force of British troops available—all told not more than 15,000, with 84 guns—against upwards of 65,000 Natives of whom 42,000 were Hindustanis), with 62 guns.* In all stations

* At Meerut, Delhi, and Rurki, and in the Punjab there were:

British Troops.

	MEN.	GUNS.
2 Regiments of Cavalry	1,410	
12 Regiments of Infantry	12,624	
9 Troops of Horse Artillery	1,017	54
5 Light Field Batteries	415	30
10 Companies of Foot Artillerymen	837	
Total	16.303	84

Native troops preponderated, and in some there were no European soldiers at all.

Edwardes and Nicholson gave it as their opinion that the only chance of keeping the Punjab and the frontier quiet lay in trusting the Chiefs and people, and in endeavouring to induce them to side with us against the Hindustanis. They undertook to communicate, regarding the raising of levies and fresh troops, with their friends and acquaintances along the border, who had proved such staunch allies in 1848-49, when we were fighting with the Sikhs. How nobly these loyal men responded to the demand made upon them, and how splendidly the frontier and Punjab soldiers whom they brought to our assistance behaved, will be seen hereafter.

Amongst other matters of importance, it was proposed by those two able soldier-civilians, Edwardes and Nicholson, that General Reed, as the senior officer in the Punjab, should join the Chief Commissioner at Rawal Pindi, leaving Brigadier Cotton in command at Peshawar; that a Movable Column, composed of reliable troops, should be organized at some convenient place in the Punjab,* prepared to move in any direction

---

Native Troops.

	MEN.	GUNS.
7 Regiments of Light Cavalry - -	3,514	
14 Regiments of Irregular Cavalry and Guides Cavalry - - -	8,519	
31 Regiments of Regular Infantry - } 15 Regiments of Irregular Infantry and } Guides Infantry - - - }	50,188	
3 Troops of Horse Artillery - -	411 -	18
6 Light Field Batteries - - -	930 -	30 (3 batteries had only 4 guns each)
2 Mountain Batteries - -	192 -	14 (1 battery had 8, the other 6 guns)
3 Companies of Foot Artillery - -	330	
Head-Quarters and 12 Companies of Sappers and Miners - - -	1,394	
Total - -	65,478 -	62

The above figures show the troops at full strength. There were probably not more than 15,000 British soldiers in the Punjab available for duty in May, 1857.

* The original proposal was that the Movable Column should be formed at Jhelum, and composed of the 24th Foot from Rawal Pindi, the 27th Foot from Nowshera, a troop of Horse Artillery from Peshawar, a Native Field Battery from Jhelum, the Guides from Murdan, the 16th Irregular Cavalry from Rawal Pindi, the Kumaon battalion from Murree, the 1st Punjab Infantry from Bannu, and a wing of the 2nd Punjab Cavalry from Kohat. But events developed so rapidly that before the column was formed every one of these troops was otherwise employed. It was thought unwise to unduly weaken the Peshawar valley; the troop of Horse Artillery, therefore, stood fast, the 27th

where its services might be required; that the Hindustani regiments should be scattered as much as possible, in order to prevent dangerous combinations; that a detachment of Punjab Infantry from Kohat should replace the Hindustani sepoys in the fort of Attock, which was a very important position, as it contained a magazine, and covered the passage of the Indus; and that a small guard of Pathan levies, under a tried and trusty frontier Native officer, should be placed in charge of the Attock ferry.

All these proposals were cordially and unanimously agreed to by the military authorities present.

The question of the command of the Movable Column was then discussed. It was considered essential that the officer selected should, in addition to other necessary qualifications, have considerable experience of the country, and an intimate knowledge of Native soldiers. It was no ordinary command. On the action of the Movable Column would depend, to a great extent, the maintenance of peace and order throughout the Punjab, and it was felt that, at such a crisis, the best man must be selected, irrespective of seniority. It was a position for which Cotton and Nicholson would have given much, and for which they were well qualified, but there was important work for them to do at Peshawar. Neville Chamberlain was available, and there was a general consensus of opinion that he should be appointed. It was necessary, however, to refer the matter to the Chief Commissioner, with a request that he would submit it for the orders of the Commander-in-Chief. This course was adopted, and in a few hours a reply was received from General Anson nominating Chamberlain to the command. My anxiety as to the Commander-in-Chief's decision was very considerable; for Brigadier Chamberlain, to my infinite delight and astonishment, had offered, in the event of his being appointed, to take me with him as his staff officer—the most wonderful piece of good fortune that could have come to me; my readers must imagine my feelings, for it is impossible for me to describe them. My most sanguine hopes seemed about to be more than realized; for though the serious aspect of affairs seemed to promise the chance of active service, I little thought that I should be lucky enough to be employed as the staff officer of such a distinguished soldier as Neville Chamberlain.

When the meeting was over I was ordered to take the several messages, which Wright and I had written out, to the telegraph office,

Foot was halted at Attock, and the 24th Foot and Kumaon battalion were kept at their stations ready to move towards the frontier. The Guides, 2nd Punjab Cavalry, and 1st Punjab Infantry were ordered to Delhi, and the 16th Irregular Cavalry and the Native Field Battery were not considered sufficiently loyal to be employed on such a duty. Eventually, the column was formed of one troop of Horse Artillery, one Field Battery, and one Infantry regiment, all British and all from Sialkot.

and see them despatched myself; as they disclosed more or less the measures that had been decided upon, it was necessary to avoid any chance of their falling into the hands of Native clerks. One of the messages* contained a summary of the proceedings of the council, and was addressed to the commanding officers of all stations in the Punjab, with the view of imparting confidence, and letting them know what steps were being taken for the protection of the British residents throughout the province. This duty having been carried out, I returned home in a not unpleasant frame of mind, for though the crisis was a grave one, the outlook gloomy, and the end doubtful, the excitement was great. There were stirring times in store for us, when every man's powers would be tested, and the hopefulness of youth inclined me to look only on the bright side of the situation.

My equanimity was somewhat disturbed later in the day by an occurrence which caused me a good deal of annoyance at the time, though it soon passed away. Nicholson came to my house and told me that the proceedings at the meeting that morning had in some unaccountable manner become known; and he added, much to my disgust, that it was thought I might perhaps have been guilty of the indiscretion of divulging them. I was very angry, for I had appreciated as much as anyone the immense importance of keeping the decisions arrived at perfectly secret; and I could not help showing something of the indignation I felt at its having been thought possible that I could betray the confidence reposed in me. I denied most positively having done so; upon which Nicholson suggested that we should proceed together to the telegraph office and see whether the information could have leaked out from there. The signaller was a mere boy, and Nicholson's imposing presence and austere manner were quite too much for him; he was completely cowed, and, after a few hesitating denials,

* The full text of the message was as follows:

'From General Reed, Peshawar.

'To Sir John Lawrence, Rawal Pindi, the Commander-in-Chief, Simla, and officers commanding all stations in the Punjab respectively; to be forwarded by the assistant in charge of the telegraph office, or post, as the case may be.

'The senior military officer in the Punjab, Major-General Reed, having this morning received news of the disarming of the troops at Mian Mir, a council of war was held, consisting of General Reed, Brigadier Cotton, Brigadier Neville Chamberlain, Colonel Edwardes, and Colonel Nicholson, and the following measures were decided on, subject to the confirmation of the Commander-in-Chief. General Reed assumes the chief military command in the Punjab; his Head-Quarters will be the Head-Quarters of the Punjab Civil Government, and a Movable Column will be formed at Jhelum at once, consisting of [the troops were here detailed]. The necessary orders for this column have been issued. The column will move on every point in the Punjab where open mutiny requires to be put down by force, and officers commanding at all stations in the Punjab will co-operate with the column.'

he admitted having satisfied the curiosity of a friend who had inquired of him how the authorities intended to deal with the crisis. This was enough, and I was cleared. The result to me of this unpleasant incident was a delightful increase of intimacy with the man for whom above all others I had the greatest admiration and most profound respect. As if to make up for his momentary injustice, Nicholson was kinder to me than ever, and I felt I had gained in him a firm and constant friend. So ended that eventful day.

At that time it was the custom for a staff officer, who had charge of any Government property, to have a guard of Native soldiers in charge of his house. That night it happened that my guard was furnished by the 64th Native Infantry, a regiment with a particularly bad reputation, and which had, in order to give effect to the measures proposed at the morning's meeting, been ordered to leave Peshawar and proceed to the outposts. The intercepted letters showed that this regiment was on the point of mutinying, and I could not help feeling, as I lay down on my bed, which, as usual in the hot weather, was placed in the verandah for the sake of coolness, how completely I was at the mercy of the sentry who walked up and down within a few feet of me. Fortunately, he was not aware that his regiment was suspected, and could not know the reason for the sudden order to march, or my career might have been ended then and there.

Within a week from that time I had started for Rawal Pindi to be ready to join the Movable Column, which was to be formed at Wazirabad as soon as the troops could be got together. I took with me only just enough kit for a hot-weather march, and left everything standing in my house just as it was, little thinking that I should never return to it or be quartered in Peshawar again.

CHAPTER VII.

BEFORE proceeding with the account of my experiences with the Movable Column, and the subsequent operations for the suppression of the rebellion, in which I was fortunate enough to take part, it will, I think, be advisable, for the better understanding of the whole situation, to devote a little time to the consideration of the progress of events from the first appearance of symptoms of disaffection in Lower Bengal, to the crisis I have just been describing, when Peshawar became involved in the general disturbance.

The substitution of a new rifle for the old musket with which the sepoys had hitherto been armed entailed a different kind of drill; and in order that this drill should be speedily learned by the whole Native army, depots were formed at convenient places for the instruction of selected men from every corps, who, on becoming proficient, were to return and instruct their own regiments. One of these depots was at Dum-Dum, and as early as the 24th January General Hearsay, commanding the Presidency division, reported to Head-Quarters that he perceived an 'unpleasant feeling' amongst the Native soldiers learning the new drill, caused by a belief instilled into them 'by designing persons, most likely Brahmins,' that they were to be forced to embrace Christianity, and that for the furtherance of this object the new ball-cartridges received from the arsenal at Fort William were greased with the fat of pigs and cows, with the intention of violating the religious prejudices and destroying the caste of those who would have to bite them.

A little later various acts of incendiarism took place at other stations in the command, and Hearsay became more than ever convinced that there was grave dissatisfaction amongst the troops. He therefore ordered a Court of Inquiry to be held to enable him to ascertain the real cause of the ill-feeling which so evidently existed.

In the General's opinion, the statements recorded in the proceedings of this Court clearly established the fact, that the Native officers and sepoys were undoubtedly imbued with the belief that an unholy mixture of cow's fat and lard had been used in the manufacture of the new cartridge, and he recommended that the rifle ammunition should in future be made up with the same description of paper that had always been used for the musket-cartridge, which, he conceived, would put an end to their suspicions and uneasiness.

The General, however, was told in reply that it was impossible to use the old paper for the new cartridge, as the bore of the rifle being much smaller than that of the musket, thinner paper was indispensable; and he was directed to inform the sepoys that the new paper, though tougher and less bulky, was made of exactly the same material as the old. With respect to the lubricating mixture, he was to announce that the Government had authorized the preparation of a grease, composed of wax and oil, which was to be made up and applied to the cartridges by the men themselves. These orders were carefully explained to the Native troops, but without any good result. Their religious objection to the new cartridge was not removed, and they frankly acknowledged their fears.

On the 6th February an officer of the 34th Native Infantry at Barrackpore was informed by a sepoy of his company that the four Native regiments at that station, fearing that they would be forced to destroy their caste and become Christians, had determined to rise against their officers, and when they had plundered and burned their bungalows, to proceed to Calcutta and try to seize Fort William, or, if that proved beyond their powers, to take possession of the treasury.

This circumstance was reported to Government by General Hearsay on the 11th February. In the same letter he said, 'We have at Barrackpore been living upon a mine ready for explosion,' and he reported a story which had reached him from Dum-Dum of a sepoy, on his way to cook his food with his *lota** full of water, meeting a low-caste man belonging to the arsenal where the Enfield cartridges were being manufactured. This man, it was said, asked the sepoy to allow him to drink from his *lota*. The sepoy, a Brahmin, refused, saying: 'I have scoured my *lota*; you will defile it by your touch.' The low-caste man replied: 'You think much of your caste, but wait a little: the *Sahib-logue*† will make you bite cartridges soaked in cow's fat, and then where will your caste be?' The sepoy no doubt believed the man, and told his comrades what was about to happen, and the report rapidly spread to other stations.

Early in March several of the Hindu sepoys belonging to the Dum-Dum School of Musketry expressed their unwillingness to bite the new cartridge, and the Commandant proposed that the drill should be altered so as to admit of the cartridge being torn instead of bitten. Hearsay supported the proposal, remarking that the new mode of loading need not be made to appear as a concession to agitation, but as part of the drill for the new weapon. Events, however, moved so quickly that, before sanction could be received to this suggestion, the troops at Berhampur had broken into open mutiny. They refused to receive their ammunition, on the ground of its being polluted, even after it was explained to them that they were not being given the new cartridges, but those which had been made up in the regiment a year before. That night they broke open the bells-of-arms, and carried off their muskets.

The Government then became aware that prompt action was necessary. They decided that such open mutiny could not be excused on the grounds of religious scruples, and ordered the regiment to be disbanded. As Berhampur was somewhat isolated, and some distance from European troops, it was arranged that the disbandment should take place at the Head-Quarters of the Presidency division, and the 19th Native Infantry was accordingly ordered to march to Barrackpore.

The revolt of this regiment brought forcibly before Lord Canning and his advisers the perilous position of Lower Bengal, owing to the paucity of European troops. Well may the authorities have been startled, for between Calcutta and Meerut, a distance of 900 miles, there were only four regiments of British infantry and a few scattered Artillerymen, numbering in all less than 5,000, while the Native troops amounted to upwards of 55,000. One of the four Infantry regiments was at Fort

* A metal drinking vessel, which the Hindu religiously guards against defilement, and to which he clings as a cherished possession when he has nothing else belonging to him in the world.

† European officers.

William; but as only a portion of it could be spared for the disbandment of the 19th, a special steamer was despatched to Rangoon to bring over the 84th Foot. This regiment reached Calcutta on the 20th March, and on the 31st the disbandment of the mutinous Native Infantry regiment was carried out. The men were paid up and escorted across th river Hughly, whence they were allowed to proceed to their homes. They behaved in the most orderly manner on the march from Berhampur and throughout the proceedings, and as they left the parade-ground they cheered General Hearsay, and wished him a long life, apparently well pleased at being let off so easily.

At Barrackpore itself an outbreak had occurred two days before in the 34th Native Infantry. As I have already related, the sepoy, Mangal Pandy, shot at the sergeant-major.* The Adjutant, on hearing what had happened, galloped to the parade-ground. As he neared the quarter-guard he was fired at, and his horse shot by the mutineer, who then badly wounded him with a sword as he was trying to disentangle himself from the fallen animal. The General now appeared on the scene, and, instantly grasping the position of affairs, rode straight at Mangal Pandy, who stood at bay with his musket loaded, ready to receive him. There was a shot, the whistle of a bullet, and a man fell to the ground—but not the General; it was the fanatic sepoy himself, who at the last moment had discharged the contents of his musket into his own breast! The wretched man had been worked up to a pitch of madness by the sepoys of his regiment, who stood by while he attacked the Adjutant, and would have allowed him to kill their Commander, but they were too great cowards to back him up openly. Mangal Pandy was not dead. He was taken to the hospital, and eventually was tried by a Court-Martial composed of Native officers, sentenced to death, and hanged in the presence of all the troops at Barrackpore. The Native officer in command of the quarter-guard met the same fate, and the regiment was then disbanded.

The orders for the disbandment of the 19th and 34th Native Infantry were directed to be read to every Native corps in the service, and it was hoped that the quick retribution which had overtaken these regiments would check the spirit of mutiny throughout the army. For a time this hope appeared to be justified. Satisfactory reports were received from different parts of Bengal, and anything like a serious or general outbreak was certainly not contemplated by the authorities. General Hearsay reported to Government that he had directed the European troops, temporarily located at Barrackpore, to return to their respective cantonments, as he did not think it probable that he would require their presence again. About the same time Sir John Lawrence, after visiting the Musketry School at Sialkot, wrote hopefully to the

* Each Hindustani regiment had a European sergeant-major and quarter-master-sergeant.

Governor-General of the aspect of affairs in the Punjab. Lord Canning and his advisers, owing to these favourable reports, were on the point of sending the 84th Foot back to Burma, when news reached them from Upper India of the calamitous occurrences at Meerut and Delhi.

The Meerut division was commanded by Major-General Hewitt, an officer of fifty years' service, and the station of Meerut by Brigadier Archdale Wilson, Commandant of the Bengal Artillery. The garrison consisted of the 6th Dragoon Guards, a troop of Horse Artillery, a battery of Field Artillery, a company of Foot Artillery, the 1st Battalion 60th Rifles, and three Native corps—the 3rd Light Cavalry, and the 11th and 20th Native Infantry.

Towards the end of April incendiary fires began to take place, and the Native soldiers evinced more or less disrespect in their manner towards their officers. These signs of disaffection were followed by the refusal of some of the troopers of the 3rd Light Cavalry to receive their cartridges, although the commanding officer carefully explained to them that they were not the new cartridges, but the very same they had always used, and that according to the new drill they were not required to bite them when loading their carbines.

A Court of Inquiry was held to investigate the matter, composed entirely of Native officers, three of whom belonged to the offending regiment. The verdict of the Court was that no adequate cause could be assigned for the disobedience of orders in refusing to receive and use the cartridges that were served out. 'The only conclusion the Court can arrive at in regard to this point is that a report seems to have got abroad which in some vague form attaches suspicion of impurity to the materials used for making these cartridges, but the Court are unanimously of opinion that there is nothing whatever objectionable in the cartridges of the 3rd Regiment Light Cavalry, and that they may be freely received and used as heretofore without in the slightest degree affecting any religious scruple of either a Hindu or Mussulman, and if any pretence contrary to that is urged, that it must be false.' This opinion, it must be remembered, was the opinion of Natives, not Europeans, and was given only sixteen days before the outbreak occurred at Meerut.

After carefully reviewing the evidence brought before the Court, and considering the opinion expressed by the Native officers who composed it, the Commander in Chief decided to try the eighty-five men who had refused to receive the cartridges by a General Court-Martial composed entirely of their own countrymen. The Court was formed of six Mahomedans and nine Hindus, six Native officers being brought over from Delhi for the purpose.

The prisoners were tried on the 8th May, found guilty, and sentenced to imprisonment with hard labour for ten years.

The following morning there was a parade of the whole of the Meerut garrison, and the finding and sentence of the Court were read to the men. The eighty-five troopers were then stripped of their uniform and fetters were fastened on their ankles. As each culprit was marched forward, he called on his comrades to rescue him, but no response came from the ranks; and when the ceremony was finished the prisoners were marched down the line and escorted to the gaol. In his report of the parade to Army Head-Quarters, General Hewitt stated that 'the majority of the prisoners seemed to feel acutely the degradation to which their folly and insubordination had brought them. The remainder of the troops are behaving steady and soldier-like.'

The action of the Meerut authorities in putting the prisoners in irons on the parade-ground, in the presence of their regiment, before being made over to the civil power, met with the disapproval of the Commander-in-Chief and the Governor-General. The former expressed his regret at the unusual procedure. The latter was more pronounced, and thus expressed himself: 'The riveting of the men's fetters on parade, occupying, as it did, several hours, in the presence of many who were already ill-disposed and many who believed in the cartridge fable, must have stung the brigade to the quick. The consigning the eighty-five prisoners after such a ceremony to gaol with no other than a Native guard over them was folly that is inconceivable.'

The procedure was no doubt unusual, and it certainly was most imprudent, under the circumstances, to trust the gaol to a Native guard. I think also, considering the number of the prisoners, and the length of time necessary for riveting the fetters, that it was not judicious to subject the troops to such a severe and protracted trial of their nerves and patience; but, before acquiescing in Lord Canning's sweeping condemnation, it should be considered that the object of the punishment was to produce a deterrent effect on those who were likely to follow the bad example that had been set them, and as the offence of the troopers had been public and ostentatious, General Hewitt no doubt thought it right to make the punishment as marked and public as possible.

The next day was Sunday, and outwardly the cantonment of Meerut had assumed its usual appearance of Sabbath calm; but there was an undercurrent of unrest—there was considerable commotion in the Native bazaars, which were unusually crowded, and had not the European officers been blinded by over-confidence in their men, signs might have been perceived amongst the Native soldiers of preparation for some untoward event.

It was late in the day before the storm burst. The Chaplain of Meerut tells us that he was about to start with his wife for evening service, when the Native nurse warned them of coming danger, beseeching her mistress to remain indoors, and, on being asked to explain, saying there would be a fight with the sepoys. The idea seemed incredible, and the Chaplain would have paid no attention to the warning had not his wife been greatly alarmed. At her earnest request he took his two children with them in the carriage, instead of leaving them in the house with the *ayah*, as had been intended. It was soon apparent that the *ayah* had not spoken without reason, for before the church was reached sounds of musketry were heard and columns of smoke were seen rising above the quarter occupied by the Native troops. As the Chaplain arrived at the church enclosure, the buglers of the 60th Rifles, who were drawn up ready to enter the church, sounded the 'alarm' and the 'assembly.' The parade was dismissed, and as the British soldiers rushed to the barracks for their arms and ammunition, the congregation rapidly dispersed, some to their homes, others to seek safety in the nearest quarter-guard.

It was the custom before the Mutiny for our soldiers to attend Divine Service unarmed, save with their side-arms. The Native soldiers were aware of this, and they no doubt calculated on the 60th Rifles being safe and almost defenceless inside the church as soon as the bells ceased tolling. What they were not aware of was the fact that, owing to the lengthening days and the increasing heat, the evening church parade had been ordered half an hour later than on the previous Sunday. The mutineers therefore showed their hand half an hour too soon, and as they galloped down the 60th Rifles lines they came upon the men fully armed and rapidly falling in. Being thus disappointed in their hope of surprising the white soldiers, the 3rd Cavalry proceeded without a moment's delay to the gaol, broke into the cells, and released their eighty-five comrades and all the other prisoners, about 1,200 in number.

While this was going on, the two Native Infantry regiments assembled on their respective parade-grounds in wild excitement, discharging their muskets at random, and setting fire to their own huts. The British officers, hearing the tumult, hastened to their lines and did their best to restore order, but in vain. The sepoys had gone too far, and were absolutely deaf to threats and entreaties. They did not attack their own officers, but warned them to get away, telling them the Company's '*raj*'* was at an end. Their clemency, however, did not extend to officers of other regiments.

Colonel Finnis, who had served forty years with the sepoys, and firmly believed in their loyalty, was the first victim; he fell riddled with bullets from a volley fired by the 20th, while exhorting the men of his own regiment (the 11th) to be true to their salt. The work of destruction then began in earnest, in which the population from the bazaars and the neighbouring villages eagerly joined, for (as the Commissioner reported) they were armed and ready for the onslaught before the sepoys commenced the attack, plainly showing how perfectly they were aware of what was about to happen. They poured forth in thousands from every direction, and in a surprisingly short time almost

* Rule.

every bungalow belonging to a British officer serving with Native troops was gutted and burnt. Besides Colonel Finnis, seven officers, three officers' wives, two children, and every stray European man, woman and child in the outskirts of the cantonments were massacred.

It was now time for the sepoys to think of themselves. They had thrown off all allegiance to the *Sarkar;** they had been guilty of murder, robbery, and incendiarism, and they knew that retribution must speedily overtake them if they remained at Meerut; they therefore lost no time in making their escape towards Delhi. They had had ample opportunity for consultation with the Native officers from that station, who had come to Meerut as members of the Court-Martial on the men of the 3rd Light Cavalry, and they knew perfectly well that the troops at Delhi were prepared to help them to seize the magazine and resuscitate the old Moghul dynasty. 'To Delhi! To Delhi!' was their cry, and off they went, leaving naught behind them in their lines but the smouldering fires of their officers' houses and the lifeless bodies of their English victims.

But it will be asked, Where were the British troops? Where indeed? On the alarm being given, the British troops got under arms 'in an incredibly short time,' but there was unaccountable delay in marching them to the spot where their help was so greatly needed. The Carabineers occupied barracks within a few hundred yards of the Native Infantry lines, the 60th Rifles were only about a mile and a half away, and the Artillery lay just beyond the 60th. The Brigadier (Wilson) despatched one company of the Rifles to guard the treasury, another he left to protect the barracks, and with the remainder, accompanied by the Carabineers and Artillery, he leisurely proceeded towards the Native Infantry lines. It was almost dark when he arrived, but there was light enough to discern, from the ruined houses and the dead bodies of the murdered officers lying about, in what a merciless spirit the revolt had been perpetrated. A few shots were fired from behind the burning huts, but not a single living being was visible, except two or three Native troopers who were dimly perceptible in the distance coming from the direction of the gaol, and it was evident that the sepoys as a body had vanished. But whither? A lengthened discussion took place as to what was the best course to pursue, which only resulted in the troops being marched back to their own end of the cantonment and bivouacking on the mall for the night. The General and Brigadier, misled by the tumult in the city, which they could distinctly hear, came to the conclusion that the sepoys had congregated within its walls and might shortly be expected to attack that part of the station where the European residents chiefly lived. It was not discovered till the next morning that all three Native regiments had made for Delhi.

* British Government.

It is easy to be wise after the event, but one cannot but feel that there was unaccountable, if not culpable, want of energy displayed by the Meerut authorities on this disastrous occasion. The officer in command was afterwards severely censured for not acting with sufficient promptitude on first hearing of the outbreak; for not trying to find out where the mutineers had gone; and for not endeavouring to overtake them before they reached Delhi. The Government of India finally signified their disapproval by removing General Hewitt from his command.

Wilson, the Brigadier, like everyone else at Meerut, appears to have been completely taken by surprise. But why this should have been the case, after the warning that had been given by the mutinous conduct of the 3rd Cavalry, and why no steps should have been taken after the exasperating parade on the 9th to guard against a possible, if not probable, outbreak, is difficult to understand; and can only be accounted for by that blind faith in the Native soldier, and disbelief in his intention or ability to revolt, which led to such unfortunate results all over India.

The following story will exemplify how completely the authorities at Meerut were blinded by this misplaced confidence. On the afternoon of the 9th the British officers of the 3rd Light Cavalry went to the gaol to pay up the prisoners belonging to their regiment. When Lieutenant Hugh Gough,* who was one of these officers, returned to his house, a Hindu Native officer, belonging to the troop Gough was temporarily commanding, told him that the men had determined to rescue their comrades, and that the Native guard over the gaol had promised to help them. Gough went at once to his commanding officer, Lieutenant-Colonel Carmichael Smyth, and reported what he had heard, but the Colonel pooh-poohed the idea as ridiculous, and told Gough he must not give credence to anything so monstrous.

Later in the day Gough met Brigadier Wilson and told him of the warning which had been given to him, without, however, producing any impression; the information was received with the same contemptuous disbelief displayed by Colonel Carmichael Smyth.

The following day (Sunday), late in the afternoon, the same Native officer, attended by two troopers, galloped to Gough's house, shouting to him that the *halat*† had begun, and that the Native Infantry were firing on their officers. Gough mounted his horse, and, accompanied by the three Cavalry soldiers, proceeded as quickly as possible to the Infantry parade-ground, where he arrived just as the wild scene of excitement and confusion I have before described was at its height. The sepoys, some in uniform, some in their own Native clothes, were rushing about in the maddest disorder, yelling, shouting, and dancing

* Now Lieutenant-General Sir Hugh Gough, V.C., G.C.B.

† Tumult.

as if possessed, while the flames from the burning huts shed a lurid light on the demoniacal proceedings.

When Gough's party appeared in sight, the sepoys called to the three troopers to get out of the way, as they wanted to shoot the *sahib*. No notice being taken of this warning, they fired straight at the whole party, but without hitting anyone. Gough, seeing things had gone too far for him to do any good, rode off with his little escort to his own lines, where he found the men busy saddling their horses, and helping themselves to ammunition from the regimental magazine, which they had broken open. He endeavoured in vain to allay the excitement; one or two shots were fired at him by recruits, but no determined attempt was made to take his life, and at last the Native officers combined to force him away, saying they could no longer answer for his safety.

It was then all but dark. Gough rode off towards the European lines, still accompanied by his trusty Native escort, and on his way came upon an enormous crowd of people from the bazaar, armed with swords, sticks, and anything they could get hold of, who tried to stop him. Through these he charged, closely followed by the Native officer and two troopers, who did not leave him until he was within sight of the Artillery mess. Then they pulled up, and said they could go no further. Gough did all he could to persuade them to remain with him, but to no purpose. They told him it was impossible for them to separate themselves from their friends and relations, and making the officer they had so carefully protected a respectful salaam, they rode off to join their mutinous comrades. Gough never heard of them again, though he tried hard to trace what had become of the men who proved themselves such 'friends in need.'

However much the authorities at Meerut deserved to be censured for their dilatoriness in dealing with the revolt in the first instance, and their lack of energy in not trying to discover in what direction the mutineers had gone, I doubt whether anything would have been gained by following them up, or whether it would have been possible to overtake them before they reached Delhi. Only a very few European Cavalry were available for pursuit, for the Carabineers, having lately arrived in India, were composed mainly of recruits still in the riding-school, and their horses for the most part were quite unbroken. These few, with the six Horse Artillery guns, might have been despatched; but the mutineers had a considerable start, the Cavalry could not have been overtaken, and as soon as the Infantry became aware that they were being followed, they would have scattered themselves over the country, the features of which were familiar to them, and, favoured by the darkness, could have defied pursuit. Delhi is forty miles from Meerut, and it would not have been possible for the 60th Rifles, marching in the terrible heat of the month of May, to have reached that place before the next evening (the 11th), and, as was afterwards ascertained, the work of murder and devastation there began on the morning of that day. The three Native Infantry regiments and the battery of Artillery stationed at Delhi were prepared to join the insurgent troopers from Meerut directly they arrived. The magazine, with its vast stores of war material, was in the hands of the King, and the 150,000 inhabitants of the city were ready to assist in the massacre of the white men and women, and the destruction of their property.

After careful consideration of all the circumstances of the revolt at Meerut, I have come to the conclusion that it would have been futile to have sent the small body of mounted troops available in pursuit of the mutineers on the night of the 10th May, and that, considering the state of feeling throughout the Native Army, no action, however prompt, on the part of the Meerut authorities could have arrested the Mutiny. The sepoys had determined to throw off their allegiance to the British Government, and the when and the how were merely questions of time and opportunity.

CHAPTER VIII.

While the events I have recounted were taking place, the Commander-in-Chief and the Head-Quarters staff were on their way up country inspecting the troops at the various stations *en route* to Simla, at which place it had been arranged that the summer of 1857 was to be spent. The Commander-in-Chief in India at that time was General the Hon. George Anson, an officer of forty-three years' service, but without much Indian experience, having been only four years in the country. He was an able, intelligent man, an excellent judge of character, a great authority on whist and on horses, and he was well known in London society, which was somewhat surprised when he accepted an appointment in India—the command of the Meerut division. He did not, however, remain long in that position, for he was soon given the command of the Madras Army, and a year and a half later became Commander-in Chief in India. General Anson was present at Waterloo as an Ensign, but had seen no service afterwards, and until he arrived in India had held no high appointment.

When the Commander-in Chief left Calcutta the previous autumn, all was apparently quiet in the Native army. He visited the principal military stations, amongst others Meerut and Delhi, and although reports of an uneasy feeling amongst the Native troops in the Presidency division had reached him from time to time, it was not until he arrived at Umballa, about the middle of March, that these reports were confirmed by personal communication with the sepoys attending the School of Musketry which had been formed at that station.

On the occasion of the Commander-in-Chief's inspection of the School, he learnt from the men of the various regiments under instruction how strongly opposed they were to using a cartridge which they believed to be injurious to their caste. Anson listened attentively to all the sepoys had to say, and then explained to them in a manly, sensible speech, that the old cartridge was not suited to the rifle about to be introduced. A new cartridge had, therefore, to be made; but they must not listen to any foolish rumour as to its being designed to destroy their caste. He assured them, 'on the honour of a soldier like themselves,' that it had never been, and never could be, the policy of the British Government to coerce the religious feeling of either the military or the civil population of India, or to interfere in any way with their caste or customs. He told the Native officers to do all in their power to allay the men's unfounded fears, and called upon them to prove themselves worthy of the high character they had hitherto maintained; he concluded by warning all ranks that the Government were determined not to yield to insubordination, which would be visited with the severest punishment.

The demeanour of the sepoys was most respectful, and when the parade was over they expressed their high sense of the Commander-in-Chief's goodness. They declared that he had removed their own objections, but that the story was universally believed by their countrymen and relations, and if they were to use the cartridge they must become social outcasts.

General Anson, feeling that the doubts and anxieties of the men with regard to the use of the new cartridges were by no means imaginary, suspended their issue until a special report had been prepared as to the composition of the paper in which they were wrapped.*

* 'I am not so much surprised,' wrote General Anson to Lord Canning on the 23rd March, 'at their objections to the cartridges, having seen them. I had no idea they contained, or, rather, are smeared with, such a quantity of grease, which looks exactly like fat. After ramming down the ball, the muzzle of the musket is covered with it. This, however, will, I imagine, not be the case with those prepared according to the late instructions. But there are now misgivings about the paper, and I think it so desirable that they should be assured that no animal grease is used in its manufacture, that I have ordered a special report to be made to me on that head from Meerut, and until I receive an answer, and am satisfied that no objectionable material is used, no firing at the depots by the sepoys will take place. It would be easy to dismiss the detachments to their regiments without any practice, on the ground that the hot weather is so advanced, and that very little progress could be made, but I do not think that would be admissible. The question, having been raised, must be settled. It would only be deferred till another year, and I trust that the measures taken by the Government when the objection was first made, and the example of the punishment of the 19th Native Infantry and of the other delinquents of the 70th, now being tried by a General Court-Martial, will have the effect we desire.'—KAYE, vol. i., p. 558.

Having thus done all that he could at the time to allay any feeling of uneasiness, and hoping that the news of the disbandment of the 19th Native Infantry would check the spirit of insubordination, General Anson continued his journey to Simla, that beautiful place in the Himalayas, 7,000 feet above the sea, which has since become the seat of the Government of India and Army Head-Quarters during the hot weather months.

The Commander-in-Chief had been at Simla rather more than a month, when, on the afternoon of Tuesday, the 12th May, an Aide-de-camp galloped in from Umballa (the Head-Quarters station of the Sirhind division), distant eighty miles, bringing with him a copy of the telegraphic message which had been despatched from Delhi the previous day to 'all stations in the Punjab,' and which had caused such consternation at Peshawar on the evening of the 11th May.

Sir Henry Barnard, commanding the Sirhind division, desired the Aide-de-camp (his own son) to inform the Commander-in-Chief that the temper of the three Native regiments at Umballa was more than doubtful, and that it seemed advisable that the three regiments of British Infantry stationed in the hills near Simla should be ordered at once to Umballa. So urgent did this seem to Barnard, that, in anticipation of sanction from the Commander-in-Chief, he told his son to warn the 75th Foot as he passed through Kasauli to be prepared for an immediate move.

General Anson at once saw the necessity for taking prompt action. That same afternoon he despatched an Aide de-camp to Kasauli to order the 75th to proceed without delay to Umballa, and the 1st Bengal Fusiliers at Dagshai to follow the 75th as soon as carriage could be collected; also to warn the 2nd Bengal Fusiliers at Subathu to be ready to move. Expresses were sent at the same to Ferozepore and Jullundur directing that a European guard should be placed in charge of the magazine at the former place, and a detachment of European Infantry thrown into the fort of Philour from the latter. The confidence reposed in the Native army before the Mutiny was so great that these two important magazines, like almost all the arsenals and magazines in India, were guarded by Native soldiers, and subsequent events proved that, but for General Anson's timely precautions, the mutineers must have obtained possession of the magazines at Ferozepore and Philour.*

* Surely those whom God has a mind to destroy, He first deprives of their senses; for not only were the magazines at Delhi and Cawnpore allowed to fall into the enemy's hands, but the great arsenal at Allahabad narrowly escaped the same fate. Up till May, 1857, this fort was garrisoned only by Native soldiers. Early in that month sixty worn-out European pensioners were brought to Allahabad from Chunar, with whose assistance, and that of a few hastily raised Volunteers, Lieutenants Russell and Tod Brown of the

Anson had not long to wait before he received confirmation of the alarming news brought by General Barnard's son. The very next afternoon a letter arrived from Meerut giving an account of the outbreak on the 10th, and a few particulars of what had occurred at Delhi. The Commander-in-Chief immediately decided on proceeding to Umballa, to superintend personally the organization of the force which, as he rightly judged, would have to be sent to Delhi. There was no hesitation on General Anson's part, or delay in issuing the necessary orders.* The 2nd Bengal Fusiliers were directed to march to Umballa, and an Artillery officer was sent express to Philour with instructions for a third-class siege-train to be got ready, and for reserve Artillery and Infantry ammunition to be despatched to Umballa. Orders were also issued for the Nasiri battalion, stationed at Jutog, near Simla, and for the company of Native Artillery at Kangra and Nurpur† to march with all expedition to Philour, for the purpose of accompanying the siege-train; and for the Sirmur battalion of Gurkhas Dehra Dun, and the Sappers and Miners at Rurki, to proceed to Meerut.

Having thus pressed forward the measures for the suppression of the revolt which to him seemed most urgent, General Anson left Simla early on the 14th May, within forty-eight hours of the receipt of the first news of the outbreak, and reached Umballa the following morning. His last act at Simla was to draft a circular which he hoped would have the effect of allaying excitement in the Native army.

The report which Sir Henry Barnard had to make to the Chief on his arrival at Umballa was not reassuring. The troops at that station consisted of Her Majesty's 9th Lancers, two troops of Horse Artillery, the 4th Bengal Light Cavalry, and two regiments of Native Infantry. The 75th Foot and 1st Bengal Fusiliers had just marched in with only thirty and seventy rounds of ammunition per man, respectively, and (from want of carriage) without tents or baggage. The Commissariat and Medical Departments were totally unprepared to meet the requirements of a force suddenly ordered to take the field; there were no doolies for the sick; supplies were difficult to collect, for the bazaars

---

Bengal Artillery, were able to overawe and disarm the Native guard on the very night on which the regiments to which they belonged mutinied in the adjoining cantonment. These two gallant officers had taken the precaution to fill the cellars below the armoury (which contained some 50,000 or 60,000 stands of arms) with barrels of powder, their intention being to blow up the whole place in the event of the sepoys getting the upper hand. This determination was known to all in the fort, and no doubt had something to say to the guard submitting to be disarmed.

* He has been accused of dilatoriness and want of decision after hearing the news.

† Places at the foot of the Himalayas.

were partially deserted; there was a scarcity of contractors, and no ammunition was available nearer than Philour, eighty miles off.

At Delhi all the Europeans who had not escaped had been massacred, and the city had been taken possession of by the Native garrison and the mutinous troops from Meerut in the name of the old King.

At Meerut the European troops were entrenching themselves; the surrounding district was in the most complete disorder, and the civil courts powerless.

At Umballa and Jullundur, although the presence of European troops had hitherto kept the Native regiments from open mutiny, it was evident that they were not in the least to be depended upon.

At Ferozepore an aggravated revolt had occurred, and at Lahore it had been found necessary to disarm all the Native troops.

From below Meerut there was no intelligence whatever, but it seemed more than probable that the spirit of rebellion had broken out in many stations, and later this was known to be the case.

To add to the Commander-in-Chief's anxieties, it was reported that the Nasiri battalion at Jutog had got out of hand for a time and refused to march to Philour, while a detachment of the same corps at Kasauli plundered the treasury, rendering it necessary to send back 100 men of the 75th Foot to reinforce the depot at that place, where a large number of European soldiers' families were collected.

The behaviour of the Gurkhas gave rise to a panic at Simla, which, however, did not last long. Lord William Hay,* who was Deputy-Commissioner at the time, induced most of the ladies, with their children, to seek a temporary asylum with the Raja of Kiunthal.† Hay himself managed to keep Simla quiet, and the men of the Nasiri battalion coming to their senses, order was restored throughout the hills. The money taken from the Kasauli treasury was nearly all voluntarily given up, and before the year was out the battalion did us good service.

It was a long list of troubles that was placed before the Commander-in-Chief. Disturbing as they all were, each requiring prompt and special action, there was one amongst them which stood out in bold relief—the situation at Delhi; and to wrest that stronghold from the hands of the mutineers was, General Anson conceived, his most pressing obligation. But could it be done with the means at his disposal? He thought not; and in this opinion he was supported by the senior officers at Umballa, with whom the question was anxiously discussed at a conference held at Sir Henry Barnard's house on the 16th May.‡ It

* Now the Marquis of Tweeddale.

† A small hill state near Simla.

‡ It is a remarkable fact that the five senior officers at this conference were all dead in less than seven weeks. General Anson, Brigadier Hallifax, commanding the Umballa station, and Colonel Mowatt, commanding the Artillery.

was nevertheless determined to push on to Delhi, and General Hewitt was asked what force he could spare from Meerut to co-operate with the Umballa column. He was warned that time was an object, and that the 23rd May was the date on which his troops would probably be required to start. All details were carefully considered. The first difficulty to be overcome was the want of carriage. No organized system of transport—one of the most essential requirements of an efficient army—existed, and, owing to the restlessness and uncertainty which prevailed throughout the country, the civil authorities were unable to collect carts and camels with the usual rapidity.*

That afternoon General Anson received a letter from Sir John Lawrence urging the importance of an immediate advance on Delhi, and giving an outline of the measures he proposed to adopt in the Punjab. He asked the Commander-in-Chief to give a general sanction to the arrangements, and concluded with these words: "I consider this to be the greatest crisis which has ever occurred in India. Our European force is so small that, unless effectively handled in the outset, and brought to bear, it will prove unequal to the emergency. But with vigour and promptitude, under the blessing of God, it will prove irresistible.'

Anson naturally hesitated to advance with an inefficient and only partially equipped force against a strongly-fortified city with an immense armed population, defended by many thousand desperate mutineers, and in his reply (dated the 17th May) he put the case plainly before Sir John Lawrence. He pointed out that the Europeans were without tents; that there were no guns at Umballa or Meerut heavier than six or nine pounders with which to batter down the walls of Delhi; that the required amount of carriage could not be provided in less than sixteen or twenty days; and that the three Native corps at Umballa could not be depended upon. He asked Sir John whether he considered 'it would be prudent to risk the small European force we have here in an enterprise against Delhi,' and he wrote: 'My own view of the state of things now is, by carefully collecting our resources, having got rid of the bad materials which we cannot trust, and having supplied their places with others of a better sort, it would not be very long before we could proceed, without a chance of failure, in whatever direction we might please.' Adding, 'this is now the opinion of all here whom I have consulted — the Major-General and Brigadier, the Adjutant-General, Quartermaster-General and Commissary-General.' Anson concluded his letter with the following words: 'It would give me

---

died within ten days; Colonel Chester, Adjutant-General of the Army, was killed at Badli-ki-Serai on the 8th June, and Sir Henry Barnard died at Delhi on the 5th July.

* See Kaye's 'History of the Indian Mutiny,' vol. ii., p. 120.

great satisfaction to have your views upon the present crisis, for I would trust to them more than to my experience.'

John Lawrence, who was straining every nerve to check the Mutiny and prevent a general rising of the population, was impatient at the idea of delay, and lost no time in giving Anson his opinion. He telegraphed it briefly on the 20th, and the following day he wrote to the effect that he knew Delhi well, having been stationed there for nearly thirteen years, and it seemed incredible to him that mutineers could hold and defend it; his belief was 'that, with good management on the part of the civil officers, it would open its gates on the approach of our troops.' He admitted that 'on military principles, in the present state of affairs, it may not be expedient to advance on Delhi until the Meerut force is prepared to act.' But he protested against European soldiers being 'cooped up in their cantonments, tamely awaiting the progress of events.' He went on to say: 'Pray only reflect on the whole history of India. Where have we failed when we acted vigorously? Where have we succeeded when guided by timid counsels? Clive with 1,200 men fought at Plassy, in opposition to the advice of his leading officers, beat 40,000 men, and conquered Bengal.'

That Sir John Lawrence greatly under-estimated the difficulties which Anson had to overcome we now know. Delhi did not open its gates on our approach, but for more than three months defied all our efforts to capture it. And in his eagerness to get the Commander-in-Chief to think as he did, the resolute Chief Commissioner forgot that Clive—not with 1,200 men, but with 3,000 disciplined troops—had to deal in the open field with an enemy little better than a rabble; whereas Anson had to attack a strong fortress, amply supplied with stores and ammunition, possessing a powerful armament, and held by soldiers who were not only well trained and equipped, but were fighting for their lives, and animated by religious fanaticism.

Still, there can be no doubt that John Lawrence's views as to the necessity for Delhi being taken at all hazards were correct. The Governor-General held the same opinion, and strongly urged it upon Anson, who loyally responded, and during the short time he remained at Umballa strenuously exerted himself to equip the troops destined for the arduous task.

While preparing for his advance on the Moghul capital, Anson did not neglect to provide, as far as lay in his power, for the safety of Umballa. The soldiers' wives and children were sent to Kasauli; a place of refuge was made for the non-combatants at the church, round which an entrenchment was thrown; a garrison, about 500 strong, was formed of the sick and weakly men of the several European regiments, assisted by some of the Patiala troops; and as an additional security half the Native corps were sent into the district, and the other half with the column to Delhi.

John Lawrence had strongly advocated the policy of trusting the Maharaja of Patiala and the Rajas of Jhind and Nabha. The attitude of these Chiefs was of extreme importance, for if they had not been well disposed towards us, our communication with the Punjab would have been imperilled. There was therefore much anxiety at Umballa as to the course Patiala, Jhind, and Nabha (the three principal members of the great Phulkian family) would elect to take. Douglas Forsyth,* Deputy-Commissioner of Umballa, who was a personal friend of the Maharaja of Patiala, at once sought an interview with him. He was beginning to explain to the Maharaja the difficulties of the situation, when he was interrupted by His Highness, who said he was aware of all that had happened; on which Forsyth asked if it was true that emissaries from the King of Delhi had come to Patiala. The Maharaja pointed to some men seated at a little distance, saying, 'There they are.' Forsyth then asked for a word in private. As soon as they were alone, he addressed the Maharaja thus: 'Maharaja *sahib*, answer me one question: Are you for us, or against us?' The Maharaja's reply was very hearty: 'As long as I live I am yours, but you know I have enemies in my own country; some of my relations are against me—my brother for one. What do you want done?' Forsyth then asked the Maharaja to send some of his troops towards Kurnal to keep open the Grand Trunk Road. The Maharaja agreed on the understanding that Europeans should soon be sent to support them—a very necessary condition, for he knew that his men could only be trusted so long as there was no doubt of our ultimate success.

Patiala was true to his word, and throughout the Mutiny the Phulkian Chiefs remained perfectly loyal, and performed the important service of keeping open communication between Delhi and the Punjab.†

On the 19th May General Anson was cheered by hearing from John Lawrence that the Corps of Guides and four trusty Punjab regiments were proceeding by forced marches to join him. On the 21st he received a message from the Governor-General informing him that European troops were coming from Madras, Bombay, and Ceylon. He also heard of the arrival of the siege-train at Umballa, and he had the satisfaction of telegraphing to the Chief Commissioner that the first detachment of the column destined for Delhi had started.

On the 23rd the Commander-in-Chief communicated his plan of operations to General Hewitt. It was as follows: Two brigades were to advance from Umballa, commanded by Brigadier Hallifax of the 75th Foot, and Colonel Jones of the 60th Rifles; and one brigade from Meerut, under the command of Brigadier Archdale Wilson. The two former were to be concentrated at Kurnal by the 30th May, and were then to advance, under General Anson, so as to arrive opposite Baghput

* The late Sir Douglas Forsyth, K.C.S.I.
† See 'The Life of Sir Douglas Forsyth.'

on the 5th June, at which place they were to be joined by the Meerut brigade, and the united force was then to proceed to Delhi.

All his arrangements being now completed, Anson left Umballa on the 24th May, and reached Kurnal the following morning. On the 26th he was struck down by cholera, and in a few hours succumbed to that fatal disease. His last words expressed a hope that his country would do him justice, and it is grievous to feel that, in estimating his work and the difficulties he had to encounter, full justice has not been done him. Anson has been undeservedly blamed for vacillation and want of promptitude. He was told to 'make short work of Delhi,' but before Delhi could be taken more men had perished than his whole force at that time amounted to. The advice to march upon Delhi was sound, but had it been rashly followed disaster would have been the inevitable result. Had the Commander-in-Chief been goaded into advancing without spare ammunition and siege Artillery, or with an insufficient force, he must have been annihilated by the overwhelming masses of the mutineers—those mutineers, who, we shall see later, stoutly opposed Barnard's greatly augmented force at Badli-ki-Serai, would almost certainly have repulsed, if not destroyed, a smaller body of troops.

On the death of General Anson the command of the Field Force devolved on Major-General Sir Henry Barnard.

CHAPTER IX.

I WILL now continue my story from the time I left Peshawar to join the Movable Column.

On the 18th May Brigadier Chamberlain and I arrived at Rawal Pindi, where we joined the Chief Commissioner, who had got thus far on his way to his summer residence in the Murree Hills when tidings of the disaster reached him. One of Sir John Lawrence's first acts after talking over matters with Chamberlain was to summon Edwardes from Peshawar, for he wished to consult with him personally about the question of raising levies and enlisting more frontier men, the only one of Edwardes's and Nicholson's proposals regarding which the Chief Commissioner had any doubt; it appeared to him a somewhat risky step to take, and he desired to give the matter very careful consideration before coming to any decision. I remember being greatly struck with the weight given by Lawrence to Edwardes's opinion. He called him his Councillor, he eagerly sought his advice, and he evidently placed the utmost reliance on his judgment.

During the six days that we remained at Rawal Pindi waiting for the

Movable Column to be assembled, I spent the greater part of my time in the Chief Commissioner's office, drafting or copying confidential letters and telegrams. I thus learned everything that was happening in the Punjab, and became aware of the magnitude of the crisis through which we were passing. This enabled me to appreciate the tremendous efforts required to cope with the danger, and to understand that the fate of Delhi and the lives of our countrymen and countrywomen in Upper India depended upon the action taken by the authorities in the Punjab. I realized that Sir John Lawrence thought of every detail, and how correct was his judgment as to which of his subordinates could, or could not, be trusted. The many European women and children scattered over the province caused him the greatest anxiety, and he wisely determined to collect them as much as possible at hill stations and the larger centres, where they would be under the protection of British troops; for this reason he ordered the families of the European soldiers at Sialkot (who were being withdrawn to join the Movable Column) to be sent to Lahore. But, notwithstanding all that had occurred, and was daily occurring, to demonstrate how universal was the spirit of disaffection throughout the Native Army, Brigadier Frederick Brind, who commanded at Sialkot, could not be brought to believe that the regiments serving under his command would ever prove disloyal, and he strongly objected to carry out an order which he denounced as 'showing a want of confidence in the sepoys.' John Lawrence, however, stood firm. Brind was ordered to despatch the soldiers' families without delay, and advised to urge the civilians and military officers to send away their families at the same time. A few of the ladies and children were sent off, but some were allowed to remain until the troops mutinied, when the Brigadier was one of the first to pay the penalty of his misplaced confidence, being shot down by one of his own orderlies.

We had not been long at Rawal Pindi before we heard that the uneasiness at Peshawar was hourly increasing, and that the detachment of the 55th Native Infantry* at Nowshera had mutinied and broken open the magazine. The military force in the Peshawar valley had been considerably weakened by the withdrawal of the 27th Foot and Corps of Guides; it was evident that disaffection was rapidly spreading, and what was still more alarming was the ominously restless feelings amongst the principal tribes on the frontier. Nicholson encountered considerable difficulty in raising local levies, and there was a general unwillingness to enlist. Our disasters in Kabul in 1841-42 had not been forgotten; our cause was considered desperate, and even Nicholson could not persuade men to join it. It was clear that this state of affairs must not be allowed to continue, and that some decisive

* The Head-Quarters of this regiment had been sent to Mardan in place of the Guides.

measures must quickly be taken, or there would be a general rising along the frontier.

Matters seemed to be drawing to a head, when it was wisely determined to disarm the Native regiments at Peshawar without delay. This conclusion was come to at midnight on the 21st May, when the news of the unfortunate occurrences at Nowshera reached Edwardes, who had returned that morning from Rawal Pindi. He and Nicholson felt that no time was to be lost, for if the sepoys heard that the regiment at Nowshera had mutinied, it would be too late to attempt to disarm them. Going forthwith to the Brigadier's house, they communicated their views to Sydney Cotton, who thoroughly appreciated the urgency of the case, and, acting with the most praiseworthy decision, summoned the commanding officers of all the Native regiments to be at his house at daybreak.

When they were assembled, the Brigadier carefully explained to the officers how matters stood. He pointed out to them that their regiments were known to be on the verge of mutiny, and that they must be disarmed forthwith, ending by expressing his great regret at having to take so serious a step.

The officers were quite aghast. They were persistent and almost insubordinate in expressing their conviction that the measure was wholly uncalled-for, that the sepoys were thoroughly loyal, and that, notwithstanding what had occurred in other places, they had perfect confidence in their men.

The Brigadier, who knew the officers well, felt that every allowance should be made for them, called upon as they were to disarm the men with whom they had been so long associated, and in whom they still implicitly believed. But although he regarded the officers' remonstrances as natural and excusable, Cotton never wavered in his decision, for he was experienced enough to see that the evil was widespread and deep-seated, and that any display of confidence or attempt at conciliation in dealing with the disaffected regiments would be worse than useless.

The parade, which was ordered for 7 a.m., was conducted with great judgment. The European troops were skilfully disposed so as to render resistance useless, and four out of the five regular Native regiments were called upon to lay down their arms. The fifth regiment—the 21st Native Infantry*—was exempted from this indignity, partly because it had shown no active symptoms of disaffection, was well commanded and had good officers, and partly because it would have been extremely difficult to carry on the military duties of the station without some Native Infantry.

The two regiments of Irregular Cavalry were also spared the disgrace

* Now the 1st Bengal Infantry.

of being disarmed. It was hoped that the stake the Native officers and men had in the service (their horses and arms being their own property) would prevent them from taking an active part in the Mutiny, and it was believed that the British officers who served with them, and who for the most part were carefully selected, had sufficient influence over their men to keep them straight. This hope proved to be not altogether without foundation, for of the eighteen regiments of Irregular Cavalry which existed in May, 1857, eight are still borne on the strength of the Bengal Army; while of the ten regiments of Regular Cavalry and seventy-four of Infantry, none of the former, and only eleven of the latter, now remain.

How immediate and salutary were the effects of the disarmament on the inhabitants of the Peshawar valley will be seen by the following account which Edwardes gave of it. 'As we rode down to the disarming a very few Chiefs and yeomen of the country attended us; and I remember judging from their faces that they came to see which way the tide would turn. As we rode back friends were as thick as summer flies, and levies began from that moment to come in.'

The Subadar-Major of the 51st—one of the four regiments disarmed—had a few days before written to the men of the 64th, who were divided amongst the outposts, calling upon them to return to Peshawar in time to join in the revolt fixed for the 22nd May. The letter ran; 'In whatever way you can manage it, come into Peshawar on the 21st instant. Thoroughly understand that point! In fact, eat there and drink here.' The rapidity with which the disarmament had been carried through spoilt the Subadar-Major's little game; he had, however, gone too far to draw back, and on the night of the 22nd he deserted, taking with him 250 men of the regiment. His hopes were a second time doomed to disappointment. However welcome 250 muskets might have been to the Afridis, 250 unarmed sepoys were no prize; and as our neighbours in the hills had evidently come to the conclusion that our *raj* was not in such a desperate state as they had imagined, and that their best policy was to side with us, they caught the deserters, with the assistance of the district police, and made them over to the authorities. The men were all tried by Court-Martial, and the Subadar-Major was hanged in the presence of the whole garrison.

On the 23rd May, the day after the disarmament, news was received at Peshawar that the 55th Native Infantry had mutinied at Mardan, and that the 10th Irregular Cavalry, which was divided between Nowshera and Mardan, had turned against us. A force was at once despatched to restore order, and Nicholson accompanied it as political officer. No sooner did the mutineers, on the morning of the 25th, catch sight of the approaching column than they broke out of the fort and fled towards the Swat hills. Nicholson pursued with his levies and mounted police, and before night 120 fugitives were killed and as many more made prisoners. The remainder found no welcome among the hill tribes, and eventually became wanderers over the country until they died or were killed. Poor Spottiswoode, the Colonel, committed suicide shortly before the Peshawar troops reached Mardan.

CHAPTER X.

WHILE I was employed in the Chief Commissioner's office at Rawal Pindi it became known that the Mutineers intended to make their stand at Delhi, and immediately urgent demands came from the Head-Quarters of the army for troops to be sent from the Punjab. Sir John Lawrence exerted himself to the uttermost, even to the extent of denuding his own province to a somewhat dangerous degree, and the Guides and 1st Punjab Infantry, which had been told off for the Movable Column, were ordered instead to proceed to Delhi.

The Guides, a corps second to none in Her Majesty's Indian Army, was commanded by Captain Daly,* and consisted of three troops of Cavalry and six companies of Infantry. The regiment had got as far as Attock, when it received the order to proceed to Delhi, and pushed on at once by double marches. The 4th Sikhs, under Captain Rothney, and the 1st Punjab Infantry, under Major Coke,† followed in quick succession, and later on the following troops belonging to the Punjab Frontier Force were despatched towards Delhi: a squadron of the 1st Punjab Cavalry, under Lieutenant John Watson (my companion in Kashmir); a squadron of the 2nd Punjab Cavalry, under Lieutenant Charles Nicholson‡ (John Nicholson's brother); a squadron of the 5th Punjab Cavalry, under Lieutenant Younghusband; and the 2nd and 4th Punjab Infantry, commanded respectively by Captains G. Green§ and A. Wilde.‖

We (Brigadier Chamberlain and I) remained at Rawal Pindi until the 24th May to give our servants and horses time to reach Wazirabad, and then started on a mail-cart for the latter place, which we reached on the 27th. Lieutenant James Walker,¶ of the Bombay Engineers, accompanied us as the Brigadier's orderly officer.

* The late General Sir Henry Daly, G.C.B.

† Now General Sir John Coke, G.C.B.

‡ Afterwards commanded by Lieutenant, now General, Sir Dighton Probyn, V.C., G.C.V.O., K.C.B.

§ The late Major-General Sir George Green, K.C.B.

‖ The late Lieutenant-General Sir Alfred Wilde, K.C.B., K.C.S.I.

¶ The late General James Walker, C.B., sometime Surveyor-General in India.

The Grand Trunk Road, which runs in a direct line from Calcutta to Peshawar, was then in course of construction through the Punjab, and in places was in rather an elementary condition. The drivers of the mail-carts sent along their half-wild and entirely unbroken ponies at racing speed, regardless alike of obstacles and consequences. With an enterprising coachman the usual pace was about twelve miles an hour, including stoppages. As we were recklessly flying along, the Brigadier, who was sitting in front, perceived that one of the reins had become unbuckled, and warned Walker and me to look out for an upset. Had the coachman not discovered the state of his tackle all might have been well, for the ponies needed no guiding along the well-known road. Unfortunately, however, he became aware of what had happened, lost his head, and pulled the reins; the animals dashed off the road, there was a crash, and we found ourselves on the ground, scattered in different directions. No great damage was done, and in a few minutes we had righted the cart, re-harnessed the ponies, and were rushing along as before.

In order that the authorities at Rawal Pindi might be able to communicate with the Movable Column while on the march and away from telegraph stations, which were few and far between in 1857, a signaller accompanied us, and travelled with his instruments on a second mail-cart, and wherever we halted for the day he attached his wire to the main line. He had just completed the attachment on our arrival at Wazirabad, when I observed that the instrument was working, and on drawing the signaller's attention to it, he read off a message which was at that moment being transmitted to the Chief Commissioner, informing him of the death of the Commander-in-Chief at Kurnal the previous day. This sad news did not directly affect the Movable Column, as it had been organized by, and was under the orders of, the Punjab Government, which for the time being had become responsible for the military, as well as the civil, administration in the north of India.

The column had marched into Wazirabad the day before we arrived. It consisted of Major Dawes' troop of European Horse Artillery, a European battery of Field Artillery, commanded by Captain Bourchier,* and Her Majesty's 52nd Light Infantry, commanded by Colonel George Campbell. In addition, and with a view to reducing the Native garrison of Sialkot, a wing of the 9th Bengal Light Cavalry and the 35th Native Infantry were attached to the column.

My first duty at Wazirabad was to call upon the senior officer, Colonel Campbell, and inform him that Brigadier Chamberlain had come to take over command of the Movable Column. I found the Colonel lying on his bed trying to make himself as comfortable as it

* Now General Sir George Bourchier, K.C.B.

was possible with the thermometer at 117° Fahrenheit. We had not met before, and he certainly received me in a very off-hand manner. He never moved from his recumbent position, and on my delivering my message, he told me he was not aware that the title of Brigadier carried military rank with it; that he understood Brigadier Chamberlain was only a Lieutenant-Colonel, whereas he held the rank of Colonel in Her Majesty's army; and that, under these circumstances, he must decline to acknowledge Brigadier Chamberlain as his senior officer. I replied that I would give his message to the Brigadier, and took my leave.

When Chamberlain heard what had occurred, he desired me to return to Campbell and explain that he had no wish to dispute the question of relative seniority, and that in assuming command of the column he was only carrying out the orders of the Commander-in-Chief in India. Campbell, who technically speaking had the right on his side, was not to be appeased, and requested me to inform the Brigadier of his determination not to serve under an officer whom he considered to be his junior.

This was not a pleasant beginning to our duties with the column, and Chamberlain thought that we had better take our departure and leave Campbell in command until the question could be settled by superior authority. Campbell was accordingly asked to march the troops to Lahore, to which place we continued our journey by mail-cart.

At the same time a reference was made to Sir John Lawrence and General Reed, which resulted in the decision that, under the peculiar circumstances of the case, it was essential that an officer of Indian experience should be in command of the column, and that Campbell, having only been a very short time in the country, did not fulfil this condition; but Campbell was told that, if he objected to serve under Chamberlain, he could remain at Lahore with the Head-Quarters of his regiment. Campbell, who at heart was really a very nice fellow and an excellent officer, would not be separated from the 52nd, and agreed to serve under the Brigadier, reserving to himself the right of protesting when the new Commander-in-Chief should arrive in India.

There was probably another reason for Campbell not wishing to serve under Chamberlain besides that of being senior to him in the army, in the fact that the Brigadier was a servant of 'John Company,' while Campbell belonged to the 'Queen's Service.' From the time of the establishment of a local army there had existed an absurd and unfortunate jealousy between the officers of the Queen's and Company's services, and one of the best results of the Mutiny was its gradual disappearance. This ill-feeling influenced not only fellow-countrymen, but relations, even brothers, if they belonged to the different services, and was distinctly prejudicial to the interests of the Government. It is difficult to understand how so puerile a sentiment could have been so long indulged in by officers who no doubt considered themselves sensible Englishmen.*

On the 31st May we arrived at Lahore, where we found everyone in a state of considerable excitement. Lahore was and is the great centre of the Punjab, and to it non-combatants and English ladies with their children were hurrying from all the outlying districts. In the city itself there was a mixed population of nearly 100,000, chiefly Sikhs and Mahomedans, many of the former old soldiers who had served in the Khalsa Army. The fort, which was within the walls of the city, was garrisoned by half a regiment of sepoys, one company of European Infantry, and a few European Artillerymen. Mian Mir, five miles off, was the Head-Quarters of the Lahore division; it was a long, straggling cantonment, laid out for a much larger force than it has ever been found necessary to place there, with the European Infantry at one end and the European Artillery at the other, separated by Native troops. This arrangement (which existed in almost every station in India) is another proof of the implicit confidence placed in the Native army—a confidence in mercenary soldiers of alien races which seems all the more surprising when we call to mind the warnings that for nearly a hundred years had been repeatedly given of the possibility of disaffection existing amongst Native troops.

There were four Native regiments at Mian Mir, one of Cavalry and three of Infantry, while the European portion of the garrison consisted of one weak Infantry regiment, two troops of Horse Artillery, and four companies of Foot Artillery. This force was commanded by Brigadier Corbett, of the Bengal Army; he had been nearly forty years in the service, was mentally and physically vigorous, and had no fear of responsibility. Robert Montgomery† was then chief civil officer at Lahore. He was of a most gentle and benevolent nature, with a rubicund countenance and a short, somewhat portly figure, which characteristics led to his being irreverently called 'Pickwick,' and probably if he had lived in less momentous times he would never have been credited with the great qualities which the crisis in the Punjab proved him to possess.

On receipt of the telegraphic news of the outbreaks at Meerut and Delhi, Montgomery felt that immediate action was necessary. He at once set to work to discover the temper of the Native troops at Mian Mir, and soon ascertained that they were disaffected to the core, and were only waiting to hear from their friends in the south to break into

* Now, except for one short interval, every officer who has joined the Indian Army since 1861 must, in the first instance, have belonged or been attached to one of Her Majesty's British regiments: the great majority have been educated at Sandhurst or Woolwich, and all feel that they are members of the same army.

† The late Sir Robert Montgomery, G.C.B.

open mutiny. He thoroughly understood the Native character, and realized the danger to the whole province of there being anything in the shape of a serious disturbance at its capital; so after consulting his various officials, Montgomery decided to suggest to the Brigadier the advisability of disarming the sepoys, or, if that were considered too strong a measure, of taking their ammunition from them. Corbett met him quite half-way; he also saw that the danger was imminent, and that prompt action was necessary, but he not unnaturally shrank from taking the extreme step of disarming men whose loyalty had never until then been doubted—a step, moreover, which he knew would be keenly resented by all the regimental officers—he therefore at first only agreed to deprive the sepoys of their ammunition; later in the day, however, after thinking the matter over, he came to the conclusion that it would be better to adopt Montgomery's bolder proposal, and he informed him accordingly that he would 'go the whole hog.'

I do not think that Corbett's action on this occasion has been sufficiently appreciated. That he decided rightly there can be no doubt, but very few officers holding commands in India at that time would have accepted such responsibility. His knowledge as to what had happened at Meerut and Delhi was based on one or two meagre telegrams, and the information Montgomery gave him as to the treacherous intentions of the sepoys at Mian Mir had been obtained by means of a spy, who, it was quite possible, might have been actuated by interested motives.

Having made up his mind what should be done, Corbett had the good sense to understand that success depended on its being done quickly, and on the Native troops being kept absolutely in the dark as to what was about to take place. A general parade was ordered for the next morning, the 13th May, and it was wisely determined not to put off a ball which was being given that evening to the officers of the 81st Foot. The secret was confided to very few, and the great majority of those who were taking part in the entertainment were ignorant of the reason for a parade having been ordered the following morning—an unusual proceeding which caused a certain amount of grumbling.

When the sepoys were drawn up, it was explained to them in their own language that they were about to be deprived of their arms, in order to put temptation out of their reach, and save them from the disgrace of being led away by the evil example of other corps. Whilst they were being thus addressed, the Horse Artillery and 81st Foot took up a second line immediately in rear of the Native regiments, the guns being quietly loaded with grape during the manœuvre. The regiments were then directed to change front to the rear, when they found themselves face to face with the British troops. The order was given to the sepoys to 'pile arms', one of the regiments hesitated, but only for a moment; resistance was hopeless, and the word of command was sullenly obeyed.

The same morning the fort of Lahore was secured. Three companies of the 81st marched into it at daylight, relieved the sepoys of their guards, and ordered them to lay down their arms. Another company of the same regiment travelled through the night in carriages to Umritsar, the holy city of the Sikhs, and occupied the fortress of Govindgarh. Montgomery had been very anxious about these two strongholds, and it was a great satisfaction to him to know that they were at length safely guarded by British bayonets.

Although, as I have said, we found Lahore in a state of considerable excitement, it was satisfactory to see how fully the situation had been grasped, and how everything that was possible had been done to maintain order, and show the people of the Punjab that we were prepared to hold our own. Montgomery's foresight and decision, and Corbett's hearty and willing co-operation, checked, if not altogether stopped, what, under less energetic management, would assuredly have resulted in very grievous trouble. Excitement was inevitable. There was a general stir throughout the province. Lahore was crowded with the families of European soldiers, and with ladies who had come there from various parts of the Punjab, all in terrible anxiety as to what might be the ultimate fate of their husbands and relatives; some of whom were with Native regiments, whose loyalty was more than doubtful; some with the Movable Column, the destination of which was uncertain; while others were already on their way to join the army hurrying to Delhi.

The difficulty with Campbell having been settled, Chamberlain assumed the command of the Movable Column, the advent of which on the 2nd June was hailed with delight by all the Europeans at Lahore. A regiment of British Infantry and two batteries of Artillery afforded a much needed support to the handful of British soldiers keeping guard over the great capital of the Punjab, and gave confidence to the Sikhs and others disposed to be loyal, but who were doubtful as to the wisdom of siding with us.

The disturbing element was the Native troops which accompanied the column. They had not shown openly that they contemplated mutiny, but we knew that they were not to be trusted, and were only watching for an opportunity to break out and escape to Delhi with their arms.

I was living with the Brigadier in a house only a few minutes' walk from the garden where the Native regiments were encamped, and the spies we were employing to watch them had orders to come to me whenever anything suspicious should occur. During the night of the 8th June one of these men awoke me with the news that the 35th Native Infantry intended to revolt at daybreak, and that some of them had already loaded their muskets. I awoke the Brigadier, who directed me to go at once to the British officers of the regiment, tell them what we had heard, and that he would be with them shortly. As soon as the Brigadier arrived the men were ordered to fall in, and on their arms being examined two of them were found to have been loaded. The sepoys to whom the muskets belonged were made prisoners, and I was ordered to see them lodged in the police-station.

Chamberlain determined to lose no time in dealing with the case, and although Drum-Head Courts-Martial were then supposed to be obsolete, he decided to revive, for this occasion, that very useful means of disposing, in time of war, of grave cases of crime.

The Brigadier thought it desirable that the Court-Martial should be composed of Native, rather than British, officers, as being likely to be looked upon by the prisoners as a more impartial tribunal, under the peculiar circumstances in which we were placed. This was made possible by the arrival of the 1st Punjab Infantry—Coke's Rifles—a grand regiment under a grand Commander. Raised in 1849, composed chiefly of Sikhs and Pathans, and possessing Native officers of undoubted loyalty, the 1st Punjab Infantry had taken part in almost every frontier expedition during the previous eight years. Its history was a glorious record of faithful and devoted service, such as can only be rendered by brave men led by officers in whom they believe and trust.* The Subadar-Major of the corps was a man called Mir Jaffir, a most gallant Afghan soldier, who entered the British service during the first Afghan war, and distinguished himself greatly in all the subsequent frontier fights. This Native officer was made president of the Court-Martial. The prisoners were found guilty of mutiny, and sentenced to death. Chamberlain decided that they should be blown away from guns, in the presence of their own comrades, as being the most awe-inspiring means of carrying the sentence into effect.† A parade was at once ordered. The troops were drawn up so as to form three sides of a square; on the fourth side were two guns. As the prisoners were being brought to the parade, one of them asked me if they were going to be blown from guns. I said, 'Yes.' He made no further remark, and they both walked steadily on until they reached the guns, to which they were bound, when one of them requested that some rupees he had on his person might be saved for his relations. The Brigadier answered: 'It is too late!' The word of command was

* During the operations in the Kohat Pass in February, 1850, within twelve months of the corps being raised, several of the men were killed and wounded. Among the latter was a Pathan named Mahomed Gul. He was shot through the body in two places, and as Coke sat by him while he was dying, he said, with a smile on his face: '*Sahib*, I am happy; but promise me one thing—don't let my old mother want. I leave her to your care.'

† Awe inspiring certainly, but probably the most humane, as being a sure and instantaneous mode of execution.

given; the guns went off simultaneously, and the two mutineers were launched into eternity.

It was a terrible sight, and one likely to haunt the beholder for many a long day; but that was what was intended. I carefully watched the sepoys' faces to see how it affected them. They were evidently startled at the swift retribution which had overtaken their guilty comrades, but looked more crest-fallen than shocked or horrified, and we soon learnt that their determination to mutiny, and make the best of their way to Delhi, was in nowise changed by the scene they had witnessed.

CHAPTER XI.

For a few days after our arrival at Lahore nothing could be settled as to the further movements of the column. It was wanted in all parts of the Punjab: Ferozepore, Multan, Jhelum, Sialkot, Umritsar, Jullundur, Philour, Ludhiana—all these places were more or less disturbed, and all were clamorous for help.

At Ferozepore the Native regiments* broke out on the 13th May, when they made a daring, but unsuccessful effort to seize the arsenal, situated inside the fort and the largest in Upper India. Had that fallen into the hands of the rebels, Delhi could not have been captured without very considerable delay, for the besieging force depended mainly upon Ferozepore for the supply of munitions of war. The fort had been allowed to fall into bad repair, and the mutineers had no difficulty in forcing their way inside; there, fortunately, they were checked by the wall which surrounded the arsenal, and this obstacle, insignificant as it was, enabled the guard to hold its own. Originally this guard consisted entirely of Native soldiers, but, as I have already recorded, after the outbreak at Meerut, Europeans had been told off for the charge of this important post; so strong, however, here as elsewhere, was the belief in the loyalty of the sepoys, and so great was the reluctance to do anything which might hurt their feelings, that the Native guard was not withdrawn. This same guard, when the attack took place, did its best to assist the assailants, and even prepared scaling-ladders to enable the latter to gain access to the magazine enclosure. The Europeans, however, were equal to the emergency; they overpowered and disarmed their treacherous companions, and then succeeded in beating off and dispersing the attacking party.

Being foiled in this attempt, the mutineers returned to the cantonment, set fire to the church and other buildings, and then started for Delhi. Ferozepore had a large European garrison, a regiment of

* One Cavalry and two Infantry.

Infantry, a battery of Field Artillery, and a company of Foot Artillery, and was supposed to be able to look after itself, although affairs had been greatly mismanaged.

Multan had next to be considered. Matters at that station were very unsettled, and indeed were causing the authorities grave anxiety, but Multan was more fortunate than many places, in being in the hands of an unusually able, experienced officer, Major Crawford Chamberlain. Consequently, the Commander-in-Chief and Chief Commissioner agreed, while fully appreciating the great value of Multan, that the presence of British troops was less urgently needed there than elsewhere, and it was decided they could not be spared from the Punjab for its protection.

The garrison at Multan consisted of a troop of Native Horse Artillery, two regiments of Native Infantry, and the 1st Irregular Cavalry, composed entirely of Hindustanis from the neighbourhood of Delhi; while in the old Sikh fort there were about fifty European Artillerymen, in charge of a small magazine. The station was nominally commanded by an officer who had been thirty-four years in the army, and had great experience amongst Natives; but he had fallen into such a bad state of health, that he was quite unfit to deal with the crisis which had now arrived. The command, therefore, was practically exercised by Chamberlain. Next to Delhi and Lahore, Multan was the most important place in Upper India, as our communication with the sea and southern India depended on its preservation.

To Chamberlain's own personality and extraordinary influence over the men of the 1st Irregular Cavalry must be attributed his success. His relations with them were of a patriarchal nature, and perfect mutual confidence existed. He knew his hold over them was strong, and he determined to trust them. But in doing so he had really no alternative—had they not remained faithful, Multan must have been lost to us. One of his first acts was to call a meeting at his house of the Native officers of the Artillery, Infantry, and his own regiment, to discuss the situation. Taking for granted the absolute loyalty of these officers, he suggested that a written bond should be given, in which the seniors of each corps should guarantee the fidelity of their men. The officers of his regiment rose *en masse*, and placing their signet-rings on the table, said: '*Kabûl sir-o-chasm*' ('Agreed to on our lives'). The Artillery Subadar declared that his men had no scruples, and would fire in whichever direction they were required; while the Infantry Native officers pleaded that they had no power over their men, and could give no guarantee. Thus, Chamberlain ascertained that the Cavalry were loyal, the Artillery doubtful, and the Infantry were only biding their time to mutiny.

Night after night sepoys, disguised beyond all recognition, attempted to tamper with the Irregular Cavalry. The Wurdi-Major,* a particularly fine, handsome *Rangar*,† begged Chamberlain to hide himself in his house, that he might hear for himself the open proposals to mutiny, massacre, and rebellion that were made to him; and the promises that, if they succeeded in their designs, he (the Wurdi-Major) should be placed upon the *gaddi*‡ of Multan for his reward. Chamberlain declined to put himself in such a position, fearing he might not be able to restrain himself.

Matters now came to a climax. A Mahomedan Subadar of one of the Native Infantry regiments laid a plot to murder Chamberlain and his family. The plot was discovered and frustrated by Chamberlain's own men, but it became apparent that the only remedy for the fast increasing evil was to disarm the two Native Infantry regiments. How was this to be accomplished with no Europeans save a few gunners anywhere near? Sir John Lawrence was most pressing that the step should be taken at once; he knew the danger of delay; at the same time, he thoroughly appreciated the difficulty of the task which he was urging Chamberlain to undertake, and he readily responded to the latter's request for a regiment of Punjab Infantry to be sent to him. The 2nd Punjab Infantry was, therefore, despatched from Dera Ghazi Khan, and at the same time the 1st Punjab Cavalry arrived from Asni,§ under Major Hughes,‖ who, hearing of Chamberlain's troubles, had marched to Multan without waiting for orders from superior authority.

The evening of the day on which these troops reached Multan, the British officers of the several regiments were directed to assemble at the Deputy-Commissioner's house, when Chamberlain told them of the communication he had received from Sir John Lawrence, adding that, having reliable information that the Native Infantry were about to mutiny, he had settled to disarm them the next morning.

* Native Adjutant.

† A name applied by the Hindus to any Rajput who has, or whose ancestors have, been converted to Islam. There were several *Rangars* in the 1st Irregulars. One day in June, Shaidad Khan, a Resaidar of this class, came to Chamberlain, and said: 'There was a rumour that he (Chamberlain) had not as much confidence in *Rangars* as in other classes of the regiment, and he came to be comforted'! Chamberlain asked him to sit down, and sent to the banker of the regiment for a very valuable sword which he had given him for safe custody. It had belonged to one of the Amirs of Sindh, was taken in battle, and given to Chamberlain by Major Fitzgerald, of the Sindh Horse. On the sword being brought, Chamberlain handed it over to Shaidad Khan and his sect for safety, to be returned when the Mutiny was over. The tears rose to the Native officer's eyes, he touched Chamberlain's knees, and swore that death alone would sever the bond of fidelity of which the sword was the token. He took his leave, thoroughly satisfied.

‡ Throne.

§ A station since abandoned for Rajanpur.

‖ Now General Sir W. T. Hughes, K.C.B.

It was midnight before the meeting broke up. At 4 a.m. the Horse Artillery troop and the two Native Infantry regiments were ordered to march as if to an ordinary parade. When they had gone about a quarter of a mile they were halted, and the Punjab troops moved quietly between them and their lines, thus cutting them off from their spare ammunition; at the same time the European Artillerymen took their places with the guns of the Horse Artillery troop, and a carefully selected body of Sikhs belonging to the 1st Punjab Cavalry, under Lieutenant John Watson, was told off to advance on the troop and cut down the gunners if they refused to assist the Europeans to work the guns.

Chamberlain then rode up to the Native Infantry regiments, and after explaining to them the reason for their being disarmed, he gave the word of command, 'Pile arms!' Thereupon a sepoy of the 62nd shouted: 'Don't give up your arms; fight for them!' Lieutenant Thomson, the Adjutant of the regiment, instantly seized him by the throat and threw him to the ground. The order was repeated, and, wonderful to relate, obeyed. The Native Infantry regiments were then marched back to their lines, while the Punjab troops and Chamberlain's Irregulars remained on the ground until the arms had been carted off to the fort.

It was a most critical time, and enough credit has never been given to Chamberlain. Considering the honours which were bestowed on others who took more or less conspicuous parts in the Mutiny, he was very insufficiently rewarded for this timely act of heroism. Had he not shown such undaunted courage and coolness, or had there been the smallest hesitation, Multan would certainly have gone. Chamberlain managed an extremely difficult business in a most masterly manner. His personal influence insured his own regiment continuing loyal throughout the Mutiny, and it has now the honour of being the 1st Regiment of Bengal Cavalry, and the distinction of wearing a different uniform from every other regiment in the service, being allowed to retain the bright yellow which the troopers wore when they were first raised by Colonel James Skinner, and in which they performed such loyal service.*

At Jhelum and Sialkot it was decided that, as the Native troops had been considerably reduced in numbers, the danger was not so great as to require the presence of the Movable Column.

Umritsar had been made safe for the time, but it was a place the

* The two disarmed regiments remained quietly at Multan for more than a year, when, with unaccountable inconsistency, a sudden spirit of revolt seized them, and in August, 1858, they broke out, tried to get possession of the guns, murdered the Adjutant of the Bombay Fusiliers, and then fled from the station. But order by that time had been quite restored, our position in the Punjab was secure and nearly all the sepoys were killed or captured by the country people.

importance of which could not be over-estimated, and it was thought that keeping a strong column in its vicinity for a few days would materially strengthen our position there. Moreover, Umritsar lay in the direct route to Jullundur, where the military authorities had proved themselves quite unfitted to deal with the emergency. It was decided, therefore, that Umritsar should be our objective in the first instance. We marched from Lahore on the 10th June, and reached Umritsar the following morning.

News of a severe fight at Badli-ki-Serai had been received, which increased our anxiety to push on to Delhi, for we feared the place might be taken before we could get there. But to our mortification it was decided that the column could not be spared just then even for Delhi, as there was still work for it in the Punjab. To add to our disappointment, we had to give up our trusted Commander; for a few hours after our arrival at Umritsar a telegram came to Neville Chamberlain offering him the Adjutant-Generalship of the Army in succession to Colonel Chester, who had been killed at Badli-ki-Serai. He accepted the offer, and I made certain I should go with him. My chagrin, therefore, can easily be understood when he told me that I must remain with the column, as it would be unfair to his successor to take away the staff officer. We were now all anxiety to learn who that successor should be, and it was a satisfaction to hear that John Nicholson was the man.

Chamberlain left for Delhi on the 13th; but Nicholson could not join for a few days, and as troops were much needed at Jullundur, it was arranged that the column should move on to that place, under the temporary command of Campbell, and there await the arrival of the new Brigadier.

On my going to Campbell for orders, he informed me that he was no longer the senior officer with the column, as a Colonel Denniss, junior to him regimentally, but his senior in army rank, had just rejoined the 52nd. Accordingly I reported myself to Denniss, who, though an officer of many years' service, had never before held a command, not even that of a regiment; and, poor man! was considerably taken aback when he heard that he must be in charge of the column for some days. He practically left everything to me—a somewhat trying position for almost the youngest officer in the force. It was under these circumstances I found what an able man Colonel Campbell really was. He correctly gauged Denniss's fitness, or rather unfitness, for the command, and appreciating the awkwardness of my position, advised me so wisely that I had no difficulty in carrying on the work.

We reached Jullundur on the 20th, Nicholson taking over command the same day. He had been given the rank of Brigadier-General, which removed all grounds for objection on the part of Campbell, and the two soon learnt to appreciate each other, and became fast friends.

Jullundur was in a state of the greatest confusion. The Native troops, consisting of a regiment of Light Cavalry and two regiments of Native Infantry, began to show signs of disaffection soon after the outbreak at Meerut, and from that time until the 7th June, when they broke into open mutiny, incendiary fires were almost of daily occurrence.

The want of resolution displayed in dealing with the crisis at Jullundur was one of the regrettable episodes of the Mutiny. The European garrison consisted of Her Majesty's 8th Foot and a troop of Horse Artillery. The military authorities had almost a whole month's warning of the mutinous intentions of the Native troops, but though they had before them the example of the prompt and successful measures adopted at Lahore and Peshawar, they failed to take any steps to prevent the outbreak.

The Brigadier (Johnstone) was on leave at the commencement of the Mutiny, and during his absence the treasure was placed in charge of a European guard, in accordance with instructions from Sir John Lawrence. This measure was reversed as soon as the Brigadier rejoined, for fear of showing distrust of the sepoys, and another wise order of the watchful Chief Commissioner—to disarm the Native troops—was never carried out. The Commissioner, Major Edward Lake, one of Henry Lawrence's most capable assistants, had also repeatedly urged upon Johnstone the advisability of depriving the sepoys of their arms, but his advice remained unheeded. When the inevitable revolt took place European soldiers were allowed to be passive spectators while property was being destroyed, and sepoys to disappear in the darkness of the night carrying with them their muskets and all the treasure and plunder they could lay their hands on.

A futile attempt at pursuit was made the following morning, but, as will be seen, this was carried out in so half-hearted a manner, that the mutineers were able to get safely across the Sutlej with their loot, notwithstanding that the passage of this broad river had to be made by means of a ferry, where only very few boats were available. Having reached Philour, the British troops were ordered to push on to Delhi, and as Jullundur was thus left without protection, Lake gladly accepted the offer of the Raja of Kapurthala to garrison it with his own troops.

There was no doubt as to the loyalty of the Raja himself, and his sincere desire to help us; but the mismanagement of affairs at Jullundur had done much to lower our prestige in the eyes of his people, and there was no mistaking the offensive demeanour of his troops. They evidently thought that British soldiers had gone never to return, and they swaggered about in swash-buckler fashion, as only Natives who think they have the upper hand can swagger.

It was clearly Lake's policy to keep on good terms with the Kapurthala people. His position was much strengthened by the arrival of our column; but we were birds of passage, and might be off at any moment, so in order to pay a compliment to the officers and principal men with the Kapurthala troops, Lake asked Nicholson to meet them at his house. Nicholson consented, and a durbar was arranged. I was present on the occasion, and was witness of rather a curious scene, illustrative alike of Nicholson and Native character.

At the close of the ceremony Mehtab Sing, a general officer in the Kapurthala Army, took his leave, and, as the senior in rank at the durbar, was walking out of the room first, when I observed Nicholson stalk to the door, put himself in front of Mehtab Sing and, waving him back with an authoritative air, prevent him from leaving the room. The rest of the company then passed out, and when they had gone, Nicholson said to Lake: 'Do you see that General Mehtab Sing has his shoes on?'* Lake replied that he had noticed the fact, but tried to excuse it. Nicholson, however, speaking in Hindustani, said: 'There is no possible excuse for such an act of gross impertinence. Mehtab Sing knows perfectly well that he would not venture to step on his own father's carpet save barefooted, and he has only committed this breach of etiquette to-day because he thinks we are not in a position to resent the insult, and that he can treat us as he would not have dared to do a month ago.' Mehtab Sing looked extremely foolish, and stammered some kind of apology; but Nicholson was not to be appeased, and continued: 'If I were the last Englishman left in Jullundur, you' (addressing Mehtab Sing) 'should not come into my room with your shoes on;' then, politely turning to Lake, he added, 'I hope the Commissioner will now allow me to order you to take your shoes off and carry them out in your own hands, so that your followers may witness your discomfiture.' Mehtab Sing, completely cowed, meekly did as he was told.

Although in the kindness of his heart Lake had at first endeavoured to smooth matters over, he knew Natives well, and he readily admitted the wisdom of Nicholson's action. Indeed, Nicholson's uncompromising bearing on this occasion proved a great help to Lake, for it had the best possible effect upon the Kapurthala people; their manner at once changed, all disrespect vanished, and there was no more swaggering about as if they considered themselves masters of the situation.

Five or six years after this occurrence I was one of a pig-sticking party at Kapurthala, given by the Raja in honour of the Commander-in-Chief, Sir Hugh Rose.† When riding home in the evening I found myself close to the elephant on which our host and the Chief were sitting. The conversation happening to turn on the events of the Mutiny, I asked what had become of General Mehtab Sing. The Raja, pointing to an elephant a little distance off on which two Native

* No Native, in Native dress, keeps his shoes on when he enters a room, unless he intends disrespect.

† The late Field Marshal Lord Strathnairn, G.C.B., G.C.S.I.

gentlemen were riding, said, 'There he is.' I recognized the General, and making him a salaam, which he politely returned, I said to him, 'I have not had the pleasure of meeting you since those hot days in June, 1857, when I was at Jullundur.' The Raja then asked me if I knew Nicholson. On my telling him I had been his staff officer, and with him at the durbar at Lake *Sahib's* house, the Raja laughed heartily, and said, 'Oh! then you saw Mehtab Sing made to walk out of the room with his shoes in his hand? We often chaff him about that little affair, and tell him that he richly deserved the treatment he received from the great Nicholson *Sahib*.'

Sir Hugh Rose was greatly interested in the story, which he made me repeat to him as soon as we got back to camp, and he was as much struck as I was with this spontaneous testimony of a leading Native to the wisdom of Nicholson's procedure.

On taking over command, Nicholson's first care was to establish an effective system of intelligence, by means of which he was kept informed of what was going on in the neighbouring districts; and, fully recognizing the necessity for rapid movement in the event of any sudden emergency, he organized a part of his force into a small flying column, the infantry portion of which was to be carried in *ekkas*.* I was greatly impressed by Nicholson's knowledge of military affairs. He seemed always to know exactly what to do and the best way to do it. This was the more remarkable because, though a soldier by profession, his training had been chiefly that of a civilian—a civilian of the frontier, however, where his soldierly instincts had been fostered in his dealing with a lawless and unruly people, and where he had received a training which was now to stand him in good stead. Nicholson was a born Commander, and this was felt by every officer and man with the column before he had been amongst them many days.

The Native troops with the column had given no trouble since we left Lahore. We were travelling in the direction they desired to go, which accounted for their remaining quiet; but Nicholson, realizing the danger of having them in our midst, and the probability of their refusing to turn away from Delhi in the event of our having to retrace our steps, resolved to disarm the 35th. The civil authorities in the district urged that the same course should be adopted with the 33rd, a Native Infantry regiment at Hoshiarpur, about twenty-seven miles from Jullundur, which it had been decided should join the column. The Native soldiers with the column already exceeded the Europeans in number, and as the addition of another regiment would make the odds against us very serious, it was arranged to disarm the 35th before the 33rd joined us.

We left Jullundur on the 24th June, and that afternoon, accom-

* A kind of light cart.

panied by the Deputy-Commissioner of the district, I rode to Philour to choose a place for the disarming parade. The next morning we started early, the Europeans heading the column, and when they reached the ground we had selected they took up a position on the right of the road, the two batteries in the centre and the 52nd in wings on either flank. The guns were unlimbered and prepared for action. On the left of the road was a serai,* behind which the officer commanding the 35th was told to take his regiment, and, as he cleared it, to wheel to the right, thus bringing his men in column of companies facing the line of Europeans. This manœuvre being accomplished, I was ordered to tell the commanding officer that the regiment was to be disarmed, and that the men were to pile arms and take off their belts. The sepoys and their British officers were equally taken aback; the latter had received no information of what was going to happen, while the former had cherished the hope that they would be able to cross the Sutlej, and thence slip off with their arms to Delhi.

I thought I could discover relief in the British officers' faces, certainly in that of Major Younghusband, the Commandant, and when I gave him the General's order, he murmured, 'Thank God!' He had been with the 35th for thirty-three years; he had served with it at the siege of Bhurtpore, throughout the first Afghan war, and in Sale's defence of Jalalabad; he had been proud of his old corps, but knowing probably that his men could no longer be trusted, he rejoiced to feel that they were not to be given the opportunity for further disgracing themselves.† The sepoys obeyed the command without a word, and in a few minutes their muskets and belts were all packed in carts and taken off to the fort.

As the ceremony was completed, the 33rd arrived and was dealt with in a similar manner; but the British officers of this regiment did not take things so quietly—they still believed in their men, and the Colonel, Sandeman, trusted them to any extent. He had been with the regiment for more than two-and-thirty years, and had commanded it throughout the Sutlej campaign. On hearing the General's order, he exclaimed: 'What! disarm my regiment? I will answer with my life for the loyalty of every man!' On my repeating the order the poor old fellow burst into tears. His son, the late Sir Robert Sandeman, who was an Ensign in the regiment at the time, told me afterwards how terribly his father felt the disgrace inflicted upon the regiment of which he was so proud.

It was known that the wing of the 9th Light Cavalry was in communication with the mutineers at Delhi, and that the men were only waiting their opportunity; so they would also certainly have been dis-

* A four-walled enclosure for the accommodation of travellers.

† It will be remembered that this was the regiment in which two men had been found with loaded muskets, and blown away from guns at Lahore.

armed at this time, but for the idea that such a measure might have a bad effect on the other wing, which still remained at Sialkot. The turn of this regiment, however, came a few days later.

Up till this time we all hoped that Delhi was our destination, but, greatly to our surprise and disappointment, orders came that morning directing the column to return to Umritsar; the state of the Punjab was causing considerable anxiety, as there were several stations at which Native corps still remained in possession of their arms.

The same afternoon I was in the Philour fort with Nicholson, when the telegraph-signaller gave him a copy of a message from Sir Henry Barnard to the authorities in the Punjab, begging that all Artillery officers not doing regimental duty might be sent to Delhi, where their services were urgently required. I at once felt that this message applied to me. I had been longing to find myself at Delhi, and lived in perpetual dread of its being captured before I could get there; now at last my hopes seemed about to be realized in a legitimate manner, but, on the other hand, I did not like the idea of leaving Nicholson—the more closely I was associated with him the more I was attracted by him—and I am always proud to remember that he did not wish to part with me. He agreed, however, that my first duty was to my regiment, and only stipulated that before leaving him I should find someone to take my place, as he did not know a single officer with the column. This I was able to arrange, and that evening Nicholson and I dined *tête-à-tête*. At dawn the next morning I left by mail-cart for Delhi, my only kit being a small bundle of bedding, saddle and bridle, my servants having orders to follow with my horses, tents, and other belongings.

CHAPTER XII.

The mail-cart rattled across the bridge of boats, and in less than an hour I found myself at Ludhiana, at the house of George Ricketts,* the Deputy Commissioner. Ricketts's bungalow was a resting-place for everyone passing through *en route* to Delhi. In one room I found Lieutenant Williams of the 4th Sikhs, who had been dangerously wounded three weeks before, while assisting Ricketts to prevent the Jullundur mutineers from crossing the Sutlej.

While I was eating my breakfast, Ricketts sat down by my side and recounted a stirring tale of all that had happened at Philour and Ludhiana consequent on the rising of the Native regiments at Jullundur. The mutineers had made, in the first instance, for Philour, a small

* George Ricketts, Esq., C.B., afterwards a member of the Board of Revenue of the North-West Provinces.

cantonment, but important from the fact of its containing a fair-sized magazine, and from its situation, commanding the passage of the Sutlej. It was garrisoned by the 3rd Native Infantry, which furnished the sole guard over the magazine—a danger which, as I have mentioned, had fortunately been recognized by the Commander-in-Chief when he first heard of the outbreak at Meerut. The men of the 3rd remained quiet, and even did good service in helping to drag the guns of the siege-train across the river, and in guarding the treasury, until the mutineers from Jullundur arrived on the 8th June. They then gave their British officers warning to leave them, saying they did not mean to injure them or their property, but they had determined they would no longer serve the *Sirkar*. Twelve British officers (there could not have been more), confronted by 3,000 sepoys, felt themselves powerless, and retired to the fort.

Ricketts had with him at that time an assistant named Thornton,* who had gone to Philour to lodge some money in the treasury. This officer had started to ride back to Ludhiana, when he suddenly became aware of what had happened, and how perilous was the position. Had he consulted his own safety, he would have returned and taken refuge in the fort, instead of which he galloped on, having to pass close by the mutineers, until he reached the bridge of boats, which, with admirable coolness and presence of mind, he cut behind him, then, hurrying on, he informed Ricketts of what had taken place; and that the rebels might shortly be expected to attempt the passage of the river. Fortunately the 4th Sikhs from Abbottabad had that very morning marched into Ludhiana, and Ricketts hoped, with their assistance, to hold the sepoys in check until the arrival of the British troops, which he believed must have been despatched from Jullundur in pursuit of the mutineers.

The garrison of Ludhiana consisted of a detachment of the 3rd Native Infantry, guarding the fort, in which was stored a large amount of powder. The detachment was commanded by Lieutenant Yorke, who, on hearing Thornton's story, went at once to the fort. He was much liked by his men, who received him quite civilly, but told him they knew that their regiment had joined the rebels from Jullundur, and that they themselves could no longer obey his orders. Ricketts then understood that he had but the 4th Sikhs and a small party of troops belonging to the Raja of Nabha to depend upon. There were only two officers with the 4th Sikhs—Captain Rothney, in command, and Lieutenant Williams, the Adjutant. Taking three companies of the regiment under Williams, and two guns of the Nabha Artillery, one dragged by camels, the other by horses, Ricketts started off towards the bridge of boats. Galloping on alone, he found that the gap in the bridge made by Thornton had not been repaired, which proved that the

* Thomas Thornton, Esq., C.S.I., afterwards Secretary to the Government of India in the Foreign Department.

rebels had not crossed by that passage, at all events. He widened the gap by cutting adrift some more boats, and then had himself ferried across the river, in order to ascertain the exact state of affairs at Philour. He learnt that no tidings had been received of any British troops having been sent from Jullundur in pursuit of the mutineers, who, having failed to get across the bridge, owing to Thornton's timely action, had gone to a ferry reported to be three miles up the river.

Ricketts recrossed the river as quickly as he could, and joined Williams. It was then getting dark, but, hoping they might still be in time to check the rebels, they pushed on in the direction of the ferry, which proved to be nearer six than three miles away. The ground was rough and broken, as is always the case on the banks of Indian rivers, swollen as they often are by torrents from the hills, which leave behind boulders and débris of all kinds. They made but little way; one of the gun-camels fell lame, the guides disappeared, and they began to despair of reaching the ferry in time, when suddenly there was a challenge and they knew they were too late. The sepoys had succeeded in crossing the river and were bivouacking immediately in front of them.

It was not a pleasant position, but it had to be made the best of; and both the civilian and the soldier agreed that their only chance was to fight. Williams opened fire with his Infantry, and Ricketts took command of the guns. At the first discharge the horses bolted with the limber, and never appeared again; almost at the same moment Williams fell, shot through the body. Ricketts continued the fight until his ammunition was completely expended, when he was reluctantly obliged to retire to a village in the neighbourhood, but not until he had killed, as he afterwards discovered, about fifty of the enemy.

Ricketts returned to Ludhiana early the next morning, and later in the day the mutineers passed through the city. They released some 500 prisoners who were in the gaol, and helped themselves to what food they wanted, but they did not enter the cantonment or the fort. The gallant little attempt to close the passage of the Sutlej was entirely frustrated, owing to the inconceivable want of energy displayed by the so-called 'pursuing force'; had it pushed on, the rebels must have been caught in the act of crossing the river, when Ricketts's small party might have afforded considerable help. The Europeans from Jullundur reached Philour before dark on the 8th; they heard the firing of Ricketts's guns, but no attempt was made by the officer in command to ascertain the cause, and they came leisurely on to Ludhiana the following day.

Having listened with the greatest interest to Ricketts's story, and refreshed the inner man, I resumed my journey, and reached Umballa late in the afternoon of the 27th, not sorry to get under shelter, for the monsoon, which had been threatening for some days past, burst with great fury as I was leaving Ludhiana.

On driving to the dâk-bungalow I found it crowded with officers, some of whom had been waiting there for days for an opportunity to go on to Delhi; they laughed at me when I expressed my intention of proceeding at once, and told me that the seats on the mail-carts had to be engaged several days in advance, and that I might make up my mind to stay where I was for some time to come. I was not at all prepared for this, and I determined to get on by hook or by crook; as a preliminary measure, I made friends with the postmaster, from whose office the mail-carts started. From him I learnt that my only chance was to call upon the Deputy-Commissioner, by whose orders the seats were distributed. I took the postmaster's advice, and thus became acquainted with Douglas Forsyth, who in later years made a name for himself by his energetic attempts to establish commercial relations with Yarkand and Kashgar. Forsyth confirmed what I had already heard, but told me that an extra cart was to be despatched that night, laden with small-arm ammunition, on which I could, if I liked, get a seat, adding: 'Your kit must be of the smallest, as there will be no room for anything inside the cart.'

I returned to the dâk-bungalow, overjoyed at my success, to find myself quite an important personage, with everyone my friend, like the boy at school who is the lucky recipient of a hamper from home. 'Take me with you!' was the cry on all sides. Only two others besides the driver and myself could possibly go, and then only by carrying our kits in our laps. It was finally arranged that Captain Law and Lieutenant Packe should be my companions. Packe was lamed for life by a shot through his ankle before we had been forty-eight hours at Delhi, and Law was killed on the 23rd July, having greatly distinguished himself by his gallantry and coolness under fire during the short time he served with the force.

We got to Kurnal soon after daybreak on the 28th. It was occupied by a few of the Raja of Jhind's troops, a Commissariat officer, and one or two civilians, who were trying to keep the country quiet and collect supplies. Before noon we passed through Panipat, where there was a strong force of Patiala and Jhind troops, and early in the afternoon we reached Alipur. Here our driver pulled up, declaring he would go no further. A few days before there had been a sharp fight on the road between Alipur and Delhi, not far from Badli-ki-Serai, where the battle of the 8th June had taken place, and as the enemy were constantly on the road threatening the rear of the besieging force, the driver did not consider it safe to go on. We could not, however, stop at Alipur, so after some consultation we settled to take the mail-cart ponies and ride on to camp. We could hear the boom of guns at intervals, and as we neared Delhi we came across several dead bodies of the enemy. It is a curious fact that most of these bodies were exactly like mummies; there was nothing disagreeable about them.

6

Why this should have been the case I cannot say, but I often wished during the remainder of the campaign that the atmospheric influences, which, I presume, had produced this effect, could assert themselves more frequently.

We stopped for a short time to look at the position occupied by the enemy at Badli-ki-Serai; but none of us were in the mood to enjoy sight-seeing. We had never been to Delhi before, and had but the vaguest notion where the Ridge (the position our force was holding) was. or how the city was situated with regard to our camp. The sound of heavy firing became louder and louder, and we knew that fighting must be going on. The driver had solemnly warned us of the risk we were running in continuing our journey, and when we came to the point where the Grand Trunk Road bifurcates, one branch going direct to the city and the other through the cantonment, we halted for a few minutes to discuss which we should take. Fortunately for us, we settled to follow that which led to the cantonment, and, as it was then getting dark, we pushed on as fast as our tired ponies could go. The relief to us when we found ourselves safe inside our own piquets may be imagined. My father's old staff-officer, Henry Norman, who was then Assistant-Adjutant-General at Head-Quarters, kindly asked me to share his tent until I could make other arrangements. He had no bed to offer me, but I required none, as I was thoroughly tired out, and all I wanted was a spot on which to throw myself down. A good night's rest quite set me up. I awoke early, scarcely able to believe in my good fortune. I was actually at Delhi, and the city was still in the possession of the mutineers.

CHAPTER XIII.

Before entering on the narrative of what came under my own observation during the three months I was at Delhi, I will relate what took place after Sir Henry Barnard succeeded General Anson in command on the 26th May, and how the little British force maintained itself against almost overwhelming odds during the first three weeks of that memorable siege.

Barnard had served as Chief of the Staff in the Crimea, and had held various staff appointments in England; but he was an utter stranger to India, having only arrived in the country a few weeks before. He fully realized the difficulties of the position to which he had so unexpectedly succeeded, for he was aware how unjustly Anson was being judged by those who, knowing nothing of war, imagined he could have started to attack Delhi with scarcely more preparation than would have been necessary for a morning's parade. The officers of the column were complete strangers to him, and he to them, and he was ignorant of the characteristics and capabilities of the Native portion of his troops. It must, therefore, have been with an anxious heart that he took over the command.

One of Barnard's first acts was to get rid of the unreliable element which Anson had brought away from Umballa. The Infantry he sent to Rohtuk, where it shortly afterwards mutinied, and the Cavalry to Meerut. That these troops should have been allowed to retain their weapons is one of the mysteries of the Mutiny. For more than two months their insubordination had been apparent, incendiarism had occurred which had been clearly traced to them, and they had even gone so far as to fire at their officers; both John Lawrence and Robert Montgomery had pressed upon the Commander-in-Chief the advisability of disarming them; but General Anson, influenced by the regimental officers, who could not believe in the disaffection of their men, had not grasped the necessity for this precautionary measure. The European soldiers with the column, however, did not conceal their mistrust of these sepoys, and Barnard acted wisely in sending them away; but it was extraordinary that they should have been allowed to keep their arms.

On the 5th June Barnard reached Alipur, within ten miles of Delhi, where he decided to await the arrival of the siege-train and the troops from Meerut.

The Meerut brigade, under Brigadier Wilson, had started on the 27th May. It consisted of two squadrons of the Carabineers, Tombs's* troop of Horse Artillery, Scott's Field Battery and two 18-pounder guns, a wing of the 1st Battalion 60th Rifles, a few Native Sappers and Miners, and a detachment of Irregular Horse.

Early on the 30th the village of Ghazi-u-din-nagar (now known as Ghaziabad) close to the Hindun river, and about eleven miles from Delhi, was reached. Thence it was intended to make a reconnaissance towards Delhi, but about four o'clock in the afternoon a vedette reported that the enemy were approaching in strength. A very careless look-out had been kept, for almost simultaneously with the report a round shot came tumbling into camp. The troops fell in as quickly as possible, and the Artillery came into action. The Rifles crossed the Hindun suspension bridge, and, under cover of our guns, attacked the enemy, who were strongly posted in a village. From this position they were speedily dislodged, and the victory was complete. Seven hundred British soldiers defeated seven times their number, capturing five guns and a large quantity of ammunition and stores. Our loss was one officer and ten men killed, and one officer and eighteen men wounded.

* The late Major-General Sir Harry Tombs, V.C., K.C.B.

The following day (Sunday) the enemy reappeared about noon, but after two hours' fighting they were again routed, and on our troops occupying their position, they could be seen in full retreat towards Delhi. The rebels succeeded in taking their guns with them, for our men, prostrated by the intense heat and parched with thirst, were quite unable to pursue. We had one officer and eleven men killed, and two officers and ten men wounded. Among the latter was an ensign of the 60th Rifles, a boy named Napier, a most gallant young fellow, full of life and spirit, who had won the love as well as the admiration of his men. He was hit in the leg, and the moment he was brought into camp it had to be amputated. When the operation was over, Napier was heard to murmur, 'I shall never lead the Rifles again! I shall never lead the Rifles again!' His wound he thought little of. What grieved him was the idea of having to give up his career as a soldier, and to leave the regiment he was so proud of. Napier was taken to Meerut, where he died a few days afterwards.*

On the 1st June Wilson's force was strengthened by the Sirmur battalion of Gurkhas,† a regiment which later covered itself with glory, and gained an undying name by its gallantry during the siege of Delhi.

On the 7th June Wilson's brigade crossed the Jumna at Baghput, and at Alipur it joined Barnard's force, the men of which loudly cheered their Meerut comrades as they marched into camp with the captured guns. The siege-train had arrived the previous day, and Barnard was now ready for an advance. His force consisted of about 600 Cavalry and 2,400 Infantry, with 22 field-guns. There were besides 150 European Artillerymen, chiefly recruits, with the siege-train, which comprised eight 18-pounders, four 8-inch and twelve 5½-inch mortars. The guns, if not exactly obsolete, were quite unsuited for the work that had to be done, but they were the best procurable. George Campbell, in his 'Memoirs of my Indian Career,' thus describes the siege-train as he saw it passing through Kurnal: 'I could not help thinking that it looked a very trumpery affair with which to bombard and take a great fortified city;' and he expressed his 'strong belief that Delhi would never be taken by that battery.'

Barnard heard that the enemy intended to oppose his march to Delhi, and in order to ascertain their exact position he sent Lieutenant Hodson (who had previously done good service for the Commander-in-Chief by opening communication with Meerut) to reconnoitre the road. Hodson reported that the rebels were in force at Badli-ki-Serai a little more than halfway between Alipur and Delhi. Orders were accordingly issued for an advance at midnight on the 7th June.

When it became known that a battle was imminent, there was great enthusiasm amongst the troops, who were burning to avenge the

* The Chaplain's Narrative of the siege of Delhi.

† Now the 1st Battalion, 2nd Gurkhas.

MAJOR-GENERAL SIR HARRY TOMBS, V.C., K.C.B.

From
a photograph by Messrs. Grillet and Co.

massacres of Meerut and Delhi. The sick in hospital declared they would remain there no longer, and many, quite unfit to walk, insisted on accompanying the attacking column, imploring their comrades not to mention that they were ill, for fear they should not be allowed to take part in the fight.*

The mutineers had selected an admirable position on both sides of the main road. To their right was a serai and a walled village capable of holding large numbers of Infantry, and protected by an impassable swamp. To their left, on some rising ground, a sand-bag battery for four heavy guns and an 8-inch mortar had been constructed. On both sides the ground was swampy and intersected by water-cuts, and about a mile to the enemy's left, and nearly parallel to the road, ran the Western Jumna Canal.

At the hour named, Brigadier Hope Grant,† commanding the Cavalry, started with ten Horse Artillery guns, three squadrons of the 9th Lancers, and fifty Jhind horsemen under Lieutenant Hodson, with the object of turning the enemy's left flank. Shortly afterwards the main body marched along the road until the lights in the enemy's camp became visible. Colonel Showers, who had succeeded Hallifax in the command of the 1st Brigade,‡ moved off to the right of the road, and Colonel Graves, who had taken Jones's place with the 2nd Brigade,§ to the left. The heavy guns remained on the road with a battery of Field Artillery on either flank. Just as day broke our guns advanced, but before they were in position the fight began by a cannonade from the rebel Artillery, which caused us severe loss. To this destructive fire no adequate reply could be made; our guns were too few and of too small calibre. To add to our difficulties, the Native bullock-drivers of our heavy guns went off with their cattle, and one of the waggons blew up. At this critical moment Barnard ordered Showers to charge the enemy's guns, a service which was performed with heroic gallantry by Her Majesty's 75th Foot, who carried the position at the point of the bayonet, with a loss of 19 officers and men killed and 43 wounded. Then, supported by the 1st Fusiliers, the same regiment dashed across the road and burst open the gates of the serai. A desperate fight ensued, but the sepoys were no match for British bayonets, and they now learnt that their misdeeds were not to be allowed to go unpunished. Graves's brigade, having passed round the *jhil*,‖ appeared on the enemy's right rear, while Grant with his Cavalry and Horse Artillery threatened their left. The defeat was complete, and the rebels retreated hastily towards Delhi, leaving their guns on the ground.

* 'Siege of Delhi: by an Officer who served there.'
† The late General Sir Hope Grant, G.C.B.
‡ 75th and 1st Bengal Fusiliers.
§ 1st Battalion 60th Rifles, 2nd Bengal Fusiliers, and Sirmur battalion.
‖ Swampy ground.

Although the men were much exhausted, Barnard determined to push on, for he feared that if he delayed the rebels might rally, and occupy another strong position.

From the cross-roads just beyond Badli-ki-Serai could be seen the Ridge on which the British force was to hold its own for more than three months during the heat of an Indian summer, and under the rain of an Indian monsoon. At this point two columns were formed, Barnard taking command of the one, which proceeded to the left towards the cantonment, and Wilson of the other, which moved along the city road. Wilson's column fought its way through gardens and enclosures until it reached the western extremity of the Ridge. Barnard, as he came under the fire of the enemy's guns, made a flank movement to the left, and then, wheeling to his right, swept along the Ridge from the Flagstaff Tower to Hindu Rao's house, where the two columns united, the rebels flying before them.

Barnard had achieved a great success and with comparatively small loss, considering the formidable position occupied by the enemy, their great strength in Artillery, and their superiority in numbers.

Our casualties were 51 killed and 131 wounded. Among the former was Colonel Chester, the Adjutant-General of the Army. Of the troops opposed to us it was reckoned that 1,000 never returned to Delhi; thirteen guns were captured, two of them being 24-pounders.

I have frequently wandered over the Ridge since 1857, and thought how wonderfully we were aided by finding a ready-made position—not only a coign of vantage for attack, but a rampart of defence, as Forrest* describes it. This Ridge, rising sixty feet above the city, covered the main line of communication to the Punjab, upon the retention of which our very existence as a force depended. Its left rested on the Jumna, unfordable from the time the snow on the higher ranges begins to melt until the rainy season is over, and of sufficient width to prevent our being enfiladed by field-guns; although, on the immediate right, bazaars, buildings, and garden-walls afforded cover to the enemy, the enclosed nature of the ground was so far advantageous that it embarrassed and impeded them in their attempts to organize an attack in force upon our flank or rear; and a further protection was afforded by the Najafgarh *jhil*, which during the rains submerges a vast area of land.

The distance of the Ridge from the city walls varied considerably. On our right, where the memorial monument now stands, it was about 1,200 yards, at the Flagstaff Tower about a mile and a half, and at the end near the river nearly two miles and a half. This rendered our left comparatively safe, and it was behind the Ridge in this direction that the main part of our camp was pitched. The Flagstaff Tower in the centre was the general rendezvous for the non-combatants, and for

* 'The Indian Mutiny,' by George W. Forrest.

those of the sick and wounded who were able to move about, as they could assemble there and hear the news from the front without much risk of injury from the enemy's fire.

The Flagstaff Tower is interesting from the fact that it was here the residents from the cantonment of Delhi assembled to make a stand, on hearing that the rebels from Meerut were murdering the British officers on duty within the city, that the three Native regiments and battery of Field Artillery had joined the mutineers, and that at any moment they themselves might expect to be attacked. The tower was 150 feet high, with a low parapet running round the top, approached by a narrow winding staircase. Here the men of the party proposed to await the attack. The ladies, who behaved with the utmost coolness and presence of mind, were, with the wives and children of the few European non-commissioned officers, placed for their greater safety on the stairs, where they were all but suffocated by the stifling heat in such a confined space. The little party on the roof consisted of some twenty British officers, the same number of half-caste buglers and drummers, and half a dozen European soldiers. Not a drop of water, not a particle of food, was to be had. No help appeared to be coming from Meerut, in the direction of which place many a longing and expectant glance had been cast during the anxious hours of that miserable 11th May. Constant and heavy firing was heard from the city and suburbs, and the Cavalry were reported to be advancing on the cantonment.

Before evening the weary watchers realized that their position was untenable, and that their only possible chance of escaping the fate which had befallen the officers within the city (whose dead bodies had been inhumanly sent in a cart to the Tower) lay in flight. Shortly before dark the move was made, the women and children were crowded into the few vehicles available, and accompanied by the men, some on foot and some on horseback, they got away by the road leading towards Umballa. They were only just in time, for before the last of the party were out of sight of the cantonment, crowds of Natives poured into it, burning, plundering, and destroying everything they could find.

Amongst the fugitives from Delhi was Captain Tytler, of the 38th Native Infantry, who, after a variety of vicissitudes, reached Umballa safely with his wife and children. When Anson's force was being formed for the advance on Delhi, Tytler was placed in charge of the military treasure chest, and through some unaccountable negligence Mrs. Tytler was allowed to accompany him. I believe that, when Mrs. Tytler's presence became known to the authorities, she would have been sent out of camp to some safe place, but at that time she was not in a fit state to travel, and on the 21st June, a few days after the force took up its position under a heavy cannonade, she gave birth to a son in the waggon in which she was accommodated. The infant, who was christened Stanley Delhi Force, seems to have been looked upon by the soldiery with quite a superstitious feeling, for the father tells us that soon after its birth he overheard a soldier say; 'Now we shall get our reinforcements; this camp was formed to avenge the blood of innocents, and the first reinforcement sent to us is a new-born infant.' Reinforcements did actually arrive the next day.

It was on the afternoon of the 8th June that the British force was placed in position on the Ridge. The main piquet was established at Hindu Rao's house, a large stone building, in former days the country residence of some Mahratta Chief. About one hundred and eighty yards further to the left was the observatory, near which our heavy gun battery was erected. Beyond the observatory was an old Pathan mosque, in which was placed an Infantry piquet with two field-guns. Still further to the left came the Flagstaff Tower, held by a party of Infantry with two more field-guns. At the extreme right of the Ridge, overlooking the trunk road, there was a strong piquet with a heavy battery.

This was the weak point of our defence. To the right, and somewhat to the rear, was the suburb of Sabzi Mandi (vegetable market), a succession of houses and walled gardens, from which the rebels constantly threatened our flank. To protect this part of the position as much as possible, a battery of three 18-pounders and an Infantry piquet was placed on what was known as the General's Mound, with a Cavalry piquet and two Horse Artillery guns immediately below. In front of the Ridge the ground was covered with old buildings, enclosures, and clumps of trees, which afforded only too perfect shelter to the enemy when making their sorties.

As described by the Commanding Engineer, 'the eastern face of Delhi rests on the Jumna, and at the season of the year during which our operations were carried on, the stream may be described as washing the face of the walls. The river front was therefore inaccessible to the besieging force, while at the same time the mutineers and the inhabitants of the city could communicate freely across the river by means of the bridge of boats and ferries. This rendered it impossible for us to invest Delhi, even if there had been a sufficient number of troops for the purpose. We were only able, indeed, to direct our attack against a small portion of the city wall, while throughout the siege the enemy could freely communicate with, and procure supplies from, the surrounding country.

'On the river front the defences consisted of an irregular wall with occasional bastions and towers, and about one half of the length of this face was occupied by the palace of the King of Delhi and its outwork, the old Moghul fort of Selimgarh.

'The remaining defences consisted of a succession of bastioned fronts, the connecting curtains being very long, and the outworks limited to one crown-work at the Ajmir gate, and Martello towers mounting a single gun, at the points where additional flanking fire to that given by the bastions themselves was required.'*

The above description will give some idea of the strength of the great city which the British force had come to capture. For more than two months, however, our energies were devoted not to capturing the city, but to defending ourselves, having to be ever on the watch to guard our communication with the Punjab, and to repel the enemy's almost daily sorties.

The defences of Delhi, which remain almost unaltered up to the present day, were modernized forms of the ancient works that existed when the city fell before Lord Lake's army in 1803. These works had been strengthened and improved some years before the Mutiny by Lieutenant Robert Napier.† How thoroughly and effectually that talented and distinguished Engineer performed the duty entrusted to him, we who had to attack Delhi could testify to our cost.

Barnard was not left long in doubt as to the intentions of the rebels, who, the very afternoon on which he occupied the Ridge, attacked Hindu Rao's house, where the Sirmur battalion, two companies of the 60th Rifles, and two of Scott's guns had been placed. The enemy were driven off before dark. The following day they began to cannonade from the city walls, and in the afternoon repeated their attack.

That same morning a welcome reinforcement reached camp, the famous Corps of Guides having arrived as fresh as if they had returned from an ordinary field day, instead of having come off a march of nearly 600 miles, accomplished in the incredibly short time of twenty-two days, at the most trying season of the year. The General, having inspected them, said a few words of encouragement to the men, who begged their gallant Commandant to say how proud they were to belong to the Delhi Force. Their usefulness was proved that same

* The bastions were small, each mounting from ten to fourteen pieces of Artillery; they were provided with masonry parapets about 12 feet in thickness, and were about 16 feet high. The curtain consisted of a simple masonry wall or rampart 16 feet in height, 11 feet thick at top, and 14 or 15 feet at bottom. This main wall carried a parapet loopholed for musketry 8 feet in height and 3 feet in thickness. The whole of the land front was covered by a faussebraye of varying thickness, ranging from 16 to 30 feet, and having a vertical scarp wall 8 feet high; exterior to this was a dry ditch about 25 feet in width. The counterscarp was simply an earthen slope, easy to descend. The glacis was very narrow, extending only 50 or 60 yards from the counterscarp, and covering barely one-half of the walls from the besiegers' view. These walls were about seven miles in circumference, and included an area of about three square miles (see Colonel Baird-Smith's report, dated September 17, 1857).

† The late Field Marshal Lord Napier of Magdala, G.C.B., G.C.S.I.

afternoon, when, in support of the piquets, they engaged the enemy in a hand-to-hand contest, and drove them back to the city.

It was close up to the walls that Quintin Battye, the dashing Commander of the Guides Cavalry, received his mortal wound. He was the brightest and cheeriest of companions, and although only a subaltern of eight years' service, he was a great loss. I spent a few hours with him on my way to Delhi, and I remember how his handsome face glowed when he talked of the opportunities for distinguishing themselves in store for the Guides. Proud of his regiment, and beloved by his men, who, grand fellows themselves, were captivated by his many soldierly qualities, he had every prospect before him of a splendid career, but he was destined to fall in his first fight. He was curiously fond of quotations, and the last words he uttered were '*Dulce et decorum est pro patriâ mori.*'

While our Infantry and Field Artillery were busily engaged with the enemy, the few heavy guns we had were put in position on the Ridge. Great things were hoped from them, but it was soon found that they were not powerful enough to silence the enemy's fire, and that our small supply of ammunition was being rapidly expended.* The rebels' guns were superior in number and some in calibre to ours, and were well served by the Native Artillerymen whom we had been at such pains to teach. Barnard discovered, too, that his deficiencies in men and *matériel* prevented regular approaches being made. There were only 150 Native Sappers and Miners with our force, and Infantry could not be spared for working parties.

On the 10th June another determined attack was made on Hindu Rao's house, which was repulsed by the Sirmur battalion of Gurkhas under its distinguished Commandant, Major Reid.† The mutineers quite hoped that the Gurkhas would join them, and as they were advancing they called out: 'We are not firing; we want to speak to you; we want you to join us.' The little Gurkhas replied, 'Oh yes; we are coming,' on which they advanced to within twenty paces of the rebels, and, firing a well-directed volley, killed nearly thirty of them.

The next day the insurgents made a third attack, and were again repulsed with considerable loss. They knew that Hindu Rao's house was the key of our position, and throughout the siege they made the most desperate attempts to capture it. But Barnard had entrusted this post of danger to the Gurkhas, and all efforts to dislodge them were unavailing. At first Reid had at his command only his own battalion and two companies of the 60th Rifles; but on the arrival of the Guides

* So badly off were we for ammunition for the heavy guns at this time, that it was found necessary to use the shot fired at us by the enemy, and a reward was offered for every 24-pounder shot brought into the Artillery Park.

† Now General Sir Charles Reid, G.C.B.

their Infantry were also placed at his disposal, and whenever he sounded the alarm he was reinforced by two more companies of the 60th. Hindu Rao's house was within easy range of nearly all the enemy's heavy guns, and was riddled through and through with shot and shell. Reid never quitted the Ridge save to attack the enemy, and never once visited the camp until carried into it severely wounded on the day of the final assault. Hindu Rao's house was the little Gurkhas' hospital as well as their barrack, for their sick and wounded begged to be left with their comrades instead of being taken to camp.*

Failing in their attempts on the centre of the position, the mutineers soon after daylight on the 12th, having concealed themselves in the ravines adjoining Metcalfe House, attacked the Flagstaff Tower, the piquet of which was composed of two Horse Artillery guns and two companies of the 75th Foot, under the command of Captains Dunbar and Knox. A heavy fog and thick mist rolling up from the low ground near the Jumna completely enveloped the Ridge and the left front of our position, hiding everything in the immediate vicinity. The piquet was on the point of being relieved by a detachment of the 2nd Bengal Fusiliers, when a large body of the enemy, who had crept up unobserved, made a rush at the Flagstaff Tower, and as nearly as possible captured the guns. The piquet was hardly pressed, Knox and several men were killed, and but for the timely arrival of two companies of the 60th, the rebels would have gained the day.

This engagement was scarcely over, when masses of insurgents advanced from the Sabzi Mandi upon Hindu Rao's house, and into the gardens on the right flank of the camp, threatening the Mound piquet. Reserves were called up, these attacks, in their turn, were repulsed and the rebels were pursued for some distance. It was most fortunate that both attacks did not take place simultaneously, as was the obvious intention of the enemy, for our strength would not have been sufficient to repel them both at the same moment.

In order to prevent the mutineers from coming to such close quarters again, a piquet was placed in Metcalfe's House, and the Mound to the rear of the ridge facing the Sabzi Mandi was strengthened. These precautions ought to, and would, have been taken before, but for the want of men. Our soldiers were scarcely ever off duty, and this fresh demand made it impossible at times to provide a daily relief for the several piquets.

Our resources in siege guns and ammunition were so limited, daily sorties, disease, and heat were making such ravages amongst our small force, there was so little hope of receiving any considerable reinforcements, and it appeared to be of such paramount importance to capture

* Forrest's 'Indian Mutiny' and Norman's 'Narrative of the Siege of Delhi,' two interesting accounts from which I shall often quote.

Delhi without further delay, that Barnard agreed to a proposal for taking it by a *coup de main.*

The particular details of the project and disposition of the troops were worked out by three young officers of Engineers, under the direct orders of the General, and were kept a profound secret; even the Commanding Engineer was not made acquainted with them. Secrecy was, of course, of vital importance, but that the officers who ought to have been chiefly concerned were kept in ignorance of the scheme, shows there was little of that confidence so essential to success existing between the Commander and those who were in the position of his principal advisers. Practically the whole force was to be engaged, divided into three columns—one to enter by the Kashmir gate, the second by the Lahore gate, and the third was to attempt an escalade. The three columns, if they succeeded in effecting an entrance, were to work their way to the centre of the city, and there unite.

It was intended that these columns should move off from camp so as to arrive at the walls just before daybreak; accordingly, at one o'clock on the morning of the 13th June the troops were suddenly paraded and ammunition served out, and then for the first time the Commanders of the three columns and the staff were made acquainted with the General's intentions. It so happened that the 75th Foot, which had followed the enemy into the grounds of Metcalfe House after the repulse on the Flagstaff Tower the previous morning, had through some oversight never been recalled; their absence was only discovered when the order was given for the regiment to turn out, and a considerable time was wasted in sending for it and bringing it back to camp. Day was breaking when this regiment received its ammunition, and all hope of an unperceived advance to the walls had to be given up. The troops were therefore dismissed, and allowed to turn in, having been uselessly disturbed from their much-needed rest.

The failure to give effect to the young Engineer officers' plan may be looked upon as a merciful dispensation of Providence, which saved us from what would almost certainly have been an irreparable disaster. When we think of the hard fighting encountered when the assault did take place under much more favourable circumstances, and how the columns at the end of that day were only just able to get inside the city, those who had practical knowledge of the siege can judge what chance there would have been of these smaller columns accomplishing their object, even if they had been able to take the enemy by surprise.

The 13th and 14th passed in comparative quiet; but early on the 15th a strong force advanced from Delhi against the Metcalfe House piquet, with the object of turning our left flank, but it was driven back with considerable loss.

On the 17th we were attacked from almost every direction—a manœuvre intended to prevent our observing a battery which was being constructed close to an Idgah,* situated on a hill to our right, from which to enfilade our position on the Ridge. As it was very important to prevent the completion of this battery, Barnard ordered it to be attacked by two small columns, one commanded by Tombs, of the Bengal Horse Artillery, the other by Reid. Tombs, with 400 of the 60th Rifles and 1st Bengal Fusiliers, 30 of the Guides Cavalry, 20 Sappers and Miners, and his own troop of Horse Artillery, moved towards the enemy's left, while Reid, with four companies of the 60th and some of his own Gurkhas, advanced through Kishenganj against their right. Tombs drove the rebels through a succession of gardens till they reached the Idgah, where they made an obstinate but unavailing resistance. The gates of the mosque were blown open, and thirty-nine of its defenders were killed. Tombs himself was slightly wounded, and had two horses killed, making five which had been shot under this gallant soldier since the commencement of the campaign. Reid's attack was equally successful. He completely destroyed the battery, and inflicted heavy loss on the enemy.

The next day but one the rebels issued from the city in great force, and threatened nearly every part of our position. The fighting was severe throughout the afternoon, the piquets having again and again to be reinforced. Towards evening, while nearly all the Infantry were thus engaged, a large party of the insurgents, passing unperceived through the suburbs and gardens on our right, reappeared about a mile and a half to our rear. Very few troops were left in camp, and all Hope Grant, who was in command at the time, could collect was four or five squadrons of Cavalry and twelve guns. He found the enemy in a strong position, against which his light guns could make but little impression, while their Artillery and well-placed Infantry did us considerable damage. Tombs's troop especially suffered, and at one time his guns were in imminent danger of being captured. Just at this moment some of the Guides Cavalry rode up. 'Daly, if you do not charge,' called out Tombs, 'my guns are taken.' Daly spurred into the bushes, followed by about a dozen of his gallant Guides. He returned with a bullet through his shoulder, but the momentary diversion saved the guns.†

As long as it was light the steady fire of the Artillery and the dashing charges of the Cavalry kept the rebels in check; but in the dusk of the evening their superior numbers told: they very nearly succeeded in turning our flank, and for some time the guns were again in great jeopardy; the 9th Lancers and Guides, bent on saving them at all hazards, charged the enemy; but, with a ditch and houses on each side, their action was paralyzed, and their loss severe. All was now in confusion, the disorder increasing as night advanced, when a small body of

* A Mahomedan place of worship and sacrifice.

† 'Siege of Delhi; by an Officer who served there.'

Infantry (about 300 of the 60th Rifles) came up, dashed forward, and, cutting a lane through the rebels, rescued the guns.*

Our loss in this affair amounted to 3 officers and 17 men killed, and 7 officers and 70 men wounded. Among the latter was Hope Grant, who had his horse shot under him in a charge, and was saved by the devotion of two men of his own regiment (the 9th Lancers) and a Mahomedan sowar of the 4th Irregular Cavalry.

It was nearly midnight before the troops returned to camp. The enemy had been frustrated in their attempt to force our rear, but they had not been driven back; we had, indeed, been only just able to hold our own. The result of the day added considerably to the anxiety of the Commander. He saw that the rebels had discovered our weak point, and that if they managed to establish themselves in our rear, our communication with the Punjab would be cut off, our small force would be invested, and without supplies and reinforcements it would be impossible to maintain our position against the daily increasing strength of the insurgents. Great was the despondency in camp when the result of the day's fighting was known; but the fine spirit which animated the force throughout the siege soon asserted itself, and our men cheerfully looked forward to the next encounter with the enemy.

At daybreak Grant was again upon the ground, but found it abandoned. Many dead men and horses were lying about, and a 9 pounder gun, left by the enemy, was brought into camp.

The troops had scarcely got back, hoping for a little rest, when the enemy again resumed their attack on the rear, and opened fire at so short a distance that their shot came right through the camp. But on this occasion they made no stand, and retreated as soon as our troops showed themselves.

In order to strengthen our position in rear a battery of two 18-pounders was constructed, supported by Cavalry and Infantry piquets, and most of the bridges over the drain from the Najafgarh *jhil* were destroyed.

For two days after the events I have just described the hard-worked little body of troops had comparative rest, but our spies informed us that the enemy were being largely reinforced, and that we might expect to be hotly attacked on the 23rd.

For some time an idea had been prevalent amongst the Natives that the English *raj* was not destined to survive its hundredth year, and that the centenary of Clive's victory on the field of Plassy on the 23rd June, 1757, would see its downfall. This idea was strengthened in the Native mind by the fact that the 23rd June, 1857, was a date propitious alike for Hindus and Mahomedans; the Jattsa, a Hindu religious festival, was to take place on that day, and there was also to be a new

* Forrest's 'The Indian Mutiny.'

moon, which the Mahomedans looked upon as a lucky omen; the astrologers, therefore, declared that the stars in their courses would fight for the mutineers. If, however, prophecies and omens alike appeared to favour the rebels, fortune was not altogether unkind to us, for on the 22nd a reinforcement reached Rhai, twenty-two miles from Delhi, consisting of six Horse Artillery guns, a small party of British Infantry, a squadron of the 2nd Punjab Cavalry, and the Head-Quarters of the 4th Sikhs, numbering in all about 850 men.

A staff officer was sent at once to Rhai to hurry on the force and tell them how urgently their assistance was required in camp; this appeal was responded to with the utmost alacrity, and early the next evening the welcome reinforcement made its appearance.

It had scarcely arrived before the Artillery on the city walls opened fire, while guns, which had been brought into the suburbs, enfiladed our right and concentrated a heavy fire on Hindu Rao's house which the few guns we had in position were quite unable to silence. The rebel Infantry occupied Kishenganj and Sabzi Mandi in force, and threatened to advance on the Mound battery, while a constant musketry fire was maintained upon the Ridge. Reid reported that the mutineers made a desperate attack at about twelve o'clock, and that no men could have fought better; they charged the Rifles, the Guides, and the Gurkhas again and again. The cannonade raged fast and furious, and at one time it seemed as though the day must be lost. Thousands were brought against a mere handful of men; but Reid knew the importance of his position, and was determined at all hazards to hold it until reinforcements arrived.*

The mutineers were checked, but not driven off. The first attempt from the Mound battery failed to repulse them, and Colonel Welchman, who was in command, was dangerously wounded. Every available man in camp had been engaged, and as a last resource the 2nd Fusiliers and the 4th Sikhs, who had just arrived from Rhai, were sent to the front. Showers was placed in command, and shortly before the day closed he succeeded in forcing the enemy to retire. So the anniversary of Plassy saw us, though hardly pressed, undefeated, and the enemy's hopes unfulfilled. They lost over 1,000 men. Our casualties were 1 officer and 38 men killed, and 3 officers and 118 men wounded. The heat all the while was terrific, and several of our men were knocked over by the sun.

The lesson taught us by this severe fighting was the importance of occupying the Sabzi Mandi, and thus preventing the enemy from approaching too close to the camp and enfilading the Ridge. This entailed more constant duty upon our already overworked soldiers, but Barnard felt that it would not do to run the risk of another such struggle.

* Reid's own report.

A piquet of 180 Europeans was accordingly placed in the Sabzi Mandi, part in a serai on one side of the Grand Trunk Road, and the rest in a Hindu temple on the opposite side. These posts were connected by a line of breastworks with the Hindu Rao piquets, and added considerably to the strength of our position.

After the 23rd there were real or threatened attacks daily; but we were left fairly undisturbed until the 27th June, when the Metcalfe and Sabzi Mandi piquets were assaulted, and also the batteries on the Ridge. These attempts were defeated without any very great loss, only 13 of our men being killed, and 1 officer and 48 men wounded.

CHAPTER XIV.

I WILL now continue my story from the 29th June, the morning after my arrival in camp, when I awoke full of excitement, and so eager to hear all my old friend Norman could tell me, that I am afraid he must have been considerably bored with my questions.

It is impossible for me to describe my pleasure at finding myself a member of a force which had already gained imperishable fame. I longed to meet and know the men whose names were in everyone's mouth. The hero of the day was Harry Tombs, of the Bengal Horse Artillery, an unusually handsome man and a thorough soldier. His gallantry in the attack on the Idgah, and wherever he had been engaged, was the general talk of the camp. I had always heard of Tombs as one of the best officers in the regiment, and it was with feelings of respectful admiration that I made his acquaintance a few days later.

Jemmy Hills,* one of the subalterns in Tombs's troop, was an old Addiscombe friend of mine; he delighted in talking of his Commander, in dilating on his merits as a soldier and his skill in handling each arm of the service. As a cool, bold leader of men Tombs was unsurpassed: no fire, however hot, and no crisis, however unexpected, could take him by surprise; he grasped the situation in a moment, and issued his orders without hesitation, inspiring all ranks with confidence in his power and capacity. He was somewhat of a martinet, and was more feared than liked by his men until they realized what a grand leader he was, when they gave him their entire confidence, and were ready to follow him anywhere and everywhere.

Another very distinguished officer of my regiment, whom I now met for the first time, and for whom I ever afterwards entertained the warmest regard, was Edwin Johnson,† Assistant-Adjutant-General of

* Now Lieutenant-General Sir James Hills-Johnes, V.C., G.C.B.
† The late General Sir Edwin Johnson, G.C.B.

LIEUTENANT-GENERAL SIR JAMES HILLS-JOHNES, V.C., G.C.B.

From
a photograph by Messrs. Bourne and Shepherd.

the Bengal Artillery, in which capacity he had accompanied Brigadier Wilson from Meerut. He had a peculiarly bright intellect—somewhat caustic, but always clever and amusing. He was a delightful companion, and invariably gained the confidence of those with whom he worked.

Johnson was the first person on whom I called to report my arrival and to find out with which troop or battery I was to do duty. He told me that the Quartermaster-General wished to keep me in his department. So, after visiting General Chamberlain,* who I knew would be anxious to hear all that had been going on in the Movable Column since his departure, I made my way to Colonel Becher, whom I found suffering from the severe wound he had received a few days before, and asked him what was to be my fate. He replied that the question had been raised of appointing an officer to help the Assistant-Adjutant-General of the Delhi Field Force, who found it impossible to carry on the daily increasing work single-handed, and that Chamberlain had thought of me for this post. Had Chamberlain's wish been carried out my career might have been quite changed, but while he was discussing the question with Sir Henry Barnard, Donald Stewart unexpectedly arrived in camp.

I was waiting outside Sir Henry Barnard's tent, anxious to hear what decision had been come to, when two men rode up, both looking greatly fatigued and half starved; one of them being Stewart. He told me they had had a most adventurous ride; but before waiting to hear his story,† I asked Norman to suggest Stewart for the new appointment—a case of one word for Stewart and two for myself, I am afraid, for I had set my heart on returning to the Quartermaster-General's department. And so it was settled, to our mutual satisfaction, Stewart becoming the D.A.A.G. of the Delhi Field Force, and I the D.A.Q.M.G. with the Artillery.

CHAPTER XV.

THAT my readers may better understand our position at the time I joined the Delhi Field Force, I might, I think, quote with advantage from a letter‡ written the very day of my arrival by General Barnard to Sir John Lawrence, in which he describes the difficulties of the situation, hitherto met by the troops with the most determined courage and endurance, but to which no end could be seen. When he took

* Chamberlain had been given the rank of Brigadier-General on his arrival at Delhi.

† The account of this adventurous ride is given in the Appendix.

‡ See Kaye's 'History of the Indian Mutiny.'

over the command, he wrote, he was expected to be able to silence at once the fire from the Mori and Kashmir bastions, and then to bring his heavy guns into play on the walls and open a way into the city, after which, it was supposed, all would be plain sailing. But this programme, so plausible in theory, was absolutely impossible to put into practice. In spite of every effort on our part, not a single one of the enemy's guns was silenced; they had four to our one, while the distance from the Ridge to the city walls was too great to allow of our comparatively light guns making any impression on them. Under these circumstances the only thing to be done was to construct batteries nearer to the city, but before these could be begun, entrenching tools, sandbags, and other necessary materials, of which the Engineers were almost entirely destitute, had to be collected. The troops were being worn out by constant sanguinary combats, and the attacks to which they were exposed required every soul in camp to repel them. It was never certain where the enemy intended to strike, and it was only by the most constant vigilance that their intentions could be ascertained, and the men were being incessantly withdrawn during the scorching heat of the day from one place to another. General Barnard concluded as follows: 'You may ask why we engage in these constant combats. The reason simply is that when attacked we must defend ourselves, and that to secure our camp, our hospitals, our stores, etc., every living being has to be employed. The whole thing is too gigantic for the force brought against it.'

Soon after Barnard wrote these lines reinforcements began to arrive, and our position was gradually improved. By the 3rd July the following troops had reached Delhi: four Horse Artillery guns (two British and two Native), a detachment of European Foot Artillery, the Head-Quarters of Her Majesty's 8th and 61st Foot, one squadron of the 5th Punjab Cavalry, the 1st Punjab Infantry, and some newly-raised Sikh Sappers and Artillery. The strength of the force was thus increased to nearly 6,600 men of all arms. The enemy's reinforcements, however, were out of all proportion to ours—mutineers from Jullundur, Nasirabad, Nimach, Kotah, Gwalior, Jhansi, and Rohilkand arrived about this time. Those from Rohilkand crossed by the bridge of boats and entered the city by the Calcutta gate; we could distinctly see them from the Ridge, marching in perfect formation, with their bands playing and colours flying. Indeed, throughout the siege the enemy's numbers were constantly being increased, while they had a practically unlimited number of guns, and the well-stocked magazine furnished them with an inexhaustible supply of ammunition.

I found myself under fire for the first time on the 30th June, when an attack was made on the Sabzi Mandi piquet and Hindu Rao's house. Eight of our men were killed and thirty wounded; amongst the latter were Yorke and Packe, both attached to the 4th Sikhs. It appeared

FIELD-MARSHAL SIR DONALD MARTIN STEWART, BART., G.C.B., G.C.S.I., C.I.E.

From
a photograph by Messrs. Elliott and Fry.

certain that these two officers were wounded by the Hindustanis of their own regiment; Packe, who was shot through the ankle, being so close up to the breastwork that it was scarcely possible for the bullet which hit him to have come from the front. Consequently all the Hindustanis in the 4th Sikhs were disarmed and turned out of camp, as it was manifestly undesirable to have any but the most loyal soldiers in our ranks.

In the afternoon of the same day I was ordered to accompany a column under Brigadier Showers, sent on reconnoitring duty towards the Idgah, where we heard that the enemy were again constructing a battery. It had not been commenced, but the intention to build one was evident, for we found a number of entrenching tools, and a quantity of sandbags.

The question of attempting to take the city by a *coup de main* was now again discussed. It was urged that our numbers, already small, were being daily reduced by casualties and sickness; that the want of proper equipment rendered it impossible to undertake regular siege operations; and that a rising in the Punjab was imminent. The chances of success were certainly more favourable than they were on the 13th June. The force to be employed was stronger; all concerned—the staff, commanders, and troops—were fully apprised of what was intended, and of the part they would have to play; above all, the details of the scheme, which was drawn up on much the same lines as the former one, were carefully worked out by Lieutenant Alex. Taylor,* who had recently come into camp, and was acting temporarily as Commanding Engineer.

Of the supreme importance of regaining possession of Delhi there can be no doubt whatever. But nevertheless the undertaking would, at that time, have been a most desperate one, and only to be justified by the critical position in which we were placed. In spite of the late reinforcements, we were a mere handful compared with the thousands within the walls. Success, therefore, depended on the completeness of the surprise; and, as we could make no movement without its being perceived by the enemy, surprise was impossible. Another strong reason against assaulting at that time was the doubtful attitude of some of the Hindustani Cavalry still with us; the whole of the effective troops, too, would have to be employed, and the sick and wounded—a large number—left to the mercy of the Native followers.

General Barnard carefully weighed all the arguments for and against the proposal, and at last reluctantly consented to the attack being made, but the discovery of a conspiracy amongst the Natives in camp caused it to be countermanded—a great disappointment to many, and there was much cavilling and discontent on the part of some, who

* Now General Sir Alexander Taylor, G.C.B.

could not have sufficiently appreciated the difficulties and risks of the undertaking, or the disastrous consequences of a repulse.

On the morning of the day on which it had been arranged that the assault should be made, the staff at Delhi received a most valuable addition in the person of Lieutenant-Colonel Baird-Smith, of the Bengal Engineers. Summoned from Rurki to take the place of the Chief Engineer, whose health had broken down, Baird-Smith was within sixty miles of Delhi on the 2nd July, when news of the intended movement reached him. He started at once, and arrived in camp early on the 3rd, but only to find that the assault had been postponed.

On the afternoon of the 3rd July the enemy came out in force (5,000 or 6,000 strong with several guns), and occupied the suburbs to our right. The troops were turned out, but instead of attacking us and returning to the city as usual when it became dark, the rebels moved off in the direction of Alipur, where we had an outpost, which was held by Younghusband's squadron of the 5th Punjab Cavalry. They reached Alipur about midnight, and had they attacked the serai at once with Infantry, Younghusband and his men could hardly have escaped, but fortunately they opened upon it with Artillery. This gave the sowars time to mount and fall back on Rhai, the next post, ten miles to the rear, which was garrisoned by the friendly troops of the Jhind Raja. The sound of the guns being heard in camp, a column under the command of Major Coke was got ready to pursue should the insurgents push up the Trunk Road, or to cut them off should they try to make their way back to the city. Besides his own corps (the 1st Punjab Infantry), Coke was given a wing of the 61st Foot, six Horse and six Field Artillery guns, one squadron of the Carabineers, one squadron of the 9th Lancers, and the Guides Cavalry; in all about 800 Infantry, 300 Cavalry, and 12 guns, and I was sent with him as staff officer.

It was generally believed that the enemy were on the look-out for treasure coming from the Punjab, which was known to be under the charge of a Native guard, and we quite expected to have a long chase after them; we were, therefore, surprised to see them, as day broke, crossing our front on their way back to Delhi.

The rebels were moving on fairly high ground, but between us and them was a swamp rendered almost impassable by recent heavy rain. It extended a considerable distance on either side, and as there was no other way of getting at the rapidly retreating foe, it had to be crossed. Our Artillery opened fire, and Coke advanced with the Cavalry and Infantry. The swamp proved to be very difficult; in it men and horses floundered hopelessly, and before we were clear the enemy had got away with their guns; they were obliged, however, to leave behind all the plunder taken from Alipur, and a considerable quantity of ammunition. My share of the loot was a nice looking, white, country-bred pony, which I found tied to a tree. I promptly annexed it, glad to save my own horse, and I congratulated myself on having made a most useful addition to my small stud. It did not, however, remain long in my possession, for a few days afterwards it was claimed by its rightful owner, Lieutenant Younghusband.

The heat was great, and as the soldiers were much distressed, having been under arms for ten hours, Coke halted the Infantry portion on the banks of the Western Jumna Canal instead of returning direct to camp. While we were enjoying a much-needed rest we were unexpectedly attacked by some fresh troops (including about 800 Cavalry) which had hurried out from the city. I was startled from a sound sleep by heavy firing, and saw the enemy advancing within a few hundred yards of our halting-place. Coke formed his Infantry along the bank of the canal, and sent a mounted officer to recall the Cavalry and Artillery. The enemy came on very boldly at first, but the steady fire of our Infantry kept them at bay, and when the guns arrived we had no difficulty in driving them off. They left 80 dead on the field; we had on our side 3 killed and 23 wounded, besides losing several British soldiers from sunstroke.

Major Coke was much grieved by the loss in this engagement of a Native friend of his, a Chief of the Kohat border, by name Mir Mubarak Shah. He was a grand specimen of a frontier Khan,* and on hearing that the 1st Punjab Infantry was ordered to Delhi expressed his determination to accompany it. He got together a troop of eighty of his own followers, and leaving Kohat on the 1st June, overtook Coke at Kurnal on the 27th, a distance of nearly 600 miles. A day or two afterwards Coke's men were approached by the Hindustanis of the 2nd Punjab Cavalry, and some Native officers of the 9th Irregulars, who tried to induce them to join in the rebellion. Advances were made in the first instance to Mir Mubarak Shah and Mir Jaffir, the Subadar-Major of the 1st Punjab Infantry, who at once informed Coke of what was going on. As soon as the regiment reached Delhi the matter was investigated, and the Native officers who had endeavoured to tamper with the men were identified, tried, and executed.

About noon on the 5th July we heard the woeful tidings that General Barnard was seized with cholera. The army had never been free from that terrible scourge since the Commander-in-Chief fell a victim to it on the 26th May, and now it had attacked his successor, who was carried off after a few hours' illness. The feeling of sadness amongst the troops at the loss of their General was universal. Throughout the six trying weeks he had been in command of the force he had never spared himself. At work from morning till night in and about the trenches, he personally attended to every detail, and had won the respect and regard of all in camp.

* Mahomedans of good family are so styled in northern India.

Few Commanders were ever placed in a more difficult position than Barnard. He arrived at Umballa when the Native troops, to whose characteristics and peculiarities (as I have already remarked) he was a complete stranger, were thoroughly disaffected, and within a week of his taking over the command of the Sirhind division the Mutiny broke out. Without any previous knowledge of Indian warfare, he found himself in front of Delhi with a force altogether too weak to effect the object for which it was intended and without any of the appliances to ensure success; while those who did not realize the extreme risk involved never ceased clamouring at a delay which was unavoidable, and urging the General to undertake a task which was impossible.

Barnard has been blamed, and not unjustly, for mistrusting his own judgment and for depending upon others for advice about matters on which an experienced Commander ought to have been the best able to decide. But every allowance must be made for the position he was so unexpectedly called upon to fill and the peculiar nature of his surroundings. Failing health, too, probably weakened the self-reliance which a man who had satisfactorily performed the duties of Chief of the Staff in the Crimea must at one time have possessed.

On the death of Sir Henry Barnard, General Reed assumed command. He had joined the force on the morning of the action of Badli-ki-Serai, but though senior to Barnard, he was too much knocked up by the intense heat of the long journey from Peshawar to take part in the action, and he had allowed Barnard to continue in command.

For the next few days we had a comparatively quiet time, of which advantage was taken to render our position more secure towards the rear. The secrecy and rapidity with which the enemy had made their way to Alipur warned the authorities how easily our communication with the Punjab might be cut off. Baird-Smith saw the necessity for remedying this, and, acting on his advice, Reed had all the bridges over the Western Jumna Canal destroyed for several miles, except one required for our own use. The Phulchudder aqueduct, which carried the canal water into the city, and along which horsemen could pass to the rear of our camp, was blown up, as was also the Bussye bridge over the drain from the Najafgarh *jhil*, about eight miles from camp.

We were not left long in peace, for on the morning of the 9th July the enemy moved out of the city in great force, and for several hours kept up an incessant cannonade on our front and right flank.

The piquet below the General's Mound happened to be held this day by two guns of Tombs's troop, commanded by Second Lieutenant James Hills, and by thirty men of the Carabineers under Lieutenant Stillman. A little beyond, and to the right of this piquet, a Native officer's party of the 9th Irregular Cavalry had been placed to watch the Trunk Road. These men were still supposed to be loyal; the regiment to which they belonged had a good reputation, and as

Christie's Horse had done excellent service in Afghanistan, where Neville and Crawford Chamberlain had served with it as subalterns. It was, therefore, believed at the Mound piquet that ample warning would be given of any enemy coming from the direction of the Trunk Road, so that the approach of some horsemen dressed like the men of the 9th Irregulars attracted little notice.

Stillman and Hills were breakfasting together, when a sowar from the Native officers' party rode up and reported that a body of the enemy's Cavalry were in sight. Hills told the man to gallop to Head-Quarters with the report, and to warn Tombs as he passed his tent. Hills and Stillman then mounted their men, neither of them having the remotest idea that the news of the enemy's advance had been purposely delayed until there was not time to turn out the troops. They imagined that the sowar was acting in good faith and had given them sufficient notice, and while Hills moved his guns towards the position from which he could command the Trunk Road, Stillman proceeded to the top of the Mound in order to get a better view of the ground over which the enemy were said to be advancing. The troop of the Carabineers was thus left by itself to receive the first rush of the rebel Cavalry; it was composed of young soldiers, some of them quite untrained, who turned and broke.

The moment Hills saw the enemy he shouted, 'Action front!' and, in the hope of giving his men time to load and fire a round of grape, he gallantly charged the head of the column single-handed, cut down the leading man, struck the second, and then was then ridden down himself. It had been raining heavily, so Hills wore his cloak; which probably saved his life, for it was cut through in many places, as were his jacket and even his shirt.

As soon as the body of the enemy had passed on, Hills, extricating himself from his horse, got up and searched for his sword, which he had lost in the mêlée. He had just found it when he was attacked by three men, two of whom were mounted; he fired at and wounded the first man; then caught the lance of the second in his left hand, and ran him through the body with his sword. The first assailant coming on again, Hills cut him down, upon which he was attacked by the third man on foot, who succeeded in wrenching his sword from him. Hills fell in the struggle, and must have been killed, if Tombs, who had been duly warned by the sowar, and had hurried out to the piquet, had not come to the rescue and saved his plucky subaltern's life.*

Notwithstanding Hills's gallant attempt to stop the sowars, his men had not time to fire a single round before they were upon them. Their object, however, was not to capture these two guns, but to induce the Native Horse Artillery to join them, and galloping past the piquet, they

* Tombs and Hills both received the Victoria Cross for their gallantry.

made straight for the troop, and called upon the men to bring away their guns. The Native Artillerymen behaved admirably: they not only refused to respond to the call, but they begged the men of the European troop, which was unlimbered close by, to fire through them on the mutineers.

Knowing nothing of what was happening, I was standing by my tent, watching my horses, which had just arrived from Philour, as they crossed the bridge over the canal cut which ran at the rear of our camp, when the enemy's Cavalry galloped over the bridge, and for a few moments my animals seemed in considerable danger; the sowars, however, having lost more than one-third of their number, and having failed in their attempt to get hold of the Native Horse Artillery guns, were bent upon securing their retreat rather than upon plunder. My servants gave a wonderful account of the many perils they had encountered—somewhat exaggerated, I dare say—but they had done me a real good service, having marched 200 miles through a very disturbed country, and arriving with animals and baggage in good order. Indeed, throughout the Mutiny my servants behaved admirably. The *khidmatgar* (table attendant) never failed to bring me my food under the hottest fire, and the *saices* (grooms) were always present with the horses whenever they were required, apparently quite indifferent to the risks they often ran. Moreover, they became imbued with such a warlike spirit that, when I was invalided in April, 1858, four of them enlisted in a regiment of Bengal Cavalry. The *khidmatgar* died soon after the Mutiny, but two of his brothers were afterwards in my service; one, who was with me during the Lushai expedition and the whole of the Afghan war, never left me for more than twenty years, and we parted with mutual regret at Bombay on board the P. and O. steamer in which I took my final departure from India in April, 1893.

Mine was not a solitary instance; not only the officers' servants, but the followers belonging to European regiments, such as cook-boys, *saices* and *bhistics* (water-carriers), as a rule, behaved in the most praiseworthy manner, faithful and brave to a degree. So much was this the case, that when the troopers of the 9th Lancers were called upon to name the man they considered most worthy of the Victoria Cross, an honour which Sir Colin Campbell purposed to confer upon the regiment to mark his appreciation of the gallantry displayed by all ranks during the campaign, they unanimously chose the head *bhistie!* Considering the peculiar position we were in at the time, it is somewhat remarkable that the conduct of the Native servants should have been so generally satisfactory. It speaks as well, I think, for the masters as the servants, and proves (what I have sometimes heard denied) that Native servants are, as a rule, kindly and considerately treated by their European masters.

To return to my story. The cannonade from within and without the city continued unceasing, and the enemy had again to be driven out of the near suburbs. This duty was entrusted to General Chamberlain, whom I accompanied as one of his staff officers. His column consisted of about 800 Infantry and six guns, a few more men joining us as we passed the Ridge. This was the first occasion on which I had witnessed fighting in gardens and walled enclosures, and I realized how difficult it was to dislodge men who knew how to take advantage of the cover thus afforded. Our soldiers, as usual, fought well against very heavy odds, and before we were able to force the enemy back into the city we had lost 1 officer and 40 men killed, and 8 officers and 163 men wounded, besides 11 poor fellows missing: every one of whom must have been murdered. The enemy had nearly 500 men killed, and considerably more than that number wounded.

The result of the day's experience was so far satisfactory that it determined General Reed to get rid of all the Hindustani soldiers still remaining in camp. It was clear that the Native officers' party near the Mound piquet had been treacherous; none of them were ever seen again, and it was generally believed that they had joined the enemy in their dash through the camp. The other Native soldiers did not hesitate to denounce their Hindustani comrades as traitors; the latter were consequently all sent away, except a few men of the 4th Irregular Cavalry who were deprived of their horses and employed solely as orderlies. It was also thought advisable to take the guns from the Native troop of Horse Artillery. A few of the younger men belonging to it deserted, but the older soldiers continued faithful, and did good work in the breaching batteries.

There was a short lull after our fight on the 9th—a sure sign that the enemy's loss was heavier than they had calculated upon. When the mutineers received reinforcements we were certain to be attacked within a few hours, but if no fresh troops arrived on the scene we could generally depend upon a day or two's respite.

Our next fight was on the 14th July. The rebels came out on that morning in great numbers, attacking Hindu Rao's house and the Sabzi Mandi piquets, and supported by a continuous fire of Artillery from the walls. For some hours we remained on the defensive, but as the enemy's numbers increased, and we were greatly harassed by their fire, a column was formed to dislodge them. It was of about the usual strength, viz., 800 Infantry and six Horse Artillery guns, with the addition of a few of the Guides Cavalry and of Hodson's newly-raised Horse. The command was given to Brigadier Showers, and I was sent as his staff officer; Reid joined in at the foot of the Ridge with all the men that could be spared, and Brigadier-General Chamberlain also accompanied the column.

We moved on under a very heavy fire until we reached an enclosure the wall of which was lined with the enemy. The troops stopped short, when Chamberlain, seeing that they hesitated, called upon them to follow him, and gave them a splendid example by jumping his horse over the wall. The men did follow him, and Chamberlain got a ball in his shoulder.

We had great difficulty in driving the enemy back; they contested every inch of the ground, the many serais and walled gardens affording them admirable cover; but our troops were not to be withstood; position after position was carried until we found ourselves in sight of the Lahore gate and close up to the walls of the city. In our eagerness to drive the enemy back we had, however, come too far. It was impossible to remain where we were. Musketry from the walls and grape from the heavy guns mounted on the Mori and other bastions committed terrible havoc. Men were falling on all sides, but the getting back was hazardous to the last degree. Numerous as the enemy were, they had not the courage to stand against us as long as we advanced, but the first sign of retreat was the signal for them to leave their shelter and press us the whole way to camp.

When the retirement commenced I was with the two advanced guns in action on the Grand Trunk Road. The subaltern in charge was severely wounded, and almost at the same moment one of his sergeants, a smart, handsome fellow, fell, shot through the leg. Seeing some men carrying him into a hut at the side of the road, I shouted: 'Don't put him there; he will be left behind; get a doolie for him, or put him on the limber.' But what with the incessant fire from the enemy's guns, the bursting of shells, the crashing of shot through the branches of the trees, and all the din and hubbub of battle, I could not have been heard, for the poor fellow with another wounded man was left in the hut, and both were murdered by the mutineers. So many of the men with the two guns were *hors de combat*, and the horses were so unsteady (several of them being wounded), that there was great difficulty in limbering up, and I was helping the drivers to keep the horses quiet, when I suddenly felt a tremendous blow on my back which made me faint and sick, and I was afraid I should not be able to remain on my horse. The powerless feeling, however, passed off, and I managed to stick on until I got back to camp. I had been hit close to the spine by a bullet, and the wound would probably have been fatal but for the fact that a leather pouch for caps, which I usually wore in front near my pistol, had somehow slipped round to the back; the bullet passed through this before entering my body, and was thus prevented from penetrating very deep.

The enemy followed us closely right up to our piquets, and but for the steadiness of the retirement our casualties must have been even more numerous than they were. As it was, they amounted to 15 men killed, 16 officers and 177 men wounded, and 2 men missing.

The enemy's loss was estimated at 1,000. For hours they were seen carrying the dead in carts back to the city.

My wound, though comparatively slight, kept me on the sick-list for a fortnight, and for more than a month I could not mount a horse or put on a sword-belt. I was lucky in that my tent was pitched close to that of John Campbell Brown, one of the medical officers attached to the Artillery. He had served during the first Afghan war, with Sale's force, at Jalalabad, and throughout both the campaigns in the Punjab, and had made a great reputation for himself as an army surgeon. He looked after me while I was laid up, and I could not have been in better hands.

The Delhi Force was fortunate in its medical officers. Some of the best in the army were attached to it, and all that was possible to be done for the sick and wounded under the circumstances was done. But the poor fellows had a bad time of it. A few of the worst cases were accommodated in the two or three houses in the cantonment that had escaped destruction, but the great majority had to put up with such shelter from the burning heat and drenching rain as an ordinary soldiers' tent could provide. Those who could bear the journey and were not likely to be fit for duty for some time were sent away to Meerut and Umballa; but even with the relief thus afforded, the hospitals throughout the siege were terribly overcrowded. Anæsthetics were freely used, but antiseptics were practically unknown, consequently many of the severely wounded died, and few amputation cases survived.

A great aggravation to the misery and discomfort in hospital was the plague of flies. Delhi is at all times noted for having more than its share of these drawbacks to life in the East, but during the siege they were a perfect pest, and for the short time I was laid up I fully realized the suffering which our sick and wounded soldiers had to endure. At night the inside of my tent was black with flies. At the first ray of light or the smallest shake to the ropes, they were all astir, and for the rest of the day there was no peace; it was even difficult to eat without swallowing one or more of the loathsome insects. I had to brush them away with one hand while I put the food into my mouth with the other, and more than once I had to rush from the table, a fly having eluded all my efforts to prevent his going down my throat.

As soon as I could get about a little, but before I was able to perform my legitimate work, I was employed in helping to look after the conservancy of the camp and its surroundings—an extremely disagreeable but most important duty, for an Indian army must always have a large following, for which sanitary arrangements are a difficulty. Then, large convoys of camels and bullock-carts arrived daily with supplies and stores, and a considerable number of transport animals had to be kept in readiness to follow up the enemy with a suitably sized force, whenever we could drive them out of the city. Without any shelter, and often with insufficient food, deaths amongst the animals were of constant occurrence, and, unless their carcases could at once be removed, the stench became intolerable. Every expedient was resorted to to get rid of this nuisance. Some of the carcases were dragged to a distance from camp, some were buried, and some were burnt, but, notwithstanding all our efforts, many remained to be gradually devoured by the jackals which prowled about the camp, and by the innumerable birds of prey which instinct had brought to Delhi from the remotest parts of India.*

At a time when the powers of each individual were taxed to the uttermost, the strain on the Commander of the force was terribly severe. Mind and body were incessantly at work. Twice in the short space of six weeks had the officer holding this responsible position succumbed, and now a third was on the point of breaking down. Major-General Reed's health, never very strong, completely failed, and on the 17th July, only twelve days after succeeding Sir Henry Barnard, he had to give up the command and leave the camp on sick certificate.

CHAPTER XVI.

General Reed was succeeded by Brigadier Archdale Wilson, the officer who commanded the Meerut column at the beginning of the campaign, and who was so successful in the fights on the Hindun. Though a soldier of moderate capacity, Wilson was quite the best of the senior officers present, three of whom were superseded by his selection. Two of these, Congreve, Acting-Adjutant-General of Queen's troops, and Graves, who had been Brigadier at Delhi when the Mutiny broke out, left the camp on being passed over; the third, Longfield, took Wilson's place as Brigadier.

Wilson's succession to the command gave great relief to the troops on account of the systematic manner in which he arranged for the various duties, and the order and method he introduced. The comparative rest to the troops; as well as the sanitary improvements he effected, did a good deal for the health of the force. Wilson also took advantage of the reinforcements we had received to strengthen our position. As far as possible he put a stop to the practice of following up the enemy close to the city walls when they were driven off after an attack (a practice which had cost us many valuable lives), contenting himself with preventing the rebels from remaining in the immediate vicinity of our advanced posts.

* 'Adjutants,' never seen in ordinary times further north than Bengal, appeared in hundreds, and were really useful scavengers.

The day after Reed's departure another sharp and prolonged attack was made upon the Ridge batteries and Sabzi Mandi piquets, and in the afternoon a column was sent to drive the enemy away. It consisted of four Horse Artillery guns, 750 Infantry, and the Guides Cavalry. Lieutenant-Colonel Jones, of the 60th Rifles, commanded the column, and, having gained experience from the lesson we had received on the 14th, he took care not to approach too near to the city walls, but cleared the Sabzi Mandi, and took up a good position, where he remained for some little time. This unusual procedure seemed to disconcert the enemy, most of whom returned to the city, while those who remained to fight did not come to such close quarters as on previous occasions. Nevertheless, we had 1 officer and 12 men killed, 3 officers and 66 men wounded, and 2 men were missing.

The four following days passed without any serious attack being made, but an unfortunate accident occurred about this time to a cousin of mine, Captain Greensill, of the 24th Foot. He was attached to the Engineer department, and was ordered to undertake some reconnoitring duty after dark. On nearing the enemy's position he halted his escort, in order not to attract attention, and proceeded alone to examine the ground. The signal which he had arranged to give on his return was apparently misunderstood, for as he approached the escort fired; he was mortally wounded, and died in great agony the next morning.

The last severe contest took place in the Sabzi Mandi on the 18th, for by this time the Engineers' incessant labour had resulted in the clearing away of the old serais and walled gardens for some distance round the posts held by our piquets in that suburb. The 'Sammy House' piquet, to the right front of Hindu Rao's house, was greatly strengthened, and cover was provided for the men occupying it—a very necessary measure, exposed as the piquet was to the guns on the Burn and Mori bastions, and within grape range of the latter, while the enemy's Infantry were enabled to creep close up to it unperceived.

The improvements we had made in this part of our position were, no doubt, carefully watched and noted by the rebels, who, finding that all attempts to dislodge us on the right ended in their own discomfiture, determined to try whether our left was not more vulnerable than they had found it in the earlier days of the siege. Accordingly early on the 23rd they sallied forth from the Kashmir gate, and, occupying Ludlow Castle and its neighbourhood, shelled Metcalfe House, the stable piquet, and the mosque piquet on the Ridge. As all attempts to silence the enemy's guns with our Artillery proved unavailing, and it was feared that if not dislodged they would establish a battery at Ludlow Castle, a small column under Brigadier Showers moved out by a cutting through the Ridge on our left, its object being (in conjunction with the Metcalfe House piquets) to turn the enemy's right and capture their guns.

The troops detailed for this duty consisted of six Horse Artillery guns, 400 British Infantry, 360 of the 1st Punjab Infantry, and a party of the Guides Cavalry, in addition to 250 men detached from the Metcalfe House piquets. The advance of the column up the road leading towards the Kashmir gate appeared to be unnoticed until it arrived close to the enemy, who then opened with grape. Our troops pressed on, and in their eagerness to capture the guns, which were being withdrawn, got too near the city walls. Here Showers was wounded, and the command devolved on Lieutenant-Colonel Jones, of the 60th, who skilfully conducted the retirement. Our loss was 1 officer and 11 men killed, 5 officers and 34 men wounded. Captain Law, one of my two companions on the mail-cart from Umballa, was the officer killed.

The enemy were fairly quiet between the 23rd and 31st July, on which date they moved out of the city in considerable strength, with the intention of making a temporary bridge across the cut in the swampy ground I have before described, and so threatening our rear. A column under Coke was sent to the other side of the cut to intercept the enemy should they succeed in getting across; this column was joined at Alipur by the Kumaon battalion (composed of Gurkhas and hill-men), about 400 strong, which had just arrived from the Punjab as escort to a large store of ammunition. The services of these troops were, however, not required, for the rain, which had been coming down in torrents for some hours, had caused such a rush of water that the bridge was carried away before it was completed. The enemy then retired towards the city. On reaching the suburbs they were reinforced by a large body of Infantry, and a most determined attack was made on the right of our position. This occurred about sunset, and all night the roar of musketry and artillery was kept up without a moment's cessation.

The next day was the anniversary of a great Mahomedan festival, when it was the custom for the King to pray and make sacrifice at the Idgah, in commemoration of Abraham's intended offering up of Ishmail.* On this particular occasion, however, the sacrifices were to be dispensed with in deference to Hindu prejudices,† and in their stead a tremendous united effort was to be made by Hindus and Mussulmans to exterminate the Feringhis. All the morning of the 1st August mosques and Hindu temples were crowded with worshippers offering up prayers for the success of the great attempt, and in the afternoon the rebels, mad with excitement and fanaticism, issued in countless numbers from the city gates, and, shouting the Moslem battle-cry, advanced and threw themselves on our defences. They were driven back by our deadly volleys, but only for a moment; they quickly re-

* According to the religion of Islam, Ishmail, not Isaac, was to have been offered up by Abraham.

† Forrest's 'The Indian Mutiny.'

formed and made a fresh attack, to be stopped again by our steady, uncompromising fire. Time after time they rallied and hurled themselves against our breastworks. All that night and well on into the next day the fight continued, and it was past noon before the devoted fanatics became convinced that their gods had deserted them, that victory was not for them, and that no effort, however heroic on their part, could drive us from the Ridge. The enemy's loss was heavy, ours trifling, for our men were admirably steady, well protected by breastworks, and never allowed to show themselves except when the assailants came close up. We had only 1 officer and 9 men killed and 36 men wounded.

The officer was Lieutenant Eaton Travers, of the 1st Punjab Infantry. He had been seven years with the regiment, and had been present with it in nearly all the many frontier fights in which it had been engaged. He was a bright, happy fellow, and a great friend of mine. As Major Coke, his commanding officer, published in regimental orders: 'This gallant soldier and true-hearted gentleman was beloved and respected by the officers and men of the regiment. His loss is an irreparable one.'

The enemy were much depressed by the failure of the Bakhra Id attack, from which they had expected great things. They began to despair of being able to drive us from our position on the Ridge, which for seven weeks had been so hotly contested. They heard that Nicholson with his Movable Column was hastening to our assistance, and they felt that, unless they could gain some signal victory before reinforcements reached us, we should take our place as the besiegers, instead of being, as hitherto, the besieged. Disaffection within the city walls was on the increase; only the semblance of authority remained to the old and well-nigh impotent King, while some of his sons, recognizing their perilous position, endeavoured to open negotiations with us. Many of the sepoys were reported to be going off to their homes, sick and weary of a struggle the hopelessness of which they had begun to realize.

Our work, however, was far from being finished. Notwithstanding losses from death and desertion, the enemy still outnumbered us by about eight or nine to one.

All this time our communication with the Punjab was maintained, and we regularly received letters and newspapers from England by the northern route; but for several weeks we had had no news from the south. Rumours of disasters occasionally reached us, but it was not until the second week in July that we heard of the fight at Agra, the retirement of our troops, and the flight of all the residents into the fort.

These scraps of intelligence, for they were mere scraps, written often in Greek character, some screwed into a quill, some sewn between the double soles of a man's shoe, and some twisted up in the messenger's hair, were eagerly looked for, and as eagerly deciphered when they came. It was cheering to learn that Allahabad was safe, that Lucknow was still holding out, that troops from Madras, Ceylon, and the Mauritius had reached Calcutta, and that Lord Elgin, taking a statesmanlike view of the situation, had diverted to India* the force intended for the China expedition, and we fondly hoped that some of the six British regiments reported by one messenger to have arrived at Cawnpore would be sent to the assistance of the Delhi Force.

Strangely enough, we knew nothing of the death of Sir Henry Lawrence or General Wheeler, and had not even heard for certain that Cawnpore had fallen and that Lucknow was besieged, while there were constant reports that Wheeler was marching up the Trunk Road. Being most anxious to get some authentic intelligence, Norman† on the 15th July wrote a letter in French addressed to General Wheeler at Cawnpore, or whoever might be in command between that place and Delhi, giving an account of our position at Delhi, and expressing a hope that troops would soon march to our assistance. The letter was entrusted to two sepoys of the Guides, who carried out their difficult task most faithfully, and on the 3rd August returned with the following reply from General Havelock, addressed to Major-General Reed:

'Cawnpore, left bank of the Ganges,
'*25th July*, 1857.

'My dear General,

'Yesterday I saw Captain Norman's letter of the 15th instant from Delhi, addressed to Sir Hugh Wheeler. That gallant officer and the whole of his force were destroyed on the 27th June by a base act of treachery. Sir Henry Somerset is Commander-in-Chief in India and Sir Patrick Grant in Bengal. Under the orders of the supreme Government I have been sent to retrieve affairs here. I have specific instructions from which I cannot depart. I have sent a duplicate of your letter to Sir P. Grant. In truth, though most anxious to march on Delhi, I have peremptory orders to relieve Lucknow. I have,

* Since writing the above it has been brought to my notice that the promptitude with which the troops were diverted to India was due in a great measure to the foresight of Sir George Grey, the Governor of the Cape, who, on hearing of the serious state of affairs in India, immediately ordered all transports which touched at the Cape on their way to take part in the China Expeditionary Force, to proceed directly to Calcutta instead of to Singapore. He also despatched as many of the Cape garrison as he could spare, with stores, etc., to India. It is right, therefore, that he should share with Lord Elgin the credit of having so quickly grasped the magnitude of the crisis through which India was passing.

† Owing to Brigadier-General Chamberlain having been placed *hors de combat* by the severe wound he received the previous day, Norman was carrying on the duties of Adjutant-General.

thank God, been very successful. I defeated the enemy at Futtehpore on the 12th, and Pandu Naddi on the 15th, and this place, which I recaptured on the 16th. On each occasion I took all the guns. Immense reinforcements are coming from England and China. Sir Patrick Grant will soon be in the field himself. Lucknow holds out. Agra is free for the present. I am sorry to hear you are not quite well. I beg that you will let me hear from you continually.'

Two days afterwards another letter was received; this time from Lieutenant-Colonel Fraser-Tytler, A.Q.M.G., with Havelock's force. It was addressed to Captain Earle, A.Q.M.G., Meerut, and ran as follows:

'Cawnpore, *July 27th.*

'General Havelock has crossed the river to relieve Lucknow, which will be effected four days hence. He has a strong force with him, and he has already thrashed the Nana and completely dispersed his force. We shall probably march to Delhi with four or five thousand Europeans and a heavy Artillery, in number, not in weight. The China force is in Calcutta, 5,000 men. More troops expected immediately. We shall soon be with you.'

These sanguine expectations were never fulfilled! Instead of Lucknow being relieved in four days, it was nearly four months before that result was achieved, and instead of troops from Cawnpore coming to help us at Delhi, the troops from Delhi formed the chief part of the force which relieved Lucknow.

While we were rejoicing at the prospect of being reinforced by a large number of British soldiers, a gloom was cast over the whole camp by the rumour that Sir Henry Lawrence was dead. As the first British Ruler of the Punjab, Henry Lawrence was known by reputation to, and respected by, every man belonging to the Delhi Force, and all realized what a serious loss his death would be to the beleaguered garrison of Lucknow. Much time, however, was not given us for lamentation, for at the end of the first week in August another attempt was made to drive us from the Metcalfe House piquets. Guns were again brought out through the Kashmir gate, and posted at Ludlow Castle and the Kudsiabagh; at the same time a number of Infantry skirmishers kept up an almost constant fire from the jungle in front of our position. The losses at the piquets themselves were not heavy, good cover having been provided; but the communications between the piquets and our main position were much exposed and extremely hazardous for the reliefs. It was felt that the enemy could not be allowed to remain in such close proximity to our outposts, and Showers (who had recovered from his slight wound) was again ordered to drive them off, for which purpose he was given a strong body of Infantry, composed of Europeans,

Sikhs, and Gurkhas, a troop of Horse Artillery, a squadron of the 9th Lancers, and the Guides Cavalry. The result was a very brilliant little affair. The orders on this occasion were to 'move up silently and take the guns at Ludlow Castle.' The small column proceeded in the deepest silence, and the first sound heard at dawn on the 12th August was the challenge of the enemy's sentry, '*Ho come dar ?*' (Who comes there ?). A bullet in his body was the reply. A volley of musketry followed, and effectually awoke the sleeping foe, who succeeded in letting off two of their guns as our men rushed on the battery. An Irish soldier, named Reegan, springing forward, prevented the discharge of the third gun. He bayoneted the gunner in the act of applying the port-fire, and was himself severely wounded. The rebel Artillerymen stood to their guns splendidly, and fought till they were all killed. The enemy's loss was severe; some 250 men were killed, and four guns were captured. On our side 1 officer and 19 men were killed, 7 officers and 85 men wounded, and 5 men missing. Amongst the wounded was the gallant Commander of the column, and that fine soldier, Major John Coke, the Commandant of the 1st Punjab Infantry. The return to camp was a stirring sight: the captured guns were brought home in triumph, pushed along by the soldiers, all madly cheering, and the horses ridden by men carrying their muskets with bayonets fixed.

The following morning the Punjab Movable Column arrived. Nicholson had preceded it by a few days, and from him I heard all about his fight with the Sialkot mutineers at Trimmu Ghat and the various marches and counter-marches which he had made since I left him at Philour.

The column was a most welcome addition to our force. It now consisted of the 52nd Light Infantry, a wing of the 61st Foot, a Field Battery, a wing of the 1st Baluch Regiment, and the 2nd Punjab Infantry, beside 200 newly-raised Multani Cavalry and 400 military police. This brought up our effective force to about 8,000 rank and file of all arms.* A more powerful siege-train than we had hitherto possessed was on its way from Ferozepore, and three companies of the 8th Foot, detachments of Artillery and the 60th Rifles, the 4th Punjab Infantry, and about 100 recruits for the 4th Sikhs were also marching towards Delhi. In addition, a small contingent from Kashmir and a few of the Jhind Raja's troops were shortly expected, after the arrival of which nothing in the shape of reinforcements could be looked for from the north.

Nor could we hope for any help from the south, for no definite news had been received from Havelock since his letter of the 25th of July, and rumours had reached us that, finding it impossible to force his way to Lucknow, he had been obliged to retire upon Cawnpore. It was felt,

* There were besides in camp at this time 1,535 sick and wounded, notwithstanding that several hundred men had been sent away.

therefore, that if Delhi were to be taken at all, it must be taken quickly, before our augmented numbers should be again diminished by sickness and casualties.

The enemy knew our position as well as we did, and appreciating the great value the siege-train would be to us, they decided on making a supreme effort to intercept it. A few days before they had been foiled by Hodson in an attempt to cut off our communication with the Punjab, and were determined to ensure success on this occasion by employing a really formidable force. This force left Delhi on the 24th August, and proceeded in the direction of the Najafgarh *jhil*.

At daybreak the following morning Nicholson started with sixteen Horse Artillery guns, 1,600 Infantry and 450 Cavalry, his orders being to overtake the enemy and bring them to action. I hoped to have been of the party, but Nicholson's request to have me as his staff officer was refused, as I had not been taken off the sick-list, though I considered my wound was practically healed.

It proved a most difficult march. The rain fell in torrents, and the roads were mere quagmires. In the first nine miles two swamps had to be got through, on crossing which Nicholson heard that the insurgents were at Najafgarh, twelve miles further off. He determined to push on, and at 4 p.m. he found them occupying a strong position about a mile and three-quarters in length. In front was an old serai which was held in force with four guns, and on either side and in rear of the serai was a village equally strongly held; while running round the enemy's right and rear was a huge drainage cut, swollen by the heavy rain. This cut, or nulla, was crossed by a bridge immediately behind the rebels' position. Nicholson advanced from a side-road, which brought him on their right with the nulla flowing between him and them. Even at the ford the water was breast-high, and it was with much difficulty and not without a good deal of delay that our troops crossed under a heavy fire from the serai. It was getting late, and Nicholson had only time to make a hasty reconnaissance. He decided to attack the serai, drive out the mutineers, and then, changing front to the left, to sweep down their line and get possession of the bridge.

As the Infantry were about to advance, Nicholson thus addressed them: 'Men of the 61st, remember what Sir Colin Campbell said at Chilianwala, and you have heard that he said the same to his gallant Highland Brigade at the Alma. I have the same request to make of you and the men of the 1st Bengal Fusiliers. Hold your fire until within twenty or thirty yards, then fire and charge, and the serai is yours.' Our brave soldiers followed these directions to the letter, and, under cover of Artillery fire, carried the serai. Front was then changed to the left as had been arranged, and the line swept along the enemy's defences, the rebels flying before them over the bridge. They confessed to a loss of more than 800 men, and they left in our hands thirteen field-pieces and a large quantity of ammunition, besides all their camp equipage, stores, camels, and horses. Our casualties were 2 officers and 23 men killed, and 3 officers and 68 men wounded—two of the officers mortally, the third dangerously.

The enemy in the city, imagining from the size of the force sent with Nicholson that we could not have many troops left in camp, attacked us in great strength on the following morning (26th), but were beaten off with a loss on our side of only 8 killed and 13 wounded.

CHAPTER XVII.

By the 6th September all the reinforcements that could be expected, including the siege train (consisting of thirty-two pieces of ordnance with ample ammunition) had arrived in camp, and the time had now come when it was necessary for Wilson to determine whether Delhi was to be assaulted, or whether the attempt must be given up. Long exposure to sun and rain began to tell terribly on the troops; sickness increased to an alarming extent, and on the 31st August there were 2,368 men in hospital—a number which, six days later, had risen to 2,977.

Norman, on whose figures implicit reliance can be placed, states that on this date the total number of effective rank and file of all arms, Artillery, Engineers, Cavalry, and Infantry, including gun-Lascars, Native drivers, newly-raised Sikh Pioneers, and recruits for the Punjab regiments, was 8,748.

The strength of the British troops was 3,217, composed of 580 Artillery, 443 Cavalry, and 2,294 Infantry. The Infantry corps were mere skeletons, the strongest being only 409 effective rank and file. The 52nd, which had arrived three weeks before with 600 healthy men, had already dwindled to 242 fit for duty.

The above numbers are exclusive of the Kashmir Contingent of 2,200 men and four guns, which had by this time reached Delhi; and several hundred men of the Jhind troops (previously most usefully employed in keeping open our communication with Kurnal) were, at the Raja's particular request, brought in to share in the glory of the capture of Delhi, the Raja himself accompanying them.

No one was more alive than the Commander of the Delhi Field Force to the fact that no further aid could be expected, and no one realized more keenly than he did that the strength of the little army at his disposal was diminishing day by day. But Wilson had never been sanguine as to the possibility of capturing Delhi without aid from

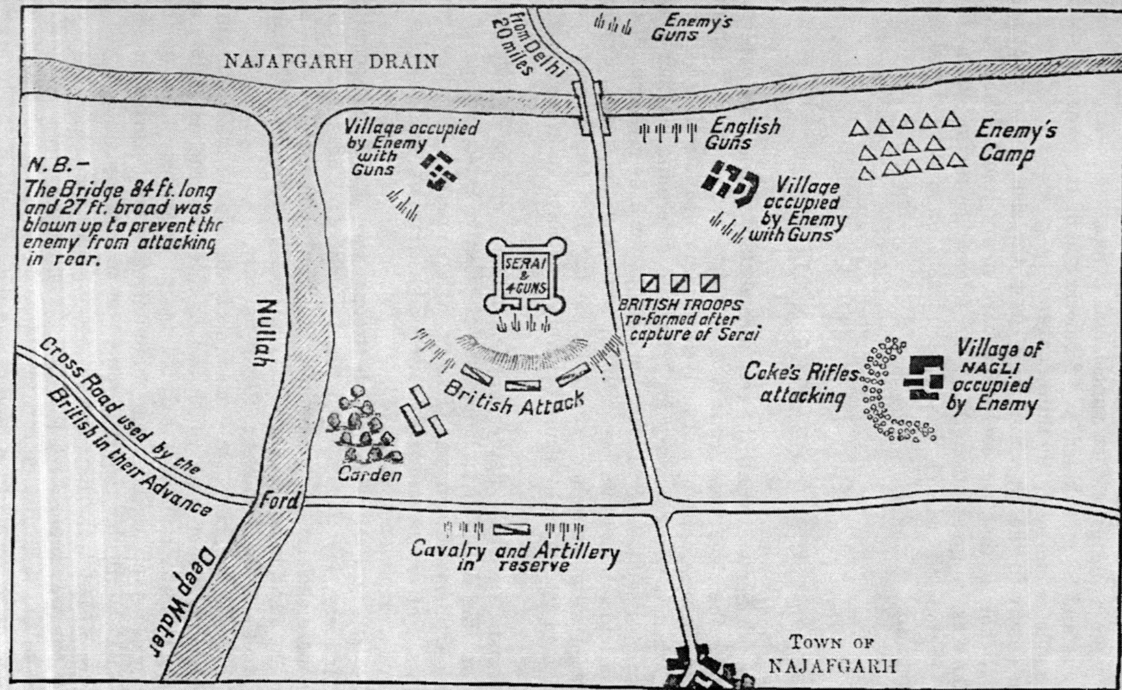

SKETCH TO ILLUSTRATE THE ENGAGEMENT AT NAJAFGARH IN AUGUST, 1857.

the south. In a letter to Baird-Smith dated the 20th August, he discussed at length his reasons for not being in a position to 'hold out any hope of being able to take the place until supported by the force from below.' He now was aware that no troops could be expected from the south, and Sir John Lawrence plainly told him that he had sent him the last man he could spare from the Punjab. On the 29th August Lawrence wrote to Wilson: 'There seem to be very strong reasons for assaulting as soon as practicable. Every day's delay is fraught with danger. Every day disaffection and mutiny spread. Every day adds to the danger of the Native Princes taking part against us.' But Wilson did not find it easy to make up his mind to assault. He was ill. Responsibility and anxiety had told upon him. He had grown nervous and hesitating, and the longer it was delayed the more difficult the task appeared to him.

Fortunately for the continuance of our rule in India, Wilson had about him men who understood, as he was unable to do, the impossibility of our remaining any longer as we were. They knew that Delhi must either be taken or the army before it withdrawn. The man to whom the Commander first looked for counsel under these conditions—Baird-Smith, of the Bengal Engineers—proved himself worthy of the high and responsible position in which he was placed. He too was ill. Naturally of a delicate constitution, the climate and exposure had told upon him severely, and the diseases from which he was suffering were aggravated by a wound he had received soon after his arrival in camp. He fully appreciated the tremendous risks which an assault involved, but, in his opinion, they were less than were those of delay. Whether convinced or not by his Chief Engineer's arguments, Wilson accepted his advice and directed him to prepare a plan of attack.

Baird-Smith was strongly supported by Nicholson, Chamberlain, Daly, Norman, and Alex. Taylor. They were one and all in communication with the authorities in the Punjab, and they knew that if 'Delhi were not taken, and that speedily, there would be a struggle not only for European dominion, but even for European existence within the Punjab itself.'*

Our position in that province was, indeed, most critical. An attempted conspiracy of Mahomedan tribes in the Murree Hills, and an insurrection in the Gogaira district, had occurred. Both these affairs were simply attempts to throw off the British yoke, made in the belief that our last hour was come. The feeling that prompted them was not confined to the Mahomedans; amongst all classes and races in the Punjab a spirit of restlessness was on the increase; even the most loyally disposed were speculating on the chances of our being able to

* Punjab Administration Report, 1857-58.

hold our own, and doubting the advisability of adhering to our cause. On the part of the Sikhs of the Manjha* there was an unwillingness to enlist, and no good recruits of this class could be obtained until after Delhi had fallen.

It was under these critical circumstances that a council of war was convened to decide definitely whether the assault should take place or not.

Nicholson was not a man of many intimacies, but as his staff officer I had been fortunate enough to gain his friendship. I was constantly with him, and on this occasion I was sitting in his tent before he set out to attend the council. He had been talking to me in confidential terms of personal matters, and ended by telling me of his intention to take a very unusual step should the council fail to arrive at any fixed determination regarding the assault. 'Delhi must be taken,' he said, 'and it is absolutely essential that this should be done at once; and if Wilson hesitates longer, I intend to propose at to-day's meeting that he should be superseded.' I was greatly startled, and ventured to remark that, as Chamberlain was *hors de combat* from his wound, Wilson's removal would leave him, Nicholson, senior officer with the force. He smiled as he answered: 'I have not overlooked that fact. I shall make it perfectly clear that, under the circumstances, I could not possibly accept the command myself, and I shall propose that it be given to Campbell, of the 52nd; I am prepared to serve under him for the time being, so no one can ever accuse me of being influenced by personal motives.'

Happily, Nicholson was not called upon to take so unusual a step. I walked with him to the Head-Quarters camp, waited in great excitement until the council of war was over, and, when Nicholson issued from the General's tent, learnt, to my intense relief, that Wilson had agreed to the assault.

That Nicholson would have carried out his intention if the council had come to a different conclusion I have not the slightest doubt, and I quite believe that his masterful spirit would have effected its purpose and borne down all opposition. Whether his action would have been right or wrong is another question, and one on which there is always sure to be great difference of opinion. At the time it seemed to me that he was right. The circumstances were so exceptional—Wilson would have proved himself so manifestly unfit to cope with them had he decided on further delay—and the consequences of such delay would have been so calamitous and far-reaching, that even now, after many years have passed, and after having often thought over Nicholson's intended action and discussed the subject with other men, I have not changed my opinion.

* The tract of country between the Sutlej and Ravi rivers.

In anticipation of an attack on Delhi, preparations had been commenced early in September, one of the first of these being to form a trench to the left of the 'Sammy House,' at the end of which a battery was constructed for four 9-pounders and two 24-pounder howitzers. The object of this battery was to prevent sorties from the Lahore or Kabul gates passing round the city wall to annoy our breaching batteries, and also to assist in keeping down the fire from the Mori bastion.* This battery, moreover, led the enemy to believe that we should attack them from our right, whereas it had been resolved to push the main attack from our left, where we could approach nearer to the walls under cover, and where our flank was completely protected by the river. The Engineers had also employed themselves in getting ready 10,000 fascines, as many gabions, and 100,000 sand-bags, besides field magazines, scaling-ladders, and spare platforms.

On the 7th September Wilson issued an order informing the force that arrangements for the assault would be commenced at once. He dwelt upon the hardships and fatigue which had been cheerfully borne by officers and men, and expressed his hope that they would be rewarded for their past labours, 'and for a cheerful endurance of still greater fatigue and exposure.' He reminded the troops of the reasons for the deadly struggle in which they were engaged, and he called upon all ranks to co-operate heart and soul in the arduous work now before them.

Ground was broken that evening. Unfortunately Baird-Smith was not able to personally superintend the construction of the breaching batteries, but he had in his second-in-command, Alex. Taylor, a thoroughly practical Engineer, who not only knew how to work himself, but how to get work out of others. Ever alert and cheerful, he was trusted and looked up to by all his subordinates, and was of all others the very man to be placed in charge of such a difficult and dangerous duty.

The first battery, known as No. 1, was traced out in two parts, about 700 yards from the Mori bastion, which the right half, with its five 18-pounders and one 8-inch howitzer, was intended to silence; while the left half, with its four 24-pounders, was to hold the Kashmir bastion in check.

All night the Engineers worked at the battery, but although before day broke it was nearly finished and armed, it was not ready to open fire until close on sunrise. The enemy did not fail to take advantage of this chance. They poured in round after round of shot and grape, causing many casualties. Their fire slackened as our guns were gradually able to make themselves felt, and by the afternoon it was silenced. Nothing remained of the Mori bastion but a heap of ruins. No. 1

* Norman's narrative.

battery was commanded by Major James Brind,* the bravest of the brave. It was said of him that he 'never slept'; and Reid (of 'Hindu Rao' fame) wrote of him: 'On all occasions the exertions of this noble officer were indefatigable. He was always to be found where his presence was most required; and the example he set to officers and men was beyond all praise.'

No. 2 battery was next taken in hand. This was erected in front of Ludlow Castle, and about 500 yards from the Kashmir gate. Like No. 1, it was formed in two parts, the right half being intended for seven heavy howitzers and two 18-pounders, and the left for nine 24-pounders, commanded respectively by Majors Kaye and Campbell. All these guns were intended to breach the Kashmir bastion, where the main assault was to be made.

Up till this time the enemy had imagined that the attack would be delivered from our right, and they were quite taken by surprise when, on the evening of the 8th September, we occupied Ludlow Castle.

Baird-Smith showed his grasp of the situation in attacking from our left, notwithstanding the greater distance of this part of our position from the city wall. No counter-attack could be made on that flank, and the comparatively open ground between the Kashmir and Mori bastions would assist us in protecting the assaulting columns.

As soon as the enemy discovered their mistake, they did their utmost to prevent our batteries being constructed; but the Engineers were not to be deterred. By the morning of the 11th No. 2 battery was completed, armed, and unmasked, and No. 3 and No. 4 batteries were marked out in the Kudsiabagh. No. 3, commanded by Major Scott, was constructed for six 18-pounders, and twelve 5½-inch mortars under Captain Blunt. Norman in his narrative says: 'The establishment of Major Scott's battery within 180 yards of the wall, to arm which heavy guns had to be dragged from the rear under a constant fire of musketry, was an operation that could rarely have been equalled in war.' During the first night of its construction 39 men were killed and wounded; but with rare courage the workmen continued their task. They were merely unarmed pioneers; and with that passive bravery so characteristic of Natives, as man after man was knocked over, they would stop a moment, weep a little over a fallen friend, place his body in a row along with the rest, and then work on as before.†

No. 4 battery, armed with ten heavy mortars, and commanded by Major Tombs, was placed under the shelter of an old building, about half-way between No. 2 and No. 3 batteries.‡

* The late General Sir James Brind, G.C.B.

† 'The Indian Mutiny,' by Forrest.

‡ When his Royal Highness the Prince of Wales was coming to India in 1875, I obtained permission from Lord Napier of Magdala, who was then Commander-in-Chief, to erect miniature embrasures to mark the gun of direction of each of the breaching batteries; and on these embrasures are recorded the number, armament, and object of the batteries.

I was posted to the left half of No. 2 battery, and had charge of the two right guns. At eight o'clock on the morning of the 11th September we opened fire on the Kashmir bastion and the adjoining curtain, and as the shots told and the stones flew into the air and rattled down, a loud cheer burst from the Artillerymen and some of the men of the Carabineers and 9th Lancers who had volunteered to work in the batteries. The enemy had got our range with wonderful accuracy, and immediately on the screen in front of the right gun being removed, a round shot came through the embrasure, knocking two or three of us over. On regaining my feet, I found that the young Horse Artilleryman who was serving the vent while I was laying the gun had had his right arm taken off.

In the evening of the same day, when, wearied with hard work and exhausted by the great heat, we were taking a short rest, trusting to the shelter of the battery for protection, a shower of grape came into us, severely wounding our commander, Campbell, whose place was taken by Edwin Johnson. We never left the battery until the day of the assault—the 14th—except to go by turns into Ludlow Castle for our meals. Night and day the overwhelming fire was continued, and the incessant boom and roar of guns and mortars, with the ceaseless rain of shot and shell on the city, warned the mutineers that their punishment was at hand. We were not, however, allowed to have it all our own way. Unable to fire a gun from any of the three bastions we were breaching, the enemy brought guns into the open and enfiladed our batteries. They sent rockets from their martello towers, and they maintained a perfect storm of musketry from their advanced trench and from the city walls. No part of the attack was left unsearched by their fire, and though three months' incessant practice had made our men skilful in using any cover they had, our losses were numerous, 327 officers and men being killed and wounded between the 7th and 14th September.

On the evening of the 13th September Nicholson came to see whether we gunners had done our work thoroughly enough to warrant the assault being made the next morning. He was evidently satisfied, for when he entered our battery he said: 'I must shake hands with you fellows; you have done your best to make my work easy to-morrow.'

Nicholson was accompanied by Taylor, who had to make certain that the breaches were practicable, and for this purpose he detailed four subaltern officers of Engineers to go to the walls as soon as it was dark, and report upon the condition they were in. Greathed and Home were told off for the Water bastion breach, and Medley and Lang* for that of the Kashmir bastion. Lang asked to be allowed to go while it was yet daylight; Taylor agreed, and with an escort of four men of the 60th Rifles he crept to the edge of the cover in the Kudsiabagh,

* Colonel Arthur Lang is the only one of the four now alive.

and then, running up the glacis, sat on top of the counterscarp for a few seconds studying the ditch and the two breaches. On his return Lang reported the breaches to be practicable; as, however, it was desirable to ascertain whether ladders would be necessary, he was sent again after dark, in company with Medley. They took a ladder and a measuring-rod with them, and were escorted by an officer and twenty-four riflemen, of whom all but six were left under cover in the Kudsia-bagh. Lang slipped into the ditch, which he found to be sixteen feet deep. Medley handed him the ladder and rod, and followed him with two riflemen, the other four remaining on the crest of the glacis to cover their retreat. With the help of the ladder they ascended the berm and measured the height of the wall. Two minutes more, and they would have reached the top of the breach, but, quiet as they had been, their movements had attracted attention, and several of the enemy were heard running towards the breach. The whole party re-ascended as rapidly as possible, and, throwing themselves on the grass, waited in breathless silence, hoping the sepoys would go away, and that they might be able to make another attempt to reach the top of the breach. The rebels, however, gave no signs of retiring, and as all needful information had been obtained, they determined to run for it. A volley was fired at the party as they dashed across the open, but no one was hit.

Greathed and Home had been equally successful, and by midnight Baird-Smith was able to report to General Wilson that both breaches were practicable.

Baird-Smith urged the importance of attacking without delay. He pointed out the impossibility of continuing the high pressure at which nearly every man* in the force had been working during the past few days;

* Nearly every man was on duty. The daily state of the several corps must have been very similar to the following one of the 75th Foot.

DAILY STATE

OF

H.M.'S 75TH REGIMENT.

Camp Delhi, 13th September, 1857.

	Sergeants.	Drummers.	Rank and File.
Fit to turn out - -	1	5	37
On duty - - - -	29	6	361

(Sd.) E. COURTENAY,
Sergt.-Major,
75th Regt.

True copy.
(Sd.) R. BAXTER, Lieut.-Adj.,
75th Regiment.

that the tension was becoming too severe to last; and that every hour that passed without assaulting was a loss to us and a gain to the enemy.

Before Wilson and Baird-Smith separated, orders had been issued for the attack to be made at daybreak the next morning, the 14th.

It was arranged that there were to be four assaulting columns and one reserve column.

The first, second and third columns, which were to operate on our left, were under the command of Brigadier-General Nicholson, who personally led No. 1 column. It consisted of:

	MEN.
Her Majesty's 75th Foot - - - -	300
1st Bengal Fusiliers - - - - -	250
2nd Punjab Infantry - - - - -	450
Total - -	1,000

and was meant to storm the breach near the Kashmir bastion.

I am indebted to the kindness of Mrs. Barter, the widow of my gallant friend and comrade, General Richard Barter, C.B., who served throughout the Mutiny with the 75th Foot, first as Adjutant and afterwards as Captain, for the above 'Daily State' and for the following extract from that officer's diary:

'In the evening the order was published for the storming of Delhi a little before daybreak the next morning, September 14, and we each of us looked carefully to the reloading of our pistols, filling of flasks, and getting as good protection as possible for our heads, which would be exposed so much going up the ladders. I wound two puggris or turbans round my old forage cap, with the last letter from the hills [Mrs. Barter was then at Kasauli, in the Himalayas] in the top, and committed myself to the care of Providence. There was not much sleep that night in our camp. I dropped off now and then, but never for long, and whenever I woke I could see that there was a light in more than one of the officers' tents, and talking was going on in a low tone amongst the men, the snapping of a lock or springing of a ramrod sounding far in the still air, telling of preparation for the coming strife. A little after midnight we fell in as quietly as possible, and by the light of a lantern the orders for the assault were then read to the men. They were to the following purport: Any officer or man who might be wounded was to be left where he fell; no one was to step from the ranks to help him, as there were no men to spare. If the assault were successful he would be taken away in the doolies, or litters, and carried to the rear, or wherever he could best receive medical assistance. If we failed, wounded and sound should be prepared to bear the worst. There was to be no plundering, but all prize taken was to be put into a common stock for fair division after all was over. No prisoners were to be made, as we had no one to guard them, and care was to be taken that no women or children were injured. To this the men answered at once, by "No fear, sir." The officers now pledged their honours on their swords to abide by these orders, and the men then promised to follow their example. At this moment, just as the regiment was about to march off, Father Bertrand came up in his vestments, and, addressing the Colonel, begged for permission to bless the regiment, saying: "We may differ some of us in matters of religion, but the blessing of an old man and a clergyman can do nothing but good." The Colonel at once assented, and Father Bertrand, lifting his hands to Heaven, blessed the regiment in a most impressive manner, offering up at the same time a prayer for our success and for mercy on the souls of those soon to die.'

No. 2 column, under Brigadier Jones, of Her Majesty's 61st Foot, consisted of:

	MEN.
Her Majesty's 8th Foot - - - -	250
2nd Bengal Fusiliers - - - -	250
4th Sikhs - - - - -	350
Total - -	850

and was intended for the storming of the breach near the Water bastion.

No. 3 column, under Colonel Campbell, of Her Majesty's 52nd Light Infantry, consisted of:

	MEN.
Her Majesty's 52nd Light Infantry - -	200
Kumaon Battalion - - - -	250
1st Punjab Infantry - - - -	500
Total - -	950

and was told off to enter the Kashmir gate after it had been blown in.

No. 4 column was to operate on our right. It was commanded by Major Reid, of the Sirmur battalion, and was composed of that regiment, the Guides Infantry, and such men from the piquets (European and Native) as could be spared. Its strength was 860 men, besides 1,200 of the Kashmir Contingent, and its orders were to attack the suburbs of Kisenganj and Paharipur, and support the main attack by effecting an entrance at the Kabul gate.

The Reserve column, under Brigadier Longfield, Her Majesty's 8th Foot, was told to await the result of the attack, and afford assistance wherever required. It consisted of:

	MEN.
Her Majesty's 61st Foot - - - -	250
4th Punjab Infantry - - - -	450
Wing Baluch battalion - - - -	300
Total - -	1,000

with 300 of the Jhind Contingent.

There were besides 200 of the 60th Rifles, who were to cover the advance of Nicholson's columns, and join the reserve as soon as the assaults had been carried out.

In order to provide these five columns, in all hardly 5,000 strong, the services of every man who could bear arms had to be put into requisition. Piquets were weakened to a dangerous extent, and many of the sick and wounded who ought to have been in hospital were utilized for the protection of the camp.

CHAPTER XVIII.

It was intended, as I have before said, that the assault should be delivered at break of day, but many of the men belonging to the regiments of the storming force had been on piquet all night, and it took some time for them to rejoin their respective corps. A further delay was caused by our having to destroy the partial repairs to the breaches which the enemy had succeeded in effecting during the night, notwithstanding the steady fire we had kept up.

While we were thus engaged, the Infantry were ordered to lie down under cover. Standing on the crenellated wall which separated Ludlow Castle from the road, I saw Nicholson at the head of his column, and wondered what was passing through his mind. Was he thinking of the future, or of the wonderful part he had played during the past four months? At Peshawar he had been Edwardes's right hand. At the head of the Movable Column he had been mainly instrumental in keeping the Punjab quiet, and at Delhi everyone felt that during the short time he had been with us he was our guiding star, and that but for his presence in the camp the assault which he was about to lead would probably never have come off. He was truly 'a tower of strength.' Any feeling of reluctance to serve under a Captain of the Company's army, which had at first been felt by some, had been completely overcome by his wonderful personality. Each man in the force, from the General in command to the last-joined private soldier, recognized that the man whom the wild people on the frontier had deified—the man of whom a little time before Edwardes had said to Lord Canning, 'You may rely upon this, that if ever there is a desperate deed to be done in India, John Nicholson is the man to do it'—was one who had proved himself beyond all doubt capable of grappling with the crisis through which we were passing—one to follow to the death. Faith in the Commander who had claimed and been given the post of honour was unbounded, and every man was prepared 'to do or die' for him.

The sun had risen high in the heavens, when the breaching guns suddenly ceased, and each soldier felt he had but a brief moment in which to brace himself for the coming conflict. Nicholson gave the signal. The 60th Rifles with a loud cheer dashed to the front in skirmishing order, while at the same moment the heads of the first and second columns appeared from the Kudsiabagh and moved steadily towards the breaches.

No sooner were the front ranks seen by the rebels than a storm of bullets met them from every side, and officers and men fell thick on the crest of the glacis. Then, for a few seconds, amidst a blaze of musketry, the soldiers stood at the edge of the ditch, for only one or two of the ladders had come up, the rest having been dropped by their killed or wounded carriers. Dark figures crowded on the breach, hurling stones upon our men and daring them to come on. More ladders were brought up, they were thrown into the ditch, and our men, leaping into it, raised them against the escarp on the other side. Nicholson, at the head of a part of his column, was the first to ascend the breach in the curtain. The remainder of his troops diverged a little to the right to escalade the breach in the Kashmir bastion. Here Lieutenants Barter and Fitzgerald, of the 75th Foot, were the first to mount, and here the latter fell mortally wounded. The breaches were quickly filled with dead and dying, but the rebels were hurled back, and the ramparts which had so long resisted us were our own.

The breach at the Water bastion was carried by No. 2 column. No sooner was its head seen emerging from the cover of the old Custom-house than it was met by a terrible discharge of musketry. Both the Engineer officers (Greathed and Hovenden) who were leading it fell severely wounded, and of the thirty-nine men who carried the ladders twenty-nine were killed or wounded in as many seconds. The ladders were immediately seized by their comrades, who, after one or two vain attempts, succeeded in placing them against the escarp. Then, amidst a shower of stones and bullets, the soldiers ascended, rushed the breach, and, slaying all before them, drove the rebels from the walls.

No. 3 column had in the meanwhile advanced towards the Kashmir gate and halted. Lieutenants Home and Salkeld, with eight Sappers and Miners and a bugler of the 52nd Foot, went forward to blow the gate open. The enemy were apparently so astounded at the audacity of this proceeding that for a minute or two they offered but slight resistance. They soon, however, discovered how small the party was and the object for which it had come, and forthwith opened a deadly fire upon the gallant little band from the top of the gateway, from the city wall, and through the open wicket.

The bridge over the ditch in front of the gateway had been destroyed, and it was with some difficulty that the single beam which remained could be crossed. Home with the men carrying the powder-bags got over first. As the bags were being attached to the gate, Sergeant Carmichael was killed and Havildar Madhoo wounded; the rest then slipped into the ditch to allow the firing party which had come up under Salkeld to carry out its share of the duty.

While endeavouring to fire the charge, Salkeld, being shot through the leg and arm, handed the slow-match to Corporal Burgess, who fell mortally wounded, but not until he had successfully performed his task.

As soon as the explosion had taken place, Bugler Hawthorne sounded the regimental call of the 52nd. Meeting with no response, he sounded twice again. The noise of firing and shouting was so great that neither the sound of the bugle nor that of the explosion reached the column, but Campbell, after allowing the firing party what he thought was sufficient time, gave the order to advance. Captain Crosse, of the 52nd, was the first to reach the gate, followed closely by Corporal Taylor of his own company, and Captain Synge of the same regiment, who was Campbell's Brigade-Major. In single file along the narrow plank they crossed the ditch in which lay the shattered remnant of the gallant little band; they crept through the wicket, which was the only part blown in, and found the interior of the gateway blocked by an 18-pounder gun, under which were lying the scorched bodies of two or three sepoys, who had evidently been killed by the explosion. The rest of the column followed as rapidly as the precarious crossing would admit, and when Campbell got inside he found himself face to face with both Nicholson's and Jones's columns, which, after mounting the three breaches, poured in a mingled crowd into the open space between the Kashmir gate and the church.

No. 4 column advanced from the Sabzi Mandi towards Kisenganj and Paharipur. Reid, the commander, was unfortunately wounded early in the day. Several other officers were either killed or wounded, and for a little time a certain amount of confusion existed owing to some misconception as to whether the command of the column should be exercised by the senior officer with the regular troops, or by the political officer with the Kashmir Contingent. The fighting was very severe. The enemy were in great numbers, and strongly posted on the banks of the canal—indeed, at one time there appeared to be a likelihood of their breaking into our weakly-guarded camp or turning the flank of our storming parties. The guns at Hindu Rao's house, however, prevented such a catastrophe by pouring shrapnel into the ranks of the rebels; and just at the critical moment Hope Grant brought up the Cavalry brigade, which had been covering the assaulting columns. The Horse Artillery dashed to the front and opened fire upon the enemy. From the gardens and houses of Kisenganj, only two or three hundred yards off, the mutineers poured a deadly fire of musketry on our men, and from the bastion near the Lahore gate showers of grape caused serious losses amongst them. Owing to the nature of the ground the Cavalry could not charge. Had they retired the guns would have been captured, and had the guns been withdrawn the position would have been lost. For two hours the troopers drawn up in battle array sat motionless, while their ranks were being cruelly raked. Not a man wavered. Hope Grant and four of his staff had their horses killed under them; two of them were wounded, and Hope Grant himself was hit by a spent shot. In Tombs's troop of Horse Artillery alone, 25 men out of 50 were wounded, and 17 horses either killed or wounded. The 9th Lancers had 38 casualties amongst the men, and lost 71 horses. 'Nothing daunted,' wrote Hope Grant, 'those gallant soldiers held their trying position with patient endurance; and on my praising them for their good behaviour, they declared their readiness to stand the fire as long as I chose. The behaviour of the Native Cavalry,' he added, 'was also admirable. Nothing could be steadier; nothing could be more soldierlike than their bearing.'

The bold front shown by the Horse Artillery and Cavalry enabled No. 4 column to retire in an orderly manner behind Hindu Rao's house, and also assisted the Kashmir Contingent in its retreat from the Idgah, where it was defeated with the loss of four guns. The repulse of this column added considerably to our difficulties by freeing many hundreds to take part in the fight which was being fiercely carried on within the city.

Meanwhile the three assaulting columns had made good their lodgment on the walls. The guns in the Kashmir and Water bastions had been turned so as to allow of their being used against the foe, and preparations were made for the next move.

Nicholson's orders were to push his way to the Ajmir gate, by the road running inside the city wall, and to clear the ramparts and bastions as he went. Jones was to make for the Kabul gate, and Campbell for the Jama Masjid.

Those three columns reformed inside the Kashmir gate, from which point the first and second practically became one. Nicholson, being accidentally separated from his own column for a short time, pushed on with Campbell's past the church, in the direction of the Jama Masjid, while the amalgamated column under Jones's leadership took the rampart route past the Kabul gate (on the top of which Jones had planted a British flag), capturing as they advanced all the guns they found on the ramparts, and receiving no check until the Burn bastion was reached by some of the more adventurous spirits. Here the enemy, taking heart at seeing but a small number of opponents, made a stand. They brought up a gun, and, occupying all the buildings on the south side of the rampart with Infantry, they poured forth such a heavy fire that a retirement to the Kabul gate had to be effected.

It was at this point that Nicholson rejoined his own column. His haughty spirit could not brook the idea of a retirement; however slight the check might be, he knew that it would restore to the rebels the confidence of which our hitherto successful advance had deprived them, and, believing that there was nothing that brave men could not achieve, he determined to make a fresh attempt to seize the Burn bastion.

The lane which was again to be traversed was about 200 yards long, with the city wall and rampart on the right, and on the left flat-roofed houses with parapets, affording convenient shelter for the enemy's sharp-shooters.

As the troops advanced up this lane the mutineers opened upon them a heavy and destructive fire. Again and again they were checked, and again and again they reformed and advanced. It was in this lane that Major Jacob, the gallant Commander of the 1st Bengal Fusiliers, fell, mortally wounded. His men wanted to carry him to the rear, but he would not allow them to remain behind for him, and refused their help, urging them to press forward against the foe. The officers, leading far ahead of their men, were shot down one after the other, and the men, seeing them fall, began to waver. Nicholson, on this, sprang forward, and called upon the soldiers to follow him. He was instantly shot through the chest.

A second retirement to the Kabul gate was now inevitable, and there all that was left of the first and second columns remained for the night.

Campbell's column, guided by Sir Theophilus Metcalfe, who from his intimate acquaintance with the city as Magistrate and Collector of Delhi was able to conduct it by the route least exposed to the enemy's fire, forced its way to the vicinity of the Jama Masjid, where it remained for half an hour, hoping that the other columns would come to its assistance. They, however, as has been shown, had more than enough to do elsewhere, and Campbell (who was wounded), seeing no chance of being reinforced, and having no Artillery or powder-bags with which to blow in the gates of the Jama Masjid, fell back leisurely and in order on the church, where he touched what was left of the Reserve column, which had gradually been broken up to meet the demands of the assaulting force, until the 4th Punjab Infantry alone remained to represent it.

While what I have just described was taking place, I myself was with General Wilson. Edwin Johnson and I, being no longer required with the breaching batteries, had been ordered to return to our staff duties, and we accordingly joined the General at Ludlow Castle, where he arrived shortly before the assaulting columns moved from the cover of the Kudsiabagh.

Wilson watched the assault from the top of the house, and when he was satisfied that it had proved successful, he rode through the Kashmir gate to the church, where he remained for the rest of the day.

He was ill and tired out, and as the day wore on and he received discouraging reports, he became more and more anxious and depressed. He heard of Reid's failure, and of Reid himself having been severely wounded; then came the disastrous news that Nicholson had fallen, and a report (happily false) that Hope Grant and Tombs were both killed. All this greatly agitated and distressed the General, until at last he began seriously to consider the advisability of leaving the city and falling back on the Ridge.

I was ordered to go and find out the truth of these reports, and to ascertain exactly what had happened to No. 4 column and the Cavalry on our right.

Just after starting on my errand, while riding through the Kashmir gate, I observed by the side of the road a doolie, without bearers, and with evidently a wounded man inside. I dismounted to see if I could be of any use to the occupant, when I found, to my grief and consternation, that it was John Nicholson, with death written on his face. He told me that the bearers had put the doolie down and gone off to plunder; that he was in great pain, and wished to be taken to the hospital. He was lying on his back, no wound was visible, and but for the pallor of his face, always colourless, there was no sign of the agony he must have been enduring. On my expressing a hope that he was not seriously wounded, he said: 'I am dying; there is no chance for me.' The sight of that great man lying helpless and on the point of death was almost more than I could bear. Other men had daily died around me, friends and comrades had been killed beside me, but I never felt as I felt then—to lose Nicholson seemed to me at that moment to lose everything.

I searched about for the doolie-bearers, who, with other camp-followers, were busy ransacking the houses and shops in the neighbourhood, and carrying off everything of the slightest value they could lay their hands on. Having with difficulty collected four men, I put them in charge of a sergeant of the 61st Foot. Taking down his name, I told him who the wounded officer was, and ordered him to go direct to the field hospital.

That was the last I saw of Nicholson. I found time to ride several times to the hospital to inquire after him, but I was never allowed to see him again.

Continuing my ride, I soon came up with Hope Grant's brigade. It had shortly before been relieved from its perilous and unpleasant position as a target for the enemy by the timely arrival of the Guides Infantry and a detachment of the Baluch battalion. I was rejoiced to find Tombs alive and unhurt, and from him and other officers of my regiment I learnt the tremendous peppering they had undergone. Hodson was also there with his newly-raised regiment, some officers of the 9th Lancers, and Dighton Probyn, Watson, and Younghusband, of the Punjab Cavalry. Probyn was in great spirits, having fallen temporarily into the command of his squadron, owing to Charles Nicholson (John Nicholson's younger brother) having been selected to take Coke's place with the 1st Punjab Infantry. Probyn retained his command throughout the campaign, for Charles Nicholson was wounded that very morning while gallantly leading his regiment. His right arm was being amputated when his heroic brother was carried mortally wounded into the same hospital, and laid on the bed next to him.

It seemed so important to acquaint the General without delay that Hope Grant and Tombs were both alive, that the Cavalry had been relieved from then exposed position, and that there was no need for further anxiety about Reid's column, that I galloped back to the church as quickly as possible.

The news I was able to give for the moment somewhat cheered the General, but did not altogether dispel his gloomy forebodings; and the failure of Campbell's column (which just at that juncture returned to the church), the hopelessness of Nicholson's condition, and, above all, the heavy list of casualties he received later, appeared to crush all spirit and energy out of him. His dejection increased, and he became more than ever convinced that his wisest course was to withdraw from the city. He would, I think, have carried out this fatal measure, notwithstanding that every officer on his staff was utterly opposed to any retrograde movement, had it not been his good fortune to have beside him a man sufficiently bold and resolute to stimulate his flagging energies. Baird Smith's indomitable courage and determined perseverance were never more conspicuous than at that critical moment, when, though suffering intense pain from his wound, and weakened by a wasting disease, he refused to be put upon the sick-list; and on Wilson appealing to him for advice as to whether he should or should not hold on to the position we had gained, the short but decisive answer, 'We *must* hold on,' was given in such a determined and uncompromising tone that it put an end to all discussion.

Neville Chamberlain gave similar advice. Although still suffering from his wound, and only able to move about with difficulty, he had taken up his position at Hindu Rao's house, from which he exercised, as far as his physical condition would allow, a general supervision and control over the events that took place on the right of the Ridge. He was accompanied by Daly and a very distinguished Native officer of the Guides, named Khan Sing Rosa, both of whom, like Chamberlain, were incapacitated by wounds from active duty. From the top of Hindu Rao's house Chamberlain observed the first successes of the columns, and their subsequent checks and retirements, and it was while he was there that he received two notes from General Wilson. In the first, written after the failure of the attacks on the Jama Masjid and the Lahore gate, the General asked for the return of the Baluch battalion, which, at Chamberlain's request, had been sent to reinforce Reid's column, and in it he expressed the hope that 'we shall be able to hold what we have got.' In the second note, written at four o'clock in the afternoon, the General asked whether Chamberlain 'could do anything from Hindu Rao's house to assist,' adding, 'our numbers are frightfully reduced, and we have lost so many senior officers that the men are not under proper control; indeed, I doubt if they could be got to do anything dashing. I want your advice. If the Hindu Rao's piquet cannot be moved, I do not think we shall be strong enough to take the city.' Chamberlain understood General Wilson's second note to imply that he contemplated withdrawing the troops from the city, and he framed his reply accordingly. In it he urged the necessity for holding on to the last; he pointed out the advantages already gained, and the demoralization thereby inflicted upon the enemy. The dying Nicholson advocated the same course with almost his latest breath. So angry and excited was he when he was told of the General's suggestion to retire, that he exclaimed, 'Thank God I have strength yet to shoot him, if necessary.' There was no resisting such a consensus of responsible and reliable opinion, and Wilson gave up all idea of retreating.

During the afternoon of the 14th, Norman, Johnson, and I, at the General's desire and for his information, visited every position occupied by our troops within the city walls. In some places there was great confusion—men without their officers, and officers without their men—all without instructions, and not knowing what was going on in their immediate neighbourhood, the inevitable result of the rapid advance We did what we could to remedy matters, and were able to report to Wilson that our troops were holding the wall from the Water bastion to the Kabul gate in sufficient strength. But this was all the comfort we could give him. The fact is, too much had been attempted on that eventful morning. We should have been satisfied with gaining possession of the Kashmir and Water bastions, and getting a lodgment within the city walls. This was as much as three such weak columns should have tried, or been asked to accomplish. No one who was present on that occasion, and experienced the difficulty, indeed impossibility, of keeping soldiers in hand while engaged in fighting along narrow streets and tortuous lanes, would ever again attempt what was expected of the assaulting columns.

While engaged in this duty we (Norman, Johnson and I) were attacked by a party of the enemy who had been hiding in considerable numbers in a side-lane watching for a chance. A fight ensued; we had only a small guard with us, but, fortunately, the firing was heard by the men of a near piquet, some of whom came to our help. With their assistance we drove off the sepoys, but in the scrimmage my poor mare was shot. She was a very useful animal, and her death was a great loss to me at the time.

At sunset on the 14th of September only a very small portion of the walls of Delhi was in our possession. The densely-populated city remained to be conquered. The magazine, the palace, and the Fort of Selimgarh, all strongly fortified, were still in the hands of the enemy. The narrow strip of ground we had gained had been won at severe loss. Three out of the four officers who commanded the assaulting columns had been disabled, and 66 officers and 1,104 men had been killed and wounded.

The night of the 14th was spent by the General and staff in

'Skinner's house,'* close to the church. Rest was badly needed, for almost everyone in the force, officers and men alike, had been hard at work, night and day, for a week. That night, luckily, we were allowed to be at peace, for whether it was that the rebels were as tired as we were, or that they were busy making preparations for further resistance, they did not disturb us; and when day broke we were all refreshed and ready to continue the struggle. At one time, indeed, early in the evening, the enemy appeared from their movements to be preparing to attack us, but just at that moment the band of the 4th Punjab Infantry struck up 'Cheer, Boys, Cheer!' upon which the men of the regiment did cheer, most lustily, and other regiments caught up and continued the inspiriting hurrahs, which apparently had the effect of disconcerting the mutineers and keeping them quiet.

CHAPTER XIX.

On the morning of the 15th the situation was reviewed, and preparations made for the conquest of the city. Order was restored amongst the troops, who, as I have shown, had become somewhat demoralized by the street fighting. Regiments and brigades were got together; raids were made on all the store shops within reach, and every bottle of beer and spirits was broken.† Some of the liquor would doubtless have been of great use in the hospitals, but there was no means of removing it, and the General wisely determined that it was best to put temptation out of the men's way. Guns and mortars were placed into

* The house belonged to the Skinner family, and was originally built by James Skinner, a Eurasian, who served the Moghul Emperor with great distinction towards the end of the last century. When Lord Lake broke up that Mahomedan Prince's power, Skinner entered the service of the East India Company and rose to the rank of Major. He was also a C.B. He raised the famous Skinner's Horse, now the 1st Bengal Cavalry. His father was an officer in one of His Majesty's regiments of Foot, and after one of Lord Clive's battles married a Rajput lady of good family, who with her father and mother had been taken prisoners. Skinner himself married a Mahomedan, so that he had an interest in the three religions, Christian, Hindu, and Mahomedan, and on one occasion, when left on the ground severely wounded, he made a vow that if his life were spared he would build three places of worship—a church, a temple, and a mosque. He fulfilled his vow, and a few years later he built the church at Delhi, and the temple and mosque which are in close proximity to it. (See Note at end of volume.)

† A report was circulated that a large number of our men had fallen into the trap laid for them by the Native shopkeepers, and were disgracefully drunk. I heard that a few men, overcome by heat and hard work, had given way to temptation, but I did not see a single drunken man throughout the day of the assault, although, as I have related, I visited every position held by our troops within the walls of the city.

position for shelling the city and palace, and a few houses near, where the enemy's sharpshooters had established themselves, were seized and occupied. We soon, however, gave up attacking such positions, for we found that street fighting could not be continued without the loss of more men than we had to spare, and that the wisest plan would be to keep the soldiers under cover as much as possible while we sapped from house to house. A battery commanding Selimgarh and part of the palace was constructed in the college gardens, and a breach was made in the wall of the magazine, which was captured the next morning with but slight loss.

On the 16th, and again on the 18th, Chamberlain took command of the troops inside the city while the General rested for a few hours. He was, as he expressed himself in a note to Chamberlain, 'completely done.'

The enemy now began to draw in their line. The suburbs were evacuated, and riding through the Sabzi Mandi, Kisenganj and Paharipur, we gazed with wonder at the size and strength of the works raised against us by the mutineers, in attacking which we had experienced such heavy loss during the early days of the siege, and from which No. 4 column had been obliged to retire on the day of the assault.

The smaller the position that had to be defended, the greater became the numbers concentrated in our immediate front, and every inch of our way through the city was stoutly disputed; but the advance, though slow, was steady, and considering the numbers of the insurgents, and the use they made at close quarters of their Field Artillery, our casualties were fewer than could have been expected.

I had been placed under the orders of Taylor, Baird-Smith's indefatigable Lieutenant, who directed the advance towards the Lahore gate. We worked through houses, courtyards, and lanes, until on the afternoon of the 19th we found ourselves in rear of the Burn bastion, the attempt to take which on the 14th had cost the life of the gallant Nicholson and so many other brave men. We had with us fifty European and fifty Native soldiers, the senior officer of the party being Captain Gordon, of the 75th Foot. A single door separated us from the lane which led to the Burn bastion. Lang, of the Engineers, burst this door open, and out dashed the party. Rushing across the lane and up the ramp, the guard was completely surprised, and the bastion was seized without our losing a man.

Early the next day we were still sapping our way towards the Lahore gate, when we suddenly found ourselves in a courtyard in which were huddled together some forty or fifty *banias*,* who were evidently as much in terror of the sepoys as they were of us. The men of our party nearly made an end of these unfortunates before their officers

* Sellers of grain and lenders of money.

could interfere, for to the troops (Native and European alike) every man inside the walls of Delhi was looked upon as a rebel, worthy of death. These people, however, were unarmed, and it did not require a very practised eye to see that they were inoffensive. We thought, however, that a good fright would do them no harm, and might possibly help us, so for a time we allowed them to believe that they were looked upon as traitors, but eventually told them their lives would be spared if they would take us in safety to some place from which we might observe how the Lahore gate was guarded. After considerable hesitation and consultation amongst themselves they agreed to two of their party guiding Lang and me, while the rest remained as hostages, with the understanding that, if we did not return within a given time, they would be shot.

Our trembling guides conducted us through houses, across courtyards, and along secluded alleys, without our meeting a living creature, until we found ourselves in an upper room of a house looking out on the Chandni Chauk,* and within fifty yards of the Lahore gate.

From the window of this room we could see beneath us the sepoys lounging about, engaged in cleaning their muskets and other occupations, while some, in a lazy sort of fashion, were acting as sentries over the gateway and two guns, one of which pointed in the direction of the Sabzi Mandi, the other down the lane behind the ramparts leading to the Burn bastion and Kabul gate. I could see from the number on their caps that these sepoys belonged to the 5th Native Infantry.

Having satisfied ourselves of the feasibility of taking the Lahore gate in rear, we retraced our steps.

The two *banias* behaved well throughout, but were in such a terrible fright of anything happening to us that they would not allow us to leave the shelter of one house until they had carefully reconnoitred the way to the next, and made sure that it was clear of the enemy. This occasioned so much delay that our friends had almost given us up, and were on the point of requiring the hostages to pay the penalty for the supposed treachery of our guides, when we reappeared on the scene.

We then discussed our next move, and it was decided to repeat the manœuvre which had been so successful at the Burn bastion. The troops were brought by the route we had just traversed, and drawn up behind a gateway next to the house in which we had been concealed. The gate was burst open, and rushing into the street, we captured the guns, and killed or put to flight the sepoys whom we had watched from our upper chamber a short time before, without losing a man ourselves.

This was a great achievement, for we were now in possession of the

* 'Silver Bazaar,' the main street of Delhi, in which were, and still are, situated all the principal jewellers' and cloth-merchants' shops.

main entrance to Delhi, and the street of the city leading direct from the Lahore gate to the palace and Jama Masjid. We proceeded up this street, at first cautiously, but on finding it absolutely empty, and the houses on either side abandoned, we pushed on until we reached the Delhi Bank. Here there was firing going on, and round shot flying about from a couple of guns placed just outside the palace. But this was evidently an expiring effort. The great Mahomedan mosque had just been occupied by a column under the command of Major James Brind; while Ensign McQueen,* of the 4th Punjab Infantry, with one of his own men had pluckily reconnoitred up to the chief gateway of the palace, and reported that there were but few men left in the Moghul fort.

The honour of storming this last stronghold was appropriately reserved for the 60th Rifles, the regiment which had been the first to engage the enemy on the banks of the Hindun, nearly four months before, and which throughout the siege had so greatly distinguished itself.

Home, of the Engineers, the hero of the Kashmir gate exploit, first advanced with some Sappers and blew in the outer gate. At this, the last struggle for the capture of Delhi, I wished to be present, so attached myself for the occasion to a party of the 60th Rifles, under the command of Ensign Alfred Heathcote. As soon as the smoke of the explosion cleared away, the 60th, supported by the 4th Punjab Infantry, sprang through the gateway; but we did not get far, for there was a second door beyond, chained and barred, which was with difficulty forced open, when the whole party rushed in. The recesses in the long passage which led to the palace buildings were crowded with wounded men, but there was very little opposition, for only a few fanatics still held out. One of these—a Mahomedan sepoy in the uniform of a Grenadier of the 37th Native Infantry—stood quietly about thirty yards up the passage with his musket on his hip. As we approached he slowly raised his weapon and fired, sending the bullet through McQueen's helmet. The brave fellow then advanced at the charge, and was, of course, shot down. So ended the 20th September, a day I am never likely to forget.

At sunrise on the 21st a royal salute proclaimed that we were again masters in Delhi, and that for the second time in the century the great city had been captured by a British force.

Later in the day General Wilson established his Head-Quarters in the Dewan-i khas (the King's private hall of audience), and, as was in accordance with the fitness of things, the 60th Rifles and the Sirmur battalion of Gurkhas† were the first troops of Her Majesty's army to

* Now Lieutenant-General Sir John McQueen, K.C.B.

† The Gurkhas became such friends with the men of the 1st Battalion 60th Rifles during the siege—the admiration of brave men for brave men—

garrison the palace of the Moghuls, in which the traitorous and treacherous massacre of English men, women and children had been perpetrated.

The importance of securing the principal members of the Royal Family was pressed upon the General by Chamberlain and Hodson, who both urged that the victory would be incomplete if the King and his male relatives were allowed to remain at large. Wilson would not consent to any force being sent after them, and it was with considerable reluctance that he agreed to Hodson going on this hazardous duty with some of his own men only. The last of the Moghul Emperors had taken refuge in Humayun's tomb, about seven miles from Delhi, where, on the afternoon of the 21st, he surrendered to Hodson on receiving a promise from that officer that his own life and the lives of his favourite wife and her son should be spared. Hodson brought them all into Delhi and placed them under a European guard in a house in the Chandni Chauk, thus adding one more to the many valuable services he had rendered throughout the siege.

I went with many others the next day to see the King; the old man looked most wretched, and as he evidently disliked intensely being stared at by Europeans, I quickly took my departure. On my way back I was rather startled to see the three lifeless bodies of the King's two sons and grandson lying exposed on the stone platform in front of the *Kotwali*. On enquiry I learnt that Hodson had gone a second time to Humayun's tomb that morning with the object of capturing these Princes, and on the way back to Delhi had shot them with his own hand—an act which, whether necessary or not, has undoubtedly cast a blot on his reputation. His own explanation of the circumstance was that he feared they would be rescued by the mob, who could easily have overpowered his small escort of 100 sowars, and it certainly would have been a misfortune had these men escaped. At the time a thirst for revenge on account of the atrocities committed within the walls of Delhi was so great that the shooting of the Princes seemed to the excited feelings of the army but an act of justice; and there were some men, whose opinions were entitled to the greatest respect, who considered the safety of the British force would have been endangered by the escape of the representatives of the house of Taimur, and that for this reason Hodson's act was justified.

My own feeling on the subject is one of sorrow that such a brilliant soldier should have laid himself open to so much adverse criticism. Moreover, I do not think that, under any circumstances, he should have done the deed himself, or ordered it to be done in that summary

---

that they made a special request to be allowed to wear the same uniform as their 'brothers' in the Rifles. This was acceded to, and the 2nd Gurkhas are very proud of the little red line on their facings.

manner, unless there had been evident signs of an attempt at a rescue.

But it must be understood that there was no breach of faith on Hodson's part, for he steadily refused to give any promise to the Princes that their lives should be spared; he did, however, undoubtedly by this act give colour to the accusations of blood-thirstiness which his detractors were not slow to make.

The news that we had occupied the palace, and were in complete possession of the city of Delhi, consoled Nicholson on his deathbed. From the first there was little hope that this valuable life could be saved. He was taken into hospital in a fainting condition from internal hemorrhage, and he endured excruciating agony; but, wrote General Chamberlain, 'throughout those nine days of suffering he bore himself nobly; not a lament or sigh ever passed his lips.' His every thought was given to his country, and to the last he materially aided the military authorities by his clear-sighted, sound, and reliable advice. His intellect remained unclouded to the end. With his latest breath he sent messages of tender farewell to his mother, hoping she would be patient under his loss, and to his oldest and dearest friend, Herbert Edwardes. After his death some frontier Chiefs and Native officers of the Multani Horse were permitted to see him, and I was told that it was touching beyond expression to see these strong men shed tears as they looked on all that was left of the leader they so loved and honoured.

Thus ended the great siege of Delhi, and to no one could the tidings of its fall have brought more intense relief and satisfaction than to the Chief Commissioner of the Punjab. Although in the first instance Sir John Lawrence certainly under-estimated the strength of the Delhi defences and the difficulties with which General Anson had to contend, he fully realized them later, and even at the risk of imperilling the safety of his own province by denuding it of troops, he provided the means for the capture of the rebel stronghold, and consequently the army of Delhi felt they owed him a deep debt of gratitude.

Like Norman when writing his narrative of the siege, I feel I cannot conclude my brief account of it without paying my small tribute of praise and admiration to the troops who bore themselves so nobly from the beginning to the end. Their behaviour throughout was beyond all praise, their constancy was unwearied, their gallantry most conspicuous; in thirty-two different fights they were victorious over long odds, being often exposed to an enemy ten times their number, who, moreover, had the advantage of ground and superior Artillery; they fought and worked as if each one felt that on his individual exertions alone depended the issue of the day; they willingly, nay, cheerfully, endured such trials as few armies have ever been exposed to for so long a time. For three months, day after day, and for the greater part of the day, every man had to be constantly under arms, exposed to a scorching Indian sun, which was almost as destructive as, and much harder to bear than, the enemy's never-ceasing fire. They saw their comrades struck down by cholera, sunstroke, and dysentery, more dispiriting a thousand times than the daily casualties in action. They beheld their enemies reinforced while their own numbers rapidly decreased. Yet they never lost heart, and at last, when it became evident that no hope of further reinforcements could be entertained, and that if Delhi were to be taken at all it must be taken at once, they advanced to the assault with as high a courage and as complete a confidence in the result, as if they were attacking in the first flush and exultation of troops at the commencement of a campaign, instead of being the remnant of a force worn out, by twelve long weeks of privation and suffering, by hope deferred (which truly 'maketh the heart sick'), and by weary waiting for the help which never came. Batteries were thrown up within easy range of the walls, than which a more heroic piece of work was never performed; and finally, these gallant few, of whom England should in very truth be everlastingly proud, stormed in the face of day a strong fortress defended by 30,000 desperate men, provided with everything necessary to defy assault.

The list of killed and wounded bears witness to the gallantry of all arms of the service. The effective force at Delhi never amounted to 10,000 men. Of these 992 were killed and 2,845 wounded, besides hundreds who died of disease and exposure. Where all behaved nobly, it is difficult to particularize; but it will not, I hope, be considered invidious if I specially draw my readers' attention to the four corps most constantly engaged: the 60th Rifles, the Sirmur battalion of Gurkhas, the Guides, and the 1st Punjab Infantry. Placed in the very front of the position, they were incessantly under fire, and their losses in action testify to the nature of the service they performed. The 60th Rifles left Meerut with 440 of all ranks; a few days before the assault they received a reinforcement of nearly 200, making a total of 640; their casualties were 389. The Sirmur battalion began with 450 men, and were joined by a draft of 90, making a total of 540; their loss in killed and wounded amounted to 319. The strength of the Guides when they joined was 550 Cavalry and Infantry, and their casualties were 303. The 1st Punjab Infantry arrived in Delhi with 3 British officers and 664 Natives of all ranks. Two of the British officers were killed, and the third severely wounded, and of the Natives, 8 officers* and 200 men were killed and wounded; while out

* Amongst the Native officers killed was Subadar Ruttun Sing, who fell mortally wounded in the glacis. He was a Patiala Sikh, and had been invalided from the service. As the 1st Punjab Infantry neared Delhi, Major

of the British officers attached to the regiment during the siege 1 was killed and 4 wounded. Further, it is a great pleasure to me to dwell on the splendid service done by the Artillery and Engineers. The former, out of their small number, had 365 killed or disabled, and the latter two-thirds of their officers and 293 of their men. I cannot more appropriately conclude this chapter than by quoting the words of Lord Canning, who, as Governor-General of India, wrote as follows in giving publication to the Delhi despatches: 'In the name of outraged humanity, in memory of innocent blood ruthlessly shed, and in acknowledgment of the first signal vengeance inflicted on the foulest treason, the Governor-General in Council records his gratitude to Major-General Wilson and the brave army of Delhi. He does so in the sure conviction that a like tribute awaits them, not in England only, but wherever within the limits of civilization the news of their well-earned triumph shall reach.'

CHAPTER XX.

THE fall of Delhi was loudly proclaimed, and the glad tidings spread like wildfire throughout the length and breadth of India, bringing intense relief to Europeans everywhere, but more especially to those in the Punjab, who felt that far too great a strain was being put upon the loyalty of the people, and that failure at Delhi would probably mean a rising of the Sikhs and Punjabis. Salutes were fired in honour

---

Coke saw the old man standing in the road with two swords on. He begged to be taken back into the service, and when Coke demurred he said: 'What! my old corps going to fight at Delhi without me! I hope you will let me lead my old Sikh company into action again. I will break these two swords in your cause.' Coke acceded to the old man's wish, and throughout the siege of Delhi he displayed the most splendid courage. At the great attack on the 'Sammy House' on the 1st and 2nd August, when Lieutenant Travers of his regiment was killed, Ruttun Sing, amidst a shower of bullets, jumped on to the parapet and shouted to the enemy, who were storming the piquet: 'If any man wants to fight, let him come here, and not stand firing like a coward! I am Ruttun Sing, of Patiala.' He then sprang down among the enemy, followed by the men of his company, and drove them off with heavy loss.

On the morning of the assault the regiment had marched down to the rendezvous at Ludlow Castle, 'left in front.' While waiting for the Artillery to fire a few final rounds at the breaches, the men sat down, and, falling in again, were doing so 'right in front.' Ruttun Sing came up to Lieutenant Charles Nicholson, who was commanding the regiment, and said: 'We ought to fall in "left in front,"' thereby making his own company the leading one in the assault. In a few minutes more Ruttun Sing was mortally wounded, and Dal Sing, the Jemadar of his company, a man of as great courage as Ruttun Sing, but not of the same excitable nature, was killed outright.

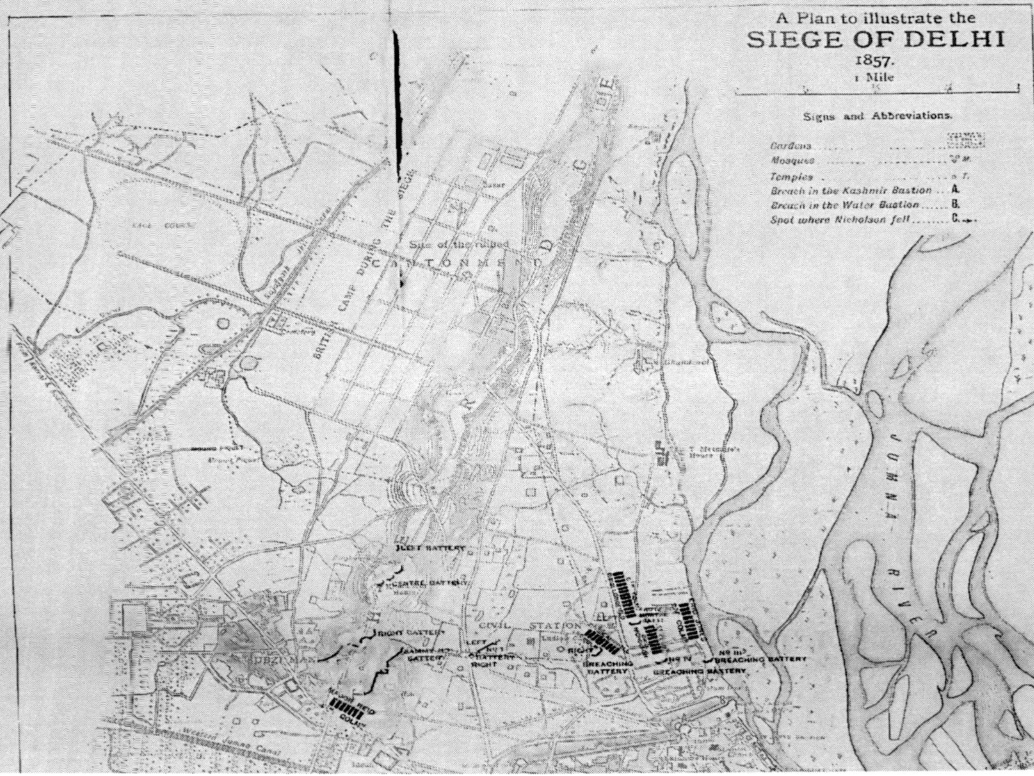
A Plan to illustrate the
SIEGE OF DELHI
1857.
1 Mile
Signs and Abbreviations.
Gardens
Mosques
Temples
Breach in the Kashmir Bastion ... A.
Breach in the Water Bastion ...... B.
Spot where Nicholson fell .... C.
BRITISH CAMP DURING THE SIEGE
Site of the ruined CANTONMENT
JUMNA RIVER
CIVIL STATION
JEET BATTERY
CENTRE BATTERY
RIGHT BATTERY
BREACHING BATTERY
Western Jumna Canal

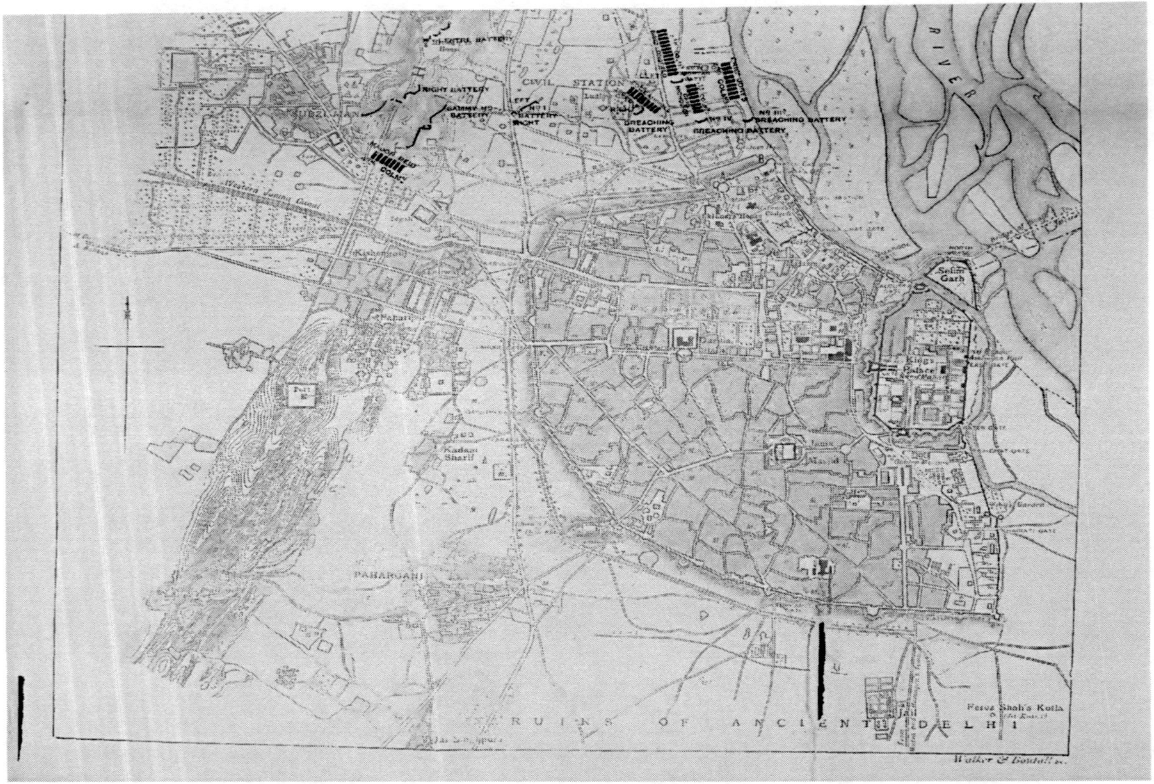

RIVER
CIVIL STATION
RIGHT BATTERY
BREACHING BATTERY
BREACHING BATTERY
Selim Garh
Kings Palace
Jama Masjid
Kadam Sharif
PAHARGANJ
RUINS OF ANCIENT DELHI
Feroz Shah's Kotla
Walker & Boutall sc.

of the victory at all the principal stations, but the Native population of the Punjab could not at first be made to believe that the Moghul capital, with its hordes of defenders, could have been captured by the small English army they saw marching through their province a few months before. Even at that time it seemed all too small for the task before it, and since then they knew it had dwindled down to less than half its numbers. It was not, indeed, until they had ocular demonstration of our success, in the shape of the loot which some of the Native followers belonging to the besieging force took back to their homes, that they became convinced of the reality of our victory.

Sir John Lawrence being painfully alive to the weakness of our position in the Punjab, as compared to the great strength of the Sikhs, on hearing the news of the capture of Delhi, begged General Wilson to send back at once a British regiment as a practical proof that our triumph was complete, and that he no longer needed so many troops. But though the city was in our possession, a great deal remained to be done before a single soldier could be spared. Above all things, it was necessary to open up communication with Cawnpore and Lucknow, in order to ascertain exactly the state of affairs in that part of the country. We had heard of the failure of Havelock's attempts to reach Lucknow, and of his having been obliged in the end to retire to Cawnpore and wait for reinforcements, but we had not been able to learn whether such reinforcements had reached him, or how long the beleaguered garrison of Lucknow was likely to hold out.

No time was wasted at Delhi. On the 21st September, the very day after the palace was occupied, it was decided to despatch a column to Cawnpore; but, on account of the weakened condition of the whole force, there was considerable difficulty in detailing the troops for its composition. The total strength of the corps* eventually selected amounted to 750 British and 1,900 Native soldiers, with sixteen field-guns.

No officer of note or high rank being available, the command of the column should have been given to the senior regimental officer serving

* Two troops of Horse Artillery, with four guns and one howitzer each, commanded respectively by Captains Remmington and Blunt. One Field Battery, with six guns, commanded by Captain Bourchier. One British Cavalry regiment, the 9th Lancers, reduced to 300 men, commanded by Major Ouvry. Two British Infantry regiments (the 8th and 75th Foot), commanded respectively by Major Hinde and Captain Gordon, which could only number between them 450 men. Detachments of three Punjab Cavalry regiments, the 1st, 2nd and 5th, commanded by Lieutenants John Watson, Dighton Probyn and George Younghusband, numbering in all 320 men. A detachment of Hodson's Horse, commanded by Lieutenant Hugh Gough, and consisting of 180 men. Two Punjab Infantry regiments, commanded by Captains Green and Wilde, each about 600 men; and 200 Sappers and Miners, with whom were Lieutenants Home and Lang.

with it, viz., Colonel Hope Grant, of the 9th Lancers; but for some unexplained motive Lieutenant-Colonel Greathed, of the 8th Foot, was chosen by General Wilson. Captain Bannatyne, of the same regiment, was appointed his Brigade-Major, and I was sent with the column as Deputy Assistant Quartermaster-General. On the fall of Delhi the whole of the Head-Quarters staff returned to Simla, except Henry Norman, whose soldierly instincts made him prefer accompanying the column, in order that he might be ready to join Sir Colin Campbell, the newly-appointed Commander-in-Chief, who had shortly before arrived in India.

Nicholson's funeral was taking place as we marched out of Delhi, at daybreak on the morning of the 24th September. It was a matter of regret to me that I was unable to pay a last tribute of respect to my loved and honoured friend and Commander by following his body to the grave, but I could not leave the column. That march through Delhi in the early morning light was a gruesome proceeding. Our way from the Lahore gate by the Chandni Chauk led through a veritable city of the dead; not a sound was to be heard but the falling of our own footsteps; not a living creature was to be seen. Dead bodies were strewn about in all directions, in every attitude that the death-struggle had caused them to assume, and in every stage of decomposition. We marched in silence, or involuntarily spoke in whispers, as though fearing to disturb those ghastly remains of humanity. The sights we encountered were horrible and sickening to the last degree. Here a dog gnawed at an uncovered limb; there a vulture, disturbed by our approach from its loathsome meal, but too completely gorged to fly, fluttered away to a safer distance. In many instances the positions of the bodies were appallingly life-like. Some lay with their arms uplifted as if beckoning, and, indeed, the whole scene was weird and terrible beyond description. Our horses seemed to feel the horror of it as much as we did, for they shook and snorted in evident terror. The atmosphere was unimaginably disgusting, laden as it was with the most noxious and sickening odours.

It is impossible to describe the joy of breathing the pure air of the open country after such a horrible experience; but we had not escaped untainted. That night we had several cases of cholera, one of the victims being Captain Wilde, the Commandant of the 4th Punjab Infantry. He was sent back to Delhi in a hopeless condition, it was thought, but he recovered, and did excellent work at the head of his fine regiment during the latter part of the campaign.

After a march of eleven miles we reached Ghazi-uddin-nagar, to find the place deserted. We halted the next day. The baggage animals were out of condition after their long rest at Delhi; and it was necessary to overhaul their loads and get rid of the superfluous kit and plunder which the followers had brought away with them. We were accompanied on our march by a few enterprising civilians, who had found their way into Delhi the day after we took possession of the palace. Amongst them was Alfred Lyall,* a schoolfellow of mine at Eton. He was on his way to take up the appointment of Assistant-Magistrate at Bulandshahr, where he was located when the Mutiny broke out. As we rode along he gave me a most interesting little history of his personal experiences during the early days of May, from the time when the first symptoms of the coming storm were felt, until that when the surrounding country rose *en masse*, and he and those with him had to seek shelter at Meerut. I should like to repeat his story for the benefit of my readers, but I refrain, as it would lose so much by my telling; and I hope that some day Sir Alfred Lyall may be induced to tell his own story in the picturesque and attractive language which is so well known and so much appreciated by the reading public.

Early on the morning of the 28th, Norman, Lyall, and I, marching with Watson's Cavalry, two or three miles in advance of the column, arrived at cross-roads, one leading to Bulandshahr, the other to Malagarh, a fort belonging to a Mahomedan of the name of Walidad Khan, who, when the British rule was in abeyance, assumed authority over the district in the name of the Emperor of Delhi. We halted, and, having put out our piquets, lay down and waited for the dawn. From information obtained by the civil officers with the column, we suspected that large numbers of mutineers were collected in the neighbourhood.

We were not left long in doubt as to the correctness of our surmisings, for we were soon rudely awakened by the rattle of shots exchanged between our vedettes and those of the enemy. Information was sent back at once to the advance guard and to our Commander, while we set to work to ascertain the enemy's exact position; this proved to be at Bulandshahr, and we were within a couple of miles of the main body.

As we advanced the rebel Cavalry fell back, and when we got under fire of their guns, our Horse Artillery came into action; our Infantry coming up, found the enemy occupying an extremely strong position, in the gaol and a walled serai at the entrance to the town, their left being covered by the enclosed gardens and ruined houses of the deserted civil station, within which they were collected in considerable force. From these points they were driven by the 75th Foot, who, in a most dashing manner, captured two 9-pounder guns, while a third was taken by the Cavalry. The rebels then began to retreat, and were followed up by a small body of Cavalry, under Drysdale,† of the 9th Lancers,

* Afterwards Sir Alfred Lyall, G.C.I.E., K.C.B., Lieutenant-Governor of the North-West Provinces, and now a member of the Indian Council.

† Now General Sir William Drysdale K.C.B.

with whom were Sarel, of the same regiment, Augustus Anson of the 84th Foot, and myself. We soon became entangled in narrow streets, but at last found ourselves in a gateway leading out of the town, which was crowded with bullock-carts, flying townspeople, and a number of the enemy, some on horseback, some on foot. There we had hard fighting; Sarel was wounded in the act of running a sepoy through the body, the forefinger of his right hand being taken off by a bullet, which then passed through his left arm; Anson was surrounded by mutineers, and performed prodigies of valour, for which he was rewarded with the Victoria Cross. I was riding a Waziri horse, which had belonged to John Nicholson, and as it had been a great favourite of his, I had commissioned a friend to buy him for me at the sale of Nicholson's effects. He was naturally impetuous, and, being now greatly excited by the firing and confusion, plunged about a good deal. He certainly was not a comfortable mount on that day, but all the same he saved my life. In the midst of the mêlée I observed a sepoy taking deliberate aim at me, and tried to get at him, but the crowd between him and me prevented my reaching him. He fired; my frightened animal reared, and received in his head the bullet which was intended for me.*

The work fell chiefly on the Cavalry and Horse Artillery. Major Ouvry, who commanded them, must have been a proud man that day, for they behaved splendidly. Two of Blunt's guns also, under an old Addiscombe friend of mine named Cracklow, did excellent service. The 9th Lancers, under Drysdale, performed wonders; and the three squadrons of Punjab Cavalry, under their gallant young leaders, Probyn, Watson, and Younghusband, and the squadron of Hodson's Horse, under Hugh Gough, showed of what good stuff they were made. Our casualties were 6 men killed, 6 officers and 35 men wounded. The enemy's loss was 300. A large quantity of ammunition and baggage fell into our hands, including many articles plundered from European men and women.

After the fight was over, the column passed through the town, and our camp was pitched about a mile beyond, on the banks of the Kali Naddi. The same afternoon Malagarh was reconnoitred, but was found to be deserted, a satisfactory result of the morning's action, for the fort, if defended, would have given us some trouble to take. Walidad Khan evidently hoped to become a power in the district, for he had begun to make gun-carriages, and we found roughly-cast guns on the lathes ready for boring out. It was decided that Malagarh Fort, which was full of articles of every description taken from the English residents, should be destroyed. Its demolition, however, took

* The horse, although badly hurt, was not killed, and eventually did me good service.

some time to effect, and as we could not move till transport came from Meerut to convey our wounded officers and men back to that place, the column halted at Bulandshahr for four days.

On the afternoon of the 1st October the fort was blown up, and most unfortunately, while superintending the operation, Lieutenant Home was killed.* The mine had been laid and the slow-match lighted, but the explosion not following as quickly as was expected, Home thought the match must have gone out, and went forward again to relight it. At that moment the mine blew up. His death was greatly felt in camp, happening as it did when all the excitement of battle was over.

We left Bulandshahr, and said good-bye to Lyall on the 3rd October, feeling that he was being placed in a position of considerable risk, thrown as he was on his own resources, with general instructions to re-establish the authority of the British Government. He was not, however, molested, and after two or three days he was joined by a small body of troops from Meerut. During the months that followed he and his escort had several alarms and some smart skirmishes; for Rohilkand, a large tract of country to the east of Bulandshahr, was held by the rebels until the following spring, and Lyall's district was constantly traversed by bodies of mutinous sepoys.

On the afternoon of the same day we reached Khurja, a fair-sized Mahomedan town, from which some of our Cavalry soldiers were recruited. The first thing that met our eyes on arrival at this place was a skeleton, ostentatiously placed against the side of a bridge leading to the encamping-ground; it was headless, and the bones were hacked and broken. It was pronounced by more than one doctor to be the skeleton of a European woman. This sight maddened the soldiery, who demanded vengeance, and at one time it seemed that the town of Khurja would have to pay the penalty for the supposed crime. The whole force was greatly excited. At length calmer counsels prevailed. The people of the town protested their innocence, and expressed their anxiety to be our humble servants; they were, as a whole, given the benefit of the doubt, but some soldiers found in the town, belonging to regiments which had mutinied, were tried, and hanged or acquitted according to the evidence given.

Some excitement was caused on reaching camp by the appearance of a fakir seated under a tree close to where our tents were pitched. The man was evidently under a vow of silence, which Hindu devotees often make as a penance for sin, or to earn a title to more than a fair share of happiness in a future life. On our addressing him, the fakir pointed to a small wooden platter, making signs for us to examine it. The platter had been quite recently used for mixing food in, and at first

* This was the Engineer officer who had such a miraculous escape when he blew in the Kashmir gate at Delhi, for which act of gallantry he had been promised the Victoria Cross.

there seemed to be nothing unusual about it. On closer inspection, however, we discovered that a detachable square of wood had been let in at the bottom, on removing which a hollow became visible, and in it lay a small folded paper, that proved to be a note from General Havelock, written in the Greek character, containing the information that he was on his way to the relief of the Lucknow garrison, and begging any Commander into whose hands the communication might fall to push on as fast as possible to his assistance, as he sorely needed reinforcements, having few men and no carriage to speak of. This decided Greathed to proceed with as little delay as might be to Cawnpore.

Just before we left Bulandshahr, a spy reported to me that an English lady was a prisoner in a village some twenty miles off, and that she was anxious to be rescued. As on cross-examination, however, the story did not appear to me to be very reliable, I told the man he must bring me some proof of the presence of the lady in the village. Accordingly, on the arrival of the column at Khurja, he appeared with a piece of paper on which was written 'Miss Martindale.' This necessitated the matter being inquired into, and I obtained the Brigadier's permission to make a détour to the village in question. I started off, accompanied by Watson and Probyn, with their two squadrons of Cavalry. We timed our march so as to reach our destination just before dawn; the Cavalry surrounded the village, and with a small escort we three proceeded up the little street to the house where the guide told us the lady was confined. Not only was the house empty, but, with the exception of a few sick and bedridden old people, there was not a soul in the village. There had evidently been a hasty retreat, which puzzled me greatly, as I had taken every precaution to ensure secrecy, for I feared that if our intention to rescue the lady became known she would be carried off. As day broke we searched the surrounding crops, and found the villagers and some soldiers hidden amongst them. They one and all denied that there was the slightest truth in the story, and as it appeared a waste of time to further prosecute the fruitless search, we were on the point of starting to rejoin our camp, when there was a cry from our troopers of '*Mem sahib hai!*' (Here is the lady), and presently an excessively dusky girl about sixteen years of age appeared, clad in Native dress. We had some difficulty in getting the young woman to tell us what had happened; but on assuring her that no harm should be done to those with whom she was living, she told us that she was the daughter of a clerk in the Commissioner's office at Sitapur; that all her family had been killed when the rising took place at that station, and that she had been carried off by a sowar to his home. We asked her if she wished to come away with us. After some hesitation she declined, saying the sowar had married her (after the Mahomedan fashion), and was kind to her, and she had no friends and relations to go to. On asking her why she had sent to let us know she was there, she replied that she thought she would like to join the British force, which she heard was in the neighbourhood, but on further reflection she had come to the conclusion it was best for her to remain where she was. After talking to her for some time, and making quite sure she was not likely to change her mind, we rode away, leaving her to her sowar, with whom she was apparently quite content.* I need hardly say we got unmercifully chaffed on our return to camp, when the result of our expedition leaked out.

At Somna, where we halted for the night, we heard that the Mahomedan insurgents, the prisoners released from gaol, and the rebel Rajputs of the neighbourhood, were prepared to resist our advance on Aligarh, and that they expected to be aided by a large number of mutineers from Delhi. We came in sight of Aligarh shortly before daybreak on the 5th October. Our advance was stopped by a motley crowd drawn up before the walls, shouting, blowing horns, beating drums, and abusing the Feringhis in the choicest Hindustani; but, so far as we could see, there were no sepoys amongst them. The Horse Artillery coming up, these valiant defenders quickly fled inside the city and closed the gates, leaving two guns in our possession. Thinking we should be sure to attack and take the place, they rushed through it to the other side, and made for the open country. But we had had enough of street fighting at Delhi. Our Cavalry and Artillery were divided into two parties, which moved round the walls, one to the right and the other to the left, and united in pursuit of the fugitives at the further side. We followed them for several miles. Some had concealed themselves in the high crops, and were discovered by the Cavalry on their return march to camp. Ouvry formed a long line, and one by one the rebels, starting up as the troopers rode through the fields, were killed, while our loss was trifling.

The inhabitants of Aligarh had apparently had a bad time of it under the rebel rule, for they expressed much joy at the result of the morning's work, and were eager in their proffers to bring in supplies for our troops and to otherwise help us.

Ill as we could afford to weaken our column, it was so necessary to keep the main line of communication open, and put a stop to the disorder into which the country had fallen, that it was decided to leave two companies of Punjabis at Aligarh, as a guard to the young civilian who was placed in charge of the district.

Fourteen miles from Aligarh on the road to Cawnpore there lived two Rajputs, twin brothers, who had taken such a prominent part in the rebellion that a price had been put on their heads, and for the

* A few years afterwards she communicated with the civil authorities of the district, and made out such a pitiful story of ill-treatment by her Mahomedan husband, that she was sent to Calcutta, where some ladies were good enough to look after her.

future peace of the district it was considered necessary to capture them. In order to surprise them the more completely, it was given out that the column was to march towards Agra, from which place disquieting news had been received, while secret orders were issued to proceed towards Cawnpore. The Cavalry went on in advance, and while it was still dark, succeeded in surrounding the village of Akrabad, where dwelt the brothers. In attempting to escape they were both killed, and three small guns were found in their house loaded and primed, but we had arrived too suddenly to admit of their being used against us. We discovered besides a quantity of articles which must have belonged to European ladies—dresses, books, photographs, and knick-knacks of every description—which made us feel that the twins had richly deserved their fate.

We halted on the 7th, and on the 8th marched across country to Bryjgarh (a prettily situated village under a fortified hill), our object being to get nearer to Agra, the reports from which place had been causing us anxiety, and likewise to put ourselves in a position to intercept the Rohilkand mutineers, who we were told were on their way to Lucknow.

No sooner had we got to Bryjgarh than we received information that the detachment we had left behind at Aligarh was not likely to be left undisturbed, and at the same time an urgent call for assistance came from Agra, where a combined attack by insurgents from Gwalior, Mhow, and Delhi was imminent. Fifty of Hodson's Horse, under a European officer, and a sufficient number of Infantry to make the detachment we had left there up to 200, were at once despatched to Aligarh. It was clear, too, that the appeal from Agra must be responded to, for it was an important place, the capital of the North-West Provinces; the troops and residents had been shut up in the fort for more than three months, and the letters, which followed each other in quick succession, showed that the authorities were considerably alarmed. It was felt, therefore, that it was imperative upon us to turn our steps towards Agra, but it entailed our marching forty-eight miles out of our way, and having to give up for the time any idea of aiding Havelock in the relief of Lucknow.

The column marched at midnight on the 8th October, the Horse Artillery and Cavalry, which I accompanied, pushing on as fast as possible. We had done thirty-six miles, when we were advised from Agra that there was no need for so much haste, as the enemy, having heard of our approach, were retiring; we accordingly halted, nothing loath, till the Infantry came up.

Early the next morning, the 10th October, we reached Agra. Crossing the Jumna by a bridge of boats, we passed under the walls of the picturesque old fort built by the Emperor Akbar nearly 300 years before.

The European residents who had been prisoners within the walls of the fort for so long streamed out to meet and welcome us, overjoyed at being free at last. We presented, I am afraid, but a sorry appearance, as compared to the neatly-dressed ladies and the spick-and-span troops who greeted us, for one of the fair sex was overheard to remark, 'Was ever such a dirty-looking lot seen?' Our clothes were, indeed, worn and soiled, and our faces so bronzed that the white soldiers were hardly to be distinguished from their Native comrades.

Our questions as to what had become of the enemy, who we had been informed had disappeared with such unaccountable celerity on hearing of the advance of the column, were answered by assurances that there was no need to concern ourselves about them, as they had fled across the Kari Naddi, a river thirteen miles away, and were in full retreat towards Gwalior. It was a little difficult to believe in the complete dispersion of the formidable rebel army, the mere rumoured approach of which had created such consternation in the minds of the Agra authorities, and had caused the many urgent messages imploring us to push on.

Our doubts, however, were met with the smile of superior knowledge. We were informed that the rebels had found it impossible to get their guns across to the Agra side of the stream, and that, feeling themselves powerless without them to resist our column, they had taken themselves off with the least possible delay. We were asked with some indignation, 'Had not the whole country round been scoured by thoroughly trustworthy men without a trace of the enemy being discovered?' And we were assured that we might take our much-needed rest in perfect confidence that we were not likely to be disturbed. We were further told by those who were responsible for the local Intelligence Department, and who were repeatedly questioned, that they had no doubt whatever their information was correct, and that there was no need to follow up the enemy until our troops were rested and refreshed.

We were then not aware of what soon became painfully apparent, that neither the information nor the opinions of the heads of the civil and military administration at Agra were to be relied upon. That administration had, indeed, completely collapsed; there was no controlling authority; the crisis had produced no one in any responsible position who understood the nature of the convulsion through which we were passing; and endless discussion had resulted (as must always be the case) in fatal indecision and timidity.

We could hardly have been expected to know that the government of so great a province was in the hands of men who were utterly unfit to cope with the difficulties of an emergency such as had now arisen, although in quieter times they had filled their positions with credit to themselves and advantage to the State.

That this was the case can be proved beyond a doubt, but I do not give it as an excuse for our being caught napping by the enemy, which we certainly were. We ought, of course, to have reconnoitred the surrounding country for ourselves, and posted our piquets as usual; and we ought not to have been induced to neglect these essential military precautions by the confident assertion of the Agra authorities that the enemy were nowhere in our neighbourhood.

The Brigadier gave orders for our camp to be pitched as soon as the tents should arrive, but he saw no necessity for posting piquets until the evening. Accordingly, I marked out the camp on the brigade parade-ground, which had been selected as best suited for the purpose —a grassy, level, open spot, a mile and a half from the fort. On the left and rear were the ruined lines of the two Native Infantry regiments which had been disarmed and sent to their homes, and the charred remains of the British officers' houses. To the right and front there was cultivation, and the high crops, almost ready to be reaped, shut out the view of the country beyond.

As the tents and baggage could not arrive for some time, I got leave to go with Norman, Watson, and a few others to breakfast in the fort. We had scarcely sat down, bent on enjoying such an unusual event as a meal in ladies' society, when we were startled by the report of a gun, then another and another. Springing to our feet, there was a general exclamation of, 'What can it mean? Not the enemy, surely!' But the enemy it was, as we were soon convinced by our host, who, having gone to a point from which he could get a view of the surrounding country, came back in hot haste, to tell us that an action was taking place.

We who belonged to the column hurried down the stairs, jumped on our horses, and galloped out of the fort and along the road in the direction of the firing. We had got but half-way to camp, when we were met and almost borne down by an enormous crowd, consisting of men, women, and children of every shade of colour, animals and baggage all mixed up in inextricable confusion. On they rushed, struggling and yelling as if pursued by demons.

The refugees from the fort, tired of their long imprisonment, had taken advantage of the security which they thought was assured by the arrival of the column to visit their deserted homes. Two-thirds of the 150,000 inhabitants of the city had also flocked out to see the troops who had taken part in the capture of Delhi (the report of which achievement was still universally disbelieved), to watch our camp being pitched, and to see what was going on generally. All this varied crowd, in terror at the first sound of firing, made for the fort and city, and were met in their flight by the heavy baggage of the column on its way to camp. Instantly, elephants, camels, led horses, doolie-bearers carrying the sick and wounded, bullocks yoked to heavily-laden carts, all becoming panic-stricken, turned round and joined in the stampede. Elephants, as terrified as their *mahouts*,* shuffled along, screaming and trumpeting; drivers twisted the tails of their long-suffering bullocks with more than usual energy and heartlessness, in the vain hope of goading them into a gallop; and camels had their nostrils rent asunder by the men in charge of them, in their unsuccessful endeavours to urge their phlegmatic animals into something faster than their ordinary stately pace.

Into this surging multitude we rushed, but for a time our progress was completely checked. Eventually, however, by dint of blows, threats, and shouts, we managed to force our way through the motley crowd and reach the scene of action. What a sight was that we came upon! I seem to see it now as distinctly as I did then. Independent fights were going on all over the parade-ground. Here, a couple of Cavalry soldiers were charging each other. There, the game of bayonet *versus* sword was being carried on in real earnest. Further on, a party of the enemy's Cavalry were attacking one of Blunt's guns (which they succeeded in carrying off a short distance). Just in front, the 75th Foot (many of the men in their shirt-sleeves) were forming square to receive a body of the rebel horse. A little to the left of the 75th, Remmington's troop of Horse Artillery and Bourchier's battery had opened fire from the park without waiting to put on their accoutrements, while the horses were being hastily harnessed by the Native drivers and *saices*. Still further to the left, the 9th Lancers and Gough's squadron of Hodson's Horse were rapidly saddling and falling in. On the right the 8th Foot and the 2nd and 4th Punjab Infantry were busy getting under arms, while beyond, the three squadrons of Punjab Cavalry, under Probyn and Younghusband, were hurrying to get on the enemy's flank.

Watson galloped off to take command of the Punjab Cavalry, and Norman and I rode in different directions to search for the Brigadier. While thus employed, I was stopped by a dismounted *sowar*, who danced about in front of me, waving his *pagri*† before the eyes of my horse with one hand, and brandishing his sword with the other. I could not get the frightened animal near enough to use my sword, and my pistol (a Deane and Adams revolver), with which I tried to shoot my opponent, refused to go off, so I felt myself pretty well at his mercy, when, to my relief, I saw him fall, having been run through the body by a man of the 9th Lancers who had come to my rescue.

Being unable to find the Brigadier, I attached myself to the next senior officer, Major Frank Turner, who commanded the Artillery. Gradually the enemy were beaten off, and the troops formed themselves up ready for pursuit, or whatever they might be called upon to do. At this juncture Greathed appeared on the ground.

* Men in charge of the elephants. † Turban.

With less experienced troops the surprise—and a thorough surprise it was—would in all probability have had serious results. Most of the men were asleep under the few tents which had already arrived, or such shelter as could be obtained near at hand, when first one round shot, then another, came right into their midst from a battery concealed in the high crops to our right front. At the same time half a dozen rebels, one of them playing the *nagàra*,* rode quietly up to the Quarter-Guard of the 9th Lancers and cut down the sentry. Being dressed, like Probyn's men, in red, they were mistaken for them, and were thus enabled to get close to the guard. This act was quickly followed by a general rush of the enemy's Cavalry, which brought about the series of fights that were going on when we appeared on the scene. The Commander was not to be found; no one knew who was the senior officer present; consequently each regiment and battery had to act according to its own discretion. The troops got ready with incredible rapidity, and set to work to drive the enemy off the ground. The Artillery replied to the insurgents' guns; the Infantry did what they could, but were hampered by the fear of doing more injury to their friends than their foes, and thus the brunt of the work fell upon the Cavalry. The 9th Lancers made a succession of brilliant charges. One troop especially distinguished itself by recovering Blunt's captured gun; the Captain (French) was killed, and the subaltern (Jones), covered with wounds, was left on the ground for dead. Watson, Probyn, and Younghusband, with their three squadrons, cleared our right flank, capturing two guns and some standards; and Hugh Gough, with his squadron, performed a similar duty on the left.

Probyn greatly distinguished himself on this occasion. In one of the charges he got separated from his men, and was for a time surrounded by the enemy, two of whom he slew. In another charge he captured a standard. For these and numerous acts of gallantry during the Mutiny, he was, to the great delight of his many friends in the column, awarded the Victoria Cross.

When Greathed arrived, the order for a general advance was given, and we were just moving off in pursuit of the rebels, when the 3rd European Regiment and a battery of Field Artillery under Lieutenant-Colonel Cotton arrived from the fort. This officer, being senior to our Brigadier, took command of the force, and untimely delay was caused while he learnt the details of our position. Having satisfied himself that the enemy must be followed up, he endorsed Greathed's order, and off we again started.

We soon overtook the retreating foe, who every now and then turned and made an ineffectual stand. At the end of about four miles we came upon their camp; it covered a considerable space, and must have

* Native kettle-drum.

taken a long time to transport and pitch—a circumstance which made the ignorance on the part of the Agra authorities as to the close proximity of the enemy appear even more unaccountable than before.

Our Infantry were now pretty well done up; they had been on the move, with one or two short intervals, for nearly sixty hours, and the 3rd Europeans were not in trim for a long and hot day's work after such a lengthened period of inactivity in the fort, and clad, as they were, in thick scarlet uniform. The enemy, however, could not be allowed to carry off their guns; so, leaving the Infantry to amuse themselves by making hay in the rebels' camp, we pushed forward with the Cavalry and Artillery. It was a most exciting chase. Property of all sorts and descriptions fell into our hands, and before we reached the Kari Naddi we had captured thirteen guns, some of them of large calibre, and a great quantity of ammunition. The enemy's loss on this occasion was not very great, owing to the extraordinary facility with which Native troops can break up and disappear, particularly when crops are on the ground.

While watching a few of the rebel Cavalry making their escape along the opposite bank of the Kari Naddi, I noticed about a dozen men belonging to the 2nd and 4th Punjab Infantry quenching their thirst in the stream. Carried away by excitement, they had managed to keep up with the pursuit, never thinking of the inevitable trudge back to Agra, which meant that, by the time they arrived there, they would have accomplished a march of not less than 70 miles without a halt, besides having had a severe fight with an enemy greatly superior in numbers.

Our casualties were slight: 12 officers and men were killed, 54 wounded, and 2 missing, besides some 20 camp-followers killed and wounded.

There is no doubt that the enemy were almost as much taken by surprise as we were. They knew that we were on our way from Aligarh, and had arranged (as we afterwards heard) with the people of the city to destroy the bridge of boats in time to prevent our crossing. But our movements were sufficiently rapid to prevent their carrying their intention into effect; and although the insurgents were informed that we had actually crossed the river they refused to believe the report, and, it was said, hanged the man who brought it. Their incredulity was strengthened by the small dimensions of the ground taken up for our camp, and the few tents which were pitched, and they made up their minds that these were only being prepared for the troops belonging to the Agra garrison, and so anticipated an easy victory. Their astonishment first became known when they were repulsed by the 75th Foot, and were heard to say to one another, '*Arrah bhai! ye Dilliwhale hain!*' (I say, brother! these are the fellows from Delhi!).

We halted at Agra on the 11th, 12th, and 13th October, partly to rest the men and transport animals, but chiefly on account of the difficulty we had in getting out of the clutches of the North-West Provinces Government, the local authorities not caring to be left to their own resources. Our wounded were taken to the fort, and lodged in the Moti Masjid,* which exquisite little building had been turned into a hospital. The men were well taken care of by the ladies, who seemed to think they could never do enough for the Delhi column.

I now for the first time saw the lovely Taj Mahal—that beautiful, world-famed memorial of a man's devotion to a woman, a husband's undying love for a dead wife. I will not attempt to describe the indescribable. Neither words nor pencil could give to the most imaginative reader the slightest idea of the all-satisfying beauty and purity of this glorious conception. To those who have not already seen it, I would say: 'Go to India. The Taj alone is well worth the journey.'

CHAPTER XXI.

During our three days' halt at Agra we were told the story of all that had happened before we came, and a sad story it was of incapacity and neglected opportunity. The Lieutenant-Governor, an able, intelligent man under ordinary circumstances, had, unfortunately, no firmness of character, no self-reliance. Instead of acting on his own convictions, he allowed himself to be entirely led by men about him, who had not sufficient knowledge of Natives to enable them to grasp how completely the latter's attitude towards us had been changed by the loss of our military hold over the country.†

Deaf to warnings from those who did understand the magnitude of the danger, the Lieutenant-Governor refused to listen to the Maharaja Scindia, who, influenced by the wise counsels of his astute and enlightened minister, Dinkar Rao, told him that the whole Native army was disloyal, and that the men of his own (the Gwalior) Contingent‡ were as bad as the rest. The authorities refused to allow

* Pearl Mosque.

† 'They regarded the Mutiny as a military revolt; the rural disturbances as the work of the mobs. The mass of the people they considered as thoroughly loyal, attached to our rule as well from gratitude as from self-interest, being thoroughly conscious of the benefits it had conferred upon them. Holding these opinions, they did not comprehend either the nature or the magnitude of the crisis. To their inability to do so, many lives and much treasure were needlessly sacrificed.'—'The Indian Mutiny,' Thornhill.

‡ The Gwalior Contingent was raised in 1844, after the battles of Punniar and Maharajpore, to replace the troops of Maharaja Scindia ordered to be reduced. It consisted of five batteries of Artillery, two regiments of Cavalry, and seven regiments of Infantry, officered by British officers belonging to the Indian Army, and paid for out of the revenues of districts transferred to British management.

the ladies and children at Gwalior to be sent into Agra for safety; they objected to arrangements being made for accommodating the non-combatants inside the walls of the fort, because, forsooth, such precautions would show a want of confidence in the Natives! and the sanction for supplies being stored in the fort was tardily and hesitatingly accorded. It was not, indeed, until the mutinous sepoys from Nimach and Nasirabad were within sixty miles of Agra that orders were given to put the fort in a state of defence and provision it, and it was not until they had reached Futtehpore Sikri, twenty-three miles from Agra, that the women and children were permitted to seek safety within the stronghold.*

Fortunately, however, notwithstanding the intermittent manner in which instructions were issued, there was no scarcity of supplies, for, owing to the foresight and energy of Lieutenant Henry Chalmers, the executive Commissariat officer, assisted by that prince of contractors, Lalla Joti Persâd, and ably supported by Mr. Reade, the civilian next in rank to the Lieutenant-Governor, food was stored in sufficient quantities, not only for the garrison, but for all the refugees from the surrounding districts.†

Mr. Drummond, the magistrate of the district, who had from the first been the chief opponent of precautionary measures for the security of the residents, had the audacity to set the Lieutenant-Governor's order for victualling the fort at defiance. He forbad grain or provisions being sold to the Commissariat contractor, whose duty it was to collect supplies, and positively imprisoned one man for responding to the contractor's demands. It was at this official's instigation that the Native police force was largely increased, instead of being done away with altogether, as would have been the sensible course; and as there was an insufficiency of weapons wherewith to arm the augmentation, a volunteer corps of Christians, lately raised, was disbanded, and their arms distributed amongst the Mahomedan police. So far was this infatuated belief in the loyalty of the Natives carried that it was proposed to disarm the entire Christian population, on the pretext that their carrying weapons gave offence to the Mahomedans! It was only on the urgent remonstrance of some of the military officers that this preposterous scheme was abandoned.‡ The two Native regiments stationed at Agra were not disarmed until one of the British officers with them had been killed and another wounded. The gaol, containing 5,000 prisoners, was left in charge of a Native guard, although the superintendent, having reliable infor-

* 'The Indian Mutiny,' Thornhill

† Throughout the campaign the Commissariat Department never failed; the troops were invariably well supplied, and, even during the longest marches, fresh bread was issued almost daily.

‡ 'The Indian Mutiny,' Thornhill.

mation that the sepoys intended to mutiny, begged that it might be replaced by European soldiers. The Lieutenant-Governor gave his consent to this wise precaution, but afterwards not only allowed himself to be persuaded to let the Native guard remain, but authorized the removal of the European superintendent, on the plea of his being an alarmist.*

On the 4th July Mr. Colvin, the Lieutenant-Governor, whose health had been very indifferent for some time, was induced, much against his will, to retire to the fort, and for the time being the management of affairs passed into the hands of Brigadier Polwhele. There was little improvement—indecision reigned supreme. Notwithstanding that the gradual approach of the mutineers from Gwalior and Nasirabad was well known, no preparations were made, no plan of action decided upon. Polwhele, who was a brave old soldier, and had seen a great deal of service, had, indeed, wisely come to the conclusion that the rebels would never venture to attack a fort like Agra, and that, if left alone, they would in all probability continue their march towards Delhi. The available troops numbered less than 1,000 effective men, and Polwhele felt that, by going out to attack the enemy, there would be a grave risk of the seat of government falling into the hands of the disaffected police and city people.

Unfortunately, however, the Brigadier allowed himself to be overruled, and when the mutineers were reported to have arrived at Shahganj, four miles from Agra, he gave way to the cry to 'Go out and do something!' and issued orders for the troops to fall in.

A series of mishaps then occurred. It was one o'clock in the afternoon of the 5th July before the column† was ready to start; the men in their thick red uniform suffered greatly from the heat and thirst; the enemy, 9,000 strong, with twelve guns, instead of being at Shahganj, were found to be strongly entrenched at Sarsia, some distance farther off. A protracted engagement then took place, and our troops, having expended all their ammunition, were obliged to retreat, leaving many dead and a gun on the field.

Meanwhile the city and cantonment were in a state of uproar. The first gun was the signal for the guard at the gaol to release the 5,000 prisoners, who, as they appeared in the streets, still wearing their fetters, caused a perfect panic amongst the respectable inhabitants; while the evil-disposed made for the cantonment, to plunder, burn, and murder. Some of the residents who had not sought shelter in the fort, confident that our troops would gain an easy

* 'The Indian Mutiny,' Thornhill.

† It consisted of the 3rd European Regiment, 568 strong, a battery of Field Artillery, with Native drivers and a few European Artillerymen, and about 100 mounted Militia and Volunteers, composed of officers, civilians and others who had taken refuge in Agra.

victory, on hearing of their defeat hurried with all speed to that place of refuge, and for the most part succeeded in reaching it; but a few were overtaken and killed by the mob, aided by the trusted police, who had early in the day broken into open mutiny.*

With one or two exceptions the officials, military and civil alike, were utterly demoralized by all these disastrous occurrences, the result of their own imbecility. For two days no one was allowed to leave the fort or approach from the outside. Within was dire confusion; without, the mob had it all their own way.

Early in August a despatch was received from the Governor-General acknowledging the receipt of the report on the fight of the 5th July, and directing that Brigadier Polwhele should be removed from the command of his brigade. On the 9th September Mr. Colvin died; he never recovered the shock of the Mutiny. As a Lieutenant-Governor in peace-time he was considered to have shown great ability in the management of his province, and he was highly respected for his uprightness of character. One cannot but feel that it was in a great measure due to his failing health that, when the time of trial came, he was unable to accept the responsibility of directing affairs himself, or to act with the promptitude and decision which were demanded from all those occupying prominent positions in 1857.

Mr. Reade, the next senior civilian, assumed charge of the government on Mr. Colvin's death, until orders were received from the Government of India vesting the supreme authority in a military officer, and appointing Colonel Hugh Fraser, of the Bengal Engineers, to be Mr. Colvin's successor with the rank and position of a Chief Commissioner. Lord Canning was doubtless induced to make this selection in consequence of the courage and ability Colonel Fraser had displayed during the Burmese War, and also on account of the sound advice he had given to the Lieutenant-Governor in the early days of the outbreak—advice which unfortunately was ignored. Mr. Reade, who had proved himself worthy of his high position, gave Colonel Fraser his cordial and unqualified support, but that officer, like his predecessor, was in bad health, and found it difficult to exercise the much-needed control. A constant state of panic continued to exist, and no reliable information could be obtained of what was going on even in the immediate neighbourhood. The relief afforded by the news of the fall of Delhi was great, but short-lived, for it was quickly followed by a report that the whole rebel army had fled from Delhi and was hastening towards Agra, and that the mutineers from Gwalior and Central India were advancing to attack the fort. Again all was confusion. Reports as to the movements of the enemy were never he same for two days together; at last what appeared to be authentic

* The police were suspected of having invited the insurgents who defeated Polwhele to Agra.

intelligence was received: the Gwalior troops were said to be close at hand, and those urgent appeals for assistance which were sent to Greathed caused us to turn our steps towards Agra.

Our object having been attained, we were all anxious to depart. The Chief Commissioner, however, was quite as anxious that we should remain; firmly believing that the Gwalior troops would reappear, he suggested that we should follow them up at least as far as Dholpur; but this proposal Greathed firmly refused to accede to. The orders he had received were to open up the country* between the Jumna and the Ganges, and he had not forgotten the little note from Havelock discovered in the fakir's platter.

At last the column was allowed to leave. The evening before our departure Norman and I called on the Chief Commissioner to say good-bye. We found Colonel Fraser greatly depressed, and inclined to take a most gloomy view of the situation, evidently thinking the restoration of our rule extremely doubtful. His last words to us were, 'We shall never meet again.'† He looked extremely ill, and his state of health probably accounted for his gloomy forebodings. We, on the contrary, were full of health and hope. Having assisted at the capture of Delhi, the dispersion of the enemy who had attempted to oppose us on our way through the Doab, and the troops we were serving with having recently achieved a decisive victory at Agra over a foe four times their number, we never doubted that success would attend us in the future as in the past, and we were now only anxious to join hands with Havelock, and assist in the relief of the sufferers besieged in Lucknow.

CHAPTER XXII.

On the 14th October we moved camp to the left bank of the Jumna, where we were joined by a small party of Artillerymen with two 18-pounder guns, and some convalescents belonging to the regiments with us, who had been left behind at Delhi—300 in all. Our camp was pitched in a pretty garden called the Rambagh, only a short distance from Agra, where we gave a picnic to the ladies who had been so kind to our wounded men—a rough sort of entertainment, as may be imagined, but much enjoyed by the easily-pleased people who had been prisoners for so long, to whom the mere getting away from the fort for a few hours was a relief.

On the morning of the 15th we commenced our march towards Mainpuri, a small station seventy miles from Agra, which we reached

* Known as the Doab.

† Colonel Fraser died within nine months of our leaving Agra.

on the 18th. While on our way there, Hope Grant, Colonel of the 9th Lancers, arrived in camp to take over the command of the column. He had remained at Delhi when superseded by Greathed, and being naturally indignant at the treatment he had received, he protested against it, and succeeded in getting the order appointing Greathed to the command cancelled.

Had an officer been specially selected on account of his possessing a more intimate acquaintance with Native soldiers and a longer experience of India, Hope Grant would no doubt have accepted the inevitable. But Greathed did not know as much of the country and Native troops as Hope Grant did; he had seen no service before he came to Delhi, and while there had no opportunity of showing that he possessed any particular qualification for command; he certainly did not exhibit any while in charge of the column, and everyone in the force was pleased to welcome Hope Grant as its leader.

The Raja of Mainpuri, who had openly joined the rebels, fled the day before we marched in, leaving behind him several guns and a quantity of powder. We halted on the 20th, blew up his fort and destroyed the powder. The European part of the station was in ruins, but a relation of the Raja had been able to prevent the Government treasury from being plundered, and he made over to us two and a half lakhs of rupees.

The civilians of the Mainpuri district were amongst the refugees at Agra, and took advantage of our escort to return to their station. We had also been joined by some officers whom the mutiny of their regiments had left without employment; they were a welcome addition to our Punjab regiments, as the limited number of British officers attached to these corps had been considerably reduced by the constantly recurring casualties. One of these officers was a Captain Carey, whose story, as he told it to me, of his escape from the massacre at Cawnpore and his subsequent experiences is, I think, worth repeating.

In the month of May Carey went into Wheeler's entrenchment with the rest of the garrison; a few days before the investment, however, Sir Henry Lawrence sent his Military Secretary, Captain Fletcher Hayes, to Cawnpore, to report on what course events were taking at that place, and, if possible, to communicate with Delhi. His escort was the 2nd Oudh Irregular Cavalry. Hayes had already made Carey's acquaintance, and, on finding him at Cawnpore, asked him to accompany him to Delhi, which invitation Carey gladly accepted. When they got close to Bewar, where the road to Mainpuri branched off, Hayes, wishing to gain information from the civil authorities as to the state of the country through which their route to Delhi lay, rode off to the latter place with Carey, having first ordered the escort to proceed towards Delhi, and having arranged with the British officers to catch them up at the end of the next day's march. The following day, as the two friends approached the encamping ground where they were to overtake the escort, they beheld the regiment marching steadily along the road in regular formation; there was nothing to warn them that it had revolted, for as there were only three British officers with the corps, whose dress was almost the same as the men's, their absence was not noticed.

Suddenly, when they had got within two or three hundred yards of the regiment, the troopers with one accord broke into shouts and yells, and, brandishing their swords, galloped towards Hayes and Carey, who, turning their horses, made with all possible speed back towards Mainpuri. Hayes, who was an indifferent rider, was soon overtaken and cut to pieces, while Carey, one of the best horsemen in the army, and beautifully mounted, escaped; the *sowars* followed him for some distance, but a wide irrigation cut, which he alone was able to clear, put an end to the pursuit. Carey reached his destination in safety, and, with the other Europeans from Mainpuri, sought refuge in the Agra fort, where he spent the following five months. It was afterwards ascertained that the three British officers with the escort had been murdered by the *sowars* shortly before Hayes and Carey came in sight.

On the 21st October we reached Bewar, the junction of the roads from Meerut, Agra, Fatehgarh, and Cawnpore, at which point the Brigadier received a communication from Sir James Outram, written in Greek character, from the Lucknow Residency, begging that aid might be sent as soon as possible, as provisions were running short.* The note was rolled up inside a quill, which the Native messenger had cunningly concealed in the heart of his thick walking-stick. Outram's urgent summons determined the Brigadier to push on. So the next day we made a march of twenty-eight miles to Goorsahaigunj, and on the 23rd we reached Miran-ki-Serai, close to the ruined Hindu city of Kanoj.

The same day I went on as usual with a small escort to reconnoitre,

* No account of the quantity and description of supplies stored in the Residency had been kept, or, if kept, it was destroyed when the Mutiny broke out. Captain James, the energetic Commissariat officer, on receiving Sir Henry Lawrence's order to provision the Residency, spent his time riding about the country buying supplies of all descriptions, which were stored wherever room could be found for them. James was very severely wounded at the fight at Chinhut, and was incapacitated the greater part of the siege. It was only by degrees that some of the supplies were discovered; no one knew how much had been collected, and no record of the quantities issued from day to day could be kept. When Outram joined hands with Inglis, his first question was, 'How much food is there?' Thanks to Sir Henry Lawrence's foresight, there was an ample supply, not only for the original garrison, but for the numbers by which it was augmented on the arrival of the relieving force. Of this, however, Outram must have been ignorant when he despatched the little note to which I have alluded in the text.

and had passed through the town, when I was fired upon by a party of the rebels, consisting of some 300 Cavalry, 500 Infantry, and four guns, who, having heard of the approach of the column, were trying to get away before it arrived. Their Cavalry and Infantry were on the opposite bank of a fairly wide stream, called the Kali Naddi, through which were being dragged some heavy pieces of cannon. I retired a short distance, and sent back word to the advance guard, which hastened to my assistance. A few rounds from our Artillery caused the enemy to abandon their guns, the Infantry dispersed and disappeared, the Cavalry fled, and we, crossing the stream, had a smart gallop after them for about four miles over a fine grassy plain. On we flew, Probyn's and Watson's squadrons leading the way in parallel lines, about a mile apart. I was with the latter, and we had a running fight till we reached the Ganges, into which plunged those of the *sowars* whom we had not been able to overtake; we reined up, and saw the unlucky fugitives struggling in the water, men and horses rolling over each other; they were gradually carried down by the swiftly running stream, and but a very few reached the opposite bank.

Our casualties were trifling, only some half-dozen men wounded, while my horse got a gash on his quarter from a sabre. Watson had the forefinger of his right hand badly cut in an encounter with a young *sowar;* I chaffed him at allowing himself to be nearly cut down by a mere boy, upon which he laughingly retorted: 'Well, boy or not, he was bigger than you.'

It was on this occasion that I first recognized the advantage of having the carbine slung on the trooper's back while in action, instead of being carried in the bucket, as is the custom with our British Cavalry. Several of the enemy's loose horses were going about with carbines on their saddles, while their dismounted riders were at an enormous disadvantage in trying to defend themselves from their mounted adversaries with only their swords. I saw, too, one of Watson's men saved from a fierce cut across the spine by having his carbine on his back. More recent experience has quite satisfied me that this is the only way this weapon should be carried when actual fighting is going on.

Three more marches brought us to Cawnpore, where we arrived on the 26th October.

We now for the first time heard the miserable 'story of Cawnpore.' We were told how, owing to Sir Hugh Wheeler's misplaced belief in the loyalty of the sepoys, with whom he had served for upwards of half a century, and to the confiding old soldier's trust in the friendship of the miscreant Nana, and in the latter's ability to defend him until succour should arrive, he had neglected to take precautionary measures for laying in supplies or for fortifying the two exposed barracks which, for some unaccountable reason, had been chosen as a place of refuge, instead of the easily defensible and well-stored magazine. Our visit to this scene of suffering and disaster was more harrowing than it is in the power of words to express; the sights which met our eyes, and the reflections they gave rise to, were quite maddening, and could not but increase tenfold the feelings of animosity and desire for vengeance which the disloyalty and barbarity of the mutineers in other places had aroused in the hearts of our British soldiers. Tresses of hair, pieces of ladies' dresses, books crumpled and torn, bits of work and scraps of music, just as they had been left by the wretched owners on the fatal morning of the 27th June, when they started for that terrible walk to the boats provided by the Nana as the bait to induce them to capitulate.* One could not but picture to one's self the awful suffering those thousand Christian souls of both sexes and of all ages must have endured during twenty-one days of misery and anxiety, their numbers hourly diminished by disease, privation, the terrific rays of a June sun, and the storm of shot, shell, and bullets which never ceased to be poured into them. When one looked on the ruined, roofless barracks, with their hastily constructed parapet and ditch (a mere apology for a defence), one marvelled how 465 men, not more than half of them soldiers by profession, could have held out for three long weeks against the thousands of disciplined troops and hordes of armed retainers whom the Nana was able to bring to the attack.

It is impossible to describe the feelings with which we looked on the Sati-Choura Ghat, where was perpetrated the basest of all the Nana's base acts of perfidy;† or the intense sadness and indignation which

* On the 25th June, after twenty-one days of intense suffering—with his numbers so reduced as to render further defence scarcely possible, with starvation staring him in the face, and with no hope of succour—Sir Hugh Wheeler most reluctantly consented to capitulate. The first overtures were made by the Nana, who, despairing of being able to capture the position, and with disaffection in his own camp, sent the following message to the General: 'All those who are in no way connected with the acts of Lord Dalhousie, and are willing to lay down their arms, shall receive a safe passage to Allahabad.' This missive, which was without signature, was in the handwriting of Azimula Khan, a Mahomedan who had been employed by the Nana as his Agent in England, and was addressed, 'To the subjects of Her Most Gracious Majesty Queen Victoria.' General Wheeler agreed to give up the fortification, the treasure, and the Artillery, on condition that each man should be allowed to carry his arms and sixty rounds of ammunition, that carriages should be provided for the conveyance of the wounded, the women, and the children, and that boats, with a sufficiency of flour, should be ready at the neighbouring *ghat* (landing-place). The Nana accepted these conditions, and three officers of the garrison were deputed to go to the river and see that the boats were properly prepared. They found about forty boats moored, and apparently ready for departure, and in their presence a show of putting supplies on board was made.

† The Nana never intended that one of the garrison should leave Cawnpore alive, and during the night of the 26th June he arranged with Tantia Topi to

overpowered us as we followed the road along which 121 women and children (many of them well born and delicately nurtured) wended their weary way, amidst jeers and insults, to meet the terrible fate awaiting them. After their husbands and protectors had been slain, the wretched company of widows and orphans were first taken to the Savada house, and then to the little Native hut, where they were doomed to live through two more weeks of intensest misery, until at length the end came, and the last scene in that long drama of foulest treachery and unequalled brutality was enacted. Our unfortunate countrywomen, with their little children, as my readers will remember, were murdered as the sound of Havelock's avenging guns was heard.

We found at Cawnpore some men who had fought their way from Allahabad with Havelock's force, from whom we heard of the difficulties they had encountered on their way, and the subsequent hardships the gallant little force had to endure in its attempts to reach Lucknow. They also told us that Havelock and Outram, with only 3,179 men of all arms, and 14 guns, had succeeded in forcing their way through that great city with a loss of 700, but only to be themselves immediately surrounded by the vast multitude of the enemy, who for three whole months had vainly endeavoured to overpower the heroic defenders of the Residency.

At Cawnpore there were very few troops. The Head-Quarters of the 64th Foot, under Colonel Wilson, and some recovered invalids belonging to regiments which had gone to Lucknow, had held it for more than a month, within an entrenchment thrown up on the river bank to protect the bridge of boats. Just before we arrived four companies of the 93rd Highlanders had marched in. It was the first time I had seen a Highland regiment, and I was duly impressed by their fine physique, and not a little also by their fine dress. They certainly looked splendid in their bonnets and kilts—a striking contrast

---

have soldiers and guns concealed at the Sati-Choura Ghat to open fire upon the Europeans he had been unable to conquer as soon as the embarkation had been effected and they could no longer defend themselves and their helpless companions in misery. The river was low and the boats were aground, having been purposely drawn close to the shore. When the last man had stepped on board, at a given signal the boatmen jumped into the water and waded to the bank. They had contrived to secrete burning charcoal in the thatch of most of the boats; this soon blazed up, and as the flames rose and the dry wood crackled, the troops in ambush on the shore opened fire. Officers and men tried in vain to push off the boats; three only floated, and of these two drifted to the opposite side, where sepoys were waiting to murder the passengers. The third boat floated down the stream, and of the number on board four eventually escaped—Lieutenants Thomson and Delafosse, both of the 53rd Native Infantry, Private Murphy of the 84th Foot, and Gunner Sullivan, of the Bengal Artillery. The rest of the officers and men were killed or drowned, and the women and children who escaped were carried off as prisoners.

to my war-worn, travel-stained comrades of the Movable Column. An *avant courier* of the Naval Brigade had also come in, sent on by Captain William Peel, of H.M.S. *Shannon*, to arrange for the rest of the blue-jackets who were about to arrive—the first naval officer, I imagine, who had ever been sent on duty so far up the country as Cawnpore.

Other troops were rapidly being pushed up, and officers who had been on leave to England were daily arriving, having hurried out to join their different regiments in various parts of India. Amongst these was an old friend and brother subaltern of mine, Augustus Otway Mayne, whom, greatly to my satisfaction, Hope Grant appointed D.A.Q.M.G. to help me, for there was now more work to be done than I could well get through.

The day after our arrival at Cawnpore we heard that the new Commander-in-Chief, Sir Colin Campbell, was to leave Calcutta that evening to take command of the force with which he hoped to effect the relief of the Lucknow garrison, and with this news came an order to Hope Grant from Sir Colin to get into communication with the Alambagh, a small garden-house not quite two miles from the city of Lucknow, built by one of the Begums of the ex-King of Oudh, in which the sick and wounded, tents and spare stores, had been left in charge of a small detachment, when Outram and Havelock advanced towards the Residency on the 25th September.

On the 30th October we left Cawnpore, and crossed the Ganges into Oudh, taking with us the four companies of the 93rd Highlanders, and the men belonging to Havelock's force, whom I have mentioned as having been left behind on account of sickness.

On the 31st we were at Bani bridge, more than half-way to the Alambagh, when a telegram reached the Brigadier directing him to halt until Sir Colin Campbell (who had got as far as Cawnpore) should arrive.

Hope Grant did not think the ground we were on well adapted for a prolonged halt; that afternoon, therefore, I went off with Mayne to reconnoitre the country for a more suitable place. We fixed upon an open plain at the village of Bhantira, about three miles nearer Lucknow. We met with no opposition that day, but the country people in the neighbourhood had shown marked hostility by killing one or two soldiers and every camp-follower who had strayed from the main road; so we were careful to examine Bhantira and all the neighbouring villages, but were unable to discover the slightest sign of an enemy.

As the next day's march was such a very short one, we did not start until 7 a.m., instead of before daybreak as usual. Mayne and I rode on ahead with a couple of *sowars*, and reached the site we had chosen for the camp without meeting a single suspicious-looking individual. We then sent back the escort to bring up the camp colour-men, and while waiting for them, we entered into conversation with some passing pilgrims, who told us they were on their way to Benares to procure holy water from the Ganges. Suddenly a bullet whizzed over our heads, fired from the direction from which we had just come. Looking back, to our amazement we saw a crowd of armed men at a distance of between three and four hundred yards, completely cutting us off from the column. The whole plain was alive with them. When they saw they were observed, they advanced towards us, shouting and firing. Fortunately for us, we had made ourselves perfectly acquainted with the country the previous day, and instantly realized that escape by our right (as we faced Lucknow) was impossible, because of a huge impassable *jhil*. There was another *jhil* to our left front, but at some little distance off, and our only chance seemed to be in riding hard enough to get round the enemy's flank before they could get close enough to this *jhil* to stop us.

Accordingly, we put spurs to our horses and galloped as fast as they could carry us to our left; the enemy turned in the same direction, and made for a village we must pass, and which we could see was already occupied. The firing got hotter and more uncomfortable as we neared this village, the walls of which we skirted at our best possible pace. We cleared the village, and hoped we had distanced the rebels, when suddenly we came upon a deep *nulla*. Mayne got safely to the other side, but my horse stumbled and rolled over with me into the water at the bottom. In the fall my hand was slightly cut by my sword, which I had drawn, thinking we might have to fight for our lives; the blood flowed freely, and made the reins so slippery when I tried to remount, that it was with considerable difficulty I got into the saddle. The enemy were already at the edge of the *nulla*, and preparing to fire, so there was no time to be lost. I struggled through the water and up the opposite bank, and ducking my head to avoid the shots, now coming thick and fast, galloped straight into some high cultivation in which Mayne had already sought shelter. Finally we succeeded in making our way to the main body of the force, where we found Hope Grant in great anxiety about us, as he had heard the firing and knew we were ahead. The dear old fellow evinced his satisfaction at our safe return by shaking each of us heartily by the hand, repeating over and over again in his quick, quaint way, 'Well, my boys, well, my boys, very glad to have you back! never thought to see you again.' The column now moved on, and we found ourselves opposed to a vast body of men, not soldiers, but country people, who in those days were all armed warriors, and who spent their time chiefly in fighting with each other. As we approached the crowd turned, opened out, and fled in every direction, spreading over the plain and concealing themselves in the long grass. We gave chase and killed many, but a large proportion escaped. Favoured by the high crops, they disappeared with that marvellous celerity with which Natives can almost instantly become invisible, leaving in our possession a 9-pounder brass gun. On this occasion we had thirty killed and wounded.

We could not at the time understand where the men had sprung from who so suddenly attacked us; but it afterwards transpired that some powerful *zemindars** in the neighbourhood had collected all the forces they could get together, and established them after dark in the very villages we had so carefully examined the previous afternoon and had found completely deserted, with the intention of falling upon the column as it passed in the early morning. The unusually late hour at which the march was made, however, disconcerted their little plan, and giving up all hope of the force coming that day, they consoled themselves by trying to get hold of Mayne and myself.

We halted on the 3rd and 4th November. On the 5th, Hope Grant sent a force to the Alambagh for the purpose of escorting a long line of carts and camels laden with provisions and ammunition, which the Commander-in-Chief was desirous of having near at hand, in case the relief of the Lucknow garrison should prove a more prolonged operation than he hoped or anticipated it was likely to be.

As we neared the Alambagh the enemy's guns opened on us from our right, while their Cavalry threatened us on both flanks. They were easily disposed of, and we deposited the stores, receiving in exchange a number of sick and wounded who were to be sent back to Cawnpore.

A curious incident happened at the Alambagh. I was employed inside the enclosure, when all at once I heard a noise and commotion some little distance off. Getting on to the roof, I looked over the plain, and saw our troops flying in every direction; there was no firing, no enemy in sight, but evidently something was wrong; so I mounted my horse and rode to the scene of confusion, where I found that the ignominious flight of our troops was caused by infuriated bees which had been disturbed by an officer of the 9th Lancers thoughtlessly thrusting a lance into their nest. There were no serious consequences, but the Highlanders were heard to remark on the unsuitability of their dress for an encounter with an enemy of that description.

On the 9th November Sir Colin Campbell joined the column, accompanied by his Chief of the Staff, Brigadier-General Mansfield.†

The following morning we were surprised to hear that a European from the Lucknow garrison had arrived in camp. All were keen to see him, and to hear how it was faring with those who had been shut up in the Residency for so long; but the new-comer was the bearer of

* Permanent occupiers of the land, either of the landlord class, as in Bengal, Oudh, and the North-West Provinces, or of the yeoman class, as in the Punjab.

† Afterwards General Lord Sandhurst, G.C.B., G.C.S.I.

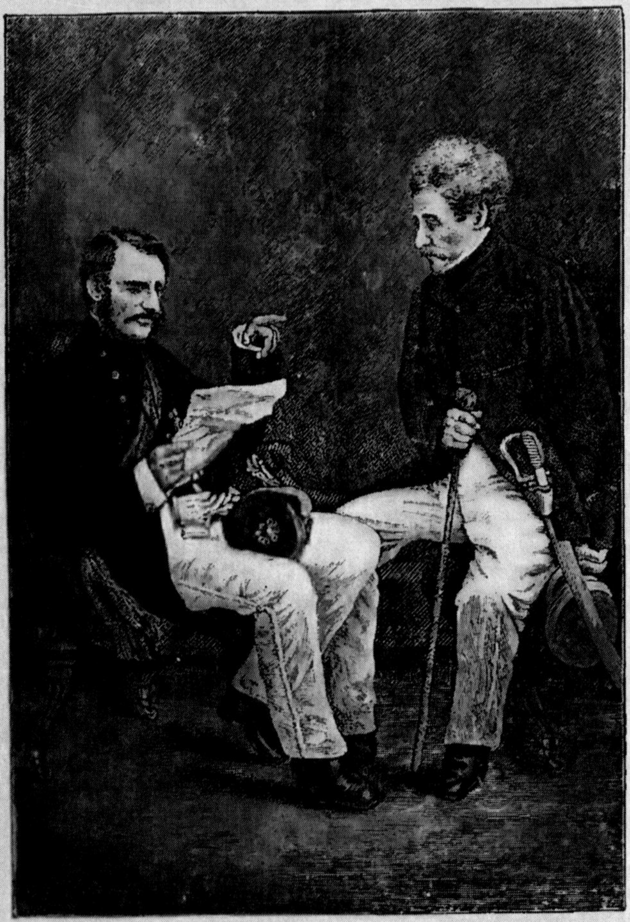

LORDS CLYDE AND SANDHURST.

(SIR COLIN CAMPBELL AND SIR WILLIAM MANSFIELD.)

From
a photograph taken in India.

very important information from Sir James Outram, and to prevent any chance of its getting about, the Commander-in-Chief kept the messenger, Mr. Kavanagh, a close prisoner in his own tent.

Outram, being anxious that the officer in command of the relieving force should not follow the same route taken by himself and Havelock, and wishing to communicate his ideas more at length than was possible in a note conveyed as usual by a spy, Kavanagh, a clerk in an office in Lucknow, pluckily volunteered to carry a letter. It was an offer which appealed to the heart of the 'Bayard of the East,' as Outram has been appropriately called, and just such an errand as he himself, had he been in a less responsible position, would have delighted to undertake. Outram thoroughly understood the risk of the enterprise, and placed it clearly before the brave volunteer, who, nothing daunted, expressed his readiness to start at once, and his confidence in being able to reach the British camp.

Disguised as a Native, and accompanied by a man of Oudh, on whose courage and loyalty he was convinced he could rely, Kavanagh left the Residency after dark on the 9th and got safely across the Gumti. He and his guide remained in the suburbs mixing with the people until the streets might be expected to be pretty well empty, when they re-crossed the river and got safely through the city. They were accosted more than once on their way, but were saved by the readiness of the Native, who it had been arranged should answer all inquiries, though Kavanagh, having been born and bred in the country, could himself speak the language fluently. On the morning of the 10th they made themselves known to a piquet of Punjab Cavalry on duty near the Alambagh.

Outram, profiting by his own experience, wished the relieving column to be spared having to fight its way through the streets of Lucknow. This was all the more necessary because the enemy, calculating on our following the same route as before, had destroyed the bridge over the canal and made extensive preparations to oppose our advance in that direction. Outram explained his views most clearly, and sent with his letter a plan on which the line he proposed we should take was plainly marked. He recommended that the advance should be made by the Dilkusha* and Martinière,† and that the canal should

* The Dilkusha house was built at the beginning of the century by a king of Oudh as a hunting-box and country residence, and close to it he cleared away the jungle and laid out a large park, which he stocked with herds of deer and other game.

† The Martinière was built by Claude Martin, a French soldier of fortune, who came out to India under Count de Lally, in the stirring days of 1757. In 1761 he was taken prisoner by the English at Pondicherry and sent to Bengal. After the conclusion of the war he enlisted in the English Army, and on attaining the rank of Captain he got permission to attach himself to the Court of the King of Oudh, where he soon obtained supreme influence, and became to all practical purposes Prime Minister. He remained an officer

be crossed by the bridge nearest the Gumti. Outram showed his military acumen in suggesting this route, as our right flank would be covered by the river, and therefore could only be molested by a comparatively distant fire. Sir Colin, appreciating all the advantages pointed out, readily accepted and strictly adhered to this plan of advance, except that, instead of crossing the canal by the bridge, we forded it a little nearer the river, a wise divergence from Outram's recommendation, and one which he would assuredly have advised had he been aware that the canal was fordable at this spot, as it kept us altogether clear of the streets.

Outram did not touch in his despatch upon any question but the all-important one of how the junction between his own and the relieving forces could best be effected. Many other matters, however, claimed the earnest consideration of the Commander-in-Chief before he could proceed. He had to determine what was to be done to secure the safety of the women and children in the Residency, after the first most pressing duty of relieving the garrison had been accomplished. Cawnpore was again in great danger from the Gwalior mutineers, who, foiled at Agra, and finding that the Maharaja Sindhia would not espouse their cause, had placed themselves under the orders of the Rani of Jhansi and Tantia Topi, the vile Mahratta whom the Nana made use of to carry out the massacre of the Sati-Choura Ghat; led by this man the rebels were seriously threatening Cawnpore, and it was necessary to take steps for its security. Then again the city of Lucknow had to be thought of; its capture and the restoration of British authority were alike essential, but our Chief knew that he had neither the time nor the means at his disposal to undertake this important operation at once. He therefore made up his mind that so soon as the Residency had been relieved he would withdraw altogether from Lucknow, and place a force at the Cawnpore side of the city, to form the nucleus of the army with which he hoped later on to take the place, and to keep open communication with his Head-Quarters, while he himself should hurry back to Cawnpore, taking with him all the non-combatants and the sick and wounded.

---

of the East India Company's Service, and at the time of his death held the rank of Major-General. He amassed a large fortune, and by his will founded colleges at Lucknow, Calcutta, and Lyons, the place of his birth. His directions that his house at the former place should never be sold, but should 'serve as a college for educating children and men in the English language and religion,' were carried out by the British Government, and Martin lies buried in its vault.

CHAPTER XXIII.

THE next morning, the 11th, I had the honour of making the Commander-in-Chief's acquaintance. The manner of my introduction was peculiarly unceremonious. I had left my own tent to be repaired at Cawnpore, and was sharing one with Norman, who was well known to, and greatly believed in by, His Excellency, whose Brigade-Major he had been at Peshawar. Before we were out of bed we heard Sir Colin's voice outside. He had come to speak to Norman about his plans for the future, and as the conversation seemed likely to be of a very confidential nature, and it was too dark for him to see me, I asked Norman to make my presence known. Sir Colin said to Norman somewhat roughly, 'Who is he?' and on my name being mentioned, he asked if I were to be trusted. Norman having vouched for my discretion, the old Chief was apparently satisfied, and then ensued an intensely interesting discussion on Outram's letter, Kavanagh's description of the state of affairs in the Residency, and the manner in which it was best to carry out Outram's recommendations.

That same afternoon the Commander-in-Chief reviewed the column, which now amounted to about 600 Cavalry and 3,500 Infantry, with 42 guns.* The parade was under the command of Hope Grant, who had been given the rank of Brigadier-General, and put in executive command of the whole force.

Sir Colin spoke a few inspiriting words to each regiment and battery, being particularly appreciative and complimentary in his remarks to

* Besides the troops from Delhi, the force consisted of Peel's Naval Brigade, with eight heavy guns and howitzers; Middleton's Field Battery of Royal Artillery (the first that had ever served in India), and two companies of garrison Royal Artillery, under Travers and Longden, equipped with heavy guns and mortars; a company of Royal Engineers under Lieutenant Lennox, V.C.;[1] a few Bengal, and two newly-raised companies of Punjab Sappers; the 93rd Highlanders, Head-Quarters and wing of the 23rd Royal Welsh Fusiliers, and of the 53rd Foot; part of the 82nd Foot, and detachments of the 5th Fusiliers, 64th, 78th, 84th, and 90th Foot, and Madras Fusiliers, regiments which had gone into the Residency with Outram and Havelock. The Infantry was brigaded as follows:

Wing 53rd Foot 93rd Highlanders Battalion of detachments 4th Punjab Infantry	Commanded by Brigadier the Hon. Adrian Hope, 93rd Highlanders.
8th Foot Battalion of detachments 2nd Punjab Infantry	Commanded by Brigadier Greathed, 8th Foot
Wing 23rd Fusiliers Two companies 82nd Foot	Commanded by Brigadier D. Russell, 84th Foot.

[1] Afterwards General Sir Wilbraham Lennox, V.C., K.C.B.

the Delhi troops, who certainly looked the picture of workmanlike soldiers; and, considering what they had accomplished, there was nothing invidious in the Chief's singling them out. The Bengal Artillery came in for a large share of praise; he had a strong liking for them, having been with them on service,* and seen of what good stuff they were made. He recognized several old acquaintances amongst the officers, and freely expressed his satisfaction at having such reliable batteries to help him in the hazardous operation he was about to undertake. He was careful also to say a few words of commendation to the four squadrons of Punjab Cavalry, and the two regiments of Punjab Infantry, the only Native troops, except the Sappers, with the column.

That evening orders were issued for a march to the Alambagh the following morning. It may perhaps seem as if Sir Colin was rather leisurely in his movements, but he had ascertained that the Lucknow garrison was in no immediate want of food, as had been reported, and he was determined to leave nothing undone to ensure the success of the undertaking. He personally attended to the smallest detail, and he had to arrange for the transport of the sick and wounded, and the women and children, shut up in the Residency, numbering in all not less than fifteen hundred souls.

Everything being ready, we began our march towards Lucknow, one and all eager to have a share in the rescue of our suffering countrywomen and their children from a most perilous position, and in relieving soldiers who had so long and so nobly performed the most harassing duty, while they cheerfully endured the greatest privations.

We had proceeded but a short distance, when the advance guard was fired upon by some guns in position on our right, near the old fort of Jalalabad. An extensive swamp protected the enemy's right flank, while on their left were a number of water-cuts and broken ground. The Infantry and Artillery wheeled round and attacked the battery in front, while Hugh Gough pushed on with his squadron of Cavalry to see if he could find a way through the apparently impassable swamp to the enemy's right and rear. Bourchier's battery coming up in the nick of time, the hostile guns were soon silenced, and Gough, having succeeded in getting through the *jhil*, made a most plucky charge, in which he captured two guns and killed a number of the enemy. For his gallant conduct on this occasion Gough was awarded the Victoria Cross, the second of two brothers to win this much coveted distinction.

The next morning Adrian Hope, who commanded a brigade, was ordered to seize the Jalalabad fort, but finding it evacuated, he blew up one of the walls, and so rendered it indefensible.

On the afternoon of the 13th I accompanied the Commander-in-

* Sir Colin Campbell had served throughout the Punjab Campaign and on the Peshawar frontier.

Chief in a reconnaissance towards the Charbagh bridge and the left front of the Alambagh, a ruse to deceive the enemy as to the real line of our advance. When riding along he told me, to my infinite pride and delight, that I was to have the honour of conducting the force to the Dilkusha. The first thing I did on returning to camp was to find a good guide. We had only about five miles to go; but it was necessary to make sure that the direction taken avoided obstacles which might impede the passage of the Artillery. I was fortunate in finding a fairly intelligent Native, who, after a great deal of persuasion, agreed, for a reward, to take me by a track over which guns could travel. I never let this man out of my sight, and made him show me enough of the road to convince me he knew the way and meant fair dealing.

The Alambagh now proved most useful; all our camp equipage was packed inside the enclosure, for we took no tents with us, and all our spare stores were left there. A rough description of semaphore, too, was constructed on the highest point of the building, by means of which we were able to communicate with the Residency. It was put in Orders that the troops were to breakfast early the next morning, and that they were to take three days' rations in their haversacks; while sufficient for fourteen days was to be carried by the Commissariat.

Just before we started on the 14th November we were strengthened by the arrival of 200 of the Military Train equipped as Cavalry, two Madras Horse Artillery guns, and another company of Madras Sappers.

Captain Moir, of the Bengal Artillery, was placed in charge of the Alambagh, with a garrison consisting of the 75th Foot, 50 of the regiment of Ferozepore,* and a few Artillerymen. The 75th was the first regiment to move down from the hills when the news of the outbreak at Meerut reached Head-Quarters; it had done grand service, had suffered heavily during the siege of Delhi, and had well earned, and badly needed, a rest. It was now only 300 strong, and had lost in six months 9 officers, in action and from disease, besides 12 wounded. The officers were all friends of mine, and I was very sorry to leave them behind, particularly Barter, the Adjutant, a jolly, good-hearted Irishman, and an excellent officer.

We marched at 9 a.m., keeping to the south of the Alambagh and the Jalalabad fort. We then struck across the fields to the ground now occupied by the Native Cavalry lines, and on to the open space upon which the present race-course is marked out. On reaching this point the Dilkusha came in sight about a mile in front. As we approached, a few shots were fired at us; but the enemy rapidly disappeared as the

* Now the 14th (Sikhs) Bengal Infantry

Cavalry and Horse Artillery, followed by the Infantry of the advance guard, in skirmishing order, passed through an opening which had been hastily made in the wall of the enclosure.

The gallop across the Dilkusha park was quite a pretty sight: deer, which had been quietly browsing, bounded away on all sides, frightened by our approach and the rattle of the guns; while the routed sepoys flew down the grassy slope leading to the Martinière. We reined up for a few seconds to look at the view which opened out before us. In front rose the fluted masonry column of the Martinière, 123 feet high; directly behind, the picturesque building itself, and in the distance the domes and minarets of the mosques and palaces within the city of Lucknow; all looked bright and fair in the morning sun.

We could see that the Martinière was occupied; a crowd of sepoys were collected round the building; and as we showed ourselves on the brow of the hill, a number of round shot came tumbling in amongst us.

Remmington's troop of Horse Artillery, Bourchier's battery, and a heavy howitzer brought up by Captain Hardy, now came into action, and under cover of their fire the 8th Foot and 1st battalion of Detachments attacked and drove the enemy out of the Martinière, while the Cavalry pursued them as far as the canal.

On this occasion my friend Watson greatly distinguished himself. Entirely alone he attacked the enemy's Cavalry, and was at once engaged with its leader and six of the front men; he fought gallantly, but the unequal contest could not have lasted much longer had not Probyn, who, with his own and Watson's squadrons, was only about 300 yards off, become aware of his comrade's critical position, and dashed to his assistance. For this 'and gallantry on many other occasions,' Hope Grant recommended Watson for the Victoria Cross, which he duly received.*

By noon on the 14th we had occupied the Dilkusha and Martinière, and placed our outposts along the right bank of the canal from the river to the point immediately opposite Banks's house. The left bank was held in force by the rebels. Early in the afternoon I went with Hope Grant, accompanied by a small force of Cavalry, to ascertain whether it would be possible to ford the canal somewhere close to the river, and we succeeded in finding a place by which the whole force crossed two days later. Our movements were fortunately not noticed by the enemy, whose attention was concentrated on the roads leading direct to the city from the Dilkusha and Martinière, by which they expected our advance to be made.

* During one of Watson's many reconnaissances he received a cut on the face from a sabre. One of the 2nd Punjab Cavalrymen, seeing what had happened, rushed to Probyn, and said: 'Watson *sahib* has got a wound which is worth a lakh of rupees!'

Sir Colin, meanwhile, had fixed his Head-Quarters in the Martinière, on the topmost pinnacle of which he caused a semaphore to be erected for communication with Outram. From this post of vantage Kavanagh was able to point out to the Commander-in-Chief the different objects of most interest to him—the positions taken up by the enemy; the group of buildings, of which the Chatta Manzil* was the most conspicuous, then occupied by the gallant troops led by Outram and Havelock, who, by overwhelming numbers alone, had been prevented from carrying their glorious enterprise to a successful issue; the Residency, where, thanks to Sir Henry Lawrence's foresight and admirable arrangements, a handful of heroic Britons had been able to defy the hordes of disciplined soldiers and armed men who, for nearly three months, day and night, had never ceased to attack the position; and the Kaisarbagh, that pretentious, garish palace of the Kings of Oudh, the centre of every kind of evil and debauchery.

Later in the day the enemy made a determined attack on our centre, which was checked by Brigadier Little advancing with the 9th Lancers and some guns. On a few rounds being fired, they retired from the immediate neighbourhood of the canal, and in the belief that there would be no further trouble that day, the Cavalry and Artillery returned to the Martinière; but the guns were hardly unlimbered before heavy firing was heard from the direction of Banks's house.

I galloped off with Mayne to ascertain the cause. Some little distance from the canal we separated, Mayne going to the left, I to the right. I found the piquets hotly engaged, and the officer in command begged me to get him some assistance. I returned to Hope Grant to report what was going on, but on the way I met the supports coming up, and presently they were followed by the remainder of Hope's and Russell's brigades. Russell had, early in the day, with soldierly instinct, seized two villages a little above the bridge to the north of Banks's house; this enabled him to bring a fire to bear upon the enemy as they advanced, and effectually prevented their turning our left. Hope opened fire with Remmington's troop, Bourchier's battery, and some of Peel's 24-pounders, and as soon as he found it had taken effect and the rebels were shaken, he proceeded to push them across the canal and finally drove them off with considerable loss.

Hope's and Russell's united action, by which our left flank was secured, was most timely, for had it been turned, our long line of camels, laden with ammunition, and the immense string of carts carrying supplies, would in all probability have been captured. As it

* Built by a king of Oudh for the ladies of his harem. It takes its name from the gilt umbrella (Chatta) with which it is adorned. Now the Lucknow Club.

was, the rear guard, under Lieutenant-Colonel Ewart,* of the 93rd Highlanders, had a hot time of it; it was frequently attacked, and its progress was so slow that it was more than twenty-four hours between the Alambagh and the Dilkusha.

At the conclusion of the fight I heard, with great grief, that my poor friend Mayne had been killed, shot through the breast a few seconds after he had left me. He was seen to turn his horse, and, after going a short distance, fall to the ground; when picked up he was quite dead. This was all I could learn. No one was able to tell me where his body had been taken, and I looked for it myself all that evening in vain.

At daybreak the next morning, accompanied by Arthur Bunny, the cheery Adjutant of Horse Artillery, I began my search afresh, and at length we discovered the body inside a doolie under the wall of the Martinière. As there was no knowing how soon our services might be required, we decided to bury the poor fellow at once. I chose a spot close by for his grave, which was dug with the help of some gunners, and then Bunny and I, aided by two or three brother officers, laid our friend in it just as he was, in his blue frock-coat and long boots, his eyeglass in his eye, as he always carried it. The only thing I took away was his sword, which I eventually made over to his family. It was a sad little ceremony. Overhanging the grave was a young tree, upon which I cut the initials 'A. O. M.'—not very deep, for there was little time: they were quite distinct, however, and remained so long enough for the grave to be traced by Mayne's friends, who erected the stone now to be seen.

The whole of that day (the 15th) was spent in preparing for the advance. The Dilkusha was turned into a general depot, where the sick and wounded were placed, also the Ordnance park and stores of every description. A rough defence was thrown up round the building, and a garrison was left to protect it, consisting of five Field guns, half the 9th Lancers, the Military Train, a squadron of Punjab Cavalry, and the 8th Foot, the whole under the command of Little, the Brigadier of Cavalry.

In the afternoon Sir Colin made a feint to the left of our position for the purpose of diverting the attention of the enemy from the real line of advance. He massed the Artillery in this direction, and ordered a constant mortar fire to be kept up during the night on the Begum palace and the barracks. To further strengthen the belief that operations would be carried on from our left, some of the piquets on our right were drawn in; this induced the enemy to make a slight demonstration in that direction. They crossed the canal, but were speedily driven back by the Madras Horse Artillery guns. They then opened

* Now General Sir John Ewart, K.C.B.

fire with a 12-pounder howitzer from the west side of the Gumti, when a really most extraordinary incident happened, which I am not sure I should have the courage to relate, were it not that Sir Dighton Probyn and Sir John Watson, who were close by and saw what took place, are able to vouch for the accuracy of my story.

A shell, fortunately a blind one, from the enemy's howitzer came into Watson's squadron, which was drawn up under the bank of the Martinière tank; it struck a trooper's saddle in front, and must have lifted the man partly out of it, for it passed between his thigh and the horse, tearing the saddle* to shreds, and sending one piece of it high into the air. The horse was knocked down, but not hurt; the man's thigh was only badly bruised, and he was able to ride again in a few days. One of Watson's officers, Captain Cosserat, having examined the man and horse, came up and reported their condition to Watson, who, of course, was expecting to be told they were both dead, and added: 'I think we had better not tell this story in England, for no one would believe it.' I myself was close to the squadron, and distinctly saw what happened.†

All that day (the 15th) I had been very hard at work, and was greatly looking forward to what I hoped would be a quiet night, when an Aide-de-camp appeared, who informed me that the Commander-in-Chief desired my presence at the Martinière.

On reporting myself to His Excellency, he told me that he was not satisfied that a sufficient reserve of small-arm ammunition had been brought with the force, and that the only chance of getting more in time was to send back to the Alambagh for it that night, adding that he could neither afford the time nor spare the troops which would be required, were the business of fetching the additional supply to be postponed until the following day. Sir Colin then asked me if I thought I could find my way back to the Alambagh in the dark. I answered, 'I am sure I can.' I might have hesitated to speak so confidently had I not taken the precaution of placing the man who had acted as my guide on the 14th in charge of some Afghan *chuprassies*‡ attached to the Quartermaster-General's department, with strict orders not to lose

* It was a Native saddle, such as Irregular Cavalry used in those days, made of felt without a tree.

† On one occasion, when I was telling this story to General Sir Samuel Browne, V.C., he said that something similar happened at the battle of Sadulapur on December 2, 1848. He (Browne) was Adjutant of his regiment (the 46th Native Infantry), which was drawn up in line, with a troop of Horse Artillery, commanded by Major Kinleside, on its right flank. Seeing that something unusual had occurred, Browne rode up to the troop, and found that one of the men had had his saddle carried away from under him by a small round shot. The man, who happened at the moment to be standing up in his stirrups, escaped with a bruise, as did the horse.

‡ A kind of more or less responsible servant or messenger, so called from wearing a chuprass, or badge of office.

sight of him. I thought, therefore, I would have him to depend upon if my own memory failed me. The Commander-in-Chief impressed very strongly upon me the great necessity for caution, and told me I could take what escort I thought necessary, but that, whatever happened, I must be back by daybreak, as he had signalled to Outram that the force would advance on the morrow. Sir Colin desired that the Ordnance officer, whose fault it was that sufficient ammunition had not been brought, should go back with me and be left at the Alambagh.

It was then dusk, and there was no time to be lost. In the first instance I went to my General, and reporting the orders I had received from the Commander-in-Chief, consulted him about my escort. Hope Grant strongly urged my taking with me a troop of the 9th Lancers, as well as some Native Cavalry, but for a night trip I thought it would be better to employ Natives only. I knew that my one chance of success depended on neither being seen nor heard, and Native Cavalry move more quietly than British, chiefly because their scabbards are of wood, instead of steel. I felt, too, that if we came across the enemy, which was not improbable, and got scattered, Natives would run less risk, and be better able to look after themselves. All this I explained to the General, but in the kindness of his heart he pressed me to take the Lancers, telling me he would feel happier about me if I had my own countrymen with me; but I stuck to my own opinion, and it was arranged that I was to be accompanied by Younghusband and Hugh Gough, with their respective squadrons of Native Cavalry. I took leave of my kind and considerate General, and hurried off first to warn the two Cavalry officers, then to the Dilkusha to tell Lieutenant Tod Brown, in charge of the Ordnance depot, that his assistant was to go with me, and lastly to arrange with the Commissariat officer for camels upon which to bring back the ammunition.

It was quite dark before I got to the place where my servants had collected, and where I expected to find my guide. What was my horror to hear that he had disappeared! He had made his escape in the confusion consequent on the enemy's attacks the previous afternoon. What was to be done now? I was in despair—and became more and more doubtful of my ability to find the Alambagh in the dark. By daylight, and with the aid of a compass, which I always carried about me, I should have had little difficulty, even though the country we had to get over was intersected by ravines and watercourses, not to speak of the uncompromising *jhil* near the Jalalabad fort. However, go I must. I could not possibly tell the Commander-in-Chief that I was unable to carry out a duty for which he had selected me—there was nothing for it but to trust to my own recollection of the route and hope for the best.

Everything having been put in train, I returned to the Artillery bivouac, managed a hasty dinner, mounted a fresh horse, and, about

9 p.m., started off, accompanied by Younghusband, Hugh Gough, the unlucky Ordnance officer, two squadrons of Cavalry, and 150 camels.

We got on well enough until we reached the broken ground near the present Native Cavalry lines, when we lost the road, or rather track, for road there was none. We could see nothing but the lights of the enemy's piquets at an uncomfortably short distance to our right. I struck a match, and made out from the compass the right direction; but that did not help us to clear the ravines, which, in our efforts to turn or get through them, made our way appear interminable. At length we found ourselves upon open ground; but, alas! having edged off too much to our right we were in close proximity to the enemy's piquets, and could distinctly hear their voices. We halted to collect the long string of camels, and as soon as they were got in order started off again. I led the way, every few minutes striking a light to see how the compass was pointing, and to take an anxious look at my watch, for I was beginning to fear I should not be able to accomplish my task by the given time. Our pace was necessarily slow, and our halts frequent, for the little party had to be carefully kept together.

At last the Jalalabad fort was reached and passed. I then told Hugh Gough, whose squadron was in front, that we had better halt, for we could not be far from the Alambagh, and I was afraid that if we approached in a body we should be fired upon, in which case the camel-drivers would assuredly run away, there would be a stampede amongst the camels, and we might find it difficult to make ourselves known. I decided it would be best for me to go on alone, and arranged with Gough that he should remain where he was until I returned.

The Alambagh proved to be farther off than I calculated, and I was beginning to fear I had lost my way, when all at once a great wall loomed in front of me, and I could just make out the figure of the sentry pacing up and down. I hailed him, and ordered him to ask the sergeant of the guard to summon the officer on duty. When the latter appeared, I explained to him my object in coming, and begged him to have the ammunition boxes ready for lading by the time I returned with the camels. I then rode back to where I had left Gough, and the whole procession proceeded to the Alambagh.

Already half the night was gone; but beyond the time required for loading the camels there was no delay; the utmost assistance was afforded us, and ere long we started on our return journey.

Day had dawned before we came in sight of the Dilkusha, and by the time I had made the ammunition over to the Ordnance officer it was broad daylight. As I rode up to the Martinière I could see old Sir Colin, only partially dressed, standing on the steps in evident anxiety at my non-arrival.

He was delighted when at last I appeared, expressed himself very pleased to see me, and, having made many kind and complimentary remarks as to the success of the little expedition, he told me to go off and get something to eat as quickly as possible, for we were to start directly the men had breakfasted. That was a very happy moment for me, feeling that I had earned my Chief's approbation and justified his selection of me. I went off to the Artillery camp, and refreshed the inner man with a steak cut off a gun bullock which had been killed by a round shot on the 14th.

At 8 a.m. the troops moved off. I was ordered to go with the advance guard.* Hope's and Russell's brigades came next, with Travers's Heavy battery, Peel's Naval Brigade, and Middleton's Field battery.

Greathed's brigade (except the 8th Foot left at the Dilkusha), with Bourchier's battery, remained to guard our left flank until mid-day, when it was ordered to follow the column and form its rear guard.

The offer of a Native who volunteered to guide us was accepted, and Sir Colin, who rode just behind the advance guard, had Kavanagh with him, whose local knowledge proved very valuable.

The enemy had been so completely taken in by the previous day's reconnaissance that they had not the slightest suspicion we should advance from our right, the result being that we were allowed to cross the canal without opposition.† We kept close along the river bank, our left being partially concealed by the high grass. About a mile beyond the canal we turned sharp to the left, and passed through the narrow street of a small village, coming immediately under fire from some houses on our right, and from the top of a high wall above and beyond them, which turned out to be the north-east corner of the Sikandarbagh.

The greatest confusion ensued, and for a time there was a complete block. The Cavalry in advance were checked by a fierce fire poured directly on them from the front: they were powerless, and the only thing for them to do was to force their way back, down the confined

* It consisted of Blunt's troop of Horse Artillery, the wing of the 53rd Foot, and Gough's squadron of Hodson's Horse.

† We had not, however, gone far, when a body of rebel Infantry, about 2,000 strong, managing to elude Greathed's brigade, crossed the canal, and, creeping quietly up, rushed the Martinière. Sir Colin had left Lieutenant Patrick Stewart, an unusually promising officer of the Bengal Engineers, on the top of the Martinière to keep Outram informed of our movements by means of the semaphore, and while Stewart was sending a message he and Watson (who was with him) observed the enemy close up to the building. They flew down the staircase, jumped on their horses, and, joining Watson's squadron and the two Madras Native Horse Artillery guns, rode to the city side of the Martinière to try and cut off the enemy, who, finding no one inside the building, and seeing their line of retreat threatened, made the best of their way back to the city. Several were killed by the Horse Artillery, which opened upon them with grape, and by Watson's *sowars*.

lane we had just passed up, which by this time was crammed with Infantry and Artillery, making 'confusion worse confounded.' As soon as the Cavalry had cleared out, the 53rd lined the bank which ran along the side of the lane nearest the Sikandarbagh, and by their fire caused all those of the rebels who had collected outside the walls to retire within the enclosure. This opened a road for Blunt, who, leading his guns up the bank with a splendid courage, unlimbered and opened fire within sixty yards of the building.

Blunt found himself under a heavy fire from three different directions—on the right from the Sikandarbagh; on the left and left front from the barracks, some huts (not twenty yards off), and a serai; and in front from the mess-house, Kaisarbagh, and other buildings. In these three directions he pointed his guns, regardless of deadly fire, especially from the huts on the left.

It would, however, have been impossible for the advance guard to have held its ground much longer, so it was with a feeling of the utmost relief that I beheld Hope's brigade coming up the lane to our assistance. A company of the 53rd, in the most brilliant manner, forced the enemy from the position they held on our left front, and the Highlanders, without a moment's hesitation, climbed on to the huts—the point, as I have already said, from which the heaviest fire proceeded; they tore off the roofs, and, leaping into the houses, drove the enemy before them right through the serai and up to the barracks, which they seized, and for the remainder of the operations these barracks were held by the 93rd.

This action on the part of the Highlanders was as serviceable as it was heroic, for it silenced the fire most destructive to the attacking force; but for all that, our position was extremely critical, and Sir Colin, perceiving the danger, at once decided that no further move could be attempted until we had gained possession of the Sikandarbagh. It was, indeed, a formidable-looking place to attack, about 130 yards square, surrounded by a thick brick wall twenty feet high, carefully loopholed, and flanked at the corners by circular bastions. There was only one entrance, a gateway on the south side, protected by a traverse of earth and masonry, over which was a double-storied guard-room. Close to the north side of the enclosure was a pavilion with a flat roof prepared for musketry, and from the whole place an incessant fire was being kept up.

Sir Colin, in order to get a better view of the position, and thus be able to decide in what direction the attack could most advantageously be made, rode up the bank and placed himself close to one of Blunt's guns. Mansfield and Hope Grant were on either side, and Augustus Anson and I were directly behind, when I heard the Commander-in-Chief exclaim, 'I am hit.' Luckily it was only by a spent bullet, which had passed through a gunner (killing him on the spot) before it struck Sir Colin on the thigh, causing a severe contusion, but nothing more. It was a moment of acute anxiety until it was ascertained that no great damage had been done.

By this time one of Travers's guns and a howitzer, which with considerable difficulty had been dragged up the bank, opened fire on the point selected by Sir Colin for the breach—the south-east corner of the wall surrounding the Sikandarbagh.* Instantly Hardy (Captain of the battery) was killed and the senior Subaltern wounded: Blunt's charger was shot, and of the few men under his command 14 Europeans and 6 Gun Lascars were killed or wounded; 20 of the troop-horses were also knocked over.†

While the heavy guns were at work on the breach, Adrian Hope, with the 53rd, cleared off a body of the enemy who had collected on our left front, and connected the barracks with the main attack by a line of skirmishers.

In less than half an hour an opening three feet square and three feet from the ground had been made in the wall. It would have been better had it been larger, but time was precious; Sir Colin would not wait, and ordered the assault to begin. The Infantry had been lying down, under such slight cover as was available, impatiently awaiting for this order. The moment it reached them, up they sprang with one accord, and with one voice uttered a shout which must have foreshadowed defeat to the defenders of the Sikandarbagh. The 93rd under Lieutenant-Colonel Ewart, and the 4th Punjab Infantry under Lieutenant Paul, led the way, closely followed by the 53rd under Lieutenant-Colonel Gordon‡ of the 93rd Highlanders, and one of the battalions of Detachments under Major Roger Barnston.

* This wall has long since been built up, and the whole place is so overgrown with jungle that it was with difficulty I could trace the actual site of the breach when I last visited Lucknow in 1893.

† Blunt's troop, when it left Umballa in May, 1857, consisted of 93 Europeans and 20 Native Gun Lascars. It suffered so severely at Delhi that only five guns could be manned when it marched from there in September, and after the fight at Agra its total loss amounted to 12 killed and 25 wounded. Four guns could then with difficulty be manned. When Blunt left the troop in January, 1858, to take command of Bourchier's Field Battery, 69 out of the 113 men with whom he had commenced the campaign had been killed or wounded! The troop would have been unserviceable, had men not volunteered for it from other corps, and drivers been posted to it from the Royal Artillery. At the commencement of the Mutiny Blunt was a subaltern, and in ten months he found himself a Lieutenant-Colonel and a C.B. Quick promotion and great rewards indeed, but nothing more than he richly deserved; for seldom, if ever, has a battery and its commander had a grander record to show.

‡ Captain Walton was the senior officer of the regiment present, and took a conspicuous part in leading it, but as in Sir Colin Campbell's opinion he was too junior to be in command, Lieutenant-Colonel Gordon was appointed as a temporary measure.

It was a magnificent sight, a sight never to be forgotten—that glorious struggle to be the first to enter the deadly breach, the prize to the winner of the race being certain death! Highlanders and Sikhs, Punjabi Mahomedans, Dogras* and Pathans, all vied with each other in the generous competition.†

A Highlander was the first to reach the goal, and was shot dead as he jumped into the enclosure; a man of the 4th Punjab Infantry came next, and met the same fate. Then followed Captain Burroughs and Lieutenant Cooper, of the 93rd, and immediately behind them their Colonel (Ewart), Captain Lumsden, of the 30th Bengal Infantry,‡ and a number of Sikhs and Highlanders as fast as they could scramble through the opening. A drummer-boy of the 93rd must have been one of the first to pass that grim boundary between life and death, for when I got in I found him just inside the breach, lying on his back quite dead —a pretty, innocent-looking, fair-haired lad, not more than fourteen years of age.

The crush now became so great in the men's eagerness to get through the opening and join the conflict within, that a regular block was the consequence, which every minute became more hopeless. One party made for the gateway and another for a barred window§ close by, determined to force an entrance by them. The traverse having been rushed by the 4th Punjab Infantry gallantly led by a Dogra Subadar,‖ a Punjabi Mahomedan of this distinguished corps behaved with the most conspicuous bravery. The enemy, having been driven out of the earthwork, made for the gateway, the heavy doors of which were in the act of being closed, when the Mahomedan (Mukarrab Khan by name) pushed his left arm, on which he carried a shield, between them, thus preventing their being shut; on his hand being badly wounded by a sword-cut, he drew it out, instantly thrusting in the other arm, when the right hand was all but severed from the wrist.¶ But he gained his

* The word 'Dogra' was originally applied to the Rajput clans in the hills and sub-montane tracts to the north of the Ravi. In later years it included hill Rajputs south of the Ravi, and in military parlance all these Rajputs who enlisted in our ranks came to be called Dogras.

† In consequence of the behaviour of the 4th Punjab Infantry on this occasion, and in other engagements in which they served with the 93rd Highlanders, the officers and men of the latter corps took a great liking to the former regiment, and some years after the Mutiny two officers of the 93rd, who were candidates for the Staff Corps, specially applied to be posted to the 4th Punjab Infantry.

‡ Attached as Interpreter to the 93rd Highlanders.

§ It was here Captain Walton, of the 53rd, was severely wounded.

‖ Subadar Gokal Sing was mentioned by the Commander-in-Chief in despatches for his conduct on this occasion.

¶ For this act of heroism Mukarrab Khan was given the Order of Merit, the Indian equivalent to the Victoria Cross, but carrying with it an increase of pay. At the end of the campaign Mukarrab Khan left the service, but when his old Commanding officer, Colonel Wilde, went to the Umbeyla expedition object—the doors could not be closed, and were soon forced open altogether, upon which the 4th Punjab Infantry, the 53rd, 93rd, and some of the Detachments, swarmed in.

This devoted action of Mukarrab Khan I myself witnessed, for, with Augustus Anson, I got in immediately behind the storming party. As we reached the gateway, Anson was knocked off his horse by a bullet, which grazed the base of the skull just behind the right ear, and stunned him for a moment—the next, he was up and mounted again, but was hardly in the saddle when his horse was shot dead.

The scene that ensued requires the pen of a Zola to depict. The rebels, never dreaming that we should stop to attack such a formidable position, had collected in the Sikandarbagh to the number of upwards of 2,000, with the intention of falling upon our right flank so soon as we should become entangled amongst the streets and houses of the Hazratganj.* They were now completely caught in a trap, the only outlets being by the gateway and the breach, through which our troops continued to pour. There could therefore be no thought of escape, and they fought with the desperation of men without hope of mercy, and determined to sell their lives as dearly as they could. Inch by inch they were forced back to the pavilion, and into the space between it and the north wall, where they were all shot or bayoneted. There they lay in a heap as high as my head, a heaving, surging mass of dead and dying inextricably entangled. It was a sickening sight, one of those which even in the excitement of battle and the flush of victory make one feel strongly what a horrible side there is to war. The wretched wounded men could not get clear of their dead comrades, however great their struggles, and those near the top of this ghastly pile of writhing humanity vented their rage and disappointment on every British officer who approached by showering upon him abuse of the grossest description.

The firing and fighting did not cease altogether for some time after the main body of the rebels were destroyed. A few got up into the guard-room above the gateway, and tried to barricade themselves in; others sought shelter in the bastions, but none escaped the vengeance of the soldiers. There were some deadly combats between the mutinous sepoys and the Sikhs. Eventually all the rebels were killed, save three or four who dropped over the wall on the city side. It is to be hoped they lived to tell the tale of the dauntless courage which carried everything before it.

Considering the tremendous odds which those who first entered through the breach were exposed to, and the desperate nature of the

in 1863, Mukarrab Khan turned up and insisted on serving with him as an orderly.

* One of the principal thoroughfares of Lucknow.

fighting, our losses were astonishingly small. The 93rd had 2 officers and 23 men (including the Sergeant-Major) killed, and 7 officers and 61 men wounded.

The 4th Punjab Infantry went into action with four British officers, of whom two were killed and one was severely wounded. Sixty-nine of the Native officers and men were also killed or wounded.*

CHAPTER XXIV.

The operation which I have tried to describe in the last chapter was not completed until well on in the afternoon, when the movement towards the Residency was at once proceeded with. To the left as we advanced the ground was fairly open (with the exception of quite a small village) for about 1,100 yards in the direction of the British Infantry mess-house. To the right also, for about 300 yards, there was a clear space, then a belt of jungle intersected by huts and small gardens extending for about 400 yards further, as far as the Shah Najaf,† a handsome white-domed tomb, surrounded by a court-yard, and enclosed by high masonry loopholed walls; and beyond the Shah Najaf rose the Kadam Rasul,‡ another tomb standing on a slight eminence.

But little opposition was experienced from the village, which was carried by the Infantry, while the Artillery were brought up to open fire on the Shah Najaf and Kadam Rasul. The latter was soon occupied by the 2nd Punjab Infantry, belonging to Greathed's brigade, which had by this time joined the main body; but the Shah Najaf proved a harder nut to crack. This building was almost concealed by dense

* Lieutenant Paul, the Commandant, was killed. Lieutenant Oldfield mortally, and Lieutenant McQueen severely, wounded. Lieutenant Willoughby, who brought the regiment out of action, was quite a lad, and was killed at Ruhiya the following April. Both he and McQueen were recommended for the V.C. for their gallantry on this occasion. After the fight was over, one of the Native officers, bemoaning the loss of the British officers, asked me who would be sent to replace them. He added: '*Sahib, ham log larai men bahut tez hain magar jang ka bandobast nahin jante*' ('Sir, we can fight well, but we do not understand military arrangements'). What the old soldier intended to convey to me was his sense of the inability of himself and his comrades to do without the leadership and general management of the British officers.

† Shah Najaf is the tomb of Ghazi-ud-din Haidar, first King of Oudh, built by himself. It derives its name from Najaf, the hill on which is built the tomb of Ali, the son-in-law of Mahomed, and of which tomb this is said to be a copy.

‡ The Kadam Rasul, or Prophet's footprint, a Mahomedan place of worship, which contained a stone bearing the impress of the foot of the Prophet, brought from Arabia by a pilgrim. During the Mutiny the holy stone was carried off.

jungle, and its great strength therefore remained unsuspected until we got quite close up to it.

Barnston's battalion of Detachments advanced in skirmishing order, under cover of our guns. One of the shells most unfortunately burst prematurely, wounding Major Barnston so severely that he died soon afterwards. Whether it was that the men were depressed by the loss of their leader, or that they were not prepared for the very damaging fire which suddenly poured upon them, I know not, but certain it is that they wavered, and for a few minutes there was a slight panic. The Commander-in-Chief, with Hope Grant, Mansfield, Adrian Hope, and their respective staffs, were sitting on their horses anxiously awaiting the result of the attack, when all at once it became apparent that there was a retrograde movement on the part of some of the men, who were emerging from the belt of jungle and hastening towards us. Norman was the first to grasp the situation. Putting spurs to his horse, he galloped into their midst, and called on them to pull themselves together; the men rallied at once, and advanced into the cover from which they had for the moment retreated. I had many opportunities for noting Norman's coolness and presence of mind under fire. On this particular occasion these qualities were most marked, and his action was most timely.

More Infantry were brought up, but without avail. The enemy evidently were determined to prevent the capture of the Shah Najaf. Fire was now opened upon us from a heavy gun on the other side of the Gumti (the first shot from which blew up one of the ammunition waggons belonging to the Naval Brigade), and all the cannon that were collected at the Kaisarbagh and mess-house were brought to bear upon us. The musketry fire was incessant, and Peel's men suffered so severely that one of his guns could not be worked.

Sir Colin was beginning to get extremely anxious, and no wonder—the position was most uncomfortable, and the prospect very gloomy. Three hours since the attack began! The day was rapidly drawing to a close, and we were no nearer our object; on the contrary, the opposition became every moment stronger, and the fire more deadly. A retreat was not to be thought of; indeed, our remaining so long stationary had been an encouragement to the enemy, and every one felt that the only chance for the little British army fighting against 30,000 desperate mutineers, with every advantage of position and intimate knowledge of locality in their favour, was to continue to advance at all hazards; and this our gallant old Chief decided to do. Placing himself at the head of the 93rd, he explained to the only too eager Highlanders the dangerous nature of the service, and called on them to follow him. There was no mistaking the response; cheer after cheer rent the air as they listened to the words of the Chief they knew so well, and believed in so thoroughly, assuring him of their readiness to follow whithersoever he should lead, do whatever he should direct. They moved off, followed by Peel's guns dragged by sailors and some of the Madras Fusiliers, the advance of the party being covered by Middleton's Field battery, which dashed to the front and opened with grape.

Almost instantaneously the narrow path along which we were proceeding was choked with wounded officers and dead and struggling horses. It was here that Sir Archibald Alison, Sir Colin's Aide-de-camp, lost his arm, and his brother (another Aide-de-camp) was wounded. Adrian Hope's horse was shot dead—indeed, very few escaped injury, either to themselves or their horses. I was one of the lucky few. On reaching the wall of the Shah Najaf enclosure, it was found to be twenty feet high, no entrance could be seen, and there were no scaling-ladders available, so there was nothing for it but to endeavour to breach the massive wall.* The 24-pounders hammered away at it for some time, but proved quite unequal to the task; though only a few yards off, they made no impression whatever, and it seemed as if the attempt to take the position must be abandoned. Peel was, therefore, ordered to withdraw his guns under cover of some rockets, which were discharged into the enclosure, and Hope was directed to retire as soon as he could collect the killed and wounded.

Captain Allgood, Sir Colin's trusted Assistant Quartermaster-General, was the bearer of the order. He and Hope, after consulting together, determined that before the latter obeyed they would try to discover if there did not exist an opening in some other part of the walls. Assisted by a sergeant of the 93rd, they set about their search, and actually did find a narrow gap, through which they could see that the enemy, terrified and thrown into confusion by the exploding rockets falling amongst them, were fast abandoning the building. The two friends helped each other through the gap, and, followed by some Highlanders, they proceeded across the now deserted enclosure to secure the only gateway, which was on the opposite side to that which we had attacked; and Allgood had the great pleasure of announcing to the Commander-in-Chief that there was no need to retire, for the formidable position was in our possession.

It was getting dark when at length we occupied the Shah Najaf; some of us got on to the top of the building to take a look round. There was just light enough to show us a sepoy sauntering unconcernedly up to the gate, evidently in happy ignorance of what had happened. He soon discovered that his comrades were no longer masters of the situation, and, letting his musket fall, he made all

* Lieutenant Salmon, R.N. (now Admiral Sir Nowell Salmon, K.C.B.), climbed up a tree overhanging this wall, in order to see what was going on behind it; he succeeded in obtaining useful information, but on being perceived, was fired at and badly wounded. He received the V.C.

haste to the river, into which he dropped, and swam to the other side.

Sir Colin and my General took up their quarters in the Shah Najaf, but only nominally, for after a scratch dinner we all joined the troops, who bivouacked where they stood.

The force was disposed in a semicircle, extending from the Shah Najaf to the barracks. The wounded were placed in the huts near the Sikandarbagh, where they passed a most comfortless night, for when the sun set it rapidly got cold, and the hospital arrangements were necessarily on a very limited scale.

By this time I was dead beat, having been for sixty hours continually in the saddle, except when I lay down for a short nap on the night of the 14th.

We were not allowed, however, to have a very long night's rest. Hours before dawn on the 17th we were roused by the beating of drums and ringing of bells (an impotent attempt on the part of the rebel leaders to excite the enthusiasm of their followers), which caused the troops to prepare for an attack and stand to their arms. But the enemy were not in a mood to encounter us in the open, small as our numbers were; they had suffered heavily the day before, and they must have begun to realize that their strongest positions were inadequate against British pluck and determination.

The mess-house was the next point to be carried, but the Commander-in-Chief thought it would be prudent to make our left quite secure in the first instance. The duty of occupying the houses and gardens situated between the barracks and Banks's house was entrusted to Brigadier Russell. Four bungalows,* in which the officers of the 32nd Foot had lived, were first seized. Russell then pushed on towards Banks's house, which it was necessary to occupy, as it commanded the crossing over the canal, by which we communicated with the Dilkusha, and by which it was thought that the people rescued from the Residency would have to be brought away. Russell, avoiding the main road, advanced under cover of his Artillery, and forced the rebels to vacate this important position, and Banks's house was held during the remainder of the operations by 50 men of the 2nd Punjab Infantry, under Lieutenant F. Keen.†

In the meantime a heavy fire from Peel's guns had been opened on the mess-house—a double-storied building, situated on slightly rising ground, surrounded by a ditch 12 feet broad, and beyond that at some little distance by a loop-holed wall.

Our losses on the previous day had been very severe, and Sir Colin,

* Marked D on the map.

† Now Major-General Keen, C.B. It was an extremely responsible charge for so young an officer with such a small party, as it was very isolated and exposed to attack.

anxious to spare his men as much as possible, decided to batter the place freely with Artillery before permitting it to be attacked. Peel's guns and Longden's mortars were therefore brought to bear upon it, and kept up a continual fire until 3 p.m., when the enemy seemed to think they had had enough, their musketry fire slackened off, and the Commander-in-Chief, considering the assault might safely be made, gave the order to advance. The attacking party was commanded by Brevet-Major Wolseley,* of the 90th Light Infantry, and consisted of a company of his own regiment, a piquet of the 53rd Foot under Captain Hopkins, and a few men of the 2nd Punjab Infantry under Captain Powlett, supported by Barnston's Detachments, under Captain Guise, of the 90th.

The building and its many outhouses were carried with a rush, and the enemy, who hastily retreated to the Moti Mahal,† were followed across the road, where our troops were stopped by the high wall which enclosed that building. Wolseley then sent for some Sappers, who quickly opened out a space through which they all passed. The Moti Mahal was hotly defended, but without avail, and ere the sun set the last position which separated the relieved from the relieving forces was in our possession.

As the party moved off to attack the mess-house, Sir Colin, who, on his white horse, was interestedly watching the proceedings, ordered me to procure a regimental colour and place it on one of the turrets of the building, that Outram might be able to judge how far we had advanced. I rode off accordingly to the 2nd Punjab Infantry, standing close by, and requested the Commandant, Captain Green, to let me have one of his colours. He at once complied, and I galloped with it to the mess-house. As I entered, I was met by Sir David Baird (one of Sir Colin's Aides-de-camp), and Captain Hopkins, of the 53rd Foot, by both of whom I was assisted in getting the flag with its long staff up the inconveniently narrow staircase, and in planting it on the turret nearest the Kaisarbagh, which was about 850 yards off. No sooner did the enemy perceive what we were about, than shot after shot was aimed at the colour, and in a very few minutes it was knocked over, falling into the ditch below. I ran down, picked it up, and again placed it in position, only for it to be once more shot down and hurled into the ditch, just as Norman and Lennox (who had been sent by Sir Colin to report what was going on in the interior of the Kaisarbagh) appeared on the roof. Once more I picked up the colour, and found that this time the staff had been broken in two. Notwithstanding, I managed to prop it up a third time on the turret, and it was not again hit, though the enemy continued to fire at it for some time.

* Now Field-Marshal Viscount Wolseley, K.P., Commander-in-Chief.

† Called the Pearl Palace from the fancied resemblance of one of its domes (since destroyed) to the curve of a pearl.

Outram, unwilling to risk unnecessary loss of men, did not greatly extend his position until he was sure we were close at hand, but he was not idle. While Sir Colin was slowly working his way towards him on the 16th, he had gradually occupied such buildings as lay in the direction of our advance. From the mess-house we could see the British flag flying on the top of the engine-house, only a short distance beyond the Moti Mahal, which satisfactory piece of intelligence Norman went down to report to Sir Colin, who, with his Chief of the Staff, had just arrived. I followed Norman, and we two made our way to the western wall of the Pearl Palace enclosure, outside which Outram and Havelock were standing together. They had run the gauntlet of the enemy's fire in coming from the engine-house; Colonel Robert Napier and two other officers who accompanied them, having been wounded, had to be carried back. Some of Lennox's Sappers set to work, and soon made a hole in the wall* large enough for these two distinguished men to pass through.

I had never before met either of them. In Afghanistan Outram had been a friend of my father, who had often spoken to me about him in terms of the warmest admiration, and his courage and chivalry were known and appreciated throughout India. It was therefore with feelings of the most lively interest that I beheld this man, whose character I so greatly admired. He was then fifty-four years of age, strong and broad-shouldered, in no way broken down by the heavy load of responsibility and anxiety he had had to bear, or the hardships he had gone through. Havelock, the hero of a hundred fights, on the contrary, looked ill, worn and depressed, but brightened up a little when Norman told him he had been made a K.C.B.

Sir Colin waited to receive these two heroes on the ground sloping down from the mess-house, and it was there that the meeting between the three veterans took place. A most impressive and memorable scene was that meeting, which has been well depicted in the historical picture by Barker.

As if to show the rage and disappointment of the enemy at this evidence of the success of our operations, every gun in the Kaisarbagh was turned upon us, and it was under a shower of shot and shell that the interview was held; it did not last long, for it was neither the time nor the place to discuss plans for the future. All Sir Colin could then say was that the troops should be removed outside Lucknow as soon as the women and children had been brought away, and he expressed his 'thankfulness that the relief of the garrison had been accomplished.'

Norman and I obtained permission to accompany Outram and Havelock back to the Residency. It was intensely but painfully interesting to visit this scene of so many acts of heroism, and of so much suffer-

* A slab let into the south-west corner of the wall marks the spot.

MAJOR-GENERAL SIR JAMES OUTRAM, G.C.B.

From
a painting by Thomas Brigstocke, R.A.

ing endured with unexampled fortitude. We first went to the posts occupied by Havelock's force in the Chatta Manzil, and in other buildings which have long since disappeared. At one of these we stopped to watch the Artillery trying to silence the enemy's guns on the opposite side of the river. We talked to the men, who were keen to hear news from the outer world and the story of our advance. It was some little time before we discovered in one of them the Commander of the battery, Captain William Olpherts,* for in his soiled and torn summer clothing, his face thin, worn, and begrimed with smoke, it was difficult to distinguish the officer from his men, and it was under these levelling circumstances that I had the honour of making the acquaintance of my distinguished brother officer, whose audacious courage on the occasion of Havelock's advance over the Charbagh bridge had won the admiration of everyone in the force, and gained for him the Victoria Cross.

We next came to the Bailey-guard; and as we looked at the battered walls and gateway, not an inch without a mark from a round shot or bullet, we marvelled that Aitken and Loughman could have managed to defend it for nearly five months. There was plenty of evidence on all the surrounding buildings of the dangerous nature of the service which they and their gallant Native comrades had so admirably performed. Although we were pressed for time, we could not resist stopping to speak to some of the Native officers and sepoys, whose magnificent loyalty throughout the siege was one of the most gratifying features of the Mutiny.

At length we came to the Residency itself, where we met a few old friends and acquaintances, who welcomed us with the most touching enthusiasm. Mrs. (afterwards Lady) Inglis and the Rev. J. P. Harris and his wife I had known at Peshawar; there were also Mrs. Fletcher Hayes, the widow of the poor fellow whose murder by the men of his own escort near Mainpuri I have related, and Mrs. Case, the widow of the brave Major of the 32nd, who lost his life at the affair of Chinhut. Mrs. Inglis showed us the tiny room which she and her children had shared with Mrs. Case all through the siege; but it was difficult to get any of them to speak of their miserable experiences, which were too sad and terrible, and too recent to be talked about, and they naturally preferred to dwell on their thankfulness for the relief that had come at last, and to listen to our account of what had happened in other places.

It was too late then to go round the position; that had to be left for another day; indeed, it was quite dark when we returned to Head-Quarters, established by our Chief in the open, his soldierly instincts prompting him to remain with his troops.

* Now General Sir William Olpherts, V.C., K.C.B.

CHAPTER XXV.

THE night of the 17th passed off quietly. Before daybreak the next morning the troops were under arms. Thousands of the enemy had collected in the Kaisarbagh, and for the protection of the mess-house, the Tara Koti, about 200 yards to the south-west, was seized and held, as from this position a flanking fire could be brought to bear upon any enemy advancing from the Kaisarbagh.

The most difficult part of Sir Colin's task had yet to be accomplished —the bringing away of the women and children, and the sick and wounded, from the Residency—and the question of how this could best be done was one which caused the Commander-in-Chief much anxious thought. Many, amongst whom were Outram and Hope Grant, pressed him to attack the Kaisarbagh and capture the city in the first instance; but 45 officers and 496 men out of our small force had been killed or wounded; Sir Colin, therefore, decided that it would be to the last degree imprudent to attempt such an undertaking with his reduced numbers, and became more than ever determined to confine his operations to the relief of the garrison.

That the Chief was right there can be no room for doubt. This force was barely strong enough for the service it had to perform. Every man was on duty day and night; there was no reserve to fall back upon; and had he listened to these proposals, and allowed himself to be drawn into complications in the city, it is more than probable that those he had come to succour would have been sacrificed. The wisdom of his decision was fully proved by subsequent events, and unreservedly acknowledged by Hope Grant and others who at the time differed from him in their ideas of the course which should be adopted.

From the Dilkusha to the Residency was not less than five miles; every yard of the way had to be guarded, and the garrison at the former place was so attenuated that it had to be reinforced by the withdrawal of part of the 75th Foot from the Alambagh. Fortunately this could be done without dangerously weakening that post, as it had been lately strengthened by the arrival of a small body of troops from Cawnpore.

It had now to be settled whether the evacuation should be effected by the route we had ourselves followed, which was circuitous and in places difficult for the wheeled vehicles necessary for the conveyance of the sick and wounded, and the women and children; or by the way past the barracks and Banks's house, which was shorter and had the advantage of a metalled road throughout. But unless Russell, whose brigade was in position at the barracks, could make the latter line secure, it would be too hazardous to adopt, and up to the present the reports from Russell had not been very promising. He had been hardly pressed on the 17th, and had sent word that he could make no impression on the enemy without heavy guns. Colonel Biddulph, the Deputy-Quartermaster-General, was therefore ordered to proceed to the barracks to ascertain how guns could best be sent to Russell's assistance, and report to the Commander-in-Chief on the whole situation. I was told to go with him and bring back the required information.

We found Russell in a very uncomfortable position, exposed to a hot fire and closely surrounded by the enemy, who were holding the British Infantry hospital and other buildings within a few yards of him.

I remained with Russell while Biddulph reconnoitred the ground between the barracks, the canal, and the Sikandarbagh. It was found covered with villages and walled enclosures, but he discovered a path secure from the enemy's fire, along which he was able to bring to Russell's assistance a 9-pounder gun, a 24-pounder howitzer, and four 5½-inch mortars. As the 9-pounder was fired, a round shot from one of the enemy's 18-pounders struck the mud wall immediately in front of it, scattering great clods of earth, which knocked over Bourchier and another officer; the round shot then hit Brigadier Russell, just grazing the back of his neck, actually cutting his watch-chain in two, and causing partial paralysis of the lower limbs for some days.

Russell being for the time *hors de combat*, Biddulph assumed command, and ordered me to return to Head-Quarters, report what had happened, and inform Sir Colin that he intended to attack the hospital and endeavour to drive the enemy out of his immediate neighbourhood.

I never saw Biddulph again. I had scarcely delivered my message to the Chief when heavy firing was heard from the direction of the barracks, and shortly afterwards a determined attack was made by the rebels on the piquets placed between the Sikandarbagh and the barracks, which was repulsed by Remmington's troop of Horse Artillery, with two companies of Infantry belonging to the 23rd and 53rd Foot, brought up by the Commander-in-Chief himself, who expressed to Remmington his warm approval of the brilliant manner in which his troop had come into action.

Sir Colin now received information that Biddulph was killed, and that Hale, who succeeded to the command of the brigade, had attacked and taken the hospital, but had been forced to abandon it. as the thatched roof had been set on fire by the shells showered upon it by the enemy, who were keeping our troops constantly on the alert. This decided Sir Colin to give up the idea of withdrawing the relieved garrison by Banks's house.

Early on the following morning, the 19th, I was sent by the Commander-in-Chief to the Residency with a note for Sir James Outram, containing the information that arrangements for the withdrawal were now complete, and that conveyances for the women, children, sick, and wounded would be sent as soon as they arrived from the Dilkusha.

When he had read the note Sir James questioned me as to the road, and asked me particularly if I had noticed the openings made in the walls of houses and enclosures, and whether I thought they were large enough for the guns, carts, and carriages to get through. I replied that I had not observed them very particularly, but I was inclined to think some of them were certainly rather small. My answer, to my astonishment, roused the ire of a wounded officer lying on a couch at the end of the room, for he wrathfully asked me whether I had measured the openings, and on my saying I had not, he added: 'You had better wait to give your opinion until you know what you are talking about; those openings were made by my orders, and I am quite sure they are the necessary size.' The officer was no other than Colonel Robert Napier, who, as I have already stated, was badly wounded on the 17th. I felt myself considerably snubbed, but Sir James kindly came to the rescue, and explained that I had merely answered his question and had not offered any opinion of my own: Colonel Napier, however, was not to be appeased, and I could plainly see that I had incurred his displeasure, and that he thought me a very bumptious youngster. I do not know whether the Chief of the Staff* ever heard of it, but it was some satisfaction to me to find afterwards that I was right in my estimation of the size of those apertures, some of which had to be enlarged before the guns and carriages could pass through.

By sunset that day the women and children had been brought away and collected in the Sikandarbagh. Not a very agreeable resting-place, for though the 2,000 dead mutineers had been got out of sight, they were merely slightly covered over in a ditch which they themselves had recently dug outside the north wall to strengthen the defences. The survivors of the siege, however, had become too inured to horrors of all kinds, and were too thankful for their deliverance from the fate which for months had constantly threatened them, to be over-sensitive.

It was a sad little assemblage; all were more or less broken down and out of health, while many were widows or orphans, having left their nearest and dearest in the Residency burial-ground. Officers and men accorded them a respectful welcome, and by their efforts to help them showed how deeply they felt for their forlorn condition, while our old Chief had a comfortable tea prepared for them. When night set in, the road having been carefully reconnoitred beforehand, the melancholy convoy with its guard of soldiers started for the Dilkusha, where it arrived in safety, and was warmly received by the officers of

* Colonel Napier was Chief of the Staff to Sir James Outram.

the 9th Lancers and the rest of the garrison, who did all that circumstances would allow to make the ladies and children comfortable.

During the 20th, 21st, and 22nd, everything that was worth removing and for which carriage could be provided was brought away. Such a miscellaneous collection it was—jewels and other valuables belonging to the ex-royal family, twenty-five lakhs of treasure, stores of all kinds, including grain, and as many of the 200 guns discovered in the palace as were considered likely to be of use.

The troops were not moved away from the Residency till midnight on the 22nd, and I had several opportunities before then of going over the position, to every point of which some thrilling story was attached, and of renewing acquaintance with many of the garrison whom I had known before. Amongst them was Sam Lawrence, of the 32nd Foot, a friend of Peshawar days, who, for his gallant defence of the Redan, was awarded the Victoria Cross. I was shown Innes's advanced post, named after McLeod Innes,* a talented Engineer officer, who also subsequently gained that coveted reward; the Cawnpore battery, where so many valuable lives had been sacrificed, and the room where Sir Henry Lawrence received his mortal wound; then I climbed up to the tower, from which a good view of the city and the posts held by the enemy could be obtained.

The more I saw, the more I wondered at what had been achieved by such a mere handful of men against such vast numbers. It was specially pleasant to me to listen to the praises bestowed on the officers of my own regiment, of whom nine were present when the siege commenced, and only one escaped to the end unwounded, while five were killed or died of their injuries. Of the other three, one was wounded three different times, and both the others once.

All were loud, too, in their praises of the Engineer officers. During the latter part of the siege the rebels, finding they could not carry the position by assault, tried hard to undermine the defences; but our Engineers were ever on the watch, and countermined so successfully that they were able to frustrate the enemy's designs on almost every occasion.

The wonderful manner in which the Hindustani soldiers held their ground, notwithstanding that they were incessantly taunted by their mutinous comrades for aiding the Feringhis against their own people, was also much dilated upon.

The casualties during the siege were extremely heavy. When it commenced on the 1st of July, the strength of the garrison was 927 Europeans and 765 Natives. Of the former, 163 were civilians—brave and useful, but untrained to arms; of the latter, 118 were pensioners, many of whom were old and decrepit. Up to the arrival

* Now Lieutenant-General McLeod Innes, V.C.

of Outram and Havelock (a period of eighty-seven days), 350 Europeans and 133 natives were either killed or died of wounds and disease. Of the noble and unselfish conduct of the ladies and soldiers' wives, everyone spoke in the highest terms and with the warmest appreciation. They suffered, without a murmur, the most terrible hardships; they devoted themselves to the sick and wounded in the hospital, and were ever ready to help in any way that was useful. Two ladies were killed, and nine died, during the siege.

The contemplation of the defence of Lucknow, and the realization of the noble qualities it called forth in the defenders, cannot but excite in the breast of every British man and woman, as it did in mine, feelings of pride and admiration. But what impressed me more than even the glorious defence was the foresight and ability of the man who made that defence possible.

Henry Lawrence was, apparently, the only European in India who, from the very first, formed an accurate estimate of the extent of the danger which threatened our rule in the early part of 1857, and who, notwithstanding his thorough appreciation of the many good qualities of Native soldiers, was not misled into a mistaken belief in the absolute loyalty of the Native army. Fourteen years before Lawrence had predicted the Mutiny* and the course it would take, and when events shaped themselves as he had foreseen, he gave it as his opinion that the disaffection would be general and widespread. But while his intimate knowledge of Native character led him to this conviction, so great was his influence with Natives—perhaps by reason of that knowledge—that he was able to delay the actual outbreak at Lucknow until his measures for the defence of the Residency were completed, and he persuaded a considerable number of sepoys, not only to continue in their allegiance, but to share with their European comrades the dangers and privations of the siege—a priceless service, for without their aid the defence could not have been made.

* *Calcutta Review*, 1843. After commenting on the habitual carelessness of Government and its disregard of ordinary military precautions and preparations, Henry Lawrence had shown how possible it was that a hostile party might seize Delhi, and, if the outbreak were not speedily suppressed, what grave consequences might ensue. 'Let this happen,' he said, 'on June 2, and does any sane man doubt that twenty-four hours would swell the hundreds of rebels into thousands, and in a week every ploughshare in the Delhi States would be turned into a sword? And when a sufficient force had been mustered, which could not be effected within a month, should we not then have a more difficult game to play than Clive at Plassy or Wellington at Assaye? We should then be literally striking for our existence at the most inclement season of the year, with the prestige of our name tarnished.' Going on to suggest that Meerut, Umballa, and Agra might say that they had no troops to spare from their own necessities, or that they had no carriage, 'Should we not, then,' he wrote, 'have to strike anew for our Indian Empire?'

BRIGADIER-GENERAL SIR HENRY LAWRENCE, K.C.B.

From
a photograph taken at Lucknow.

In no part of India was there greater need for the services of a strong, enlightened, and sympathetic Ruler and Statesman. Difficult as were the positions in which many men in authority were placed in 1857, none was more difficult than that in which Henry Lawrence found himself when he took over the Chief Commissionership of Oudh in the spring of that year. His colleagues in the administration were at feud with each other, and by their ignorance of the proper methods of dealing with the people they had succeeded in alienating all classes.

While Lawrence was engaged in pouring oil on those troubled waters, and in earning the gratitude of the people by modifying the previous year's undue assessment, signs appeared of the disaffection, which had begun amongst the troops at Barrackpore, having spread to the cantonments in Oudh. Sir Henry met this new trouble in the same intelligent and conciliatory spirit as that in which he had dealt with his civil difficulties. He summoned to a durbar some Native officers who had displayed a very proper feeling of loyalty by arresting several fanatics who had tried to tamper with the soldiery, and he liberally rewarded them, pointing out at the same time in forcible language the disgrace to a soldier of being faithless to his salt. But while doing everything in his power to keep the Natives loyal, and with a certain amount of success, he did not neglect to take every possible precaution.

When first he heard of the outbreak at Meerut, he telegraphed to the Governor-General advising him to send for British troops to China and Ceylon, and to call on the Nepalese to assist; at the same time he applied to Lord Canning for, and obtained, the rank of Brigadier-General, which gave him military as well as civil control—a very necessary measure, for none of the senior military officers in Oudh were men to be relied upon; indeed, as in so many other places, they had to be effaced when the troubles began.

Very early in the day Henry Lawrence commenced his preparations for the defence of the Residency; he cleared the ground of all cover in its immediate vicinity, as far as it was possible to do so; he fortified it, mounted guns, stored ammunition, powder, and firewood; arranged for a proper supply of water; collected food, which proved sufficient, not only for the original number of refugees, but for the 3,000 additional mouths belonging to Outram and Havelock's force; in fact, he did everything which forethought and ingenuity could suggest to enable the garrison to hold out in what he foresaw would be a long and deadly struggle against fearful odds. There was no fort, as there was at Agra, capable of sheltering every European in Oudh, and strong enough to defy any number of mutineers, nor was there, as at Cawnpore, a well-stocked and strongly-fortified magazine to depend upon. But Henry Lawrence was not cast down by the difficulties which surrounded him; he was fully alive to the danger, but he recognized that his best, indeed, his only, chance of delaying the inevitable rebellion until (as he hoped) assistance might arrive, was to show a bold front.

On the 27th May Lawrence wrote to Lord Canning as follows: 'Hitherto the country has been kept quiet, and we have played the Irregulars against the line regiments; but being constituted of exactly the same material, the taint is fast pervading them, and in a few weeks, if not days—unless Delhi be in the interim captured—there will be but one feeling throughout the army, a feeling that our prestige is gone, and that feeling will be more dangerous than any other. Religion, fear, hatred, one and all have their influence; but there is still a reverence for the Company's *ikbál**—when it is gone we shall have few friends indeed. The tone and talk of many have greatly altered during the last few days, and we are now asked, almost in terms of insolence, whether Delhi is captured, or when it will be. It was only just after the Kabul massacre, and when we hesitated to advance through the Khyber, that, in my memory, such a tone ever before prevailed.'†

Feeling all this so strongly, it is the more remarkable that Henry Lawrence never lost heart, but struggled bravely on 'to preserve the soldiery to their duty and the people to their allegiance,' while at the same time he was, as I have shown, making every conceivable preparation to meet the outbreak whenever it should come.

There is no doubt that Henry Lawrence was a very remarkable man; his friendly feeling for Natives, and his extraordinary insight into their character, together with his military training and his varied political experience, peculiarly fitted him to be at the head of a Government at such a crisis.‡

All this, however, is a digression from my narrative, to which I must now return.

While the withdrawal was being effected, Peel's guns distracted the enemy's attention from the proceedings by keeping up a perpetual and destructive fire on the Kaisarbagh, thus leading the rebels to believe that our whole efforts were directed to taking that place. By the evening of the 22nd three large breaches had been made, and the enemy naturally expected an assault to take place the next morning. But the

* Prestige, or, rather, good luck. † 'Life of Sir Henry Lawrence.'

‡ In Sir Henry Lawrence's 'Life' two memoranda appear, one by Lieutenant (now Lieutenant-General) McLeod Innes, Assistant Engineer at Lucknow in 1857, the other by Sir Henry Lawrence himself. They are worthy of perusal, and will give the reader some insight into Lawrence's character; they will also exemplify how necessary it is for anyone placed in a position of authority in India to study the peculiarities of the people and gain their confidence by kindness and sympathy, to which they readily respond, and, above all, to be firm and decided in his dealings with them. Firmness and decision are qualities which are appreciated more than all others by Natives; they expect them in their Rulers, and without them no European can have any power over them, or ever hope to gain their respect and esteem.

object of that heavy fire had already been accomplished; the women and children, the sick and wounded, were all safe in the Dilkusha; no one was left in the Residency but the garrison, on duty for the last time at the posts they had so long and so bravely defended, and they were to leave at midnight.

As the clock struck twelve, in the deepest silence and with the utmost caution, the gallant little band evacuated the place, and passed down the long line of posts, first those held by Outram's and Havelock's men, and then those occupied by the relieving force, until they reached the Martinière Park. As they moved on, Outram's and Havelock's troops fell in behind, and were followed by the relieving force, which brought up the rear. The scheme for this very delicate movement had been most carefully considered beforehand by General Mansfield, the clever Chief of the Staff, who clearly explained to all concerned the parts they had to play, and emphatically impressed upon them that success depended on his directions being followed to the letter, and on their being carried out without the slightest noise or confusion.

Sir Colin Campbell and Hope Grant, surrounded by their respective staffs, watched the movement from a position in front of the Sikandarbagh, where a body of Artillery and Infantry were held in readiness for any emergency. When the time arrived for the advanced piquets to be drawn in, the enemy seemed to have become suspicious, for they suddenly opened fire with guns and musketry from the Kaisarbagh, and for a moment we feared our plans had been discovered. Fortunately, one of Peel's rocket-carts was still in position beyond the Moti Mahal, and the celerity with which the officer in charge replied to this burst of fire apparently convinced the enemy we were holding our ground, for the firing soon ceased, and we breathed again.

Mansfield had taken the precaution to have with him an officer from Hale's brigade, which was on the left rear of our line of posts, that he might go back and tell his Brigadier when the proper time came for the latter to move off in concert with the rest of the force; but this officer had not, apparently, understood that he would have to return in the dark, and when Mansfield directed him to carry out the duty for which he had been summoned, he replied that he did not think he could find his way. Mansfield was very angry, and with reason, for it was of supreme importance that the retirement should be simultaneous, and turning to me, he said: 'You have been to Hale's position: do you think you could find your way there now?' I answered: 'I think I can.' Upon which he told me to go at once, and ordered the officer belonging to the brigade to accompany me. I then asked the General whether he wished me to retire with Hale's party or return to him. He replied: 'Return to me here, that I may be sure the order has been received.'

I rode off with my companion, and soon found I had undertaken to perform a far from easy, and rather hazardous duty. I had only been over the ground twice—going to and returning from the position on the 18th—and most of the villages then standing had since been burnt. There was no road, but any number of paths, which seemed to lead in every direction but the right one; at last, however, we arrived at our destination, I delivered the order to Colonel Hale, and set out on my return journey alone. My consternation was great on reaching the Sikandarbagh, where I had been ordered to report myself to Mansfield, to find it deserted by the Generals, their staffs, and the troops; not a creature was to be seen. I then began to understand what a long time it had taken me to carry out the errand upon which I had been sent, much longer, no doubt, than Mansfield thought possible. I could not help feeling that I was not in at all a pleasant position, for any moment the enemy might discover the force had departed, and come out in pursuit. As it turned out, however, happily for me, they remained for some hours in blissful ignorance of our successful retirement, and, instead of following in our wake, continued to keep up a heavy fire on the empty Residency and other abandoned posts. Turning my horse's head in the direction I knew the troops must have taken, I galloped as fast as he could carry me until I overtook the rear guard just as it was crossing the canal, along the right bank of which the greater part of the force had been placed in position. When I reported myself to Mansfield, he confessed that he had forgotten all about me, which somewhat surprised me, for I had frequently noticed how exactly he remembered the particulars of any order he gave, no matter how long a time it took to execute it.

CHAPTER XXVI.

The Relief of the Lucknow garrison was now accomplished—a grand achievement indeed, of which any Commander might well be proud, carried out as it had been in every particular as originally planned, thus demonstrating with what care each detail had been thought out, and how admirably movement after movement had been executed.

November the 23rd was spent in arranging for the march to Cawnpore, and in organizing the division which was to be left in position, under Outram, in and about the Alambagh; it was to be strong enough to hold its own, and to keep open communication with Head-Quarters.

My time was chiefly occupied in assisting in the distribution of transport, and in carrying out Hope Grant's directions as to the order in which the troops were to march. Round the Dilkusha the scene of confusion was bewildering in the extreme; women, children, sick and

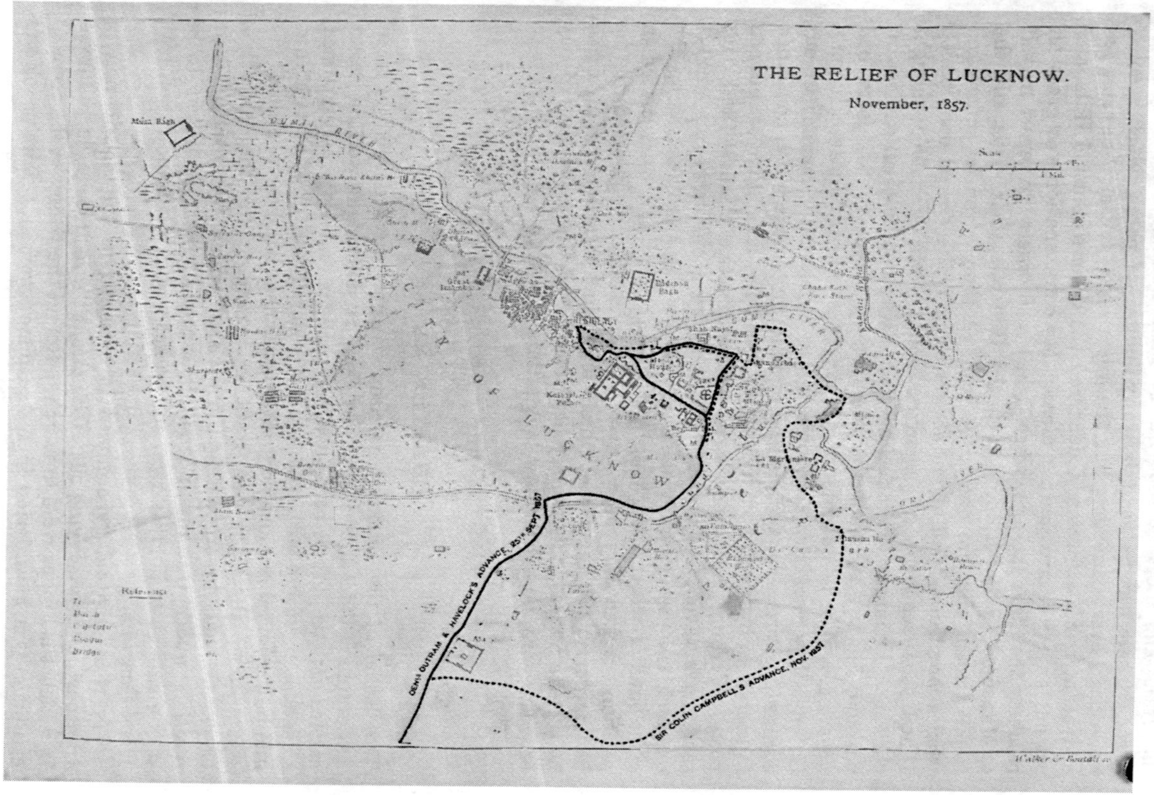
THE RELIEF OF LUCKNOW.
November, 1857.
GEN^LS OUTRAM & HAVELOCK'S ADVANCE, 25TH SEPT 1857
SIR COLIN CAMPBELL'S ADVANCE, NOV. 1857
CITY OF LUCKNOW
GUMTI RIVER
Walker & Boutall sc.

wounded men, elephants, camels, bullocks and bullock-carts, grass-cutters' ponies, and doolies with their innumerable bearers, all crowded together. To marshal these incongruous elements and get them started seemed at first to be an almost hopeless task. At last the families were got off in two bodies, each under a married officer whose wife was of the party, and through whom all possible arrangements for their comfort were to be made, and their place on the line of march, position in camp, etc., determined.

In the afternoon the force was gratified by the issue of a General Order by the Commander-in-Chief thanking the troops for the manner in which the very difficult and harassing service of the Relief had been performed. Alluding to the withdrawal, he said it was a model of discipline and exactitude, the result of which was that the rebels were completely thrown off their guard, and the retirement had been successfully carried out in the face of 50,000 of the enemy along a most inconveniently narrow and tortuous lane—the only line of retreat open.

The following morning Hope Grant's division marched to the Alambagh. On arrival there, our transport was sent back for Outram's division, which joined us the morning after, bringing with it General Havelock's dead body. He had died the previous day—'a martyr to duty,' as the Commander-in-Chief expressed it in his General Order. The brave old soldier, who had served with distinction in four campaigns before the Mutiny—Burma, Afghanistan, Gwalior, and the Sutlej—was buried inside the Alambagh enclosure, respected and honoured by the whole army, but more especially by those who had shared in his noble efforts to rescue the Lucknow garrison.

A wash and change of clothes, in which we were now able to indulge, were much-appreciated luxuries. From the time we had left the Alambagh every officer and man had been on duty without cessation, and slept, if they slept at all, on the spot where the close of day found them fighting.

It was a rough experience, but, notwithstanding the exposure, hard work, and a minimum of sleep, there was no great sickness amongst the troops. The personal interest which every man in the force felt in the rescue of his countrymen and countrywomen, in addition to the excitement at all times inseparable from war, was a stimulant which enabled all ranks to bear up in a marvellous manner against long-continued privations and hardships—for body and mind are equally affected by will—and there was no doubt about the will in this instance to endure anything that was necessary for the speedy achievement of the object in view. Personally, I was in the best of health, and though I almost lived on horseback, I never felt inconvenience or fatigue.

The 25th and 26th were busy days, spent in allotting camp equipage and making the necessary arrangements for fitting out Outram's force —4,000 strong, with 25 guns and howitzers and 10 mortars.

At 11 a.m. on the 27th we started on our return march towards Cawnpore.* It was a strange procession. Everything in the shape of wheeled carriage and laden animals had to keep to the road, which was narrow, and for the greater part of the way raised, for the country at that time of the year was partly under water, and *jhils* were numerous. Thus, the column was about twelve miles in length, so that the head had almost reached the end of the march before the rear could start. Delays were constant and unavoidable, and the time each day's journey occupied, as well as the mode of conveyance—country carts innocent of springs—must have been most trying to delicate women and wounded men. Fortunately there was no rain; but the sun was still hot in the daytime, causing greater sensitiveness to the bitter cold at night.

My place was with the advance guard, as I had to go on ahead to mark out the camp and have ramps got ready to enable the carts to be taken off the raised roads. Soon after leaving the Alambagh we heard the sound of guns from the direction of Cawnpore, and when we reached Bani bridge (about thirteen miles on, where a small post had been established) the officer in command told us that there had been heavy firing all that day and the day before.

Camp was pitched about two miles further on late in the afternoon; but my work was not over till midnight, when the rear guard arrived, for it took all that time to form up the miscellaneous convoy.

Next morning we made an early start, in order to reach our destination, if possible, before dark. Having received no information from Cawnpore for more than ten days, the Commander-in-Chief was beginning to feel extremely anxious, and the firing we had heard the previous day had greatly increased his uneasiness, for there seemed little room for doubt that the Gwalior rebels were making an attack on that place. The probability that this would happen had been foreseen by Sir Colin, and was one of his reasons for determining to limit the operations at Lucknow to the withdrawal of the garrison.

* Our force consisted of the troops which Sir Colin had reviewed on the Alambagh plain on the 11th instant, with the exception of the 75th Foot, which was transferred to Outram's division. We had, however, in their place, the survivors of the 32nd Foot, and of the Native regiments who had behaved so loyally during the siege. These latter were formed into one battalion, called the Regiment of Lucknow—the present 16th Bengal Infantry. The 32nd Foot, which was not up to full strength (1,067) when the Mutiny broke out, had in 1857-58 no less than 610 men killed and wounded, exclusive of 169 who died from disease. We had also with us, and to them was given an honoured place, 'the remnant of the few faithful pensioners who had alone, of many thousands in Oudh, responded to the call of Sir Henry Lawrence to come in to aid the cause of those whose salt they had eaten.'—Lecture on the Relief of Lucknow, by Colonel H. W. Norman.

We had not proceeded far, when firing was again heard, and by noon all doubt as to its meaning was ended by a Native who brought a note marked 'Most urgent,' written in Greek character, and addressed to 'General Sir Colin Campbell, or any officer commanding troops on the Lucknow road.' This turned out to be a communication from General Windham, who had been placed in command at Cawnpore when the Commander-in-Chief left for Lucknow on the 9th of November. It was dated two days earlier, and told of an attack having been made, that there had been hard fighting, and that the troops were sorely pressed; in conclusion Windham earnestly besought the Chief to come to his assistance with the least possible delay.

Two other letters followed in quick succession, the last containing the disappointing and disheartening intelligence that Windham, with the greater part of his troops, had been driven into the entrenchment, plainly showing that the city and cantonment were in the possession of the enemy, and suggesting the possibility of the bridge of boats having been destroyed.

Sir Colin, becoming impatient to learn the exact state of the case, desired me to ride on as fast as I could to the river; and if I found the bridge broken, to return at once, but if it were still in existence to cross over, try and see the General, and bring back all the information I could obtain.

I took a couple of sowars with me, and on reaching the river I found, under cover of a hastily-constructed *tête-de-pont*, a guard of British soldiers, under Lieutenant Budgen, of the 82nd Foot, whose delight at seeing me was most effusively expressed. He informed me that the bridge was still intact, but that it was unlikely it would long remain so, for Windham was surrounded except on the river side, and the garrison was 'at its last gasp.'

I pushed across and got into the entrenchment, which was situated on the river immediately below the bridge of boats. The confusion inside was great, and I could hardly force my way through the mass of men who thronged round my horse, eager to learn when help might be expected; they were evidently demoralized by the ill-success which had attended the previous days' operations, and it was not until I reassured them with the news that the Commander-in-Chief was close at hand that I managed to get through the crowd and deliver my message to the General.

The 'hero of the Redan,' whom I now saw for the first time, though the fame of his achievement had preceded him to India, was a handsome, cheery-looking man of about forty-eight years of age, who appeared, in contrast to the excited multitude I had passed, thoroughly calm and collected; and notwithstanding the bitter disappointment it must have been to him to be obliged to give up the city and retire with his wholly inadequate force into the entrenchment, he was not dispirited, and had all his wits about him. In a few words he told me what had happened, and desired me to explain to the Commander-in-Chief that, although the city and cantonment had to be abandoned, he was still holding the enemy in check round the assembly-rooms (which were situated outside and to the west front of the entrenchment), thus preventing their approaching the bridge of boats near enough to injure it.

I was about to start back to Head-Quarters, when suddenly loud cheers broke from the men, caused by the appearance in their midst of the Commander-in-Chief himself. After I had left him, Sir Colin became every minute more impatient and fidgety, and ere long started off after me, accompanied by Mansfield and some other staff officers. He was recognized by the soldiers, some of whom had known him in the Crimea, and they at once surrounded him, giving enthusiastic expression to their joy at seeing him again.

The Chief could now judge for himself as to how matters stood, so, as there was plenty of work in camp for me, I started back to rejoin my own General. On my way I stopped to speak to Budgen, whom I found in a most dejected frame of mind. Unfortunately for him, he had used exactly the same words in describing the situation at Cawnpore to Sir Colin as he had to me, which roused the old Chief's indignation, and he flew at the wretched man as he was sometimes apt to do when greatly put out, rating him soundly, and asking him how he dared to say of Her Majesty's troops that they were 'at their last gasp.'

I found Hope Grant about four miles from the river bank, where the camp was being pitched. Sir Colin did not return till after dark, when we were told that the rest of Windham's troops had been driven inside the entrenchment, which only confirmed what we had suspected, for flames were seen mounting high into the air from the direction of the assembly-rooms, which, it now turned out, had been set on fire by the enemy—an unfortunate occurrence, as in them had been stored the camp equipage, kits, clothing, etc., belonging to most of the regiments which had crossed the Ganges into Oudh. But what was more serious still was the fact that the road was now open for the rebels' heavy guns, which might be brought to bear upon the bridge of boats at any moment.

Owing to the length of the march (thirty-two or thirty-three miles), some of the carts and the heavy guns did not arrive till daybreak. Scarcely had the bullocks been unyoked, before the guns were ordered on to the river bank, where they formed up, and so effectually plied the enemy with shot and shell that the passage of the river was rendered comparatively safe for our troops.

When the men had breakfasted, the order was given to cross over. Sir Colin accompanied the column as far as the bridge, and then directed Hope Grant, with the Horse Artillery and most of the Cavalry,

Bourchier's battery and Adrian Hope's brigade, to move to the south-east of the city and take up a position on the open ground which stretched from the river to the Grand Trunk Road, with the canal between us and the enemy. By this arrangement communication with Allahabad, which had been temporarily interrupted, was restored, a very necessary measure, for until the road was made safe, reinforcements, which on account of the paucity of transport had to be sent up in small detachments, could not reach us, nor could the families and sick soldiers be sent down country.

The passage of the huge convoy over the bridge of boats, under the protection of Greathed's brigade, was a most tedious business, occupying thirty hours, from 3 p.m. on the 29th till about 9 p.m. on the 30th, when Inglis brought over the rear guard. During its transit the enemy fired occasionally on the bridge, and tried to destroy it by floating fire-rafts down the river; fortunately they did not succeed, and the convoy arrived without accident on the ground set apart for it in the rear of our camp.

For the three first days of December I was chiefly employed in reconnoitring with the Native Cavalry the country to our left and rear, to make sure that the rebels had no intention of attempting to get round that flank, and in making arrangements for the despatch of the families, the sick, and the wounded, to Allahabad *en route* to Calcutta. We improvised covers for some of the carts, in which we placed the women and children and the worst cases amongst the men; but with all our efforts to render them less unfit for the purpose, these carts remained but rough and painful conveyances for delicate women and suffering men to travel in.

We were not left altogether unmolested by the enemy during these days. Round shot kept continually falling in our midst, particularly in the neighbourhood of the Commander-in-Chief's tent, the exact position of which must have somehow been made known to the rebels, otherwise they could not have distinguished it from the rest of the camp, as it was an unpretentious hill tent, such as was then used by subaltern officers.

Until the women left camp on the night of the 3rd December, we were obliged to act on the defensive, and were not able to stop the enemy's fire completely, though we managed to keep it under control by occupying the point called Generalganj, and strengthening the piquets on our right and left flank. On the 4th a second unsuccessful attempt was made to destroy the bridge of boats by means of fire-rafts, and on the 5th there were several affairs at the outposts, all of which ended in the discomfiture of the rebels without any great loss to ourselves; Lieutenant-Colonel Ewart of the 93rd Highlanders, who lost his arm on the 1st, and Captain Crutchley of the same regiment, who was severely wounded, being the only casualties amongst the officers.

CHAPTER XXVII.

THE time had now arrived to give the Gwalior troops a repetition of the lesson taught them at Agra on the 10th October. They had had it all their own way since then; and having proved too strong for Windham, they misunderstood the Commander-in-Chief remaining for so long on the defensive, and attributed his inaction to fear of their superior prowess.

Sunday, the 6th December, was one of those glorious days in which the European in northern India revels for a great part of the winter, clear and cool, with a cloudless sky. I awoke refreshed after a good night's rest, and in high spirits at the prospect before us of a satisfactory day's work; for we hoped to drive the enemy from Cawnpore, and to convince those who had witnessed, if not taken part in, the horrible brutalities perpetrated there, that England's hour had come at last.

The 42nd Highlanders, a battery of Royal Artillery, and detachments of several different corps, had quite lately been added to the force, so that the Commander-in-Chief had now at his disposal about 5,000 Infantry, 600 Cavalry, and 35 guns. The Infantry were divided into four brigades, commanded respectively by Greathed, Adrian Hope, Inglis, and Walpole.* The Cavalry brigade, consisting of the same regiments which had come with us from Delhi, was commanded by Brigadier Little, the Artillery† by Major-General Dupuis, and the Engineers by Colonel Harness, General Windham being placed in charge of the entrenchments.

Opposed to this force there were 25,000 men, with 40 guns, not all disciplined soldiers, but all adepts in the use of arms, and accustomed to fighting. They were divided into two distinct bodies, one composed of the Gwalior Contingent, the Rani of Jhansi's followers, and the mutinous regiments which had been stationed in Bundelkand, Central India, and Rajputana, which occupied the right of the enemy's position, covering their line of retreat by the Kalpi road. The other consisted of the troops—regular and irregular—which had attached themselves to the Nana, and held the city and the ground which lay between it and the Ganges, their line of retreat being along the Grand

* Greathed's brigade consisted of the 8th and 64th Foot and 2nd Punjab Infantry. Adrian Hope's brigade consisted of the 53rd Foot, 42nd and 93rd Highlanders, and 4th Punjab Infantry. Inglis's brigade consisted of the 23rd Fusiliers, 32nd and 82nd Foot. Walpole's brigade consisted of the 2nd and 3rd Battalions Rifle Brigade and a detachment of the 38th Foot.

† The Artillery consisted of Peel's Naval Brigade, Blunt's, Bridge's and Remmington's troops of Horse Artillery, Bourchier's, Middleton's, and Smith's Field batteries, and Longden's Heavy battery.

Trunk Road to Bithur. Tantia Topi was in command of the whole force, while the Nana remained with his own people on the left flank.

On the centre and left the enemy were very strongly posted, and could only be approached through the city and by way of the difficult broken ground, covered with ruined houses, stretching along the river bank.

While the men were eating their breakfasts, and the tents were being struck, packed, and sent to the rear, Sir Colin carefully explained his plan of operations to the Commanding officers and the staff; this plan was, to make a feint on the enemy's left and centre, but to direct the real attack on their right, hoping thus to be able to dispose of this portion of Tantia Topi's force, before assistance could be obtained from any other part of the line.

With this view Windham was ordered to open with every gun within the entrenchment at 9 a.m.; while Greathed, supported by Walpole, threatened the enemy's centre. Exactly at the hour named, the roar of Windham's Artillery was heard, followed a few minutes later by the rattle of Greathed's musketry along the bank of the canal. Meanwhile, Adrian Hope's brigade was drawn up in fighting formation behind the Cavalry stables on our side of the Trunk Road, and Inglis's brigade behind the racecourse on the other side. At eleven o'clock the order was given to advance. The Cavalry and Horse Artillery moved to the left with instructions to cross the canal by a bridge about two miles off, and to be ready to fall upon the enemy as they retreated along the Kalpi road. Walpole's brigade, covered by Smith's Field battery, crossed the canal by a bridge immediately to the left of Generalganj, cleared the canal bank, and, by hugging the wall of the city, effectually prevented reinforcements reaching the enemy's right.

Peel's and Longden's heavy guns, and Bourchier's and Middleton's Field batteries, now opened on some brick-kilns and mounds which the enemy were holding in strength on our side of the canal, and against which Adrian Hope's and Inglis's brigades advanced in parallel lines, covered by the 4th Punjab Infantry in skirmishing order.

It was a sight to be remembered, that advance, as we watched it from our position on horseback, grouped round the Commander-in-Chief. Before us stretched a fine open grassy plain; to the right the dark green of the Rifle Brigade battalions revealed where Walpole's brigade was crossing the canal. Nearer to us, the 53rd Foot, and the 42nd and 93rd Highlanders in their bonnets and kilts, marched as on parade, although the enemy's guns played upon them and every now and then a round shot plunged through their ranks or ricocheted over their heads; on they went without apparently being in the least disconcerted, and without the slightest confusion.

As the brick-kilns were neared, the 4th Punjab Infantry, supported by the 53rd Foot, charged the enemy in grand style, and drove them across the canal. Here there occurred a slight check. The rebels, having been reinforced, made a stand, and bringing guns to bear upon the bridge within grape range, they must have done us great damage but for the timely arrival of Peel and his sailors with a heavy gun. This put new life into the attacking party; with a loud cheer they dashed across the bridge, while Peel poured round after round from his 24-pounder on the insurgents with most salutary effect. The enemy faced about and retired with the utmost celerity, leaving a 9-pounder gun in our possession.

The whole of Hope's brigade, followed by Inglis's, now arrived on the scene and proceeded to cross the canal, some by the bridge, while others waded through the water. Having got to the other side, both brigades re-formed, and moved rapidly along the Kalpi road. We (the Commander-in-Chief, Hope Grant, and their respective staffs) accompanied this body of troops for about a mile and a half, when the rebels' camp came in sight. A few rounds were fired into it, and then it was rushed.

We were evidently unexpected visitors; wounded men were lying about in all directions, and many sepoys were surprised calmly cooking their frugal meal of unleavened bread. The tents were found to be full of property plundered from the city and cantonment of Cawnpore—soldiers' kits, bedding, clothing, and every description of miscellaneous articles; but to us the most valuable acquisition was a quantity of grain and a large number of fine bullocks, of which those best suited for Ordnance purposes were kept, and the rest were made over to the Commissariat.

That portion of the rebel force with which we had been engaged was now in full retreat, and Sir Colin wished to follow it up at once; but the Cavalry and Horse Artillery had not arrived, so that considerable delay occurred; while we were waiting the Chief arranged to send Mansfield with a small force* round to the north of Cawnpore, and, by thus threatening the road along which the Nana's troops must retreat, compel them to evacuate the city. The 23rd Royal Welsh Fusiliers and a detachment of the 38th Foot were to be left to look after the deserted camp, and Inglis's brigade was to move along the Kalpi road in support of the Cavalry and Horse Artillery. But where were the much-needed and anxiously-expected mounted troops? It was not like them to be out of the way when their services were required; but it was now nearly two o'clock, they had not appeared, and the days were very short. What was to be done? The enemy could not be allowed to carry off their guns and escape punishment. Suddenly the old Chief announced that he had determined to follow them up himself with Bourchier's battery and his own escort.

* Mansfield was given the two Rifle Brigade battalions, the 93rd Highlanders, Longden's Heavy, and Middleton's Field battery.

What a chase we had! We went at a gallop, only pulling up occasionally for the battery to come into action, 'to clear our front and flanks.' We came up with a goodly number of stragglers, and captured several guns and carts laden with ammunition. But we were by this time overtaking large bodies of the rebels, and they were becoming too numerous for a single battery and a few staff officers to cope with. We had outstripped the Commander-in-Chief, and Hope Grant decided to halt, hoping that the missing Cavalry and Horse Artillery might soon turn up. We had not to wait long. In about a quarter of an hour they appeared among some trees to our left, even more put out than we were at their not having been to the front at such a time. Their guide had made too great a détour, but the sound of our guns showed them his mistake, and they at once altered their course and pushed on in the direction of the firing. Sir Colin had also come up, so off we started again, and never drew rein until we reached the Pandu Naddi, fourteen miles from Cawnpore. The rout was complete. Finding themselves pressed, the sepoys scattered over the country, throwing away their arms and divesting themselves of their uniform, that they might pass for harmless peasants. Nineteen guns, some of them of large calibre, were left in our hands. Our victory was particularly satisfactory in that it was achieved with but slight loss to ourselves, the casualties being 2 officers and 11 men killed, and 9 officers and 76 men wounded.

Hope Grant now desired me to hurry back to Cawnpore before it got too dark, and select the ground for the night's bivouac. As there was some risk in going alone, Augustus Anson volunteered to accompany me. We had got about half-way, when we came across the dead body of Lieutenant Salmond, who had been acting Aide-de-camp to my General, and must have got separated from us in the pursuit. His throat was cut, and he had a severe wound on the face. Soon after we met Inglis's brigade, which, in accordance with my instructions, I turned back. On reaching the Gwalior Contingent camp, we heard that an attempt had been made to recapture it, which had been repulsed by the troops left in charge.

It was dusk by the time we reached the junction of the Kalpi and Grand Trunk roads, and we agreed that this would be a good place for a bivouac, the city being about a mile in front, and Mansfield's column less than two miles to the left. I marked out the ground, and showed each corps as it came up the position it was to occupy. When all this was over I was pretty well tired out and ravenously hungry; but food there was none, so I had made up my mind to lie down, famished as I was. Just then I came across some sleeping men, who to my joy turned out to be Dighton Probyn and the officers of the 2nd Punjab Cavalry, who were magnanimous enough to forgive the abrupt interruption to their slumbers, and to supply me with some cold mutton, bread, and a bottle of beer. Never was man more grateful for a meal, and never was a meal more thoroughly enjoyed. I lay down beside my friends and was soon fast asleep, in spite of the bitter cold and being much troubled about my horse; neither for him nor myself was there a vestige of covering to be found.

The next morning I was astir by cockcrow. Patrols who had been sent forward to ascertain the truth of a rumour which had reached the Commander-in-Chief the previous evening, to the effect that the city had been evacuated, returned with confirmation of the report; but the news in other respects was far from satisfactory. Mansfield's movement had caused the enemy to retire, but they had got away without loss, and had succeeded in carrying off all their guns; so that only one half of Tantia Topi's force had really been dealt with; the other half still remained to be disposed of, and to Hope Grant's great satisfaction and my delight, the duty of following them up was entrusted to him.

His orders were to go to Bithur, as it was thought likely that the Nana's troops would retire on that place. But as the news was not very reliable, Hope Grant was told to use his own discretion, and act according to circumstances.

For several days I had been trying unsuccessfully to get hold of some Natives upon whom I could rely to bring me trustworthy information as to the enemy's movements. It is always of the utmost importance that a Quartermaster-General on service should have the help of such men, and I was now more than ever in need of reliable intelligence. In this emergency I applied to Captain Bruce, the officer in charge of the Intelligence Department which had been established at Cawnpore for the purpose of tracing the whereabouts of those rebels who had taken a prominent part in the atrocities. I was at once supplied with a first-rate man, Unjur Tiwari by name,* who from that moment until I left

* Unjur Tiwari's career was a very remarkable one. A sepoy in the 1st Bengal Native Infantry, he was at Banda when the Mutiny broke out, and during the disturbances at that place he aided a European clerk and his wife to escape, and showed his disinterestedness by refusing to take a gold ring, the only reward they had to offer him. He then joined Havelock's force, and rendered excellent service as a spy; and although taken prisoner more than once, and on one occasion tortured, he never wavered in his loyalty to us. Accompanying Outram to Lucknow, he volunteered to carry a letter to Cawnpore, and after falling into the hands of the rebels, and being cruelly ill-treated by them, he effected his escape, and safely delivered Outram's message to Sir Colin Campbell. He then worked for me most faithfully, procuring information which I could always thoroughly rely upon; and I was much gratified when he was rewarded by a grant of Rs. 3,000, presented with a sword of honour, and invested with the Order of British India, with the title of Sirdar Bahadur. I was proportionately distressed some years later to find that, owing to misrepresentations of enemies when he was serving in the Oudh Military Police, Unjur Tiwari had been deprived of his rewards, and learning he was paralyzed and in want, I begged Lord Napier to interest

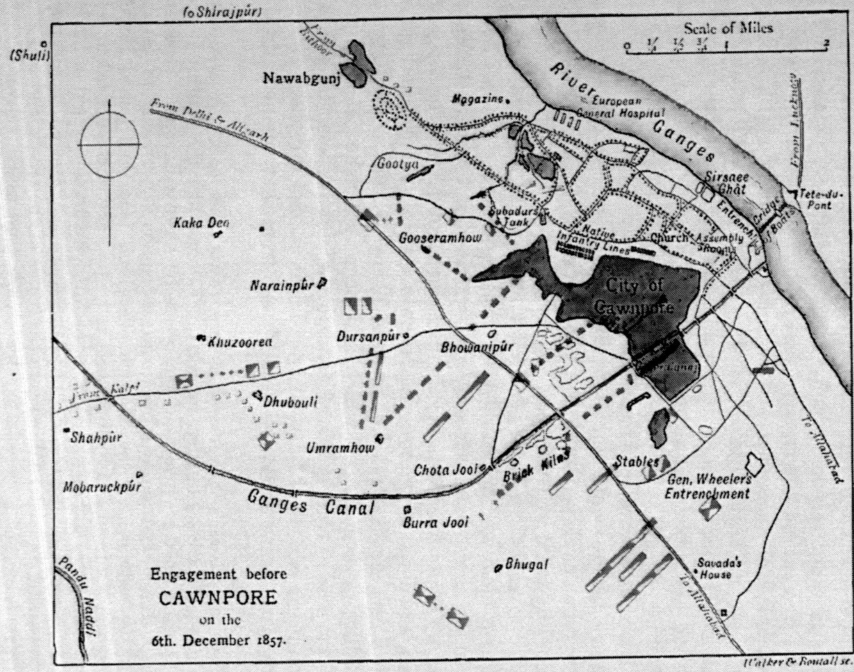

Engagement before
CAWNPORE
on the
6th. December 1857.

India for England in April, 1858, rendered me most valuable service. He was a Brahmin by caste, and belonged to the 1st Native Infantry. In a few words I explained what I required of him, and he started at once for Bithur, promising to meet me the next day on the line of march.

Early on the afternoon of the 8th we marched out of Cawnpore, and at sunset Unjur Tiwari, true to his promise, made his appearance at the point where the road turns off to Bithur. He told me that the Nana had slept at that place the night before, but hearing of our approach, had decamped with all his guns and most of his followers, and was now at a ferry some miles up the river, trying to get across and make his way to Oudh. We had come thirteen miles, and had as many more to go before we could get to the ferry, and as there was nothing to be gained by arriving there in the dark, a halt was ordered for rest and refreshment. At midnight we started again, and reached Sheorajpur (three miles from the ferry) at daybreak. Here we left our impedimenta, and proceeded by a cross-country road. Presently a couple of mounted men belonging to the enemy, not perceiving who we were, galloped straight into the escort. On discovering their mistake, they turned and tried to escape, but in vain; one was killed, the other captured, and from him we learnt that the rebels were only a short distance ahead. We pushed on, and soon came in sight of them and of the river; crowds were collected on the banks, and boats were being hurriedly laden, some of the guns having already been placed on board. Our troops were ordered to advance, but the ground along the river bank was treacherous and very heavy. Notwithstanding, the Artillery managed to struggle through, and when the batteries had got to within 1,000 yards of the ferry, the enemy appeared suddenly to discover our presence, and opened upon us with their Artillery. Our batteries galloped on, and got considerably nearer before they returned the fire; after a few rounds the rebels broke and fled. The ground was so unfavourable for pursuit, being full of holes and quicksands, that nearly all escaped, except a few cut up by the Cavalry. Fifteen guns were captured, with one single casualty on our side—the General himself—who was hit on the foot by a spent grape-shot, without, happily, being much hurt.

Hope Grant's successful management of this little expedition considerably enhanced the high opinion the Commander-in-Chief had already formed of his ability. He was next ordered to proceed to Bithur and complete the destruction of that place, which had been

---

himself in the matter, the result being that the brave old man was given a yearly pension of Rs. 1,200 for his life. He was alive when I left India, and although he resided some distance from the railway he always had himself carried to see me whenever I travelled in his direction.

begun by Havelock in July. We found the palace in good order—there was little evidence that it had been visited by an avenging force, and in one of the rooms which had been occupied by the treacherous Azimula Khan, I came across a number of letters, some unopened, and some extremely interesting, to which I shall have to refer later on.

We left Adrian Hope's brigade at Bithur to search for treasure reported to have been buried near the palace, and returned to Cawnpore, where we remained for about ten days, not at all sorry for the rest.

During this time of comparative idleness, I went over the ground where the troops under Windham had been engaged for three days, and heard many comments on the conduct of the operations. All spoke in high terms of Windham's dash and courage, but as a Commander he was generally considered to have failed.

Windham was without doubt placed in an extremely difficult position. The relief of the garrison at Lucknow was of such paramount importance that Sir Colin Campbell was obliged to take with him every available man,* and found it necessary to order Windham to send all reinforcements after him as soon as they arrived, although it was recognized as probable that Tantia Topi, with the large force then assembled near Kalpi, would advance on Cawnpore as soon as the Commander-in-Chief was committed to his difficult undertaking. Windham's orders were to improve the defences of the entrenchment; to carefully watch the movements of the Gwalior army; and to make as much display as possible of the troops at his command by encamping them in a conspicuous position outside the city; but he was not on any account to move out to attack, unless compelled to do so in order to prevent the bombardment of the entrenchment. The safety of this entrenchment was of great importance, for it contained a number of guns, quantities of ammunition and other warlike stores, and it covered, as already shown, the bridge of boats over the Ganges.

Windham loyally carried out his instructions, but he subsequently asked for and obtained leave to detain any troops arriving at Cawnpore after the 14th of November, as he did not feel himself strong enough, with the force at his disposal, to resist the enemy if attacked. But even after having received this sanction he twice despatched strong reinforcements to Lucknow, thus weakening himself considerably in order to give Sir Colin all possible help.

* The garrison left at Cawnpore consisted of:

Four companies of the 64th Foot, and small detachments of other regiments	450 men.
Sailors	47 men.
Total	497

With a hastily organized bullock battery of four field guns, manned partly by Europeans and partly by Sikhs.

Windham eventually had at his disposal about 1,700 Infantry and eight guns, the greater part of which were encamped as directed, outside the city, close to the junction of the Delhi and Kalpi roads, while the rest were posted in and around the entrenchment. Meanwhile the rebels were slowly approaching Cawnpore in detachments, with the evident intention of surrounding the place. On the 17th two bodies of troops were pushed on to Shuli and Shirajpur, within fifteen miles of the city, and a little less than that distance from each other. Windham thought that if he could manage to surprise either of these, he could prevent the enemy from concentrating, and he drew up a scheme for giving effect to this plan, which he submitted for the approval of the Commander-in-Chief. No reply came, and after waiting a week he gave up all idea of attempting to surprise the detachments, and determined to try and arrest the rebels' advance by attacking the main body, still some distance off. Accordingly he broke up his camp, and marched six miles along the Kalpi road, on the same day that the Gwalior force moved some distance nearer to Cawnpore. The next morning, the 25th, the enemy advanced to Pandu Naddi, within three miles of Windham's camp.

Windham now found himself in a very critical position. With only 1,200 Infantry* and eight light guns, he was opposed to Tantia Topi with an army of 25,000 men and forty guns. He had to choose whether he would fight these enormous odds or retire; he decided that to fight was the least of the two evils, and he was so far successful that he drove back that portion of the opposing force immediately in his front, and captured three guns; but being unable to press his advantage on account of the paucity of men and the total absence of Cavalry, he had perforce to fall back—a grievous necessity. He was followed the whole way, insulted and jeered at, by the rebel horsemen. The result of the day was to give confidence to the wily Mahratta leader; he pushed on to Cawnpore, and attacked Windham with such vehemence that by nightfall on the 28th the British troops were driven inside the entrenchment, having had 315 men killed and wounded, and having lost all their baggage and camp equipage.

Windham undoubtedly laid himself open to censure. His defence was that, had he received the Commander-in-Chief's authority to carry out his plan for surprising the rebels, he would certainly have broken up their army, and the disaster could not have occurred. But surely when he decided that circumstances had so changed since Sir Colin's orders were given as to justify him in disregarding them, he should have acted on his own responsibility, and taken such steps as appeared

* The force was composed of the 34th Foot, and portions of the 82nd and 88th Foot, and 2nd Battalion Rifle Brigade; with four 9-pounders, manned partly by Royal and Bengal gunners and partly by Sikhs; and four 6-pounders, manned by Madras Native gunners.

to him best, instead of applying for sanction to a Commander far from the scene of action, and so entirely ignorant of the conditions under which the application was made, as to render it impossible for him to decide whether such sanction should be given. The march which Windham made towards the enemy on the 24th was quite as grave a disobedience of orders as would have been the surprise movement he contemplated on the 17th; but while the former placed him in a most dangerous position, and one from which it was impossible to deal the enemy a decisive blow, the latter, if successful, would have deserved, and doubtless would have received, the highest praise.

CHAPTER XXVIII.

Our stay at Cawnpore was more prolonged than the Commander-in-Chief intended or wished it to be, but want of transport made it impossible for us to move until the carts returned which had gone to Allahabad with the women and children and the sick soldiers. We were thus delayed until the 23rd December, on which date we commenced our march towards Fatehgarh.

At Chobipur, two marches from Cawnpore, where we spent Christmas Day, we were joined by the troops who had been left behind at Bithur; they had not succeeded in discovering any considerable quantity of treasure, some silver vessels of various kinds being the only result of their labours.

The Commander-in-Chief's object in moving on Fatehgarh was to restore order throughout the Doab and open communication between the Punjab and Bengal.

A brigade under Brigadier Walpole had been despatched on the 16th, with orders to clear the country along the left bank of the Jumna up to Mainpuri, where he was to be joined by Brigadier Seaton with a strong column from Delhi, and whence the united force was to advance on Fatehgarh.

We reached Gursahaiganj, where the road turns off to Fatehgarh, on the 31st, and here the main body of the army halted on New Year's Day, 1858; but information having been received that 5,000 rebels under the Nawab of Farakabad had partly destroyed the suspension bridge over the Kali Naddi, about five miles ahead, and had then gone off towards Fatehgarh, Adrian Hope's brigade was sent forward to repair the damage and watch the bridge.

Early the following morning Sir Colin, with Mansfield and the rest of his staff, went on to inspect progress, leaving orders for the rest of the force to follow later in the day. Very soon, however, Hope Grant received an urgent message from the Chief of the Staff, telling him to push on the troops with all possible speed, as the enemy had returned, and were now in strength on the other side of the Kali Naddi.

We (Sir Hope and his staff) started off with the Horse Artillery and Cavalry, and found, on reaching the bridge, that the rebels were occupying the village of Khudaganj, just across the river, and only about 300 yards off, from which advantageous position they were pouring a heavy fire on Hope's brigade. Our piquets on the further side of the stream had been strengthened by a wing of the 53rd Foot, and a wing of the 93rd Highlanders had been placed in reserve behind the bridge on the nearer side, the rest of the regiment having been despatched to watch a ford some distance down the river, while a battery of Field Artillery had been brought into action in reply to the enemy's guns. Immediately on the arrival of the main body, three of Peel's guns, under Vaughan, his First Lieutenant, were pushed across the bridge to the further side, and getting under shelter of a convenient building, opened fire on the village, and on a toll-bar directly in its front, about which the enemy were collected in considerable numbers. Our Infantry now crossed over, followed by the Cavalry and Horse Artillery—a tedious operation, as there had not been time to fully repair the bridge, and in one place planks had only been laid for half its width, necessitating horses being led, and Infantry passing over in sections. Moreover, the enemy had got the exact range. and several casualties occurred at this spot; one round shot alone killed and wounded six men of the 8th Foot. Vaughan at last succeeded in silencing the gun which had troubled us most, and preparations were made for an attack on the village. While we were watching the proceedings, the Interpreter to the Naval Brigade, Henry Hamilton Maxwell, a brother officer of mine who had been standing close to me, was very badly wounded in the leg, and both Sir Colin and Sir Hope were hit by spent bullets, luckily without being much hurt.

There was a feeling throughout the army that Sir Colin was inclined to favour Highlanders unduly; and a rumour got about that the 93rd were to be allowed the honour of delivering the assault on Khudaganj, which was highly resented by the 53rd, and they determined that on this occasion, at any rate, the Highlanders should not have it all their own way. The 53rd was composed of a remarkably fine set of fellows, chiefly Irish, and it was Mansfield's own regiment; wishing, therefore, to do an old comrade a good turn, he had placed Major Payn,* one of the senior officers, in command of the piquets. Payn was a fine dashing soldier, and a great favourite with the men, who calculated on his backing them up if they upset Sir Colin's little plan. Whether what happened was with or without Payn's permission, I cannot say, but we were all waiting near the bridge for the attacking party to form,

* The late General Sir William Payn, K.C.B.

when suddenly the 'advance' was sounded, then the 'double,' followed by a tremendous cheer, and we saw the 53rd charge the enemy. Sir Colin was very angry, but the 53rd could not be brought back, and there was nothing for it but to support them. Hope's and Greathed's troops were instantly pushed on, and the Cavalry and Horse Artillery were ordered to mount.

The ground gradually sloped upwards towards Khudaganj, and the regiments moving up to the attack made a fine picture. The 93rd followed the impulsive 53rd, while Greathed's brigade took a line to the left, and as they neared the village the rebels hastily limbered up their guns and retired. This was an opportunity for mounted troops such as does not often occur; it was instantly seized by Hope Grant, who rode to the Cavalry, drawn up behind some sand hills, and gave the word of command, 'Threes left, trot, march.' The words had hardly left his lips before we had started in pursuit of the enemy, by this time half a mile ahead, the 9th Lancers leading the way, followed by Younghusband's, Gough's, and Probyn's squadrons. When within 300 yards of the fugitives, the 'charge' was sounded, and in a few seconds we were in their midst. A regular mêlée ensued, a number of the rebels were killed, and seven guns captured in less than as many minutes. The General now formed the Cavalry into a long line, and, placing himself at the head of his own regiment (the 9th Lancers), followed up the flying foe. I rode a little to his left with Younghusband's squadron, and next to him came Tyrrell Ross, the doctor.* As we galloped along, Younghusband drew my attention with great pride to the admirable manner in which his men kept their dressing.

On the line thundered, overtaking groups of the enemy, who every now and then turned and fired into us before they could be cut down, or knelt to receive us on their bayonets before discharging their muskets. The chase continued for nearly five miles, until daylight began to fail and we appeared to have got to the end of the fugitives, when the order was given to wheel to the right and form up on the road. Before, however, this movement could be carried out, we overtook a batch of mutineers, who faced about and fired into the squadron at close quarters. I saw Younghusband fall, but I could not go to his assistance, as at that moment one of his *sowars* was in dire peril from a sepoy who was attacking him with his fixed bayonet, and had I not

* Tyrrell Ross was well known as a skilful surgeon, and much esteemed as a staunch friend. He had just returned from England, and had that very morning been placed in medical charge of the Cavalry Brigade. When the order to mount was given, Ross asked the General where he wished him to be, pointing out that he would not be of much use in the rear if there were a pursuit across country. Hope Grant replied: 'Quite so; I have heard that you are a good rider and can use your sword. Ride on my left, and help to look after my third squadron.' This Ross did as well as any Cavalry officer could have done.

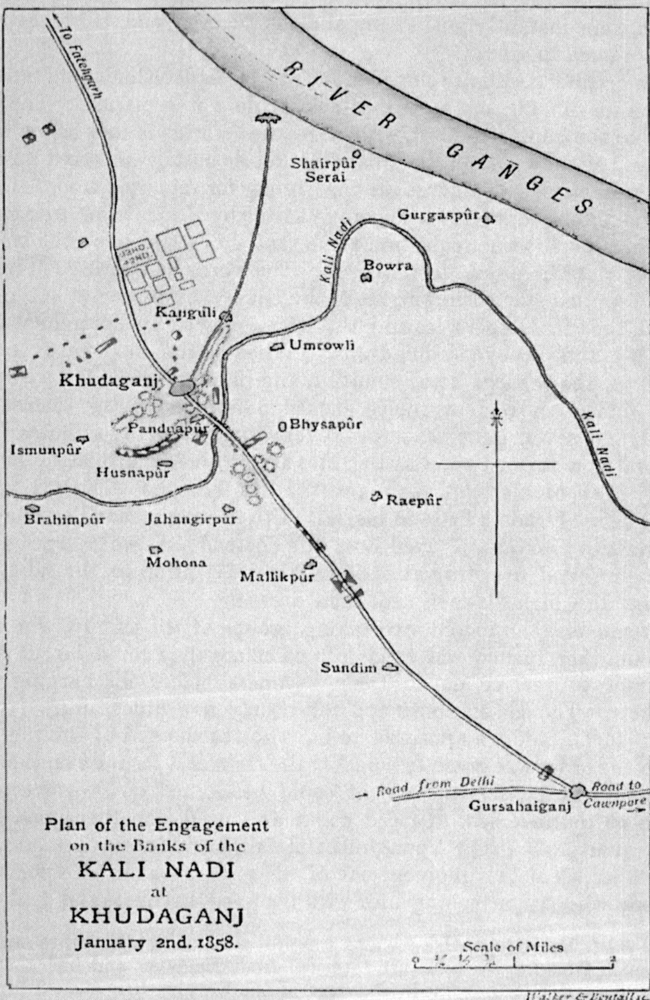

Plan of the Engagement
on the Banks of the
KALI NADI
at
KHUDAGANJ
January 2nd. 1858.

helped the man and disposed of his opponent, he must have been killed. The next moment I descried in the distance two sepoys making off with a standard, which I determined must be captured, so I rode after the rebels and overtook them, and while wrenching the staff out of the hands of one of them, whom I cut down, the other put his musket close to my body and fired; fortunately for me it missed fire, and I carried off the standard.*

Tyrrell Ross, attracted by a party of men in the rear of the squadron bending over the fallen Younghusband, now came up, and, to everyone's great grief, pronounced the wound to be mortal. From the day that I had annexed Younghusband's pony at the siege of Delhi we had been so much together, and had become such fast friends, that it was a great shock to me to be told that never again would my gallant comrade lead the men in whom he took such soldierly pride.†

When the wounded had been attended to, we returned to camp, where we found Sir Colin waiting to welcome us, and we received quite an ovation from our comrades in the Infantry and Artillery. We must have presented a curious spectacle as we rode back, almost every man carrying some trophy of the day, for the enemy had abandoned everything in their flight, and we found the road strewn with laden carts and palankins, arms, Native clothing, etc. Our losses were surprisingly small—only 10 men killed, and 30 men and 2 officers wounded.

The next day the column marched to Fatehgarh, which we found deserted. The rebels had fled so precipitately that they had left the bridge over the Ganges intact, and had not attempted to destroy the valuable gun-carriage factory in the fort, which was then placed in the charge of Captain H. Legeyt Bruce.‡

We remained a whole month at Fatehgarh, and loud were the complaints in camp at the unaccountable delay. It was the general opinion that we ought to move into Rohilkand, and settle that part of the country before returning to Lucknow; this view was very strongly held by Sir Colin Campbell, and those who accused him of "indecision, dilatoriness, and wasting the best of the cold weather" could not have known how little he deserved their censure. The truth was, that the Governor-General and the Commander-in-Chief were not in accord as

* For these two acts I was awarded the Victoria Cross.

† Younghusband met with an extraordinary accident during the fight at Agra. While pursuing one of the Gwalior rebels, he fell with his horse into a disused well, fifty feet deep, and was followed by two of his men, also mounted. Ropes were brought, and the bodies were hauled up, when, to the astonishment of everyone, Younghusband was found to be alive, and, beyond being badly bruised, uninjured. He had fallen to the bottom in a sitting position, his back resting against the side of the well, and his legs stretched out in front of him, while his horse fell standing and across him. He was thus protected from the weight of the other two horses and their riders, who were all killed.

‡ Now Major-General H. L. Bruce, C.B.

to the order in which the several military operations should be taken in hand; the latter urged that Rohilkand should be dealt with first, and settled before the end of the cold weather; he thought that the troops would then be the better for a rest, and that Lucknow could very well wait till the following autumn. Lord Canning opined, on the other hand (and I entirely agree with him), that, while it was most desirable that order should be restored in Rohilkand, and indeed throughout the whole of the North-West Provinces, the possession of Lucknow was of 'far greater value.' 'Every eye,' Lord Canning wrote, 'is upon Oudh as it was upon Delhi: Oudh is not only the rallying-place of the sepoys, the place to which they all look, and by the doings in which their own hopes and prospects rise or fall; but it represents a dynasty; there is a king of Oudh "seeking his own."' He pointed out that there was an uneasy feeling amongst the Chiefs of Native States, who were intently watching our attitude with regard to Lucknow, and that even in 'far-off Burma' news from Lucknow was anxiously looked for. The Governor-General laid great stress also upon the advisability of employing as soon and as close to their own country as possible the troops from Nepal which, at Sir Henry Lawrence's suggestion, had been applied for to, and lent us by, the Nepalese Government.

The visit of Jung Bahadur (the Prime Minister of Nepal) to England a few years before had opened his eyes to our latent power, and he had been able to convince his people that time alone was required for us to recover completely from the blow which had been dealt us by the Mutiny, and that it was therefore to their advantage to side with us. Lord Canning wisely judged, however, that it would be highly imprudent to allow the province immediately adjoining Nepal to continue in a state of revolt, and he felt that neither Jung Bahadur nor his Gurkhas would be satisfied unless they were allowed to take an active part in the campaign.

CHAPTER XXIX.

Our prolonged stay at Fatehgarh was not altogether without advantage. Such a large force being concentrated in the neighbourhood secured the safety of the Doab for the time being, and as Fatehgarh was equally conveniently situated for an advance, either into Rohilkand or upon Lucknow, the rebels were kept in a state of uncertainty as to the direction of our next move.

At length it was decided that Lucknow was to be our first objective, and Sir Colin at once communicated with Outram and Napier as to the best means of conducting the siege. Then, leaving Hope Grant to take the division across the Ganges, the Chief went to Allahabad, the temporary Head-Quarters of the supreme Government, to discuss the situation with the Governor-General.

We marched through Cawnpore, and on the 8th February reached Unao, where we found encamped the 7th Hussars, a troop of Royal Horse Artillery, the 38th Foot and the 79th Highlanders.

Sir Colin on his return from Allahabad on the 10th issued a General Order detailing the regiments, staff, and Commanders who were to take part in the 'Siege of Lucknow.'* Hope Grant, who had been made a Major-General for the 'Relief of Lucknow,' was appointed to the command of the Cavalry division, and I remained with him as D.A.Q.M.G.

Rumours had been flying about that the Nana was somewhere in the neighbourhood, but 'Wolf!' had been cried so often with regard to him, that but little notice was taken of the reports, until my faithful spy, Unjur Tiwari, brought me intelligence that the miscreant really was hiding in a small fort about twenty-five miles from our camp. Hope Grant started off at once, taking with him a compact little force, and reached the fort early next morning (17th February), just too late to catch the Nana, who, we were told, had fled precipitately before day-break. We blew up the fort, and for the next few days moved by short marches towards Lucknow, clearing the country as we went of rebels, small parties of whom we frequently encountered. On the 23rd we reached Mianganj, a small fortified town on the old Cawnpore and Lucknow road, where some 2,000 of the enemy had ensconced themselves. Our advance guard having been fired upon as we approached, the column was halted and the baggage placed in safety, while Hope Grant reconnoitred the position in order to see where it could most advantageously be attacked. We found the town enclosed by a high

* The Infantry portion of the army was divided into three divisions, commanded respectively by Outram, Lugard, and Walpole. This was exclusive of Franks's column, which joined at Lucknow and made a fourth division. The Artillery was placed under Archdale Wilson, and the Engineers under Robert Napier. Sir Colin's selection of Commanders caused considerable heart-burnings, especially amongst the senior officers who had been sent out from England for the purpose of being employed in the field. But, as the Chief explained to the Duke of Cambridge, the selection had been made with the greatest care, it having been found that 'an officer unexperienced in war in India cannot act for himself . . . it is quite impossible for him to be able to weigh the value of intelligence . . . he cannot judge what are the resources of the country, and he is totally unable to make an estimate for himself of the resistance the enemy opposed to him is likely to offer.' Sir Colin wound up his letter as follows: 'I do not wish to undervalue the merits of General or other officers lately arrived from England, but merely to indicate to your Royal Highness the difficulties against which they have to contend. What is more, the state of things at present does not permit of trusting anything to chance, or allowing new-comers to learn, except under the command of others.' —Shadwell's 'Life of Lord Clyde.'

loop-holed wall with circular bastions at the four corners and at regular intervals along the sides, the whole being surrounded by a wet ditch, while the gateways had been strengthened by palisades. Large bodies of the enemy's Cavalry hovered about our reconnoitring party, only to retire as we advanced, apparently not liking the look of the 7th Hussars and 9th Lancers, who formed the General's escort.

After a careful inspection, Hope Grant decided to breach the north-west angle of the wall, as from a wood near the Infantry could keep down the fire of the enemy's sharpshooters, and the heavy guns would be in a measure protected while the walls were being bombarded. A sufficiently good breach was made in about two hours, and the 53rd Regiment, having been selected for the honour of leading the assault, was told to hold itself in readiness. Hope Grant then spoke a few words of encouragement to the men, and their Colonel (English) replied on their behalf that they might be depended upon to do their duty. The signal was given; the Horse Artillery, under Lieutenant-Colonel Frank Turner, galloped to within grape range of the town, and covered by their fire the 53rd marched on steadily until they got within 100 yards of the walls, when, with a ringing cheer, they dashed through the water in the ditch and entered the breach. Hopkins, the plucky Captain of the light company, was the first inside the walls, followed closely by Augustus Anson and an adventurous Post-Captain of the Royal Navy, who, being unemployed, came to see what 'a winter's campaign in India' was like.* There was a good deal of hand-to-hand fighting, and the enemy lost about 500 men, those who tried to escape being cut down by the Cavalry outside the walls. We took about the same number of prisoners, but as none of these were soldiers, and vowed they had been forced to take up arms against us, the General, as much to their astonishment as to their delight, ordered them to be set free. Our losses were small.

Next day we halted while the walls were being destroyed and the place rendered indefensible. As I was superintending the work of destruction, the horrors of war were once more brought very forcibly before me by the appearance of an infirm old man, who besought me to spare his house, saying: 'Yesterday I was the happy father of five sons: three of them lie there' (pointing to a group of dead bodies); 'where the other two are, God only knows. I am old and a cripple, and if my house is burned there is nothing left for me but to die.' Of course I took care that his house and property were left untouched.

On the 25th February we marched to Mohan, a picturesquely situated village on the bank of the Sai Naddi, which stream we crossed the next day and encamped on a fine grassy plain, there to remain until it should be time to join the army before Lucknow.

* The late Captain Oliver Jones, who published his experiences under that title.

While we were halting at this place, Watson and I had rather a curious adventure. During a morning's ride my greyhound put up a *nilghai** so close to us that Watson, aiming a blow at him with his sword, gashed his quarter. Off he started, and we after him at full speed; the chase continued for some miles without our getting much nearer, when, all at once, we beheld moving towards us from our right front a body of the enemy's Cavalry. We were in an awkward position; our horses were very nearly dead beat, and we could hardly hope to get away if pursued. We pulled up, turned round, and trotted back, very quietly at first, that our horses might recover their breath before the enemy got to closer quarters and we should have to ride for our lives. Every now and then we looked back to see whether they were gaining upon us, and at last we distinctly saw them open out and make as if to charge down upon us. We thought our last hour was come. We bade each other good-bye, agreeing that each must do his best to escape, and that neither was to wait for the other, when lo! as suddenly as they had appeared, the horsemen vanished, as though the ground had opened and swallowed them; there was nothing to be seen but the open plain, where a second before there had been a crowd of mounted men. We could hardly believe our eyes, or comprehend at first that what we had seen was simply a mirage, but so like reality that anyone must have been deceived. Our relief, on becoming convinced that we had been scared by a phantom enemy, was considerable; but the apparition had the good effect of making us realize the folly of having allowed ourselves to be tempted so far away from our camp without escort of any kind in an enemy's country, and we determined not to risk it again.†

While we were occupied in clearing the country to the north of the Cawnpore-Lucknow road, the main body of the army, with the siege-train, Engineer park, Naval Brigade,‡ ammunition, and stores of all kinds, had gradually been collecting at Bhantira, to which place we were ordered to proceed on the 1st March. We had a troublesome march across country, and did not reach the Head-Quarters camp until close on midnight. There was much difficulty in getting the guns through the muddy nullas and up the steep banks, and but for the assistance of the elephants the task could hardly have been accomplished. It was most curious and interesting to see how these sagacious creatures watched for and seized the moment when their help was needed to get the guns up the steep inclines; they waited till the

* Literally 'blue cow,' one of the bovine antelopes.

† A few days afterwards, when we were some miles from the scene of our adventure, I was awakened one morning by the greyhound licking my face; she had cleverly found me out in the midst of a large crowded camp.

‡ Peel had changed his 24-pounders for the more powerful 64-pounders belonging to H.M.S. *Shannon.*

horses dragging the gun could do no more and were coming to a standstill, when one of them would place his forehead against the muzzle and shove until the gun was safely landed on the top of the bank.

We started early on the morning of the 2nd for Lucknow, Hope Grant taking command of the Cavalry division for the first time.

On nearing the Alambagh, we bore to our right past the Jalalabad fort, where Outram's Engineers were busily engaged in constructing fascines and gabions for the siege, and preparing spars and empty casks for bridging the Gumti. As we approached the Mahomedbagh we came under the fire of some of the enemy's guns placed in a grove of trees; but no sooner had the Artillery of our advance guard opened fire than the rebels retired, leaving a gun in our hands. We moved on to the Dilkusha, which we found unoccupied. The park had been greatly disfigured since our last visit, most of the finest trees having been cut down.

My General was now placed in charge of the piquets, a position for which he was admirably fitted and in which he delighted. He rode well, without fatigue to himself or his horse, so that any duty entailing long hours in the saddle was particularly congenial to him. I invariably accompanied him in his rounds, and in after-years I often felt that I owed Hope Grant a debt of gratitude for the practical lessons he gave me in outpost duty.

Strong piquets with heavy guns were placed in and around the Dilkusha, as well as in the Mahomedbagh. The main body of the army was encamped to the rear of the Dilkusha, its right almost on the Gumti, while its left stretched for two miles in the direction of the Alambagh. Hope Grant, wishing to be in a convenient position in case of an attack, spent the night in the Mahomedbagh piquet, and Anson, the D.A.A.G., and I kept him company.

On the 3rd some of the troops left at Bhantira came into camp, and on the 5th General Franks arrived. His division, together with the Nepalese Contingent, 9,000 strong, brought the numbers at the Commander-in-Chief's disposal up to nearly 31,000 men, with 164 guns;* not a man too many for the capture of a city twenty miles in circumference, defended by 120,000 armed men, who for three months and a half had worked incessantly at strengthening the defences, which con-

* Naval Brigade	431
Artillery	1,745
Engineers	865
Cavalry	3,169
Infantry	12,498
Franks's Division	2,880
Nepalese Contingent	9,000
	30,588

sisted of three lines, extending lengthwise from the Charbagh bridge to the Gumti, and in depth from the canal to the Kaisarbagh.

In Napier's carefully prepared plan, which Sir Colin decided to adopt, it was shown that the attack should be made on the east, as that side offered the smallest front, it afforded ground for planting our Artillery, which the west side did not, and it was the shortest approach to the Kaisarbagh, a place to which the rebels attached the greatest importance; more than all, we knew the east side, and were little acquainted with the west. Napier further recommended that the attack should be accompanied by a flank movement on the north, with the object of taking in reverse the first and second lines of the enemy's defences.* A division was accordingly sent across the Gumti for this purpose, and the movement, being entirely successful, materially aided in the capture of the city. The passage of the river was effected by means of two pontoon bridges made of empty barrels, and thrown across the stream a little below the Dilkusha. They were completed by midnight on the 5th March, and before day broke the troops detailed for this service had crossed over.

Outram, who, since the 'Relief of Lucknow,' had been maintaining his high reputation by keeping the enemy in check before the Alambagh, commanded this division, with Hope Grant as his second in command. As soon as it was light we moved away from the river to be out of reach of the Martinière guns, and after marching for about two miles we came in view of the enemy; the Artillery of the advance guard got to within a thousand yards and opened fire, upon which the rebels broke and fled. The Bays pursued them for a short distance, but with very little result, the ground being intersected with nullas, and the enemy opening upon them with heavy guns, they had to retire precipitately, with the loss of their Major, Percy Smith, whose body, unhappily, had to be abandoned.

About noon we encamped close to Chinhut, and Hope Grant took special care that day to see the piquets were well placed, for the rebels were in great numbers, and we were surrounded by ravines and wooded enclosures. It was thought by some that he was unnecessarily anxious and careful, for he rode several times over the ground; but the next morning proved how right he was to leave nothing to chance.

While we were at breakfast, information was brought in that the enemy were advancing in force, and directly afterwards half a dozen

* Kaye, in his 'History of the Indian Mutiny,' gives the credit for originating this movement to the Commander-in-Chief himself: but the present Lord Napier of Magdala has letters in his possession which clearly prove that the idea was his father's, and there is a passage in General Porter's 'History of the Royal Engineers,' vol. ii., p. 476, written after he had read Napier's letters to Sir Colin Campbell, which leaves no room for doubt as to my version being the correct one.

round shot were sent into our camp; the troops fell in, the Infantry moved out, and Hope Grant took the Horse Artillery and Cavalry to our right flank, where the mutineers were collected in considerable numbers. In less than an hour we had driven them off, but we were not allowed to follow them up, as Outram did not wish to get entangled in the suburbs until heavy guns had arrived. The piquets were strengthened and pushed forward, affording another opportunity for a useful lesson in outpost duty.

All that day and the next I accompanied my General in his reconnaissance of the enemy's position, as well as of the ground near the Gumti, in order to determine where the heavy guns could best be placed, so as effectually to enfilade the enemy's first line of defences along the bank of the canal. On returning to report progress to Outram at mid-day on the 8th, we found Sir Colin Campbell and Mansfield with him, arranging for a joint attack the following day; after their consultation was over, they all rode with us to see the site Hope Grant had selected for the battery. It was a slightly elevated piece of ground about half a mile north of the Kokrel nulla, fairly concealed by a bend of the river; but before it could be made use of it was considered necessary to clear the rebels out of the position they were occupying between the nulla and the iron bridge, the key to which was the Chakar Kothi, and Outram was directed to attack this point the next morning.

At 2 a.m. on the 9th the heavy guns, escorted by the 1st Bengal Fusiliers, were sent forward to within 600 yards of the enemy. The troops then moved off in two parties, that on the right being commanded by Hope Grant. We marched along the Fyzabad road, the two Rifle Brigade battalions leading the way in skirmishing order, with the Cavalry well away to the right. The rebels retired as we advanced, and Walpole, commanding one of our brigades, by wheeling to his left on reaching the opposite bank of the nulla, was enabled to enfilade their position. The column was then halted, and I was sent to inform Outram as to our progress.

When I had delivered my message, and was about to return, Outram desired me to stay with him until the capture of the Chakar Kothi (which he was just about to attempt) should be accomplished, that I might then convey to Hope Grant his orders as to what further action would be required of him; meanwhile Outram sent a messenger to tell my General what he was about to do, in view of his co-operating on the right.*

* Outram's division consisted of the 23rd Royal Welsh Fusiliers, 79th Highlanders, 2nd and 3rd battalions of the Rifle Brigade, 1st Bengal Fusiliers, 2nd Punjab Infantry, D'Aguilar's, Remmington's and Mackinnon's troops of Horse Artillery, Gibbon's and Middleton's Field Batteries, and some Heavy guns, 2nd Dragoon Guards, 9th Lancers, 2nd Punjab Cavalry, and Watson's and Sandford's squadrons of the 1st and 5th Punjab Cavalry.

The Chakar Kothi was attacked and taken, and the enemy, apparently having lost heart, fled precipitately. One of the 1st Bengal Fusiliers' colours was placed on the top of this three-storied building by Ensign Jervis to show the Commander-in-Chief that it was in our possession, and that the time had come for him to attack the first line of the enemy's defences. We then continued our advance to the river, where the parties united, and I rejoined Hope Grant.

It was now only 2 p.m., and there was plenty of time to place the heavy guns in position before dark. Major Lothian Nicholson,* Outram's Commanding Engineer, was superintending this operation, when he thought he perceived that the enemy had abandoned their first line, but he could not be quite sure. It was most necessary to ascertain for certain whether this was the case, as the Infantry of Hope's brigade, which had attacked and driven the rebels out of the Martinière, could be seen preparing to assault the works at the other side of the river. A discussion ensued as to how this knowledge could be obtained, and a young subaltern of the 1st Bengal Fusiliers, named Butler,† offered to swim across the Gumti, and, if he found the enemy had retired, to communicate the fact to Hope's men. This feat was successfully accomplished by the plucky young volunteer; he found the enemy had retired, and, on giving the information to Hope, the brigade advanced, and before nightfall the whole of the enemy's first line was in our possession—a success which had been achieved with but slight loss to us, the chief casualty during the day being William Peel, the gallant Commander of the Naval Brigade, who had been seriously wounded while in command of a battery near the Dilkusha.

The next day, the 10th, Outram's camp was moved close up to the Gumti, and batteries were constructed from which fire could be poured on the mess-house and the Kaisarbagh. For the protection of these works, and to prevent an attack in force being made on the main part of the column, Hope Grant kept moving about with the Horse Artillery and Cavalry between the river and the Sitapur road, our reconnaissance extending beyond the old cantonment. We had several little fights, in one of which a very promising officer named Sandford, who had succeeded Younghusband in command of the 5th Punjab Cavalry squadron, was killed.

At daybreak on the morning of the 11th the batteries opened fire on the enemy's second line of defence; at the same time Outram himself led a strong body of Infantry along the river with the object of securing the approaches to the bridges. On reaching the Fyzabad road, about half a mile from the iron bridge, Outram placed the 1st Bengal Fusiliers in a mosque, with orders to entrench themselves and hold the post.

* The late Lieutenant-General Sir Lothian Nicholson, K.C.B.

† Now Colonel Thomas Butler, V.C.

while he pushed on to the stone bridge about a mile away. Outram's advance was covered by Hope Grant's Horse Artillery and Cavalry, but we had to keep at some distance away to the right, in order to avoid houses and walled enclosures. Soon after crossing the Sitapur road we heard guns to our left, and proceeding at a smart trot, came up with Outram just as he was about to attack a large body of the rebels, who, finding themselves in an awkward position, with the river in their rear and their retreat by the iron bridge cut off, made but a feeble resistance before they broke and fled. Some few escaped by the stone bridge, but the greater number, including the whole of the mutinous 15th Irregular Cavalry, made for the old cantonment. We pursued with our Cavalry, and very few of them got away. A couple of guns and a quantity of plunder were left behind by the enemy, who evidently had not expected us and were quite unprepared for our attack. Outram pushed on to the stone bridge, but finding he was losing men from the fire poured upon us by the rebels from the opposite side of the river, he fell back to the mosque where he had left the Fusiliers.

That afternoon, as there was nothing particular for the Cavalry to do, the General, Anson, and I rode across the river to see how matters were progressing on the left of the attack. We reached the Head-Quarters camp just as Sir Colin was about to receive a visit of ceremony from the Nepalese General, the famous Jung Bahadur. Our old Chief, in honour of the occasion, had doffed his usual workman-like costume, and wore General's full-dress uniform, but he was quite thrown into the shade by the splendour of the Gurkha Prince, who was most gorgeously attired, with magnificent jewels in his turban, round his neck, and on his coat.

I looked at Jung Bahadur with no small interest, for his deeds of daring had made him conspicuous amongst probably the bravest race of men in the world, and the fact that a high-born Hindu, such as he was, should, fifty years ago, have so far risen superior to caste prejudice as to cross the sea and visit England, proved him to be a man of unusually strong and independent mind. He was about five feet eight inches high—tall for a Gurkha—with a well-knit, wiry figure, a keen, dauntless eye, and a firm, determined mouth—in every respect a typical, well-bred Nepalese. The interview did not last long, for Sir Colin disliked ceremonial, and, shortly after the Nepalese Prince had taken his seat, news was brought in that the assault on the Begum Kothi had been successfully completed, upon which Sir Colin made the necessity for attending to business an excuse for taking leave of his distinguished visitor, and the interview came to an end.

I then obtained leave to go to the scene of the recent fight, and, galloping across the canal by the bridge near Banks's house, soon found myself at the Begum Kothi. There I was obliged to dismount, for even on foot it was a difficult matter to scramble over the breach. The place was most formidable, and it was a marvel that it had been taken with comparatively so little loss on our side. The bodies of a number of Highlanders and Punjabis were lying about, and a good many wounded men were being attended to, but our casualties were nothing in proportion to those of the enemy, 600 or 700 of whom were buried the next day in the ditch they had themselves dug for their own protection. A very determined stand had been made by the sepoys when they found there was no chance of getting away. There were many tales of hair-breadth escapes and desperate struggles, and on all sides I heard laments that Hodson should have been one of those dangerously, if not mortally, wounded in the strife. Hodson had been carried to Banks's house, and to the inquiry I made on my way back to camp, as to his condition, the answer was, 'Little, if any, hope.'

A great stride in the advance had been made on this day. Outram had accomplished all that was expected of him, and he was now busy constructing additional batteries for the bombardment of the Kaisarbagh; while Lugard,* from his newly-acquired position at the Begum Kothi, was also able to bring fire to bear upon that doomed palace.

Hodson died the following day (the 12th). As a soldier, I had a very great admiration for him, and, in common with the whole army, I mourned his early death.†

On the 13th Lugard's division was relieved by Franks's, and to Jung Bahadur and his Gurkhas, only too eager for the fray, was entrusted the conduct of operations along the line of the canal between Banks's house and the Charbagh bridge. On our side of the river nothing of importance occurred.

* Now General the Right Hon. Sir Edward Lugard, G.C.B.

† It was current in camp, and the story has often been repeated, that Hodson was killed in the act of looting. This certainly was not the case. Hodson was sitting with Donald Stewart in the Head-Quarters camp, when the signal-gun announced that the attack on the Begum Kothi was about to take place. Hodson immediately mounted his horse, and rode off in the direction of the city. Stewart, who had been ordered by the Commander-in-Chief to accompany the troops, and send an early report to his Excellency of the result of the assault, had his horse ready, and followed Hodson so closely that he kept him in sight until within a short distance of the fighting, when Stewart stopped to speak to the officer in charge of Peel's guns, which had been covering the advance of the troops. This delayed Stewart for a few minutes only, and as he rode into the court-yard of the palace a Highland soldier handed him a pistol, saying, 'This is your pistol, sir; but I thought you were carried away mortally wounded a short time ago?' Stewart at once conjectured that the man had mistaken him for Hodson. In face they were not much alike, but both were tall, well made and fair, and Native soldiers had frequently saluted one for the other. It is clear from this account that Hodson could not have been looting, as he was wounded almost as soon as he reached the palace.

The capture of the Imambara (a mosque situated between the Begum Kothi and the Kaisarbagh) was accomplished early next morning. The assault was led by Brasyer's Sikhs and a detachment of the 10th Foot, supported by the remainder of that regiment and the 90th Light Infantry. After a short but very severe struggle, the enemy were forced to retire, and were so closely pursued that the storming party suddenly found themselves in a building immediately overlooking the Kaisarbagh.

It had not been intended to advance that day beyond the Imambara, but, recognizing the advantage of the position thus gained, and the demoralized condition of the rebels, Franks wisely determined to follow up his success. Reinforcements were hurried forward, the troops holding the Sikandarbagh and the Shah Najaf were ordered to act in concert, and before nightfall the Kaisarbagh, the mess-house, and the numerous buildings situated between those places and the Residency, were in our possession.

By means of the field telegraph, Outram was kept accurately informed as to the movements of Franks's division, and he could have afforded it valuable assistance had he been allowed to cross the Gumti with his three brigades of Infantry. Outram, with his soldierly instinct, felt that this was the proper course to pursue; but in reply to his request to be allowed to push over the river by the iron bridge, he received from the Commander-in-Chief through Mansfield the unaccountably strange order that he must not attempt it, if it would entail his losing 'a single man.' Thus a grand opportunity was lost. The bridge, no doubt, was strongly held, but with the numerous guns which Outram could have brought to bear upon its defenders its passage could have been forced without serious loss; the enemy's retreat would have been cut off, and Franks's victory would have been rendered complete, which it certainly was not, owing to Outram's hands having been so effectually tied.

Lucknow was practically in our hands on the evening of the 14th March, but the rebels escaped with comparatively slight punishment, and the campaign, which should have then come to an end, was protracted for nearly a year by the fugitives spreading themselves over Oudh, and occupying forts and other strong positions, from which they were able to offer resistance to our troops until towards the end of May, 1859, thus causing the needless loss of thousands of British soldiers.* Sir Colin saw his mistake when too late. The next day orders were issued for the Cavalry to follow up the mutineers, who were understood to have fled in a northerly direction. One brigade under Campbell (the Colonel of the Bays) was directed to proceed to

* In the month of May, 1858, alone, not less than a thousand British soldiers died of sunstroke, fatigue and disease, and about a hundred were killed in action.

Sandila, and another, under Hope Grant, towards Sitapur. But the enemy was not seen by either. As usual, they had scattered themselves over the country and entirely disappeared, and many of the rebels who still remained in the city seized the opportunity of the Cavalry being absent to get away.

Outram's command on the left bank of the Gumti was now broken up, with the view to his completing the occupation of the city. Accordingly, on the 16th, he advanced from the Kaisarbagh with Douglas's brigade* and Middleton's battery, supported by the 20th Foot and Brasyer's Sikhs, and occupied in quick succession, and with but slight resistance, the Residency, the Machi Bhawan, and the great Imambara, thus taking in reverse the defences which had been thrown up by the enemy for the protection of the two bridges. As Outram pushed on, the rebels retreated, some across the stone bridge towards Fyzabad, and some through the city towards the Musabagh. They made two attacks to cover their retirement, one on Walpole's piquets, which enabled a large number (20,000 it was said) to get away in the Fyzabad direction, and another on the Alambagh, which was much more serious, for the garrison had been reduced to less than a thousand men, and the rebels' force was considerable, consisting of Infantry, Cavalry and Artillery. They attacked with great determination, and fought for four hours and a half before they were driven off.

It was not a judicious move on Sir Colin's part to send the Cavalry miles away from Lucknow just when they could have been so usefully employed on the outskirts of the city. This was also appreciated when too late, and both brigades were ordered to return, which they did on the 17th. Even then the Cavalry were not made full use of, for instead of both brigades being collected on the Lucknow bank of the river, which was now the sole line of retreat left open to the enemy (the bridges being in our possession), one only (Campbell's) was sent there Hope Grant being directed to take up his old position on the opposite side of the Gumti, from which we had the mortification of watching the rebels streaming into the open country from the Musabagh, without the smallest attempt being made by Campbell to stop or pursue them. His brigade had been placed on the enemy's line of retreat on purpose to intercept them, but he completely failed to do what was expected of him. We, on our side, could do nothing, for an unfordable river flowed between us and the escaping mutineers.†

* Consisting of the 23rd Fusiliers, 79th Highlanders, and 1st Bengal Fusiliers.

† Captain Wale, a gallant officer who commanded a newly raised corps of Sikh Cavalry, lost his life on this occasion. He persuaded Campbell to let him follow up the enemy, and was shot dead in a charge. His men behaved extremely well, and one of them, by name Ganda Sing, saved the life of the late Sir Robert Sandeman, who was a subaltern in the regiment. The same

There was one more fight in Lucknow. The Moulvie* of Fyzabad (who from the first was one of the prominent leaders of the rebellion) had returned at the head of a considerable force, and had placed himself in a strongly-fortified position in the very centre of the city. It was not without a severe struggle that he was dislodged by the 93rd Highlanders and 4th Punjab Infantry under Lugard. The brunt of the fighting fell upon the last-named regiment, the gallant Commander (Wilde) of which, and his second in command,† were severely wounded. The Moulvie made his escape, but his followers were pursued, and many of them were cut up. Thus at last the city was cleared of rebels, and we were once more masters in Lucknow.

On the 22nd March Hope Grant was ordered to proceed to Kursi, a small town about twenty-five miles off between the Sitapur and Fyzabad roads, reported to be occupied in force by the enemy.

We started at midnight with a brigade of Infantry, 1,000 Cavalry, two troops of Horse Artillery, and eight heavy guns and mortars. We were delayed some hours by the heavy guns and their escort (the 53rd Foot) taking a wrong turn when leaving the city, which resulted in the enemy being warned of our approach in time to clear out before we arrived.

On hearing they had gone, Hope Grant pushed on with the mounted portion of the force, and we soon came in sight of the enemy in full retreat. The Cavalry, commanded by Captain Browne,‡ was ordered to pursue. It consisted of Browne's own regiment (the 2nd Punjab Cavalry), a squadron of the 1st Punjab Cavalry under Captain Cosserat, and three Horse Artillery guns. At the end of two miles, Browne came upon a body of the mutineers formed up on an open plain. The

---

man, two years later, saved the late Sir Charles Macgregor's life during the China war, and when I was Commander-in-Chief in India I had the pleasure of appointing him to be my Native Aide-de-Camp. Granda Sing, who has now the rank of Captain and the title of *Sirdar Bahadur*, retired last year with a handsome pension and a small grant of land.

* A Mahomedan Priest.

† Now General Cockburn Hood, C.B.

‡ Now General Sir Samuel Browne, V.C., G.C.B. This popular and gallant officer, well known to every Native in Upper India as '*Sām Brūn Sahib*,' and to the officers of the whole of Her Majesty's army as the inventor of the sword-belt universally adopted on service, distinguished himself greatly in the autumn of 1858. With 230 sabres of his own regiment and 350 Native Infantry, he attacked a party of rebels who had taken up a position at Nuria, a village at the edge of the Terai, about ten miles from Pilibhit. Browne managed to get to the rear of the enemy without being discovered; a hand-to-hand fight then ensued, in which he got two severe wounds—one on the knee, from which he nearly bled to death, the other on the left shoulder, cutting right through the arm. The enemy were completely routed, and fled, leaving their four guns and 300 dead on the ground. Browne was deservedly rewarded with the V.C.

GENERAL SIR SAMUEL BROWNE, V.C., G.C.B., K.C.S.I.

From
a photograph by Messrs. Elliott and Fry.

Cavalry charged through them three times, each time thinning their ranks considerably, but they never wavered, and in the final charge avenged themselves by killing Macdonnell (the Adjutant of the 2nd Punjab Cavalry), and mortally wounding Cosserat. I arrived on the ground with Hope Grant just in time to witness the last charge and the fall of these two officers, and deplorable as we felt their loss to be, it was impossible not to admire the gallantry and steadiness of the sepoys, every one of whom fought to the death.

As soon as Browne could get his men together, the pursuit of the enemy was continued; no further opposition was met with, and fourteen guns fell into our hands.

On the 24th we retraced our steps, halting for the night at the old cantonment of Muriao, where we buried poor Macdonnell. On the 25th we crossed the Gumti, and pitched our camp near the Dilkusha.

Lucknow was now completely in our possession, and our success had been achieved with remarkably slight loss, a result which was chiefly due to the scientific manner in which the siege operations had been carried on under the direction of our talented Chief Engineer, Robert Napier, ably assisted by Colonel Harness; and also to the good use which Sir Colin Campbell made of his powerful force of Artillery. Our casualties during the siege amounted to only 16 British officers, 3 Native officers, and 108 men killed; 51 British officers, 4 Native officers, and 540 men wounded, while 13 men were unaccounted for.

The capture of Lucknow, though not of such supreme importance in its consequences as the taking of Delhi, must have convinced the rebels that their cause was now hopeless. It is true than Jhansi had not yet fallen, and that the rest of Oudh, Rohilkand, and the greater part of Central India remained to be conquered, but there was no very important city in the hands of the enemy, and the subjugation of the country was felt to be merely a matter of time. Sir Hugh Rose, after a brilliant campaign, had arrived before Jhansi, columns of our troops were traversing the country in every direction, and the British Army had been so largely increased that, on the 1st of April, 1858, there were 96,000 British soldiers in India, besides a large body of reliable Native troops, some of whom, although hurriedly raised, had already shown that they were capable of doing good service—a very different state of affairs from that which prevailed six months before.

For some time I had been feeling the ill effects of exposure to the climate and hard work, and the doctor, Campbell Browne, had been urging me to go on the sick-list; that, of course, was out of the question until Lucknow had fallen. Now, however, I placed myself in Browne's hands, hoping that a change to the Hills was all that was needed to set me up; but the doctors insisted on a trip to England. It was a heavy blow to me to have to leave while there was still work to be done, but I had less hesitation than I should have had if most of my own immediate friends had not already gone. Several had been killed, others had left sick or wounded; Watson had gone to Lahore, busily engaged in raising a regiment of Cavalry;* Probyn was on his way home, invalided; Hugh Gough had gone to the Hills to recover from his wounds; and Norman and Stewart were about to leave Lucknow with Army Head-Quarters.

On the 1st April, the sixth anniversary of my arrival in India, I made over my office to Wolseley, who succeeded me as Deputy-Assistant Quartermaster-General on Hope Grant's staff, and towards the middle of the month I left Lucknow.

The Commander-in-Chief was most kind and complimentary when I took leave of him, and told me that, in consideration of my services, he would bestow upon me the first permanent vacancy in the Quartermaster-General's Department, and that he intended to recommend that I should be given the rank of Brevet Major so soon as I should be qualified by becoming a regimental Captain. I was, of course, much gratified by his appreciative words and kindly manner; but the brevet seemed a long way off, for I had only been a First Lieutenant for less than a year, and there were more than a hundred officers in the Bengal Artillery senior to me in that rank!

I marched to Cawnpore with Army Head-Quarters. Sir William Peel, who was slowly recovering from his wound, was of the party. We reached Cawnpore on the 17th, and the next day I said good-bye to my friends on the Chief's staff. Peel and I dined together on the 19th, when to all appearances he was perfectly well, but on going into his room the next morning I found he was in a high fever, and had some suspicious looking spots about his face. I went off at once in search of a doctor, and soon returned with one of the surgeons of the 5th Fusiliers, who, to my horror—for I had observed that Peel was nervous about himself—exclaimed with brutal frankness the moment he entered the room, 'You have got small-pox.' It was only too true. On being convinced that this was the case, I went to the chaplain, the Rev. Thomas Moore, and told him of Peel's condition. Without an instant's hesitation, he decided the invalid must come to his house to be taken care of. That afternoon I had the poor fellow carried over, and there I left him in the kind hands of Mrs. Moore, the *padre's* wife, who had, as a special case, been allowed to accompany her husband to Cawnpore. Peel died on the 27th. On the 4th May I embarked at Calcutta in the P. and O. steamer *Nubia*, without, alas! the friend whose pleasant companionship I had hoped to have enjoyed on the voyage.

* The present 13th Bengal Lancers

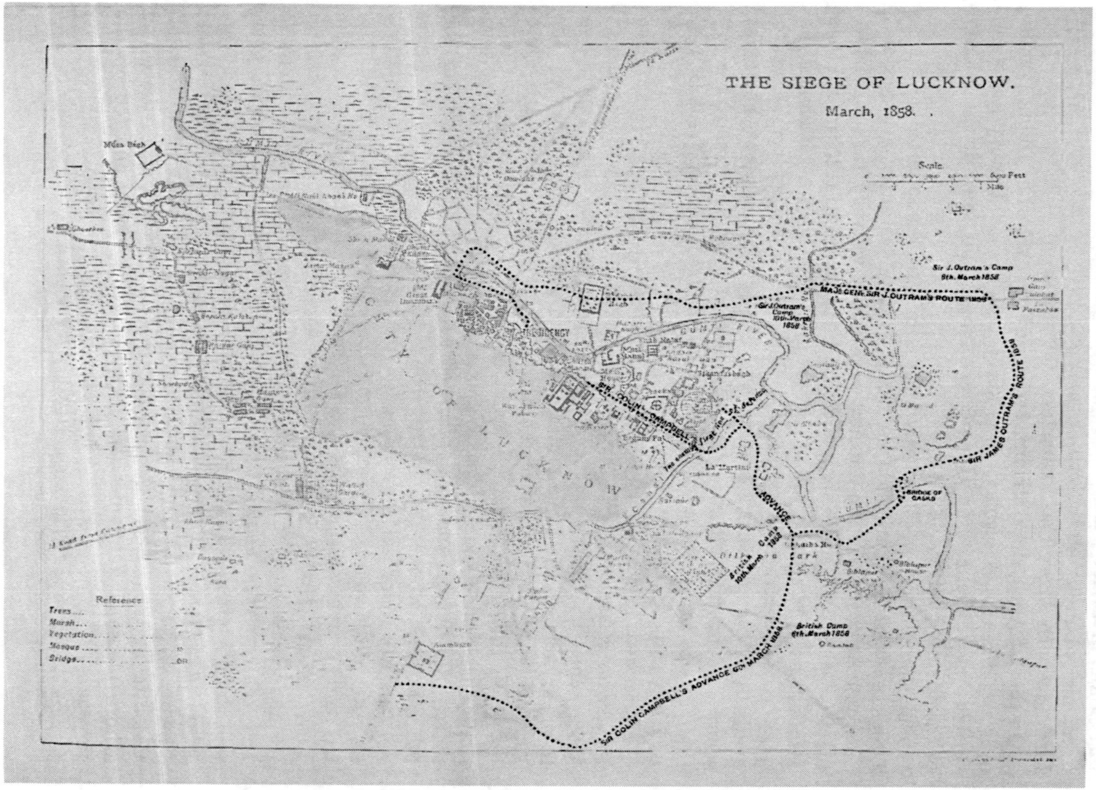
THE SIEGE OF LUCKNOW.
March, 1858.
Scale
Sir J. Outram's Camp 9th. March 1858
MAJ. GEN. SIR J. OUTRAM'S ROUTE 1858
SIR JAMES OUTRAM'S ROUTE 1858
GUMTI RIVER
BRIDGE OF CASAS
SIR COLIN CAMPBELL
ADVANCE
British Camp 10th. March 1858
British Camp 6th. March 1858
SIR COLIN CAMPBELL'S ADVANCE 6th MARCH 1858
CITY OF LUCKNOW
Reference
Trees
Marsh
Vegetation
Mosque
Bridge

CHAPTER XXX.

'What brought about the Mutiny?' and 'Is there any chance of a similar rising occurring again?' are questions which are constantly being put to me; I will now endeavour to answer them, though it is not a very easy task—for I feel that my book will be rendered more interesting and complete to many if I endeavour to give them some idea of the circumstances which, in my opinion, led to that calamitous crisis in the history of our rule in India, and then try to show how I think a repetition of such a disaster may best be guarded against.

The causes which brought about the Mutiny were so various, and some of them of such long standing, that it is difficult to point them out as concisely as I could wish; but I will be as brief as possible.

During the first years of our supremacy in India, Hindus and Mahomedans alike were disposed to acquiesce in our rule—the blessings of rest and peace after a long reign of strife and anarchy were too real not to be appreciated; but as time went by, a new generation sprang up by whom past miseries were forgotten, and those who had real grievances, or those who were causelessly discontented, were all ready to lay the blame for their real or fancied troubles on their foreign rulers. Mahomedans looked back to the days of their Empire in India, but failed to remember how completely, until we broke the Mahratta power, the Hindus had got the upper hand. Their Moulvies taught them that it was only lawful for true Mussulmans to submit to the rule of an infidel if there was no possibility of successful revolt, and they watched for the chance of again being able to make Islam supreme. The Hindus had not forgotten that they had ousted the Mahomedans, and they fancied that the fate of the British *raj* might also be at their mercy.

The late Sir George Campbell, in his interesting memoirs, says: 'The Mutiny was a sepoy revolt, not a Hindu rebellion.' I do not altogether agree with him; for, although there was no general rising of the rural population, the revolt, in my judgment, would never have taken place had there not been a feeling of discontent and disquiet throughout that part of the country from which our Hindustani sepoys chiefly came, and had not certain influential people been thoroughly dissatisfied with our system of government. This discontent and dissatisfaction were produced by a policy which, in many instances, the Rulers of India were powerless to avoid or postpone, forced upon them as it was by the demands of civilization and the necessity for a more enlightened legislation. Intriguers took advantage of this state of affairs to further their own ends. Their plan of action was to alienate the Native army, and to increase the general feeling of uneasiness and suspicion, by spreading false reports as to the intentions of the authorities in regard to the various measures which had been adopted to promote the welfare and prosperity of the masses. It can hardly be questioned that these measures were right and proper in themselves, but they were on that account none the less obnoxious to the Brahmin priesthood, or distasteful to the Natives generally. In some cases also they were premature, and in others they were not carried out as judiciously as they might have been, or with sufficient regard to the feelings and prejudices of the people.

The prohibition of *sati* (burning widows on the funeral pyres of their husbands); the putting a stop to female infanticide; the execution of Brahmins for capital offences; the efforts of missionaries and the protection of their converts; the removal of all legal obstacles to the remarriage of widows; the spread of western and secular education generally; and, more particularly, the attempt to introduce female education, were causes of alarm and disgust to the Brahmins, and to those Hindus of high caste whose social privileges were connected with the Brahminical religion. Those arbiters of fate, who were until then all-powerful to control every act of their co-religionists, social, religious or political, were quick to perceive that their influence was menaced, and that their sway would in time be wrested from them, unless they could devise some means for overthrowing our Government. They knew full well that the groundwork of this influence was ignorance and superstition, and they stood aghast at what they foresaw would be the inevitable result of enlightenment and progress. Railways and telegraphs were specially distasteful to the Brahmins: these evidences of ability and strength were too tangible to be pooh-poohed or explained away. Moreover, railways struck a direct blow at the system of caste, for on them people of every caste, high and low, were bound to travel together.

The fears and antagonism of the Brahmins being thus aroused, it was natural that they should wish to see our rule upset, and they proceeded to poison the minds of the people with tales of the Government's determination to force Christianity upon them, and to make them believe that the continuance of our power meant the destruction of all they held most sacred.

Nor was opportunity wanting to confirm, apparently, the truth of their assertions. In the gaols a system of messing had been established which interfered with the time-honoured custom of every man being allowed to provide and cook his own food. This innovation was most properly introduced as a matter of gaol discipline, and due care was taken that the food of the Hindu prisoners should be prepared by cooks of the same or superior caste. Nevertheless, false reports were disseminated, and the credulous Hindu population was led to believe that the prisoners' food was in future to be prepared by men of inferior caste, with the object of defiling and degrading those for whom it was prepared. The news of what was supposed to have happened in the gaols spread from town to town and from village to village, the belief gradually gaining ground that the people were about to be forced to embrace Christianity.

As the promiscuous messing story did not greatly concern the Mahomedans, other cries were made use of to create suspicion and distrust amongst the followers of the Prophet. One of these, which equally affected the Hindu and Mahomedan, was the alleged unfairness of what was known in India as the land settlement, under which system the right and title of each landholder to his property was examined, and the amount of revenue to be paid by him to the paramount Power, as owner of the soil, was regulated.

The rapid acquisition of territory by the East India Company, and the establishment of its supremacy as the sovereign Power throughout India, were necessarily effected by military operations; but as peace and order were established, the system of land revenue, which had been enforced in an extremely oppressive and corrupt manner under successive Native Rulers and dynasties, had to be investigated and revised. With this object in view, surveys were made, and inquiries instituted into the rights of ownership and occupancy, the result being that in many cases it was found that families of position and influence had either appropriated the property of their humbler neighbours, or evaded an assessment proportionate to the value of their estates. Although these inquiries were carried out with the best intentions, they were extremely distasteful to the higher classes, while they failed to conciliate the masses. The ruling families deeply resented our endeavours to introduce an equitable determination of rights and assessment of land revenue. They saw that it would put an end to the system of pillage and extortion which had been practised from time immemorial; they felt that their authority was being diminished, and that they would no longer be permitted to govern their estates in the same despotic manner as formerly. On the other hand, although the agricultural population generally benefited materially by our rule, they could not realize the benevolent intentions of a Government which tried to elevate their position and improve their prospects. Moreover, there were no doubt mistakes made in the valuation of land, some of it being assessed at too high a rate, while the revenue was sometimes collected in too rigid a manner, sufficient allowance not being made for the failure of crops. Then the harsh law for the sale of proprietary rights in land to realize arrears of land-tax was often enforced by careless revenue authorities in far too summary a manner. The peasantry of India were, and still are, ignorant and apathetic. Accustomed from the earliest days to spoliation and oppression, and to a periodical change of masters, they had some reason to doubt whether the rule of the Feringhis would be more permanent than that of the Moghuls or the Mahrattas. Much as a just and tolerant Government would have been to their advantage, they were unable to appreciate it, and if they had appreciated it, they were too timid and too wanting in organization to give it their open support. Under these social and political conditions, the passive attitude of the rural population failed to counterbalance the active hostility of a large section of the upper classes, and of their predatory followers, who for centuries had lived by plunder and civil war.

Another weighty cause of discontent, chiefly affecting the wealthy and influential classes, and giving colour to the Brahmins' accusation that we intended to upset the religion and violate the most cherished customs of the Hindus, was Lord Dalhousie's strict enforcement of the doctrine of the lapse of property in the absence of direct or collateral heirs, and the consequent appropriation of certain Native States, and the resumption of certain political pensions by the Government of India. This was condemned by the people of India as grasping, and as an unjustifiable interference with the institutions of the country, and undoubtedly made us many enemies.*

Later on, the annexation of Oudh, which was one of those measures forced on the Rulers of India in the interests of humanity and good government, and which could hardly have been longer delayed, created suspicion and apprehension amongst all the Native States. For more than sixty years Governor-General after Governor-General had pointed out the impossibility of a civilized Government tolerating in the midst of its possessions the misrule, disorder, and debauchery which were desolating one of the most fertile and thickly-populated districts in India.

As early as 1801 Lord Wellesley wrote: 'I am satisfied that no effectual security can be provided against the ruin of the province of Oudh until the exclusive management of the civil and military govern-

* In this matter it seems to me that Lord Dalhousie's policy has been unfairly criticized. The doctrine of lapse was no new-fangled theory of the Governor-General, but had been recognized and acted upon for many years by the Native dynasties which preceded the East India Company. Under the Company's rule the Court of Directors had investigated the subject, and in a series of despatches from 1834 to 1846 had laid down that, in certain cases, the selection and adoption of an heir by a Native Ruler was an incontestable right, subject only to the formal sanction of the suzerain Power, while in other cases such a procedure was optional, and could only be permitted as a special favour. Lord Dalhousie concurred in the view that each case should be considered and decided on its merits. His words were: 'The Government is bound in duty, as well as in policy, to act on every such occasion with the purest integrity, and in the most scrupulous observance of good faith. Where even a shadow of doubt can be shown, the claim should at once be abandoned. But where the right to territory by lapse is clear, the Government is bound to take that which is justly and legally its due, and to extend to that territory the benefits of our sovereignty, present and prospective.'

ment of that country shall be transferred to the Company under suitable provisions for the Nawab and his family.'

In 1831 Lord William Bentinck warned the King of Oudh that, unless he would consent to rule his territories in accordance with the principles of good government and the interest of the people, the East India Company would assume the entire administration of the province, and would make him a state prisoner.

In 1847 Lord Hardinge went in person to Lucknow and solemnly reiterated the warning, giving the King two years to reform his administration.

In 1851 Colonel Sleeman, the Resident at Lucknow, whose sympathy with the Rulers of Native States was thought to be even too great, and who was the last person to exaggerate the misrule existing in Oudh, reported to Lord Dalhousie that the state of things had become intolerable, and that, if our troops were withdrawn from Oudh, the landholders would in one month's time overrun the province and pillage Lucknow. It is true Sleeman, with his Native proclivities, did not contemplate annexation; his advice was to 'assume the administration,' but not to 'grasp the revenues of the country.' The same mode of procedure had been advocated by Henry Lawrence six years before in an article which appeared in the *Calcutta Review*. His words were: 'Let Oudh be at last governed, not for one man, the King, but for the King and his people. Let the administration of the country be Native; let not one rupee come into the Company's coffers.'

Sleeman was followed in 1854 by Colonel Outram, than whom he could not have had a more admirable successor, or one less likely to be unnecessarily hard upon a State which, with all its shortcomings, had been loyal to us for nearly a century. Colonel Outram, nevertheless, fully endorsed the views of his predecessor. General Low, the then Military Member of Council, who twenty years before, when Resident at Lucknow, had deprecated our assuming even temporarily the administration of Oudh, thinking our action would be misunderstood by the people, now also stated his conviction that 'it was the paramount duty of the British Government to interfere at once for the protection of the people of Oudh.

In summing up the case, Lord Dalhousie laid three possible courses of action before the authorities in England. The King of Oudh might be forced to abdicate, his province being incorporated in the British dominions; or he might be maintained in his royal state as a subsidized Prince, the actual government being permanently transferred to the East India Company; or the transfer of the government to the East India Company might be for a limited period only. The Governor-General recommended the second course, but the Court of Directors and Her Majesty's Ministers decided to adopt the first, and requested Lord Dalhousie to carry out the annexation before he resigned his office.

This measure, so long deferred and so carefully considered, could hardly, in my opinion, have been avoided by a civilized and civilizing Government. It was at last adopted with the utmost reluctance, and only after the experiment of administering a province for the benefit of the Natives, without annexing it, had been tried in the Punjab and had signally failed. To use Lord Dalhousie's words, it was amply justified on the ground that 'the British Government would be guilty in the sight of God and man if it were any longer to aid in sustaining by its countenance an administration fraught with suffering to millions.' But the Natives generally could not understand the necessity for the measure, or believe in the reasons which influenced us; many of them, therefore, considered it an unprovoked usurpation, and each Ruler of a Native State imagined that his turn might come next.

Thus, the annexation of Oudh in one sense augmented that weakness in our position as an eastern Power which, so to speak, had its source in our strength. So long as there was a balance of power between ourselves and Native States—Mahratta, Rajput, Sikh, or Mahomedan—they were prevented by their mutual jealousies and religious differences from combining against us; but when that balance was destroyed and we became the paramount Power in India, the period of danger to us began, as was prophesied by the far-seeing Malcolm in the early days of our first conquests. We had now become objects of suspicion and dread to all the lesser Powers, who were ready to sink their own disputes in the consideration of the best means to check the extension of our rule and overthrow our supremacy; while we, inflated by our power and satisfied with our apparent security, became more dogmatic and uncompromising in enforcing principles which, though sound and just in themselves, were antipathetic to Native ideas and traditions. By a great many acts and measures we made them feel how completely our ideas differed from theirs. They preferred their own, and strongly resented our increasing efforts to impose ours upon them. Even those amongst the Native Princes who were too enlightened to believe that we intended to force our religion upon them and change all their customs, felt that their power was now merely nominal, and that every substantial attribute of sovereignty would soon disappear if our notions of progress continued to be enforced.

At a time when throughout the country there existed these feelings of dissatisfaction and restless suspicion, it was not to be expected that the most discontented and unfriendly of the Native Rulers would not seize the opportunity to work us mischief. The most prominent of these amongst the Mahomedans were the royal family of Delhi and the ex-King of Oudh, and, amongst the Hindus, Dundu Pant, better known by English people as the 'Nana Sahib.'

All three considered themselves badly treated, and no doubt, from their point of view, their grievances were not altogether groundless.

The King of Oudh's I have already indicated, and when his province was annexed, he was removed to Calcutta. Having refused the yearly pension of twelve lakhs* of rupees, offered to him, and declined to sign the treaty by which his territory was made over to the British Government, he sent his mother, his son, and his brother to England to plead his cause for him.

The most influential of the three discontented Rulers, or, at all events, the one whom the rebellious of all castes and religions were most inclined to put forward as their nominal leader, was the head of the Delhi royal family, by name Bahadur Shah. He was eighty years old in 1857, and had been on the throne for twenty years. His particular grievance lay in the fact of our decision that on his death the title of King, which we had bestowed on the successors of the Moghul Emperor, should be abolished, and his family removed from Delhi.

In the early part of the century Lord Wellesley pointed out the danger of allowing a Mahomedan Prince, with all the surroundings of royalty, to remain at the seat of the old Moghul government, but the question was allowed to remain in abeyance until 1849, when Lord Dalhousie reconsidered it, and obtained the sanction of the authorities in England to the removal of the Court from Delhi to a place about fourteen miles off, where the Kutub tower stands. At the same time the Heir Apparent was to be told that on his father's death the title of King of Delhi would cease.

Lord Dalhousie had been only a short time in India when he took up this question, and he could not properly have appreciated the estimation in which the Natives held the King of Delhi, for he wrote in support of his proposals 'that the Princes of India and its people had become entirely indifferent to the condition of the King or his position.' But when the decision of the British Government on the subject reached India, he had been more than two years in the country, and although his views as to the desirability of the measure remained unchanged, the experience he had gained enabled him to gauge more accurately the feelings of the people, and, with the advice of his Council, he came to the conclusion that it would be wiser to let affairs remain *in statu quo* during Bahadur Shah's lifetime. The royal family were informed accordingly, and an agreement was drawn up, signed, sealed, and witnessed, by which the Heir Apparent accepted the conditions to be imposed upon him on the death of his father, who was to be allowed to remain in Delhi during his lifetime, with all the paraphernalia of royalty.

However satisfactory this arrangement might be to the Government of India, to every member of the Delhi royal family it must have seemed oppressive and humiliating to the last degree. Outwardly

* In those days £120,000.

they appeared to accept the inevitable quietly and submissively, but they were only biding their time, and longing for an opportunity to throw off the hated English yoke. The war with Persia in 1856 seemed to offer the chance they wanted. On the pretence that the independence of Herat was threatened by the Amir of Kabul, the Persians marched an army to besiege that place. As this act was a violation of our treaty with Persia made three years before, Her Majesty's Government directed that an army should be sent from India to the Persian Gulf. The troops had scarcely left Bombay before the Lieutenant-Governor of the North-West Provinces was warned by a Native correspondent that the King of Delhi was intriguing with the Shah of Persia. At the same time a proclamation was posted on the walls of the Jama Masjid (Shah Jehan's famous mosque at Delhi), to the effect that a Persian army was coming to relieve India from the presence of the English, and calling on all true believers to rise and fight against the heretics. Reports were also diligently circulated of our being defeated on the shores of the Persian Gulf, and the people were made to believe that their opportunity had arrived, and that the time was now favourable for a successful rebellion.

Of the three principal movers in the events which immediately preceded the Mutiny, the Nana Sahib was by far the most intelligent, and had mixed most with Europeans. He was the adopted son and heir of the last of the Peshwas, the Chiefs of the Mahratta confederacy. His cause of dissatisfaction was the discontinuance to him of a pension which, at the close of the Mahratta war in 1818, was granted to the Peshwa, on the clear understanding that it was to cease at his death. The Peshwa died in 1851, leaving the Nana an enormous fortune; but he was not content. The lapse of the pension, to which he was not entitled, rankled in his breast, and when all his efforts to get it restored to him proved of no avail, he became thoroughly disgusted and disaffected. After failing to obtain in India a reconsideration of the decision of the Government on the subject, he sent to England as confidential agent a Mahomedan of the name of Azimula Khan, who remained three years in Europe, residing for the most part in London; but he also visited Paris, Constantinople, and the Crimea, arriving at the latter place when we, in alliance with the French, were besieging Sebastopol. He was a man of no rank or position in his own country, a mere agent of the Nana's, but he was received into the best English society, was everywhere treated as a royal Prince, and became engaged to a young English girl, who agreed to follow him to India to be married. All this was revealed by the correspondence to which I have referred as having been found in the Nana's palace of Bithur. The greater number of these letters were from people in England—not a few from ladies of rank and position. One elderly dame called him her dear eastern son. There were numerous letters from his English *fiancée*, and two from a Frenchman of the name of Lafont,* relating to some business with the French settlement of Chandernagore, with which he had been entrusted by Azimula Khan, acting for the Nana. Written, as these letters were, immediately before the Mutiny, in which the Nana was the leading spirit, it seems probable that '*les principales choses*,' to which Lafont hopes to bring satisfactory answers, were invitations to the disaffected and disloyal in Calcutta, and perhaps the French settlers at Chandernagore, to assist in the effort about to be made to throw off the British yoke. A portion of the correspondence was unopened, and there were several letters in Azimula's own handwriting which had not been despatched. Two of these were to Omar Pasha at Constantinople, and told of the sepoys' discontent and the troubled state of India generally. That the Nana was intriguing with the King of Delhi, the Nawab of Oudh, and other great personages, has been proved beyond a doubt, although at the time he was looked upon by the British residents at Cawnpore as a perfectly harmless individual, in spite of its being known that he considered himself

* 'Benares,
'*April* 4, 1857.

'MON CHER AZIMULA KHAN,

'Je suis parti de Cawnpore le premier du mois et suis arrivé ici ce matin, je partirai ce soir et serai à Chandernagore le 7 au matin, dans la journée je ferai une visite au Gouverneur et le lendemain irai à Calcutta, je verrai notre Consul Général. Ecrivez-moi et adressez-moi vos lettres, No. 123, Dhurumtollah. Je voudrais que vous puissiez m'envoyer des fonds au moins 5 ou 600 Rs. sans retard, car je ne resterai à Calcutta que le temps nécessaire pour tout arranger et *le bien arranger*. Je suppose 48 heures à Calcutta et deux ou trois jours au plus à Chandernagore, ne perdez pas de temps mais répondez de suite. Pour toutes les principales choses les réponses seraient satisfaisantes, soyez-en assuré.

'Faites en sorte de me répondre sans délai afin que je ne sois pas retenu à Calcutta.

'Présentez mes compliments respectueux.

'Rappelez-moi au souvenir de Baba Sahib, et croyez moi,

'Votre bien dévoué
'A. LAFONT.

'Mon adresse à Chandernagore, "Care of Mesdames Albert."

'N.B.—Mais écrivez-moi à *Calcutta*, car je serai chaque jour là, en chemin de fer, je fais le trajet en 20 minutes. Si vous avez quelque chose de pressé à me communiquer vous le pouvez faire par télégraph en Anglais seulement.
'A. L.'

'Chandernagore,
'*April* 9, 1857.

'MON CHER AZIMULA KHAN,

'J'ai tout arrangé, *j'apporterai une lettre*, et elle sera satisfaisante *cette lettre* me sera donnée le 14 et le 15 je partirai pour Cawnpore. Mes respects à son Altesse,

'Votre tout dévoué
'A. LAFONT.'

aggrieved on account of his having been refused the continuance of the pension, and because a salute of guns (such as it is the custom to give to Native Princes on entering British territory) had not been accorded to him.

While the spirit of rebellion was thus being fostered and stirred into active existence throughout the country, it was hardly to be hoped that the Native army would be allowed to remain unaffected by a movement which could not easily attain formidable proportions without the assistance of the Native soldiers, who themselves, moreover, had not remained unmoved spectators of all that had happened during the previous thirty or forty years. The great majority of the sepoys were drawn from the agricultural classes, especially in the province of Oudh, and were therefore directly interested in all questions connected with rights of property, tenure of land, etc.; and questions of religion and caste affected them equally with the rest of the population.

Quietly, but surely, the instigators of rebellion were preparing the Native army for revolt. The greatest cunning and circumspection were, however, necessary to success. There were so many opposing interests to be dealt with, Mahomedans and Hindus being as violently hostile to each other, with regard to religion and customs, as they were to us. Soldiers, too, of all ranks had a great stake in their profession. Some had nearly served their time for their pensions, that greatest of all attractions to the Native to enter the army, for the youngest recruit feels that, if he serves long enough, he is sure of an income sufficient to enable him to sit in the sun and do nothing for the rest of his days—a Native's idea of supreme happiness. The enemies of our rule generally, and the fanatic in particular, were, however, equal to the occasion. They took advantage of the widespread discontent to establish the belief that a systematic attack was to be made on the faith and habits of the people, whether Hindu or Mahomedan, and, as a proof of the truth of their assertions, they alleged that the Enfield cartridges which had been recently issued to the army were greased with a mixture of cows' fat and lard, the one being as obnoxious to the Hindu as the other is to the Mahomedan. The news spread throughout the Bengal Presidency; the sepoys became alarmed, and determined to suffer any punishment rather than pollute themselves by biting the contaminating cartridge, as their doing so would involve loss of caste, which to the Hindu sepoy meant the loss of everything to him most dear and sacred in this world and the next. He and his family would become outcasts, his friends and relations would look on him with horror and disgust, while eternal misery, he believed, would be his doom in the world to come.

It has been made quite clear that a general belief existed amongst the Hindustani sepoys that the destruction of their caste and religion had been finally resolved upon by the English, as a means of forcing them to become Christians, and it seems extraordinary that the English officers with Native regiments were so little aware of the strength of this impression amongst their men.

The recent researches of Mr. Forrest in the records of the Government of India prove that the lubricating mixture used in preparing the cartridges was actually composed of the objectionable ingredients, cows' fat and lard, and that incredible disregard of the soldiers' religious prejudices was displayed in the manufacture of these cartridges. When the sepoys complained that to bite them would destroy their caste, they were solemnly assured by their officers that they had been greased with a perfectly unobjectionable mixture. These officers, understanding, as all who have come in contact with Natives are supposed to understand, their intense abhorrence of touching the flesh or fat of the sacred cow or the unclean pig, did not believe it possible that the authorities could have been so regardless of the sepoys' feelings as to have allowed it to be used in preparing their ammunition: they therefore made this statement in perfect good faith. But nothing was easier than for the men belonging to the regiments quartered near Calcutta to ascertain, from the low-caste Native workmen employed in manufacturing the cartridges at the Fort William arsenal, that the assurances of their officers were not in accordance with facts, and they were thus prepared to credit the fables which the sedition-mongers so sedulously spread abroad, to the effect that the Government they served and the officers who commanded them had entered into a deliberate conspiracy to undermine their religion.

Notwithstanding all the evil influence brought to bear on the Native army, I do not think that the sepoys would have proved such ready instruments in the hands of the civilian intriguers, had that army been organized, disciplined, and officered in a satisfactory manner, and had there been a sufficient proportion of British troops in India at the time. To the great preponderance of Native, as compared with British, troops may be attributed the fact that the sepoys dared to break into open mutiny. Moreover, the belief of the Natives in the invincibility of the British soldier, which formerly enabled small numbers of Europeans to gain victories over large Native armies, had been seriously weakened by the lamentable occurrences at Kabul during the first Afghan war, terminating in the disastrous retreat in the winter of 1841-42.

To add to the exalted idea the sepoys were beginning to entertain of their own importance, they were pampered by their officers and the civil Government to a most absurd extent, being treated under all circumstances with far greater consideration than the European soldiers. For instance, in the time of Lord William Bentinck flogging was abolished in the Native army,* while still in full swing amongst

* Flogging was re-introduced in 1845.

British soldiers, and sepoys were actually allowed to witness the humiliation of their white comrades when this degrading form of punishment was inflicted upon them.

In the early days of our connexion with India, we had no need for an army. Living, as we were, on sufferance in a foreign land for commercial purposes, armed men were only required to guard the factories. As these factories increased in size and importance, these armed men were given a semi-military organization, and in time they were formed into levies as a reserve to the few Europeans entertained by the merchants, to enable them to hold their own against the French, who were then beginning to dispute with us for supremacy in southern India. When employed in the field, the Native troops were associated with a varying proportion of British soldiers, but the number of the latter was limited by the expense of their maintenance, the difficulty of supplying them from England, and the unadvisability of locking up a part of the British army in distant stations, which at that time were very inaccessible and generally unhealthy. Native troops were therefore raised in continually increasing numbers, and after the battle of Plassey the Native army was rapidly augmented, especially in the Bengal Presidency; and, trained and led as it was by British officers, it achieved remarkable successes.

During the thirteen years preceding the Mutiny, the Native army, numbering 217,000 men and 176 guns, was increased by 40,000 men and 40 guns, but no addition was made to the small British force of 38,000 until 1853, when one regiment was added to each Presidency, or less than 3,000 soldiers in all. This insignificant augmentation was subsequently more than neutralized by the withdrawal of six British regiments from India to meet the requirements of the Crimean and Persian wars. Lord Dalhousie, Governor-General in 1854, saw the danger of this great preponderance of Native troops. He represented that the annexations and conquests which had taken place during his tenure of office necessitated a proportional increase of British soldiers; he protested against the withdrawal of a single European regiment, either on account of the war with Russia or for operations in the Persian Gulf, and he solemnly warned Her Majesty's Government that the essential element of our strength in India was the presence of a large number of British troops.

No attention, however, was paid to Lord Dalhousie's representations by the authorities in England, who doubtless thought they understood the requirements of India better than the Governor-General, with his more than six years' experience of the country. In spite of his remonstrances, two regiments were ordered to England, and four were sent later to the Persian Gulf, with the result which I have already stated.

When the Mutiny broke out, the whole effective British force in

India only amounted to 36,000 men, against 257,000 Native soldiers,* a fact which was not likely to be overlooked by those who hoped and strived to gain to their own side this preponderance of numerical strength, and which was calculated to inflate the minds of the sepoys with a most undesirable sense of independence. An army of Asiatics, such as we maintain in India, is a faithful servant, but a treacherous master; powerfully influenced by social and religious prejudices with which we are imperfectly acquainted, it requires the most careful handling; above all, it must never be allowed to lose faith in the prestige or supremacy of the governing race. When mercenaries feel that they are indispensable to the maintenance of that authority which they have no patriotic interest in upholding, they begin to consider whether it would not be more to their advantage to aid in overthrowing that authority, and if they decide that it would be, they have little scruple in transferring their allegiance from the Government they never loved, and have ceased to fear, to the power more in accordance with their own ideas, and from which, they are easily persuaded, they will obtain unlimited benefits.

A fruitful cause of dissatisfaction in our Native army, and one which pressed more heavily upon it year by year, as our acquisitions of territory in northern India became more extended, was the sepoy's liability to service in distant parts of India, entailing upon him a life amongst strangers differing from him in religion and in all their customs, and far away from his home, his family, and his congenial surroundings—a liability which he had never contemplated except in the event of war, when extra pay, free rations and the possibility of loot, would go far to counterbalance the disadvantages of expatriation. Service in Burma, which entailed crossing the sea, and, to the Hindu, consequent loss of caste, was especially distasteful. So great an objection, indeed, had the sepoys to this so-called 'foreign service,' and so difficult did it become to find troops to relieve the regiments, in consequence of the bulk of the Bengal army not being available for service beyond the sea, that the Court of Directors sanctioned Lord Canning's proposal that, after the 1st September, 1856, 'no Native recruit shall be accepted who does not at the time of his enlistment undertake to serve beyond the sea whether within the territories of the Company or beyond them.' This order, though absolutely necessary, caused the greatest dissatisfaction amongst the Hindustani sepoys, who looked upon it as one of the measures introduced by the *Sirkar* for the forcible, or rather fraudulent, conversion of all the Natives to Christianity.†

* This does not include the bodies of armed and trained police, nor the lascars attached to the Artillery as fighting men. These amounted to many thousands.

† In a letter to Lord Canning, which Sir Henry Lawrence wrote on the 9th May, 1857, he gave an interesting account of a conversation he had had

That the long-existing discontent and growing disloyalty in our Native army might have been discovered sooner, and grappled with in a sufficiently prompt and determined manner to put a stop to the Mutiny, had the senior regimental and staff officers been younger, more energetic, and intelligent, is an opinion to which I have always been strongly inclined. Their excessive age, due to a strict system of promotion by seniority which entailed the employment of Brigadiers of seventy, Colonels of sixty, and Captains of fifty, must necessarily have prevented them performing their military duties with the energy and activity which are more the attributes of younger men, and must have destroyed any enthusiasm about their regiments, in which there was so little hope of advancement or of individual merit being recognized. Officers who displayed any remarkable ability were allowed to be taken away from their own corps for the more attractive and better-paid appointments appertaining to civil employ or the Irregular service. It was, therefore, the object of every ambitious and capable young officer to secure one of these appointments, and escape as soon as possible from a service in which ability and professional zeal counted for nothing.*

So far as I understand the causes which led to the rebellion of 1857, I have now answered the question, 'What brought about the Mutiny?' The reply to the second question, 'Is there any chance of a similar rising occurring again?' must be left to another chapter.

---

with a Brahmin Native officer of the Oudh Artillery, who was most persistent in his belief that the Government was determined to make the people of India Christians. He alluded especially to the new order about enlistment, our object being, he said, to make the sepoys go across the sea in order that they might be obliged to eat what we liked; and he argued that, as we had made our way through India, had won Bhartpur, Lahore, etc., by fraud, so it might be possible that we would mix bone-dust with grain sold to Hindus. Sir Henry Lawrence was quite unable to convince the Native officer; he would give us credit for nothing, and although he would not say that he himself *did* or did *not* believe, he kept repeating, 'I tell you Natives are all like sheep; the leading one tumbles, and down all the rest roll over him.'

* It is curious to note how nearly every military officer who held a command or high position on the staff in Bengal when the Mutiny broke out, disappeared from the scene within the first few weeks, and was never heard of officially again. Some were killed, some died of disease, but the great majority failed completely to fulfil the duties of the positions they held, and were consequently considered unfit for further employment. Two Generals of divisions were removed from their commands, seven Brigadiers were found wanting in the hour of need, and out of the seventy-three regiments of Regular Cavalry and Infantry which mutinied, only four Commanding officers were given other commands, younger officers being selected to raise and command the new regiments.

CHAPTER XXXI.

THE India of to-day is altogether a different country from the India of 1857. Much has been done since then to improve the civil administration, and to meet the legitimate demands of the Native races. India is more tranquil, more prosperous, and more civilized than it was before the Mutiny, and the discipline, efficiency, and mobility of the Native army have been greatly improved. Much, however, still remains to be done, and a good deal might with advantage be undone, to secure the contentment of the Natives with our rule.

Our position has been materially strengthened by the provision of main and subsidiary lines of communication by road and railway; by the great network of telegraphs which now intersects the country; and by the construction of canals. These great public works have largely increased the area of land under cultivation, minimized the risk of famine, equalized the prices of agricultural produce, and developed a large and lucrative export trade. Above all, while our troops can now be assembled easily and rapidly at any centre of disturbance, the number of British soldiers has been more than doubled and the number of Native soldiers has been materially reduced. Moreover, as regards the Native equally with the British army of India, I believe that a better feeling never existed throughout all ranks than exists at present.

Nevertheless, there are signs that the spirit of unrest and discontent which sowed the seeds of the Mutiny is being revived. To some extent this state of things is the natural result of our position in India, and is so far unavoidable, but it is also due to old faults reappearing—faults which require to be carefully watched and guarded against, for it is certain that, however well disposed as soldiers the men in our ranks may be, their attitude will inevitably be influenced by the feelings of the people generally, more especially should their hostility be aroused by any question connected with religion.

For a considerable time after the Mutiny we became more cautious and conciliatory in administrative and legislative matters, more intent on doing what would keep the Chiefs and Rulers satisfied, the masses contented, and the country quiet, than on carrying out our own ideas. Gradually this wholesome caution is being disregarded. The Government has become more and more centralized, and the departmental spirit very strong. Each department, in its laudable wish for progress and advancement, is apt to push on measures which are obnoxious to the Natives, either from their not being properly understood, or from their being opposed to their traditions and habits of life, thus entailing the sacrifice of many cherished customs and privileges. Each department admits in theory the necessity for caution, but in practice presses for liberty of action to further its own particular schemes.

Of late years, too, the tendency has been to increase the number of departments and of secretariat offices under the supreme Government, and this tendency, while causing more work to devolve on the supreme Government than it can efficiently perform, results in lessening the responsibility of provincial Governments by interference in the management of local concerns. It is obvious that in a country like India, composed as it is of great provinces and various races differing from one another in interests, customs, and religions, each with its own peculiar and distinct necessities, administrative details ought to be left to the people on the spot. The Government of India would then be free to exercise a firm and impartial control over the Empire and Imperial interests, while guiding into safe channels, without unduly restraining, intelligent progress.

In times of peace the administration is apt to fall too exclusively into the hands of officials whose ability is of the doctrinaire type; they work hard, and can give logical and statistical reasons for the measures they propose, and are thus able to make them attractive to, and believed in by, the authorities. But they lack the more perfect knowledge of human nature, and the deeper insight into, and greater sympathy with, the feelings and prejudices of Asiatics, which those possessed in a remarkable degree who proved by their success that they had mastered the problem of the best form of government for India. I allude to men like Thomas Munro, Mountstuart Elphinstone, John Malcolm, Charles Metcalfe, George Clerk, Henry and John Lawrence, William Sleeman, James Outram, Herbert Edwardes, John Nicholson, and many others. These administrators, while fully recognizing the need for a gradual reform, understood the peculiarities of our position in the east, the necessity for extreme caution and toleration, and a 'live and let live' policy between us and the Natives. The sound and broad views of this class of public servant are not always appreciated either in India or England, and are too often put aside as unpractical, obstructive, and old-fashioned.

Amongst the causes which have produced discontent of late years, I would mention our forest laws and sanitary regulations, our legislative and fiscal systems—measures so necessary that no one interested in the prosperity of India could cavil at their introduction, but which are so absolutely foreign to Native ideas, that it is essential they should be applied with the utmost gentleness and circumspection.

I think, also, that the official idea of converting the young Princes and Nobles of India into English gentlemen by means of English tutors and English studies should be carried out with great care and caution. It has not hitherto invariably succeeded, and the feeling in many States is strongly opposed to it. The danger of failure lies in the wholesome restraint of the tutor being suddenly removed, and in the young Prince being left at too early an age to select his advisers and companions. The former, perhaps not unnaturally, are interested in proving that the training of their young Ruler by his European governor or tutor has not resulted in good either to himself or his people, while the latter are too often of the lowest class of European adventurers.

The proceedings and regulations of the Forest Department, desirable as they may be from a financial and agricultural point of view, have provoked very great irritation in many parts of India. People who have been accustomed from time immemorial to pick up sticks and graze their cattle on forest lands, cannot understand why they should now be forbidden to do so, nor can they realize the necessity for preserving the trees from the chance of being destroyed by fire, a risk to which they were frequently exposed from the Native custom of making use of their shelter while cooking, and of burning the undergrowth to enrich the grazing.

The action taken by the Government in sanitary matters has also aroused much ill-feeling and apprehension. Sanitary precautions are entirely ignored in eastern countries. The great majority of the people can see no good in them, and no harm in using the same tank for drinking purposes and for bathing and washing their clothes. The immediate surroundings of their towns and villages are most offensive, being used as the general receptacles for dead animals and all kinds of filth. Cholera, fever, and other diseases, which carry off hundreds of thousands every year, are looked upon as the visitation of God, from which it is impossible, even were it not impious to try, to escape; and the precautionary measures insisted upon by us in our cantonments. and at the fairs and places of pilgrimage, are viewed with aversion and indignation. Only those who have witnessed the personal discomfort and fatigue to which Natives of all ages and both sexes willingly submit in their struggle to reach some holy shrine on the occasion of a religious festival, while dragging their weary limbs for many hundreds of miles along a hot, dusty road, or being huddled for hours together in a crammed and stifling railway carriage, can have any idea of the bitter disappointment to the pilgrims caused by their being ordered to disperse when cholera breaks out at such gatherings, without being given the opportunity of performing their vows or bathing in the sacred waters.*

* Few acts have been more keenly resented than the closing of the great Hurdwar Fair in the autumn of 1892, on account of a serious outbreak of cholera. It was looked upon by the Natives as a direct blow aimed at their religion, and as a distinct departure from the religious tolerance promised in Her Majesty's proclamation of 1858. The mysterious mud marks on mango-trees in Behar have been attributed by some to a self-interested motive on the part of certain priests to draw the attention of Hindus to the sanctity of some temple outside the limits of British jurisdiction, where the devotees would be

Further, our legislative system is based on western ideas, its object being to mete out equal justice to the rich and poor, to the Prince and peasant. But our methods of procedure do not commend themselves to the Indian peoples. Eastern races are accustomed to a paternal despotism, and they conceive it to be the proper function of the local representatives of the supreme Power to investigate and determine on the spot the various criminal and civil cases which come under the cognizance of the district officials. Legal technicalities and references to distant tribunals confuse and harass a population which, with comparatively few exceptions, is illiterate, credulous, and suspicious of underhand influence. An almost unlimited right of appeal from one court to another, in matters of even the most trivial importance, not only tends to impair the authority of the local magistrate, but gives an unfair advantage to the wealthy litigant whose means enable him to secure the services of the ablest pleader, and to purchase the most conclusive evidence in support of his claims. For it must be remembered than in India evidence on almost any subject can be had for the buying, and the difficulty, in the administration of justice, of discriminating between truth and falsehood is thereby greatly increased. Under our system a horde of unscrupulous pleaders has sprung up, and these men encourage useless litigation, thereby impoverishing their clients, and creating much ill-feeling against our laws and administration.

Another point worthy of consideration is the extent to which, under the protection of our legal system, the peasant proprietors of India are being oppressed and ruined by village shop-keepers and money-lenders. These men advance money at a most exorbitant rate of interest, taking as security the crops and occupancy rights of the cultivators of the soil. The latter are ignorant, improvident, and in some matters, such as the marriage ceremonies of their families, inordinately extravagant. The result is that a small debt soon swells into a big one, and eventually the aid of the law courts is invoked to oust the cultivator from a holding which, in many cases, has been in the possession of his ancestors for hundreds of years. The money-lender has his accounts to produce, and these can hardly be disputed, the debtor as a rule being unable to keep accounts of his own, or, indeed, to read or write. Before the British dominion was established in India, the usurer no doubt existed, but his opportunities were fewer, his position more precarious, and his operations more under control than they are at present. The money-lender then knew that his life would not be safe if he exacted too high

at liberty to assemble in any numbers without being troubled by officious inspectors, and where they could remain as long as they pleased, irrespective of the victims daily claimed by cholera, that unfailing avenger of the neglect of sanitary laws in the east.

interest for the loans with which he accommodated his customers, and that if he became too rich, some charge or other would be trumped up against him, which would force him to surrender a large share of his wealth to the officials of the State in which he was living. I do not say that the rough-and-ready methods of Native justice in dealing with money-lenders were excusable or tolerable, but at the same time I am inclined to think that, in granting these men every legal facility for enforcing their demands and carrying on their traffic, we may have neglected the interests of the agriculturists, and that it might be desirable to establish some agency under the control of Government, which would enable the poorer landholders to obtain, at a moderate rate of interest, advances proportionate to the security they had to offer.*

Another danger to our supremacy in India is the license allowed to the Native press in vilifying the Government and its officials, and persistently misrepresenting the motives and policy of the ruling Power. In a free country, where the mass of the population is well educated, independent, and self-reliant, a free press is a most valuable institution, representing as it does the requirements and aspirations of important sections of the community, and bringing to light defects and abuses in the social and political system. In a country such as Great Britain, which is well advanced in the art of self-government, intolerant and indiscriminate abuse of public men defeats its own object, and misstatements of matters of fact can be at once exposed and refuted. Like most of the developments of civilization which are worth anything, the English press is a plant of indigenous growth, whereas in India the Native press is an exotic which, under existing conditions, supplies no general want, does nothing to refine, elevate, or instruct the people, and is used by its supporters and promoters—an infinitesimal part of the population—as a means of gaining its selfish ends, and of fostering sedition, and racial and religious animosities. There are, I am afraid, very few Native newspapers actuated by a friendly or impartial spirit towards the Government of India, and to Asiatics it seems incredible that we should permit such hostile publications to be scattered broadcast over the country, unless the assertions were too true to be disputed, or unless we were too weak to suppress them. We gain neither credit nor gratitude for our tolerant attitude towards the Native press—our forbearance is misunderstood; and while the well-disposed are amazed at our inaction, the disaffected rejoice at being allowed to promulgate baseless insinuations and misstatements

* The proposal would seem to be quite a practical one, for I read in the *Times* of the 28th November, 1894, that the Government of New Zealand invited applications for Consols in connexion with the scheme for granting loans at a reasonable rate of interest to farmers on the security of their holdings.

which undermine our authority, and thwart our efforts to gain the goodwill and confidence of the Native population.

Yet another danger to the permanence of our rule in India lies in the endeavours of well-intentioned faddists to regulate the customs and institutions of eastern races in accordance with their own ideas. The United Kingdom is a highly civilized country, and our habits and convictions have been gradually developed under the influences of our religion and our national surroundings. Fortunately for themselves, the people of Great Britain possess qualities which have made them masters of a vast and still expanding Empire. But these qualities have their defects as well as their merits, and one of the defects is a certain insularity of thought, or narrow-mindedness—a slowness to recognize that institutions which are perfectly suitable and right for us may be quite unsuited, if not injurious, to other races, and that what may not be right for us to do is not necessarily wrong for people of a different belief, and with absolutely different traditions and customs.

Gradually the form of Government in the United Kingdom has become representative and democratic, and it is therefore assumed by some people, who have little, if any, experience of the east, that the Government of India should be guided by the utterances of self-appointed agitators who pose as the mouth-pieces of an oppressed population. Some of these men are almost as much aliens* as ourselves, while others are representatives of a class which, though intellectually advanced, has no influence amongst the races in whom lies the real strength of India. Municipal self-government has been found to answer well in the United Kingdom, and it is held, therefore, that a similar system must be equally successful in India. We in England consume animal food and alcoholic liquors, but have no liking for opium; an effort has accordingly been made to deprive our Asiatic fellow-subjects, who, as a rule, are vegetarians, and either total abstainers or singularly abstemious in the matter of drink, of a small and inexpensive stimulant, which they find necessary to their health and comfort. British institutions and ideas are the embodiment of what long experience has proved to us to be best for ourselves; but suddenly to establish these institutions and enforce these ideas on a community which is not prepared for them, does not want them, and cannot understand them, must only lead to suspicion and discontent. The Government of India should, no doubt, be progressive in its policy, and in all things be guided by the immutable principles of right, truth, and justice; but these principles ought to be applied, not necessarily as we should apply them in England, but with due regard to the social peculiarities and religious prejudices of the people whom it ought to be our aim to make better and happier.

* I allude to the Parsis, who came from Persia, and whose religion and customs are as distinct from those of the Natives of India as are our own.

It will be gathered from what I have written that our administration, in my opinion, suffers from two main defects. First, it is internally too bureaucratic and centralizing in its tendencies; and, secondly, it is liable to be forced by the external pressure of well-meaning but irresponsible politicians and philanthropists to adopt measures which may be disapproved of by the authorities on the spot, and opposed to the wishes, requirements, and interests of the people. It seems to me that for many years to come the best form of government for India will be the intelligent and benevolent despotism which at present rules the country. On a small scale, and in matters of secondary importance, representative institutions cannot perhaps do much harm, though I am afraid they will effect but little good. On a large scale, however, such a system of government would be quite out of place in view of the fact that ninety-nine out of every hundred of the population are absolutely devoid of any idea of civil responsibility, and that the various races and religious sects possess no bond of national union.

In reply, then, to the question, 'Is there any chance of a Mutiny occurring again?' I would say that the best way of guarding against such a calamity is—

By never allowing the present proportion of British to Native soldiers to be diminished or the discipline and efficiency of the Native army to become slack.

By taking care that men are selected for the higher civil and military posts whose self-reliance, activity, and resolution are not impaired by age, and who possess a knowledge of the country and the habits of the peoples.

By recognizing and guarding against the dogmatism of theorists and the dangers of centralization.

By rendering our administration on the one hand firm and strong, on the other hand tolerant and sympathetic; and last, but not least, by doing all in our power to gain the confidence of the various races, and by convincing them that we have not only the determination, but the ability to maintain our supremacy in India against all assailants.

If these cardinal points are never lost sight of, there is, I believe, little chance of any fresh outbreak disturbing the stability of our rule in India, or neutralizing our efforts to render that country prosperous, contented, and thoroughly loyal to the British Crown.

CHAPTER XXXII.

I TRAVELLED home *viâ* Corfu, Trieste, Venice, and Switzerland, arriving in England towards the end of June. The intense delight of getting 'home' after one's first term of exile can hardly be exaggerated, and certainly cannot be realized, save by those who have gone through the exile, and been separated, as I had been for years, from all that made the happiness of my early life. Every English tree and flower one comes across on first landing is a distinct and lively pleasure, while the greenness and freshness are a delicious rest to the eye, wearied with the deadly whitey-brown sameness of dried-up sandy plains, or the all-too gorgeous colouring of eastern cities and pageants.

My people were living in Ireland, in the county of Waterford, so after only a short sojourn in London, for the very necessary re-equipment of the outer man, I hastened over there. I found my father well and strong for a man of seventy-four, and to all appearance quite recovered from the effects of his fifty years of Indian service, and, to my great joy, my mother was looking almost as young, and quite as beautiful, as I had left her six years before. My little sister, too, always an invalid, was very much as when I had parted from her—full of loving-kindness for everyone, and, though unable to move without help, perfectly happy in the many resources she had within herself, and the good she was able to do in devoting those resources to the benefit of others.

There, too, I found my fate, in the shape of Nora Bews, a young lady living with a married sister not far from my father's place, who a few months later consented to accompany me on my return to India. The greater part of my leave was, therefore, spent in Ireland.

During the winter months I hunted with the Curraghmore hounds, and was out with them the day before Lord Waterford was killed. We had no run, and at the end of the day, when wishing us good-bye, he said: 'I hope, gentlemen, we shall have better luck next time.' 'Next time' there was 'better luck' as regarded the hunting, but the worst of all possible luck for Lord Waterford's numerous friends; in returning home after a good run, and having killed two foxes, his horse stumbled over quite a small ditch, throwing his rider on his head; the spinal cord was snapped and the fine sportsman breathed his last in a few moments.

I was married on the 17th May, 1859, in the parish church of Waterford. While on our wedding tour in Scotland, I received a command to be present on the 8th June at Buckingham Palace, when the Queen proposed to honour the recipients of the Victoria Cross by presenting the decoration with Her Majesty's own hands.

Being anxious that my wife should be spared the great heat of a journey to India in July, the hottest month of the year in the Red Sea, and the doctors being very decided in their opinion that I should not return so soon, I had applied for a three months' extension of leave, and quite calculated on getting it, so our disappointment was great when the answer arrived and I found that, if I took the extension, I should lose my appointment in the Quartermaster-General's Depart-

LADY ROBERTS.

(WIFE OF SIR ABRAHAM ROBERTS).

From
a sketch by Carpenter.

ment. This, we agreed, was not to be thought of, so there was nothing for it but to face the disagreeable necessity as cheerfully as we could. We made a dash over to Ireland, said good-bye to our relations, and started for India on the 27th June.

The heat in the Red Sea proved even worse than I had anticipated. Our captain pronounced it the hottest trip he had ever made. Twice was the ship turned round to steam against the wind for a short time in order to revive some of the passengers, who were almost suffocated.

We passed the wreck of the *Alma*, a P. and O. vessel which had struck on a coral reef not far from Mocha. The wreck had happened in the dead of night, and there had been only time to get the passengers into the boats, in which they were rowed to another reef near at hand; there they had remained for eighty hours in their scanty night garments, and without the smallest shelter, until rescued by a friendly steamer. The officers and crew were still on the rock when we passed, endeavouring to get up the mails and the passengers' property. We supplied them with provisions and water, of which they were badly in need, and then had to leave them in their extremely uncomfortable position.

We could not complain of lack of air after we passed Aden, for we forthwith encountered the south-west monsoon, then at its height, and on entering the Bay of Bengal we experienced something very nearly akin to a cyclone. We broke our rudder; the lightships, on which a certain number of pilots were always to be found, had all been blown out to sea; and as we had only just sufficient coal to take us up the Hugli when the pilot should appear, we did not dare to keep up steam. Thus we had to remain at the mercy of the winds and waves for some days, until at length a brig with a pilot on board was sent to look for us, and eventually we arrived in Calcutta, in rather a dilapidated condition, on the 30th July.

We were not cheered by the orders I found awaiting me, which were to proceed to Morar and join Brigadier-General Sir Robert Napier, then in command of the Gwalior district. Morar in the month of August is one of the hottest places in India, and my wife was considerably the worse for our experiences at sea. However, a Calcutta hotel never has many attractions, and at that time of year was depressing and uncomfortable to the last degree; in addition, I had rather a severe attack of my old enemy, Peshawar fever, so we started on our journey 'up country' with as little delay as possible.

The railway at that time was not open further than Raniganj; thence we proceeded for a hundred miles in a 'dâk-ghari,' when, changing into doolies, we continued our journey to Hazaribagh, a little cantonment about twenty miles off the main road, where some relations of mine were living; but a day or two after our arrival at their hospitable house, I was ordered back to Calcutta.

I left my wife with our kind friends, and retraced my steps in considerable elation of spirits, for the China expedition was even then being talked about, and I hoped this sudden summons might possibly mean that I was to be sent with it in some capacity. On reaching Calcutta, however, I was told that I had been appointed to organize and take charge of the large camp to be formed for the triumphal progress which Lord Canning proposed to make through Oudh, the North-West Provinces, and the Punjab, with the view of meeting the principal feudatory Chiefs, and rewarding those who had been especially loyal during the rebellion. I was informed that the tents were in store in the arsenal at Allahabad, and that the camp must be ready at Cawnpore on the 15th October, on which date the Viceroy would arrive, and a day or two later commence his stately procession towards Lucknow.

While I was in England a Royal Proclamation had announced to the people of India that the Queen had taken over the government of their country, which had hitherto been held in trust for Her Majesty by the Honourable East India Company. This fact had been publicly proclaimed, with befitting ceremony, throughout the length and breadth of the land, on the 1st November, 1858. At the same time it was announced that Her Majesty's representative in India was henceforth to be styled Viceroy and Governor-General of India, and it was with the object of emphasizing this Proclamation, and impressing the Native mind with the reality of Queen Victoria's power and authority, that Lord Canning decided on undertaking this grand tour.

While in Calcutta on this occasion, I was offered a post in the Revenue Survey Department. I refused it, for, although as a married man the higher pay was a tempting bait, the recollection of the excitement and variety of the year of the Mutiny was still fresh upon me, and I had no wish to leave the Quartermaster-General's Department. I therefore started for Allahabad, picking up my wife *en route.*

It was then the middle of the rains, and the bridge of boats over the Jumna had been taken down, so we had to cross in ferry-boats—dâk-gharis, horses, and all—rather a perilous-looking proceeding, for the river was running at a tremendous pace, and there was some difficulty in keeping the boat's head straight. At Allahabad we stayed with a brother officer of mine in the fort, while I was getting the camp equipage out of store, and the tents pitched for inspection. There had not been a large camp for many years, and everything in India deteriorates so rapidly, that I found most of the tents in such a state of mildew and decay as to render it necessary to renew them almost entirely before they could be used for such a splendid occasion as that of the first Viceroy's first march through the re-conquered country.

From Allahabad we proceeded to Cawnpore, where I had a busy time arranging for the multifarious requirements of such an enormous camp; and sometimes I despaired of its being completed by the appointed date. However, completed it was; and on the 15th October Lord and

Lady Canning arrived, and expressed themselves so pleased with all the arrangements, and were so kindly appreciative of the exertions I had made to be ready for them by the appointed time, that I felt myself fully rewarded for all my trouble.

The next day I took my wife to call upon Lady Canning, whose unaffected and simple, yet perfectly dignified manner completely charmed her, and from that day she was devoted, in common with everyone who was at all intimately associated with Lady Canning, to the gentle, gracious lady, who was always kindness itself to her.

On the 18th the Viceroy made his first march towards Lucknow. The camp equipage was in duplicate, so that everyone on arriving at the new halting-place found things exactly the same as in the tents they had left.

The camp occupied a considerable space, for, in addition to the Viceroy's large *entourage*, ground had to be provided for the Commander-in-Chief and the officers of Army Head-Quarters, who were marching with us; then there were the post-office, telegraph, workshops, *toshikhana*,* commissariat, and a host of other offices to be accommodated, beside the escort, which consisted of a battery of Horse Artillery, a squadron of British Cavalry, a regiment of British Infantry, a regiment of Native Cavalry, a regiment of Native Infantry, and the Viceroy's Bodyguard. For the Viceroy, his staff, guests, and secretaries alone, 150 large tents were pitched in the main street, and when we came to a station the duplicate tents were also pitched. For the transport of this portion of the camp equipage 80 elephants and 500 camels were required.†

It is very difficult to give any idea of the extraordinary spectacle a big camp like this presents on the line of march. The followers, as a rule, are accompanied by their wives and families, who are piled upon the summits of laden carts, or perched on the loads borne by the baggage animals. In the two camps marching together (Lord Canning's and Lord Clyde's) there could not have been less than 20,000 men, women, and children—a motley crowd streaming along about four-and-twenty miles of road, for the day's march was usually about twelve miles, and before every one had cleared out of the camp occupied the night before, the advance guard had begun to arrive on the ground to

* The depository for jewels and other valuables kept for presentation to Native Chiefs at durbars.

† The following details will give some idea of the magnitude of the arrangements required for the Viceroy's camp alone. Besides those above mentioned there were 500 camels, 500 bullocks and 100 bullock carts for transport of camp equipage, 40 *sowari* (riding) elephants, 527 coolies to carry the glass windows belonging to the larger tents, 100 *bhistics*, and 40 sweepers for watering and keeping the centre street clean. These were in addition to the private baggage animals, servants, and numberless riding and driving horses, for all of which space and shelter had to be provided.

be occupied the next day. The strictest discipline had to be maintained, or this moving colony would have been a serious calamity to the peasantry, for the followers would have spread themselves over the country like a flight of locusts, and taken anything they could lay their hands on, representing themselves as *Mulk-i-Lord-Sahib-Ke-Naukar*,* whom according to immemorial tradition it was death to resist. The poor, frightened country-people, therefore, hardly ventured to remonstrate at the *mahouts* walking off with great loads of their sugar-cane, or to object to the compulsory purchase of their farm produce for half its value. There was a great deal of this kind of raiding at the commencement of the march, and I was constantly having complaints made to me by the villagers; but after I had inflicted on the offenders a few summary and tolerably severe punishments, and made the peasants to understand it was not the *Mulk-i-Lord-Sahib's* wish that they should submit to such treatment from his servants, order was established, and I had very rarely any trouble.

Our first halt was at Lucknow. Sir Hope Grant was commanding the division, and had established himself very comfortably in the Dilkusha. He had written asking me to bring my wife straight there and stay with him during the Viceroy's visit, as it was still very hot in tents during the day. An invitation which I gladly accepted, for it was pleasant to think of being with my old General again, and I wanted to introduce him to my wife.

The next day, the 22nd October, the state entry was made into Lucknow. It must have been an imposing sight, that long array of troops and guns, with Lord Canning in the centre, accompanied by the Commander-in-Chief, and surrounded by their respective staffs in full uniform. Lord Canning, though at that time not given to riding, looked remarkably well on horseback; for he had a fine head and shoulders, and sat his horse well; on foot, his height, not being quite in proportion, rather detracted from the dignity of his presence.

I headed the procession, leading it across the Charbagh bridge, the scene of Havelock's fiercest encounter, past the Machi Bhawan, and the Residency, to the Kaisarbagh, in front of which were drawn up in a body the Talukdars of Oudh, who had with difficulty been persuaded to come and make their obeisance, for, guiltily conscious of their disloyalty during the rebellion, they did not feel at all sure that the rumours that it was intended to blow them all away from guns, or to otherwise summarily dispose of them, were not true. They salaamed respectfully as the Viceroy passed, and the cavalcade proceeded to the Martinière park, where the camp, which I had pitched the previous day, lay spread before us, in all the spotless purity of new white tents glistening in a flood of brilliant sunshine. The streets through which

* Servants of the Lord of the Country, or Governor-General.

we passed were crowded with Natives, who—cowed, but not tamed—looked on in sullen defiance, very few showing any sign of respect for the Viceroy.

Sir William and Lady Mansfield, and several other people from our camp were also staying with Sir Hope Grant, and that evening the whole Dilkusha party went to a state dinner given by Lord and Lady Canning. The latter was a delightful hostess; the shyest person was set at ease by her kindly, sympathetic manner, and she had the happy knack of making her guests feel that her entertainments were a pleasure to herself—the surest way of rendering them enjoyable to those she entertained.

I made use of the next week, which was for me a comparatively idle time, to take my wife over the ground by which we had advanced two years before, and explain to her the different positions held by the enemy. She was intensely interested in visiting the Sikandarbagh, the Shah Najaf, the mess-house, and, above all, that glorious memorial of almost superhuman courage and endurance, the Residency, ruined, roofless, and riddled by round shot and bullets. Very little had then been done towards opening out the city, and the surroundings of the Residency were much as they had been during the defence—a labyrinth of streets and lanes; it was therefore easier for the stranger to realize exactly what had taken place than it is now that the landmarks have been cleared away, and well-laid-out gardens and broad roads have taken the place of jungle and narrow alleys.

On the 26th the Viceroy held a grand durbar for the reception of the Talukdars. It was the first function of the sort I had witnessed, and was an amusing novelty to my wife, who, with Lady Canning and some of the other ladies in camp, viewed the proceedings from behind a semi-transparent screen, it not being considered at that time the thing for ladies to appear at ceremonials when Natives were present. The whole scene was very impressive, though not as brilliant in colouring as it would have been in any other part of India, owing to the Chiefs of Oudh being clad in simple white, as is the custom amongst Rajputs.

The Talukdars, to the number of one hundred and sixty, were ushered to their places in strict order of seniority, the highest in rank being the last to arrive. They were arranged in a half semicircle on the right of the Viceroy's chair of state, while on the left the Europeans were seated according to their official rank. When all was ready, the words 'Attention! Royal salute! Present arms!' were heard without, warning those within of the Viceroy's approach, and, as the bugles sounded and the guns thundered forth their welcome, Lord Canning, accompanied by the Commander-in-Chief, and preceded by their staffs, entered the tent.

Everyone rose, and remained standing until the great man took his seat, when the Foreign Secretary came forward, and, making a low bow, informed His Excellency that all who had been summoned to attend the durbar were present. The Chiefs were then brought up and introduced to the Viceroy one by one; each made a profound obeisance, and, as a token of allegiance, presented an offering of gold mohurs, which, according to etiquette, the Viceroy just touched by way of acknowledgment. The presents from the Government to the Chiefs were then handed in on trays, and placed on the ground in front of each, the value of the present being regulated according to the rank and position of the recipient. This part of the ceremony being over, the Viceroy rose and addressed the Talukdars.

After expressing his pleasure at meeting them in their own country, he gave them an assurance that, so long as they remained faithful to the Government, they should receive every consideration; he told them that a new era had commenced in Oudh, and that henceforth they would be allowed to revert to the conditions under which they had held their estates prior to the annexation of the province. When Lord Canning had finished speaking, a translation of his address in Urdu was read to the Talukdars by Mr. Beadon, the Foreign Secretary; *atar* and *pan** were then handed round, and the Viceroy took his departure with the same formalities as those with which the durbar had been opened.

There is some excuse to be made for the attitude of the Talukdars, who, from their point of view, had little reason to be grateful to the British Government. These powerful Chiefs, whose individual revenues varied from £10,000 to £15,000 a year, and who, in their jungle fastnesses, often defied their sovereign's troops, had suddenly been deprived of all the authority which in the confusion attending a long period of misgovernment they had gradually usurped, as well as of a considerable proportion of the landed property which, from time to time, they had forcibly appropriated. The conversion of feudal Chiefs into ordinary law-abiding subjects is a process which, however beneficial to the many, is certain to be strenuously resisted by the few.

In March, 1858, when Lucknow was captured, a Proclamation was issued by the Government of India confiscating the proprietary rights in the soil. The object in view was not merely to punish contumacious Chiefs, but also to enable the Government to establish the revenue system on a sounder and firmer footing. Talukdars who submitted were to receive their possessions as a free gift direct from the Government; while those who had done good service, whether men of Oudh or strangers, might be rewarded by grants of confiscated property.

The Proclamation was considered in many influential quarters too

* A few drops of attar of roses are given to each person, and a small packet of *pan*, which is composed of slices of betel-nut smeared with lime and wrapped in a leaf of the betel-tree.

arbitrary and sweeping a measure; Outram protested against it, and Lord Ellenborough (the President of the Board of Control) condemned it; but Lord Canning was backed up by the British public, and Lord Ellenborough resigned to save his Cabinet from being wrecked. That Outram and Ellenborough took the right view of the case is, I think, shown by the fact that Lord Canning cancelled the Proclamation on his first visit to Lucknow. By that time he had come to recognize that the Talukdars had reasonable grounds for their discontent, and he wisely determined to take a step which not only afforded them the greatest relief and satisfaction, but enlisted their interest on the side of Government. From that day to this, although, from time to time, subsequent legislation has been found necessary to save the peasantry from oppression, the Chiefs of Oudh have been amongst the most loyal of Her Majesty's Indian subjects.

We remained a few days longer at Lucknow. Lord and Lady Canning entertained all the residents, while a ball was given by the latter in the Chatta Manzil to the strangers in camp, and the city and principal buildings were illuminated in the Viceroy's honour with those curious little oil-lamps which are the most beautiful form of illumination, the delineation of every line, point, and pinnacle with myriads of minute lights producing a wonderfully pretty effect.

On the 29th the first march was made on the return journey to Cawnpore. My duty was to go on ahead, select the best site for the next day's camping-ground, and make all necessary arrangements for supplies, etc. I waited till the Viceroy had given his orders, and then my wife and I started off, usually in the forenoon; sometimes we remained till later in the day, lunching with one or other of our friends in camp, and on very rare occasions, such as a dinner-party at the Viceroy's or the Commander-in-Chief's, we drove on after dinner by moonlight. But that was not until we had been on the march for some time and I felt that the head Native in charge of the camp was to be trusted to make no mistake. It was a life of much interest and variety, and my wife enjoyed the novelty of it all greatly.

Lord Canning held his second durbar at Cawnpore on the 3rd November, when he received the principal Chiefs of Bundelkand, the Maharaja of Rewa, the Maharaja of Benares, and a host of lesser dignitaries.

It was on this occasion that, in accordance with the Proclamation which had already announced that the Queen had no desire to extend her territorial possessions, and that the estates of Native Princes were to be scrupulously respected, the Chiefs were informed that the right of adoption was conceded to them. This meant that, in default of male issue, they were to be allowed to adopt sons according to the Indian custom of adoption, and that the British Government would recognize the right of the chosen heir to succeed as Ruler of the State as well as to inherit the personal property of the Chief by whom he had been adopted. There had been no clear rule on this point previously, each case having been considered on its own merits, but the doctrine that adoption should not be recognized, and that, in default of natural heirs, the State should lapse and be annexed by the supreme Government, had been enforced in a good many instances. Lord Canning's announcement therefore caused the liveliest satisfaction to certain classes throughout India, and did more than any other measure to make the feudatory Princes believe in the sincerity of the amnesty Proclamation.*

Our next move was to Fatehgarh, eight marches from Cawnpore, where, on the 15th November, a third durbar was held, at which was received, amongst other leading men of Rohilkand whose services were considered worthy of acknowledgment, the Nawab of Rampur, who had behaved with distinguished loyalty in our time of trouble. This Mahomedan Nobleman's conduct was the more meritorious in that the surrounding country swarmed with rebels, and was the home of numbers of the mutinous Irregular Cavalry, while the close proximity of Rampur to Delhi, whence threats of vengeance were hurled at the Nawab unless he espoused the King's cause, rendered his position extremely precarious.

From Fatehgarh we proceeded to Agra, nine marches, only halting on Sundays, and consequently everyone appreciated being stationary there for a few days. The camp was pitched on the parade-ground, the scene of the fight of the 10th October, 1857. Here the Viceroy

* The question of Native Rulers having the right to adopt heirs was first brought to Lord Canning's notice by the three Phulkian chiefs—Patiala, Jhind and Nabha—who jointly requested in 1858 that the right of adoption might be accorded to them as a reward for the services they had rendered during the Mutiny. The request was refused at the time on the ground that it had never been the custom of the country, though it had occasionally been done. Since then, however, Lord Canning had come to see that the uncertainty which prevailed as to the rights of succession was harassing to the owners of land, and undesirable in many ways, and he urged upon the Secretary of State that some distinct rule on the subject might with advantage be laid down. He wrote as follows: 'The crown of England stands forth the unquestioned Ruler and paramount Power in all India, and is now for the first time brought face to face with its feudatories. There is a reality in the suzerainty of the Sovereign of England which has never existed before, which is not only felt, but eagerly acknowledged by the Chiefs. A great convulsion has been followed by such a manifestation of our strength as India has never seen; and if this in its turn be followed by an act of general and substantial grace, over and above the special rewards which have already been given to those whose services deserve them, the measure will be seasonable and appreciated.' Lord Canning's proposals met with the cordial approval of Her Majesty's Government, and his announcement at Cawnpore rejoiced the hearts of the Chiefs, one of whom, the Maharaja of Rewa, was a leper and had no son. He said, on hearing the Viceroy's words, 'They dispel an evil wind which has long been blowing upon me.'

received some of the bigger potentates, who were accompanied by large retinues, and, as far as the *spectacle* went, it was one of the grandest and most curious gatherings we had yet witnessed.

The occasions are rare on which a Viceroy has the opportunity of receiving in durbar the great vassals of our Indian Empire, but when these assemblies can be arranged they have a very useful effect, and should not be looked upon as mere empty ceremonials. This was especially the case at a time when the country had so recently been convulsed by intestine war, and when the Native Princes were anxiously considering how their prospects would be affected by Her Majesty's assumption of the administration of India.

The Chief of highest rank on this occasion was the Maharaja of Gwalior, who, as I have already stated, influenced by his courageous Minister, Dinkar Rao, had remained faithful to us. Like most Mahratta Princes of that time, he was very imperfectly educated. Moreover, he was possessed of a most wayward disposition, frequently threatening, when thwarted in any way, to throw up the reins of government, and take refuge in the jungle; manners he had none.

Next came the enlightened head of the Princely house of Jaipur, the second in importance of the great Chiefs of Rajputana.

He was succeeded by the Karaoli Raja, whose following was the most quaint of all. Amongst the curious signs of his dignity he had on his escort four tigers, each chained on a separate car, and guarded by strange-looking men in brass helmets.

The Maharao Raja of Ulwar was the next to arrive, seated on a superb elephant, eleven feet high, magnificently caparisoned with cloth-of-gold coverings, and chains and breastplates of gold. He was a promising-looking lad who had succeeded to his estate only two years before; but he soon fell into the hands of low intriguers, who plundered his pominions and so oppressed his people that the British Government had to take over the management of his State.

After Ulwar came the Nawab of Tonk, the descendant of an adventurer from Swat, on the Peshawar border, who had become possessed of considerable territory in Rajputana. The Nawab stood by us in the Mutiny, when his capital was plundered by Tantia Topi.

The sixth in rank was the Jât Ruler of Dholpur, a bluff, coarse-looking man, and a very rude specimen of his race.

Last of all arrived the Nawab of Jaora, a handsome, perfectly-dressed man of considerable refinement of manner, and with all the courtesy of a well-bred Mahomedan. Though a feudatory of the rebellious Holkar of Indore, he kept aloof from all Mahratta intrigues, and behaved well to us.

Some of the highest of the Rajput Chiefs declined to attend, alleging as an excuse the distance of their capitals from Agra; but the truth is that these Rulers, the best blood of India, had never bowed their heads to any Power, not even that of the Moghul, and they considered it would be derogatory to their dignity to obey the summons of the representative of a sovereign, of whom they considered themselves the allies and not the mere feudatories.*

Those of the Chieftains attending this durbar who had shown conspicuous loyalty during the rebellion were not allowed to leave without receiving substantial rewards. Sindhia had territory bestowed on him to the value of £30,000 a year. Jaipur was given the confiscated property of Kôt Kāsim, yielding £5,000 a year, while others were recompensed according to the importance of the services rendered.

CHAPTER XXXIII.

We remained at Agra until the 9th December. There was so much of beauty and interest in and around the place, that Lady Canning found a wealth of subjects for her facile pencil, and was well content to remain there. There were the usual banquets to the residents, and entertainments given by the Agra people to those in camp, one of them being a party in the Taj gardens, to give us an opportunity of seeing the tomb by moonlight, when it certainly looks its loveliest. My wife was more delighted even than I had anticipated with the perfect beauty of the Taj and the exquisite little mosque in the fort, the Moti-Masjid. I greatly enjoyed showing her all that was worth seeing, and witnessing her pleasure on first viewing these wonderful works of art.

There was no halt again, except the usual one on Sunday, until we reached Meerut on the 21st December.

Three marches from Agra a fire broke out in Lady Canning's tent soon after she had retired for the night, caused by the iron pipe of the stove, which passed through the side of the tent, becoming over-heated. Lady Canning's tents were on one side of the big dining-tent, and the Viceroy's on the other. Immediately on perceiving the fire, Lady Canning ran across to awaken her husband, but the Native sentry, who did not know her or understand a word of what she was saying, would not let her in, and, in despair of being able to make anyone hear, she rushed off to the tent of Sir Edward Campbell, the Military Secretary, which was nearest her own. She succeeded in awaking him, and then flew back to try and save some of her own treasures. The first thing she thought of was her portfolio of drawings, which she dragged out-

* These Rajput Chiefs, however, accepted Lord Lytton's invitation to attend the Imperial Assemblage at Delhi on the 1st January, 1877, and having once given their allegiance to the 'Empress of India,' they have since been the most devotedly loyal of Her Majesty's feudatory Princes.

side; but it had already been partially burned, and most of the valuable and characteristic sketches she had made at the different durbars were destroyed. She next tried to rescue her jewels, many of which she had worn the night before; her pearls were lying on the dressing-table, and she was only just in time to save them; one of the strings had caught fire, and several of the pearls were blackened. She swept them off the table into a towel, and threw them into a tub of water standing outside. Her wardrobe was completely destroyed. More damage would have been done had not the Private Secretary, Mr. Lewin Bowring, on the alarm being given, hurried to the dining-tent, and, with great presence of mind, ordered the Native Cavalry sentry to cut the ropes, causing it to fall at once, and preventing the fire from spreading. Some office boxes and records were destroyed, but nothing more. We were as usual in the advance camp, and did not hear what had happened until next morning, when Lady Canning arrived dressed in Lady Campbell's clothes; and as Lady Canning was tall, and Lady Campbell was short, the effect was rather funny.

Christmas was spent at Meerut, where I met several of my brother officers, amongst others my particular friend Edwin Johnson, whom I had the great pleasure of introducing to my wife. With scarcely an exception, my friends became hers, and this added much to the happiness of our Indian life.

Delhi, our next halting-place, was certainly not the least interesting in our tour. Lord Canning was anxious to understand all about the siege, and visited the different positions; the Ridge and its surroundings, the breaches, and the palace, were the chief points of interest. There were two 'Delhi men' besides myself to explain everything to him, Sir Edward Campbell, who was with the 60th Rifles throughout, and one of the best officers in the regiment, and Jemmy Hills, who had now become the Viceroy's Aide-de-camp; while in Lord Clyde's camp there were Norman, Stewart, and Becher.

I had, of course, taken my wife to the scenes of the fights at Agra, Aligarh, and Bulandshahr, but Delhi had the greatest fascination for her. It is certainly an extraordinarily attractive place, setting aside the peculiar interest of the siege. For hundreds of years it had been the seat of Government under Rulers of various nationalities and religions; few cities have the remains of so much pomp and glory, and very few bear the traces of having been besieged so often, or could tell of so much blood spilt in their defence, or of such quantities of treasure looted from them. When Tamerlane captured Delhi in 1398 the city was given over to massacre for five days, 'some streets being rendered impassable by heaps of dead'; and in 1739 the Persian conqueror, Nadir Shah, after sacking the place for fifty-eight days and massacring thousands of its inhabitants, carried off thirty-two millions sterling of booty.

Although the fierce nature of the struggle that Delhi had gone through in 1857 was apparent everywhere, the inhabitants seemed now to have forgotten all about it. The city was as densely populated as it had ever been; the Chandni Chauk was gay as formerly with draperies of bright-coloured stuffs; jewellers and shawl-merchants carried on their trades as briskly as ever, and were just as eager in their endeavours to tempt the *Sahib log* to spend their money as if trade had never been interrupted; so quickly do Orientals recover from the effects of a devastating war.

We left Delhi on the 3rd January, 1860, marching *viâ* Karnal. When at this place my wife went to see Lady Canning, as she often did if we remained at all late in camp. On this particular occasion she found her busy with the English mail, which had just arrived, so she said she would not stay then, but would come next day instead. Lady Canning, however, would not let my wife go until she had read her part of a letter from Lady Waterford, which she thought would amuse her. It was in answer to one from Lady Canning, in which she had described the camp, and given her sister a list of all the people in it. Lady Waterford wrote: 'Your Quartermaster-General must be the son of General Roberts, who lives near Waterford; he came home on leave last year. I must tell you an amusing little anecdote about his father. One night, when the General was dining at Curraghmore, he found himself sitting next the Primate of Ireland, with whom he entered into conversation. After some time they discovered they had known each other in the days of their youth, but had never met since a certain morning on which they went out to fight a duel on account of some squabble at a mess; happily the quarrel was stopped without any harm being done, each feeling equally relieved at being prevented from trying to murder the other, as they had been persuaded they were in honour bound to do. The two old gentlemen made very merry over their reminiscences.'

For some time I had been indulging a hope that I might be sent to China with my old General, Hope Grant, who had been nominated to the command of the expedition which, in co-operation with the French, was being prepared to wipe out the disgrace of the repulse experienced early in the year, by the combined French and English naval squadrons in their attack on the Taku forts. My hope, however, was doomed to disappointment. Lord Clyde decided to send Lumsden and Allgood as A.Q.M.G.'s with the force, and I was feeling very low in consequence. A day or two afterwards we dined with the Cannings, and Lord Clyde took my wife in to dinner. His first remark to her was: 'I think I have earned your gratitude, if I have not managed to satisfy everyone by these China appointments.' On my wife asking for what she was expected to be grateful, he said: 'Why, for not sending your husband with the expedition, of course. I suppose you would rather not be left in a foreign country alone a few months after your marriage? If Roberts had not been a newly-married man, I would have sent him.' This was too much for my wife, who sympathized greatly with my disappointment, and she could not help retorting: 'I am afraid I cannot be very grateful to you for making my husband feel I am ruining his career by standing in the way of his being sent on service. You have done your best to make him regret his marriage.' The poor old Chief was greatly astonished, and burst out in his not too refined way: 'Well, I'll be hanged if I can understand you women! I have done the very thing I thought you would like, and have only succeeded in making you angry. I will never try to help a woman again.' My wife saw that he had meant to be kind, and that it was, as he said, only because he did not 'understand women' that he had made the mistake. She was soon appeased, and in the end she and Lord Clyde became great friends.

The middle of January found us at Umballa, where Lord Canning met in state all the Cis-Sutlej Sikh Chiefs. Fine, handsome men they most of them were, and magnificently attired. The beautifully delicate tints which the Sikhs are so fond of, the warlike costumes of some of the Sirdars, the quiet dignity of these high-born men who had rendered us such signal service in our hour of need, made the scene most picturesque and impressive. The place of honour was given to the Maharaja of Patiala (the grandfather of the present Maharaja), as the most powerful of the Phulkian Princes; and he was followed by his neighbours of Nabha and Jhind, all three splendid specimens of well-bred Sikhs, of stately presence and courtly manners. They were much gratified at having the right of adoption granted to their families, and at being given substantial rewards in the shape of extension of territory.

The Sikh Chiefs were followed by Rajas of minor importance, chiefly from the neighbouring hills, whom the Viceroy had summoned in order to thank them for assistance rendered during the Mutiny. Many of them had grievances to be redressed; others had favours to ask; and the Viceroy was able to more or less satisfy them by judiciously yielding to reasonable demands, and by bestowing minor powers on those who were likely to use them well. The wisdom of this policy of concession on Lord Canning's part was proved in after years by its successful results.

On the 29th January the Raja of Kapurthala came out to meet the Viceroy one march from Jullundur. He had supplemented the valuable assistance rendered to Colonel Lake in the early days of the Mutiny by equipping and taking into Oudh a force of 2,000 men, which he personally commanded in six different actions. The Viceroy cordially thanked him for this timely service, and in recognition of it, and his continued and conspicuous loyalty, bestowed upon him large estates in Oudh, where he eventually became one of the chief Talukdars. This Raja was the grandfather of the enlightened nobleman who came to England three years ago.

After visiting Umritsar, gay with brilliant illuminations in honour of the Viceroy, and crowded with Sikhs come to welcome the Queen's representative to their sacred city, we arrived at Lahore on the 10th February.

Early the following morning Lord Canning made his state entry. As we approached the citadel the long line of mounted Chiefs drawn up to receive the Viceroy came into view. A brilliant assemblage they formed, Sikh Sirdars, stately Hill Rajputs, wildly picturesque Multanis and Baluchis with their flowing locks floating behind them, sturdy Tawanas from the Salt range, all gorgeously arrayed in every colour of the rainbow, their jewels glittering in the morning sun, while their horses, magnificently caparisoned in cloth-of-gold saddle cloths, and gold and silver trappings, pranced and curvetted under pressure of their severe bits. As the procession appeared in sight they moved forward in one long dazzling cavalcade, each party of Chiefs being headed by the Commissioner of the district from which they came; they saluted as they approached the Viceroy, and then passing him fell in behind, between the Body Guard and the Artillery of the escort. A royal salute was fired from the fort as we passed under the city walls; we then wound through the civil station of Anárkáli, and on to camp where the garrison of Mian Mir, under the command of Major-General Sir Charles Windham, was drawn up to receive the Viceroy.

At nightfall there were illuminations and a procession of elephants; the Viceroy, seated in a superb howdah, led the way through the brilliantly lighted city. Suddenly a shower of rockets was discharged which resulted in a stampede of the elephants, who rushed through the narrow streets, and fled in every direction, to the imminent peril and great discomfort of the riders. In time they were quieted and brought back, only to become again unmanageable at a fresh volley of fireworks; a second time they were pacified, and as they seemed to be getting accustomed to the noise and lights, the procession proceeded to the garden of the old palace. Here the elephants were drawn up, when all at once a fresh discharge of rockets from every side drove them mad with fright, and off they bolted under the trees, through gates, and some of them could not be pulled up until they had gone far into the country. Howdahs were crushed, hats torn off, but, strange to say, there was only one serious casualty; an officer was swept out of his howdah by the branch of a tree, and falling to the ground, had his thigh broken. Lord Clyde declared that a general action was not half so dangerous, and he would much sooner have been in one!

The Lahore durbar, at which the Punjab Chiefs were received, surpassed any former ceremonials in point of numbers and splendour of effect. Many of Runjit Singh's Sirdars were present, and many who had fought against us in the Sutlej and Punjab campaigns, but had now become our fast friends. The Chiefs quite spontaneously prepared and presented Lord Canning with an address, and, in reply, his Excellency made an eloquent and telling speech, commenting in terms of the highest appreciation on the courage and loyalty displayed by the Nobles and people of the Punjab during the Mutiny.

While the camp was marching to Sialkot, where the Maharaja of Kashmir and some of the leading men of the Punjab were to be received, the Viceroy, accompanied by Lady Canning, Lord Clyde, and a small staff, went on a flying visit to Peshawar, with the object of satisfying himself, by personal examination of our position there, as to the advisability or otherwise of a retirement cis-Indus—a retrograde movement which John Lawrence was still in favour of. The visit, however, only served to strengthen Lord Canning in his preconceived opinion that Peshawar must be held on to as our frontier station.

My wife remained at Mian Mir with our good friends Doctor and Mrs. Tyrrell Ross until it was time for her to go to Simla, and the kind thoughtfulness of Lord Canning, who told me the camp now worked so well that my presence was not always necessary, enabled me to be with her from time to time.

Lord Canning's tour was now nearly over, and we marched without any halt of importance from Sialkot to Kalka at the foot of the hills, where, on the 9th April, the camp was broken up. It was high time to get into cooler regions, for the heat of the tents in the day had become very oppressive.

Thus ended a six months' march of over a thousand miles—a march never likely to be undertaken again by any other Viceroy of India, now that railway trains run from Calcutta to Peshawar, and saloon carriages have taken the place of big tents.

This progress through India had excellent results. The advantages of the representative of the Sovereign meeting face to face the principal feudatories and Chiefs of our great dependency were very considerable, and the opportunity afforded to the Viceroy of personally acknowledging and rewarding the services of those who had helped us, and of showing that he was not afraid to be lenient to those who had failed to do so, provided they should remain loyal in the future, had a very good effect over the whole of India. The wise concessions also announced at the different durbars as regards the adoption by Native Rulers of successors to their estates, and the grant to Native gentlemen of such a share as they were fitted for in the government of the country, were undoubtedly more appreciated than any other description of reward given for assistance in the Mutiny.

My duty with the Viceroy being ended, I returned to Mian Mir to fetch my wife and the little daughter, who had made her appearance on the 10th March, and escort them both to Simla. The journey up the hill was a tedious one. Carriages were not then used as they are now, and my wife travelled in a *jampan*, a kind of open, half-reclining sedan chair, carried by relays of four men, while I rode or walked by her side. She had been greatly exhausted by the heat of the journey from Mian Mir, but as we ascended higher and higher up the mountain side, and the atmosphere became clearer and fresher, she began to revive. Four hours, however, of this unaccustomed mode of travelling in her weak state had completely tired her out, so on finding a fairly comfortable bungalow at the end of the first stage, I decided to remain there the next day. After that we went on, stage by stage, until we reached Simla. Our house, 'Mount Pleasant,' was on the very top of a hill; up and up we climbed through the rhododendron forest, along a path crimson with the fallen blossom, till we got to the top, when a glorious view opened out before our delighted eyes. The wooded hills of Jakho and Elysium in the foreground, Mahasu and the beautiful Shalli peaks in the middle distance, and beyond, towering above all, the everlasting snows glistening in the morning sun, formed a picture the beauty of which quite entranced us both. I could hardly persuade my wife to leave it and come into the house. Hunger and fatigue, however, at length triumphed. Our servants had arranged everything in our little abode most comfortably; bright fires were burning in the grates, a cosy breakfast was awaiting us, and the feeling that at last we had a home of our own was very pleasant.

Lord Canning did not remain long at Simla. His Council in Calcutta was about to lose its President, Sir James Outram, who was leaving India on account of failing health; and as the suggestion to impose an income-tax was creating a good deal of agitation, the Viceroy hurried back to Calcutta, deeming it expedient to be on the spot.

The measures necessary for the suppression of the Mutiny had emptied the Government coffers; and although a large loan had been raised, the local authorities found it impossible to cope with the increased expenditure. Lord Canning had, therefore, applied to the Government in England for the services of a trained financier; and Mr. Wilson, who had a great reputation in this respect, was sent out. He declared the only remedy to be an income-tax, and he was supported in this view by the merchants of Calcutta. Other Europeans, however, who were intimately acquainted with India, pointed out that it was not advisable to ignore the dislike of Natives to such direct taxation; and Sir Charles Trevelyan, Governor of Madras, argued well and wisely against the scheme. Instead, however, of confining his action in the matter to warning and advising the supreme Government, he publicly proclaimed his opposition, thus giving the signal for agitation to all the malcontents in India. Lord Elphinstone, the Governor of Bombay, followed Trevelyan's example, but in a less pronounced manner, and these attacks from the minor Presidencies proved a serious embarrassment to the action of the Government. In spite of all this antagonism, the income-tax was passed, and Sir Charles Trevelyan's unusual procedure led to his recall.

Lord Canning left Simla for his long and trying journey in May, about the hottest time of the year. On my taking leave of him, he told me that Sir Hugh Rose, then commanding the Bombay army, had been appointed to succeed Lord Clyde, who had long been anxious to return to England, and that Sir Hugh, though he intended to go to Calcutta himself, wished the Head-Quarters of the Army to remain at Simla; a question about which we had been rather anxious, as it would have been an unpleasant breaking up of all our plans, had I been ordered to Calcutta.

Life at Simla was somewhat monotonous. The society was not very large in those days; but there were a certain number of people on leave from the plains, who then, as at present, had nothing to do but amuse themselves, consequently there was a good deal of gaiety in a small way; but we entered into it very little. My wife did not care much about it, and had been very ill for the greater part of the summer. She had made two or three kind friends, and was very happy in her mountain home, though at times, perhaps, a little lonely, as I had to be in office the greater part of each day.

In the autumn we made a trip into the interior of the hills, beyond Simla, which was a new and delightful experience for my wife. We usually started in the morning, sending our servants on about half way, when they prepared breakfast for us in some pretty, shady spot; there we remained, reading, writing, or resting, until after lunch, and it was time to move on, that we might get to our halting place for the night before dinner.

It was a lovely time of the year, when the autumn tints made the forest gorgeous, and the scarlet festoons of the Himalayan vine stood out in brilliant contrast to the dark green of the solemn deodar, amongst the branches of which it loves to twine itself.

CHAPTER XXXIV.

In 1860 an important alteration was made in the organization of the army in India, by the passing of a Bill for the amalgamation of the local European Forces with the Royal Army.

On the transfer of the administration of India from the Honourable East India Company to the Crown, a question arose as to the conditions under which the European soldiers had enlisted. The Government contended that the conditions were in no way affected by the abolition of the Company. The soldiers, on the other hand, claimed to be re-enlisted, and on this being refused they asked for their discharge. This was granted, and 10,000 out of the 16,000 men serving in the local army had to be sent to England. These men were replaced and the local Forces were kept up to strength by fresh drafts from England; but, from the date of the amalgamation, enlistment to serve solely in India was to cease.

There was great difference of opinion as to the advisability of this measure; officers of the Queen's service for the most part, and notably Sir Hugh Rose, were in favour of it, but it was not generally popular in India. It was feared that the change would result in a great increase to the military charges which the Indian Government would be called upon to pay; that, notwithstanding such increase, there would be a serious diminution in the control exercised by that Government over the administration and organization of the British Army in India; and that, under the pressure of political emergency in Europe, troops might be withdrawn and Indian requirements disregarded. On the other hand, those in favour of the Bill thought that, after the transfer of India to the Crown, the maintenance of a separate Force uncontrolled by the Horse Guards would be an anomaly. There was, no doubt, much to be said on both sides of the question, but, although it has been proved that the fears of those opposed to the change were not altogether without foundation, in my opinion it was unavoidable, and has greatly benefited both services.

The amalgamation considerably accelerated my promotion, for, in order to place the Indian Ordnance Corps on the same footing as those of the Royal service, the rank of Second Captain had to be introduced into the former, a rank to which I attained in October, 1860, only, however, to hold it for one day, as the next my name appeared in the *Gazette* as a Brevet Major.

The same year saw the introduction of the Staff Corps. This was the outcome of the disappearance during the Mutiny of nearly the whole of the Regular regiments of the Bengal Army, and their replacement by Irregular regiments. But, as under the Irregular system the number of British officers with each corps was too limited to admit of their promotion being carried on regimentally, as had been done under the Regular system,* some organization had to be devised by which

* Under the Regular system, which was modelled on the Royal Army organization, each regiment of Native Cavalry had 22, and each regiment of Native Infantry 25 British officers, who rose to the higher grades by seniority. From this establishment officers were taken, without being seconded, for the multifarious extra-regimental duties on which the Indian Army was, and is still, employed, viz., Staff, Civil, Political, Commissariat, Pay, Public Works, Stud, and Survey. With the Irregular system this was no longer possible,

the pay and promotion of all officers joining the Indian Army in future could be arranged. Many schemes were put forward; eventually one formulated by Colonel Norman was, with certain modifications, accepted by the Secretary of State, the result being that all officers about to enter the Indian Army were to be placed on one list, in which they would be promoted after fixed periods of service;* and all those officers who had been thrown out of employment by the disbandment of their regiments, or by the substitution of the Irregular for the Regular system, were to have the option of joining it. The term Staff Corps, however, was a misnomer, for the constitution of the Corps and the training of its officers had no special connection with staff requirements.

Towards the end of the summer the Viceroy announced his intention of making a march through Central India, and I was again ordered to take charge of his camp, which was to be formed at Benares. My wife and her baby remained at Simla with our friends the Donald Stewarts, and I left her feeling sure that with them she would be happy and well taken care of.

Sir Hugh Rose was at Allahabad, and as I passed through that place I availed myself of the opportunity to pay my respects to the new Chief, being anxious to meet an officer whom I had held in great admiration from the time when, as *Chargé d'affaires* at Constantinople, his pluck and foresight practically saved Turkey in her time of peril from Russia's threatened attack—admiration increased by the masterly manner in which he had conducted the Central India campaign, in spite of almost overwhelming difficulties from want of transport and other causes, and a severe attack of sunstroke, which would have incapacitated many men. Sir Hugh Rose, when I first met him at Allahabad, was fifty-nine years of age, tall, slight, with refined features, rather delicate-looking, and possessing a distinctly distinguished appearance. He received me most kindly, and told me that he wished me to return to Head-Quarters when the Viceroy could dispense with my services.

The camp this year was by no means on so grand a scale as the preceding one. The escort was much smaller, and the Commander-in-Chief with Army Head-Quarters did not march with us as on the previous occasion.

Lord and Lady Canning arrived by steamer at Benares on the 6th November, and I went on board to meet them. Lord Canning was

although the number of British officers with each corps was (after the Mutiny) increased from 3 to 9 with a Cavalry, and 3 to 8 with an Infantry regiment.

* Captain after twelve years,[1] Major after twenty years, and Lieutenant-Colonel after twenty-six years.

[1] Since reduced to eleven years.

cordial and pleasant as usual, but I did not think he looked well. Lady Canning was charming as ever; she reproached me for not having brought my wife, but when I told her how ill she had been, she agreed that camp was not quite the place for her.

Benares, to my mind, is a most disappointing city; the streets are narrow and dirty, there are no fine buildings, and it is only interesting from its being held so sacred by the Hindus. The view of the city and burning ghâts from the river is picturesque and pretty, but there is nothing else worth seeing.

Two days were occupied in getting the camp to Mirzarpur, on the opposite bank of the Ganges. There was no bridge, and everything had to be taken over in boats; 10,000 men, 1,000 horses, 2,000 camels, 2,000 bullocks, besides all the tents, carts, and baggage, had to be ferried across the great river. The 180 elephants swam over with their *mahouts* on their backs to keep their heads straight and urge them on; the stream was rapid, and it was a difficult business to land them safely at the other side, but at last it was accomplished, and our only casualty was one camel, which fell overboard.

The march to Jubbulpur lay through very pretty scenery, low hills and beautiful jungle, ablaze with the flame-coloured blossom of the dhâk-tree. Game abounded, and an occasional tiger was killed. Lord Canning sometimes accompanied the shooting expeditions, but not often, for he was greatly engrossed in, and oppressed by, his work, which he appeared unable to throw off. Even during the morning's drive he was occupied with papers, and on reaching camp he went straight to his office tent, where he remained the whole day till dinner-time, returning to it directly the meal was over, unless there were strangers present with whom he wished to converse.

At Jubbulpur the Viceroy held a durbar for the Maharaja Tukaji Holkar of Indore, and some minor Chiefs of that part of the country. Holkar's conduct during the Mutiny was not altogether above suspicion, but, considering that the only troops at his disposal belonged to the mutinous Indore Contingent, which consisted mainly of Hindustanis enlisted by English officers, over whom he could not be expected to exercise much control, Lord Canning gave him the benefit of the doubt, and was willing to attribute his equivocal behaviour to want of ability and timidity, rather than to disloyalty, and therefore allowed him to come to the durbar.

Another potentate received at this time by the Viceroy was the Begum of Bhopal, who, being a powerful and skilful Ruler, and absolutely loyal to the British Government, had afforded us most valuable assistance during the rebellion. She was one of those women whom the East has occasionally produced, endowed with conspicuous talent and great strength of character, a quality which, from its rarity amongst Indian women, gives immense influence to those who possess it. Lord

Canning congratulated the Begum on the success with which she had governed her country, thanked her for her timely help, and bestowed upon her a large tract of country as a reward. She was a determined-looking little woman, and spoke fluently in her own language; she personally managed the affairs of her State, and wrote a remarkably interesting account of her travelling experiences during a pilgrimage to Mecca.

Just as the Begum took her departure, news was brought in of the presence of a tiger two or three miles from the cantonment, and as many of us as could get away started off in pursuit. Not considering myself a first-rate shot, I thought I should be best employed with the beaters, but, as good luck would have it, the tiger broke from the jungle within a few yards of my elephant: I could not resist having a shot, and was fortunate enough to knock him over.

While at Jubbulpur, I visited the famous marble rocks on the Nerbudda. We rowed up the river for about a mile, when the stream began to narrow, and splendid masses of marble came into view. The cliffs rise to about a hundred feet in height, pure white below, gradually shading off to gray at the top. The water at their base is of a deep brown colour, perfectly transparent and smooth, in which the white rocks are reflected with the utmost distinctness. In the crevices hang numerous beehives, whose inmates one has to be careful not to disturb, for on the bank are the graves of two Englishmen who, having incautiously aroused the vicious little creatures, were attacked and drowned in diving under the water to escape from their stings.

A few days later the Viceroy left camp, and proceeded to Lucknow, where he held another durbar for the Talukdars of Oudh. Lady Canning continued to march with us to Mirzapur, where I took her on board her barge, and bade her farewell—a last farewell, for I never saw this good, beautiful, and gifted woman again.

The camp being broken up, I returned towards the end of February to my work in the Quartermaster-General's Office at Simla. I found the place deep in snow; it looked very beautiful, but the change of temperature, from the great heat of Central India to several degrees of frost, was somewhat trying. My wife had benefited greatly from the fine bracing air, and both she and our baby appeared pictures of health; but a day or two after my arrival the little one was taken ill, and died within one week of her birthday—our first great sorrow.

We passed a very quiet, uneventful summer, and in the beginning of October we left Simla for Allahabad, where I had received instructions to prepare a camp for the Viceroy, who had arranged to hold an investiture of the Star of India, the new Order which was originally designed to honour the principal Chiefs of India who had done us good service, by associating them with some of the highest and most distinguished personages in England, and a few carefully selected

Europeans in India. Lord Canning was the first Grand Master, and Sir Hugh Rose the first Knight.

The durbar at which the Maharajas Sindhia and Patiala, the Begum of Bhopal, and the Nawab of Rampur were invested, was a most imposing ceremony. The Begum was the cynosure of all eyes—a female Knight was a novelty to Europeans as well as to Natives—and there was much curiosity as to how she would conduct herself; but no one could have behaved with greater dignity or more perfect decorum, and she made a pretty little speech in Urdu in reply to Lord Canning's complimentary address. She was dressed in cloth-of-gold, and wore magnificent jewels: but the effect of her rich costume was somewhat marred by a funny little wreath of artificial flowers, woollen mittens, and black worsted stockings with white tips. When my wife visited the Begum after the durbar, she showed her these curious appendages with great pride, saying she wore them because they were 'English fashion.' This was the first occasion on which ladies were admitted to a durbar, out of compliment to the Begum.

That evening my wife was taken in to dinner by a man whose manner and appearance greatly impressed her, but she did not catch his name when he was introduced; she much enjoyed his conversation during dinner, which was not to be wondered at, for, before she left the table, he told her his name was Bartle Frere.* She never saw him again, but she always says he interested her more than almost any of the many distinguished men she has since met.

From Allahabad the Viceroy again visited Lucknow, this time with the object of urging upon the Talukdars the suppression of the horrible custom of female infanticide, which had its origin in the combined pride and poverty of the Rajputs. In various parts of India attempts had been made, with more or less success, to put a stop to this inhuman practice. But not much impression had been made in Oudh, in consequence of the inordinately large dowries demanded from the Rajput fathers of marriageable daughters. Two hundred Talukdars attended Lord Canning's last durbar, and, in reply to his feeling and telling speech, declared their firm determination to do their best to discourage the evil.

The Commander-in-Chief had decided to pass the winter in marching through the Punjab, and inspecting the different stations for troops in the north of India. The Head-Quarters camp had, therefore, been formed at Jullundur, and thither we proceeded when the gathering at Allahabad had dispersed. We had but just arrived, when we were shocked and grieved beyond measure to hear of Lady Canning's death. Instead of accompanying the Viceroy to Allahabad she had gone to Darjeeling, and on her return, anxious to make sketches of the beautiful

* The late Sir Bartle Frere, Bart, G.C.B., G.C.S.I.

jungle scenery, she arranged, alas! contrary to the advice of those with her, to spend one night in the *terai*,* where she contracted jungle-fever, to which she succumbed ten days after her return to Calcutta. Her death was a real personal sorrow to all who had the privilege of knowing her; what must it have been to her husband, returning to England without the helpmate who had shared and lightened the burden of his anxieties, and gloried in the success which crowned his eventful career in India.

The Commander-in-Chief arrived in the middle of November, and all the officers of the Head-Quarters camp went out to meet him. I was mounted on a spirited nutmeg-gray Arab, a present from Allgood. Sir Hugh greatly fancied Arabian horses, and immediately noticed mine. He called me up to him, and asked me where I got him, and of what caste he was. From that moment he never varied in the kindness and consideration with which he treated me, and I always fancied I owed his being well disposed towards me from the very first to the fact that I was riding my handsome little Arab that day; he loved a good horse, and liked his staff to be well mounted. A few days afterwards he told me he wished me to accompany him on the flying tours he proposed to make from time to time, in order to see more of the country and troops than would be possible if he marched altogether with the big camp.

We went to Umritsar, Mian Mir, and Sialkot; at each place there were the usual inspections, mess dinners, and entertainments. The Chief's visit made a break in the ordinary life of a cantonment, and the residents were glad to take advantage of it to get up various festivities; Sir Hugh, too, was most hospitably inclined, so that there was always a great deal to do besides actual duty when we arrived at a station.

Jamu, where the Ruler of Kashmir resides during the winter, is not far from Sialkot, so Sir Hugh was tempted to accept an invitation from the Maharaja to pay him a visit and enjoy some good pig-sticking, to my mind the finest sport in the world. His Highness entertained us right royally, and gave us excellent sport, but our pleasure was marred by the Chief having a bad fall: he had got the first spear off a fine boar, who, feeling himself wounded, turned and charged, knocking over Sir Hugh's horse. All three lay in a heap together; the pig was dead, the horse was badly ripped up, and the Chief showed no signs of life. We carried him back to Jamu on a *charpoy*,† and when he regained consciousness we found that no great harm was done beyond a severely bruised face and a badly sprained leg, which, though still very painful two or three days later, did not prevent the plucky old fellow from riding over the battle-field of Chilianwalla.

* The fever-giving tract of country at the foot of the Himalayas.
† Native string bed.

Very soon after this Norman, who was then Adjutant-General of the Army, left Head-Quarters to take up the appointment of Secretary to the Government of India in the Military Department. Before we parted he expressed a hope that I would soon follow him, as a vacancy in the Department was about to take place, which he said he was sure Lord Canning would allow him to offer to me. Norman was succeeded as Adjutant-General of the Indian Army by Edwin Johnson, the last officer who filled that post, as it was done away with when the amalgamation of the services was carried into effect.

Two marches from Jhelum my wife was suddenly taken alarmingly ill, and had to remain behind when the camp moved on. Sir Hugh Rose most kindly insisted on leaving his doctor (Longhurst) in charge of her, and told me I must stay with her as long as was necessary. For three whole weeks we remained on the encamping ground of Sahawar; at the end of that time, thanks (humanly speaking) to the skill and care of our Doctor, she was sufficiently recovered to be put into a doolie and carried to Lahore, I riding a camel by her side, for my horses had gone on with the camp.

While at Lahore I received a most kind letter from Norman, offering me the post in the Secretariat which he had already told me was about to become vacant. After some hesitation—for the Secretariat had its attractions, particularly as regarded pay—I decided to decline the proffered appointment, as my acceptance of it would have taken me away from purely military work and the chance of service in the field. I left my wife on the high-road to recovery, and hurried after the camp, overtaking it at Peshawar just in time to accompany the Commander-in-Chief on his ride along the Derajat frontier, a trip I should have been very sorry to have missed. We visited every station from Kohat to Rajanpur, a ride of about 440 miles. Brigadier-General Neville Chamberlain, who was still commanding the Punjab Frontier Force, met us at Kohat, and remained with us to the end. We did from twenty-five to forty miles a day, and our baggage and servants, carried on riding-camels, kept up with us.

This was my first experience of a part of India with which I had later so much to do, and which always interested me greatly. At the time of which I am writing it was a wild and lawless tract of country. As we left Kohat we met the bodies of four murdered men being carried in, but were told there was nothing unusual in such a sight. On one occasion General Chamberlain introduced to Sir Hugh Rose two young Khans, fine, handsome fellows, who were apparently on excellent terms. A few days later we were told that one of them had been murdered by his companion, there having been a blood-feud between their families for generations; although these two had been brought up together, and liked each other, the one whose clan had last lost a member by the feud felt himself in honour bound to sacrifice his friend.

When I rejoined my wife at the end of the tour, I found her a great deal worse than her letters had led me to expect, but she had been much cheered by the arrival of a sister who had come out to pay us a visit, and who lived with us until she married an old friend and brother officer of mine named Sladen. We remained at Umballa till the end of March; the only noteworthy circumstance that occurred there was a parade for announcing to the troops that Earl Canning had departed, and that the Earl of Elgin and Kincardine was now Viceroy of India.

There are few men whose conduct of affairs has been so severely criticized as Lord Canning's, but there are still fewer who, as Governors or Viceroys, have had to deal with such an overwhelming crisis as the Mutiny. While the want of appreciation Lord Canning at first displayed of the magnitude of that crisis may, with perfect justice, be attributed to the fact that most of his advisers had gained their experience only in Lower Bengal, and had therefore a very imperfect knowledge of popular feeling throughout India, the very large measure of success which attended his subsequent action was undoubtedly due to his own ability and sound judgment.

That by none of Lord Canning's responsible councillors could the extent of the Mutiny, or the position in Upper India, have been grasped, was evident from the telegram* sent from Calcutta to the Commander-in-Chief on the 31st May, three weeks after the revolt at Meerut had occurred; but from the time Lord Canning left Calcutta in January, 1858, and had the opportunity of seeing and judging for himself, all that he did was wise and vigorous.

Outwardly Lord Canning was cold and reserved, the result, I think, of extreme sensitiveness; for he was without doubt very warm-hearted, and was greatly liked and respected by those about him, and there was universal regret throughout India when, three months after his departure, the news of his death was received.

We returned to Simla early in April. The season passed much as other seasons had passed, except that there was rather more gaiety. The new Viceroy remained in Calcutta; but Sir Hugh Rose had had quite enough of it the year before, so he came up to the Hills, and established himself at 'Barnes Court.' He was very hospitable, and having my sister-in-law to chaperon, my wife went out rather more than she had cared to do in previous years. We spent a good deal of our time also at Mashobra, a lovely place in the heart of the Hills, about six miles from Simla, where the Chief had a house, which he was good enough to frequently place at our disposal, when not making use of it

* 'Your force of Artillery will enable us to dispose of Delhi with certainty. I therefore beg that you will detach one European Infantry regiment and a small force of European Cavalry to the south of Delhi, without keeping them for operations there, so that Aligarh may be recovered and Cawnpore relieved immediately.'

himself. It was an agreeable change, and one which we all greatly enjoyed. But at the best one gets very tired of the Hills by the close of the summer, and I was glad to start off towards the end of October with my wife and her sister for Agra, where this year the Head-Quarters camp was to be formed, as the Chief had settled the cold-weather tour was to begin with a march through Bundelkand and Central India, the theatre of his successful campaign.

The second march out we were startled by being told, when we awoke in the morning, that Colonel Gawler, the Deputy-Adjutant-General of Queen's troops, had been badly wounded in the night by a thief, who got into his tent with the object of stealing a large sum of money Gawler had received from the bank the previous day, and for greater safety had placed under his pillow when he went to bed. In the middle of the night his wife awoke him, saying there was someone in the tent, and by the dim light of a small oil-lamp he could just see a dark figure creeping along the floor. He sprang out of bed and seized the robber; but the latter, being perfectly naked and oiled all over, slipped through his hands and wriggled under the wall of the tent. Gawler caught him by the leg just as he was disappearing, and they struggled outside together. When despairing of being able to make his escape, the thief stabbed Gawler several times with a knife, which was tied by a string to his wrist. By this time Mrs. Gawler had been able to arouse two Kaffir servants, one of whom tried to seize the miscreant, but in his turn was stabbed. The second servant, however, was more wary, and succeeded in capturing the thief; Kaffir fashion, he knocked all the breath out of his body by running at him head down and butting him in the stomach, when it became easy to bind the miscreant hand and foot. It was a bad part of the country for thieves; and when some four weeks later I went off on a flying tour with the Commander-in-Chief, I did not leave my wife quite as happily as usual. But neither she nor her sister was afraid. Each night they sent everything at all valuable to be placed under the care of the guard, and having taken this precaution, were quite easy in their minds.

When the camp reached Gwalior, the Maharaja Sindhia seemed to think he could not do enough to show his gratitude to Sir Hugh Rose for his opportune help in June, 1858,* when the Gwalior troops mutinied, and joined the rebel army under the Rani of Jhansi and

* After the capture of Kalpi in May, 1858, Sir Hugh Rose, worn out with fatigue and successive sunstrokes, was advised by his medical officer to return at once to Bombay; his leave had been granted, and his successor (Brigadier-General Napier) had been appointed, when intelligence reached him to the effect that the rebel army, under Tantia Topi and the Rani of Jhansi, had been joined by the whole of Sindhia's troops and were in possession of the fort of Gwalior with its well-supplied arsenal. Sir Hugh Rose at once cancelled his leave, pushed on to Gwalior, and by the 30th of June had re-captured all Sindhia's guns and placed him again in possession of his capital.

THE EARL CANNING, K.G., G.C.B., G.M.S.I.,
VICEROY AND GOVERNOR-GENERAL OF INDIA.

From
a photograph by Messrs. Mayall.

Tantia Topi. The day after our arrival Sindhia held a grand review of his new army in honour of our Chief. The next day there was an open-air entertainment in the Phulbagh (garden of flowers); the third a picnic and elephant fight, which, by the way, was a very tame affair. We had nerved ourselves to see something rather terrific, instead of which the great creatures twisted their trunks about each other in quite a playful manner, and directly the play seemed to be turning into earnest they were separated by their *mahouts*, being much too valuable to be allowed to injure themselves. Each day there was some kind of entertainment: pig-sticking or shooting expeditions in the morning, and banquets, fireworks, and illuminations in the evening.

Gwalior is an interesting place. The fort is picturesquely situated above a perpendicular cliff; the road up to it is very steep, and it must have been almost impregnable in former days. It was made doubly interesting to us by Sir Hugh Rose explaining how he attacked it, and pointing out the spot where the Rani of Jhansi was killed in a charge of the 8th Hussars.

Our next halt was Jhansi. Here also Sir Hugh had a thrilling tale to tell of its capture, and of his having to fight the battle of the Betwa against a large force brought to the assistance of the rebels by Tantia Topi, while the siege was actually being carried on.

From Jhansi the big camp marched to Lucknow, *viâ* Cawnpore; while the Chief with a small staff (of which I was one) and light tents, made a detour by Saugor, Jubbulpur, and Allahabad. We travelled through pretty jungle for the most part, interspersed with low hills, and we had altogether a very enjoyable trip. Sir Hugh was justly proud of the splendid service the Central India Field Force had performed under his command; and, as we rode along, it delighted him to point out the various places where he had come in contact with the rebels.

While at Allahabad, on the 13th January—quite the coolest time of the year—I had a slight sunstroke, which it took me a very long time to get over completely. The sensible custom introduced by Lord Clyde, of wearing helmets, was not always adhered to, and Sir Hugh Rose was rather fond of cocked hats. On this occasion I was wearing this—for India—most unsuitable head-dress, and, as ill-luck would have it, the Chief kept me out rather late, going over the ground where the present cantonment stands. I did not feel anything at the time, but an hour later I was suddenly seized with giddiness and sickness, and for a short time I could neither see nor hear. Plentiful douches of cold water brought me round, and I was well enough in the afternoon to go with the Chief to inspect the fort; but for months afterwards I never lost the pain in my head, and for many years I was very susceptible to the evil influence of the sun's rays.

We reached Lucknow towards the middle of January. Here, as elsewhere, we had constant parades and inspections, for Sir Hugh carried out his duties in the most thorough manner, and spared himself no trouble to secure the efficiency and the well-being of the soldier. At the same time, he was careful not to neglect his social duties; he took a prominent part in all amusements, and it was mainly due to his liberal support that we were able to keep up a small pack of hounds with Head-Quarters, which afforded us much enjoyment during the winter months.

From Lucknow we marched through Bareilly, Meerut, and Umballa, and the 30th March saw us all settled at Simla for the season.

Early in April Lord Elgin arrived in Simla for the hot weather, and from that time to the present, Simla has continued to be the Head-Quarters of the Government during the summer months.

About this time the changes necessitated by the amalgamation of the services took place in the army staff. Edwin Johnson lost his appointment in consequence, and Colonel Haythorne,* Adjutant-General of Queen's troops, became Adjutant-General of the Army in India, with Donald Stewart as his deputy. The order limiting the tenure of employment on the staff in the same grade to five years was also now introduced, which entailed my good friend Arthur Becher vacating the Quartermaster-Generalship, after having held it for eleven years. He was succeeded by Colonel Paton, with Lumsden as his deputy, and Charles Johnson (brother of Edwin Johnson) and myself as assistants in the Department.

CHAPTER XXXV.

In the autumn of 1863, while we were preparing for the usual winter tour, Sir Hugh Rose, who had accompanied Lord Elgin on a trip through the hills, telegraphed to the Head-Quarters staff to join him at Mian Mir without delay.

The news which greeted us on our arrival was indeed disturbing. Lord Elgin was at Dharmsala in a dying condition, and the Chief had been obliged to leave him and push on to Lahore, in consequence of unsatisfactory reports from Brigadier-General Chamberlain, who was just then commanding an expedition which had been sent into the mountains near Peshawar, and had met with unexpected opposition. The civil authorities on the spot reported that there existed a great deal of excitement all along the border, that the tribes were collecting in large numbers, that emissaries from Kabul had appeared amongst them, and that, unless reinforcements could be sent up at once, the Government would be involved in a war which must inevitably lead to the most serious complications, not only on the frontier, but with

* The late General Sir Edmund Haythorne, K.C.B.

Afghanistan. In so grave a light did the Lieutenant-Governor, Sir Robert Montgomery, view the position, that he contemplated the force being withdrawn and the undertaking abandoned.

Sir Hugh had had nothing to do with the despatch of this expedition; it had been decided on by the Government of India in consultation with the Lieutenant-Governor of the Punjab. When the Commander-in-Chief was communicated with, he expressed himself adverse to the proposal, and placed his views at length before the Government, pointing out the inexpediency of entering a difficult and unknown country, unless the troops were properly equipped with transport, supplies, and reserve ammunition; that time did not permit of their being so equipped before the winter set in; and that, to provide a force of 5,000 men (the strength considered necessary by the Government), the frontier would have to be dangerously weakened. Moreover, he gave it as his opinion that it would be better to postpone operations until the spring, when everything could be perfectly arranged. Subsequent events proved how sound was this advice. But before proceeding with my narrative it will be as well to explain the circumstances with led the authorities to undertake this expedition.

In 1857, when all our resources were required to quell internal tumult, the Hindustani fanatics* took the opportunity to stir up disturbances all along the Yusafzai frontier of the Peshawar district, and, aided by the rebel sepoys who had fled to them for protection, they made raids upon our border, and committed all kinds of atrocities. We were obliged, therefore, to send an expedition against them in 1858, which resulted in their being driven from their stronghold, Sitana, and in the neighbouring tribes being bound down to prevent them re-occupying that place. Three years later the fanatics returned to their former haunts and built up a new settlement at Malka; the old troubles recommenced, and for two years they had been allowed to go on raiding, murdering, and attacking our outposts with impunity. It was, therefore, quite time that measures should be taken to effectually rid the frontier of these disturbers of the peace, provided such measures could have been decided upon early enough in the year to ensure success.

* In 1825 a religious adventurer from Bareilly made his appearance on the Yusafzai frontier with about forty Hindustani followers, and gave out that he was a man of superior sanctity, and had a divine command to wage a war of extermination, with the aid of all true believers, against the infidel. After studying Arabic at Delhi, he proceeded to Mecca by way of Calcutta, and during this journey his doctrines had obtained so great an ascendency over the minds of the Mahomedans of Bengal that they have ever since supplied the colony which Syad Ahmed Shah founded in Yusafzai with money and recruits. The Syad was eventually slain fighting against the Sikhs, but his followers established themselves at Sitana, and in the neighbourhood of that place they continue to flourish, notwithstanding that we have destroyed their settlements more than once during the last forty years.

The Punjab Government advocated the despatch of a very strong force. Accordingly, two columns were employed, the base of one being in the Peshawar valley, and that of the other in Hazara. The Peshawar column was to move by the Umbeyla Pass, the Buner frontier, and the Chamla valley, thus operating on the enemy's line of retreat. This route would not have been chosen, had not Chamberlain been assured by the civil authorities that no hostility need be feared from the Bunerwals, even if their country had to be entered, as they had given no trouble for fifteen years, and their spiritual head, the Akhund of Swat,* had no sympathy with the fanatics. It was not, therefore, considered necessary to warn the Buner people of our approach until preparations were completed; indeed, it was thought unadvisable to do so, as it was important to keep the proposed line of advance secret. The strength of the force was 6,000 men, with 19 guns, but to make up these numbers the stations in Upper India had to be considerably weakened, and there was no reserve nearer than Lahore.

The Peshawar column† being all ready for a start, a Proclamation was forwarded to the Buner and other neighbouring tribes, informing them of the object of the expedition, and stating that there was no intention of interfering with them or their possessions.

On the following morning, the 20th October, the Umbeyla Pass was entered, and by noon the kotal‡ was reached without any resistance to speak of; but, from information brought in, it was evident that any further advance would be stoutly opposed. The road turned out to be much more difficult than had been anticipated, and the hurriedly collected transport proved unequal to the strain. Not a single baggage animal, except the ammunition mules, got up that night; indeed, it was not until the morning of the 22nd—more than forty-eight hours after they started—that the rear guard reached the kotal, a distance of only six miles. As soon as it arrived Colonel Alex. Taylor, R.E., was sent off with a body of Cavalry, under Lieutenant-Colonel Probyn, to reconnoitre the road in front. The delay in reaching the top of the

* The Akhund of Swat was a man of seventy years of age at the time of the Umbeyla expedition; he had led a holy life, and had gained such an influence over the minds of Mahomedans in general, that they believed he was supplied by supernatural means with the necessaries of life, and that every morning, on rising from his prayers, a sum of money sufficient for the day's expenditure was found under his praying carpet.

† The Peshawar column consisted of half of 19th Company Royal Artillery, No. 3 Punjab Light Field Battery, the Peshawar and Hazara Mountain Batteries, the 71st and 101st Foot, the Guides, one troop 11th Bengal Lancers, one company Bengal Sappers and Miners, 14th Sikhs, 20th Punjab Infantry, 32nd Pioneers, 1st, 3rd, 5th and 6th Punjab Infantry, and 4th and 5th Gurkhas. The Hazara column consisted of a wing of the 51st Foot, 300 Native Cavalry, a regiment of Native Infantry and eight guns, holding Darband, Torbela, and Topi on the Indus.

‡ The highest point of a pass crossing a mountain range.

pass had given the tribes time to collect, and when the reconnoitring party entered the Chamla valley the Bunerwals could be seen about two miles and a half off, occupying in force the range which separates Buner and Chamla. Whatever may have been their first intention, they apparently could not resist the temptation to try and cut off this small body of Cavalry, for our horsemen on their return journey found a large number of the trusted Buner tribe attempting to block the mouth of the pass. A charge was made, but mounted men could not do much in such a hilly country; the proceedings of the Bunerwals, however, had been observed from the kotal, and Major Brownlow,* with some of his own regiment (the 20th Punjab Infantry), was sent to the assistance of the party. A hand-to-hand fight ensued, and the enemy pressed our troops closely on their way back, coming right in amongst them with the utmost daring.

There was now brought in to the Commissioner by a spy the copy of a letter from the Hindustani fanatics, addressed to the Bunerwals, telling them not to be taken in by our assurances that our only object was to punish the fanatics, for our real intentions were to annex Chamla, Buner, and Swat. This letter no doubt aroused the suspicions of the tribes, and, encouraged by the slowness of our movements, they all joined against us from Buner, Mahaban, and the Black Mountain.

On the 23rd large bodies of men with numerous standards were to be seen approaching the mouth of the pass, and a day or two later a report was received that our foes were to have the support of the Akhund of Swat, which meant a most formidable accession of moral as well as material strength, and put a stop, for the time being, to any possibility of a successful advance being made with the force at Chamberlain's disposal.

The position occupied by our troops was enclosed on the left (west) by the Guru Mountain, which separates Umbeyla from Buner, and on the right (east) by a range of hills, not quite so high. The main piquet on the Guru occupied a position upon some precipitous cliffs known as the Eagle's Nest, while that on the right was designated the 'Crag piquet.' The Eagle's Nest was only large enough to accommodate 110 men, so 120 more were placed under the shelter of some rocks at its base, and the remainder of the troops told off for the defence of the left piquet were drawn up on and about a rocky knoll, 400 feet west of the Eagle's Nest.

Some 2,000 of the enemy occupied a breastwork on the crest of a spur of the Guru Mountain; and about noon on the 26th they moved down, and with loud shouts attacked the Eagle's Nest. Their matchlock men posted themselves to the greatest advantage in a wood, and opened a galling fire upon our defences, while their swordsmen made

* Now General Sir Charles Brownlow, G.C.B.

a determined advance. The nature of the ground prevented our guns from being brought to bear upon the assailants, and they were thus able to get across the open space in front of the piquet, and plant their standards close under its parapet. For some considerable time they remained in this position, all our efforts to dislodge them proving of no avail. Eventually, however, they were forced to give way, and were driven up the hill, leaving the ground covered with their dead, and a great many wounded, who were taken into our hospitals and carefully treated, while a still greater number were carried off by their friends. Our losses were, 2 British officers, 1 Native officer, and 26 men killed; and 2 British officers, 7 Native officers, and 86 men wounded.

The day following the fight the Bunerwals were told they might carry away their dead, and we took advantage of their acceptance of this permission to reason with them as to the uselessness of an unnecessary sacrifice of their tribesmen, which would be the certain result of further opposition to us. Their demeanour was courteous, and they conversed freely with General Chamberlain and Colonel Reynell Taylor, the Commissioner, but they made it evident that they were determined not to give in.

Our position had now become rather awkward; there was a combination against us of all the tribes between the Indus and the Kabul rivers, and their numbers could not be less than 15,000 armed men. Mutual animosities were for the time allowed to remain in abeyance, and the tribes all flocked to fight under the Akhund's standard in the interests of their common faith. Moreover, there was trouble in the rear from the people along the Yusafzai border, who assisted the enemy by worrying our lines of communication. Under these changed conditions, and with such an inadequate force, Chamberlain came to the conclusion that, for the moment, he could only remain on the defensive, and trust to time, to the discouragement which repeated unsuccessful attacks were sure to produce on the enemy, and to the gradual decrease of their numbers, to break up the combination against us; for, as these tribesmen only bring with them the quantity of food they are able to carry, as soon as it is finished they are bound to suspend operations till more can be procured.

For three weeks almost daily attacks were made on our position; the enemy fought magnificently, some of them being killed inside our batteries, and twice they gained possession of the 'Crag piquet,' the key of the position, which it was essential should be retaken at all hazards. On the second occasion General Chamberlain himself led the attacking party, and was so severely wounded that he was obliged to relinquish the command of the force.

The Lieutenant-Governor of the Punjab, being convinced that reinforcements were necessary, in consultation with Colonels Durand* and

* The late Sir Henry Marion Durand, K.C.S.I., C.B., afterwards Lieutenant-Governor of the Punjab.

Norman (the Foreign and Military Secretaries, who had come to Lahore to meet the Viceroy), and without waiting for the sanction of the Commander-in-Chief, ordered to the frontier the three regiments which had been detailed for the Viceroy's camp,* as well as the 93rd Highlanders, then at Sialkot; and when Sir Hugh Rose on his arrival at Lahore heard of the heavy losses the expeditionary force had sustained, and of General Chamberlain being *hors de combat* from his wound, further reinforcements from every direction were hurried to the front. Subsequently, however, it became a question whether the troops should not be withdrawn altogether, and the punishment of the fanatics given up, the Government of India and the Punjab Government being completely in accord in favouring this view, while the Commissioner of Peshawar, Major James (who had succeeded Reynell Taylor),† and Sir Hugh Rose were as strongly opposed to a retrograde movement. The Commander-in-Chief pointed out to the Government that the loss of prestige and power we must sustain by retiring from the Umbeyla Pass would be more disastrous, both from a military and political point of view, than anything that could happen save the destruction of the force itself, and that General Chamberlain, on whose sound judgment he could rely, was quite sure that a retirement was unnecessary.

Unfortunately at this time the Viceroy died at Dharmsala, and the question remained in abeyance pending the arrival of Sir William Denison, Governor of Madras, who was coming round to take over the reins of Government until a successor to Lord Elgin should be sent from England.

In the meantime Sir Hugh Rose was most anxious to obtain exact information respecting our position at Umbeyla, the means of operating from it, the nature of the ground—in fact, all details which could only be satisfactorily obtained by sending someone to report on the situation, with whom he had had personal communication regarding the points about which he required to be enlightened. He therefore determined to despatch two officers on special service, whose duty it would be to put the Commander-in-Chief in possession of all the facts of the case; accordingly, Colonel Adye‡ (Deputy-Adjutant-General of Royal Artillery) and I were ordered to proceed to Umbeyla without delay.

Adye proved a most charming travelling companion, clever and entertaining, and I think we both enjoyed our journey. We reached the pass on the 25th November.

There had been no fighting for some days, and most of the wounded had been removed. Sir Neville Chamberlain was still in camp, and I was sorry to find him suffering greatly from his wound. We were

* 7th Royal Fusiliers, 23rd Pioneers, and 24th Punjab Native Infantry.

† Reynell Taylor remained with the force as political officer.

‡ General Sir John Adye, G.C.B.

much interested in going over the piquets and listening to the story of the different attacks made upon them, which had evidently been conducted by the enemy with as much skill as courage.* The loyalty of our Native soldiers struck me as having been most remarkable. Not a single desertion had occurred, although all the Native regiments engaged, with the exception of the Gurkhas and Punjab Pioneers, had amongst them members of the several tribes we were fighting, and many of our soldiers were even closely related to some of the hostile tribesmen; on one occasion a young Buner sepoy actually recognized his own father amongst the enemy's dead when the fight was over.†

We listened to many tales of the gallantry of the British officers. The names of Brownlow, Keyes,‡ and Hughes § were on everyone's lips, and Brownlow's defence of the Eagle's Nest on the 26th October, and of the 'Crag piquet' on the 12th November, spoke volumes for his coolness and pluck, and for the implicit faith reposed in him by the men of the 20th Punjab Infantry, the regiment he had raised in 1857 when but a subaltern. In his official report the General remarked that 'to Major Brownlow's determination and personal example he attributed the preservation of the "Crag piquet."' And Keyes's recapture of the same piquet was described by Sir Neville as 'a most brilliant exploit, stamping Major Keyes as an officer possessing some of the highest military qualifications.' Brownlow and Keyes were both recommended for the Victoria Cross.

* The expedition was an admirable school for training men in outpost duty. The Pathans and Gurkhas were quite at home at such work, and not only able to take care of themselves, but when stalked by the enemy were equal to a counter-stalk, often most successful. The enemy used to joke with Brownlow's and Keyes's men on these occasions, and say, 'We don't want you. Where are the *lal pagriwalas?* [as the 14th Sikhs were called from their *lal pagris* (red turbans)] or the *goralog* [the Europeans]? They are better *shikar* [sport]!' The tribesmen soon discovered that the Sikhs and Europeans, though full of fight, were very helpless on the hill-side, and could not keep their heads under cover.

† Colonel Reynell Taylor, whilst bearing like testimony to the good conduct of the Pathan soldiery, said the personal influence of officers will always be found to be the only stand-by for the Government interests when the religious cry is raised, and the fidelity of our troops is being tampered with. Pay, pensions, and orders of merit may, and would, be cast to the winds when the honour of the faith was in the scale; but to snap the associations of years, and to turn in his hour of need against the man whom he has proved to be just and worthy, whom he has noted in the hour of danger, and praised as a hero to his family, is just what a Pathan will not do—to his honour be it said. The fact was that the officers in camp had been so long and kindly associated with their soldiers that the latter were willing to set them before their great religious teacher, the Akhund of Swat ('Records of Expeditions against the North-West Frontier Tribes').

‡ The late General Sir Charles Keyes, G.C.B.

§ The late Major-General T. E. Hughes, C.B., Royal Artillery.

We (Adye and I) had no difficulty in making up our minds as to the course which ought to be taken. The column was daily being strengthened by the arrival of reinforcements, and although the combination of the tribesmen was still formidable, the enemy were showing signs of being disheartened by their many losses, and of a wish to come to terms.

Having consulted the civil and military authorities on the spot, we informed the Commander-in-Chief that they were of opinion a withdrawal would be most unwise, and that it was hoped that on the arrival of General Garvock* (Chamberlain's successor) an advance would be made into the Chamla valley, for there would then be a sufficient number of troops to undertake an onward move, as well as to hold the present position, which, as we told the Chief, was one of the strongest we had ever seen.

Sir William Denison reached Calcutta on the 2nd December. A careful study of the correspondence in connexion with the Umbeyla expedition satisfied him that the Commander-in-Chief's views were correct, and that a retirement would be unwise.

Sir Hugh Rose had previously requested to be allowed to personally conduct the operations, and in anticipation of the Government acceding to his request, he had sent a light camp to Hasan Abdal, from which place he intended to push on to Umbeyla; and with the object of collecting troops near the frontier, where they would be available as a reserve should the expedition not be soon and satisfactorily settled, he desired me to select an encamping-ground between Rawal Pindi and Attock suitable for 10,000 men.

Leaving Adye in the pass, I started for Attock, where I spent three days riding about in search of a promising site for the camp. I settled upon a place near Hasan Abdal, which, however, was not in the end made use of. The people of the country were very helpful to me; indeed, when they heard I had been a friend of John Nicholson, they seemed to think they could not do enough for me, and delighted in talking of their old leader, whom they declared to be the greatest man they had ever known.

On my return I marched up the pass with the Rev. W. G. Cowie† and Probyn, who, with 400 Cavalry, had been ordered to the front to be in readiness for a move into the Chamla valley. James, the Commissioner, had been working to detach the Bunerwals from the combination against us, and on the afternoon of our arrival a deputation of their headmen arrived in camp, and before their departure the next morning they promised to accompany a force proceeding to destroy Malka, and to expel the Hindustani fanatics from the Buner country.

* The late General Sir John Garvock, G.C.B.

† Now Bishop of Auckland and Primate of New Zealand.

Later, however, a messenger came in to say they could not fulfil their promise, being unable to resist the pressure brought to bear upon them by their co-religionists. The man further reported that large numbers of fresh tribesmen had appeared on the scene, and that it was intended to attack us on the 16th. He advised the Commissioner to take the initiative, and gave him to understand that if we advanced the Bunerwals would stand aloof.

Sir Hugh Rose had been accorded permission to take command of the troops in the field, and had sent word to General Garvock not 'to attempt any operations until further orders.' James, however, thinking that the situation demanded immediate action, as disturbances had broken out in other parts of the Peshawar valley, deprecated delay, and pressed Garvock to advance, telling him that a successful fight would put matters straight. Garvock consented to follow the Commissioner's advice, and arranged to move on the following day.

The force was divided into three columns. The first and second—consisting of about 4,800 men, and commanded respectively by Colonel W. Turner, C.B.,* and Lieutenant-Colonel Wilde, C.B.—were to form the attacking party, while the third, about 3,000 strong, under the command of Lieutenant-Colonel Vaughan,† was to be left for the protection of the camp.

At daybreak, on the 15th, the troops for the advance, unencumbered by tents or baggage, and each man carrying two days' rations, assembled at the base of the 'Crag piquet.' Turner, an excellent officer, who during the short time he had been at Umbeyla had inspired great confidence by his soldierly qualities, had on the previous afternoon reconnoitred to the right of the camp, and had discovered that about 4,000 men were holding the village of Lalu, from which it was necessary to dislodge them before Umbeyla could be attacked. On being told to advance, therefore, Turner moved off in the direction of Lalu, and, driving the enemy's piquets before him, occupied the heights overlooking the valley, out of which rose, immediately in front about 200 yards off, a conical hill which hid Lalu from view. This hill, which was crowded with Hindustani fanatics and their Pathan allies, was a most formidable position; the sides were precipitous, and the summit was strengthened by *sangars*.‡ No further move could be made until the enemy were dislodged, so Turner lined the heights all round with his Infantry, and opened fire with his Mountain guns. Meanwhile, Wilde's column had cleared off the enemy from the front of the camp, and formed up on Turner's left. On the advance being sounded, Turner's Infantry rushed down the slopes, and in ten minutes could be seen driving the enemy from the heights on his right; at the

* The late Brigadier-General Sir W. W. Turner, K.C.B.
† General Sir T. L. Vaughan, K.C.B.
‡ Stone breastworks.

THE STORMING OF THE CONICAL HILL AT UMBEYLA BY THE 101st FOOT (BENGAL FUSILIERS).

From a sketch by General Sir John Adye, G.C.B., R.A.

same time the 101st Fusiliers, the leading regiment of Wilde's column, made straight for the top of the conical hill, and, under cover of the fire from the Mountain guns of both columns, and supported by the Guides, 4th Gurkhas, and 23rd Pioneers, they climbed the almost perpendicular sides. When near the top a short halt was made to give the men time to get their breath; the signal being then given, amidst a shower of bullets and huge stones, the position was stormed, and carried at the point of the bayonet. It was a grand sight as Adye and I watched it from Hughes's battery; but we were considerably relieved when we perceived the enemy flying down the sides of the hill, and heard the cheers of the gallant Fusiliers as they stood victorious on the highest peak.

Now that the enemy were on the run it was the time to press them, and this Turner did so effectually that the leading men of his column entered Lalu simultaneously with the last of the fugitives. The rapidity of this movement was so unexpected that it threw the enemy inside the walls into confusion; they made no stand, and were soon in full retreat towards Umbeyla and the passes leading into Buner.

While affairs were thus prospering on our right, the enemy, apparently imagining we were too busy to think of our left, came in large numbers from the village of Umbeyla, threatening the camp and the communications of the second column. Wilde, however, was prepared for them, and held his ground until reinforced by Turner, when he made a forward movement. The Guides, and detachments of the 5th Gurkhas and 3rd Sikhs, charged down one spur, and the 101st down another; the enemy were driven off with great slaughter, leaving a standard in the hands of the Gurkhas, and exposing themselves in their flight to Turner's guns. During the day they returned, and, gathering on the heights, made several unsuccessful attacks upon our camp. At last, about 2 p.m., Brownlow, who was in command of the right defences, assumed the offensive, and, aided by Keyes, moved out of the breastworks and, by a succession of well-executed charges, completely cleared the whole front of the position, and drove the tribesmen with great loss into the plain below.

All opposition having now ceased, and the foe being in full retreat, the force bivouacked for the night. We had 16 killed and 67 wounded; while our opponents admitted to 400 killed and wounded.

The next morning we were joined by Probyn with 200 sabres of the 11th Bengal Lancers and the same number of the Guides; and after a hasty breakfast the order was given to march into the Chamla valley. My duty was to accompany the Mountain batteries and show them the way. As we debouched into comparatively open country, the enemy appeared on a ridge which completely covered our approach to Umbeyla, and we could descry many standards flying on the most prominent points. The road was so extremely difficult that it was half-past two o'clock before the whole force was clear of the hills.

General Garvock, having made a careful reconnaissance of the enemy's position, which was of great strength and peculiarly capable of defence, had decided to turn their right, a movement which was to be entrusted to the second column, and I was told to inform Turner that he must try and cut them off from the Buner Pass as they retreated. I found Turner close to Umbeyla and delivered my message. He moved forward at once with the 23rd Pioneers and a wing of the 32nd Pioneers in line, supported by the second wing, having in reserve a wing of the 7th Royal Fusiliers.

When we had passed the village of Umbeyla, which was in flames, having been set fire to by our Cavalry, the wing of the 32nd was brought up in prolongation of our line to the right. The advance was continued to within about 800 yards of the Buner Pass, when Turner, observing a large body of the enemy threatening his left flank, immediately sent two companies of the Royal Fusiliers in that direction. Just at that moment a band of *Ghazis* furiously attacked the left flank, which was at a disadvantage, having got into broken ground covered with low jungle. In a few seconds five of the Pioneer British officers were on the ground, one killed and four wounded; numbers of the men were knocked over, and the rest, staggered by the suddenness of the onslaught, fell back on their reserve, where they found the needed support, for the Fusiliers stood as firm as a rock. At the critical moment when the *Ghazis* made their charge, Wright, the Assistant-Adjutant-General, and I, being close by, rushed in amongst the Pioneers and called on them to follow us; as we were personally known to the men of both regiments, they quickly pulled themselves together and responded to our efforts to rally them. It was lucky they did so, for had there been any delay or hesitation, the enemy, who thronged the slopes above us, would certainly have come down in great numbers, and we should have had a most difficult task. As it was, we were entirely successful in repulsing the *Ghazis*, not a man of whom escaped. We counted 200 of the enemy killed; our losses were comparatively slight—8 killed and 80 wounded.

We bivouacked for the night near the village of Umbeyla, and the next morning the Bunerwals, who, true to their word, had taken no part in the fighting on the 15th or 16th, came in and made their submission.

The question which now had to be decided was, whether a force fully equipped and strong enough to overcome all opposition should be sent to destroy the fanatic settlement of Malka, or whether the work of annihilation should be entrusted to the Bunerwals, witnessed by British officers. The latter course was eventually adopted, chiefly on account of the delay which provisioning a brigade would entail—a delay which the Commissioner was anxious to avoid—for although for the present the combination had broken up, and most of the tribesmen were dispersing to their homes, the Akhund of Swat and his followers were still hovering about in the neighbourhood, and inaction on our part would in all probability have led to a fresh gathering and renewed hostilities.

The terms which were drawn up, and to which the Bunerwals agreed, were:

The breaking-up of the tribal gathering in the Buner Pass.

The destruction of Malka; those carrying out the work to be accompanied by British officers and such escort as might be considered necessary by us.

The expulsion of the Hindustanis from the Buner, Chamla, and Amazai countries.

And, finally, it was stipulated that the headmen of their tribe should be left as hostages until such time as the requirements should have been fulfilled.

On the afternoon of Saturday, the 19th December, the little party of British officers who were to witness the destruction of Malka assembled at Umbeyla. Its members were Reynell Taylor (who was in charge), Alex. Taylor (Commanding Engineer), two Survey officers, Wright, Adye, and myself. Twenty-five Cavalry and 4 companies of the Guides Infantry, under four officers, formed our escort, and it had been arranged that we were to be accompanied by four leading Buner Khans, with 2,000 followers, who would be responsible for our safety, and destroy the fanatics' stronghold in our presence. Rain was falling heavily, but as all our arrangements had been made, and delay was considered undesirable, it was settled that we should make a start. It was rough travelling, and it was almost dark when we reached Kuria, only eight miles on our way, where we halted for the night, and where we had to remain the next day, as the Bunerwals declared they could not continue the journey until they had come to an understanding with the Amazais, in whose territory Malka was situated.

We had noticed on leaving Umbeyla that, instead of 2,000 Bunerwals, there were only about sixty or seventy at the most, and in reply to our repeated questions as to what had become of the remainder, we were told they would join us later on. It soon became evident, however, that no more were coming, and that the Khans thought it wiser to trust to their own influence with the Amazais rather than to intimidation.

We made a fresh start on the morning of the 21st. Malka was only twelve miles off, but the way was so difficult, and our guides stopped so often to consult with the numerous bands of armed men we came across, that it was sunset before we arrived at our destination.

Malka was perched on a spur of the Mahabun mountain, some distance below its highest peak. It was a strong, well-built place, with accommodation for about 1,500 people. The Amazais did not attempt to disguise their disgust at our presence in their country, and they gathered in knots, scowling and pointing at us, evidently discussing whether we should or should not be allowed to return.

The next morning Malka was set on fire, and the huge column of smoke which ascended from the burning village, and was visible for miles round, did not tend to allay the ill-feeling so plainly displayed. The Native officers of the Guides warned us that delay was dangerous, as the people were becoming momentarily more excited, and were vowing we should never return. It was no use, however, to attempt to make a move without the consent of the tribesmen, for we were a mere handful compared to the thousands who had assembled around Malka, and we were separated from our camp by twenty miles of most difficult country. Our position was no doubt extremely critical, and it was well for us that we had at our head such a cool, determined leader as Reynell Taylor. I greatly admired the calm, quiet manner in which he went up and spoke to the headmen, telling them that, the object of our visit having been accomplished, we were ready to retrace our steps. At this the Amazais became still further excited. They talked in loud tones, and gesticulated in true Pathan fashion, thronging round Taylor, who stood quite alone and perfectly self-possessed in the midst of the angry and dangerous-looking multitude. At this crisis the Bunerwals came to our rescue. The most influential of the tribe, a grey-bearded warrior, who had lost an eye and an arm in some tribal contest, forced his way through the rapidly increasing crowd to Taylor's side, and, raising his one arm to enjoin silence, delivered himself as follows: 'You are hesitating whether you will allow these English to return unmolested. You can, of course, murder them and their escort; but if you do, you must kill us Bunerwals first, for we have sworn to protect them, and we will do so with our lives.' This plucky speech produced a quieting effect, and taking advantage of the lull in the storm, we set out on our return journey; but evidently the tribesmen did not consider the question finally or satisfactorily settled, for they followed us the whole way to Kuria. The slopes of the hills on both sides were covered with men. Several times we were stopped while stormy discussions took place, and once, as we were passing through a narrow defile, an armed Amazai, waving a standard above his head, rushed down towards us. Fortunately for us, he was stopped by some of those less inimically disposed; for if he had succeeded in inciting anyone to fire a single shot, the desire for blood would quickly have spread, and in all probability not one of our party would have escaped.

On the 23rd December we reached our camp in the Umbeyla Pass, when the force, which had only been kept there till our return, retired to the plains and was broken up.

During my absence at Umbeyla my wife remained with friends at

Mian Mir for some time, and then made her way to Peshawar, where I joined her on Christmas Day. She spent one night *en route* in Sir Hugh Rose's camp at Hasan Abdal, and found the Chief in great excitement and very angry at such a small party having been sent to Malka, and placed at the mercy of the tribes. He did not know that my wife had arrived, and in passing her tent she heard him say: 'It was madness, and not one of them will ever come back alive.' She was of course dreadfully frightened. As soon as Sir Hugh heard she was in camp, he went to see her, and tried to soften down what he knew she must have heard; but he could not conceal his apprehension; and my poor wife's anxiety was terrible, for she did not hear another word till the morning of the day I returned to her.

CHAPTER XXXVI.

Early in the New Year (1864) Sir Hugh Rose, with the Head-Quarters camp, marched into Peshawar, where we remained until the middle of February. The time was chiefly spent in inspections, parades, and field-days, varied by an occasional run with the hounds. The hunting about Peshawar was very fair, and we all, the Chief included, got a great deal of fun out of our small pack.

On the 25th January a full-dress parade was held to announce to the garrison that Sir John Lawrence had been appointed Viceroy of India, and soon afterwards we left Peshawar and began our return march to Simla.

We changed our house this year and took one close to the Stewarts, an arrangement for which I was very thankful later, when my wife had a great sorrow in the death of her sister, Mrs. Sladen, at Peshawar. It was everything for her at such a time to have a kind and sympathizing friend close at hand, when I was engaged with my work and could be very little with her during the day. At this time, as at all others, Sir Hugh Rose was a most considerate friend to us; he placed his house at Mashobra at my wife's disposal, thus providing her with a quiet resort which she frequently made use of and which she learned to love so much that, when I returned to Simla as Commander-in-Chief, her first thought was to secure this lovely 'Retreat' as a refuge from the (sometimes) slightly trying gaiety of Simla.

The Commander-in-Chief was good enough to send in my name for a brevet for the Umbeyla expedition, but the Viceroy refused to forward the recommendation, for the reason that I was 'too junior to be made a Lieutenant-Colonel.' I was then thirty-two!

Throughout the whole of 1864 I was more or less ill; the office work (which never suited me quite as well as more active employment) was excessive, for, in addition to the ordinary routine, I had undertaken to revise the 'Bengal Route-Book,' which had become quite obsolete, having been compiled in 1837, when Kurnal was our frontier station. A voyage round the Cape was still considered the panacea for all Indian ailments, and the doctors strongly advised my taking leave to England, and travelling by that route.

We left Simla towards the end of October, and, after spending the next three months in Calcutta, where I was chiefly employed in taking up transports and superintending the embarkation of troops returning to England, I was given the command of a batch of 300 time-expired men on board the *Renown*, one of Green's frigate-built ships which was chartered for their conveyance. Two hundred of the men belonged to the 2nd and 3rd Battalions of the Rifle Brigade, the remainder to the Artillery and various other corps; they had all been twelve years in the army, and most of them were decorated for service in the Crimea and Indian Mutiny.

At the inspection parade before we embarked, a certain number of men were brought up for punishment for various offences committed on the way down country; none of the misdemeanours appeared to me very serious, so I determined to let the culprits off. I told the men that we had now met for the first time and I was unwilling to commence our acquaintance by awarding punishments; we had to spend three or four months together, and I hoped they would show, by their good behaviour while under my command, that I had not made a mistake in condoning their transgressions. The officers seemed somewhat surprised at my action in this matter, but I think it was proved by the men's subsequent conduct that I had not judged them incorrectly, for they all behaved in quite an exemplary manner throughout the voyage.

We had been on board more than six weeks, when one of the crew was attacked by small pox—an untoward circumstance in a crowded ship. The sailor was placed in a boat which was hung over the ship's side, and a cabin-boy, the marks on whose face plainly showed that he had already suffered badly from the disease, was told off to look after him. The man recovered, and there was no other case. Shortly before we reached St. Helena, scurvy appeared amongst the troops, necessitating lime-juice being given in larger quantities, but what proved a more effectual remedy was water-cress, many sacks of which were laid in before we left the island.

On the 29th May, 1865, we sighted the 'Lizard,' and took a pilot on board, who brought with him a few newspapers, which confirmed the tidings signalled to us by an American ship that the war between the Federals and Confederates was at an end. How eagerly we scanned the journals, after having heard nothing from home for four months, but the only piece of news we found of personal interest to ourselves was that my father had been made a K.C.B.

On the 30th May we reached Portsmouth, and landed between two showers of snow! I had a final parade of the men before leaving the ship, and I was quite sorry to say good-bye to them; some of the poor fellows were already beginning to be anxious about their future, and to regret that their time with the colours was over.

My father, mother, and sister came up to London to meet us, very little changed since I had left them six years before. I remained in England till March, 1866, when I returned to India, leaving my wife behind to follow in the autumn.

While I was at home, Sir Hugh Rose's term of the chief command in India came to an end, and his place had been taken by Sir William Mansfield. On my arrival in Calcutta, I received orders to join the Allahabad division, and thither I proceeded. In October I went to Calcutta to meet my wife and take her to Allahabad, where we remained for nearly a year, her first experience of a hot season in the plains, and a very bad one it was. Cholera was rife; the troops had to be sent away into camps, more or less distant from the station, all of which had to be visited once, if not twice, daily; this kept me pretty well on the move from morning till night. It was a sad time for everyone. People we had seen alive and well one day were dead and buried the next; and in the midst of all this sorrow and tragedy, the most irksome—because such an incongruous—part of our experience was that we had constantly to get up entertainments, penny readings, and the like, to amuse the men and keep their minds occupied, for if once soldiers begin to think of the terrors of cholera, they are seized with panic, and many get the disease from pure fright.

My wife usually accompanied me to the cholera camps, preferring to do this rather than be left alone at home. On one occasion, I had just got into our carriage after going round the hospital, when a young officer ran after us to tell me a corporal in whom I had been much interested was dead. The poor fellow's face was blue; the cholera panic had evidently seized him, and I said to my wife, 'He will be the next.' I had no sooner reached home than I received a report of his having been seized.

We were fortunate in having at Allahabad as Chaplain the present Bishop of Lahore, who, with his wife, had only lately come to India; they never wearied in doing all that was possible for the soldiers. Bishop Matthew is still one of our closest friends; his good, charming, and accomplished wife, alas! died some years ago.

We remained at Allahabad until August, 1867, when we heard that a brigade from Bengal was likely to be required to take part in an expedition which would probably be sent from Bombay to Abyssinia for the relief of some Europeans whom the King, Theodore, had imprisoned, and that the Mountain battery, on the strength of which my name was still borne, would in such case be employed. I therefore thought I had better go to Simla, see the authorities, and arrange for rejoining my battery, if the rumour turned out to be true. The cholera had now disappeared, so I was at liberty to take leave, and we both looked forward to a cooler climate and a change to brighter scenes after the wretched experience we had been through. On my arrival at Simla I called upon the Commander-in-Chief and told him that, if my battery was sent on service, I wished to join it and was quite ready to resign my staff appointment.

Sir William Mansfield was particularly kind in his reception of me, from which I augured well; but I could learn nothing definite, and it was not until quite the end of September that it was announced that Colonel Donald Stewart was to have command of the Bengal Brigade with the Abyssinian Force, and that I was to be his Assistant-Quartermaster-General. We at once hastened back to Allahabad, where we only remained long enough to pack up what we wanted to take with us, and arrange for the disposal of our property; thence we proceeded to Calcutta, where, for the next two months, I had a busy time taking up transports and superintending the equipment of the force.

I had often read and heard of the difficulties and delays experienced by troops landing in a foreign country, in consequence of their requirements not being all shipped in the same vessels with themselves—men in one ship, camp equipage in another, transport and field hospital in a third, or perhaps the mules in one and their pack-saddles in another; and I determined to try and prevent these mistakes upon this occasion. With Stewart's approval, I arranged that each detachment should embark complete in every detail, which resulted in the troops being landed and marched off without the least delay as each vessel reached its destination.*

* The average strength of the regiments was as follows: 10th and 12th Bengal Cavalry, each 9 British officers, 13 Native officers, 450 non-commissioned officers and men, 3 Native doctors, 489 horses, 322 mules, 590 followers. 21st and 23rd Punjab Infantry, each 9 British officers, 16 Native officers, 736 non-commissioned officers and men, 3 Native doctors, 10 horses, 350 mules, 400 followers. I found that six ships were required for the conveyance of a Cavalry and four for that of an Infantry regiment; for the Mountain battery three ships were necessary, and for the coolie corps (1,550 strong) four; in all twenty-seven ships, besides nine tugs. In selecting ships, care was taken to secure those intended for Artillery or Cavalry as high 'tween-decks as possible; a sufficient number of these were procurable at Calcutta, either iron clippers from Liverpool or large North American built traders with decks varying from 7 feet 6 inches to 8 feet 2 inches high. I gave the preference to wooden ships, as being cooler and more easily ventilated. The vessels taken up were each from 1,000 to 1,400 tons, averaging in length from 150 to 200 feet, with a beam varying from 30 to 35 feet, and usually they had a clear upper deck, where from forty to fifty animals were accommodated.

We were living with the Stewarts in the Commander-in-Chief's quarters in Fort William, which His Excellency had placed at our disposal for the time being. On the 1st November Calcutta was visited by the second cyclone within my experience. We had arranged to go to the opera that evening, but when it was time to start the wind was so high that there seemed every chance of the carriage being blown over before we could get there, so we decided not to attempt it. It was well we did, for the few adventurous spirits who struggled through the storm had the greatest difficulty in getting back to their homes. The opera-house was unroofed before the performance was half over, and very little of the building remained standing the next day. At bedtime we still thought it was only a bad storm, but towards midnight the wind increased to an alarming extent, and my wife awoke me, and begged me to get up, as the windows were being burst open and deluges of rain coming in. Stewart and I tried to reclose the windows, but the thick iron bars had been bent in two and forced out of their sockets; a heavy oak plate-chest and boxes, which we with much difficulty dragged across the windows, were blown into the middle of the dining-room, like so much cardboard, and the whole place was gradually flooded. We were driven out of each room in turn, till at length we all took refuge in a small box room, about ten feet wide, right in the middle of the house, where we remained the rest of the night and 'hoped for the day.'

Towards morning the wind abated, but what a scene of desolation was that upon which we emerged! The rooms looked as if they could never be made habitable again, and much of our property was floating about in a foot of water.

My first thought was for the shipping, and I hurried down to the river to see how my transports had fared. Things were much better than I expected to find them—only two had been damaged. Most fortunately the cyclone, having come from a different direction, was not accompanied by a storm-wave such as that which worked so much mischief amongst the shipping on a former occasion, but the destruction on land was even greater: all the finest trees were torn up by the roots, a great part of the Native bazaar was levelled, and lay from two to three feet deep in water, while many houses were wholly or partly demolished. We came across most curious sights when driving round Calcutta in the evening; some of the houses were divided clean down the centre, one half crumbled into a heap of ruins, the other half still standing and displaying, as in a doll's house, the furniture in the different stories.

The work of filling up and loading the vessels was greatly retarded, owing to a large number of cargo boats having been sunk, consequently it was the 5th December before the first transport got off: from that date the others started in quick succession, and on the 9th

January, 1868, Stewart and his staff left Calcutta in the P. and O. steamer *Golconda*. The officers and men of the Mountain battery were also on board, Captain Bogle in command, my friend Jemmy Hills in my place as second Captain, and Collen* and Disney as subalterns. Mrs. Stewart and my wife accompanied us as far as Aden, where they were left to the kind care of Major-General Russell,† commanding there at the time, until the arrival of the mail-steamer in which they were to proceed to England.

On the 3rd February we anchored in Annesley Bay and landed at Zula.

CHAPTER XXXVII.

It will, perhaps, be as well to recall to the reader's mind that the object of the expedition in which we were taking part was to rescue some sixty Europeans, who, from one cause or another, had found their way to Abyssinia, and been made prisoners by the King of that country. Amongst these were four English officials, Mr. Rassam, and Captain Cameron, who had at different times been the bearers of letters from Queen Victoria to King Theodore, and Lieutenant Prideaux and Dr. Blanc of the Bombay Army; the rest were chiefly French and German missionaries, and artisans, with their wives and children. The prisoners were confined in a fort built on the Magdāla plateau, 9,150 feet above sea-level, and 379 miles inland from Annesley Bay.

The repeated demands of the British Government for the restoration of the prisoners having been treated with contemptuous silence by the King, Colonel Merewether, the Political Agent at Aden, who in July, 1867, had been directed to proceed to Massowa and endeavour to obtain the release of the captives, and to make inquiries and collect information in case of an expedition having to be sent, reported to the Secretary of State that he had failed to communicate with the King, and urged the advisability of immediate measures being taken to prepare a force in India for the punishment of Theodore and the rescue of the prisoners. Colonel Merewether added that in Abyssinia the opinion had become very general that England knew herself to be too weak to resent insult, and that amongst the peoples of the neighbouring countries, even so far as Aden, there was a feeling of contemptuous surprise at the continued long-suffering endurance of the British Government.

On receipt of this communication, Her Majesty's Government,

* Now Major-General Sir Edwin Collen, K.C.I.E., Military Member of the Governor-General's Council.

† Now General Sir Edward Lechmere Russell, K.C.S.I.

having exhausted all their resources for the preservation of peace, decided to send an expedition from India under the command of Lieutenant-General Sir Robert Napier, the Commander-in-Chief of the Bombay Army. After carefully considering the distance along which operations would have to be prosecuted, and the necessity for holding a number of detached posts, Napier gave it as his opinion that the force should consist of not less than 12,000 men.*

Profiting by the experience of the Crimean War, the Government was determined that the mobility of the force should not be hampered by want of food and clothing. Stores of all descriptions were despatched in unstinted quantities from England, and three of the steamers in which they were conveyed were fitted up as hospital ships. But food, clothing, and stores, however liberally supplied, would not take the army to Magdāla without transport.

The question as to the most suitable organization for the Land Transport Corps occupied a good deal of Sir Robert Napier's attention while the expedition was being fitted out, and caused a considerable amount of correspondence between him and the Bombay Government. The Commissary-General wished to keep the corps under his own orders, and objected to its being given an entirely military organization. Sir Robert Napier preferred to establish the corps on an independent basis, but was at first overruled by the Bombay Government. While acting in accordance with their orders, the Commander-in-Chief wrote: 'I believe that the success of systems depends more on the men who work them than on the systems themselves; but I cannot accept without protest a decision to throw such a body of men as the drivers of our transport animals will be (if we get them) on an expedition in a foreign country without a very complete organization to secure order and discipline.' Eventually Sir Robert got his own way, but much valuable time had been lost, and the corps was organized on too small a scale;† the officers and non-commissioned officers were not sent to Zula in sufficient time or in sufficient numbers to take charge of the transport animals as they arrived.

A compact, properly-supervised train of 2,600 mules, with serviceable, well-fitting pack-saddles, was sent from the Punjab; and from Bombay came 1,400 mules and ponies and 5,600 bullocks, but these numbers proving altogether inadequate to the needs of the expedition, they were supplemented by animals purchased in Persia, Egypt, and

* The numbers actually despatched from India were 13,548, of whom 3,786 were Europeans. In addition, a company of Royal Engineers was sent from England.

† At first it was thought that 10,000 mules, with a coolie corps 3,000 strong, would suffice, but before the expedition was over, it was found necessary to purchase 18,000 mules, 1,500 ponies, 1,800 donkeys, 12,000 camels, and 8,400 bullocks.

on the shores of the Mediterranean. The men to look after them were supplied from the same sources, but their number, even if they had been efficient, was insufficient, and they were a most unruly and unmanageable lot. They demanded double the pay for which they had enlisted, and struck work in a body because their demand was not at once complied with. They refused to take charge of the five mules each man was hired to look after, and when that number was reduced to three, they insisted that one should be used as a mount for the driver. But the worst part of the whole organization, or, rather, want of organization, was that there had been no attempt to fit the animals with pack-saddles, some of which were sent from England, some from India, and had to be adjusted to the mules after they had been landed in Abyssinia, where there was not an establishment to make the necessary alterations. The consequence was that the wretched animals became cruelly galled, and in a few weeks a large percentage were unfit for work, and had to be sent to the sick depot.

Other results of having no properly arranged transport train, and no supervision or discipline, were that mules were lost or stolen, starved for want of food, or famished from want of water. The condition of the unfortunate animals was such that, though they had been but a few weeks in the country, when they were required to proceed to Senafe, only sixty-seven miles distant, a very small proportion were able to accomplish the march; hundreds died on the way, and their carcases, quickly decomposing in the hot sun, became a fruitful source of dangerous disease to the force.

On arrival at Zula, we were told that Sir Robert Napier was at Senafe, the first station in the Hills, and the advanced depot for supplies. We of the Bengal brigade were somewhat disconcerted at the orders which awaited us, from which we learned that our brigade was to be broken up; the troops were to proceed to the front; while Stewart was to take command at Senafe, and I myself was to remain at Zula, as senior staff officer. The disappointment was great, but, being the last-comer, I had no unfairness to complain of, and I had plenty to do. I spent the greater part of each day amongst the shipping, superintending the embarkation and disembarkation of men, animals, and stores.

Zula was not an attractive place of residence. The heat was intense —117° in the daytime in my tent. The allowance of fresh water was extremely limited,* while the number of scorpions was quite the reverse, and the food, at the best, was not appetizing. Few who remained there as long as I did escaped scurvy and horrible boils or sores. I was fortunate, however, in finding in charge of the transport

* Fresh water was obtained by condensing the sea-water; there were few condensers, and no means of aërating the water.

arrangements afloat, my old friend and Eton schoolfellow, George Tryon,* to whom I owed many a good dinner, and, what I appreciated even more, many a refreshing bath on board the *Euphrates*, a transport belonging to the British India Steam Navigation Company which had been fitted up for Captain Tryon and his staff. Indeed, all the officers of the Royal Navy were most helpful and kind, and I have a very pleasant recollection of the hospitality I received from Commodore Heath† and those serving under him.

During the four months I remained at Zula, Tryon and I were constantly together, and I had plenty of opportunity for observing the masterly manner in which he could grasp a situation, his intimate knowledge of detail, and the strong hold he had over all those working with him, not only the officers of the Royal Navy, but also the commanders of the merchant vessels taken up as transports, and lying in Annesley Bay.

On the 17th April news reached us that four days before Sir Robert Napier had successfully attacked Magdāla and released the prisoners, having experienced but very slight opposition; and that King Theodore, deserted by his army, which had apparently become tired of his brutalities, had committed suicide.‡ A few days later Major-General Russell, who had come from Aden to take over the command at Zula, received orders to prepare for the embarkation of the force. Arrangements were accordingly made to enable regiments and batteries to be embarked on board the transports told off for them directly they arrived from the front—a matter of the utmost importance, both on account of the fearful heat at Zula, and the absence of a sufficient water-supply.

On the 2nd June the Commander-in-Chief returned to Zula, and on the 10th he embarked on board the old Indian marine steamer *Feroze* for Suez. Sir Robert was good enough to ask me to accompany him, as he wished to make me the bearer of his final despatches. My work was ended, the troops had all left, and as I was pretty well knocked up, I felt extremely grateful for the offer, and very proud of the great honour the Chief proposed to confer upon me.

We reached Alexandria on the 20th June, and the next day I started in the mail-steamer for Brindisi, arriving in London on the evening of Sunday, the 28th. I received a note at my club from Edwin Johnson (who was at that time Assistant Military Secretary to H.R.H. the Duke of Cambridge), directing me to take the despatches without delay to the Secretary of State for India. I found Sir Stafford and Lady Northcote at dinner; Sir Stafford looked through the despatches,

* The late Admiral Sir George Tryon, K.C.B.

† Now Admiral Sir Leopold Heath, K.C.B.

‡ He is said to have killed in one month, or burnt alive, more than 3,000 people. He pillaged and burnt the churches at Gondur, and had many priests and young girls cast alive into the flames.

and when he had finished reading them, he asked me to take them without delay to the Commander-in-Chief, as he knew the Duke was most anxious to see them. There was a dinner-party, however, that night at Gloucester House, and the servant told me it was quite impossible to disturb His Royal Highness; so, placing my card on the top of the despatches, I told the man to deliver them at once, and went back to my club. I had scarcely reached it when the Duke's Aide-de-camp made his appearance and told me that he had been ordered to find me and take me back with him. The Commander-in-Chief received me very kindly, expressing regret that I had been sent away in the first instance; and Their Royal Highnesses the Prince and Princess of Wales, who were present, were most gracious, and asked many questions about the Abyssinian Expedition.

The next day I joined my wife, who was staying with my people at Clifton, and on the 14th August, when the rewards for the Abyssinian Expedition were published, my name appeared for a brevet Lieutenant-Colonelcy.

I was now anxious to ascertain in what manner I was to be employed. My five years as A.Q.M.G. were about to expire, and I thought I should like to go back to my regiment for a time. I therefore applied for the command of a battery of Horse Artillery. I was told, in answer to my application, that it was not the custom to appoint an officer who had been in staff employment for some time to the mounted branch, but that, in consideration of my services, the Duke of Cambridge was pleased to make an exception in my favour. I was posted to a battery at Meerut, and warned to be ready to start in an early troopship. Before the time for our departure arrived, however, I received a letter from Lumsden, who had now become Quartermaster-General, informing me that the Commander-in-Chief had recommended, and the Government had approved of, the formation of a fresh grade —that of First A.Q.M.G.—and that he was directed by Sir William Mansfield to offer the new appointment to me—an offer which I gratefully accepted; for though the command of a Horse Artillery battery would have been most congenial, this unexpected chance of five years' further staff employ was too good to be refused.

On the 4th January, 1869, having said good-bye to those dear to us, two of whom I was never to see again, my wife and I, with a baby girl who was born the previous July, embarked at Portsmouth on board the s.s. *Helvetia*, which had been taken up for the conveyance of troops to Bombay, the vessel of the Royal Navy in which we were to have sailed having suddenly broken down. The *Helvetia* proved most unsuitable as a transport, and uncomfortable to the last degree for passengers, besides which it blew a gale the whole way to Alexandria. We were all horribly ill, and our child caught a fatal cold. We thoroughly appreciated a change at Suez to the Indian trooper, the

Malabar, where everything possible was done for our comfort by our kind captain (Rich, R.N.), and, indeed, by everyone on board; but, alas! our beautiful little girl never recovered the cruel experience of the *Helvetia*, and we had the terrible grief of losing her soon after we passed Aden. She was buried at sea.

It was a very sad journey after that. There were several nice, kind people amongst our fellow-passengers; but life on board ship at such a time, surrounded by absolute strangers, was a terrible trial to us both, and, what with the effects of the voyage and the anxiety and sorrow she had gone through, my wife was thoroughly ill when we arrived at Simla towards the end of February.

CHAPTER XXXVIII.

In January, 1869, Sir John Lawrence, after a career which was altogether unique, he having risen from the junior grades of the Bengal Civil Service to the almost regal position of Governor-General,* left India for good. He was succeeded as Viceroy by Lord Mayo, one of whose first official acts was to hold a durbar at Umballa for the reception of the Amir Sher Ali, who, after five years of civil war, had succeeded in establishing himself on the throne of Afghanistan, to which he had been nominated by his father, Dost Mahomed Khan.†

Sher Ali had passed through a stormy time between the death of the Dost, in June, 1863, and September, 1868. He had been acknowledged as the rightful heir by the Government of India, and for the first three years he held the Amirship in a precarious sort of way. His two elder brothers, Afzal and Azim, and his nephew, Abdur Rahman (the present Ruler of Afghanistan), were in rebellion against him. The death of his favourite son and heir-apparent, Ali Khan, in

* I should have mentioned that Sir John Lawrence was not the only instance of a Bengal civilian rising to the position of Governor-General, as a predecessor of his, Sir John Shore, afterwards Lord Teignmouth, was appointed Governor-General in 1792, and held that office until 1798.

† Dost Mahomed had several sons. Mahomed Akbar and Ghulam Haidar, the two heirs-designate in succession, died before their father. Sixteen other sons were alive in 1863, of whom the following were the eldest:

1. Mahomed Afzal Khan, aged	52 years	By a wife not of Royal blood.
2. Mahomed Azim Khan	,, 45 ,,	
3. Sher Ali Khan	,, 40 ,,	By a favourite Popalzai wife.
4. Mahomed Amir Khan	,, 34 ,,	
5. Mahomed Sharif Khan	,, 30 ,,	
6. Wali Mahomed Khan	,, 33 ,,	By a third wife.
7. Faiz Mahomed Khan	,, 25 ,,	

Afzal Khan had a son Abdur Rahman Khan, the present Amir of Afghanistan, and Sher Ali had five sons—Ali Khan, Yakub Khan, Ibrahim Khan, Ayub Khan, and Abdulla Jan.

action near Khelat-i-Ghilzai, in 1865, grieved him so sorely that for a time his reason was affected. In May, 1866, he was defeated near Ghazni (mainly owing to the treachery of his own troops) by Abdur Rahman, who, releasing his father, Afzal, from the prison into which he had been cast by Sher Ali, led him in triumph to Kabul, and proclaimed him Amir of Afghanistan.

The new Amir, Afzal, at once wrote to the Government of India detailing what had occurred, and expressing a hope that the friendship of the British, which he so greatly valued, would be extended to him. He was told, in reply, that the Government recognized him as Ruler of Kabul, but that, as Sher Ali still held Kandahar and Herat, existing engagements with the latter could not be broken off. The evident preference thus displayed for Sher Ali caused the greatest vexation to the brothers Afzal and Azim, who showed their resentment by directing an Envoy who had come from Swat to pay his respects to the new Amir to return to his own country and set on foot a holy war against the English; the Waziri *maliks** in attendance at the court were dismissed with presents and directions to harass the British frontier, while an emissary was despatched on a secret mission to the Russians.

After his defeat near Ghazni, Sher Ali fled to Kandahar, and in the January of the following year (again owing to treachery in his army) he met with a second defeat near Khelat-i-Ghilzai, and lost Kandahar.

On this fact being communicated to the Government of India, Afzal Khan was in his turn recognized as Amir of Kabul and Kandahar. But he was at the same time informed that the British Government intended to maintain a strict neutrality between the contending parties in Afghanistan. John Lawrence, in his letter of the 20th of February, said that 'neither men, nor arms, nor money, nor assistance of any kind, have ever been supplied by my Government to Amir Sher Ali. Your Highness and he, both equally unaided by me, have fought out the battle, each upon your own resources. I purpose to continue the same policy for the future. If, unhappily, the struggle for supremacy in Afghanistan has not yet been brought to a close, and hostilities are again renewed, I shall still side with neither party.'

This reply altogether failed to satisfy Afzal and Azim. They answered it civilly, but at the same time they sent a copy of it to General Romanofski, the Russian Governor of Tashkent, who was informed by the new Amir that he had no confidence in the 'Lord *sahib's* fine professions of friendship, and that he was disgusted with the British Government for the ingratitude and ill-treatment shown towards his brother Azim.† He looked upon the Russians as his real

* The headmen of villages in Afghanistan are styled *maliks*.

† Azim Khan behaved well towards the Lumsden Mission, and it was reported that he encouraged his father, Dost Mahomed Khan, not to disturb the Peshawar frontier during the Mutiny.

and only friends, hoped soon to send a regular Ambassador to the Russian camp, and would at all times do his utmost to protect and encourage Russian trade.'

In October of this year (1867) Afzal Khan died, and his brother Azim, hastening to Kabul, took upon himself the Amirship. Abdur Rahman had hoped to have succeeded his father, but his uncle having forestalled him, he thought it politic to give in his allegiance to him, which he did by presenting his dead father's sword, in durbar, to the new Amir, who, like his predecessor, was now acknowledged by the Government of India as Ruler of Kabul and Kandahar.

The tide, however, was beginning to turn in favour of Sher Ali. Azim and Abdur Rahman quarrelled, and the former, by his extortions and cruelties, made himself detested by the people generally.

In March, 1868, Sher Ali's eldest son, Yakub Khan, regained possession of Kandahar for his father. In July father and son found themselves strong enough to move towards Ghazni, where Azim Khan's army was assembled. The latter, gradually deserted by his soldiers, took to flight, upon which Sher Ali, after an absence of forty months, entered Kabul on the 8th of September, and re-possessed himself of all his dominions, with the exception of Balkh, where Azim and Abdur Rahman (now reconciled to each other) still flew the flag of rebellion.

One of the newly-installed Amir's first acts was to inform the Viceroy of his return to Kabul, and of the recovery of his kingdom. He announced his desire to send some trusted representatives, or else proceed himself in person, to Calcutta, 'for the purpose of showing his sincerity and firm attachment to the British Government, and making known his real wants.'

Sir John Lawrence, in his congratulatory reply, showed that a change had come over his policy of non-interference in the internal affairs of Afghanistan, for he stated that he was 'prepared, not only to maintain the bonds of amity and goodwill which were established between Dost Mahomed and the British Government, but, so far as may be practicable, to strengthen those bonds'; and, as a substantial proof of his goodwill, the Viceroy sent Sher Ali £60,000, aid which arrived at a most opportune moment, and gave the Amir that advantage over his opponents which is of incalculable value in Afghan civil war, namely, funds wherewith to pay the army and bribe the opposite side.

The energetic and capable Abdur Rahman Khan had in the meantime collected a sufficient number of troops in Turkestan to enable him to move towards Kabul with his uncle Azim. On nearing Ghazni, he found himself confronted by Sher Ali; the opposing forces were about equal in strength, and on both sides there was the same scarcity of ready money. Suddenly the report was received that money was being sent from India to Sher Ali, and this turned the scale in his favour. Abdur Rahman's men deserted in considerable numbers, and a battle fought on the 3rd January, 1869, resulted in the total defeat of uncle and nephew, and in the firmer consolidation of Sher Ali's supremacy.

The change in policy which induced the Government of India to assist a struggling Amir with money, after its repeated and emphatic declarations that interference was impossible, was undoubtedly brought about by an able and elaborate memorandum written by the late Sir Henry Rawlinson on the 28th July, 1868. In this paper Rawlinson pointed out that, notwithstanding promises to the contrary, Russia was steadily advancing towards Afghanistan. He referred to the increased facilities of communication which would be the result of the recent proposal to bring Turkestan into direct communication, *viâ* the Caspian, with the Caucasus and St. Petersburg. He dwelt at length upon the effect which the advanced position of Russia in Central Asia would have upon Afghanistan and India. He explained that by the occupation of Bokhara Russia would gain a pretext for interfering in Afghan politics, and 'that if Russia once assumes a position which, in virtue either of an imposing military force on the Oxus, or of a dominant political influence in Afghanistan, entitles her, in Native estimation, to challenge our Asiatic supremacy, the disquieting effect will be prodigious.'

'With this prospect before us,' Sir Henry asked, 'are we justified in maintaining what has been sarcastically, though perhaps unfairly, called Sir John Lawrence's policy of "masterly inaction"? Are we justified in allowing Russia to work her way to Kabul unopposed, and there to establish herself as a friendly power prepared to protect the Afghans against the English?' He argued that it was contrary to our interests to permit anarchy to reign in Afghanistan; that Lord Auckland's famous doctrine of 'establishing a strong and friendly Power on our North-West Frontier' was the right policy for India, 'that Dost Mahomed's successful management of his country was in a great measure due to our aid, and that, if we had helped the son as we had helped the father, Sher Ali would have summarily suppressed the opposition of his brothers and nephews.' Rawlinson then added: 'Another opportunity now presents itself. The fortunes of Sher Ali are again in the ascendant; he should be secured in our interests without delay.'

Rawlinson's suggestions were not at the time supposed to commend themselves to the Government of India. In the despatch in which they were answered,* the Viceroy and his Councillors stated that they still objected to any active interference in the affairs of Afghanistan; they foresaw no limits to the expenditure which such a move would entail,

* Dated 4th January, 1869.

and they believed that the objects that they had at heart might be attained by an attitude of readiness and firmness on the frontier. It is worthy of note, however, that, after Sir Henry Rawlinson's memorandum had been received by the Indian Government, and notwithstanding these protests, the sum of £60,000 was sent to Sher Ali, that Sir John Lawrence invited him 'to come to some place in British territory for a personal meeting in order to discuss the best manner in which a limited support might be accorded,' and that five days from the time of writing the above-mentioned despatch, John Lawrence sent a farewell letter to Sher Ali, expressing the earnest hope of the British Government that His Highness's authority would be established on a solid and permanent basis, and informing him that a further sum of £60,000 would be supplied to him during the next few months, and that future Viceroys would consider, from time to time, what amount of practical assistance in the shape of money or war materials should periodically be made over to him as a testimony of their friendly feeling, and to the furtherance of his legitimate authority and influence.

Sher Ali expressed himself as most grateful, and came to Umballa full of hope and apparently thoroughly well disposed towards the British Government. He was received with great state and ceremony, and Lord Mayo was most careful to demonstrate that he was treating with an independent, and not a feudatory, Prince.

At this conference Sher Ali began by unburdening himself of his grievances, complaining to Lord Mayo of the manner in which his two elder brothers had each in his turn been recognized as Amir, and dwelling on the one-sided nature of the treaty made with his father, by which the British Government only bound itself to abstain from interfering with Afghanistan, while the Amir was to be 'the friend of the friends and the enemy of the enemies of the Honourable East India Company.' His Highness then proceeded to make known his wants, which were that he and his lineal descendants on the throne that he had won 'by his own good sword' should be acknowledged as the *de jure* sovereigns of Afghanistan; that a treaty offensive and defensive should be made with him; and that he should be given a fixed subsidy in the form of an annual payment.

It was in regard to the first of these three demands that Sher Ali was most persistent. He explained repeatedly and at some length that to acknowledge the Ruler *pro tempore* and *de facto* was to invite competition for a throne, and excite the hopes of all sorts of candidates; but that if the British Government would recognize him and his dynasty, there was nothing he would not do in order to evince his gratitude.

These requests, the Amir was informed, were inadmissible. There could be no treaty, no fixed subsidy, no dynastic pledges. He was further told that we were prepared to discourage his rivals, to give him warm countenance and support, and such material assistance as we considered absolutely necessary for his immediate wants, if he, on his part, would undertake to do all he could to maintain peace on our frontier and to comply with our wishes in matters connected with trade.

As an earnest of our goodwill, the Amir was given the second £60,000 promised him by Sir John Lawrence, besides a considerable supply of arms and ammunition,* and was made happy by a promise that European officers should not be required to reside in any of his cities. Before the conference took place, Lord Mayo had contemplated British agents being sent to Kabul in order to obtain accurate information regarding events in Central Asia, but on discovering how vehemently opposed Sher Ali was to such an arrangement, he gave him this promise. Saiyad Nur Mahomed, the Minister who accompanied the Amir, though equally averse to European agents, admitted that 'the day might come when the Russians would arrive, and the Amir would be glad, not only of British officers as agents, but of arms and troops to back them.'

One request which the Amir made towards the close of the meeting the Viceroy agreed to, which was that we should call Persia to account for her alleged encroachments on the debatable ground of Sistan. This, which seemed but an unimportant matter at the time, was one of the chief causes of Sher Ali's subsequent estrangement; for the committee of arbitration which inquired into it decided against the Amir, who never forgave what he considered our unfriendly action in discountenancing his claims.

The Umballa conference was, on the whole, successful, in that Sher Ali returned to his own country much gratified at the splendour of his reception, and a firm personal friend of Lord Mayo, whose fine presence and genial manner had quite won the Amir's heart, although he had not succeeded in getting from him everything he had demanded.

CHAPTER XXXIX.

We spent a very quiet year at Simla. My wife was far from strong, and we had another great sorrow in the death of a baby boy three weeks after his birth.

That winter I was left in charge of the Quartermaster-General's

* Besides the remainder of the aggregate sum of twelve lakhs, 6,500 more rifles were forwarded to the frontier for transmission to the Amir, and in addition four 18-pounder smooth-bore guns, two 8-inch howitzers, and a Mountain battery of six 3-pounders complete, with due proportion of ammunition and stores, together with draught bullocks and nine elephants.

office, and we moved into 'Ellerslie,' a larger and warmer house than that in which we had lived during the summer.

Simla in the winter, after a fresh fall of snow, is particularly beautiful. Range after range of hills clothed in their spotless garments stretch away as far as the eye can reach, relieved in the foreground by masses of reddish-brown perpendicular cliffs and dark-green ilex and deodar trees, each bearing its pure white burden, and decked with glistening fringes of icicles. Towards evening the scene changes, and the snow takes the most gorgeous colouring from the descending rays of the brilliant eastern sun—brilliant even in mid-winter—turning opal, pink, scarlet, and crimson; gradually, as the light wanes, fading into delicate lilacs and grays, which slowly mount upwards, till at last even the highest pinnacle loses the life-giving tints, and the whole snowy range itself turns cold and white and dead against a background of deepest sapphire blue. The spectator shivers, folds himself more closely in his wraps, and retreats indoors, glad to be greeted by a blazing log-fire and a hot cup of tea.

In the spring of the next year (1870) Sir William Mansfield's term of command came to an end, and he was succeeded by Lord Napier of Magdāla. The selection of this distinguished officer for the highest military position in India was greatly appreciated by the Indian army, as no officer of that army had held it since the days of Lord Clive.

In September a daughter was born, and that winter we again remained at Simla. I amused myself by going through a course of electric telegraphy, which may seem rather like a work of supererogation; but during the Umbeyla campaign, when the telegraph office had to be closed in consequence of all the clerks being laid up with fever, and we could neither read nor send messages, I determined that I would on the first opportunity learn electric signalling, in order that I might be able to decipher and send telegrams should I ever again find myself in a similar position.

In May my wife and I went for a march across the hills to Chakrata, and thence to Mussoórie and back by way of Dehra Dun and the plains. The object of this trip was to settle the boundary of Chakrata, and my wife took the opportunity of my being ordered on this duty to get away from Simla, as we had now been there for more than two years, and were consequently rather longing for a change. Our route lay through most beautiful scenery, and notwithstanding that the trip was a little hurried, and that some of the marches were therefore rather long, we enjoyed it immensely. When passing along the ridge of a very high hill one afternoon, we witnessed rather a curious sight—a violent thunderstorm was going on in the valley below us, while we ourselves remained in the mildest, most serene atmosphere, enjoying bright sunshine and a blue sky. Dense black clouds filled up the valley a thousand feet beneath us, the thunder roared, the lightning flashed, and soon we could hear the rush of waters in the streams below from the torrents of rain which the clouds were discharging; but it was not until we had crossed over the mountain, and descended to a low level on the other side, that we fully realized the effects of the heavy storm.

On our return to Simla we had the pleasure of a visit from Major-General Donald Stewart, who had come up to receive Lord Mayo's instructions before taking over his appointment as Superintendent of the Andaman Islands. In September he and I travelled together to Calcutta, to which place I was directed to proceed in order to make arrangements for a military expedition into the country of the Lushais, having been appointed senior staff officer to the force.

Lushai, situated between south-eastern Bengal and Burma, was a *terra incognita* to me, and I had only heard of it in connexion with the raids made by its inhabitants upon the tea-gardens in its vicinity, which had now spread too far away from Cachar for the garrison of that small military station to afford them protection. From time to time the Lushais had done the planters much damage, and carried off several prisoners, and various attempts had been made in the shape of small military expeditions to punish the tribesmen and rescue the captives; but from want of proper organization, and from not choosing the right time of the year, these attempts had hitherto been unsuccessful, and our failures had the inevitable result of making the Lushais bolder. Raids became more frequent and more destructive; until at last a little European girl, named Mary Winchester, was carried off, and kept by them as a prisoner; on this the Lieutenant-Governor of Bengal declared that a punitive expedition was 'absolutely necessary for the future security of the British subjects residing on the Cachar and Chittagong frontiers.'

The despatch of a force was therefore decided upon; it was to consist of two small columns*—one having its base at Cachar, the other at Chittagong—commanded respectively by Brigadier-Generals Bourchier, C.B., and C. Brownlow, C.B., supreme political power being also vested in these two officers. Long experience had taught Lord Napier the wisdom of having only one head in time of war, and he impressed upon the Government his opinion that the civil officers, while acting as advisers and as the channels of communication with the tribes, should be subordinate to the control of the two Commanders, who, after having been put in possession of the views and wishes of

* The Cachar column consisted of half of the Peshawar Mountain battery, one company of Bengal Sappers and Miners, the 22nd Punjab Infantry, 42nd and 44th Assam Light Infantry. The Chittagong column consisted of the other half of the Mountain battery, the 27th Punjab Infantry, and the 2nd and 4th Gurkhas. Each regiment was 500 strong, and each column was accompanied by 100 armed police.

the Government, should be held responsible for carrying them out loyally so far as circumstances and the safety of the force would permit.

As the existence of the tea industry was at stake, the Lushais having established a perfect terror on all the estates within their reach, it was essential that they should be given a severe lesson, and this could only be done by their principal villages, which lay at some considerable distance from the base of operations, being visited in force. The difficult country and the paucity of transport necessitated the columns being lightly equipped; no tents were to be allowed, and baggage and followers were to be reduced to a minimum. My instructions were to fit out and despatch the two columns, and then join Brigadier-General Bourchier at Cachar.

I was kept in Calcutta all October—not a pleasant month, the climate then being very muggy and unhealthy. Everyone who could get away had gone to the Hills or out to sea; and the offices being closed for the Hindu holidays of the *Durga Puja*, it was extremely difficult to get work done. Everything for the Chittagong column had to be sent by sea. The shipping of the elephants was rather interesting: they clung desperately to the ground, trying hard to prevent themselves being lifted from it; and when at last, in spite of all their struggles, they were hoisted into the air, the helpless appearance of the huge animals and their despairing little cries and whines were quite pathetic. I found it trying work being on the river all day; my eyes suffered from the glare, and I became so reduced that before I left Calcutta I weighed scarcely over eight stone—rather too fine a condition in which to enter on a campaign in a mountainous country, so thickly covered with jungle as to make riding out of the question.

By the 3rd November the equipment and stores for both columns had been despatched, and on the 16th I joined General Bourchier at the house of that most hospitable of hosts, Mr. Edgar,* Deputy-Commissioner of Cachar, who accompanied the left column as civil officer.

We left Cachar on the 23rd, and from the outset we had to make our own roads, a labour which never ceased until the end of January, by which date 110 miles had been completed. There was not the vestige of a track to direct us; but I got hold of some people of the country, with whom I made friends, and induced them to act as guides. Many a long and weary reconnaissance had to be executed, however, before the line of advance could be decided upon. The troops worked with a will, and, notwithstanding the vapour-bath-like atmosphere of the valleys and the difficult nature of the country, which was a succession of hill-ranges covered with jungle forests, made almost impenetrable from the huge creepers, and intersected by rivers and

* Now Sir John Edgar, K.C.S.I.

watercourses, a good road, from six to eight feet wide, was constructed, with a sufficiently easy gradient for laden elephants to travel over. Cutting one's way day after day through these dense, gloomy forests, through which hardly a ray of light penetrates, was most stifling and depressing. One could hardly breathe, and was quite unable to enjoy the beauty of the magnificent trees, the graceful bamboos and canes, and the wonderful creepers, which abounded, and under other circumstances would have been a source of pleasure; the difficulties we encountered, and the consequent delay in our progress, quite prevented me from being in a frame of mind to appreciate my picturesque surroundings.

It became evident from the first that our onward movements would be greatly impeded by want of transport. Notwithstanding the experience which ought to have been gained in many small mountain wars, the Government had not been taught that a properly organized transport corps was an absolute necessity, and that it was a mere waste of money to collect a number of men and animals without providing trained supervision. Fourteen hundred of our coolies were attached to the Commissariat Department without anyone to look after them, consequently officers and non-commissioned officers, who could ill be spared from their regimental duties, had to be told off to organize and work them.

To add to our troubles, cholera broke out amongst some Nepalese coolies on their way to join us; out of 840, 251 died in a few days, and a number deserted panic-stricken, while the rest were so weakened and shaken that, notwithstanding the care bestowed upon them by their able and energetic Commandant, Major H. Moore, only 387 joined the column. We were not much better off in the matter of elephants, which had been so carelessly selected that only 33 out of the 157 sent with our column were of any use. All this resulted in our being obliged to still further reduce our already small kits. Officers were allowed only forty pounds of baggage, and soldiers twenty-four pounds, limits within which it was rather difficult to keep. A couple of blankets were essential, as we should have to operate over mountains five and six thousand feet high; so was a waterproof sheet, for even if we should be lucky enough to escape rain, the dew is so heavy in those parts that it wets one just as thoroughly as a shower of rain. These three items with my cloak and cork mattress—which is also a very necessary adjunct in such a damp climate—amounted to thirty-one pounds, leaving only nine pounds for a change of clothes, plate, knife, fork, etc.—not too much for a four months' campaign. However, 'needs must,' and it is surprising how many things one considers absolute necessities under ordinary circumstances turn out to have been luxuries when we are obliged to dispense with them.

The advance portion of the column did not arrive at Tipai Mukh, only eighty-four miles from Cachar, until the 9th December, which will give an idea of the enforced slowness of our progress. Tipai Mukh proved a very suitable place for our depot: it was situated at the junction of two rivers, the Tipai and the Barak; thickly-wooded hills rose precipitously on all sides, but on the right bank of the Barak there was sufficient level space for all our requirements. With the help of local coolies, the little Gurkhas were not long in running up hospitals and storesheds; bamboo, the one material used in Lushailand for every conceivable purpose, whether it be a house, a drinking vessel, a bridge, a woman's ear-ring, or a musical instrument, grew in profusion on the hillside. A trestle bridge was thrown across the Tipai in a few hours, and about that bridge I have rather an amusing story to relate. On my telling the young Engineer officer in charge of the Sapper company that a bridge was required to be constructed with the least possible delay, he replied that it should be done, but that it was necessary to calculate the force of the current, the weight to be borne, and the consequent strength of the timber required. Off he went, urged by me to be as quick as he could. Some hours elapsed, and nothing was seen of the Engineer, so I sent for him and asked him when the bridge was to be begun. He answered that his plans were nearly completed, and that he would soon be able to commence work. In the meantime, however, and while these scientific calculations were being made, the headman of the local coolies had come to me and said, if the order were given, he would throw a good bridge over the river in no time. I agreed, knowing how clever Natives often are at this kind of work, and thinking I might just as well have two strings to this particular bow. Immediately, numbers of men were to be seen felling the bamboos on the hillside a short distance above the stream: these were thrown into the river, and as they came floating down they were caught by men standing up to their necks in water, who cut them to the required length, stuck the uprights into the river-bed, and attached them to each other by pieces laid laterally and longitudinally; the flooring was then formed also of bamboo, the whole structure was firmly bound together by strips of cane, and the bridge was pronounced ready. Having tested its strength by marching a large number of men across it, I sent for my Engineer friend. His astonishment on seeing a bridge finished ready for use was great, and became still greater when he found how admirably the practical woodmen had done their work; from that time, being assured of their ability to assist him, he wisely availed himself when difficulties arose of their useful, if unscientific, method of engineering.

By the 14th December matters had so far progressed as to warrant an advance. As our route now lay away from the river, scarcity of water entailed greater care being taken in the selection of encamping grounds, so on arriving at our halting-place each day I had to reconnoitre ahead for a suitable site for our next resting-ground, a considerable addition to the day's work. Road-making for the passage of the elephants became more difficult, and transport was so deficient that the troops could only be brought up very gradually. Thus, it was the 22nd of the month before we reached the Tuibum river, only twenty miles from Tipai Mukh. On our way we were met by some scouts from the villages ahead of us, who implored of us to advance no further, saying, if we would only halt, their headmen would come in and submit to whatever terms we chose to make. The villagers were informed in reply that our quarrel was not with them, and so long as we remained unmolested, not the slightest injury should be done to them, their villages, or their crops; but that we were determined to reach the country of Lalbura, the Chief who had been the ringleader in the raids upon the tea-gardens.

We pushed on as fast as the dense undergrowth would permit until within about a mile of the river, where we found the road blocked by a curious erection in the form of a gallows, from which hung two grotesque figures, made of bamboo. A little further on it was a felled tree which stopped us; this tree was studded all over with knife like pieces of bamboo, and from the incisions into which these were stuck exuded a red juice, exactly the colour of blood. This was the Lushai mode of warning us what would be our fate if we ventured further. We, however, proceeded on our way, bivouacked for the night, and early the next morning started off in the direction of some villages which we understood lay in the road to our destination.

For the first thousand feet the ascent was very steep, and the path so narrow that we could only march in single file. Suddenly we entered upon a piece of ground cleared for cultivation, and as we emerged from the forest we were received by a volley from a position about sixty yards off. A young police orderly, who was acting as our guide, was knocked over by my side, and a second volley wounded one of the sepoys, on which we charged and the enemy retired up the hill. We came across a large number of these *jooms* (clearings), and at each there was a like effort to oppose us, always with the same result. After advancing in this way for the greater part of the day, alternately through dense jungle and open spaces, and occasionally passing by scattered cottages, we sighted a good-sized village, where it was decided we should remain for the night. The day's march had been very severe, the village being 4,000 feet above the river; and the troops were so worn out with their exertions that it was with difficulty the piquets could be got to construct proper shelter for themselves out of the plentiful supply of trees and underwood ready at hand. Throughout the night the enemy's sharpshooters kept up an annoying fire under cover of the forest which surrounded the village, and so as soon as day dawned a party moved out to clear the ground all round.

It was most aggravating to find from the view we got of the country from this elevated position that the previous day's harassing march had been an absolutely useless performance and an unnecessary waste of time and strength. We could now distinctly see that this village did not lead to Lalbura's country, as we had been led to believe it would, and that there was no alternative but to retrace our steps as far as the river. The men and animals were too tired to march that day, and the next being Christmas, we made another halt, and commenced our retirement on the 26th. This was an extremely nasty business, and had to be carried out with very great caution. The ground, as I said before, necessitated our proceeding in single file, and with only 250 fighting men (all that our deficient transport admitted of being brought on to this point) it was difficult to guard the long line of sick, wounded, and coolies. As soon as we began to draw in our piquets, the Lushais, who had never ceased their fire, perceiving we were about to retire, came down in force, and entered one end of the village, yelling and screaming like demons, before we had got out at the other. The whole way down the hill they pressed us hard, endeavouring to get amongst the baggage, but were invariably baffled by the Gurkhas, who, extending rapidly whenever the ground was favourable, retired through their supports in admirable order, and did not once give the enemy the chance of passing them. We had 3 men killed and 8 wounded during the march, but the Lushais confessed afterwards to a loss of between 50 and 60.

As we were given to understand that our short retrograde movement had been interpreted into a defeat by the Lushais, the General wisely determined to pay the village of Kholel another visit. Our doing so had the best possible effect. A slight resistance was offered at the first clearance, but by the time the ridge was reached the Chief, having become convinced of the uselessness of further opposition, submitted, and engaged to give hostages and keep open communication with our depot at Tipai Mukh, a promise which he most faithfully performed.

1872 opened auspiciously for me. On New Year's Day I was agreeably surprised by a communication from the Quartermaster-General informing me that, a vacancy having unexpectedly occurred, Lord Napier had appointed me Deputy-Quartermaster-General. This was an important step in my department, and I was proportionately elated.

A few days later I received the good news of the birth of a son at Umballa on the 8th.

Paucity of transport and difficulty about supplies kept us stationary on the Tuibum for some time, after which we moved on as before, the Lushais retiring in front of us until the 25th, when they attacked us while we were moving along a narrow ravine, with a stream at the bottom and steep hills on either side. The first volley wounded the

General in the arm and hand, and killed his orderly. The enemy's intention was evidently to push past the weak column along the hill-side and get amongst the coolies; but this attempt was again foiled by the Gurkhas, who, flinging off their great-coats, rushed into the stream and engaged the Lushais before they could get at the baggage, pressing them up the mountain, rising 2,500 feet above us, as fast as the precipitous nature of the ascent would allow. On the crest we found the enemy occupying a good-sized village, out of which we cleared them and took possession of it ourselves. On this occasion we had only 4 killed and 8 wounded, including the General, while the enemy lost about 60. In one place we found a heap of headless bodies. The Lushais, if unable to remove their dead. invariably decapitate them to prevent their adversaries from carrying off the heads, their own mode of dealing with a slain enemy, as they believe that whoever is in possession of the head will have the man to whom it belonged as a slave in the next world.

To complete the success we had gained, the General sent me the next day with a small party to burn the village of Taikum, belonging to the people who had attacked us. It was past noon before we could make a start, owing to the non-arrival of the elephants with the guns. When they did come in, the poor huge creatures were so fatigued by their climb that it was considered advisable to transfer their loads to coolies, particularly as the route we had to traverse was reported to be even more difficult than anything we had yet encountered. When we had proceeded a short distance, we perceived that our way was blocked a mile ahead by a most formidable-looking stockade, on one side of which rose perpendicular cliffs, while on the other was a rocky ravine. As the nature of the ground did not admit of my approaching near enough to discover whether the Artillery could be placed so as to cover the Infantry advance, and being anxious to avoid losing many of my small party, I settled to turn the stockade by a detour up the hillside. This manœuvre took some time, owing to the uncompromising nature of the country; but it was successful, for when we struck the track, we found ourselves about a mile on the other side of the stockade. The Lushais, on realizing what we were about, retired to Taikum, which place came into view at 5 p.m. It was situated on the summit of a hill 1,200 yards in front, and was crowded with men. The guns were brought at once into action, and while Captain Blackwood* was preparing his fuses, I advanced towards the village with the Infantry. The first shell burst a little beyond the village, the second was lodged in its very centre, for a time completely paralyzing the Lushais. On recovering from the shock, they took to their heels and scampered off

* Major Blackwood, who was killed at Maiwand, in command of E Battery, R.H.A.

in every direction, the last man leaving the village just as we entered it. The houses, as usual, were made of bamboo, and after it had been ascertained that there was no living creature inside any of them, the place was set on fire, and we began our return journey. There was a bright moon, but even aided by its light we did not reach our bivouac until midnight. This ended the campaign so far as opposition was concerned, for not another shot was fired either by us or against us during the remaining six weeks we continued in the country.

Soon after this we heard that some of the captives we had come to relieve had been given up to the Chittagong column, and that Mary Winchester was safe in General Brownlow's hands—very satisfactory intelligence, showing as it did that the Lushais were beginning to understand the advisability of acceding to our demands. The work of our column, however, was not over, for although, from the information we received of his whereabouts, we had given up hope of joining hands with Brownlow, Bourchier determined that Lalbura's country must be reached; he (Lalbura) being the chief offender, it would never have done to let him think his stronghold lay beyond our power.

In order that we might be well out of Lushailand before the rains, which usually begin in that part of the world about the middle of March, and are extremely heavy, it was decided not to wait until a road could be made for elephants, but to trust to coolie-carriage alone, and to push on rapidly as soon as supplies sufficient for twelve days could be collected. Kits were still further reduced, officers and soldiers alike being only allowed a couple of blankets and one or two cooking utensils.

We resumed our march on the 12th February; the route in many places was strongly and skilfully stockaded, but the tidings of our successes had preceded us, and our advance was unopposed. In five days we reached the Chamfai valley, at the end of which, on a high hill, Lalbura's village was situated.* Although Lalbura's father, Vonolel, had been dead some years, the people still called the place Vonolel's country. Vonolel had been a famous warrior, and they were evidently very proud of his reputation. We were shown his tomb, which, like that of all great Lushai braves, was decorated with the heads of human beings (his slaves in paradise) and those of animals, besides drinking-vessels and various kinds of utensils for his use in another life.

Lalbura had taken himself off; but his headmen submitted to us and accepted our terms. We remained at this place till the 21st, in accordance with an agreement we had made with Brownlow to send up signals on the night of the 20th in case his column should be anywhere in the neighbourhood. During the three days we stayed amongst

* Latitude 23° 26′ 32″, longitude (approximately) 93° 25′ ; within a short distance of Fort White, lately built in the Chin Hills.

them we mixed freely with the Lushais, who were greatly delighted and astonished with all we had to show them. The telescope and the burning-glass amused them greatly; our revolvers excited their envy; and for the little Mountain guns they displayed the highest veneration. But what seemed to astonish them more than anything was the whiteness of our skins, particularly when on closer inspection they discovered that our arms and bodies were even fairer than our faces and hands, which to our eyes had become from long exposure so bronzed as to make us almost unrecognizable as Europeans.

We were all glad that the duty entrusted to us had been satisfactorily ended, and we were hoping that the Viceroy, who had taken a keen personal interest in our proceedings, would be satisfied with the result, when we were shocked and startled beyond measure by hearing that Lord Mayo had been murdered by a convict while visiting the Andaman Islands. The disastrous news arrived as we were in the midst of firing signal-rockets, burning blue-lights, and lighting bonfires to attract the attention of the Chittagong column. I could not help thinking of the heavy loss India had sustained, for the manly, open-hearted Governor-General had impressed the Native Chiefs in quite an exceptional manner, and he was liked as well as respected by all classes of Europeans and Natives. I felt also much for Donald Stewart, to whom, I knew, such a terrible tragedy, happening while he was Superintendent at Port Blair, would be a heavy blow.

On the 6th March we reached Tipai Mukh, where we bade farewell to our Lushai friends, numbers of whom accompanied us to get possession of the empty tins, bags, and casks which were got rid of at every stage. The hostages and those who had assisted us were liberally rewarded, and we parted on the best of terms, with promises on their part of future good behaviour—promises which were kept for nearly twenty years.

No one was sorry that the marching was at an end, and that the rest of the journey back was to be performed in boats. Constant hard work and exposure in a peculiarly malarious and relaxing climate had told upon the whole force; while our having to depend for so long on tinned meats, which were not always good, and consisted chiefly of pork, with an occasional ration of mutton and salt beef, had been very trying to the officers. One and all were 'completely worn out,' as the principal medical officer reported; two out of our small number died, and the General's condition gave cause for grave anxiety. For myself, having a perfect horror of pork, I think I should have starved outright but for the extraordinary culinary talent of Mr. Edgar, who disguised the presence of the unclean animal in such a wonderful way in soups, stews, etc., that I frequently partook of it without knowing what I was eating. My wife and some anonymous kind friend sent by post small tins of Liebig's extract, which were highly appreciated.

Cholera pursued us up to and beyond Cachar; the wretched coolies suffered most, and it is a disease to which Gurkhas are peculiarly susceptible, while a feast on a village pig from time to time probably helped to make matters worse for them. Many of these grand little soldiers and some of the Sikhs also fell victims to the scourge. My orderly, a very smart young Gurkha, to my great regret, was seized with it the day after I reached Cachar, and died next morning.

On my way to Simla, I spent a few days with Norman at Calcutta. The whole place was in mourning on account of the terrible catastrophe which had happened at Port Blair.

CHAPTER XL.

LORD NAPIER OF MURCHISTON, the Governor of Madras, had been summoned to Calcutta to act as Viceroy until Lord Northbrook, Lord Mayo's successor, should arrive. He seemed interested in what I had to tell him about Lushai, and Lord Napier of Magdāla spoke in laudatory terms of the manner in which the expedition had been carried out.

I reached Simla on the 1st of April, the twentieth anniversary of my arrival in India. I found my wife, with the two children, settled in Snowdon,* a house I had recently purchased. She had had much trouble in my absence, having been at death's door herself, and having very nearly lost our little son at Umballa three weeks after his birth from a Native wet-nurse having tried to kill him. The English nurse's suspicions had been aroused by one day finding a live coal in the cradle, but she did not mention this discovery at the time for fear of frightening my wife; but she determined to watch. A few days later, while with our little girl in the next room, she heard the baby boy choking, and rushed in to find, to her horror, blood on his lips, and that he was struggling violently, as if to get rid of something in his throat! She pushed down her finger and pulled out a sharp piece of cane about two inches long; but other pieces had evidently gone down, for the poor little fellow was in terrible agony for many days. It turned out that the wretched woman hated the unwonted confinement of her new life, and was determined to get away, but was too much afraid of her husband to say so. He wanted her to remain for the sake of the high pay this class of servant receives, so it appeared to the woman that her only chance of freedom was to get rid of the child, and to carry out her purpose she first attempted to set fire to the

* We lived in this house whenever we were in Simla, till we left it in 1892. It has since been bought by Government for the Commander-in-Chief's residence.

cradle, and finding this did not succeed, she pulled some pieces of cane off the chair upon which she was sitting, and shoved them down the child's throat. She was, as my wife described her, a pretty, innocent, timid-looking creature, to whom no one would ever have dreamt of attributing such an atrocity. The boy was made extremely delicate for several months by this misadventure, as his digestion had been ruined for the time being, but eventually he completely recovered from its effects.

In September the C.B. was conferred upon me for the Lushai Expedition. Lord Napier informed me of the fact in a particularly kind little note. I was very proud of being a member of the Bath, although at the time a brevet would have been a more useful reward, as want of rank was the reason Lord Napier had given for not allowing me to act as Quartermaster-General, on Lumsden being temporarily appointed Resident at Hyderabad.

We began our usual winter tour in the middle of October. At Mian Mir I made the acquaintance of the Adjutant of the 37th Foot, the late Sir Herbert Stewart, who was then a smart, good-looking subaltern, and I recollect his bemoaning bitterly his bad luck in never having had a chance of seeing service. How little at that time could it have been anticipated that within twelve years he would see hard fighting in Africa, and be killed as a Major-General in command of a column!

We visited several of the stations in the Punjab, and spent a few days at Jamu as guest of the Maharaja of Kashmir, who treated us royally, and gave us some excellent pig-sticking; and on the 21st December we joined Head-Quarters at Lawrencepur for a large Camp of Exercise, to be held on the identical ground which I had selected for the camp which Sir Hugh Rose proposed to have eleven years before.

Lord Napier of Magdāla did much to improve the efficiency of the army by means of Camps of Exercise. He held one at Delhi in the winter of 1871-72, and the Camp of which I am writing was most successful and instructive. No Commander-in-Chief ever carried out inspections with more thoroughness than did Lord Napier of Magdāla. He spared himself no trouble. On the hottest day he would toil through barrack after barrack to satisfy himself that the soldiers were properly cared for; Europeans and Natives were equally attended to, and many measures conducive to the men's comfort date from the time he was in command in India.

At the close of this camp Lumsden, who had returned to his appointment from Hyderabad, gave up the Quartermaster-Generalship for good. We had been greatly thrown together during the twenty-one years I had been in India, and my wife and I were very sorry to bid farewell to him and Mrs. Lumsden. He was succeeded by Edwin Johnson, pending whose arrival I was now allowed to officiate.

From Lawrencepur I went with the Commander-in-Chief to Calcutta. Soon after we arrived there I was asked by Sir Douglas Forsyth to accompany him on his Mission to Yarkand and Kashgar. I should have much liked to have done so, for the idea of a trip to these, at that time unknown, regions possessed great fascinations for me. I was therefore well pleased when Lord Napier told me he would not stand in the way of my going, and proportionately disappointed when, the next day, His Excellency said that on consideration he did not think I could be spared just then, for the Quartermaster-General would be new to the work at first, and he thought he would need my assistance.

The end of April saw us back in Simla, and in July Edwin Johnson arrived.

During the summer of 1873 important events occurred which had much to do with our subsequent relations with Afghanistan. The inquiries which Sher Ali had begged Lord Mayo to make about Persian encroachments in Sistan, had resulted in General Goldsmid* and Colonel Pollock† being deputed in 1871 to proceed to Sistan to decide the question. The settlement arrived at by these officers, which assigned to Afghanistan the country up to the right bank of the Helmand, but nothing beyond, satisfied neither the Shah nor the Amir, and the latter sent his confidential Minister, Saiyad Nur Mahomed, the Afghan Commissioner in the Sistan arbitration, to meet Lord Northbrook on his arrival in Bombay for the purpose of appealing to him against the decision. It could not, however, be reversed; but in a subsequent interview which the new Viceroy accorded the Envoy, the latter was told that as soon as Persia and Afghanistan had signified their acceptance of the settlement, the Government of India would present the Amir with five lakhs of rupees as compensation for the ceded territory which had for a time belonged to Afghanistan.

The action of Her Majesty's Ministers in communication with Russia regarding the northern boundary of Afghanistan was another matter about which the Amir was greatly exercised; and Lord Northbrook, thinking that all such vexed questions could be more satisfactorily explained by personal communication than by letter, proposed to the Amir that His Highness should consent to receive at Kabul a British officer 'of high rank and dignity, in whom I have full confidence' (Mr. Macnabb),‡ 'who will also explain to Your Highness,' wrote the Viceroy, 'the negotiations which have now been satisfactorily concluded with the Government of His Majesty the Emperor of Russia, whereby the Russian Government have agreed to recognize and respect the integrity and independence of the territories now in Your Highness's possession.'

To this request Sher Ali replied that he considered it advisable that

* General Sir Frederick Goldsmid, K.C.M.G.

† Major-General Sir Frederick Pollock, K.C.S.I.

‡ Sir Donald Macnabb, K.C.S.I., then Commissioner of Peshawar.

one of his agents should first wait on the Viceroy to ascertain the real views of the British Government on these important matters. This was agreed to, and Saiyad Nur Mahomed was again selected to represent the Amir. He reached Simla towards the end of June. On being informed that Persia had unreservedly accepted the decision as to the Sistan question, the Envoy declared that, whatever opinion the Amir might hold as to his rights, His Highness would also scrupulously respect that decision. With regard to the northern frontier, the Envoy begged it to be clearly understood that the Afghan Government wished to be allowed to make their own laws and follow their own customs within their territories; that the internal affairs of the country should be free from interference; and that the acknowledgment by Russia of the Amir's claim to land south of the Oxus should be confirmed by Bokhara. He further requested 'that the British Government would distinctly promise that, in the event of any aggression on the Amir's territories, they would consider the perpetrator of such aggression as their own enemy.' It was explained to the Saiyad that the British Government did not share the Amir's apprehension of Russia; that under such circumstances as he contemplated, it would be the duty of the Amir to refer to the British Government, who would decide whether it was an occasion for assistance to be rendered by them, and what the nature and extent of the assistance should be; moreover, that their help must be conditional upon the Amir himself abstaining from aggression, and on his unreserved acceptance of the advice of the British Government in regard to his external relations.

Two other questions were discussed:

(1) The location in certain towns in Afghanistan of British officers as representatives of the British Government.

(2) The present assistance to be rendered to the Amir for the purpose of strengthening his country against foreign aggression.

On the first point the Envoy said he had no instructions, but that, in his opinion, to ask Sher Ali to allow British officers to be located in Afghanistan would give rise to mistrust and apprehension. He recommended that a letter should be addressed to the Amir, pointing out the desirability of a British officer being sent to inspect the western and northern boundaries of Afghanistan, proceeding *viâ* Kandahar and returning *viâ* Kabul, where he might confer personally with His Highness. This suggestion was carried out.

With regard to the second point under discussion, the Envoy stated that 20,000 stand-of-arms were desired, laying very particular stress on 5,000 Sniders being included in this number, and that hopes were entertained by the Amir that he would be largely assisted with money. In answer to this, the Saiyad was told that there was not then a sufficient reserve supply of Sniders for the English troops in India, and that it was impossible to spare more than 5,000 Enfields; that this number should at once be placed at the Amir's disposal, and that the remainder should be forwarded as soon as they were received from England. He was further informed that five lakhs of rupees (exclusive of the five lakhs promised the year before, as indemnification for the loss of territory) would be given to Sher Ali.

A final letter from the Viceroy was sent to the Amir through Saiyad Nur Mahomed, dated 6th September, 1873, summing up the result of the conference. His Highness was told, with reference to a fear expressed by the Envoy lest Russia should press for the establishment of a Russian Mission and agents in Afghanistan, that Prince Gortschakoff had officially intimated that, while he saw no objection to British officers going to Kabul, he engaged that Russian agents should abstain from doing so, and that, far from apprehending a Russian invasion of Afghanistan, the British Government believed that the effect of the recent arrangements had been to render the occurrence of such a contingency more remote than ever. At the same time, being desirous of seeing the Amir strong and his rule firmly established, the Government were prepared to give him any reasonable assistance.

Sher Ali was greatly annoyed and disappointed at the result of his Envoy's visit to Simla. He was of a very impulsive, passionate disposition; his reply to the Viceroy's letter was discourteous and sarcastic; he declined to receive a British officer at Kabul, and although he condescended to accept the arms presented to him, he left the ten lakhs of rupees untouched in the Peshawar treasury. Colonel Valentine Baker, who was at that time travelling through Central Asia, was forbidden by the Amir to pass through Afghanistan on his way to India; and a few months later he refused to allow Sir Douglas Forsyth's Mission to return to India by way of Afghanistan.

CHAPTER XLI.

In the beginning of October my wife and I started for a fortnight's trip to the top of the Chor, a fine mountain sixty-two miles from Simla, and close on 12,000 feet high. We were accompanied by a very dear friend of ours—now no more—Colonel Baigrie, who was soon afterwards made Quartermaster-General in Bombay. He was a talented artist and delightful companion, and notwithstanding the old adage that two are company and three none, we three enjoyed our holiday immensely.

After crossing a stream called the Ghiri, below Fagu, the road passes through beautiful forest and cliff scenery, and for the most part was fairly easy, until the foot of the mountain was reached about six miles from the top, when it became very precipitous and difficult. We were the whole day doing this march, breakfasting in one place and lunching in another higher up. There was a good deal of snow in the shady spots. A few days before we had noticed that the top of the mountain was white, but the sun was still too strong in the day-time for the snow to lie long in exposed parts. The way being too steep for my wife to ride or go in a dandy, we all three walked, or rather climbed, up to the shoulder where our tents were pitched, about a mile from the summit.

The forest through which we passed was very beautiful, commencing with dark-green ilex, glistening holly, and sombre brown oak, interspersed with groups of the dainty, graceful, white-stemmed birch, and wreathed with festoons of the scarlet Himalayan vine. As we mounted higher, trees became fewer and the foliage less luxuriant, till at length only oaks were to be seen, their branches twisted into all sorts of weird, fantastic shapes from the strength of the south-west monsoon. Huge rocks became more frequent, covered with lichens and mosses of every shade, from dark-green to brilliant crimson. At length trees and shrubs were left behind, except the red-berried juniper, which grows at a higher elevation here than any other bush, and flourishes in the clefts of the rocks, where nothing else will exist. We got up in time to see the most glorious sunset; the colours were more wonderful than anything I had ever seen before, even in India. My wife urged Baigrie to make a rough sketch, and note the tints, that he might paint a picture of it later. He made the sketch, saying: 'If I attempted to represent truly what we see before us, the painting would be rejected by the good people at home as absurdly unreal, or as the work of a hopeless lunatic.' There was such a high wind that our small tents had a narrow escape of being blown away. That night the water was frozen in our jugs, and it was quite impossible to keep warm.

We were up betimes the next morning, and climbed to the highest peak, where we found breakfast awaiting us and a magnificent view of the Himalayan ranges, right down to the plains on one side and up to the perpetual snows on the other. We descended to the foot of the mountain in the afternoon, and then returned, march by march, to Simla.

Towards the end of the month Lord Napier began his winter tour, visiting the hill stations first. At Chakrata I made the acquaintance of the 92nd Highlanders, that distinguished corps which stood me in such good stead a few years later in Afghanistan. At the end of November we found ourselves at Lucknow, in time to take part in Lord Northbrook's state entry, and be present at a fête given to the Viceroy in the Wingfield Park by Sir George Cooper, the Chief Commissioner.

From Lucknow we went for a brief visit to a small Camp of Exercise near Rurki, where Lord Napier left the Adjutant-General, Thesiger,* in command, while he himself proceeded to visit some of the stations in the Madras Presidency, and I returned for a short time to Simla.

While riding up the hill from Kalka, I had a novel experience. One of those tremendous thunder-storms which are not uncommon in the Himalayas came on; the rain was blinding and incessant, and the peals of thunder were simultaneous with the lightning. At last there was a tremendous crash; a flash, more vivid than the rest, passed right in front of my horse's head, accompanied by a whizzing noise and a sulphurous smell, completely blinding me for a second. Two Natives travelling a few yards ahead of me fell flat on their faces, and I thought they were killed, but it turned out they were only knocked over and very much frightened.

Early in January, 1874, we received by telegram the infinitely sad news of my father's death. We ought, I suppose, to have been prepared for such an event, seeing that he was within a few months of his ninetieth birthday; but he was so well and active, and took such a keen interest in all that was going on, especially anything connected with India, that we hardly realized his great age, and always hoped we might see him once more. He had received the G.C.B. from Her Majesty's hands at Windsor on the 8th December, and two days afterwards he wrote me an account of the ceremony, and expressed himself much pleased and gratified at the Queen's gracious manner to him. He said nothing about his health, but we heard later that he had taken cold in the train on his way home, and never recovered from the effects; he died on the 30th of December. His love for India had not been weakened by his twenty years' absence from the country, and he never wearied of being told of the wonderful changes which had taken place since his day—changes which, for the most part, dated from the Mutiny, for up till 1857 life in India was much the same as when my father first landed in the beginning of the century.

A continued drought in Behar was at this time causing grave fears of a famine, such as from time to time had desolated various parts of India. Nine years before such a drought, and the absence of means of communication, which prevented grain being thrown into the famine-stricken districts in sufficient quantities, resulted in one-fourth of the population of Orissa being carried off by starvation, or disease consequent on starvation. So on this occasion Lord Northbrook was determined, at all costs, to ward off such a calamity. He sent Sir Richard Temple to Behar in the confident hope that his unbounded resource and energy would enable him to cope with the difficulties of the situation, a hope that was fully realized. Relief works were at

* Now General Lord Chelmsford, G.C.B.

once commenced; a transport train was quickly improvised, worked chiefly by military and police officers; and one million tons of rice were distributed amongst the people. Not a life was lost, but the cost to the State was enormous—six millions and a half sterling.

In the beginning of February I was ordered by Government to proceed to the famine districts to help Temple. I started at once; but I had not been long in Behar before I was required to join the Commander-in-Chief in Calcutta, His Excellency having determined to nominate me Quartermaster-General, in succession to Johnson, who was about to become Adjutant-General. Being only a Lieutenant-Colonel in the army, I could not, according to the rules, be put at once permanently into the appointment, which carried with it the rank of Major-General. The difficulty was overcome, however, by my being allowed to officiate till the following January, when, in the ordinary course of promotion, I should become a Colonel.

Lord Northbrook spent the summer of 1874 in Calcutta, in consequence of the famine necessities having to be met; and as the Commander-in-Chief determined to follow his example, I took a house in Calcutta, and my wife joined me in the middle of March—rather a bad time of year to come down to the plains after spending the winter amongst the snows of Simla. But she did not fancy Simla in the season as a grass-widow, and had had quite enough of being alone.

We continued in Calcutta until August, when the Head-Quarters returned to Simla, where we remained till November.

We had a standing camp at Umballa during the winter of 1874-75, doing our inspections from there, and returning to the camp at intervals. There was the usual visit to Calcutta in March, towards the end of which month another daughter was born.

In October, 1875, I spent some time at Delhi, arranging for the Camp of Exercise to be held there in January for His Royal Highness the Prince of Wales. The camp was formed in the beginning of December, and consisted of 17,000 men, in four divisions, commanded by Major-Generals Sir Charles Reid, Macdonnell, the Hon. Arthur Hardinge, and Donald Stewart.

The country round Delhi is particularly well suited for extended manœuvres, and full advantage was taken of the facilities it afforded during the two months the Camp of Exercise lasted. The Prince of Wales landed at Calcutta on the 23rd December; and Lord Napier with his staff went down to meet His Royal Highness, whose reception was loyal and hearty to a degree. As the *Serapis*, with the Prince on board, steamed slowly up the Hughli, salutes were fired from Fort William and three ships of the Royal Navy. All the vessels in the river were gay with flags, their yards were manned, and good hearty English cheers resounded from stem to stern of each ship as the Indian troopship, carrying the heir to England's throne, came in sight. As soon as the *Scrapis* was moored, the Viceroy went on board to greet the Prince and conduct His Royal Highness to the gaily-decorated landing-stage, where the principal officials, Native Princes, and chief inhabitants of Calcutta were assembled. Troops lined the road from the river to Government House, and the *maidan* (the great open space in front) was thronged with a dense crowd of Natives in their most brilliant gala attire, eager to catch a glimpse of the son of the great Queen of England.

That evening Lord Northbrook gave a State banquet. The next day there was a reception of the Princes and Chiefs, followed by a levée, and after dark the whole place was most beautifully illuminated. The week that followed was taken up with entertainments of various kinds —balls, races, and garden-parties, interspersed with official visits— which I am afraid the Prince could not have found amusing—and on New Year's Day, 1876, His Royal Highness held a Chapter of the Order of the Star of India, after which the Commander-in-Chief returned to Delhi to arrange to receive the Prince in that historical city on the 11th January.

His Royal Highness's camp, and that of the Commander-in-Chief, were pitched on the ground occupied by the British army during the siege. The road, five miles in length, from the station to the camp was lined with troops, and on the Ridge itself were placed six Rifle corps, three of which had taken part in the siege.* The 2nd Gurkhas were very appropriately drawn up immediately under Hindu Rao's house, and when this point was reached, the Prince stopped and warmly complimented the men on the distinguished service the regiment had performed.

The next day there was a parade of all the troops in review order for the inspection of the Prince, who was pleased to express his complete satisfaction and approval of 'the steadiness under arms, soldier-like bearing, and precision of movement, which distinguish the corps of the three armies assembled at the camp at Delhi.'

That evening the Prince was present at a ball in the *diwan-i-khas* (private audience hall) in the palace. given in His Royal Highness's honour by the officers of the army.

The next few days were taken up with manœuvres, which the Prince attended, accompanied by Lumsden† and myself. The defence was commanded by Reid, the attack by Hardinge, the latter's object being to gain possession of the Ridge, with a view to future operations against the city on the arrival of the main army from the Punjab. But the attack did not meet with the success which attended Barnard in 1857, while the Commander of the defence proved himself as skilful

* 60th Rifles, 2nd Gurkhas, and 1st Punjab Infantry.

† Lumsden returned to Head-Quarters as Adjutant-General on Edwin Johnson being appointed a member of the Indian Council in London.

in protecting the Ridge against an enemy advancing from the north as he had been, twenty years before, in repulsing one coming from the opposite direction.

The Prince of Wales held another investiture of the Star of India on the 7th of March at Allahabad, which Lord Napier and the staff attended. At its close we took our leave of His Royal Highness, who started that night for England.

In less than a fortnight our dear old Chief followed, and I saw him off from Bombay on the 10th April. I was very low at parting with him, for though in the earlier days of our acquaintance I used to think he was not very favourably disposed towards me, when I became more intimately associated with him nothing could exceed his kindness. He was universally regretted by Europeans and Natives alike. The soldiers recognized that he had carefully guarded their interests and worked for their welfare, and the Native Princes and people felt that he was in sympathy with them, and to this day they speak of *Lat Napier Sahib* with the deepest respect and affection.

Lord Napier was succeeded in the command by Sir Frederick Haines.

CHAPTER XLII.

WITH a new Commander-in-Chief came a new Viceroy, and it was while we were in Bombay seeing the last of Lord Napier that the *Orontes* steamed into the harbour with Lord Lytton on board. Little did I imagine when making Lord Lytton's acquaintance how much he would have to say to my future career.

His Excellency received me very kindly, telling me he felt that I was not altogether a stranger, as he had been reading during the voyage a paper I had written for Lord Napier, a year or two before, on our military position in India, and the arrangements that would be necessary in the event of Russia attempting to continue her advance south of the Oxus. Lord Napier had sent a copy of this memorandum to Lord Beaconsfield, by whom it had been given to Lord Lytton.

During the summer of 1876 our frontier policy was frequently under discussion. Sir Bartle Frere wrote two very strong letters after the Conservative Government came into power in 1874, drawing attention to the danger of our being satisfied with a policy of aloofness, and pointing out the necessity for coming into closer relations with the Amir of Afghanistan and the Khan of Khelat. Soon afterwards the Secretary of State communicated with the Government of India

FIELD-MARSHAL LORD NAPIER OF MAGDALA, G.C.B., G.C.S.I.

From
a photograph by Messrs. Maull and Fox.

as to the advisability of establishing British agents in Afghanistan. and of persuading the Amir to receive a temporary Embassy at Kabul, as had originally been proposed by Lord Northbrook.

The members of Lord Northbrook's Council were unanimously opposed to both these proposals, but they did not succeed in convincing Lord Salisbury that the measures were undesirable; and on the resignation of Lord Northbrook, the new Viceroy was furnished with special instructions as to the action which Her Majesty's Government considered necessary in consequence of the activity of Russia in Central Asia, and the impossibility of obtaining accurate information of what was going on in and beyond Afghanistan.

The question of the Embassy was dealt with at once; Lord Lytton directed a letter to be sent to the Amir announcing his assumption of the Viceroyalty, and his intention to depute Sir Lewis Pelly to proceed to Kabul for the purpose of discussing certain matters with His Highness.

To this communication a most unsatisfactory reply was received, and a second letter was addressed to the Amir, in which he was informed that, should he still decline to receive the Viceroy's Envoy after deliberately weighing all the considerations commended to his serious attention, the responsibility of the result would rest entirely on the Government of Afghanistan, which would thus alienate itself from the alliance of that Power which was most disposed and best able to befriend it.

This letter was the cause of considerable excitement in Kabul, excitement which ran so high that the necessity for proclaiming a religious war was mooted; and, to complicate matters, the Amir at this time received overtures from General Kauffmann, the Russian Governor-General in Turkestan.

A delay of six weeks occurred before Sher Ali replied to Lord Lytton's letter, and then he altogether ignored the Viceroy's proposal to send a Mission to Kabul, merely suggesting that the British Government should receive an Envoy from him, or that representatives from both countries should meet and hold a conference on the border, or, as another alternative, that the British Native Agent at Kabul should return and discuss affairs with the Viceroy.

The last suggestion was accepted by the Government of India, and the agent (Nawab Ata Mahomed Khan) arrived in Simla early in October. The Nawab gave it as his opinion that the Amir's attitude of estrangement was due to an accumulation of grievances, the chief of which were—the unfavourable arbitration in the Sistan dispute; the want of success of Saiyad Nur Mahomed's mission to India in 1873, when it was the desire of the Amir's heart to enter into an offensive and defensive alliance with the British Government; the interposition of Lord Northbrook's Government on behalf of Yakub

Khan;* the recent proceedings in Khelat,† which the Amir thought were bringing us objectionably near Kandahar; the transmission of presents through Afghanistan, to his vassal, the Mir of Wakhan, without the Amir's permission;‡ and, above all, the conviction that our policy was exclusively directed to the furtherance of British interests without any thought for those of Afghanistan.

As regarded the proposed Mission to Kabul, the Envoy said that His Highness objected to it for many reasons. Owing to local fanaticism, he could not insure its safety, and it seemed probable that, though of a temporary nature to begin with, it might only be the thin end of the wedge, ending in the establishment of a permanent Resident, as at the courts of the Native Rulers in India. Furthermore, the Amir conceived that, if he consented to this Mission, the Russians would insist upon their right to send a similar one, and finally, he feared a British Envoy might bring his influence to bear in favour of the release of his son, Yakub Khan, with whom his relations were as strained as ever.

In answer, the Viceroy enumerated the concessions he was prepared to make, and the conditions upon which alone he would consent to them; and this answer the agent was directed to communicate to the Amir.

The concessions were as follows:

(1) That the friends and enemies of either State should be those of the other.

(2) That, in the event of unprovoked aggression upon Afghanistan from without, assistance should be afforded in men, money, and arms; and also that to strengthen the Amir against such aggression, the British Government was willing to fortify Herat and other points on the frontier, and, if desired, to lend officers to discipline the army.

(3) That Abdulla Jan should be recognized as the Amir's successor to the exclusion of any other aspirant; and that the question of material aid in support of such recognition should be discussed by the Plenipotentiaries.

(4) That a yearly subsidy should be paid to the Amir on the following conditions:

That he should refrain from external aggression or provocation of his neighbours, and from entering into external relations without our knowledge.

* The Amir's eldest son, who had rebelled on his younger brother, Abdulla Jan, being nominated heir to the throne.

† Before Lord Northbrook left India he sent Major Sandeman on a Mission to Khelat to re-open the Bolan Pass, and endeavour to settle the differences between the Khan and the Baluchistan tribes, and between the tribes themselves, who were all at loggerheads.

‡ Presents given by the British Government to the Mir of Wakhan in recognition of his hospitable reception of the members of the Forsyth Mission on their return from Yarkund.

That he should decline all communication with Russia, and refer her agents to us.

That British agents should reside at Herat and elsewhere on the frontier.

That a mixed commission of British and Afghan officers should determine and demarcate the Amir's frontier.

That arrangements should be made, by allowances or otherwise, for free circulation of trade on the principal trade routes.

That similar arrangements should be made for a line of telegraph, the direction of which was to be subsequently determined.

That Afghanistan should be freely opened to Englishmen, official and non-official, and arrangements made by the Amir, as far as practicable, for their safety, though His Highness would not be absolutely held responsible for isolated accidents.

The Viceroy concluded by suggesting that, if the Amir agreed to these proposals, a treaty might be arranged between the agents of the respective Governments, and ratified either at Peshawar, by the Amir meeting Lord Lytton there, or at Delhi if the Amir accepted His Excellency's invitation to be present at the Imperial Assemblage.

The Amir at the time vouchsafed no reply whatever to these proposals or to the invitation to come to Delhi.

In the autumn of 1876 preparations were commenced for the 'Imperial Assemblage,' which it was announced by the Viceroy would be held at Delhi on the first day of January, 1877, for the purpose of proclaiming to the Queen's subjects throughout India the assumption by Her Majesty of the title of 'Empress of India.' To this Assemblage Lord Lytton further announced that he proposed 'to invite the Governors, Lieutenant-Governors, and Heads of Administration from all parts of the Queen's Indian dominions, as well as the Princes, Chiefs, and Nobles in whose persons the antiquity of the past is associated with the prosperity of the present, and who so worthily contribute to the splendour and stability of this great Empire.'

Delhi was selected as the place where the meeting between the Queen's representative and the great nobles of India could most appropriately be held, and a committee was appointed to make the necessary arrangements. As a member of the committee I was deputed to proceed to Delhi, settle about the sites for the camps, and carry out all details in communication with the local authorities. The Viceroy impressed upon me that the Assemblage was intended to emphasize the Proclamation Lord Canning issued eighteen years before, by which the Queen assumed the direct sovereignty of her eastern possessions, and that he wished no trouble or expense to be spared in making the ceremony altogether worthy of such a great historical event.

I returned to Simla in October, when my wife and I accompanied the Commander-in-Chief on a very delightful march over the Jalauri Pass through the Kulu valley, then over the Bubbu Pass and through the Kangra valley to Chamba and Dalhousie. Our party consisted of the Chief, his Doctor (Bradshaw), Persian interpreter (Moore), General and Mrs. Lumsden, and ourselves. The first slight shower of snow had just fallen on the Jalauri Pass, and as we crossed over we disturbed a number of beautiful snow-pheasants and minals busily engaged in scratching it away to get at their food. The scenery on this march is very fine and varied; for the most part the timber and foliage are superb, and the valleys are very fertile and pretty, lying close under the snow-capped mountains.

Having inspected the 'Hill stations,' we proceeded to Peshawar, where the Viceroy had arranged to hold a conference with the Lieutenant-Governor of the Punjab and the Commissioner of Peshawar about frontier affairs.

Early in December I was back again at Delhi, where I found the arrangements for the several camps progressing most satisfactorily, and canvas cities rising up in every direction. I had previously chosen the site of the old cantonment for the camps of the Viceroy, the Commander-in-Chief, and the principal officials, while for the Assemblage itself I had selected ground about three miles off.

The Chiefs and Princes were all settled in their several camps ready to meet the Viceroy, who, on his arrival, in a few graceful words welcomed them to Delhi, and thanked them for responding to his invitation. He then mounted, with Lady Lytton, on a state elephant, and a procession was formed, which, I fancy, was about the most gorgeous and picturesque which has ever been seen even in the East. The magnificence of the Native Princes' retinues can hardly be described; their elephant-housings were of cloth of gold, or scarlet-and-blue cloths embroidered in gold and silver. The howdahs were veritable thrones of the precious metals, shaded by the most brilliant canopies, and the war-elephants belonging to some of the Central India and Rajputana Chiefs formed a very curious and interesting feature. Their tusks were tipped with steel; they wore shields on their foreheads, and breastplates of flashing steel; chain-mail armour hung down over their trunks and covered their backs and sides; and they were mounted by warriors clad in chain-mail, and armed to the teeth. Delhi must have witnessed many splendid pageants, when the Rajput, the Moghul, and the Mahratta dynasties, each in its turn, was at the height of its glory; but never before had Princes and Chiefs of every race and creed come from all parts of Hindustan, vying with each other as to the magnificence of their *entourage*, and met together with the same object—that of acknowledging and doing homage to one supreme Ruler.

The next few days were spent by Lord Lytton in receiving the sixty-three* Ruling Princes of India according to the strictest etiquette. Each Prince, with his suite, was met at the entrance to the camp, and conducted up the street to the durbar tent by mounted officers, the salute to which he was entitled being fired while the procession moved on. He was then presented by the Foreign Secretary to the Viceroy, who placed him on a chair on his right, immediately below a full-length portrait of Her Majesty. A satin banner, richly embroidered with the Chief's armorial bearings, surmounted by the Imperial crown, was next brought in by Highland soldiers and planted in front of the throne, when the Viceroy, leading the particular Chief towards it, thus addressed him: 'I present Your Highness with this banner as a personal gift from Her Majesty the Queen, in commemoration of her assumption of the title of Empress of India. Her Majesty trusts that it may never be unfurled without reminding you not only of the close union between the throne of England and your loyal and princely house, but also of the earnest desire of the paramount power to see your dynasty strong, prosperous, and permanent.'

His Excellency then placed round the Chief's neck a crimson ribbon, to which was attached a very handsome gold medal† with the Queen's head engraved on it, adding: 'I further decorate you, by command of Her Majesty. May this medal be long worn by yourself, and long kept as an heirloom in your family in remembrance of the auspicious date it bears.'

The 1st January, 1877, saw the Queen proclaimed Empress of India, The ceremony was most imposing, and in every way successful. Three tented pavilions had been constructed on an open plain. The throne-pavilion in the centre was a very graceful erection, brilliant in hangings and banners of red, blue, and white satin magnificently embroidered in gold, with appropriate emblems. It was hexagonal in shape, and rather more than 200 feet in circumference. In front of this was the pavilion for the Ruling Chiefs and high European officials, in the form of a semicircle 800 feet long. The canopy was of Star of India blue-and-white satin embroidered in gold, each pillar being surmounted by an Imperial crown. Behind the throne was the stand for the spectators, also in the form of a semicircle divided in the middle, and likewise canopied in brilliant colours. Between these two blocks was the entrance to the area.

Each Chief and high official sat beneath his own banner, which was planted immediately behind his chair, and they were all mixed up as

* 'Besides the sixty-three Ruling Chiefs, there were nearly three hundred titular Chiefs and persons of distinction collected at the Imperial Assemblage, besides those included in the suites of Ruling Chiefs.—J. Talboys Wheeler, 'History of the Delhi Assemblage.'

† These gold medals were also presented to the Governors, Lieutenant-Governors, and other high officials, and to the members of the Imperial Assemblage Committee.

much as possible to avoid questions of precedence, the result being the most wonderful mass of colour, produced from the intermingling of British uniforms and plumes with gorgeous eastern costumes, set off by a blaze of diamonds and other precious stones.

All the British troops brought to Delhi for the occasion were paraded to the north, and the troops and retainers belonging to the Native Chiefs to the south, of the pavilion. Guards of Honour were drawn up on either side of the throne and at each opening by which the Ruling Chiefs were to enter the pavilion.

The guests being all seated, a flourish of trumpets by the heralds exactly at noon announced the arrival of the Viceroy. The military bands played a march, and Lord Lytton, accompanied by Lady Lytton, their daughters, and his staff, proceeded to the pavilion. His Excellency took his seat upon the throne, arrayed in his robes as Grand Master of the Star of India, the National Anthem was played, the Guards of Honour presented arms, while the whole of the vast assemblage rose as one man. The Chief Herald was then commanded to read the Proclamation. A flourish of trumpets was again sounded, and Her Majesty was proclaimed Empress of India.

When the Chief Herald had ceased reading, the Royal Standard was hoisted, and a salute of 101 salvoes of artillery was fired, with a *feu de joie* from the long line of troops. This was too much for the elephants. As the *feu de joie* approached nearer and nearer to them they became more and more alarmed, and at last scampered off, dispersing the crowd in every direction. When it ceased they were quieted and brought back by their *mahouts*, only to start off again when the firing recommenced; but, as it was a perfectly bare plain, without anything for the great creatures to come in contact with, there was no harm done beyond a severe shaking to their riders. As the sound of the last salvo died away the Viceroy addressed the assemblage. When he had ceased speaking, the assembly again rose *en masse* and joined the troops in giving several ringing cheers.

His Highness the Maharaja Sindhia then spoke as follows: '*Shah in Shah Padishah.* May God bless you. The Princes of India bless you, and pray that your sovereignty and power may remain steadfast for ever.'

Sir Salar Jung rose on behalf of the boy Nizam, and said: 'I am desired by His Highness the Nizam to request your Excellency to convey to Her Majesty, on the part of himself and the Chiefs of India, the expression of their hearty congratulations on the assumption of the title of Empress of India, and to assure the Queen that they pray for her, and for the enduring prosperity of her Empire, both in India and England.'

The Maharajas of Udaipur and Jaipur, in the name of the united Chiefs of Rajputana, begged that a telegram might be sent to the

THE EARL OF LYTTON, G.C.B., G.M.S.I., G.M.I.E.,
VICEROY OF INDIA.

From
a photograph by Messrs. Maull and Fox.

Queen, conveying their dutiful and loyal congratulations; and the Maharaja of Kashmir expressed his gratification at the tenor of the Viceroy's speech, and declared that he should henceforth consider himself secure under the shadow of Her Majesty's protecting care.*

It is difficult to overrate the political importance of this great gathering. It was looked upon by most of the Ruling Chiefs as the result of the Prince of Wales's visit, and rejoiced in as an evidence of Her Majesty's increased interest in, and appreciation of, the vast Empire of India with its many different races and peoples.

I visited all the camps, and conversed with every one of the Princes and Nobles, and each in turn expressed the same intense gratification at the Viceroy's reception of him, the same fervent loyalty to the Empress, and the same satisfaction that the new title should have been announced with such appropriate splendour and publicity.

General rejoicings in honour of the occasion took place all over India, in Native States as well as British cantonments. School-houses, town halls, hospitals, and dispensaries were founded, large numbers of prisoners were released, substantial additions were made to the pay of all ranks in the Native Army, as well as a considerable increase in numbers to the Order of British India; and the amnesty granted in 1859 was extended to all but murderers and leaders in the Mutiny.

When the Assemblage broke up, I started with Sir Frederick Haines for a tour along the Derajat frontier. We visited Kohat, Bannu, Dera Ismail Khan, and Multan; proceeded by steamer down the Indus to Sukkur, and thence rode to Jacobabad. Then on to Kotri, from which place we went to see the battle-field of Miani, where Sir Charles Napier defeated the Amirs of Sind in 1843. From Kotri we travelled to Simla *viâ* Karachi and Bombay, where we were most hospitably entertained by the Commander-in-Chief of Bombay (Sir Charles Stavely) and his wife.

Afghan affairs were this year again giving the Viceroy a great deal of anxiety. The Amir had eventually agreed to a discussion of Lord Lytton's proposals being held, and for this purpose Saiyad Nur Mahomed and Sir Lewis Pelly had met at Peshawar in January, 1877. The meeting, unfortunately, ended in a rupture, owing to Sher Ali's agent pronouncing the location of European officers in any part of Afghanistan an impossibility; and what at this crisis complicated matters to a most regrettable extent was the death of Saiyad Nur Mahomed, who had been in failing health for some time.

On learning the death of his most trusted Minister, and the failure of the negotiations, Sher Ali broke into a violent fit of passion, giving vent to his fury in threatenings and invectives against the British Govern-

* In endeavouring to describe this historical event, I have freely refreshed my memory from Talboys Wheeler's 'History of the Imperial Assemblage,' in which is given a detailed account of the proceedings.

ment. He declared it was not possible to come to terms, and that there was nothing left for him but to fight; that he had seven crores of rupees, every one of which he would hurl at the heads of the English, and he ended by giving orders for a *jahad* (a religious war) to be proclaimed.

For the time being nothing more could be done with Afghanistan, and the Viceroy was able to turn his attention to the following important questions: the transfer of Sind from Bombay to the Punjab, a measure which had been unanimously agreed to by Lord Northbrook's Government; the removal from the Punjab government of the trans-Indus tract of country, and the formation of the latter into a separate district under the control of a Chief Commissioner, who would be responsible to the Government of India alone for frontier administration and trans-frontier relations. This post Lord Lytton told me, as much to my surprise as to my gratification, that he meant to offer to me, if his views were accepted by the Secretary of State. It was above all others the appointment I should have liked. I delighted in frontier life and frontier men, who, with all their faults, are men, and grand men, too. I had felt for years what an important factor the trans-Indus tribes are in the defence of India, and how desirable it was that we should be on better terms with them than was possible so long as our policy consisted in keeping them at arm's length, and our only intercourse with them was confined to punitive expeditions or the visits of their head-men to our hard-worked officials, whose whole time was occupied in writing long reports, or in settling troublesome disputes to the satisfaction of no one.

I now hoped to be able to put a stop to the futile blockades and inconclusive reprisals which had been carried on for nearly thirty years with such unsatisfactory results, and I looked forward to turning the wild tribesmen from enemies into friends, a strength instead of a weakness, to our Government, and to bringing them by degrees within the pale of civilization. My wife quite shared my feelings, and we were both eager to begin our frontier life.

As a preliminary to my engaging in this congenial employment, Lord Lytton proposed that I should take up the command of the Punjab Frontier Force. I gladly acquiesced; for I had been a long time on the staff, and had had three years of the Quartermaster-Generalship. My friends expressed surprise at my accepting the position of Brigadier-General, after having filled an appointment carrying with it the rank of Major-General; but this was not my view. I longed for a command, and the Frontier Force offered opportunities for active service afforded by no other post.

We were in Calcutta when the question was decided, and started very soon afterwards to make our arrangements for the breaking up of our home at Simla. I took over the command of the Force on the

15th March, 1878. My wife accompanied me to Abbottabad—the pretty, quiet little place in Hazara, about 4,000 feet above the sea, which was to be henceforth our winter head-quarters. For the summer months we were to be located in the higher hills, and my wife was anxious to see the house which I had purchased from my predecessor, General Keyes, at Natiagali. So off we set, nothing daunted by being told that we were likely to find snow still deep in places.

For the first part of the way we got on well enough, my wife in a dandy, I riding, and thirteen miles were accomplished without much difficulty. Suddenly the road took a bend, and we found ourselves in deep snow. Riding soon proved to be impossible, and the dandy-bearers could not carry my wife further; so there was nothing for it but to walk. We were seven miles from our destination, and at each step we sank into the snow, which became deeper and deeper the higher we ascended. On we trudged, till my wife declared she could go no further, and sat down to rest, feeling so drowsy that she entreated me to let her stay where she was. Fortunately I had a small flask with me filled with brandy. I poured a little into the cup, mixed it with snow, and administered it as a stimulant. This restored her somewhat, and roused her from the state of lethargy into which she had fallen. Again we struggled on. Soon it became dark, except for such light as the stars, aided by the snow, afforded. More than once I despaired of reaching the end of our journey; but, just as I had become quite hopeless, we saw lights on the hill above us, and heard our servants, who had preceded us, shouting to attract our attention. I answered, and presently they came to our assistance. Half carrying, half dragging her, we got my wife up the steep mountain-side; and at length, about 9 p.m., we arrived at the little house buried in snow, into which we crept through a hole dug in the snow wall which encircled it. We were welcomed by a blazing wood-fire and a most cheering odour of dinner, to which we did full justice, after having got rid of our saturated garments. Next morning we started on our return journey at daybreak, for it was necessary to get over the worst part of the road before the sun had had time to soften the snow, which the night's frost had so thoroughly hardened that we slipped over it without the least difficulty.

This was our only visit to our new possession, for very soon afterwards I was informed that Lord Lytton wished me to spend the summer at Simla, as the Lieutenant-Governor of the Punjab would be there, and His Excellency was anxious to discuss the details of the proposed Chief Commissionership. My wife, therefore, returned to Simla at once, and I joined her at the end of May, having in the meanwhile inspected every regiment and visited every post held by the Frontier Force between Sind and Hazara—a most interesting experience, which I thoroughly enjoyed.

CHAPTER XLIII.

BEFORE continuing my story, it will, I think, be as well to recall to the minds of my readers the train of events which led to England and Russia becoming at the same moment solicitous for the Amir's friendship, for it was this rivalry which was the immediate cause of the second Afghan war.

Less than two hundred years ago the British Empire in the East and Russia were separated from each other by a distance of 4,000 miles. Russia's most advanced posts were at Orenburg and Petropaulovsk, while England had obtained but an uncertain footing on the seaboard of southern India. The French were our only European rivals in India, and the advance of Russia towards the Oxus was as little anticipated as was England's advance towards the Indus.

Thirty years later Russia began to absorb the hordes of the Kirghiz steppes, which gave her occupation for more than a hundred years, during which time England was far from idle. Bengal was conquered, or ceded to us, the Madras Presidency established, and Bombay had become an important settlement, with the result that, in the early part of this century, the distance between the Russian and English possessions had been diminished to less than 2,000 miles.

Our progress wa now more rapid. While Russia was laboriously crossing a barren desert, the North-West Provinces, the Carnatic, the territories of the Peshwa, Sind, and the Punjab, successively came under our rule, and by 1850 we had extended our dominions to the foot of the mountains beyond the Indus.

Russia by this time, having overcome the difficulties of the desert, had established herself at Aralsk, near the junction of the Syr Daria with the waters of Lake Aral; so that in fifty years the distance between the outposts of the two advancing Powers in Asia had been reduced to about 1,000 miles.

Repeated successful wars with Persia, and our desertion of that Power owing to the conviction that we could no longer defend her against the Russians, had practically placed her at their mercy, and they had induced Persia, in 1837, to undertake the siege of Herat. At the same time, the Russian Ambassador at Teheran had despatched Captain Vitkievitch to Kabul with letters from himself and from the Czar to the Amir, in the hope of getting Dost Mahomed Khan to join the Russians and Persians in their alliance against the English.

Vitkievitch's arrival at Kabul towards the end of 1837 had been anticipated by Captain (afterwards Sir Alexander) Burnes, who had been sent three months before by Lord Auckland on a Mission to the Amir, ostensibly to improve our commercial relations with the Afghans, but in reality to prevent them from joining the Russo-Persian alliance.

Burnes had been most cordially received by Dost Mahomed, who hoped, with the help of the Indian Government, to recover the district of Peshawar, which had been wrested from him by the Sikhs. Vitkievitch's reception was proportionately discouraging, and for some weeks he could not obtain an interview with the Amir.

The Dost's hopes, however, were not fulfilled. We declined to give him any assistance towards regaining possession of Peshawar or defending his dominions, should his refusal to join with Persia and Russia draw down upon him the enmity of those Powers.

Vitkievitch, who had been patiently biding his time, was now taken into favour by the Amir, who accorded him a reception which fully compensated for the neglect with which he had previously been treated.

Burnes remained at Kabul until the spring of 1838, and then returned to India to report that Dost Mahomed had thrown himself heart and soul into the Russo-Persian alliance.

Under pressure from the English Ministry the Governor-General of India determined to take the extreme measure of deposing an Amir who had shown himself so hostilely inclined, and of placing on the throne of Kabul a Ruler who, it was hoped, would feel that it was to his interest to keep on good terms with us. It was for this object that the first Afghan war* was undertaken, which ended in the murder of our nominee, Shah Shuja, and the triumphant return of Dost Mahomed. The disastrous failure of our action in this matter taught the British Government that our frontier on the Sutlej was too far removed for us to think of exercising any real influence in Afghanistan, and that the time had not arrived to warrant our interfering in Afghan affairs.

After this came our war with the Sikhs, resulting in our conquest of the Punjab, and our frontier becoming conterminous with that of Afghanistan on the banks of the Indus.

There was a lull in the movements of Russia in Central Asia until after the Crimean War of 1854-56, which, while temporarily checking the designs of Russia in Europe, seems to have stimulated her progress in the East. After the passage of the great desert, Russia found herself in the midst of fertile and settled countries, whose provinces fell under her control as rapidly as those of India had fallen under ours, until in 1864 Chimkent was occupied, the point beyond which Prince Gortchakoff stated that there was no intention on the part of Russia to make further advances.

Notwithstanding these assurances, Tashkent was captured on the 29th June of the following year. In 1866 Khojent was successfully

* It is instructive to note how remarkably similar were the circumstances which brought about the first and second Afghan wars, viz., the presence of Russian officers at Kabul.

assaulted. Tisakh fell on the 30th October; and in the spring of 1867 the fort of Yani-Kargan in the Nurata mountains was seized and occupied.

Bokhara alone remained unconquered, but the Ruler of that State, after vainly endeavouring to gain assistance from Afghanistan and to enlist the sympathies of the Indian Government, was compelled to sue for peace.

Important as these acquisitions were, they attracted but little attention in England, owing partly to the policy of non-interference which had been adopted as regards Central Asian affairs, and partly to the British public being absorbed in European politics, until 1868, when the occupation of Samarkand by Russia caused considerable excitement, not to say consternation, amongst the authorities in England.

Conferences took place in the spring of 1870 between Lord Clarendon, the Secretary of State for Foreign Affairs, and Baron Brunow, the Russian Ambassador, with the object of determining a neutral zone, which should be the limit of the possessions of England and Russia in Central Asia. For nearly three years, Russia was persistent in her endeavours to have Afghanistan placed outside the pale of British influence; but the Indian Government were equally persistent in pointing out the danger of agreeing to such an arrangement, and it was not until the 31st January, 1873, that the boundary, which neither England nor Russia might cross, was finally agreed upon.

Six months later the conquest of Khiva by Russia was effected. It was at first given out that the expedition was to punish acts of brigandage, and to rescue fifty Russian prisoners, but was on no account to lead to a prolonged occupancy of the Khanate. Count Schouvaloff, the Russian Statesman who was deputed to communicate the object of the expedition to the British Government, declared that a positive promise to this effect might be given to the British public, as a proof of the friendly and pacific intentions of his master the Czar; but, notwithstanding these assurances, the Russians never left Khiva, and it has been a Russian possession from that time.

Thus, in a little more than twenty years, Russia had made a stride of 600 miles towards India, leaving but 400 miles between her outposts and those of Great Britain. Russia's southern boundary was now, in fact, almost conterminous with the northern boundary of Afghanistan, near enough to cause the Ruler of that country considerable anxiety, and make him feel that Russia had become a dreaded neighbour, and that the integrity of his kingdom could not be maintained save by the aid of one of the two great Powers between whose fire he now found himself.

I have endeavoured to show how it was that Sher Ali, notwithstanding his soreness and disappointment at the many rebuffs he had received from us in the earlier part of his career, gratefully remembered the timely aid afforded him by Sir John Lawrence, and the princely reception accorded to him by Lord Mayo, and was still quite prepared in 1873 to enter into friendly relations with us, provided we would recognize his favourite son as his heir, and give a direct promise of aid in the event of Russian aggression. Our refusal to accede to these terms, added to our adverse decision in regard to the Sistan boundary, turned Sher Ali from a friend into an enemy, and he decided, as his father had done forty years before, to throw in his lot with Russia.

CHAPTER XLIV.

In 1877 Russia declared war with Turkey; for more than a year fighting had been going on between the two countries, and as it seemed possible to the British Government that England might in the end be drawn into the contest, it was deemed expedient to obtain help from India, and a force of about 5,000 Native soldiers was despatched from Bombay to Malta in response to the demand from home.

Russia answered this move on our part by increased activity in Central Asia; and in June, 1878, it was reported by Major Cavagnari, Deputy-Commissioner of Peshawar, that a Russian Envoy of the same rank as the Governor-General of Tashkent was about to visit Kabul, and that General Kauffmann had written to the Amir that the Envoy must be received as an Ambassador deputed by the Czar himself. A few days later further reports were received of Russian troops being mobilized, and of the intention of Russia to establish cantonments on the ferries of Kilif and Kerki on the Oxus.

The Amir, it was said, summoned a council of the leading Chiefs, to discuss the question whether it would be most advantageous for Afghanistan at this juncture to side with Russia or with England; it was decided apparently in favour of the former, for from the moment General Stolietoff's Mission set foot on Afghan territory it met with an enthusiastic reception. Five miles from the capital Stolietoff and his companions were welcomed by the Foreign Secretary. They were then mounted on richly-caparisoned elephants, and escorted by a large body of troops to the Bala Hissar, where the following morning they were received in state by Sher Ali, and the nobles of highest degree in his kingdom.*

* On the 13th June, the day on which the Berlin Congress held its first sitting, the news of the approach of General Stolietoff's Mission reached Kabul. The Russians hoped that the Mission might influence the decision of the Berlin Congress, and although its despatch was repudiated by the Imperial Government at St. Petersburg, it was subsequently ascertained on excellent authority that the project of sending a Mission to Kabul was discussed three times at the Council of Ministers, and, according to a statement in the

On the eve of the day that the Mission entered Kabul, Stolietoff received a despatch from General Kauffmann giving him the heads of the Berlin Treaty, with the following commentary in the handwriting of the Governor-General himself: 'If the news be true, it is indeed melancholy;' adding, however, that the Congress had finished its sittings, and that, therefore, the Envoy in his negotiations with the Amir had better refrain from arranging any distinct measures, or making any positive promises, and '*not go generally as far as would have been advisable if war with England had been threatened.*' Evidently these instructions greatly modified the basis of Stolietoff's negotiations with Sher Ali; for, although the Russians deny that an offensive and defensive alliance with the Afghan Ruler was contemplated, it seems probable, from the tone of Kauffmann's despatch, that the Envoy's instructions were elastic enough to admit of such an arrangement had the circumstances of the case made it desirable—*e.g.*, had the Berlin Congress failed to establish peace in Europe.

In telegraphing to the Secretary of State an account of these proceedings at Kabul, the Viceroy requested explicit instructions from Her Majesty's Government as to whether this conduct on the part of Russia and Afghanistan was to be left to the Government of India to deal with as a matter between it and the Amir, or whether, having regard to Russia's formal promises, it would be treated as an Imperial question 'In the former case,' he concluded, 'I shall propose, with your approval, to insist on an immediate suitable reception of a British Mission.'

Lord Lytton's proposition was approved of by Her Majesty's Ministers, and a letter* was at once written by the Viceroy to the

---

Journal de St. Petersbourg, orders were sent in April, 1878, to General Kauffmann regarding its despatch. About the same time, the Russian Minister of War proposed that the Army of the Caucasus should be transferred bodily across the Caspian to Astrabad, whence the troops would march in two columns on Herat; while three columns, amounting in the aggregate to 14,000 men, were to move direct upon the Oxus from Turkestan. The main part of this scheme was never carried into effect, probably from its being found too great an undertaking at a time when Russia had scarcely obtained a footing beyond the Caspian, but the minor movement was partially carried out. The largest of the three columns, under Kauffmann's own command, moved from Tashkent, through Samarkand, to Jam, the most southern point of the Russian possessions at that time, and within ten marches of Kilif, the main ferry over the Oxus. There it remained for some weeks, when it returned to Tashkent, the Afghan expedition being abandoned in consequence of the Treaty of Berlin having been signed.

* 'SIMLA,
'*14th August*, 1878.

'The authentic intelligence which I have lately received of the course of recent events at Kabul and in the countries bordering on Afghanistan has rendered it necessary that I should communicate fully and without reserve with your Highness upon matters of importance which concern the interests

Amir, announcing that a Mission would shortly be despatched to Kabul with General Sir Neville Chamberlain, at that time Commander-in-Chief in Madras, as its responsible head.

Major Cavagnari was at the same time directed to inform the authorities at Kabul that the object of the Mission was altogether friendly, and that a refusal to grant it a free passage and safe conduct, such as had been accorded to the Russian Envoy, would be considered as an act of open hostility.

Intimation of the Viceroy's intentions reached Kabul on the 17th August, the day on which the Amir's favourite son, Abdulla Jan, died. This untoward event was taken advantage of to delay answering the Viceroy's letter, but it was not allowed in any way to interfere with the progress of the negotiations with Russia. When these were completed, Stolietoff inquired from Sher Ali whether he meant to receive the English Mission, whereupon the Amir asked for the General's advice in the matter. Stolietoff, while replying somewhat evasively, gave Sher Ali to understand that the simultaneous presence of Embassies from two countries in almost hostile relations with each other would not be quite convenient, upon which His Highness decided not to allow the British Mission to enter Afghanistan. This decision, however, was not communicated to the Viceroy, and on the 21st September the Mission* marched out of Peshawar and encamped at Jamrud, three miles short of the Kyber Pass.

---

of India and of Afghanistan. For this reason, I have considered it expedient to depute a special and confidential British Envoy of high rank, who is known to your Highness—his Excellency General Sir Neville Bowles Chamberlain, Knight Grand Cross of the Most Honourable Order of the Bath, Knight Grand Commander of the Most Exalted Order of the Star of India, Commander-in-Chief of the Madras Army—to visit your Highness immediately at Kabul, in order that he may converse personally with your Highness regarding these urgent affairs. It appears certain that they can best be arranged for the welfare and tranquillity of both States, and for the preservation of friendship between the two Governments, by a full and frank statement of the present position. This letter is therefore sent in advance to your Highness by the hand of Nawab Gholam Hussein Khan, C.S.I., a faithful and honoured Sirdar of my Government, who will explain all necessary details as to the time and manner of the Envoy's visit. It is asked that your Highness may be pleased to issue commands to your Sirdars, and to all other authorities in Afghanistan, upon the route between Peshawar and Kabul, that they shall make, without any delay, whatever arrangements are necessary and proper for effectively securing to my Envoy, the representative of a friendly Power, due safe conduct and suitable accommodation according to his dignity, while passing with his retinue through the dominions of your Highness.

'I beg to express the high consideration I entertain for your Highness, and to subscribe myself.'

* The Mission was composed of General Sir Neville Chamberlain, G.C.B., G.C.S.I.; Major Cavagnari, C.S.I.; Surgeon-Major Bellew, C.S.I.; Major O. St. John, R.E.; Captain St. V. Hammick, 43rd Foot; Captain F. Onslow,

In consequence of the extremely hostile attitude of the Amir, and the very unsatisfactory reply received from General Faiz Mahomed Khan, commanding the Afghan troops in the Kyber Pass, to a letter* he had written a few days before, Sir Neville Chamberlain suspected that the advance of the Mission would be opposed, and, in order 'to reduce to a minimum any indignity that might be offered to our Government,' he deputed Major Cavagnari to ride on with a few sowars to Ali Masjid, a fort ten miles beyond the mouth of the Pass, and demand leave for the Mission to proceed.

Madras Cavalry; Lieutenant Neville Chamberlain, Central India Horse; Maharaj Pertap Sing of Jodhpur; and Sirdar Obed Ulla Khan, of Tonk. Lieutenant-Colonel F. Jenkins and Captain W. Battye were with the escort.

* 'PESHAWAR,
'*15th September*, 1878.

(After compliments.) 'I write to inform you that, by command of His Excellency the Viceroy and Governor-General of India, a friendly Mission of British officers, with a suitable escort, is about to proceed to Kabul through the Khyber Pass, and intimation of the despatch of this Mission has been duly communicated to His Highness the Amir by the hand of the Nawab Ghulam Hussein Khan.

'I hear that an official from Kabul has recently visited you at Ali Masjid, and he has doubtless instructed you in accordance with His Highness the Amir's commands. As, however, information has now been received that you have summoned from Peshawar the Khyber headmen with whom we were making arrangements for the safe conduct of the British Mission through the Khyber Pass, I therefore write to inquire from you whether, in accordance with the instructions you have received, you are prepared to guarantee the safety of the British Mission to Daka or not: and I request that a clear reply to this inquiry may be speedily communicated by the hand of the bearer of this letter, as I cannot delay my departure from Peshawar. It is well known that the Khyber tribes are in receipt of allowances from the Kabul Government, and also, like other independent tribes on this frontier, have relations with the British Government. It may be well to let you know that when the present negotiations were opened with the Khyber tribes, it was solely with the object of arranging with them for the safe conduct of the British Mission through the Khyber Pass, in the same manner as was done in regard to the despatch of our Agent, the Nawab Ghulam Hussein Khan; and the tribes were given clearly to understand that these negotiations were in no way intended to prejudice their relations with His Highness the Amir, as it was well known that the object of the British Mission was altogether of a friendly character to His Highness the Amir and the people of Afghanistan.

'I trust that, in accordance with the instructions you have received from His Highness the Amir, your reply to this letter will be satisfactory, and that it will contain the required assurances that the Mission will be safely conducted to Daka. I shall expect to receive your reply to this letter not later than the 18th instant, so please understand that the matter is most urgent.

'But at the same time, it is my duty to inform you, in a frank and friendly manner, that if your answer is not what I trust it will be, or if you delay to send an early reply, I shall have no alternative but to make whatever arrangements may seem to me best for carrying out the instructions I have received from my own Government

When within a mile of the fort, Cavagnari was met by a body of Afridis, who warned him that the road ahead was blocked by Afghans, and that if he ventured further he would be fired upon. On this Cavagnari halted, and while in the act of writing a letter to Faiz Mahomed, complaining of the treatment he had met with, and informing him that he and his companions intended to proceed until fired upon, an act the responsibility for which would rest with the Amir's representatives, a message was brought him from Faiz Mahomed to the effect that he was coming to meet him, and would hear anything he had to communicate.

The interview took place near a water-mill on the right bank of the stream which flows under Ali Masjid. I have several times since ridden past the spot and pictured to myself the meeting between the British political officer and the Afghan General. It was a meeting of most portentous moment, for its result would mean peace or war.

Faiz Mahomed's bearing was perfectly courteous, but he made it clear that he did not intend to permit the Mission to pass, explaining that he was only acting as a sentry under instructions from Kabul, and that he was bound to resist the entrance of the Mission into Afghan territory with all the force at his disposal. He spoke with considerable warmth, and told Cavagnari that but for their personal friendship he would, in obedience to the Amir's orders, have shot down him and his escort.

Faiz Mahomed's followers were not so respectful in their bearing as their Chief, and their manner warned Cavagnari that it was unadvisable to prolong the conversation; he, therefore, took leave of the Afghan General, and returned to Jamrud. The Mission was dissolved,* our Agent at Kabul was ordered to return to India, and Cavagnari was instructed to remain at Peshawar and arrange for alienating the Afridis in the Khyber from the Amir's interests.

In reporting these circumstances to the Secretary of State, the Government of India expressed their regret that this final endeavour on their part to arrive at some definite understanding with the Amir of Kabul should have been thus met with repudiation and affront, and concluded their despatch in the following words: 'The repulse of Sir Neville Chamberlain by Sher Ali at his frontier while the Russian

* In a letter to Lord Lytton reporting the rebuff the Mission had encountered, General Chamberlain wrote: 'No man was ever more anxious than I to preserve peace and secure friendly solution, and it was only when I plainly saw the Amir's fixed intention to drive us into a corner that I told you we must either sink into a position of merely obeying his behests on all points or stand on our rights and risk rupture. Nothing could have been more distinct, nothing more humiliating to the dignity of the British Crown and nation; and I believe that but for the decision and tact of Cavagnari at one period of the interview, the lives of the British officers and the Native following were in considerable danger.'

emissaries are still at his capital has proved the inutility of diplomatic expedients, and has deprived the Amir of all claim upon our further forbearance.'

It had been arranged that, if it were unfortunately found to be necessary to support political efforts by military measures, two columns should be mobilized, one at Sukkur on the Indus, for an advance in the direction of Kandahar, the other at Kohat for operations in the Kuram valley, and that I was to have command of the latter. As soon, therefore, as the tidings of Sir Neville's repulse was received, I started from Simla to be on the spot in case the proposal to employ force should be sanctioned by the authorities in England.

Between the time of my leaving Simla and my arrival at Kohat on the 9th October, it was decided to employ a third column to make a demonstration in the direction of the Khyber for the purpose of clearing the Amir's troops out of the pass.*

The formation of this column was no doubt a wise move, as the Afghans were holding Ali Masjid, the spot on which the insult had been offered to our Envoy, and the presence of a force on this line would tend to relieve the pressure against my column; but looked at from my point of view, this third column was not quite so desirable, as it involved the withdrawal of three of my most efficient regiments, and the transfer of a large number of my transport animals to the Khyber for its use. There was some consolation, however, in the fact that my old friend Major-General Sir Samuel Browne, who had been named for the command in the Khyber, was to be the gainer by my loss.

Major-General Donald Stewart, who was in England, was telegraphed for to command the Kandahar column, the advanced portion of which, it was intended, should push on under Major-General Biddulph to strengthen Quetta.

The long-expected reply† from the Amir to the Viceroy's letter of

* The approximate strength of the three columns was as follows:

	Officers.	*Men.*	*Guns.*
I. The Kandahar Field Force	265	12,599	78
II. The Kuram Field Force	116	6,549	18
III. The Peshawar Valley Field Force ...	325	15,854	48
	706	35,002	144

† 'KABUL,
'*6th October*, 1878.

(After compliments.) 'Your Excellency's despatch regarding the sending of a friendly Mission has been received through Nawab Gholam Hussein Khan; I understand its purport, but the Nawab had not yet an audience, nor had your Excellency's letters been seen by me when a communication was received to the address of my servant, Mirza Habibulla Khan, from the Commissioner of Peshawar, and was read. I am astonished and dismayed by the 14th August was received at Simla on the 19th October. Its tone was considered extremely discourteous; it contained no apology for the public affront offered to the British Government, and indicated no desire for improved relations.

The reply was at once communicated to the Secretary of State, who was further informed that the Government of India proposed the following measures:—

The immediate issue of a manifesto which should define the cause of offence, declare a friendly disposition towards the Afghan people and reluctance to interfere in their internal affairs, and should fix the whole responsibility of what might happen upon the Amir.

An advance into the Kuram valley as soon as the force at Kohat was ready to move.

The expulsion of the Afghan troops holding the Khyber Pass.

An advance from Quetta into Pishin, or, if necessary, to Kandahar.

Lord Cranbrook (who had succeeded the Marquis of Salisbury as Secretary of State for India) replied* that he did not consider matters to be at present ripe for taking the extreme measures recommended by the Government of India, and that, before crossing the frontiers of Afghanistan, a letter should be addressed to the Amir demanding, in temperate language, an apology, and the acceptance of a permanent Mission within Afghan limits; that sufficient time should be given for

---

this letter, written threateningly to a well-intentioned friend, replete with contentions, and yet nominally regarding a friendly Mission. Coming thus by force, what result, or profit, or fruit, could come of it? Following this, three other letters from above-mentioned source, in the very same strain, addressed to my officials, have been perused by me. Thus, during a period of a few days several letters from that quarter have all been before me, and none of them have been free from harsh expressions and hard words, repugnant to courtesy and politeness, and in tone contrary to the ways of friendship and intercourse. Looking to the fact that I am at this time assaulted by affliction and grief at the hand of fate, and that great trouble has possessed my soul, in the officials of the British Government patience and silence would have been specially becoming. Let your Excellency take into consideration this harsh and breathless haste with which the desired object and place of conference have been seized upon, and how the officials of the Government have been led into discussion and subjection to reproach. There is some difference between this and the pure road of friendship and goodwill. In alluding to those writings of the officials of the opposite Government which have emanated from them, and are at this time in the possession of my own officials, the latter have in no respect desired to show enmity or opposition towards the British Government, nor, indeed, do they with any other Power desire enmity or strife; but when any other Power, without cause or reason, shows animosity towards this Government, the matter is left in the hands of God, and to His will. The esteemed Nawab Gholam Hussein Khan, the bearer of this despatch, has, in accordance with written instructions received from the British Government, asked for permission to retire, and it has been granted.'

* 25th October.

the receipt of a reply to this letter (the text of which was to be telegraphed to Lord Cranbrook for approval before despatch), and that meanwhile the massing of troops should be continued, and adequate forces assembled at the various points where the frontier would be crossed if war were declared. The Secretary of State went on to say: 'There must be no mistake at to our show of power to enforce what we require; this *locus penitentiæ* should be allowed before hostile acts are committed against the Amir.'

These instructions were carried out, and on the 30th October the ultimatum was despatched to Sher Ali, informing him that, unless his acceptance of the conditions were received by the Viceroy not later than the 20th November, he would be treated by the British Government as a declared enemy.

CHAPTER XLV.

It was a proud, albeit a most anxious, moment for me when I assumed command of the Kuram Field Force; though a local Major-General, I was only a Major in my regiment, and save for a short experience on one occasion in Lushai, I had never had an opportunity of commanding troops in the field. Earnestly longing for success, I was intensely interested in ascertaining the qualities of those who were to aid me in achieving it. To this end I lost no time in taking stock of the several officers and corps who were to be associated with me, some of whom were personally known to me, while others I had never met before; and in endeavouring to satisfy myself as to their qualifications and fitness for their several posts, I could not help feeling that they must be equally anxious as to my capability for command, and that the inspection must be of nearly as great moment to them as to me.

The results of a very close investigation were tolerably satisfactory, but there were weak points in my armour which gave me grave cause for anxiety.

I came to the conclusion that the force was not numerically strong enough for the very difficult task before it—in the first instance, the occupation of the Kuram valley and the expulsion of all Afghan garrisons south of the Shutargardan Pass, and in the second, as opportunity might offer, the pushing my reconnaissances into the Khost valley, and, if military considerations would admit, the dislodging the Amir's administration from that tract of country, so as to prevent the Kabul Government drawing supplies from it. Finally, I was directed to explore the roads leading to the unknown region beyond Khost.

The Shutargardan was not less than 180 miles from Kohat, the garrison of which station would, on my departure, be reduced to a minimum, and Rawal Pindi, the nearest place from which aid could be procured, was 130 miles still further off, separated from Kohat by an execrable road and the swiftly-flowing river Indus, crossed by a precarious bridge of boats. It had to be taken into account also that the various Afridi tribes were watching their opportunity, and at the first favourable moment, in common with the tribesmen nearer Kuram, they might be expected to take advantage of our weakness and attack our convoys and the small posts which had necessarily to be established along our line of communication.

The attitude of the Mahomedan sepoys, of whom there were large numbers in four out of my six Native Infantry regiments, was also a cause of considerable anxiety; for I was aware that they were not altogether happy at the prospect of taking part in a war against their co-religionist, the Ruler of Afghanistan, and that the mullas were already urging them to desert our cause.

Furthermore, I discovered that my only British Infantry Regiment, the 2nd Battalion of the 8th Foot, was sickly to a degree, and therefore in an unserviceable condition. It was largely composed of quite young, unacclimatized soldiers, peculiarly susceptible to fever—that terrible scourge which fills the hospitals of our Punjab stations in the autumn of each year. I rode out to meet the battalion on its way into Kohat, and was horrified to see the long line of doolies and ambulance-carts by which it was accompanied.

The inefficient state of the transport added to my anxieties. Notwithstanding the difficulties experienced in former campaigns from the same cause, the Government had neglected to take any steps for the organization of a proper transport service while we were at peace; consequently, when everything should have been ready for a start, confusion reigned supreme in this all-important department. Large numbers of camels, mules, and bullocks arrived daily, picked up at exorbitant prices from anyone who would supply them; but most of these animals were quite unfit to enter upon the hard work of a campaign, and with a totally inexperienced and quite insufficient staff of officers to supervise them, it was evident that the majority must succumb at an early date.

Hardly had I realized these shortcomings in the constitution and equipment of my column than I received intelligence which led me to believe that the Afghans would hold the Peiwar Kotal (the pass leading into Afghanistan over the range of mountains bounding the Kuram valley) in great strength, and were determined to oppose our advance at this point. Under these circumstances I felt myself justified in representing to the powers at Simla that I considered the number of troops at my disposal inadequate for the task they were expected to perform, which representation resulted in the 23rd Pioneers, whose transfer to the Khyber column had been under consideration, being left with me, and the 72nd Highlanders, a battery of Field Artillery, and the 28th Punjab Infantry, being sent to Kohat. Of these, however, I was allowed to take on with me only one wing of the 72nd, half the battery, and the 28th Punjab Infantry; and the last-named regiment I could hardly consider as part of my force, for when we should arrive at Thal, our furthest frontier post, it would have to be dropped, with a wing of the 5th Punjab Cavalry and No. 2 Mountain Battery, to garrison that place.

This small reinforcement was not given to me without considerable demur on the part of the military authorities, who had made up their minds that the Kuram column would meet with slight, if any, opposition, and that the chief stand would be made in the Khyber. Lord Lytton, however, supported my appeal, as did Sir Neville Chamberlain, who was then acting as Military Member of Council, and who had personal knowledge of the great natural strength of the Peiwar Kotal position.

I next turned my attention to the transport, and endeavoured by all the means I could think of to render it more efficient. A certain portion of it I placed in regimental charge; I had the men instructed in loading and unloading, and I took great care that the animals were not overladen.

Happily, I had a very able staff. Major Galbraith, the Assistant-Adjutant-General, though new to the work, proved exceptionally good, and Captain Badcock, the chief Commissariat officer, and Major Collett and Captain 'Dick' Kennedy, officers of the Quartermaster-General's department, whom I had myself selected, I could thoroughly depend upon.

As regards my own personal staff I was equally lucky, Captain Pretyman of the R.A. being my A.D.C., and Lieutenant Neville Chamberlain, of the Central India Horse, and Lieutenant-Colonel George Villiers, of the Grenadier Guards, my Orderly officers.

As political adviser I had with me an old friend and schoolfellow, Colonel Garrow Waterfield, Commissioner of Peshawar, who brought with him a large following of Native gentlemen connected with the frontier, by whom he thought our intercourse with the tribesmen would be assisted. With scarcely an exception they proved loyal, and throughout the campaign helped me materially.

Knowing how important it was to secure the interest of the Chiefs and Khans of the border on our side, especially those who had influence in the Kuram valley, we lost no opportunity of becoming acquainted with them while we were at Kohat. They were friendly and full of promises, but it was clear that the amount of assistance to be given by them depended on whether or not our occupation of Kuram was to be permanent, and on this important point I solicited definite instructions. I reported to the Commander-in-Chief that, from all I had learnt, the advent of a British force would be welcomed by the people, provided they understood that it was the forerunner of annexation; that in this case we should be regarded as deliverers, and all the resources of the country would be placed at our disposal; but if the people were led to believe that the force would be withdrawn when our work was finished, and that they would be again handed over to the tender mercies of the Kabul Government, we must expect no aid from them, as they would naturally dread the resentment of their Afghan rulers.

In reply, I was informed that I could assure the people of Kuram that our occupation would be permanent; and my being enabled to make this promise was undoubtedly the explanation of the friendly reception we met with on entering the valley, and the cause of my receiving at the same time a letter from the Chief of the Turis (the inhabitants of the Kuram valley), inquiring when we might be expected, as they were suffering greatly from the tyranny of the Afghan Government, and were anxiously waiting the arrival of the British.

CHAPTER XLVI.

By the 15th November my column* (consisting of 1,345 British and 3,990 Native soldiers, with 13 guns) was concentrated at Thal, and on the 20th—the limit of time given to the Amir—no reply having been vouchsafed to the Viceroy's ultimatum, orders were issued to the three columns to advance the next day.†

* The details of the column are given in the Appendix.

† On the 30th November a subordinate officer of the Kabul Government reached Sir Samuel Browne's camp at Daka, and delivered the following letter from the Amir to the address of the Viceroy:

'FROM HIS HIGHNESS THE AMIR OF KABUL TO THE VICEROY OF INDIA.

'KABUL, *19th November*, 1878.

'Be it known to your Excellency that I have received, and read from beginning to end, the friendly letter which your Excellency has sent, in reply to the letter I despatched by Nawab Ghulam Hussein Khan. With regard to the expressions used by your Excellency in the beginning of your letter, referring to the friendly character of the Mission and the goodwill of the British Government, I leave it to your Excellency, whose wisdom and justice are universally admitted, to decide whether any reliance can be placed upon goodwill, if it be evidenced by words only. But if, on the other hand, goodwill really consists of deeds and actions, then it has not been manifested by the various wishes that have been expressed, and the proposals that have been made by British officials during the last few years to officials of this God-granted Government—proposals which, from their nature, it was impossible for them to comply with.

'One of these proposals referred to my dutiful son, the ill-starred wretch,

The Kuram valley, from which my force received its designation, is about 60 miles long, and from 3 to 10 miles wide. On every side rise high and magnificently-wooded mountains, those on the north and east being the most lofty and precipitous, while on the north-west projects the spur which runs down from Sika Ram, the highest peak of the

---

Mahomed Yakub Khan, and was contained in a letter addressed by the officials of the British Government to the British Agent then residing in Kabul. It was written in that letter that, "if the said Yakub Khan be released and set at liberty, our friendship with the Afghan Government will be firmly cemented, but that otherwise it will not."

'There are several other grounds of complaint of similar nature, which contain no evidence of goodwill, but which, on the contrary, were effective in increasing the aversion and apprehension already entertained by the subjects of this God-granted Government.

'With regard to my refusal to receive the British Mission, your Excellency has stated that it would appear from my conduct that I was actuated by feelings of direct hostility towards the British Government.

'I assure your Excellency that, on the contrary, the officials of this God-granted Government, in repulsing the Mission, were not influenced by any hostile or inimical feelings towards the British Government, nor did they intend that any insult or affront should be offered. But they were afraid that the independence of this Government might be affected by the arrival of the Mission, and that the friendship which has now existed between the two Governments for several years might be annihilated.

'A paragraph in your Excellency's letter corroborates the statement which they have made to this Government. The feelings of apprehension which were aroused in the minds of the people of Afghanistan by the mere announcement of the intention of the British Government to send a Mission to Kabul, before the Mission itself had actually started or arrived at Peshawar, have subsequently been fully justified by the statement in your Excellency's letter, that I should be held responsible for any injury that might befall the tribes who acted as guides to the Mission, and that I should be called upon to pay compensation to them for any loss they might have suffered; and that if, at any time, these tribes should meet with ill-treatment at my hands, the British Government would at once take steps to protect them.

'Had these apprehensions proved groundless, and had the object of the Mission been really friendly, and no force or threats of violence used, the Mission would, as a matter of course, have been allowed a free passage, as such Missions are customary and of frequent occurrence between allied States. I am now sincerely stating my own feelings when I say that this Government has maintained, and always will maintain, the former friendship which existed between the two Governments, and cherishes no feelings of hostility and opposition towards the British Government.

'It is also incumbent upon the officials of the British Government that, out of respect and consideration for the greatness and eminence of their own Government, they should not consent to inflict any injury upon their well-disposed neighbours, and to impose the burden of grievous troubles upon the shoulders of their sincere friends. But, on the contrary, they should exert themselves to maintain the friendly feelings which have hitherto existed towards this God-granted Government, in order that the relations between the two Governments may remain on the same footing as before; and if, in accordance with the custom of allied States, the British Government should

Sufed Koh range, upwards of 14,000 feet high. This spur forms the boundary between Kuram and Afghanistan, and is crossed by the Peiwar Kotal. A river, which varies from 100 to 500 yards in width, flows through the valley, and the road, or, rather, track, which existed in 1878, ran for the most part along its rocky bed. In the winter months the depth of the water nowhere exceeded three feet, except after heavy rain, and although the stream was rather swift, it could usually be forded with very little risk. The valley itself had a bleak and deserted appearance, save in the immediate vicinity of the few and widely-scattered villages, around which were clustered fruit trees and patches of cultivation.

For six weeks the thoughts of every one in the force had been turned towards Kuram, consequently there was considerable excitement when at 3 a.m. on the 21st November the leading troops crossed the river into Afghan territory and encamped eight miles from Thal. The next morning we marched fifteen miles farther up the valley to Hazir Pir, where we halted for one day to improve the road (in some places impracticable for guns and transport) and to allow of the rear part of the column closing up. As we proceeded on our way, the headmen from the different villages came out to welcome us, and on arriving at Hazir Pir we found a plentiful repast awaiting us spread under the shade of some trees. Knives and forks were evidently considered unnecessary adjuncts by our entertainers, so I unhesitatingly took my first lesson in eating roast kid and pillaued chicken without their aid.

On the 24th we marched to the Darwazai defile, and the next day proceeded through it to Kuram, forty-eight miles from Thal. We found the fort evacuated by the Afghans, who had left behind one 6-pounder gun.

Notwithstanding the proffers of assistance I had received, I could get no reliable information as to the whereabouts of the enemy; from one account I was led to believe that they were in full retreat, from another that they were being strongly reinforced. So, to find out the truth, I reconnoitred as far as the cantonment of Habib Kila, fifteen miles

---

desire to send a purely friendly and temporary Mission to this country, with a small escort, not exceeding twenty or thirty men, similar to that which attended the Russian Mission, this servant of God will not oppose its progress.'

It was ascertained that this messenger had come to Basawal on the 22nd November, when, hearing of the capture of Ali Masjid by British troops, he immediately returned to Kabul. The Amir's letter, though dated the 19th November, was believed to have been re-written at Kabul after the news of the fall of Ali Masjid. The text of this letter was telegraphed to the Secretary of State on the 7th December; in reply Lord Cranbrook pointed out that the letter evaded all the requirements specified in the Viceroy's ultimatum, and could not have been accepted even if it had reached him before the 20th November.

ahead, and there ascertained that the Afghan army, consisting (it was said) of 18,000 men and eleven guns, had left the place only a short time before, and was then moving into position on the Peiwar Kotal.

Depot hospitals were formed at Kuram, and all our surplus stores and baggage were left there with the following garrison: Two guns of F/A, Royal Horse Artillery, half of G/3, R.A., the squadron 10th Hussars, one squadron 12th Bengal Cavalry, and the company of Bengal Sappers and Miners, besides all the sick and weakly men of the column.

At 5 a.m. on the 28th the remainder of the force, with the exception of the troops who had been dropped at the several halting-places to keep open our line of communication, marched towards the Peiwar.

The stars were still shining when we started, but it was very dark, and we were chilled to the bone by a breeze blowing straight off the snows of the Sufed Koh; towards sunrise it died away, and was followed by oppressive heat and clouds of dust. Our progress was slow, for the banks of the numerous nullas which intersect the valleys had to be ramped before the guns and baggage could pass over them.

On reaching Habib Kila, intelligence was again brought that the Amir's troops were in disorderly retreat, and had abandoned their guns at the foot of the pass. I at once pushed a reconnaissance in force up the south-eastern slopes of the mountain under the command of Colonel Gordon,* of the 29th Punjab Infantry, who discovered that, so far from the enemy having abandoned their guns, they had taken up an extremely strong position on the pass, from which they fired on the reconnaissance party as it advanced, wounding one British, one Native officer† and nine men.

As the Afghans seemed inclined to press Gordon, two guns were brought into action, and, to cover his retirement, I sent out the 5th Gurkhas, under Lieutenant-Colonel Fitz-Hugh, who skilfully effected this object with the loss of only one Gurkha wounded.

Gordon brought me back the valuable piece of information that no further advance in that direction was possible, save in single file—valuable because, had I attempted a front attack, the sacrifice of life

* Now General J. Gordon, C.B., Assistant Military Secretary, Horse Guards.

† The Native officer was Subadar-Major Aziz Khan, a fine old soldier who had seen hard work with his regiment during the Mutiny, and in many a frontier expedition. He twice obtained the Order of Merit for bravery in the field, and for his marked gallantry on one occasion he had received a sword of honour and a *khilat* (a dress of honour or other present bestowed as a mark of distinction). Aziz Khan was shot through the knee, and after a few days the wound became so bad the Doctors told him that, unless he submitted to amputation, or consented to take some stimulants in the shape of wine, he would die of mortification. Aziz Khan, who was a strict and orthodox Mahomedan, replied that, as both remedies were contrary to the precepts of the religion by which he had guided his life, he would accept death rather than disobey them. He died accordingly.

must have been enormous, even if the attack had proved successful, the possibility of which I still greatly doubt.

Our tents not having arrived, the force prepared to bivouac; but our position proving untenable, from being within range of the Afghan shells, we moved a mile to the rear. Strong piquets were posted on the neighbouring heights, and the night passed without further interruption.

We halted the two following days. Men and cattle were exhausted from their fatiguing marches, and supplies had to be brought up before we could advance further; besides, I required time to look about me before making up my mind how the Peiwar Kotal could most advantageously be attacked.

It was, indeed, a formidable position—a great deal more formidable than I had expected—on the summit of a mountain rising abruptly 2,000 feet above us, and only approachable by a narrow, steep, and rugged path, flanked on either side by precipitous spurs jutting out like huge bastions, from which an overwhelming fire could be brought to bear on the assailants. The mountain on the enemy's right did not look much more promising for moving troops, and I could only hope that a way might be found on their left by which their flank could be turned. The country, however, in that direction was screened from view by spurs covered with dense forests of deodar.

I confess to a feeling very nearly akin to despair when I gazed at the apparently impregnable position towering above us, occupied, as I could discern through my telescope, by crowds of soldiers and a large number of guns.

My Chief Engineer, Colonel Perkins,* made a reconnaissance, which only too surely confirmed Gordon's opinion; and he further ascertained that a deep ravine lay between the ground occupied by our piquets on the north and the kotal, so that an attack on the enemy's immediate left seemed as hopeless as on his right, or to his front.

On the afternoon of the 29th I sent my Quartermaster-General, Major Collett, with his assistant, Captain Carr, and a small escort, to the top of a hill, which lay to the right rear of our camp, from which they were able to get a fairly good view of the surrounding country. Collett reported that, so far as he could judge, it seemed likely that, as I had hoped, the enemy's left might be turned by a route over what was known as the Spingawi Kotal, where it had been ascertained that some Afghan troops were posted. This was encouraging, but before I could finally decide on adopting this line of attack, it was expedient to find out whether it was practicable for troops, and whether the kotal itself was held in great strength. Accordingly, early next morning, Collett was again despatched to make a closer reconnaissance of the Spingawi approaches.

* Now General Sir Æneas Perkins, K.C.B.

While all this was going on, I did everything I could think of to prevent what was in my mind being suspected by the enemy or, indeed, by my own troops. Each day more than once, accompanied by an imposing number of officers and a considerable escort, I climbed the lofty spur by which a direct attack would have to be covered, and everyone in camp was made to believe that an attack in this direction was being prepared for. I was particularly careful to have this idea impressed on the Turis and the Afghan camel-drivers, by whom the enemy were pretty sure to be informed of what was going on; and also on the Mahomedan sepoys, whom I suspected of being half-hearted. I confided my real plan to only three people, my two senior staff-officers, Galbraith and Collett, and my A.D.C., Pretyman, for I knew, from the nature of the country, that, under the most favourable circumstances, the way must be difficult and circuitous, and its passage must occupy several hours; and that if the Afghans got wind of the contemplated movement, and should attack my small force while on the march and divided, defeat if not annihilation would be inevitable, for the surrounding tribes would be certain to join against us if once they believed us to be in difficulties.

I had heard that the smallness of the column was being freely commented on and discussed; indeed, people in Kuram did not care to disguise their belief that we were hastening to our destruction. Even the women taunted us. When they saw the little Gurkhas for the first time, they exclaimed: 'Is it possible that these beardless boys think they can fight Afghan warriors?' They little suspected that the brave spirits which animated those small forms made them more than a match for the most stalwart Afghan. There was no hiding from ourselves, however, that the force was terribly inadequate for the work to be done. But done it must be. A retirement was not to be thought of, and delay would only add to our difficulties, as the Afghans were daily being reinforced from Kabul, and we heard of still further additions of both Artillery and Infantry being on their way.

Collett returned soon after noon on the 30th; he had done admirably and brought me most useful information, the result of which was that I determined to adopt the Spingawi route. The nights were long, and I calculated that by starting at 10 p.m., and allowing for unforeseen delays, we should reach the foot of the pass while it was still dark.

Fresh efforts were now made to distract the enemy's attention from the real point of attack. In addition to the reconnoitring parties which were ostentatiously moved towards the Peiwar, batteries were marked out at points commanding the kotal, and a great display was made of the arrival of the two Horse and three Field Artillery guns, which I had left at Kuram till the last moment on account of scarcity of forage at the front, and of the two squadrons of Bengal Cavalry, which for the same reason I had sent back to Habib Killa. Even with these

THE ATTACK ON THE PEIWAR KOTAL.

From
a painting by Vercker Hamilton.

additions the total strength of the force in camp, including British officers, amounted to only 889 Europeans and 2,415 Natives, with 13 guns.

These attempts to mislead the enemy were entirely successful, for the Afghans shelled the working parties in the batteries, and placed additional guns in position on the south side of the pass, showing distinctly that they were preparing for a front attack, while in our camp also it was generally believed that this was the movement which would be carried out the next morning.

When it became sufficiently dark to conceal our proceedings, all the commanding and staff officers assembled in my tent, and I disclosed to them my scheme for the attack, impressing upon them that success depended upon our being able to surprise the enemy, and begging of them not even to whisper the word 'Spingawi' to each other.

I had had sufficient time since I took over the command to test the capabilities of the officers and regiments upon whom I had to depend, so that I had now no difficulty in disposing the troops in the manner most likely to ensure success.

For the turning movement I selected:

4 guns F/A, R.H.A.,
The wing 72nd Highlanders,
No 1 Mountain Battery (4 guns),
2nd and 29th Punjab Infantry,
5th Gurkhas,
23rd Pioneers—
Total strength 2,263 men with 8 guns;

and I determined to command the attack myself, with Brigadier-General Thelwall as second in command.

For the feint and for the defence of our camp I left under the command of Brigadier-General Cobbe:

2 guns F/A, R.H.A.,
3 guns G/3, R.A.,
2nd Battalion 8th Foot,*
12th Bengal Cavalry,
5th Punjab Infantry.

In all, a little more than 1,000 men with 5 guns.

At 10 p.m. on Sunday, the 1st December, the little column fell in, in absolute silence, and began its hazardous march. Tents were left standing and camp-fires burning; and so noiselessly were orders carried out that our departure remained unsuspected even by those of our own people who were left in camp.

The track (for there was no road) led for two miles due east, and then, turning sharp to the north, entered a wide gorge and ran along

* The strength of this battalion had now dwindled down to 348 men.

the bed of a mountain stream. The moonlight lit up the cliffs on the eastern side of the ravine, but made the darkness only the more dense in the shadow of the steep hills on the west, underneath which our path lay, over piles of stones and heaps of glacier débris. A bitterly cold wind rushed down the gorge, extremely trying to all, lightly clad as we were in anticipation of the climb before us. Onward and upwards we slowly toiled, stumbling over great boulders of rock, dropping into old water-channels, splashing through icy streams, and halting frequently to allow the troops in the rear to close up.

In spite of the danger incurred, I was obliged every now and then to strike a match and look at my watch to see how the time was going. I had calculated that, by starting as early as ten o'clock, there would be an hour or two to spare for rest. The distance, however, proved rather greater than was expected and the road much rougher, but these facts were, to my mind, not sufficient to account for the slowness of our progress, and I proceeded to the head of the column, anxious to discover the true cause of the delay.

I had chosen the 29th Punjab Infantry to lead the way, on account of the high reputation of Colonel John Gordon, who commanded it, and because of the excellent character the regiment had always borne; but on overtaking it my suspicions were excited by the unnecessarily straggling manner in which the men were marching, and to which I called Gordon's attention. No sooner had I done so than a shot was fired from one of the Pathan companies, followed in a few seconds by another. The Sikh companies of the regiment immediately closed up, and Gordon's Sikh orderly whispered in his ear that there was treachery amongst the Pathans.

It was a moment of intense anxiety, for it was impossible to tell how far we were from the Spingawi Kotal, or whether the shots could be heard by the enemy; it was equally impossible to discover by whom the shots had been fired without delaying the advance, and this I was loath to risk. So, grieved though I was to take any steps likely to discredit a regiment with such admirable traditions, I decided to change the order of the march by bringing one company of the 72nd Highlanders and the 5th Gurkhas to the front, and I warned Lieutenant-Colonel Brownlow, in command of the 72nd, to keep a watch over the Pathans with his three remaining companies, for I felt that our enterprise had already been sufficiently imperilled by the Pathans, and that hesitation would be culpable; for, unless we could reach the kotal while our approach was still concealed by the darkness, the turning movement would in all probability end in disaster.

On the Gurkhas coming up, I told Major Fitz-Hugh, who commanded them, that the moment he reached the foot of the kotal, he must front form company, fix bayonets, and charge up the slope without waiting for further orders.

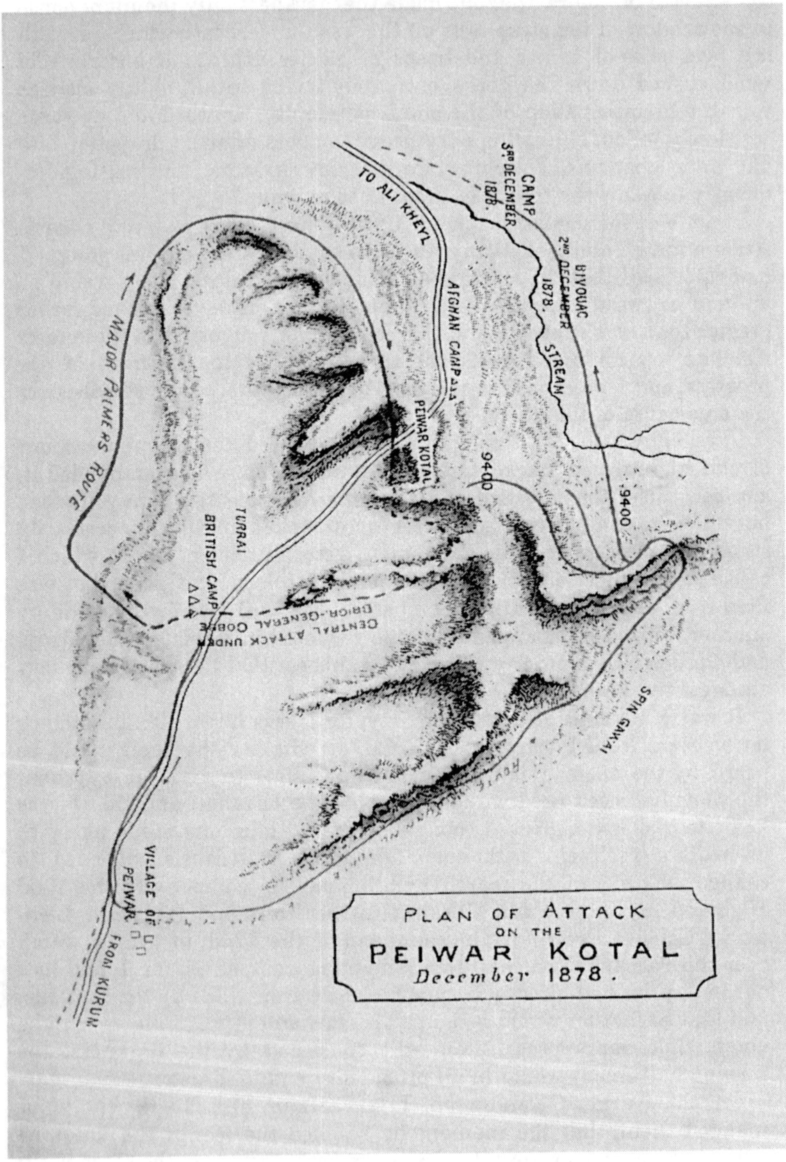

PLAN OF ATTACK ON THE PEIWAR KOTAL December 1878.

Soon afterwards, and just as the first streak of dawn proclaimed the approach of day, the enemy became aware of our presence, and fired into us, when instantly I heard Fitz-Hugh give the word to charge. Brownlow, at the head of his Highlanders, dashed forward in support, and two guns of the Mountain battery coming up at the moment, I ordered its Commandant, Captain Kelso, to come into action as soon as he could find a position.

I was struck by the smile of satisfied pride and pleasure with which he received the order. He was delighted, no doubt, that the opportunity had arrived to prove what the battery—to perfect which he had spared neither time nor labour—could do; but it was the last time that gallant soldier smiled, for a few seconds later he was shot dead.

The Gurkhas, forgetting their fatigue, rapidly climbed the steep side of the mountain, and, swarming into the first entrenchment, quickly cleared it of the enemy; then, guided by the flashes of the Afghan rifles, they pressed on, and, being joined by the leading company of the 72nd, took possession of a second and larger entrenchment 200 yards higher up. Without a perceptible pause, the Highlanders and Gurkhas together rushed a third position, the most important of all, as it commanded the head of the pass.

The Spingawi Kotal was won; but we were surrounded by woods, which were crowded with Afghans, some 400 of whom made a dashing but ineffectual attempt to carry off their guns, left behind in the first scare of our sudden attack. These men were dressed so exactly like some of our own Native soldiers that they were not recognized until they got within 100 yards of the entrenchment, and they would doubtless have succeeded in accomplishing their purpose—as the Highlanders and Gurkhas were busy pursuing the fugitives—had not Galbraith, whom I had sent with an order to the front, hurriedly collected a certain number of stragglers and met the Afghans with such a murderous fire that they broke and fled, leaving seventy dead in a space of about fifty yards square.

As the rising sun lighted up the scene of the conflict, the advantages of a night attack became more apparent. The pass lay across the shoulder of a mountain (9,400 feet above the sea), and through a magnificent pine forest. Its approaches were commanded by precipitous heights, defended by breastworks of felled trees, which completely screened the defenders, who were quite comfortably placed in wide ditches, from which they could fire deadly volleys without being in the least exposed themselves. Had we not been able to surprise the enemy before the day dawned, I doubt whether any of us could have reached the first entrenchment. As it was, the regiment holding it fled in such a hurry that a sheepskin coat and from sixty to a hundred rounds of ammunition were left behind on the spot where each man had lain.

We had gained our object so far, but we were still a considerable distance from the body of the Afghan army on the Peiwar Kotal.

Immediately in rear of the last of the three positions on the Spingawi Kotal was a *murg*, or open grassy plateau, upon which I re-formed the troops who had carried the assault. The 2nd Punjab Infantry, the 23rd Pioneers, and the battery of Royal Horse Artillery were still behind; but as the guns were being transported on elephants, I knew the progress of this part of the force must be slow, and thinking it unwise to allow the Afghans time to recover from their defeat, I determined to push on with the troops at hand.

A field hospital was formed on the *murg*, and placed under a guard, ammunition-pouches were re-filled, and off we started again, choosing as our route the left of two hog-backed, thickly-wooded heights running almost longitudinally in the direction of the Peiwar Kotal, in the hope that from this route communication might be established with our camp below. I was not disappointed, for very soon Captain Wynne, in charge of the signalling, was able to inform Brigadier-General Cobbe of our progress, and convey to him the order to co-operate with me so far as his very limited numbers would permit.

Our advance was at first unopposed, but very slow, owing to the density of the forest, which prevented our seeing any distance, and made it difficult to keep the troops together.

At the end of two hours we arrived at the edge of a deep hollow, on the further side of which, 150 yards off, the enemy were strongly posted, and they at once opened fire upon us.

Fancy my dismay at this critical moment on discovering that the Highlanders, Gurkhas, and the Mountain battery, had not come up! They had evidently taken a wrong turn in the almost impenetrable forest, and I found myself alone with the 29th Punjab Infantry. Knowing that the missing troops could not be far off, I hoped that they would hear the firing, which was each moment becoming heavier; but some time passed, and there were no signs of their approach. I sent staff officer after staff officer to search for them, until one only remained, the Rev. J. W. Adams, who had begged to be allowed to accompany me as Aide-de-camp for this occasion, and him I also despatched in quest of the missing troops. After some time, which seemed to me an age, he returned to report that no trace could he find of them; so again I started him off in another direction. Feeling the situation was becoming serious, and expecting that the Afghans, encouraged by our inaction, would certainly attack us, I thought it advisable to make a forward movement; but the attitude of the 29th was not encouraging. I addressed them, and expressed a hope that they would now by their behaviour wipe out the slur of disloyalty which the firing of the signal shots had cast upon the regiment, upon

MY GURKHA ORDERLIES.

From
a water-colour sketch by the late General Woodthorpe, C.B., R.E.

which Captain Channer,* who was just then in command, stepped forward, and said he would answer for the Sikhs; but amongst the Pathans there was an ominous silence, and Channer agreed with me that they did not intend to fight. I therefore ordered Channer and his subaltern, Picot, to advance cautiously down the slope with the Sikhs of the regiment, following myself near enough to keep the party in sight. I had not gone far, however, before I found that the enemy were much too strongly placed to be attacked successfully by so few men; accordingly I recalled Channer, and we returned to the position at the top of the hill.

My orderlies† during this little episode displayed such touching devotion that it is with feelings of the most profound admiration and gratitude I call to mind their self-sacrificing courage. On this (as on many other occasions) they kept close round me, determined that no shot should reach me if they could prevent it; and on my being hit in the hand by a spent bullet, and turning to look round in the direction it came from, I beheld one of the Sikhs standing with his arms stretched out trying to screen me from the enemy, which he could easily do, for he was a grand specimen of a man, a head and shoulders taller than myself.

To my great relief, on my return to the edge of the hollow, Adams met me with the good tidings that he had found not only the lost troops, but the Native Infantry of the rear portion of the column, and had ascertained that the elephants with the guns were close at hand.

Their arrival was most opportune, for the enemy had been reinforced, and, having discovered our numerical weakness, were becoming bolder; they charged down the hill, and were now trying to force their way up to our position, but our Mountain guns were quickly brought into action, and under their cover another attempt was made to drive the Afghans from their position. The 23rd Pioneers, under the command of Colonel Currie, the two front companies led by Captain Anderson, moved down the slope, and were soon lost to view in the thick wood at the bottom of the dell; when they reappeared it was, to my great disappointment, on the wrong side of the hollow: they had

* Now Major-General Channer, V.C., C.B.

† I had six orderlies attached to me—two Sikhs, two Gurkhas, and two Pathans. The Sikhs and Gurkhas never left me for a day during the two years I was in Afghanistan. The Pathans behaved equally well, but they fell sick, and had to be changed more than once. Whenever I emerged from my tent, two or more of the orderlies appeared and kept close by me. They had always good information as to what was going on, and I could generally tell whether there was likely to be trouble or not by the number in attendance; they put themselves on duty, and decided how many were required. One of the Gurkhas is since dead, but the other and the two Sikhs served with me afterwards in Burma, and all three now hold the high position of Subadar in their respective regiments.

failed in the attack, and Anderson and some men had been killed. The enemy's position, it was found, could only be reached by a narrow causeway, which was swept by direct and cross fires, and obstructed by trunks of trees and a series of barricades.

It was evident to me that under these circumstances the enemy could not be cleared out of their entrenchment by direct attack without entailing heavy loss, which I could ill afford and was most anxious to avoid. I therefore reconnoitred both flanks to find, if possible, a way round the hill. On our left front was a sheer precipice; on the right, however, I discovered, to my infinite satisfaction, that we could not only avoid the hill which had defeated us, but could get almost in rear of the Peiwar Kotal itself, and threaten the enemy's retreat from that position.

At this juncture I was further cheered by the arrival of Lieutenant-Colonel Perkins and Major McQueen, who, with the 5th Punjab Infantry, had worked their way up the steep mountain-side, in the hope of getting near to the Peiwar Kotal and co-operating with me. They were, however, checked by the deep ravine I have before described, and, guided by the sound of firing, pushed higher up the hill. They brought me word that the Artillery left in camp had opened fire on the kotal soon after daybreak, and had succeeded in silencing two of the enemy's guns; that our Infantry had crept up within 1,400 yards of the kotal, but were met by such a destructive fire that they could not advance further; that Brigadier-General Cobbe had been severely wounded, and that Colonel Barry Drew had assumed the command. Perkins also gave me the useful information that he had observed on his way up a spur from which the kotal position could be fired upon at a distance of 1,100 yards. To this spot I ordered Lieutenant Shirres, who had succeeded poor Kelso in command of the Mountain battery, to take his guns, and I asked Perkins to return and tell Drew to press on to the kotal, in the hope that Sherries's fire and the turning movement I was about to make would cause the enemy to retreat.

I sent the 29th Punjab Infantry back to the Spingawi to protect the wounded. I left the 2nd Punjab Infantry in the position we had up till now been occupying, and I took McQueen's regiment with me.

A few rounds from the Mountain battery, and the fact that their rear was threatened and their retreat about to be cut off, soon produced signs of wavering amongst the Afghans. Their Artillery fire slackened, their Infantry broke, and about 2 p.m. Drew and Hugh Gough found it possible to make a move towards the Peiwar Kotal. Gough was the first to reach the crest, closely followed by Lieutenant Brabazon, his orderly officer, and a fine plucky Dogra named Birbul. They were soon joined by some hundreds of Turi levies collected by Waterfield and by the 8th Foot. Another body of levies under Major Palmer,*

* Now Major-General Sir Arthur Palmer, K.C.B.

MY SIKH ORDERLIES.

From
a water-colour sketch by the late General Woodthorpe, C.B., R.E.

24

who had done good service by making a feint on the right of the Afghan position, arrived about the same time. Plunder was of course the sole object of the Turis, but their co-operation at the moment was useful, and helped to swell our small numbers. The enemy having evacuated their stronghold and retreated by the Alikhel road, abandoning in their headlong flight guns, waggons, and baggage, were pursued by Hugh Gough, whose Cavalry had by this time come up.

The Peiwar Kotal was not visible from the route we had taken, but just before daylight had quite gone I could make out with the aid of my telescope a large body of Afghans moving towards the Shutargardan, which made me feel quite satisfied that the enemy's position was in our possession.

Night overtook us before we could reach the kotal, and as everyone was thoroughly tired out, having been hard at work since 10 p.m. the night before, with but little food, I thought it better to bivouac where we were, on the southern slope of the Sika Ram mountain. It was hardly a pleasant experience lying on the ground without even cloaks at an elevation of 9,000 feet, and with the thermometer marking twenty degrees of frost; but spite of cold and hunger, thoroughly content with the day's work, and with my mind at rest, I slept as soundly as I had ever done in the most luxurious quarters, and I think others did the same. At any rate, no one that I could hear of suffered from that night's exposure.

We continued our march at daybreak, and reached the kotal in an hour.

The examination of the enemy's position was very interesting. It was of enormous natural strength, the dispositions made for its defence were most complete and judicious, and the impossibility of taking it by other than a turning movement was proved beyond a doubt; it extended from the Spingawi to some commanding heights nearly a mile south of the Peiwar Kotal; thus having a front of about four miles facing due east. From right to left the position ran along a lofty and rugged range of mountains, clothed with dense pine-forests. Towards the eastern side the range was precipitous, but descended on the west by a succession of upland meadows to the valley of the Hariab; it was crossed by only two roads, viz., the Peiwar and Spingawi Kotals; at a few other points there were paths, but too narrow and precipitous for the passage of troops.

The Peiwar Kotal is a narrow depression in the ridge, commanded on each side by high pine-clad mountains. The approach to it from the Kuram valley was up a steep, narrow, zigzag path, commanded throughout its entire length from the adjacent heights, and difficult to ascend on account of the extreme roughness of the road, which was covered with large fragments of rocks and boulders. Every point of the ascent was exposed to fire from both guns and rifles, securely placed behind breastworks constructed of pine-logs and stones. At the top of the path was a narrow plateau, which was again commanded from the thickly-wooded heights on each side, rising to an elevation of 500 feet.

The Afghan Commander had been quite confident of success, and was only waiting for reinforcements to attack our camp; but these reinforcements did not arrive until the afternoon of the 1st December, just too late for him to carry out his intention. He had under his command eight Regular regiments of the Afghan army, and eighteen guns; while these numbers were augmented by hordes of neighbouring tribesmen, who were only too glad to respond to the cry of a *jahad* against the infidel, firmly believing that as true believers their cause would be victorious.

Our loss at the Peiwar was not great—2 officers and 18 men killed, and 3 officers and 75 men wounded. The Afghans suffered much more severely, besides leaving in our possession all their guns, with quantities of ammunition and other warlike stores.

CHAPTER XLVII.

Perceiving that further pursuit of the enemy would be useless, I decided to halt a few days to admit of our overtaxed transport bringing up supplies and tents, and to arrange for the occupation of the Peiwar position during the winter months. But I considered that my work would be incomplete if we stopped short of the Shutargardan Pass. Moreover, it was very desirable that we should investigate this route, and, if possible, get into friendly communication with some of the sections of the Ghilzai tribe. The Jajis, through whose territory the first part of the road ran, now showed themselves to be as well disposed as the Turis; they readily brought in supplies, and volunteered to labour for us, and from the information obtained by the political officers, the inhabitants of the Hariab valley seemed equally anxious to be friendly. The dislodgment of the Afghan army by a much smaller force, from a position they had themselves chosen, had evidently had a salutary effect.

As soon as I had leisure, I inquired from Colonel Gordon whether he had been able to discover the men who had fired the signal shots on the night of the 2nd, and whether he did not think that the Pathan Native officers ought to be able to point out the offenders. Gordon replied that he suspected the Jemadar of the Pathan company knew who the culprits were, and that one soldier had confessed to firing the second shot; moreover, he told me that eighteen Pathans had left the regiment during the fight. On receiving this unpleasant information,

ONE OF MY PATHAN ORDERLIES.

From
a water-colour sketch by the late General Woodthorpe, C.B., R.E.

I assembled a Court of Inquiry, with orders to have the proceedings ready for my consideration by the time I returned from the Shutargardan.

Having despatched the sick and wounded to Kuram and made all necessary arrangements, I marched on the 6th December to Alikhel, twelve miles on the road to the Shutargardan. Before starting, I issued an order thanking the troops for the efforts they had made to ensure success, and I had the honour of communicating to them at the same time a congratulatory message from the Queen.*

We reached the foot of the Shutargardan on the 8th, and reconnoitred to the top of the pass the next morning. This point was 11,000 feet above the sea, commanded a fine view of the Logar valley, and I discovered from it that there was nothing between us and the immediate vicinity of Kabul to prevent a force moving rapidly on that place.

We returned to Alikhel on the 10th, and, as it was important to retain control of this advanced post, I decided to leave Captain Rennick in political charge, a duty for which his nerve and determination of character eminently fitted him. Colonel Waterfield, as a temporary arrangement, remained there also with a battery of Artillery and two regiments of Punjab Infantry, for the purpose of establishing friendly relations with the neighbouring tribesmen.

From Alikhel there were said to be two roads leading to Kuram, besides the difficult path over the Peiwar Kotal; and as it was of great importance to gain a knowledge of an alternative line of communication, in view of further trouble, I determined to explore one of them, choosing that which appeared to be the shortest, and which I heard had been used some time before by an Afghan Mountain battery. This route was described as practicable for camels, and ran through lands belonging to tribes whose headmen were with me, a fact which should, I thought, ensure our being free from attack.

I left Alikhel on the 12th December, taking with me No. 1 Mountain Battery, a wing 72nd Highlanders, the 5th Gurkhas, and the 23rd Pioneers. The route lay for four miles along the banks of the Hariab stream, a tribatary of the Kuram river, through a valley which gradually narrowed into a thickly-wooded ravine, three miles long:

* 'FROM THE VICEROY, LAHORE, TO GENERAL ROBERTS.

'*6th December*, 1878.

'I have much pleasure in communicating to you and the force under your command the following telegram just received from Her Majesty, and desire at the same time to add my warm congratulations on the success achieved. Message begins: "I have received the news of the decisive victory of General Roberts, and the splendid behaviour of my brave soldiers, with pride and satisfaction, though I must ever deplore the unavoidable loss of life. Pray inquire after the wounded in my name. May we continue to receive good news."

at the end of this ravine the road, turning sharply to the left, ascended till it reached an open grassy plateau, on which stood the hamlet of Sapari. The inhabitants turned out to welcome us, bringing supplies, and appearing so friendly that I settled to halt there for the night. I had been warned, however, by the *maliks* of some of the villages we had passed through in the morning, that we should probably be attacked on the march the next day, and that a defile which lay at the other side of a mountain over which we had to cross would be particularly dangerous to us. I determined, therefore, to send on troops that evening to occupy the pass over this mountain, and to start the baggage off long before daybreak, so that it should be out of the way of the main body, which would also have to march at an early hour in order to reach the kotal before the tribesmen had time to collect.

This could have been accomplished without difficulty, but for the machinations of our false friends in the village, who directed on to the precipitous path we had to ascend a stream of water which soon turned into a sheet of ice, and when I arrived on the spot I found the road blocked by fallen animals vainly struggling to regain their footing. This caused so much delay that it was nearly noon before the last camel had got over the pass.

The descent on the other side was scarcely less difficult, though free from ice. We dropped 3,000 feet in the first two miles, down a way which can only be described as a ruined staircase, with the steps missing at intervals, ending in the defile against the dangers of which we had been warned. This defile was certainly a nasty place to be caught in, being five miles long, and so narrow that the camels' loads struck against the rocks on either side; and it was impossible to move flanking parties along the cliffs above, as they were intersected by wide chasms running back for long distances.

It was important to secure the exit from this gorge without delay, and for this purpose I pushed on four companies of the 23rd Pioneers, and in support, when the ravine began to widen out a little, I hurried on the Highlanders and the Mountain battery, leaving the Gurkhas to protect the baggage and bring up the rear.

We only got possession of the exit just in time. The Pioneers, by occupying commanding positions on either side of the opening, effectually checkmated several large bodies of armed men who were approaching from different directions, and whose leaders now declared they had only come to help us! Later on we discovered still more formidable gatherings, which doubtless would have all combined to attack us, had they been in time to catch us in the ravine.

The tail of the column was followed and much harassed by the enemy; but they were kept at bay by the steadiness of the gallant Gurkhas, and so successful were they in safe-guarding the baggage, that, although many of the drivers ran away at the first shot, leaving

ONE OF MY PATHAN ORDERLIES.

From
a water-colour sketch by the late General Woodthorpe, C.B., R.E.

the soldiers to lead the animals as well as defend them, not a single article fell into the hands of the tribesmen. The regiment lost three men killed, and Captain Powell and eleven men wounded. Captain Goad, of the Transport Department, was also badly hurt.*

On Goad being knocked over, Sergeant Greer, of the 72nd Highlanders, assisted by three privates, picked him up, and having placed him under cover of a rock, they turned their attention to the enemy. They were only four against large numbers, but by their cool and steady use of the Martini-Henry rifle, which had shortly before been issued to the British soldiers in India, they were enabled to hold their ground until help arrived, when they succeeded in carrying the wounded officer away.

I had observed in the advance on the Peiwar Kotal the skill and gallantry displayed by Sergeant Greer, and noted him as a man fitted for promotion. His distinguished conduct in rescuing and defending Goad confirmed me in my opinion, and I accordingly recommended him for a commission, which, to my great gratification, Her Majesty was graciously pleased to bestow upon him.

That night we halted at the village of Keria; thence the route was easy enough, so, leaving the troops to rest and recover from the last hard march, I rode on to Kuram, where there was much to be done.

The ejectment of the Afghan ruler of Khost and the exploration of that valley formed, it will be remembered, part of the programme given to me to carry through, and it was very desirable that this service should be completed before the winter rains set in. Peace and order now reigned in Upper Kuram and in the neighbourhood of the Peiwar; but there was a good deal of excitement in the lower part of the valley and in Khost, our line of communication was constantly harassed by raiders, convoys were continually threatened, outposts fired into, and telegraph-wires cut. The smallness of my force made it difficult for me to deal with these troubles, so I applied to the Commander-in-Chief for the wing of the 72nd Highlanders left at Kohat, and the 5th Punjab Cavalry at Thal to be ordered to join me at Kuram. At the same time I moved up No. 2 Mountain Battery and the 28th Punjab Infantry, sending the 29th Punjab Infantry to take the place of the 28th at Thal.

I was greatly hampered by want of transport. Arrangements had to be made for sending the sick and wounded, as well as the captured guns, to Kohat (the sight of the latter, I fancied, would have a good effect on the tribes in our rear); but hard work, scarcity of forage, and absence of supervision, had told, as was to be expected, on animals in bad condition at the outset. Mules and camels died daily, reducing our all too small numbers to such an extent that it was with considerable difficulty the convoy was at last despatched.

* Both officers died of their wounds soon afterwards.

From the first I foresaw that want of transport would be our greatest difficulty, and so it proved; very few supplies could be obtained in the vicinity of Kuram; the troops at Kohat had been drawing on the adjacent districts ever since October, so that the purchasing agents had every day to go further away to procure necessaries, and consequently an increased number of animals were required for their conveyance. My Commissary-General reported to me that only a few days' provisions for the troops remained in hand, and that it was impossible to lay in any reserve unless more transport could be provided. About this reserve I was very anxious, for the roads might soon become temporarily impassable from the rising of the rivers after the heavy rain to be expected about Christmas. Contractors were despatched to all parts of the country to procure camels, and I suggested to Government that pack-bullocks should be bought at Mirzapur, and railed up country, which suggestion being acted upon, the danger of the troops having to go hungry was warded off.

The treacherous soldiers of the 29th Punjab Infantry had now to be dealt with—a necessary, but most unpleasant, duty. A perusal of the proceedings of the Court of Inquiry satisfied me that the two men who discharged their rifles during the night-march, the Jemadar of their company who failed to report their criminal action, and the eighteen who deserted their colours during the engagement, should all be tried by Court-Martial.

The prisoners were found guilty. The sepoy who fired the first shot was sentenced to death, and the one who discharged the second to two years' imprisonment with hard labour; the court, recognizing a possibility that the latter, being a young soldier, might have loaded and fired without intending treachery, gave him the benefit of the doubt. The Jemadar was awarded seven years' transportation, and the eighteen deserters terms varying from ten years to one year.

It was with deep regret that I confirmed these several sentences, but it was necessary that a deterrent example should be made. Treachery was altogether too grave a crime to be lightly dealt with, and desertions amongst the Pathans were becoming of much too frequent occurrence, particularly as the deserters invariably carried away with them their rifles and ammunition.

The effect of these sentences was most salutary; there was not a single desertion subsequent to the Court-Martial for more than a year, although during that time the Mahomedan portion of my force were severely tried by appeals from their co-religionists.

On Christmas Eve authentic intelligence was brought to me that, on hearing of the defeat of the Afghan army, Sher Ali, with the members of the Russian Mission then at Kabul, had fled to Turkestan, and that his son, Yakub Khan, had been released from prison, and had assumed the reins of Government.

About this time, also, Sir Samuel Browne, who was at Jalalabad, received a letter* from the Amir, in which he announced his intention of proceeding to St. Petersburg to lay his case before the Czar and obtain the aid of Russia.

Sher Ali's disappearance and Yakub Khan's assumption of authority suggested new possibilities to the Viceroy, who at once instructed Major Cavagnari, the political officer with the Khyber column, to communicate, if possible, with Yakub Khan, and explain to him that our quarrel was with Sher Ali alone, that he might rest assured of the friendly disposition of the British Government towards him personally, and that, unless he took the initiative, hostilities would not be resumed.

Before proceeding to Kuram, I invited all the Turis and Jajis who had afforded us assistance to meet me in durbar that they might be suitably rewarded. A goodly number responded to the invitation, and were told, in accordance with the instructions I had received from the Government of India, that they would henceforth be under British protection; that no Amir of Afghanistan should ever again be permitted to tyrannize over them; that while they would be expected to live peaceably, neither their religion nor their customs would be interfered with; that roads would be made and markets established, and that whatever supplies they could provide for the use of the troops would be liberally paid for.

* 'From Amir Sher Ali Khan to the Officers of the British Government.

'Be it known to the officers of the British Government that this suppliant before God never supposed, nor wished, that the matters [in dispute] between you and myself should come to this issue [literally, "should come out from the curtain"], or that the veil of friendship and amity, which has for many years been upheld between two neighbours and adjoining States, should, without any cause, be thus drawn aside.

'And since you have begun the quarrel and hostilities, and have advanced on Afghan territory, this suppliant before God, with the unanimous consent and advice of all the nobles, grandees, and of the army in Afghanistan, having abandoned his troops, his realm, and all the possessions of his crown, has departed with expedition, accompanied by a few attendants, to St. Petersburg, the capital of the Czar of Russia, where, before a congress, the whole history of the transactions between myself and yourselves will be submitted to all the Powers [of Europe]. If you have anything in dispute with me regarding State affairs in Afghanistan, you should institute and establish your case at St. Petersburg, and state and explain what you desire, so that the questions in dispute between us may be made known and clear to all the Powers. And surely the side of right will not be overlooked. If your intentions are otherwise, and you entertain hostile and vindictive feelings towards the people of Afghanistan, God alone is their Protector and real Preserver. Upon the course of action here above stated this suppliant before God has resolved and decided.'

After this I started for Khost, accompanied by Colonel Waterfield, the political officer.

The column I took with me consisted of the squadron of the 10th Hussars, 200 of the 72nd Highlanders, a wing of the 5th Punjab Cavalry, the 21st and 28th Punjab Infantry, and Nos. 1 and 2 Mountain Batteries. The corps were so weak that their total strength only amounted to 2,000 men.

We reached Matun, the name given to some three villages grouped round a small fort in the centre of the valley, on the 6th January, 1879. The Afghan Governor, with whom I had been in communication, met me and arranged to surrender the fort, on condition that his personal safety should be guaranteed, and that he should be allowed to go either to Kabul or India, as he might desire.

About half a mile from the fort I halted the column, and taking a small escort of the 10th Hussars, I rode on with the Governor, who invited me with my staff into his house. While tea was being handed round, the Governor (Akram Khan by name) warned me that we should be attacked, and that he could do nothing to prevent it, having only some 200 local militia and no regular troops. He further said that the inhabitants of the valley were not directly opposed to the British Government, and, if left to themselves, would give no trouble; but he doubted their being able to resist the pressure put upon them by a large number of tribesmen who had collected from the adjacent districts, attracted by the smallness of the force, which they believed 'had been delivered into their hands.'

This intelligence showed me I must be prepared for a scrimmage, so I ordered the camp to be pitched in the form of a square as compactly as possible, with the transport animals and impedimenta in the centre, and strong piquets at the four angles. Cavalry patrols were sent out as far as the broken and hilly nature of the ground would permit, and every endeavour was made to ascertain the strength and whereabouts of the enemy, but to no purpose: the enemy were invisible, and the patrols reported that they had come across numbers of peaceable-looking husbandmen, but no one else.

The night passed off quietly, but when advancing day made them visible, multitudes of tribesmen were descried collecting on the slopes of the neighbouring hills. Some friendly Natives were sent to ascertain their intentions, followed by a Cavalry reconnoitring party, when suddenly a number of camel-drivers and mule-men, who had gone to the nearest village to procure fodder for their animals, came rushing back to camp in the wildest terror and excitement, declaring that the enemy seemed to rise as if by magic out of the ground, and that several thousands were already in the village. No doubt some of these were 'the peaceable-looking husbandmen' the patrols had encountered the previous day. I now became somewhat anxious, not only for the safety of the reconnoitring party, which appeared to be in danger of being cut off, but for that of the whole force; such a mere handful as we were compared to the numbers arrayed against us.

Vigorous action was evidently necessary. Accordingly, I ordered all the available Cavalry (only 70 men of the 10th Hussars, and 155 of the 5th Punjab Cavalry), under Colonel Hugh Gough, to follow the reconnoitring party in case of their being so hard pressed as to have to retire, and Captain Swinley's Mountain battery, with six companies of the 28th Punjab Infantry, under Colonel Hudson,* to move out in support. Colonel Drew I left in charge of the camp, with 200 Highlanders, the 21st Punjab Infantry, and a Mountain battery. I myself joined Gough, who, by dismounted fire and several bold charges, notwithstanding the difficult nature of the ground, succeeded in driving the enemy to the highest ridges, over which Swinley's well-directed fire eventually forced them to retreat.

Heavy firing was now heard in the direction of our camp, and I hurried back, taking with me a troop of the 5th Punjab Cavalry. I found that during my absence Drew had been attacked on two sides; he had been able to prevent the enemy from coming to close quarters, but they were still hovering about at no great distance, and I thought it advisable to clear them away by moving out against them with all the troops at my disposal. As we approached, they disappeared with their usual rapidity; the 5th Punjab Cavalry, however, got in amongst some of them, and we returned to camp with 100 prisoners, 500 head of cattle, some sheep, and a large quantity of grain.

The tribesmen, however, had not been sufficiently punished to prevent a repetition of the attack, probably with largely increased numbers; so I ordered the destruction of the hamlets nearest us, in which they had been sheltered and some of our camp followers had been murdered.

The next night a most unfortunate occurrence took place, resulting in the death of six of our prisoners; but it was just one of those things which could hardly have been foreseen or guarded against, and for which, however lamentable, no one was to blame. The headmen of the particular Waziri tribe to which the captives belonged had been summoned during the day, and told that the men would be released on payment of a sum of fifty rupees each. The money was paid down at once for a certain number, who were immediately set free; but there was not quite enough for all, and the headmen went off to procure what was required for the ransom of the remainder. Soon after dark, however, some of the enemy† were discovered creeping up the banks of a nulla at the back of the camp, where the unransomed

* The late Lieutenant-General Sir John Hudson, K.C.B., who died as Commander-in-Chief of the Bombay Army.

† No doubt friends of the prisoners, who had come to help them to escape.

men were detained under a guard; the nearest sentry instantly fired, and the piquets all round took up the firing, thinking that another attack on the camp had commenced. At the sound of the first shot the prisoners all jumped to their feet, and calling to each other to escape, attempted to seize the rifles belonging to the guard, upon which the Native officer in command (a Pathan like themselves) told them that if they persisted in trying to escape, they would be shot. His words had no effect, and to prevent his men being overpowered, he gave the order to fire. Six of the prisoners were killed and thirteen wounded. It was a most regrettable affair, but a Court of Inquiry decided that the Native officer had no option, and completely exonerated the guard from acting with undue severity. The wounded were, of course, taken to our hospital, and well cared for by our Doctors.*

The remainder of our sojourn in Khost was not marked by any incident of particular interest. We marched to the end of the valley, and made a careful survey of it and of the surrounding hills.

The instructions I received with regard to Khost were, to occupy the valley and dislodge the Afghan administration therefrom. To my great chagrin, the smallness of my force made it impossible for me to give effect to these instructions as I could have wished. To have remained in Khost under the circumstances would have been to court disaster; the numbers of the enemy were daily increasing, and it would have been impossible to hold our own. It was, however, of great importance, if practicable, to retain some control over the valley, a peculiarly productive district, which, if left alone by us, I feared would become a centre of dangerous intrigue against any settled government in Kuram. Accordingly I determined to try how placing Khost in charge of one of our own Native officials would answer, and I selected for the position Shahzada Sultan Jan, a Saddozai gentleman of good birth, and a Sunni Mahomedan in religion, who, I thought, would be a *persona grata* to the Khostwals, and, if supported by some Native levies, and associated in his administrative duties with the chief *maliks* of Khost, would be more likely to hold his own than anyone else I could place there. This was, however, a mere experiment, and I did not disguise from myself that its success was very doubtful; but it was the only way in which I could attempt to carry out the orders of Government, my hands being so completely tied by

* This occurrence was made great capital of by the anti-war party at home. A member of the House of Commons, in commenting upon it, said that 'some ninety prisoners, who had been taken, had been tied together with ropes'; that 'on their making some attempt to escape they were set upon, and many of them slaughtered in their bonds'; and that 'the dead, the living, the dying, and the wounded were left tied together, and lying in one confused mass of bodies.'

paucity of troops. I had no fear for the Shahzada's personal safety, and I felt that, if in the end I should be obliged to abandon Khost altogether for the present, it could later, if necessary, be easily re-occupied with a somewhat larger force.

Having decided on the course to be adopted, I held a durbar, which was numerously attended, and addressed the people of Khost in much the same way I had spoken to the Turis in Kuram, expressing a hope that they would support the Shahzada's authority until a more permanent form of government could be established.

On the 27th January we left Khost and made one march; the next day I halted, so as to be near the Shahzada in case of need. The intelligence brought to me that evening satisfied me that my experiment would not answer, and that without troops (which I could not spare) to support the newly-established authority at first starting off, we could not hope to maintain any hold over the country; for though the Khostwals themselves were perfectly content with the arrangements I had made, they could not resist the tribesmen, who directly our backs were turned began to show their teeth. Accordingly, I decided to bring the Shahzada away while I could do so without trouble. I marched back to Matun the next morning with 1,000 men (Cavalry and Infantry) and four Mountain guns. We found Sultan Jan in anything but a happy frame of mind, and quite ready to come away. So having formally made the place over to the *maliks*, we started on our return journey. As we departed, a collection of our tribal enemies (about 3,000) who had been watching the proceedings took the opportunity to attack us; but two weak squadrons of Cavalry, skilfully handled by Hugh Gough, kept them in check, and we reached camp without further molestation.

The next day, the last of January, we returned to Hazir Pir in Kuram. There I received a visit from Sirdar Wali Mahomed Khan, brother of Sher Ali, who was accompanied by several leading men of the Logar valley, some of whom were of great assistance to me a few months later. Wali Mahomed was a man of about fifty years of age; he had a pleasing countenance, of the same Jewish type as the majority of the Afghan nation, but he had a weak face and was evidently wanting in character. He told me that he had fled from Kabul to escape the vengeance of his nephew, Yakub Khan, who attributed his long imprisonment by his father to the Sirdar's influence. Sir Samuel Browne and Major Cavagnari, on the Khyber line, were conducting all political negotiations with the Afghans, so I passed Wali Mahomed Khan on to them.

During the month of February my time was chiefly employed in inspecting the roads and the defensive posts which my talented and indefatigable Chief Engineer was constructing, examining the arrangements for housing the troops, and looking after the transport animals and Commissariat depots. No more military demonstrations were necessary, for the people were quietly settling down under British rule. Convoys were no longer molested nor telegraph wires cut; but I had one rather unpleasant incident with regard to a war Correspondent, which, until the true facts of the case were understood, brought me into disrepute with one of the leading London newspapers, the representative of which I felt myself compelled to dismiss from the Kuram Field Force.

Judging from his telegrams, which he brought to me to sign, the nerves of the Correspondent in question must have been somewhat shaken by the few and very distant shots fired at us on the 28th November. These telegrams being in many instances absolutely incorrect and of the most alarming nature, were of course not allowed to be despatched until they had been revised in accordance with truth; but one, evidently altered and added to after I had countersigned it, was brought to me by the telegraph master. I sent for the Correspondent, who confessed to having made the alterations, not apparently realizing that he had done anything at all reprehensible, but he promised that he would never do such a thing again. This promise was not kept; telegrams appeared in his paper which I had not seen before despatch, and which were most misleading to the British public. Moreover, his letters, over which I could have no control, and which I heard of for the first time when the copies of his paper arrived in Kuram, were most subversive of the truth. It was on the receipt of these letters that I felt it to be my duty to send the too imaginative author to the rear.

No one could be more anxious than I was to have all details of the campaign made public. I considered it due to the people of Great Britain that the press Correspondents should have every opportunity for giving the fullest and most faithful accounts of what might happen while the army was in the field, and I took special pains from the first to treat the Correspondents with confidence, and give them such information as it was in my power to afford. All I required from them in return was that the operations should be truthfully reported, and that any Correspondent who did not confine himself to the recording of facts, and felt himself competent to criticize the conduct of the campaign, should be careful to acquaint himself with the many and varied reasons which a Commander must always have to consider before deciding on any line of action.

What to my mind was so reprehensible in this Correspondent's conduct was the publication, in time of war, and consequent excitement and anxiety at home, of incorrect and sensational statements, founded on information derived from irresponsible and uninformed sources, and the alteration of telegrams after they had been countersigned by the recognized authority, the result of which could only be to keep the public in a state of apprehension regarding the force in the field, and, what is even more to be deprecated, to weaken the confidence of the troops in their Commander. It was satisfactory to me that my action in the matter met with the fullest approval of the Viceroy.

About this time my column was strengthened by the arrival of the Contingent provided by the Punjab Chiefs, under the command of Brigadier General John Watson, my comrade of the Mutiny days. The Contingent consisted of 868 Cavalry, and 2,685 Infantry with 13 guns, which were placed in position along the line of communication, and proved of great use in relieving the Regular army of escort duty. The senior Native officer with the Punjabis was Bakshi Ganda Sing, Commander-in-Chief of the Patiala army, a particularly handsome, gentlemanly Sikh, with whom I have ever since been on terms of friendly intercourse.

Towards the end of February I paid a visit to Kohat, where my wife met me; we spent a week together, and I had the pleasure of welcoming to the frontier that grand regiment, the 92nd Highlanders, which had been sent up to be in readiness to join my column in the event of an advance on Kabul becoming necessary.

CHAPTER XLVIII.

I was informed by the Viceroy's Private Secretary in the beginning of March that, unless satisfactory arrangements could soon be come to with Yakub Khan, an onward move would have to be made. Accordingly I now set about preparing for such a contingency.

Sher Ali had died in Afghan Turkestan on the 21st February, and, in communicating the event to the Viceroy, Yakub Khan wrote that he was anxious matters might be so arranged that 'the friendship of this God-granted State with the illustrious British Government may remain constant and firm.'

The new Amir was told in reply that Lord Lytton was prepared to enter into negotiations for the conclusion of peace, and for the restoration of a friendly alliance between the two Governments, provided that His Highness renounced all claim to authority over the Khyber and Michni Passes, and the independent tribes inhabiting the territory directly connected with the main routes leading to India; that the district of Kuram from Thal to the crest of the Shutargardan Pass, and the districts of Pishin and Sibi, should remain under the control of the British Government; that the foreign relations of Afghanistan should be conducted in accordance with the advice and wishes of the British Government; and that British officers should be accredited to the Kabul Government, and permitted to reside at such places as might hereafter be decided upon.

Yakub Khan's reply was not altogether satisfactory. He agreed to British officers being deputed to Afghanistan on the understanding that they should reside in Kabul, and abstain from interference in State affairs; but he declined to renounce his authority over the Khyber and Michni Passes and the tribes in their vicinity, and refused to consent to Kuram, Pishin, and Sibi being placed under British protection.

The Viceroy now determined to try what a personal conference between the Amir and Cavagnari could effect towards a settlement of these vexed questions, so in answering the Amir Cavagnari was directed to convey a hint that an invitation to him to visit Kabul might be productive of good results, and to point out that the places we desired to occupy were looked upon as essential to the permanent security of the Indian frontier. The Amir replied, expressing his readiness to receive Cavagnari in his capital, and laying stress on his determination to regulate his future conduct in strict conformity with his professions of loyalty, but begged that he might not be called upon to cede any portion of his territory.

Hardly had this letter, dated the 29th March, been received, than a proclamation addressed by Yakub to the Khagianis, a tribe which had been giving much trouble, was intercepted and brought to Cavagnari; in it the Amir praised and complimented the Khagianis for their religious zeal and fidelity to himself. He exhorted them to have no fear of the infidels, against whom he was about to launch an irresistible force of troops and *Ghazis*, and wound up as follows: 'By the favour of God, and in accordance with the verse "Verily God has destroyed the powerful ones," the whole of them will go to the fire of hell for evermore. Therefore kill them to the extent of your ability.' A curious commentary this on the Amir's protestation of loyalty.

Notwithstanding this piece of treachery, it was decided not to break off negotiations, and Yakub Khan was informed by Cavagnari that a Mission would proceed to Kabul so soon as the necessary arrangements could be made for its reception. At the same time Lord Lytton himself wrote to the Amir, telling him that, as he was willing to receive an Envoy, Cavagnari would be deputed to visit Kabul, and communicate unreservedly with him upon the questions at issue between the two States.

I, personally, was not at all satisfied that the time had come for negotiation, for I felt that the Afghans had not had the sense of defeat sufficiently driven into them to convince them of our strength and ability to punish breach of treaty, and, therefore, that a peace made now, before they had been thoroughly beaten, would not be a lasting one, and would only end in worse trouble in the near future. The Afghans are an essentially arrogant and conceited people; they had not forgotten our disastrous retreat from Kabul, nor the annihilation of our army in the Khurd Kabul and Jagdalak Passes in 1842, and believed themselves to be quite capable of resisting our advance on Kabul. No great battle had as yet been fought; though Ali Masjid and the Peiwar Kotal had been taken, a small force of the enemy had been beaten by Charles Gough's brigade, near Jalalabad, and a successful Cavalry skirmish had occurred near Kandahar, the Afghans had nowhere suffered serious loss, and it was not to be wondered at if the fighting men in distant villages, and in and around Kabul, Ghazni, Herat, Balkh, and other places, still considered themselves undefeated and capable of defying us. They and their leaders had to depend for information as to recent events upon the garbled accounts of those who had fought against us, and it was unlikely they would be shaken in their belief in their superiority by such one-sided versions of what had occurred. On many occasions I had been amused, in listening to Afghan conversation, to find that, while they appeared thoroughly conversant with and frequently alluded to their triumphs over us, they seemed to know nothing, or had no recollection, of Sale's successful defence of Jalalabad, or of Pollock's victorious march through the Khyber Pass and the destruction by him of the chief bazaar in Kabul.

My ideas about the negotiations being premature were freely expressed to Colonel Colley,* Lord Lytton's Private Secretary, who paid me a visit in Kuram at this time, and had been a constant correspondent of mine from the commencement of the war. Colley, however, explained to me that, right or wrong, the Viceroy had no option in the matter; that there was the strongest feeling in England against the continuance of the war; and that, unless the new Amir proved actively hostile, peace must be signed. He expressed himself sanguine that the terms of the treaty which Cavagnari hoped to conclude with Yakub Khan would give us an improved frontier, and a permanent paramount influence at Kabul, the two points about which he said the Viceroy was most anxious, and to which he assigned the first place in his political programme. Lord Lytton foresaw that, whatever might be the future policy of the two European Powers concerned, the contact of the frontiers of Great Britain and Russia in Asia was only a matter of time, and his aim was to make sure that the conterminous line, whenever it might be reached, should be of our choosing, and not one depending on the exigencies of the moment, or on the demands of Russia.

The Native agent (Bukhtiar Khan), who was the bearer of the Viceroy's and Cavagnari's letters to the Amir, reached Kabul at the moment when the Afghan officials who had accompanied Sher Ali in his flight returned to that place from Turkestan. Counsel was held with these men as to the manner of receiving the British Mission; but

* The late Major-General Sir George Colley, K.C.B.

there was an influential military party averse to peace, and the Amir was strongly advised to abandon the English alliance and trust to Russia. Upon hearing this, our agent became alarmed for the safety of the Mission, and being apprehensive that Yakub Khan would not have the power to protect its members from insult, he suggested to the Amir that he should visit our camp instead of the British Mission coming to Kabul, a suggestion which was ultimately adopted, the Viceroy considering that it was infinitely the best arrangement that could be made.

On the 8th May the Amir arrived in Sir Samuel Browne's camp at Gandamak, thirty miles on the Kabul side of Jalalabad, and on the 26th, owing to the tact and diplomatic skill of Louis Cavagnari, the Treaty of Gandamak was signed, and so ended the first phase of the second Afghan war.

Under the terms of the treaty, Yakub Khan agreed to the cession of territory considered necessary by us, and bound himself to conduct his foreign policy in accordance with the advice of the British Government; while, on our side, we promised to support him against external aggression. It was further arranged that a British representative, with a suitable escort, should reside at Kabul;* that the Amir should in like manner (if he desired it) depute an agent to the Viceregal Court; that British agents with sufficient escorts should be at liberty to visit the Afghan frontiers whenever, in the interests of both countries, it was considered necessary by the British Government; that there should be no hindrance to British subjects trading peaceably within the Amir's dominions; that traders should be protected, the transit of merchandise facilitated, and roads kept in good order; that a line of telegraph should be constructed from India to Kabul, at the expense of the British, but under the protection of the Afghan Government; and that an annual subsidy of six lakhs of rupees should be paid to the Amir and his successors.

The Khyber column was now withdrawn, with the exception of two brigades, and orders were sent to the Kandahar column to prepare to withdraw on the 1st September, the earliest date at which the troops could safely march through the Bolan Pass. I was told to stay where I was, as Kuram, by the treaty conditions, was to remain under our control and be administered by the British Government.

On the 24th May I held a parade in honour of the Queen's birthday, at which 6,450 officers and men were present.† They were thoroughly

* Kabul was expressly selected by Yakub Khan as the place where he wished the Embassy to reside.

† At this parade I had the great pleasure of decorating Captain Cook with the Victoria Cross, and Subadar Ragobir Nagarkoti, Jemadar Pursoo Khatri, Native Doctor Sankar Dass, and five riflemen of the 5th Gurkhas, with the Order of Merit, for their gallant conduct in the attack on the Spingawi Kotal,

fit and workmanlike, and being anxious that the tribesmen should see what grand soldiers I had at hand should an advance be necessary, I invited all the neighbouring clans to witness the display. The Afghans were seated in picturesque groups round the flag-staff, when suddenly, as the first round of the *feu-de-joie* was fired, they started to their feet, thinking that treachery was intended, and that they were caught in a trap: they took to their heels, and we had considerable difficulty in bringing them back, and in making them understand that the firing which had so upset their equanimity was only a sign of rejoicing on that auspicious anniversary. By degrees they became assured that there was no thought of taking an unfair advantage of them, and at the conclusion of the ceremony they were made happy by a present of sheep. In the afternoon an impromptu rifle meeting was got up. The matchlock men could not hold their own against our good shots armed with Martini-Henry rifles, a fact which evidently greatly impressed the tribesmen, some of whom then and there came forward and promised that if I should be required to advance on Kabul they would not oppose me.

I took advantage of our improved relations with the Afghans, consequent on the ratification of the treaty, to enlarge our geographical knowledge of the passes which lead from Kuram towards Kabul, and the independent territories in the neighbourhood. The presence of the troops, no doubt, had something to say to the cheerful acquiescence of the tribesmen in these explorations, which they appeared to look upon as the result of a wish to make ourselves acquainted with the country assigned to us by the treaty, and having, to use their own expression, lifted for us the *purdah* (curtain) of their country, they became most friendly, and took a curious pleasure in pointing out to us the points of defence at which they would have opposed us, had we been advancing as enemies.

Towards the end of June I heard from Lord Lytton that he wished me to be one of the military members of a Commission of Inquiry into army expenditure and organization which was about to be convened at Simla, if I thought I could be spared from my post at Kuram. The people of the valley had by this time settled down so contentedly, and the tribesmen showed themselves so peacefully disposed, that I thought I could safely leave my post for a time, before returning to take up my abode in the neighbourhood for some years, as I hoped to do, when my appointment as Frontier Commissioner should have received the sanction of the authorities in England.

---

and during the passage of the Mangior defile. It was a happy circumstance that Major Galbraith, who owed his life to Captain Cook's intrepidity, and Major Fitz-Hugh, whose life was saved by Jemadar (then Havildar) Pursoo Khatri, should both have been present on the parade.

Meanwhile, however, some temporary arrangement was necessary for the administration of Kuram, and I wrote to the Foreign Secretary (Alfred Lyall), pointing out my views upon the subject.

Seeing how much could be done with these wild people by personal influence, and how ready they were to submit to my decisions when disputes arose amongst them—decisions at times literally given from the saddle—I was very adverse to their being handed over to some official who, from his training, would not be able to understand dealing out the rough-and-ready justice which alone was suited to these lawless beings, and who could not imagine any question being properly settled without its having undergone the tedious process of passing through the law courts. Such a rule would, I knew, disgust a people accustomed to decide their quarrels at the point of the sword—a people to whom law and order had been hitherto unknown, and must be distasteful, until they had had time to realize their beneficial effects. Profitable employment and judicious management would in time, no doubt, turn them into peaceful subjects. Friendly intercourse had already done much towards this end, and tribes who for generations had been at feud with each other now met, when visiting our camp, on common ground, without (much I think to their own astonishment) wanting to cut each other's throats. What was further required, I conceived, was the opening up of the country by means of roads, which would facilitate intercommunication and give remunerative employment to thousands who had hitherto lived by plunder and bloodshed.

In answering my letter, the Foreign Secretary informed me that the future of Kuram would be settled when I reached Simla, whither I was to proceed so soon as I had seen the British Mission across the frontier.

On the 15th July Major Cavagnari, who had been selected as 'the Envoy and Plenipotentiary to His Highness the Amir of Kabul,' arrived in Kuram, accompanied by Mr. William Jenkins, C.I.E., of the Civil Service, and Lieutenant Hamilton, V.C., Surgeon-Major Kelly, 25 Cavalry and 50 Infantry of the Guides Corps. I, with some fifty officers who were anxious to do honour to the Envoy and see the country beyond Kuram, marched with Cavagnari to within five miles of the crest of the Shutargardan Pass, where we encamped, and my staff and I dined that evening with the Mission. After dinner I was asked to propose the health of Cavagnari and those with him, but somehow I did not feel equal to the task; I was so thoroughly depressed, and my mind was filled with such gloomy forebodings as to the fate of these fine fellows, that I could not utter a word. Like many others, I thought that peace had been signed too quickly, before, in fact, we had instilled that awe of us into the Afghan nation which would have been the only reliable guarantee for the safety of the Mission. Had we shown our strength by marching to Kabul in the first instance, whether opposed or not, and there dictated the terms of the treaty, there would have been some assurance for its being adhered to; as it was, I could not help feeling there was none, and that the chances were against the Mission ever coming back.

Cavagnari, however, showed no sign of sharing my forebodings; he and his companions were in the best of spirits; he spoke most hopefully of the future, and talked of a tour he hoped to make with me in the cold weather along the northern and western frontiers of Afghanistan. Other matters of intense interest to us both were discussed, and before separating for the night it was arranged that Mrs. Cavagnari should either join him in Kabul the following spring, or come and stay with my wife and me in Kuram, where I had already laid the foundations of a house near the beautifully situated village of Shalufzan.

Early next morning the Sirdar, who had been deputed by the Amir to receive the Mission, came into camp, and soon we all started for the top of the pass. We had gone about a mile, when we were joined by an escort of Afghan Cavalry, dressed something like British Dragoons, with the exception of their head-gear, which consisted of the discarded helmets of the old Bengal Horse Artillery. They were mounted on small, useful-looking horses, and were armed with smooth-bore carbines and *tulwars* (Native swords).

As we ascended, curiously enough, we came across a solitary magpie, which I should not have noticed had not Cavagnari pointed it out and begged me not to mention the fact of his having seen it to his wife, as she would be sure to consider it an unlucky omen.

On reaching the Afghan camp, we were received in a large, tastefully decorated tent, where tea was served, and we were afterwards conducted to the top of the mountain, where carpets were spread and more tea passed round, while we gazed on the fine view of the Logar valley which stretched out beneath us.

On descending to the camp, we were invited to partake of dinner, served in Oriental fashion on a carpet spread on the ground. Everything was done most lavishly and gracefully, and nothing was omitted that was calculated to do us honour. Nevertheless, I could not feel happy as to the prospects of the Mission, and my heart sank as I wished Cavagnari good-bye. When we had proceeded a few yards in our different directions, we both turned round, retraced our steps, shook hands once more, and parted for ever.

I did not delay at Kuram; there was nothing to keep me there, and the prospect of getting back to my belongings and to civilization, now that all active work was at an end, was too alluring to be withstood. My wife met me at the foot of the Hills, and we drove up to Simla together. I was greeted by Lord Lytton and many kind friends most warmly, and had the gratification of hearing that I had been made a K.C.B., and that I had been accorded the thanks of both Houses of Parliament.

I was soon deep in the work of the Army Commission, which met for the first time under the presidency of the Hon. Sir Ashley Eden,* K.C.S.I., on the 1st August. The heavy loss to the revenues of India, consequent on the unfavourable rate of exchange, rendered extensive reductions in public expenditure imperative, and the object of this Commission was to find out how the cost of the army could be reduced without impairing its efficiency.

Very little was done at the first meeting, and at its close Eden confessed to me that he did not at all see his way, and that he was somewhat aghast at the difficulties of the task before the Commission. To me it seemed clear that the maintenance of a separate army for each presidency, Bengal, Bombay, and Madras, was at the root of the evils it was our duty to consider and try to reform; and I promised the President that, before the Commission again assembled, I would prepare a scheme which might form a basis for them to work upon.

I considered it an anachronism, since railways and telegraphs had annihilated distance, to keep up three Commanders-in-Chief, and separate departments, each having an independent head, in the three different presidencies. I put my ideas on paper, and Eden announced himself in favour of my scheme, which substituted for the three presidential armies four army corps, all subordinate to the Commander-in-Chief in India. Portions of my recommendation began to be carried into effect directly they had received the sanction of the authorities in England—such as the amalgamation of the Commissariat, Pay, Ordnance, and Stud departments—but it was not until April, 1895, sixteen years after the proposal had been recommended by the Government of India, and although, during that period, four successive Viceroys, each backed up by a unanimous Council, had declared themselves strongly in favour of the change, that the finishing touch was given to the new organization, by the abolition of the offices of Commanders-in-Chief of Madras and Bombay, and the creation of four Army Corps, namely, the Punjab, the Bengal, the Madras, and the Bombay, each commanded by a Lieutenant-General.

CHAPTER XLIX.

My wife and I thought and talked much over our new life on the frontier, to which we both looked forward with great interest and pleasure, but, before entering upon it, we settled to go home for a time to place our boy at school and see our friends, and we were arranging our plans accordingly, when suddenly our 'castles in the air' were

* Lieutenant-Governor of Bengal.

dashed to the ground by a ruthless blow from the hand of Fate, and the whole of India, the whole of the civilized world, was struck with grief, horror, and indignation at the awful news of the massacre at Kabul of Cavagnari and his gallant companions.

Throughout the month of August telegrams and letters constantly came from Cavagnari (now a Lieutenant-Colonel and a K.C.B.) to the Viceroy, the Foreign Secretary, and myself, in which he always expressed himself in such a manner as to lead to the belief that he was perfectly content with his position, and felt himself quite secure; and in his very last letter, dated the 30th August, received after his death, he wrote: 'I personally believe that Yakub Khan will turn out to be a very good ally, and that we shall be able to keep him to his engagements.' His last telegram to the Viceroy, dated the 2nd September, concluded with the words, 'All well.' Cavagnari mentioned in one of his letters that the Afghan soldiers were inclined to be mutinous, and in another that a dispute had arisen in the bazaar between them and the men of the British escort, but at the same time he expressed his confidence in the Amir's ability and determination to maintain order; I could not, however, help being anxious about Cavagnari, or divest myself of the feeling that he might be over-estimating Yakub Khan's power, even if His Highness had the will, to protect the Mission.

Between one and two o'clock on the morning of the 5th September, I was awakened by my wife telling me that a telegraph man had been wandering round the house and calling for some time, but that no one had answered him.* I got up, went downstairs, and, taking the telegram from the man, brought it up to my dressing-room, and opened it; it proved to be from Captain Conolly, Political Officer at Alikhel, dated the 4th September. The contents told me that my worst fears—fears I had hardly acknowledged to myself—had been only too fully realized. The telegram ran:

> 'One Jelaladin Ghilzai, who says he is in Sir Louis Cavagnari's secret service, has arrived in hot haste from Kabul, and solemnly states that yesterday morning the Residency was attacked by three regiments who had mutinied for their pay, they having guns, and being joined by a portion of six other regiments. The Embassy and escort were defending themselves when he left about noon yesterday. I hope to receive further news.'

I was paralyzed for the moment, but was roused by my wife calling out, 'What is it? Is it bad news from Kabul?' She had divined my fears about Cavagnari, and had been as anxious about him as I had been myself. I replied, 'Yes, very bad, if true. I hope it is not.' But I felt it was. I woke my A.D.C., and sent him off at once to the Viceroy with the telegram. The evil tidings spread rapidly. I was

* There are no such things as bells or knockers in India.

no sooner dressed than Mr. Alfred Lyall arrived. We talked matters over, I despatched a telegram* to Captain Conolly, and we then went off to Lord Lytton.

Early as it was, I found the Council assembled. The gravity of the situation was thoroughly appreciated, and it was unanimously decided that, should the disastrous report prove to be true, troops must proceed to Kabul with the least possible delay to avenge or, if happily incorrect or exaggerated, to support the Mission.

Sir Samuel Browne's force had been broken up, Sir Donald Stewart was in far-off Kandahar, and his troops had, all but a small number, left on their return march to India; the Kuram force was, therefore, the only one in a position to reach Kabul quickly, and I was ordered to proceed at once to Kuram and resume my command.

As a preliminary measure, Brigadier-General Massy, who had been placed in temporary command during my absence, was directed to move troops to the Shutargardan, where they were to entrench themselves and await orders, while Stewart was directed to stop all regiments on their way back to India, and himself hold fast at Kandahar.

During the day further telegrams were received confirming the truth of the first report, and telling of the Mission having been overwhelmed and every member of it cruelly massacred; and later Captain Conolly telegraphed that messengers had arrived from the Amir bringing two letters addressed to me giving his version of what had occurred.

During the few hours I remained at Simla I was busily engaged in discussing with Sir Frederick Haines the formation of the Kabul Field Force,† as my new command was designated, and the many

* 'Lose no time and spare no money to obtain reliable information of what is going on in Kabul, and keep me constantly informed by urgent telegrams. I am in hopes that Jelaladin's report will turn out to be greatly exaggerated, if not untrue. As, however, his intelligence is sure to spread and cause a certain amount of excitement, warn General Massy and Mr. Christie (the Political Officer in Kuram) to be on the alert.'

† The Kabul Field Force was composed as follows:

ARTILLERY.

Lieutenant-Colonel B. L. Gordon, commanding.
Captain J. W. Inge, Adjutant.
F/A, Royal Horse Artillery, Major J. C. Smyth-Windham.
G/3, Royal Artillery, Major Sydney Parry.
No. 1 (Kohat) Mountain Battery (four guns), Captain Morgan.
No. 2 (Derajât) Mountain Battery (four guns), Captain Swinley.
Two Gatling guns, Captain Broadfoot.

ENGINEERS.

Lieutenant-Colonel Æ. Perkins, C.B., commanding.
Lieutenant F. Spratt, Adjutant.

important matters which had to be considered. More troops had to be hurried up, for it would be necessary to hold Kuram in strength while I moved on to Kabul, and, as communication by the Shutargardan could not be depended upon after December, on account of snow, the Khyber route would have to be opened out.

At the commencement of the last year's campaign my anxiety had been so largely increased by having been given officers totally inexperienced in war to fill the higher posts in the Kuram column, that I did not hesitate to press upon the Commander-in-Chief, now that I had a far more difficult operation to carry through, the importance of my senior officers being tried men on whom I could implicitly rely; and I succeeded in getting for the command of my two Infantry brigades Herbert Macpherson* and T. D. Baker,† the Viceroy's Military Secretary, both of whom had seen a good deal of service, while the former had already commanded a brigade in the field.

To the command of the Artillery and Cavalry, Lieutenant-Colonel B. Gordon and Brigadier-General Massy were appointed, neither of whom had much experience of war. Gordon had served in Central India during the Mutiny, and Massy by his pluck as a subaltern of Infantry

---

Captain Woodthorpe, R.E., in charge of surveying.
Captain Stratton, 22nd Regiment, in charge of signalling.
Lieutenant F. Burn-Murdoch, R.E., Royal Engineer Park.

CAVALRY.

Brigadier-General W. D. Massy, commanding.
Lieutenant J. P. Brabazon, 10th Hussars, Brigade-Major.
9th Lancers, Lieutenant-Colonel R. S. Cleland.
5th Punjab Cavalry, Major B. Williams.
12th Bengal Cavalry, Major Green.
14th Bengal Lancers, Lieutenant-Colonel Ross.

1ST INFANTRY BRIGADE.

Brigadier-General H. Macpherson, C.B., V.C., commanding.
Captain G. de C. Morton, 6th Foot, Brigade-Major.
67th Foot, Lieutenant-Colonel C. B. Knowles.
92nd Highlanders, Lieutenant-Colonel G. H. Parker.
28th Punjab Infantry, Lieutenant-Colonel J. Hudson.

2ND INFANTRY BRIGADE.

Brigadier-General T. D. Baker, C.B., 18th Foot, commanding.
Captain W. C. Farwell, 26th Punjab Infantry, Brigade-Major.
72nd Highlanders, Lieutenant-Colonel Brownlow.
5th Gurkhas, Lieutenant-Colonel Fitz-Hugh.
5th Punjab Infantry, Lieutenant-Colonel J. Macqueen.
3rd Sikhs, Lieutenant-Colonel G. N. Money.
23rd Pioneers, Lieutenant-Colonel Currie.

* The late Lieutenant-General Sir Herbert Macpherson, V.C., K.C.B., who died as Commander-in-Chief of Madras.

† The late Sir Thomas Baker, K.C.B., who died as Quartermaster-General at the Horse Guards.

in the Crimea had gained for himself the *sobriquet* of 'Redan' Massy. But he had not served with Cavalry in the field, and from my slight acquaintance with him I could not say whether he possessed the very exceptional qualities required in a Cavalry Commander.

My staff had proved themselves so capable and reliable that I had no wish to make any change; it was, however, materially strengthened by the addition of Colonel MacGregor,* as 'Chief of the Staff,' with Captain Combe,† 10th Hussars, and Lieutenant Manners Smith‡ as Deputy-Assistant Quartermaster-Generals.

Mr. H. M. Durand § was attached to me as Political Secretary, and Major Hastings as Political Officer, in place of Colonel Waterfield, who was *hors de combat* from a broken leg. Hugh Gough, with the rank of Brigadier-General, and Major Mark Heathcote as his assistant, were placed in charge of the lines of communication.

Before leaving Simla I paid a farewell visit to Lord Lytton. I found him in a state of deep distress and depression. To a man of his affectionate disposition, the fate of Cavagnari, for whom he had a great personal regard, was a real grief. But on public grounds he felt still more strongly the collapse of the Mission and the consequent heavy blow to the policy he had so much at heart, viz., the rectification of our defective frontier, and the rendering India secure against foreign aggression—a policy which, though scouted at the time by a party which later became all-powerful, has since been justified by the action of successive Governments, Liberal and Conservative alike, until at the present moment our frontier is gradually becoming what Lord Lytton, with his clear foresightedness and intelligent appreciation of our responsibilities and India's requirements, would then have made it.

In answer to my request for instructions as to the line I should take about our future relations with the Afghans, Lord Lytton said: 'You can tell them we shall never again altogether withdraw from Afghanistan, and that those who help you will be befriended and protected by the British Government.'

While I was with Lord Lytton, a telegram‖ was brought in from

* The late Sir Charles MacGregor, K.C.B.

† Now Major-General Combe, C.B.

‡ This promising young officer greatly distinguished himself at Kabul, and died a few years afterwards of cholera.

§ Now Sir Mortimer Durand, K.C.S.I., K.C.I.E., British Minister at Teheran.

‖ Telegram dated 6th September, 1879.

From	*To*
Captain Conolly, Alikhel.	Foreign Secretary, Simla.

'*Clear the Line.*—Sirkai Khan, bearer of the Amir's first letter, confirms previous reports of disaster, and describes how Badshah Khan visited the

Captain Conolly, reporting the details of the attack upon the Embassy, as given to him by the messenger who had been entrusted by the Amir to deliver the two letters addressed to me. In this telegram Conolly solicited instructions as to what he was to communicate to the Amir in reply to His Highness's request for aid, and inquired whether he was at liberty to make terms with one Badshah Khan, an influential Ghilzai Chief, who had come to Alikhel to offer his services.

The following telegram was sent in reply by the Foreign Secretary:

'Your telegram 6th. Reply to the Amir at once from the Viceroy that a strong British force under General Roberts will march speedily on Kabul to his relief, from the Shutargardan, and that he should use all his resources to co-operate with, and facilitate, the advance of the troops through his country. Your proposal to subsidize Badshah Khan and accept his services is approved. Roberts will send detailed instructions.'

Late in the afternoon of the same day (September 6th) I left Simla, accompanied by my wife as far as Umballa, where I found my staff waiting for me. She saw us off in the train, bidding us a cheery good-bye and good luck, but I am afraid the return journey must have been a sad one for her.

Thought for the immediate future filled my mind as we sped on our way to the front, and not a few difficulties connected with the proposed advance on Kabul presented themselves to me. My chief causes for anxiety were the insufficiency of transport, and the great extent of the lines of communication which would have to be guarded. It would be necessary to hold the country in strength from Thal to the Shutargardan, a distance of 115 miles, until such time as the Khyber route could be opened, and I felt that the force at my disposal (7,500 men and 22 guns) was none too large for the work before it, considering

---

spot, and saw the dead bodies of the Envoy, staff, and escort. Of the latter, some nine sowars are said to have been out getting grass that day, and were not killed with the rest; defence was very stubborn, and the loss of the Kabulis heavy, put down at one hundred, or more. Finding they could not storm the place, the mutineers set fire to the doorway below, and, when that gave way, swarmed in and up to the upper story, overwhelmed the defenders, and sacked the place.

'The second letter was brought by another messenger, servant of the Embassy *Mehmandar*, whose story in all but a few unimportant details is the same as that first received.

'If an advance on Kabul is decided on to revenge massacre of Embassy, and also to quiet surrounding tribes, whom any (?) action would tempt to break out, it appears to me all-important to secure safe passage of the Shutargardan, and with this object to subsidize Badshah Khan handsomely.

'I have detained the Kabul messengers pending receipt of instructions as to the line of policy to follow, and what to communicate to the Amir or Badshah Khan. The former invokes our aid; the latter expresses himself, through his messenger, anxious to serve us. Once in Logar valley, where they have had a bumper harvest, we could live on the country.'

that I should have to provide a garrison for the Shutargardan, if not for other posts between that place and Kabul.

My Commissariat arrangements, too, caused me many misgivings, increased by the fact that Major Badcock, my chief Commissariat Officer, and Major Collett, my Assistant Quartermaster-General, who had afforded such valuable aid in Kuram, thinking the war was at an end, had taken leave to England. My doubts vanished, however, and my spirits rose at the sight of my brave troops, and the enthusiastic welcome they gave me as I rode through Kuram on the 12th September on my way to Alikhel. A splendid spirit pervaded the whole force; the men's hearts were on fire with eager desire to press on to Kabul, and be led against the miscreants who had foully massacred our countrymen, and I felt assured that whatever it was possible for dauntless courage, unselfish devotion, and firm determination to achieve, would be achieved by my gallant soldiers.

On reaching Alikhel, Captain Conolly handed to me the Amir's letters,* to which I replied at once, and the next day, under instructions

* TRANSLATION OF A LETTER FROM THE AMIR OF KABUL TO GENERAL ROBERTS, DATED KABUL, 8 A.M., THE 3RD SEPTEMBER, 1879.

(After compliments.) The troops who had assembled for pay at the Bala Hissar suddenly broke out and stoned their officers, and then all rushed to the Residency and stoned it, receiving in return a hail of bullets. Confusion and disturbance reached such a height that it was impossible to quiet it. People from Sherpur and country around the Bala Hissar, and city people of all classes, poured into the Bala Hissar and began destroying workshops, Artillery park, and magazine; and all the troops and people attacked the Residency. Meanwhile, I sent Daud Shah[1] to help the Envoy. On reaching the Residency, he was unhorsed by stones and spears, and is now dying. I then sent Sirdar Yahia Khan and my own son, the heir-apparent, with the Koran to the troops; but no use. I then sent well-known Syads and Mullahs of each class, but of no avail; up till now, evening, the disturbance continues. It will be seen how it ends. I am grieved with this confusing state of things. It is almost beyond conception. (Here follow the date and the Amir's seal.)

SECOND LETTER FROM THE AMIR, DATED KABUL, THE 4TH SEPTEMBER, 1879.

Yesterday, from 8 a.m. till evening, thousands assembled to destroy the Embassy. There has been much loss of life on both sides. At evening they set fire to the Residency. All yesterday and up till now, I with five attendants have been besieged. I have no certain news of the Envoy, whether he and his people have been killed in their quarters, or been seized and brought out. Afghanistan is ruined; the troops, city, and surrounding country have thrown off their yoke of allegiance. Daud Shah is not expected to recover; all his attendants were killed. The workshops and magazine are totally gutted—in fact, my kingdom is ruined. After God, I look to the Government for aid and advice. My true friendship and honesty of purpose will be proved as clear as daylight. By this misfortune I have lost my friend,

[1] The Commander-in-Chief of the Afghan army.

from the Government of India, I wrote to His Highness that, in conformity with his own special request that an English officer should be deputed as Envoy to his Court, and on condition that he would himself be responsible for the protection and honourable treatment of such an Envoy, Major Cavagnari and three British officers had been allowed to go to Kabul, all of whom within six weeks had been ruthlessly murdered by his troops and subjects; that his inability to carry out the treaty engagements, and his powerlessness to establish his authority, even in his own capital, having thus become apparent, an English army would now advance on Kabul with the double object of consolidating his Government, should he himself loyally do his best to fulfil the terms of the treaty, and of exacting retribution from the murderers of the British Mission. But that, although His Highness laid great stress in his letter of the 4th September on the sincerity of his friendship, my Government had been informed that emissaries had been despatched from Kabul to rouse the country people and tribes against us, and as this action appeared inconsistent with friendly intentions, I considered it necessary for His Highness to send a confidential representative to confer with me and explain his object.

I had little doubt as to the truth of the report that the Amir was using every effort to incite the Ghilzais and other tribes to oppose us, and I was confirmed in my conviction by a Native gentleman, Nawab Ghulam Hussein Khan,* at one time our agent at Kabul, who told me that, although he did not believe that Yakub Khan had actually planned the massacre of the Embassy, he had certainly taken no steps to prevent it, and that he, Ghulam Hussein Khan, was convinced that the Amir was now playing us false. It was, therefore, a relief to find awaiting me at Alikhel several of the leading men from the neighbouring districts, to whom I had telegraphed, before leaving Simla, asking them to meet me.

These men were profuse in their proffers of assistance, and, although I did not place a great deal of faith in their promises, I came to the conclusion that, notwithstanding Yakub Khan's treacherous efforts to stir up the tribes, if I could only push on rapidly with a fairly strong force, I need not anticipate any opposition that I could not overcome. Everything depended on speed, but rapidity of movement depended on the condition of the transport service, and my inspection of the animals, as I passed through Kuram, was not calculated to raise hopes of being able to make a very quick advance; for, owing to continuous hard work and the want of a staff of trained transport attendants, the

the Envoy, and also my kingdom. I am terribly grieved and perplexed. (Here follow the date and the Amir's seal.)

* The Nawab was on his way from Kandahar to Kabul, but on hearing of the massacre he came to Alikhel.

numbers of animals had steadily diminished, and those that remained were for the most part sickly and out of condition.

On the 16th of September I issued a Proclamation,* copies of which I caused to be sent to the people of Kabul, Ghazni, and all the neighbouring tribes; this, I hoped, would facilitate our advance, and reassure those who had taken no part in the attack on the Residency. I also wrote a letter† to the *maliks* of the Logar valley, whose territory we

* TRANSLATION OF A PROCLAMATION ISSUED BY MAJOR-GENERAL SIR FREDERICK ROBERTS.

Alikhel, 16th September, 1879.

Be it known to all the Chiefs and the people of the country of Kabul and its dependencies that, in accordance with the Treaty concluded in May, 1879, corresponding to Jamdi-ul-Akhir 1296 Hijri, between the two great Governments, and to the terms of which His Highness the Amir expressed his assent, and agreed to the location of an Envoy of Her Imperial Majesty the Empress, a British Envoy was, at the special request of His Highness the Amir, located at the Kabul Court, and the Amir guaranteed that he should be treated honourably and protected.

Within six weeks after the said Envoy was received at and entered Kabul the whole Embassy was besieged and massacred in the very citadel of His Highness the Amir, who could not save or protect them from the hands of the soldiers and the people. From this, the lack of power of the Amir and the weakness of his authority in his capital itself are quite apparent and manifest. For this reason the British troops are advancing for the purpose of taking a public vengeance on behalf of the deceased as well as of obtaining satisfaction (*lit.*, consolidation) of the terms entered into in the Treaty concluded. The British troops are entering Afghanistan for the purpose of strengthening the royal authority of His Highness the Amir on condition that His Highness loyally uses those powers for the maintenance of friendship and of amicable relations with the British Government. This is the only course by which the Amir's kingdom can remain intact, and (by which) also the friendly sentiments and sincerity expressed in his letter of the 4th September, 1879, after the occurrence of the (said) event can be proved.

For the purpose of removing any doubt about the concord of the two Governments, the Amir has been addressed to depute a confidential agent to my camp. The British force will not punish or injure anyone except the persons who have taken part or joined in the massacre of the Embassy unless they offer opposition. All the rest, the small and great, who are unconcerned (therein) may rest assured of this. Carriage and supplies of every description should be brought into the British camp. Full price and hire shall be paid for everything that may be taken. Whereas mercy and humanity are the characteristics of this great Government, this proclamation is issued beforehand for the information of the people at large.

† TRANSLATION OF A LETTER FROM MAJOR-GENERAL SIR FREDERICK ROBERTS TO CERTAIN *maliks* OF THE LOGAR VALLEY.

From the Proclamation already issued by me, you will have learnt the reasons for the march of the British troops to Kabul. Her Majesty's Government, by the movement of troops, intends to exact retribution for the massacre of the Embassy and to aid His Highness the Amir in restoring order.

Let all those not concerned in the massacre rest assured, provided no opposition is shown.

must enter directly we had crossed the Shutargardan, and whose co-operation I was most anxious to obtain. On the 18th I again wrote* to the Amir, enclosing copies of these two documents, and informing him that I was still awaiting a reply to my first letter and the arrival of His Highness's confidential representative; that I hoped he would soon issue the necessary orders for the furtherance of our plans, and that he might rest assured of the support of the British Government.

On the 19th September matters had so far progressed that I was able to tell the Viceroy that Brigadier-General Baker was entrenched with his brigade on the Shutargardan, and engaged in improving the road to Kushi, the first halting-place in the Logar valley; that supplies were being collected by means of local transport; that I was bringing up reserve ammunition and treasure from the rear on Artillery waggons; and that every possible effort was being made to render the force mobile.

On the 20th I received the Amir's reply. He expressed regret that he was unable to come to Alikhel himself, but intimated that he was sending two confidential agents, his Mustaufi (Finance Minister), Habibulla Khan, and his Wazir (Prime Minister), Shah Mahomed Khan, who accordingly arrived the next day.

At each interview I had with these gentlemen during the three days they remained in my camp, they impressed upon me that the Amir was inclined to be most friendly, and that his only wish was to be guided by the advice of the British Government. But, notwithstanding these plausible assurances, I soon discovered that Yakub Khan's real object in sending these two high officials was to stop the advance of the force, and induce me to leave the punishment of the troops who had committed the massacre in the hands of the Afghan authorities, or else to delay us long enough to give time for the whole country to rise against us.

As the conversations which were carried on at the meetings with the Afghan agents are interesting, and have an important bearing on the subsequent proceedings, I give in the Appendix the notes taken at the time by my Political Secretary.

I was anxious to keep one of the Amir's representatives with me,

His Highness the Amir, in communications received by me, expresses his friendship, and wishes to continue amicable relations. As the British troops under my command will shortly enter the Logar valley, I write to reassure you, and expect that you will inform all the residents of the valley not concerned in the late hateful massacre the purport of the Proclamation, and give every assistance in providing carriage and supplies required for the troops, for which adequate hire and payment will be made. I hope that after the above assurance all the headmen will come to meet me in my camp, where I shall be glad to see them.

* This letter is given in full in the Appendix.

but neither of them was willing to remain, so I felt bound to let them both depart, taking with them the following letter to the Amir:

To His Highness the Amir of Kabul.

Camp, Alikhel, 25th September, 1879.

(After compliments.) I have received Your Highness's two letters of the 19th and 20th September (1st and 2nd Shawal), delivered to me by the hands of Your Highness's two confidential representatives, Mustaufi Habibulla Khan and Wazir Shah Mahomed.

I am much obliged to Your Highness for sending me two such well-known men, and of such character as the Mustaufi and the Wazir. They have informed me of Your Highness's wishes, and I quite understand all they have told me. It is unfortunate that the season is so late, and that winter will soon be here; but there is yet time for a British army to reach Kabul before the great cold sets in.

The Viceroy of India is much concerned that there should have been any delay in promptly acceding to Your Highness's request for advice and assistance, as conveyed in Your Highness's letters of the 3rd and 4th instant. It was His Excellency's earnest wish that troops should march on Kabul at once, so as to ensure Your Highness's personal safety and aid Your Highness in restoring peace and order at your capital.

Unfortunately, the want of transport, and the necessity for collecting a certain amount of supplies, have caused a few weeks' delay; it is, however, a source of gratification and happiness to the Viceroy to learn that Your Highness's safety is not at present endangered, and His Excellency trusts Your Highness will be able to keep everything quiet in your kingdom, until such time as British troops may reach Kabul.

I am glad to be able to inform Your Highness that news reached me yesterday of the departure of a considerable force from Kandahar under the command of a brave and distinguished officer, and that a large body of troops, under command of General Bright, were advancing rapidly from Peshawar to Jalalabad and onwards *viâ* Gandamak to Kabul. My own force will, I hope, be in a state to march before long. As Your Highness is aware, the Shutargardan has been occupied for some days. Meanwhile regiments of Cavalry and Infantry and batteries of Artillery have reached Kuram to replace those I am taking on with me, and to reinforce my own column should a necessity for more troops arise—a contingency I do not in the least expect.

The Viceroy of India, in His Excellency's anxiety for Your Highness's welfare and safety, issued orders that each of the three armies, now advancing from Kandahar, Kuram, and the Khyber, should be strong enough to overcome any opposition Your Highness's enemies could possibly offer. That each is strong enough there can be no doubt.

I understand that there is no one at Kelat-i-Ghilzai or Ghazni to stop the progress of the troops *en route* from Kandahar. There is no reason, therefore, why they should not reach Kabul in a very short time.

The Khyber tribes, having understood and appreciated the Treaty of peace made by Your Highness with the British Government in May last, have unanimously agreed to assist the troops from Peshawar in every way, and are now eager to keep the road through the Khyber safe, and to place all their transport animals at the disposal of the British Commander, who will thus be enabled to concentrate his force rapidly at Kabul. Through the kindness of Your Highness I have experienced much less difficulty than I could have expected, and I may now reasonably hope to be with Your Highness at least as soon as either the Kandahar or Khyber column.

I look forward with great pleasure to the meeting with Your Highness, and trust that you will continue your kind assistance to obtain for me supplies and transport.

I have carefully considered Your Highness's proposal that you yourself should be permitted to administer just punishment to the mutinous troops and others who shared in the treacherous and cruel attack on the British Envoy and his small escort, and thus save Her Majesty's troops the trouble, hardship, and privation which must necessarily be encountered by an advance on Kabul at this season of the year. I thank Your Highness most cordially, on the part of the Viceroy and Government of India, for this further proof of Your Highness's friendly feelings. Under ordinary circumstances such an offer would be gratefully and willingly accepted, but after what has recently occurred, I feel sure that the great British nation would not rest satisfied unless a British army marched to Kabul and there assisted Your Highness to inflict such punishments as so terrible and dastardly an act deserves.

I have forwarded Your Highness's letters in original to the Viceroy; a copy of this, my reply, will be submitted by to-day's post for His Excellency's consideration. Meanwhile I have permitted Mustaufi Habibulla Khan and Wazir Shah Mahomed to take their leave and rejoin Your Highness.

I delayed my own departure from Alikhel until a sufficiency of supplies had been collected at Kushi, and everything was ready for as rapid an advance on Kabul as my limited transport would admit of; for, so long as I remained behind, the people of Afghanistan could not be sure of my intentions, and no doubt hoped that the Amir's remonstrances would have the desired effect, and prevent our doing more than occupying the Shutargardan, or making a demonstration toward Kushi. My crossing the pass would, I knew, be the signal for all those determined on opposition to assemble; it was politic, therefore, to remain behind until the last moment.

When all arrangements were complete, so far as was possible with the means at my disposal, I issued the following Field Force Order:

'The Government of India having decided that a force shall proceed with all possible despatch to Kabul, in response to His Highness the Amir's appeal for aid, and with the object of avenging the dastardly murder of the British representative and his escort, Sir Frederick Roberts feels sure that the troops under his command will respond to the call with a determination to prove themselves worthy of the high reputation they have maintained during the recent campaign.

'The Major-General need address no words of exhortation to soldiers whose courage and fortitude have been so well proved. The Afghan tribes are numerous, but without organization; the regular army is undisciplined, and whatever may be the disparity in numbers such foes can never be formidable to British troops. The dictates of humanity require that a distinction should be made between the peaceable inhabitants of Afghanistan and the treacherous murderers for whom a just retribution is in store, and Sir Frederick Roberts desires to impress upon all ranks the necessity for treating the unoffending population with justice, forbearance, and clemency.

'The future comfort and well being of the force depend largely on the friendliness of our relations with the districts from which supplies must be drawn; prompt payment is enjoined for all articles purchased by departments and individuals, and all disputes must be at once referred to a political officer for decision.

'The Major-General confidently looks forward to the successful accomplishment of the object of the expedition, and the establishment of order and a settled Government in Afghanistan.'

CHAPTER L.

On the 27th September I made over the Kuram command to Brigadier-General T. Gordon, and set out for Kushi, where Baker was now encamped.

Just before I started I had the pleasure of welcoming my old friend and brother officer, Major-General J. Hills, V.C., C.B., who had been with Sir Donald Stewart as Assistant Adjutant-General from the beginning of the campaign, and who had, the moment he heard there was to be an advance on Kabul, come with all speed to place his services at my disposal. Although I had no employment for Hills at the time, there would be plenty for all to do at Kabul, and I was delighted to have so good a soldier with me.

My escort consisted of the Head-Quarters of the Cavalry brigade, one squadron 9th Lancers, 5th Punjab Cavalry, and detachments of the 5th and 28th Punjab Infantry. We had only gone about halfway through the pass when I pushed on with the Cavalry, in the hope of reaching the camp on the top before dark, and was very soon met by twenty-five men of the 92nd Highlanders, who brought me a note from Colonel Perkins, R.E., in command on the Shutargardan, warning me that we were sure to be attacked. We had not proceeded far, when at the narrowest part of the defile we found the passage blocked by some 2,000 Afghans, and as we approached a volley was fired from a party concealed by some rocks on our left. I was told afterwards that it was intended for me, but I remained unscathed, and the principal medical officer, Dr. Townsend, who was riding on my right, and to whom I was talking at the moment, was severely wounded. The Highlanders, supported by some dismounted Cavalry, cleared away the enemy to the north, but as they clung to the precipitous hills on the south, we had to wait till the main body of the escort came up, when they were speedily dispersed.

Meanwhile, a sharp little engagement had taken place further up the gorge, and as we advanced we could see the enemy retiring before a detachment of the 92nd Highlanders, under Colour-Sergeant Hector Macdonald, and of the 3rd Sikhs, under Jemadar Sher Mahomed, a Native of Kabul. The manner in which the Colour-Sergeant and the Native officer handled their men gave me a high opinion of them both.*

* Macdonald, having subsequently further distinguished himself, was given a commission, and is now commanding a regiment in the Egyptian Army. Sher Mahomed was rewarded with the Order of Merit.

On the top of the Shutargardan Pass that evening I received the Amir's reply* to my last letter, in which he expressed his gratitude for the sympathy and support afforded him by the British Government, and informed me that he had given orders to the Governor of Jalalabad that the Khyber column should not meet with any opposition. I was also given a letter from Sirdar Wali Mahomed Khan, and several other Sirdars, professing loyalty to the British Government, and expressing pleasure at my approach. And at the same time the rather embarrassing information reached me that the Amir, desiring personal communication with me, had already arrived in Baker's camp at Kushi, attended by his son Musa Khan, a lad about seven years old, his father-in-law, and the Commander-in-Chief of the Afghan army (Daud Shah), with a suite of 45 members and an escort of 200 men.

Although I had met with but slight opposition hitherto, it was evident from the secret information I received that the Ghilzais were inclined to be hostile, and intended to oppose us, and as it was important to keep open communication with Alikhel through their country, I arranged for the Shutargardan to be held by a Mountain battery, the 3rd Sikhs, and the 21st Punjab Infantry, under the command of Lieutenant-Colonel G. N. Money, an officer on whose judgment and coolness I knew I could rely.

The next morning I rode to Kushi, where my first interview with the Amir of Afghanistan took place.

I cannot say that I was favourably impressed by his appearance. He was an insignificant-looking man, about thirty-two years of age, with a receding forehead, a conical-shaped head, and no chin to speak

* FROM THE AMIR OF KABUL, DATED KUSHI, 27TH SEPTEMBER, 1879.

(After compliments.) Your friendly letter has reached me just at this moment, 8 p.m., the 10th Shawal (27th September), and opened the doors of joy and happiness on the face of my heart marked with affection. I feel perfectly certain and confident that the movements of Her Imperial Majesty's victorious troops are merely for the purpose of consolidating the foundation of my kingdom and strengthening the basis of my government.

In truth, the sympathy of friends with friends is fitting and proper, and the indulgence and kindness of a great Government to a sincere and faithful friend are agreeable and pleasing. I am exceedingly gratified with, and thankful to, the representatives of the illustrious British Government for their expression of sympathy and their support of my cause. Your friendly and wise suggestion that none of the ignorant tribes of Afghanistan should oppose the British troops, so that the officers of the British Government should be the better able to support and protect me, is very acceptable and reasonable. Before I received your letter, I had sent orders repeatedly to the Governors of Jalalabad and Lalpura not to let anyone oppose or resist the British troops, and stringent orders have again been issued to the Governor of Jalalabad to use his utmost endeavours and efforts in this respect. The order in question to the address of the Governor of Jalalabad will be shown you to-morrow, and sent by an express courier.

of, and he gave me the idea of being entirely wanting in that force of character without which no one could hope to govern or hold in check the warlike and turbulent people of Afghanistan. He was possessed, moreover, of a very shifty eye, he could not look one straight in the face, and from the first I felt that his appearance tallied exactly with the double-dealing that had been imputed to him. His presence in my camp was a source of the gravest anxiety to me. He was constantly receiving and sending messages, and was no doubt giving his friends at Kabul all the information he could collect as to our resources and intentions. He had, however, come ostensibly as our ally, seeking refuge from his mutinous soldiers, and whatever suspicions I might secretly entertain, I could only treat him as an honoured guest, so long as there was nothing proved against him.

My first visit to Yakub Khan was of a formal character. Nevertheless, he seized the opportunity to urge strongly upon me the advisability of delaying my advance, that he might have time, he said, to restore order amongst his troops, and to punish those who had participated in the attack on the Embassy. I replied that my orders were peremptory, and that it was my duty, as it was my determination, to press on to Kabul with all possible speed. Finding that his arguments had no effect, he changed his tactics, and declared that he was much alarmed for the safety of his family, whom he had left in the Bala Hissar; that he had only one regiment on which he could depend; that he feared when the others should hear of our approach they would break out and attack the citadel; and that the innocent people in Kabul, not considering it possible that a British force could get there so quickly, had made no arrangements to convey their families away.

Feeling that anxiety for the safety of the families was not the true cause for the Amir's efforts to delay us, and that his sole object was to gain time for the development of plans for opposing our advance—which subsequent events proved had been made with great care—I told him it was impossible to accede to his wishes, but that time would be given for all women and children to clear out of the city if it should prove necessary to attack it. This necessity, however, I was most anxious to avoid, and earnestly hoped that our fighting would be over before we entered Kabul, for I had not forgotten Delhi, and I dreaded the idea of the troops having to force their way through narrow streets and crowded bazaars.

Yakub Khan was evidently much chagrined at my decision. He had left Kabul hurriedly, his movements probably being hastened by hearing that his uncle, Wali Mahomed Khan, and several other Sirdars with whom he was at enmity, were on their way to join me. He had not even brought a tent with him, and, had he succeeded in inducing me to delay our advance, he would without doubt have returned to Kabul at once. As it was, he was accommodated with a tent in the centre of the camp, and the best arrangements possible, under the circumstances, made for his entertainment.

When his own tents arrived, he asked leave to have them pitched outside camp limits. To this I consented, at the same time ordering that a guard of the same strength as my own should be detailed as his escort, ostensibly to do him honour, but in reality that I might be kept informed as to his movements. Unwelcome guest as he was, I thought the least of two evils was to keep him now that we had got him, as his presence in Kabul would be sure to increase the opposition I felt certain we should encounter.

In response to the fears expressed by the Amir as to the safety of the non-combatants, I issued the following Proclamation to the people of Kabul:

'Be it known to all that the British Army is advancing on Kabul to take possession of the city. If it be allowed to do so peacefully, well and good; if not, the city will be seized by force. Therefore, all well-disposed persons, who have taken no part in the dastardly murder of the British Envoy, or in the plunder of the Residency, are warned that, if they are unable to prevent resistance being offered to the entrance of the British army, and the authority of His Highness the Amir, they should make immediate arrangements for their own safety, either by coming to the British camp, or by such other measures as may seem fit to them. And as the British Government does not make war on women and children, warning is given that all women and children should be removed from the city beyond the reach of harm. The British Government desires to treat all classes with justice, and to respect their religion, feelings, and customs, while exacting full retribution from offenders. Every effort will, therefore, be made to prevent the innocent suffering with the guilty, but it is necessary that the utmost precaution should be taken against useless opposition.

'After receipt of this Proclamation, therefore, all persons found armed in or about Kabul will be treated as enemies of the British Government; and, further, it must be distinctly understood that, if the entry of the British force is resisted, I cannot hold myself responsible for any accidental injury which may be done to the persons or property of even well-disposed people, who may have neglected this warning.'

At the same time, the matter having been brought to my notice by Lord Lytton, and bearing in my mind that my father had told me one of the chief causes of the outbreak in Kabul in 1841 was the Afghans' jealousy of their women, and resentment at the European soldiers' intimacy with them, I thought it well to impress upon all the necessity for caution in this respect by publishing the following Order:

'Sir Frederick Roberts desires General officers, and officers commanding corps, to impress upon all officers under their command the necessity for constant vigilance in preventing irregularities likely to arouse the personal jealousies of the people of Kabul, who are, of all races, most susceptible as regards their women.

'The deep-seated animosity of the Afghans towards the English has been mainly ascribed to indiscretions committed during the first occupation of Kabul, and the Major-General trusts that the same excellent discipline so long exhibited by the troops under his command will remove the prejudices of past years, and cause the British name to be as highly respected in Afghanistan as it is throughout the civilized world.*

On the 30th September (my forty-seventh birthday), all arrangements which it was possible for me to make having been completed, the Cavalry brigade marched eight miles to Zargunshahr, the first halting-place on the way to Kabul. I accompanied it, for I was informed that Wali Mahomed Khan and the Sirdars had arrived so far, and I could not let them come on to my camp so long as the Amir was still in it. I wished, also, to interview the Logar *maliks* and ascertain whether I could procure supplies from their valley. There was bread-stuff with the force sufficient for fourteen days, but for the transport of so much grain a large number of animals was required, which could ill be spared, for carriage was so short that I could only move a little more than half the troops at one time, and instead of being able to march direct on Kabul with 6,000 men, a halt would have to be made every other day to admit of the animals going back to bring up the rear brigade, which practically meant my only having at my disposal rather more than half that number at any one time. How fervently I wished that those in authority, who never can see the necessity for maintaining transport in time of peace, could be made to realize the result of their short-sightedness—the danger of having to divide a none too large force in an enemy's country, the consequent risk of failure, the enormous increase of anxiety to the Commander, the delay in achieving the object of the campaign, and the additional labour to all concerned in an undertaking, arduous enough under the most favourable circumstances, in a difficult country, and under a burning eastern sun, even if possessed of good and sufficient transport.

Stores had been collected at Kushi partly by means of local carriage, and partly by our own animals doing the journey twice over from Alikhel, a distance of thirty-six miles. So hard pressed was I for transport that I had to make the Cavalry soldiers march on foot and lead their horses laden with grain—an unusual piece of duty, which was, however, performed with the cheerful alacrity which the troops of the Kabul Field Force always displayed.

But all this is a digression. To return to my story. The *maliks* of Logar, greatly to my relief, agreed to bring a certain amount of supplies; while Wali Mahomed Khan and the other Sirdars were full of protestations of loyalty and devotion. Most of them remained with me all the time I was in Kabul, and some of them afforded me considerable assistance. The Sirdars warned me to place no trust in the

* It was a matter of intense gratification to me that the whole time we remained in Afghanistan, nearly two years, not a single complaint was made by an Afghan of any soldier in my force having interfered with the women of the country.

Amir, and enlarged on the treachery of his conduct, but as I knew they looked upon Yakub Khan as their own deadly enemy, I accepted their counsel with some reservation. I was not, however, able to feel quite at ease about the proceedings of my Royal guest, so I returned to Kushi that same evening.

On the 1st October the whole of the Kabul Field Force was assembled in the Logar valley.*

I waited at Kushi with the last of the Infantry until the morning of the 2nd. Just as I was leaving camp, I became aware that firing was going on in the direction of the Shutargardan, and later in the day I received a report from Colonel Money as to what had happened there.

The enemy, emboldened by the diminished numbers of the garrison, and undervaluing what might be accomplished by a small number of good soldiers, had assembled in force, and occupied the crest of the mountain, the only place from which heliographic communication with me could be kept up. Money very properly decided that this could not be permitted, and considered it best to take the initiative before the enemy should become still stronger, so ordered an advance. Under cover of the Mountain battery's fire, Major Griffiths, of the 3rd Sikhs, with 200 of his own men and 50 of the 21st Punjab Infantry, supported by 150 rifles of the latter corps, stormed the Afghans' position. The assault, delivered in a most spirited manner, was perfectly successful.

* The force was made up as follows:

	British Officers.	Other Ranks. British.	Other Ranks. Native.
Divisional, Brigade, and Departmental Staff	60		
F/A, R.H.A.	7	118	
G/3, R.A.	7	137	
No. 2 Mountain Battery	3		223
Two Gatling guns	1	34	
9th Lancers (one squadron)	4	118	
5th Punjab Cavalry	7		325
12th Bengal Cavalry	6		328
14th Bengal Lancers	7		407
67th Foot	18	686	
72nd Highlanders	23	746	
92nd Highlanders	17	717	
5th Punjab Infantry	8		610
5th Gurkhas	7		574
23rd Pioneers	6		671
28th Punjab Infantry	8		636
7th Company Bengal Sappers and Miners	3	2	93
	192	2,558	3,867

Major Griffiths, however, was wounded, also a signalling sergeant of the 67th Foot and five men of the 3rd Sikhs, while the enemy left thirty dead on the ground, and were pursued down the slope of the hill without making any attempt to rally.

On the 3rd we marched fifteen miles to Zahidabad, where we first came in sight of the fortified hill above Kabul. The rear guard was fired into on the way, and we had considerable difficulty in crossing the Logar river, as the water from a large irrigation cut had been directed back into the stream just above the ford. Our only casualty on this day was Captain 'Dick' Kennedy, who was wounded in the hand.

It was plain from these occurrences, and from the attack on the Shutargardan, that the people generally were not disposed to be friendly. From the Amir I could extract no information on this head, although he must have been fully aware of the feelings and intentions of his subjects. He was in constant communication with Kabul, and was frequently being met by mounted messengers, who, from the haste with which they travelled, as evidenced by the exhausted state of their horses and the eagerness with which the Amir read the letters they brought, appeared to be the bearers of important tidings.

It may be imagined how irritating and embarrassing was Yakub Khan's presence, since his position in my camp enabled him to give the leaders at Kabul accurate information as to our numbers and movements. That he felt pretty sure of our discomfiture was apparent from his change of manner, which, from being at first a mixture of extreme cordiality and cringing servility, became as we neared Kabul distant, and even haughty.

On the 5th October, one month from the receipt at Simla of the evil tidings of the fate of the British Embassy, we reached the pretty little village of Charasia, nestling in orchards and gardens, with a rugged range of hills towering above it about a mile away. This range descended abruptly on the right to permit the exit of the Logar river, and rose again on its other side in precipitous cliffs, forming a fine gorge* about halfway between our camp and Kabul city, now only from ten to twelve miles distant.

An uncle of the Amir (Sirdar Nek Mahomed Khan), and a General in the Afghan army, came out to meet Yakub Khan at this place; he remained some time in earnest conversation with his nephew, and, as he was about to remount his horse, called out in so loud a tone that it was evidently meant for us all to hear, that he was 'now going to disperse the troops.'† Very different, however, was the story brought

* Known as the *sang-i-nawishta* (inscribed stone).

† Shortly after I was settled at Kabul, the following letter, written by Nek Mahomed on the evening of the day he had been with the Amir, to some person whom he wished to acquaint with the state of affairs, was brought to me:

to me by an escaped Native servant of Cavagnari's, who came into our camp later in the day. This man declared that preparations for fighting were steadily being carried on; that the soldiers and towns-people were streaming into the arsenal and supplying themselves with cartridges; that large bodies of troops were moving out in our direction; and that, when we advanced next day, we should certainly be opposed by a formidable force. The Amir, on having this intelligence communicated to him, pretended to disbelieve it utterly, and assured me that all was at peace in the city, that Nek Mahomed would keep the troops quiet, and that I should have no trouble; but I was not taken in by his specious assurances.

Now more than ever I felt the want of sufficient transport! Had it been possible to have the whole of my force with me, I should have advanced at once, and have occupied that evening the range of hills I have described; but Macpherson's brigade was still a march behind, and all I could do was, immediately on arrival, to send back every available transport animal to bring it up. I pushed forward Cavalry patrols along the three roads leading to Kabul, and rode out myself to reconnoitre the position in front. It was sufficiently strong to make me wish I had a larger force. Towards evening groups of men appeared on the skyline all round, giving unmistakable warning that the tribes were gathering in large numbers.

From the information brought me by the Cavalry, and from my own examination of the ground, I decided to advance along the left bank of the river: and to facilitate this movement I determined to seize the heights on either side of the gorge at daybreak, whether Macpherson's brigade had arrived or not. That night strong piquets were thrown out round the camp, and Cavalry patrols were ordered to proceed at dawn to feel for the enemy. *L'homme propose, mais Dieu dispose.*

'My kind Friend,—The truth is that to-day, at sunrise, I went to the camp, the Amir having summoned me. When I arrived, Mulla Shah Mahomed [the Wazir] first said to me, "Go back and tell the people to raise a holy war." I did not feel certain about what he said [or was not satisfied with this], [but] the Amir afterwards told me to go back that very hour and rouse the people to a *ghaza*. I got back to Kabul about 7 o'clock, and am collecting the people. Salaam.'

The letter was not addressed, but it was sealed with Nek Mahomed's seal, and there was no reason to doubt its authenticity.

CHAPTER LI.

THE Cavalry having reported that the road through the *sang-i-nawishta* gorge was impassable, I started off a party* before it was fully light on the 6th, to work at it and make it practicable for guns. I was preparing to follow with an escort of Cavalry to examine the pass and the ground beyond, when the growing daylight discovered large numbers of Afghan troops in regular formation crowning the hills that I ought to have been in a position to occupy the preceding evening. No hurry, no confusion was apparent in their movements; positions were taken up and guns placed with such coolness and deliberation that it was evident regularly trained troops were employed. Very soon I received reports of our Cavalry patrols having been fired upon, and of their having been obliged to retire.

Immediate action was imperatively necessary; the Afghans had to be dislodged from their strong position at any cost, or we should have been surrounded by overwhelming numbers. Their occupation of the heights was, I felt, a warning that must not be disregarded, and a menace that could not be brooked.

Behind this range of hills lay the densely-crowded city of Kabul, with the scarcely less crowded suburbs of Chardeh, Deh-i-Afghan, and numberless villages thickly studded over the Kabul valley, all of which were contributing their quota of warriors to assist the Regular troops in disputing the advance of the British. It did not require much experience of Asiatics to understand that, if the enemy were allowed to remain undisturbed for a single night in the position they had taken up, their numbers would increase to an extraordinary extent.

I now received a report from the rear that the road was blocked, and that the progress of Macpherson's brigade would certainly be opposed; while, on the crests of the hills to the right and left of my camp, bodies of men began to assemble, who, I surmised (which surmise I afterwards learnt was correct), were only waiting for the sun to go down to make a general attack upon the camp under cover of dusk.

The situation was one of great anxiety. The whole force with me was not more than 4,000 men and eighteen guns. The treacherous Amir and his equally treacherous Ministers had, of course, kept the Afghan Commander fully informed as to the manner in which my troops were perforce divided; the position of every man and every gun with me was known; and I feared that, as soon as we were engaged

* Twenty sabres, 9th Lancers, one squadron 5th Punjab Cavalry, two guns, No. 2 Mountain battery, 284 rifles, 92nd Highlanders, and 450 rifles, 23rd Pioneers.

with the enemy, the opportunity would be taken to attack my weakly-defended camp and to engage Macpherson's small brigade, encumbered as it was with its large convoy of stores and ammunition.

The numbers of the enemy were momentarily increasing, so delay would assuredly make matters worse; the only chance of success, therefore, was to take the initiative, and attack the Afghan main position at once. Accordingly, I sent an officer with orders to the troops who were moving towards the gorge not to commence work, but to take up a defensive position until my plans were further developed. I sent another messenger to Macpherson, informing him of my intention to take immediate action, and telling him to keep a good look-out, and push on to Charasia with all possible speed, and at the same time I reinforced him by a squadron of Cavalry.

The Afghan position formed the arc of a circle, extending from the *sang-i-nawishta* gorge to the heights above Chardeh. Both sides of the gorge were occupied by the enemy, as was a semi-detached hill to the south of it, and sixteen guns were observed in position. The line they had taken up occupied nearly three miles of country; and their main position was the ridge, which, close to the gorge, rose 1,000 feet above the plain, running up at its western extremity to a peak 2,200 feet high. Thence the line stretched along the edge of some lower heights to a rugged hill, the summit of which was about 1,800 feet above Charasia. In front of this formidable position were a succession of sandy hills, forming a series of easily defensible posts, and at the foot of these hills ran a bare stony belt, sloping down to the cultivated land surrounding Charasia and the hamlet of Khairabad.

My movements and reconnaissances up till now having led the enemy to believe that I intended to deliver my attack on their left at the *sang-i-nawishta*, they were seen to be concentrating their forces in that direction. But this position could only have been carried with such damaging loss to us that I determined to make the real attack by an outflanking movement to their right.

The men having made a hasty breakfast, I despatched General Baker in this direction, and placing at his disposal the troops noted below,* I entrusted to him the difficult task of dislodging the enemy, while I continued to distract their attention towards the gorge by making a feint to their left.

Baker's little column assembled in a wooded enclosure close to Charasia, where he left his field hospital and reserve ammunition, for the safe guarding of which I sent him the 5th Punjab Infantry, while he was further reinforced by 450 men of the 23rd Pioneers and three Field Artillery guns. I was thus left with only six Horse Artillery

* Two guns, No. 2 Mountain battery, two Gatling guns, detachment 12th Bengal Cavalry, 72nd Highlanders, 5th Gurkhas (300 rifles), 5th Punjab Infantry (200 rifles), No. 7 Company Sappers and Miners.

guns, 450 Cavalry, and between 600 and 700 Infantry for the protection of the camp, where I was still handicapped by the presence of the Amir and his untrustworthy following.

While Baker advanced to the left, the party near the *sang-i-nawishta* gorge, commanded by Major White, of the 92nd Highlanders, was ordered to threaten the pass and to prevent the enemy occupying any portion of the Charasia village, to advance within Artillery range of the enemy's main position above the gorge, and when the outflanking movement had been thoroughly developed and the enemy were in full retreat, but not before, to push the Cavalry through the gorge and pursue.

At about 11.30 a.m. Baker's leading troops emerged into the open, and were immediately engaged with a crowd of armed Afghans, supported by a considerable body of Regular troops. The General now sent one company of the 72nd, under Captain Hunt, to turn the Afghans off a succession of peaks situated at right angles to the ridge they were occupying on their extreme right. Running along this ridge, and stretching across the Indiki road to the sandhills, the Afghan right wing held a line considerably in advance of their left on the hill above the *sang-i-nawishta* gorge, and one which could not easily be turned, for the peaks the 72nd were sent to occupy were almost inaccessible, and the fire from them swept the slopes up which our troops must advance. These peaks, therefore, formed the key of the position, and their defenders had to be dislodged from them at all hazards before anything else could be attempted. The company of the 72nd with much difficulty fought their way up, and gained a footing on the first peak, where they were obliged to pause, until reinforced by two companies of the 5th Gurkhas under Captain Cook, V.C., when they advanced all together, clearing the enemy from each successive point. while the remainder of the 72nd breasted the hill, and, under cover of the Mountain guns, attacked the position in front. But the enemy were obstinate, and the extremely difficult nature of the ground somewhat checked the gallant Highlanders. Seeing their dilemma, Baker despatched two companies of the 5th Gurkhas, under Lieutenant-Colonel Fitz-Hugh, and 200 men of the 5th Punjab Infantry, under Captain Hall, to their assistance; while the 23rd Pioneers were brought up on the right, in support, and a detachment of the 5th Punjab Infantry echeloned in rear, on the left of the line.

The engagement now became hot, and the firing fast and furious. My readers will, I am sure, be able to realize with what intense excitement and anxiety I watched the proceedings. It was evident to me that little progress could be made so long as the enemy retained possession of the ridge, which the Afghan Commander apparently had just begun to appreciate was the real point of attack, for his troops could now be seen hurrying to this point, and it became more urgently necessary than ever to carry the position before it could be reinforced. At 2 p.m. it was seized; the Highlanders and Gurkhas could no longer be resisted; the Afghans wavered, and then began to retreat, exposed to a cross-fire that effectually prevented their rallying.

The brunt of this affair was borne by the 72nd, admirably led by their company officers, under the skilful direction of Lieutenant-Colonel Clarke and his Adjutant, Lieutenant Murray. I closely watched their movements, and particularly observed one man pushing up the precipitous hillside considerably in advance of everyone else, and apparently utterly regardless of the shower of bullets falling round him. I inquired about him later on, and found that he was a young Irish private of the 72nd, named MacMahon, to whose coolness and daring was in a great measure due the capture of this very strong post. Her Majesty, I am glad to be able to relate, subsequently rewarded this intrepid soldier by bestowing on him the Victoria Cross.

The general advance was now sounded, and gallantly was it responded to. The main position was stormed by the Highlanders, Gurkhas, and Punjab Infantry, each trying hard to be the first to close with its defenders. The enemy fought desperately, charging down on the Gurkhas, by whom, under the leadership of Lieutenant-Colonel Fitz-Hugh and his Adjutant, Lieutenant Martin, they were repulsed and driven over the crest with heavy loss.

The Afghans now took up a position some 600 yards in the rear of that from which they had just been dislodged, where they made an obstinate stand for half an hour, but they were again forced back on the attacking party being strengthened by the arrival of two companies of the 92nd Highlanders, sent to their assistance by Major White, who had already successfully engaged the Afghan left above the *sang-i-nawishta* gorge. As the enemy's advanced posts on the hill to the south, and directly in front of the gorge, prevented our guns from coming within range of their position on the heights above, these posts had to be disposed of as a preliminary to effective co-operation with Baker; accordingly, about noon the hill was captured by two companies of the 92nd, under Captain Cotton, and half a battery of Field Artillery was advanced to a point whence Major Parry was able to engage the Afghan guns posted above the gorge.

It was at this juncture, when Baker's troops, having carried the main position, were proceeding to attack that to which the enemy had retreated, that White despatched two companies of the 92nd, under Captain Oxley, by whose timely aid the determined foe were at length driven from this point of vantage also. The troops followed up their success and advanced at the double, while our guns shelled the shaken masses.

The Afghan right and centre now gave way completely; the enemy broke, and fled down the slopes on the further side in a north-westerly direction, eventually taking refuge in the Chardeh villages.

By 3.45 we were in possession of the whole of the main ridge. The first objective having been thus gained, the troops, pivoting on their right, brought round their left and advanced against the now exposed flanks of the enemy's left wing, and simultaneously with this movement White advanced from his position by the hill in front of the gorge, and a little after four o'clock had gained possession of the pass and twelve Afghan guns.

Completely outflanked and enfiladed by Baker's fire, the left wing of the Afghan force made but little resistance; they rapidly abandoned the height, and retired across the river toward the north-east, pursued by the small body of Cavalry attached to White's force, under Major Hammond, and a party of the 92nd, under Major Hay.

Baker now paused to allow of the Infantry's ammunition being replenished, and then advanced along the ridge towards the pass, which he reached in time to help the Cavalry who were engaged with the enemy's rear guard at the river; the latter were driven off and forced to retreat; but by this time the growing darkness made further pursuit impossible. We were therefore compelled to rest satisfied with holding the ground in advance by piquets and occupying both ends of the *sang-i-nawishta* defile, where the troops bivouacked for the night. I was able to supply them with food from Charasia, and they were made as comfortable as they could be under the circumstances.

While the fighting was taking place on the heights in front of Charasia, the hills on both flanks of my camp were crowded with the enemy, anxiously watching the result; they did not approach within the Cavalry patrols, but one party caused so much annoyance to a picquet by firing into it that it became necessary to dislodge it, a service which was performed in a very daring manner by a few of the 92nd, under Lieutenant Grant and Colour-Sergeant Hector Macdonald, the same non-commissioned officer who had a few days before so distinguished himself in the Hazardarakht defile.

Our casualties were wonderfully few, only 18 killed and 70 wounded,* while the enemy left 300 dead behind them, and as they succeeded in carrying numbers of their killed and wounded off the field, their loss must have been heavy. I subsequently ascertained that we had

* During the fight the Infantry expended 41,000 rounds, of which over 20,000 were fired by the 72nd Highlanders. The half-battery G/3 R.A. fired 6 common shell (percussion fuses) and 71 shrapnel (time fuses); total, 77 rounds. No. 2 Mountain Battery fired 10 common shell and 94 shrapnel, total, 104 rounds. The two Gatlings fired 150 rounds.

At the tenth round one of the Gatlings jammed, and had to be taken to pieces. This was the first occasion on which Gatling guns were used in action. They were not of the present improved make, and, being found unsatisfactory, were made but little use of.

opposed to us, besides thirteen Regular regiments, between eight and ten thousand Afghans. Ghilzais from Tezin and Hisarak had hurried up in large numbers to join the enemy, but, luckily for us, arrived too late. Of these some returned to their homes when they found the Afghan army had been beaten, but the greater number waited about Kabul to assist in any further stand that might be made by the Regular troops.

The heliograph, worked by Captain Stratton, of the 22nd Foot, had been of the greatest use during the day, and kept me fully informed of all details. The last message as the sun was sinking behind the hills, confirming my own observations, was a most satisfactory one, to the effect that the whole of the enemy's position was in our possession, and that our victory was complete.

Throughout the day my friend (!) the Amir, surrounded by his Sirdars, remained seated on a knoll in the centre of the camp watching the progress of the fight with intense eagerness, and questioning every-one who appeared as to his interpretation of what he had observed. So soon as I felt absolutely assured of our victory, I sent an Aide-de-camp to His Highness to convey the joyful intelligence of our success. It was, without doubt, a trying moment for him, and a terrible dis-appointment after the plans which I subsequently ascertained he and his adherents at Kabul had carefully laid for our annihilation. But he received the news with Asiatic calmness, and without the smallest sign of mortification, merely requesting my Aide-de-camp to assure me that, as my enemies were his enemies, he rejoiced at my victory.

Macpherson's brigade, with its impedimenta, arrived before it was quite dark, so altogether I had reason to feel satisfied with the day's results. But the fact still remained that not more than twelve miles beyond stood the city of Kabul, with its armed thousands ready to oppose us should an assault prove necessary. I had besides received information of a further gathering of Ghilzais bent upon another attack on the Shutargardan, and that reinforcements of Regular troops and guns were hastening to Kabul from Ghazni. Prompt action was the one and only means of meeting these threatened difficulties. My troops had had more than enough for one day, and required rest, but needs must when the devil (in the shape of Afghan hordes) drives. I resolved to push on, and issued orders for tents to be struck at once and an advance to be made at break of day.

At the first streak of dawn on the 7th I started, leaving Macpherson to come on with the heavy baggage as quickly as he could. I marched by the *sang-i-nawishta* defile, where Major White met me and ex-plained to me his part in the victory of the previous day. From my inspection of the ground, I had no difficulty in coming to the conclusion that much of the success which attended the operations on this side was due to White's military instincts and, at one supreme moment, his extreme personal gallantry. It afforded me, therefore, very great pleasure to recommend this officer for the Victoria Cross, an honour of which more than one incident in his subsequent career proved him to be well worthy.

Our rapid advance, following on the defeat of the previous day, had the effect I hoped it would have. On arriving at Beni Hissar, a considerable village, surrounded by orchards and gardens, only two miles south of the far-famed citadel of the Bala Hissar, I sent out Cavalry patrols to reconnoitre, who brought me the pleasing news that the Bala Hissar had been evacuated, and the only part of the city visible seemed to be deserted.

During the day I received visits from some of the chief merchants of Kabul, who each told a different tale regarding the movements of the defeated Afghan army and the intentions of the Afghan Commander. From their conflicting accounts, however, I gathered that, fresh troops having arrived from Kohistan, the remnants of the Charasia army had joined them, and that the combined forces were then occupying the range of hills immediately above Kabul, to the west, and had determined to make another stand.

Having received intelligence that the enemy, if again defeated, intended to retire towards Turkestan, I directed Brigadier-General Massy, on the morning of the 8th October, to move out with the Cavalry brigade and place himself across their line of retreat.* The brigade started at 11 a.m., and, in order to avoid the city and adjacent heights, made a considerable detour by Siah Sang and Sherpur, the new Afghan cantonment. On reaching the latter place, Massy heliographed to me that he had found it deserted, the magazine blown up, and seventy-five guns† abandoned inside the enclosure, and that the enemy were now occupying a ridge‡ which seemed to him to be a prolongation of the Shahr-i-Darwaza range above Kabul; then, continuing his march, he crossed a depression in this ridge called the Nanachi Kotal, and wheeling to his left, and skirting the Asmai heights on the western side, he soon came in sight of the Afghan camp, pitched on the slope of the hills about a mile from Deh-i-Mazang.

Brigadier-General Massy was informed, in reply to his heliogram, that Baker would be despatched at once to drive the enemy from their position and force them to fall back upon the Cavalry, upon which Massy immediately made the arrangements which appeared to him

* The troops available for this purpose were: One squadron 9th Lancers, 5th Punjab Cavalry, 12th Bengal Cavalry, and 14th Bengal Lancers; total, 720 of all ranks.

† The guns included four English 18-pounders, one English 8-inch howitzer and two Afghan imitations of this weapon, and forty-two bronze Mountain guns.

‡ The Asmai heights.

most advisable for blocking, with the limited number of sabres at his disposal, the several roads by which the enemy might attempt to escape.

I could only spare to Baker a very small force (1,044 rifles, two Mountain guns and one Gatling), for Macpherson's and White's troops had not yet come up. He started off without a moment's delay, and, driving the enemy's scouts before him, worked his way along the Shahr-i-Darwaza heights to the west; but his progress was very slow, owing to the extreme difficulty of the ground, and the day was far spent before he found himself near enough to the enemy to use his Artillery. To his delight, Baker perceived that he commanded the Afghan camp and the rear of their main position; but his satisfaction was considerably allayed when he discovered that between him and them lay a deep gorge* with precipitous sides, through which ran the Kabul river, and that before he could attack he would have to descend 1,600 feet, and then climb up the opposite side, which was nearly as high and quite as steep.

Anxious as Baker was that there should be no delay in delivering the assault, by the time his dispositions were made it had become too dark to attempt it, and most reluctantly he had to postpone the movement till daybreak the next day. He had ascertained that the Kabul river was not fordable for Infantry except at a point which was commanded by the enemy's camp, and was too far from support to warrant piquets being pushed across at night. Nothing whatever could be seen, but a very slight noise as of stealthy movement in the Afghan camp was heard, and the fear seized Baker that the enemy might escape him. Soon after 11 p.m., therefore, when the rising moon began in a measure to dispel the darkness, Baker sent a strong patrol under a British officer to feel for the enemy. The patrol came into contact with the Afghan scouts on the river-bank, from some of whom, taken prisoners in the struggle, they learned that the enemy had crept away under cover of the night, and the greater number had dispersed to their own homes; but about 800, mounted on Artillery horses, were reported to have accompanied their Commander, Mahomed Jan, and to have escaped in the direction of Bamian.

Meanwhile, Brigadier-General Massy, from his point of observation beneath the Asmai heights, had perceived that it was impossible for Baker to carry the enemy's main position by daylight; he tried to communicate with Baker and ascertain his plans, but the party despatched on this service were unable to get through the villages and woods, which were all held by the enemy, and returned unsuccessful. Massy then collected his scattered squadrons and bivouacked for the night, being anxious that his men and horses should have food and rest,

* The Deh-i-Mazang gorge.

and it not having struck him that the enemy might attempt to escape during the hours of darkness.

The information that in very truth they had escaped was brought to Baker at 4.30 a.m. He at once communicated it to Massy, telling him at the same time that any movement the Cavalry might make in pursuit would be supported by the troops under his immediate command, and also by a brigade under Brigadier-General Macpherson, which I had despatched to reinforce Baker; Macpherson and White, with their respective troops, having arrived at Beni Hissar shortly after Baker had started.

I joined Baker at this time, and great was my disappointment at being told that the Afghans had given us the slip. I went carefully over the ground, however, and satisfied myself that Baker had done all that was possible under the circumstances, and that the enemy having eluded us could not in any way be attributed to want of care or skill on his part.

Massy scoured the country until nightfall on the 9th, but with very little success, only one small party of fugitives being overtaken about four-and-twenty miles on the road to Ghazni. Numbers, doubtless, found shelter in the city of Kabul, others in the numerous villages with which the richly-cultivated Chardeh valley was thickly studded, and whose inhabitants were hostile to a man; others escaped to the hills; and the remainder, having had ten hours' start, could not be overtaken.

The enemy's camp was left standing, and twelve guns, some elephants, camels, mules, and ponies, fell into our possession.

During that day our camp was moved nearer the city to Siah Sang, a commanding plateau between the Kabul and Logar rivers, close to their confluence, and less than a mile east of the Bala Hissar. The 5th Gurkhas and two Mountain guns were left to hold the heights on which Brigadier-General Baker had been operating, and the rest of the force was concentrated on Siah Sang.

CHAPTER LII.

At last I was at Kabul, the place I had heard so much of from my boyhood, and had so often wished to see! The city lay beneath me, with its mud-coloured buildings and its 50,000 inhabitants, covering a considerable extent of ground. To the south-east corner of the city appeared the Bala Hissar, picturesquely perched on a saddle just beneath the Shahr-i-Darwaza heights, along the top of which ran a fortified wall, enclosing the upper portion of the citadel and extending to the Deh-i-Mazang gorge.

Kabul was reported to be perfectly quiet, and numbers of traders came into our camp to dispose of their wares; but I forbade anyone to enter the city until I had been able to decide upon the best means of maintaining order amongst a population for the most part extremely fanatical, treacherous, and vindictive.

So far our success had been complete: all opposition had been overcome, Kabul was at our mercy, the Amir was in my camp ready to agree to whatever I might propose, and it had been all done with extraordinarily little loss to ourselves. Nevertheless, I felt my difficulties were very far from being at an end—indeed, the part of my duty still remaining to be accomplished was surrounded with far greater difficulty, and was a source of much more anxiety to me than the military task I had undertaken; for, with regard to the latter, I possessed confidence in myself and my ability to perform it, whereas, with respect to the political and diplomatic side of the question, actual personal experience I had none, and I could only hope that common-sense and a sense of justice would carry me through.

The instructions I had received from the Government of India were very general in their character, for the Viceroy felt that any proceedings must necessarily depend on the state of affairs obtaining at Kabul, the acts and attitude of the Amir and his people, and the various conditions impossible to foresee when the Foreign Office letter was written to me on the 29th September. But, though general, they were very comprehensive.

The troops were to be placed in strong and secure positions, such as would give me complete control over the Amir's capital; any Afghan soldiers remaining at Kabul, and the whole of the city population, were to be disarmed; supplies were to be collected in sufficient quantities to render my force independent in case of interruption along the line of communication; Yakub Khan's personal safety was to be secured, and adequate supervision maintained over his movements and actions; a close investigation was to be instituted into all the causes and circumstances connected with the 'totally unprovoked and most barbarous attack by the Amir's soldiery and the people of his capital upon the representative of an allied State, who was residing under the Amir's protection in the Amir's fortress, in very close proximity to the Amir himself, and whose personal safety and honourable treatment had been solemnly guaranteed by the Ruler of Afghanistan.'

The retribution to be exacted was to be adapted to the twofold character of the offence, and was to be imposed upon the Afghan nation in proportion as the offence was proved to be national, and as the responsibility should be brought home to any particular community. Further, the imposition of a fine, it was suggested upon the city of Kabul 'would be in accordance with justice and precedent,' and the demolition of fortifications and removal of buildings within range of my defences, or which might interfere with my control over the city, might be 'necessary as a military precaution.'

In forming my plans for the removal of obstructive buildings, I was to consider 'whether they can be combined with any measures compatible with justice and humanity for leaving a memorial of the retribution exacted from the city in some manner and by some mark that will not be easily obliterated.'

I was told that 'in regard to the punishment of individuals, it should be swift, stern, and impressive, without being indiscriminate or immoderate; its infliction must not be delegated to subordinate officers of minor responsibility acting independently of your instructions or supervision; and you cannot too vigilantly maintain the discipline of the troops under your orders, or superintend their treatment of the unarmed population, so long as your orders are obeyed and your authority is unresisted. You will deal summarily in the majority of cases with persons whose share in the murder of anyone belonging to the British Embassy shall have been proved by your investigations, but while the execution of justice should be as public and striking as possible, it should be completed with all possible expedition, since the indefinite prolongation of your proceedings might spread abroad unfounded alarm.'

The despatch concluded with the words: 'It will probably be essential, not only for the protection of your own camp from annoyance, but also for the security of the well-affected population and for the general maintenance of order, that you should assume and exercise supreme authority in Kabul, since events have unfortunately proved that the Amir has lost that authority, or that he has conspicuously failed to make use of it.'

On the 10th I visited Sherpur, and the next day I went to the Bala Hissar, and wandered over the scene of the Embassy's brave defence and cruel end. The walls of the Residency, closely pitted with bullet-holes, gave proof of the determined nature of the attack and the length of the resistance. The floors were covered with blood-stains, and amidst the embers of a fire were found a heap of human bones. It may be imagined how British soldiers' hearts burned within them at such a sight, and how difficult it was to suppress feelings of hatred and animosity towards the perpetrators of such a dastardly crime. I had a careful but unsuccessful search made for the bodies of our ill-fated friends.

The Bala Hissar, at one time of great strength, was now in a somewhat dilapidated condition. It contained eighty-five guns, mortars and howitzers, some of them of English manufacture, upwards of 250 tons of gunpowder, stowed away in earthen vessels, many millions of Enfield and Snider cartridges, and a large number of arms, besides quantities of saddlery, clothing for troops, musical instruments, shot.

ENTRANCE TO THE BALA HISSAR, KABUL.

From a photograph by J. Burke.

shell, caps, and accoutrements, and a vast amount of lead, copper and tin. It would not have given us much trouble to storm the Bala Hissar, had we been obliged to do so, for Artillery could have opened on it within easy range, and there was cover for Infantry close up to the walls.

The reading of the Proclamation announcing the intentions of the British Government with regard to the punishment of the city was to take place in the Bala Hissar next day. The Amir had agreed to accompany me. The leading people were invited to attend, and I had given orders that all the troops were to take part in the procession, so as to render as impressive as possible the ceremony, at which were to be made known to the inhabitants of Kabul the terms imposed upon them by the British Government. The object of my visit was to decide how the troops might best be disposed so as to make the most imposing display on the occasion.

I decided to detain in custody two Sirdars, Yahia Khan* and his brother Zakariah Khan, the Mustaufi, and the Wazir, as these four were Yakub Khan's principal advisers, and I was satisfied that their influence was being used against us, and that so long as they were at large a mine might be sprung upon me at any moment.

The Commander-in-Chief, Daud Shah, was also in the Amir's confidence; but I determined to leave him at liberty, for, from what I could learn, he had made an effort (not a very strong one, perhaps) to help our unfortunate countrymen, and he had on several occasions since he had been in my camp given me useful information; moreover, I hoped to obtain further help from him, in which hope I was not altogether disappointed.

As to what I ought to do with the Amir I was considerably puzzled. Lord Lytton had urged upon me the necessity for weighing well the advisability of prematurely breaking with him, as it was very possible he might become a useful instrument in our hands, an eventuality which I thoroughly understood; but I was not at all sure that Yakub Khan would not break with me when he learnt my decision with regard to his Ministers, and I had received more than one warning that, if he failed to keep me from entering Kabul, he contemplated flight and a supreme effort to raise the country against me.

Yakub Khan certainly did not deserve much consideration from us; for, though no absolute proof was forthcoming of his having instigated the attack upon the Embassy, he most certainly made not the slightest effort to stop it or to save the lives of those entrusted to his care, and throughout that terrible day showed himself to be, if not a deliberate traitor, a despicable coward. Again, his endeavours to delay the march of my force for the sole purpose of gaining sufficient time to organize

* Yahia Khan was Yakub Khan's father-in-law.

the destruction of the army to whose protection he had appealed deprived him, to my mind, of the smallest claim to be treated as an honourable ally.

My doubts as to what policy I ought to pursue with regard to Yakub Khan were all solved by his own action on the morning of the 12th October. He came to my tent before I was dressed, and asked for an interview, which was, of course, accorded. The only chair I possessed I offered to my Royal visitor, who seated himself, and then and there announced that he had come to resign the Amirship, and that he was only carrying out a determination made before he came to Kushi; he had then allowed himself to be over-persuaded, but now his resolution was fixed. His life, he said, had been most miserable, and he would rather be a grass-cutter in the English camp than Ruler of Afghanistan; he concluded by entreating me to allow his tent to be pitched close to mine until he could go to India, to London, or wherever the Viceroy might desire to send him. I placed a tent at his disposal, ordered breakfast to be prepared for him, and begged him not to decide at once, but think the matter over for some hours, adding that I would see him again at ten o'clock, the hour appointed for him to accompany me to the Bala Hissar in order that he might be present at the reading of the Proclamation. At this time, it must be remembered, the Amir did not know what the terms of the Proclamation were, and was entirely ignorant of my intentions regarding his Ministers.

As arranged, I had another interview with Yakub Khan at ten o'clock, when I found him unshaken in his resolve to abdicate, and unwilling, under the circumstances, to be present at the ceremony which was about to take place. He said, however, that he would send his eldest son, and that all his Ministers should attend me. I begged him again to reconsider the decision he had come to, and to think well over the results to himself; but finding that he had finally* made up his mind, I told His Highness I would telegraph his determination to

* At an interview which Major Hastings, the Political Officer, and Mr. Durand, my Political Secretary, had with His Highness at my request on the 23rd October, he said, referring to the subject of the Amirship: 'I call God and the Koran to witness, and everything a Mussulman holds sacred, that my only desire is to be set free, and end my days in liberty. I have conceived an utter aversion for these people. I always treated them well, and you see how they have rewarded me. So long as I was fighting in one place or another, they liked me well enough. Directly I became Amir, and consulted their own good by making peace with you, they turned on me. Now I detest them all, and long to be out of Afghanistan for ever. It is not that I am unable to hold the country; I have held it before and could hold it again, but I have no further wish to rule such a people, and I beg of you to let me go. If the British Government wish me to stay, I will stay, as their servant or as the Amir, if you like to call me so, until my son is of an age to succeed me, or even without that condition; but it will be wholly against my own inclination, and I earnestly beg to be set free.'

the Viceroy and ask for instructions; that he would not, of course, be forced to continue to reign at Kabul against his will, but that I would ask him to retain his title until I could receive a reply from Simla.

At noon I proceeded to the Bala Hissar, accompanied by my staff, the Heir-Apparent, the Ministers, and a large gathering of the chief Sirdars of Kabul. Both sides of the road were lined with troops, of whom I felt not a little proud that day. Notwithstanding that the duty required of them had been severe and continuous, now that they were required to take part in a ceremonial parade, they turned out as clean and smart as one could wish to see them.

As the head of the procession entered the main gateway, the British flag was run up, the bands played the National Anthem, and a salute of thirty-one guns was fired.

On arriving at the public Hall of Audience, I dismounted, and ascending the steps leading to it, I addressed the assembled multitude, and read to them the following Proclamation, containing the orders of the British Government:

'In my Proclamation dated the 3rd October, I informed the people of Kabul that a British army was advancing to take possession of the city, and I warned them against offering any resistance to the entry of the troops and the authority of His Highness the Amir. That warning has been disregarded. The force under my command has now reached Kabul and occupied the Bala Hissar, but its advance has been pertinaciously opposed, and the inhabitants of the city have taken a conspicuous part in the opposition offered. They have therefore become rebels against His Highness the Amir, and have added to the guilt already incurred by them in abetting the murder of the British Envoy and his companions—a treacherous and cowardly crime which has brought indelible disgrace upon the Afghan people. It would be but a just and fitting reward for such misdeeds if the city of Kabul were now totally destroyed and its very name blotted out; but the great British Government ever desires to temper justice with mercy, and I now announce to the inhabitants of Kabul that the full retribution for their offence will not be exacted, and that the city will be spared.

'Nevertheless, it is necessary that they should not escape all penalty, and, further, that the punishment inflicted should be such as will be felt and remembered. Therefore, such portions of the city buildings as now interfere with the proper military occupation of the Bala Hissar, and the safety and comfort of the British troops to be quartered in it, will be at once levelled with the ground; and, further, a heavy fine, the amount of which will be notified hereafter, will be imposed upon the inhabitants of Kabul, to be paid according to their several capacities. I further give notice to all, that, in order to provide for the restoration and maintenance of order, the city of Kabul and the surrounding country, to a distance of ten miles, are placed under martial law. With the consent of His Highness the Amir, a military Governor of Kabul will be appointed, to administer justice and punish with a strong hand all evil-doers. The inhabitants of Kabul and of the neighbouring villages are hereby warned to submit to his authority.

'This punishment, inflicted upon the whole city, will not, of course, absolve from further penalties those whose individual guilt may be hereafter proved. A full and searching inquiry into the circumstances of the late outbreak will be held, and all persons convicted of having taken part in it will be dealt with according to their deserts.

'With the view of providing effectually for the prevention of crime and disorder, and the safety of all well-disposed persons in Kabul, it is hereby notified that for the future the carrying of dangerous weapons, whether swords, knives, or firearms, within the streets of the city or within a distance of five miles from the city gates, is forbidden. After a week from the date of this Proclamation, any person found armed within those limits will be liable to the penalty of death. Persons having in their possession any articles whatsoever which formerly belonged to members of the British Embassy are required to bring them forthwith to the British camp. Anyone neglecting this warning will, if found hereafter in possession of any such articles, be subject to the severest penalties.

'Further, all persons who may have in their possession any firearms or ammunition formerly issued to or seized by the Afghan troops, are required to produce them. For every country-made rifle, whether breech or muzzle loading, the sum of Rs. 3 will be given on delivery, and for every rifle of European manufacture Rs. 5. Anyone found hereafter in possession of such weapons will be severely punished. Finally, I notify that I will give a reward of Rs. 50 for the surrender of any person, whether soldier or civilian, concerned in the attack on the British Embassy, or for such information as may lead directly to his capture. A similar sum will be given in the case of any person who may have fought against the British troops since the 3rd September (Shawal) last, and therefore become a rebel against His Highness the Amir. If any such person so surrendered or captured be a captain or subaltern officer of the Afghan army, the reward will be increased to Rs. 75, and if a field officer to Rs. 120.'

The Afghans were evidently much relieved at the leniency of the Proclamation, to which they listened with the greatest attention. When I had finished reading it, I dismissed the assembly, with the exception of the Ministers whom I had decided to make prisoners. To them I explained that I felt it to be my duty to place them under restraint, pending investigation into the part they had taken in the massacre of the Embassy.

The following day I made a formal entry into the city, traversing all its main streets, that the people might understand that it and they were at our mercy. The Cavalry brigade headed the procession; I followed with my staff and escort, and five battalions of Infantry brought up the rear; there were no Artillery, for in some places the streets were so narrow and tortuous that two men could hardly ride abreast.

It was scarcely to be expected the citizens would give us a warm welcome; but they were perfectly respectful, and I hoped the martial and workmanlike appearance of the troops would have a salutary effect.

I now appointed Major-General James Hills, V.C., to be Governor of Kabul for the time being, associating with him the able and respected Mahomedan gentleman, Nawab Ghulam Hussein Khan, as the most likely means of securing for the present order and good government in the city. I further instituted two Courts—one political, consisting of Colonel Macgregor, Surgeon-Major Bellew,* and Mahomed Hyat Khan, a Mahomedan member of the Punjab Commission, and an excellent Persian and Pushtu scholar, to inquire into the complicated circumstances which led to the attack on the Residency, and to ascertain, if possible, how far the Amir and his Ministers were implicated. The other, a military Court, with Brigadier-General Massy as president, for the trial of those Chiefs and soldiers accused of having taken part in the actual massacre.†

Up to this time (the middle of October) communication with India had been kept up by way of the Shutargardan, and I had heard nothing of the approach of the Khyber column. It was so very necessary to open up the Khyber route, in view of early snow on the Shutargardan, that I arranged to send a small force towards Jalalabad, and to move the Shutargardan garrison to Kabul, thus breaking off communication with Kuram.

Colonel Money had beaten off another attack made by the tribesmen on his position, but as they still threatened him in considerable numbers, I despatched Brigadier-General Hugh Gough with some troops to enable him to withdraw. This reinforcement arrived at a most opportune moment, when the augmented tribal combination, imagining that the garrison was completely at its mercy, had sent a message to Money offering to spare their lives if they laid down their arms! So sure were the Afghans of their triumph that they had brought 200 of their women to witness it. On Gough's arrival, Money dispersed the gathering, and his force left the Shutargardan, together with the Head-Quarters and two squadrons of the 9th Lancers, which had been ordered to join me from Sialkot, and afterwards proved a most valuable addition to the Kabul Field Force.

I was sitting in my tent on the morning of the 16th October, when I was startled by a most terrific explosion in the upper part of the Bala Hissar, which was occupied by the 5th Gurkhas, while the 67th Foot were pitched in the garden below. The gunpowder, stored in a detached building, had somehow—we never could discover how—become ignited, and I trembled at the thought of what would be the

* Dr. Bellew was with the brothers Lumsden at Kandahar in 1857.

† My action in endorsing the proceedings of this court, and my treatment of Afghans generally, were so adversely and severely criticized by party newspapers and periodicals, and by members of the Opposition in the House of Commons, that I was called upon for an explanation of my conduct, which was submitted and read in both Houses of Parliament by the Secretary of State for India, Viscount Cranbrook, and the Under-Secretary of State for India, the Hon. E. Stanhope. In the Parliamentary records of February, 1880, can be seen my reply to the accusations, as well as an abstract statement of the executions carried out at Kabul in accordance with the findings of the military Court.

consequences if the main magazine caught fire, which, with its 250 tons of gunpowder, was dangerously near to the scene of the explosion. I at once sent orders to the Gurkhas and the 67th to clear out, and not to wait even to bring away their tents, or anything but their ammunition, and I did not breathe freely till they were all safe on Siah Sang. The results of this disaster, as it was, were bad enough, for Captain Shafto, R.A. (a very promising officer), a private of the 67th, the Subadar-Major of the 5th Gurkhas, and nineteen Natives, most of them soldiers, lost their lives.

A second and more violent explosion took place two hours and a half after the first, but there was no loss of life amongst the troops, though several Afghans were killed at a distance of 400 yards from the fort.

There was given on this occasion a very practical exemplification of the good feeling existing between the European soldiers and the Gurkhas. The 72nd and the 5th Gurkhas had been much associated from the commencement of the campaign, and a spirit of *camaraderie* had sprung up between them, resulting in the Highlanders now coming forward and insisting on making over their greatcoats to the little Gurkhas for the night—a very strong proof of their friendship, for at Kabul in October the nights are bitterly cold.

Two telegrams received about this time caused the greatest gratification throughout the force. One was from the Commander-in-Chief, conveying Her Majesty's expression of 'warm satisfaction' at the conduct of the troops; the other was from the Viceroy, expressing his 'cordial congratulations' and His Excellency's 'high appreciation of the ability with which the action was directed, and the courage with which it was so successfully carried out.' I was informed at the same time by Lord Lytton that, on the recommendation of the Commander-in-Chief, I was given the local rank of Lieutenant-General, to enable me to be placed in command of all the troops in eastern Afghanistan, a force of 20,000 men and 46 guns, in two divisions. The first division remained under my own immediate command, and Major-General R. O. Bright, C.B.,* was appointed to the command of the other. I was, of course very much pleased at this proof of the confidence reposed in me.

CHAPTER LIII.

I HAD given much thought to the question of housing the troops during the winter, which was now fast approaching. Some of the senior officers were in favour of quartering them in the Bala Hissar, as being the place with most prestige attached to it; but the fact that there was

* Afterwards General Sir Robert Bright, G.C.B.

not accommodation in it for the whole force, and that, therefore, the troops would have to be separated, as well as the dangerous proximity of the huge store of gunpowder, which could only be got rid of by degrees, decided me to occupy in preference the partly-fortified cantonment of Sherpur, about a mile north-east of the city, and close to the ruins of the old British entrenchment. It was enclosed on three sides by a high and massive loop-holed wall, and on the fourth by the Bimaru heights, while it possessed the advantage of having within its walls sufficient shelter in long ranges of brick buildings for the British troops, and good hospital accommodation, and there was ample space for the erection of huts for the Native soldiers.

The drawback was that the great extent of its perimeter, more than four and a half miles, made it a very difficult place to defend; but, remembering the grievous results of General Elphinstone's force being scattered in 1841, I thought the advantage of being able to keep my troops together outweighed the disadvantage of having to defend so long a line.

Materials for the Native soldiers' huts were brought from the Bala Hissar, the demolition of which, as an act of retributive justice, I had recommended to the Government of India, as it appeared to me that the destruction of the fortified palace in which the massacre had taken place, and which was the symbol of the power of the Afghans and their boasted military strength, would be a more fitting punishment for treachery and insult than any other we could inflict, and a more lasting memorial of our ability to avenge our countrymen than any we could raise. The tidings that their ancient citadel had been levelled to the ground would, I felt sure, spread throughout the length and breadth of Afghanistan, bearing with them a political significance that could hardly be over-estimated.

I now set to work to collect supplies for the winter. Al *khalsa*, or State grain, we took as our right, the justice of this being recognized both by the Amir and the people, but what was the property of private individuals was purchased at a price the avaricious Afghan could not resist. There had been a good harvest, and supplies were abundant; but the people from the outlying districts were chary of assisting us, for they knew from experience that all who befriended the British would be sure to suffer when we took our departure.

I had repeated complaints brought to me of the harshness and injustice with which those who had shown themselves well disposed towards us were treated by the Amir on his return from signing the Treaty at Gandamak, and most of the Afghans were so afraid of the Amir's vengeance when they should again be left to his tender mercies, that they held aloof, except those who, like Wali Mahomed Khan and his following, were in open opposition to Yakub Khan, and some few who were still smarting from recent injury and oppression.

I was frequently asked by the Afghans, when requiring some service to be rendered, 'Are you going to remain?' Could I have replied in the affirmative, or could I have said that we should continue to exercise sufficient control over the Government of the country to prevent their being punished for helping us, they would have served us willingly. Not that I could flatter myself they altogether liked us, but they would have felt it wise in their own interests to meet our requirements; and, besides, the great mass of the people were heartily sick and tired of a long continuance of oppression and misrule, and were ready to submit (for a time, at least) to any strong and just Government.

Lord Lytton, in the hope of saving from the resentment of the Amir those who had been of use to us in the early part of the war, had expressly stipulated in Article II. of the Gandamak Treaty that 'a full and complete amnesty should be published, absolving all Afghans from any responsibility on account of intercourse with the British Forces during the campaign, and that the Amir should guarantee to protect all persons, of whatever degree, from punishment or molestation on that account.'

But this stipulation was not adhered to. Yakub Khan more than once spoke to me about it, and declared that it was impossible to control the turbulent spirits in Afghanistan without being supreme, and that this amnesty, had it been published, would have tied his hands with regard to those who had proved themselves his enemies.

His neglect to carry out this Article of the treaty added considerably to my difficulty, as will be seen from the following letter from Asmatula Khan, a Ghilzai Chief, to whom I wrote, asking him to meet me at Kabul.

'I received your kind letter on the 8th of Shawal [28th September], and understood its contents, and also those of the enclosed Proclamation to the people of Kabul. I informed all whom I thought fit of the contents of the Proclamation.

'Some time ago I went to Gandamak to Major Cavagnari. He instructed me to obey the orders of the Amir, and made me over to His Highness. When Major Cavagnari returned to India, the Amir's officials confiscated my property, and gave the Chiefship to my cousin* [or enemy], Bakram Khan.

'The oppression I suffered on your account is beyond description. They ruined and disgraced every friend and adherent of mine. On the return of Major Cavagnari to Kabul, I sent my Naib [deputy] to him, who informed him of my state. Major Cavagnari sent a message to me to the effect that I should recover my property by force if I could, otherwise I should go to the hills, and not come to Kabul until I heard from him. In the meantime I received news of the murder of the Envoy, and I am still in the hills.'

---

* In Pushtu the word *tarbur* signifies a cousin to any degree, and is not unfrequently used as 'enemy' the inference being that in Afghanistan a cousin is necessarily an enemy.

The thought of what might be in store for those who were now aiding me troubled me a good deal. No doubt their help was not disinterested, but they were 'friends in need,' and I could not be quite indifferent to their future.

I had several interesting conversations with Yakub Khan, and in discussing with him Sher Ali's reasons for breaking with us, he dwelt on the fact that his father, although he did not get all he wished out of Lord Mayo, was fairly satisfied and content with what had been done for him, but when Saiyad Nur Mahomed returned from Simla in 1873, he became thoroughly disgusted, and at once made overtures to the Russians, with whom constant intercourse had since been kept up.

Yakub Khan's statements were verified by the fact that we found Kabul much more Russian than English. The Afghan Sirdars and officers were arrayed in Russian pattern uniforms, Russian money was found in the treasury, Russian wares were sold in the bazaars, and although the roads leading to Central Asia were certainly no better than those leading to India, Russia had taken more advantage of them than we had to carry on commercial dealings with Afghanistan.*

When I inquired of Yakub Khan what had become of the correspondence which must have been carried on between his father and the Russians, he declared that he had destroyed it all when on his way to Gandamak; nevertheless, a certain number of letters† from Generals Kauffmann and Stoliatoff came into my possession, and a draft of the treaty the latter officer brought from Tashkent was made for me from memory by the man who had copied it for Sher Ali, aided by the

* As I reported at the time, the magnitude of Sher Ali's military preparations was, in my opinion, a fact of peculiar significance. He had raised and equipped with arms of precision sixteen regiments of Cavalry and sixty-eight of Infantry, while his Artillery amounted to nearly 300 guns. Numbers of skilled artisans were constantly employed in the manufacture of rifled cannon and breech-loading small arms. Swords, helmets, uniforms, and other articles of military equipment, were stored in proportionate quantities. Upon the construction of the Sherpur cantonment Sher Ali had expended an astonishing amount of labour and money. The size and cost of this work may be judged from the fact that the main line of rampart, with barrack accommodation, extended to a length of nearly two miles under the western and southern slopes of the Bimaru hills, while the original design was to carry the wall entirely round the hills, a distance of four and a half miles, and the foundations were laid for a considerable portion of this length. All these military preparations must have been going on for some years, and were quite unnecessary, except as a provision for contemplated hostilities with ourselves. Sher Ali had refused during this time to accept the subsidy we had agreed to pay him, and it is difficult to understand how their entire cost could have been met from the Afghan treasury, the annual gross revenue of the country at that time amounting only to about 80 lakhs of rupees.

† These letters, as well as my report to the Secretary to the Government of India in the Foreign Department, with an account of my conversation with Yakub Khan, are given in the Appendix.

Afghan official who was told off to be in attendance on Stoliatoff, and who had frequently read the treaty.

In one of my last conversations with Yakub Khan, he advised me 'not to lose sight of Herat and Turkestan.' On my asking him whether he had any reason to suppose that his representatives in those places meant to give trouble, he replied: 'I cannot say what they may do; but, remember, I have warned you.' He, no doubt, knew more than he told me, and I think it quite possible that he had some inkling of his brother's* (Ayub Khan's) intentions, in regard to Kandahar, and he probably foresaw that Abdur Rahman Khan would appear on the scene from the direction of Turkestan.

I duly received an answer to my telegram regarding the abdication of Yakub Khan, in which I was informed that His Highness's resignation was accepted by Her Majesty's Government, and I was directed to announce the fact to the people of Afghanistan in the following terms:

> 'I, General Roberts, on behalf of the British Government, hereby proclaim that the Amir, having by his own free will abdicated, has left Afghanistan without a Government. In consequence of the shameful outrage upon its Envoy and suite, the British Government has been compelled to occupy by force of arms Kabul, the capital, and to take military possession of other parts of Afghanistan.
>
> 'The British Government now commands that all Afghan authorities, Chiefs, and Sirdars do continue their functions in maintaining order, referring to me whenever necessary.
>
> 'The British Government desire that the people shall be treated with justice and benevolence, and that their religious feelings and customs be respected.
>
> 'The services of such Sirdars and Chiefs as assist in preserving order will be duly recognized, but all disturbers of the peace and persons concerned in attacks upon the British authority will meet with condign punishment.
>
> 'The British Government, after consultation with the principal Sirdars, tribal Chiefs, and others representing the interests and wishes of the various provinces and cities, will declare its will as to the future permanent arrangements to be made for the good government of the people.'

This manifesto was issued on the 28th October, and the same day I informed Yakub Khan that his abdication had been accepted, and acquainted him with the orders passed by the British Government in connexion with this fact.†

Yakub Khan showed no interest either in the Proclamation, a Persian translation of which was read to him, or the Government's decision as to himself, and made no comment beyond a formal '*bisyar khub*' ('very good') and an inclination of the head.

I then told Yakub Khan that, as I was now charged with the govern-

* Sirdar Ayub Khan was Governor of Herat in 1879.

† There were present at the interview, besides myself, Colonel Macgregor, Major Hastings, Surgeon-Major Bellew, Nawab Sir Ghulam Hussein Khan, and Mr. H. M. Durand.

ment of the country, it was necessary that I should take possession of the treasury and all moneys therein. He signified his assent, but demurred to certain sums being considered as public property, contending that they formed part of his father's wealth, and that the British Government might as well take from him his *choga*,* this also having come from the pockets of the people. 'My father was *Padishah*,' he said; 'there was no distinction between public and private money. However,' he went on, 'I have given up the crown, and I am not going to dispute about rupees. You may take all I have, down to my clothes; but the money was my father's, and is mine by right.'

I replied that it was necessary that all money in his possession should be given up, but that his private effects should not be touched; that he would be given a receipt for the money, and that, if the Government of India decided it to be his personal property, it should be returned to him.

This Yakub Khan at first declined to accept, with some show of temper. Eventually he came round, and said, 'Yes, give me a receipt, so that no one may say hereafter that I carried off State money to which I had no right. It can be easily made sure that I have no money when I go.'†

Spite of all his shortcomings, I could not help feeling sorry for the self-deposed Ruler, and before leaving him I explained that he would be treated with the same consideration that had always been accorded to him, that Nawab Sir Ghulam Hussein Khan‡ should have a tent next to his, and that it should be the Nawab's care to look after his comfort in every way, and that I should be glad to see him whenever he wished for an interview. That same day, under instructions, I issued the following further manifesto:

'In my Proclamation of yesterday I announced that His Highness the Amir had of his own free will abdicated, and that for the present the government of Afghanistan would be carried on under my supervision. I now proclaim that, in order to provide for the cost of administration, I have taken possession of the State treasury, and that, until the British Government shall declare its will as to the permanent arrangements to be made for the future good government of the country, the collection of revenue and the expenditure of public money will be regulated by me. All persons concerned

---

* A kind of mantle worn by Afghans.

† As Yakub Khan refused under one pretext or another to deliver up any money, Major Moriarty, the officer in charge of the Kabul Field Force treasure-chest, and Lieutenant Neville Chamberlain, accompanied by an escort, searched a house in the city in which a portion of Yakub Khan's money was said to be concealed. Upwards of eight and a half lakhs of rupees, and a certain amount of jewellery and gold coins, tillas and Russian five-rouble pieces, in all amounting to nine and a half lakhs, were found. This sum was subsequently refunded to the Afghan Government.

‡ The Nawab had been made a K.C.S.I.

are hereby informed that they must obey without dispute or delay such orders as may be issued by me in regard to the payment of taxes and other connected matters; and I give plain warning that anyone resisting or obstructing the execution of such orders will be treated with the utmost severity as an enemy to the British Government.'

CHAPTER LIV.

On the 1st November my Head-Quarters and the 1st division moved into Sherpur, which the Engineers had prepared for winter quarters, and where stores of provisions and forage were assuming satisfactory proportions. The same day Brigadier-General Macpherson left Kabul with a brigade of about 1,800 men and four guns to join hands with the troops which I had lately heard were advancing from the Khyber, and had reached Gandamak. I joined Macpherson the following morning at Butkhak, about eleven miles from Kabul, where our first post towards the Khyber had already been established. It was very important that our communication with India should be by a route good enough for wheeled carriages; I was therefore anxious to see for myself if it were not possible to avoid the Khurd-Kabul Pass, which was said to be very difficult. I had, besides, a strong wish to visit this pass, as being the scene of Sir Robert Sale's fight with the tribesmen in 1841, and of the beginning of the massacre of General Elphinstone's unfortunate troops in 1842.* The Afghan Commander-in-Chief, Daud Shah, and several Ghilzai Chiefs, accompanied me; from them I learned that an easier road did exist, running more to the east, and crossing over the Lataband mountain. Personal inspection of the two lines proved that Daud Shah's estimate of their respective difficulties was correct; the Lataband route was comparatively easy, there was no defile as on the Khurd-Kabul side, and the kotal, 8,000 feet above the sea, was reached by a gradual ascent from Butkhak. However, I found the Khurd-Kabul much less difficult than I had imagined it to be; it might have been made passable for carts, but there was no object in using it, as the Lataband route possessed the additional advantage of being some miles shorter; accordingly I decided upon adopting the latter as the line of communication with India.

Macpherson reported that the country beyond Khurd-Kabul was fairly settled, and that, on the 7th, he had been able to open communication with Brigadier-General Charles Gough, commanding Bright's leading brigade. I was thus again brought into communication with India, and in a position to clear my hospitals of those

* A most thrilling account of Elphinstone's retreat through this pass is given in Kaye's 'History of the War in Afghanistan,' vol. ii., p. 229.

THE LATABAND PASS.

From a photograph by J. Burke.

amongst the sick and wounded who were not progressing favourably, and could not soon be fit for duty.

By this time the Inquiry Commission had completed its difficult task of trying to sift the truth concerning the fate of Cavagnari and his companions from the mass of falsehood with which it was enveloped. The progress had been slow, particularly when examination touched on the part Yakub Khan had played in the tragedy; witnesses were afraid to give evidence openly until they were convinced that he would not be re-established in a position to avenge himself. The whole matter had been gone into most fully, and a careful perusal of the proceedings satisfied me that the Amir could not have been ignorant that an attack on the Residency was contemplated. He may not have foreseen or desired the massacre of the Embassy, but there was no room for doubt as to his having connived at a demonstration against it, which, had it not ended so fatally, might have served him in good stead as a proof of his inability to guarantee the safety of foreigners, and thus obtain the withdrawal of the Mission.

It was impossible, under these circumstances, that Yakub Khan could ever be reinstated as Ruler of Kabul, and his remaining in his present equivocal position was irksome to himself and most embarrassing to me. I therefore recommended that he should be deported to India, to be dealt with as the Government might decide after reviewing the information elicited by the political Court of Inquiry, which to me appeared to tell so weightily against the ex-Amir, that, in my opinion, I was no longer justified in treating as rebels to his authority Afghans who, it was now evident, had only carried out his secret, if not his expressed, wishes when opposing our advance on Kabul. I decided, therefore, to proclaim a free and complete amnesty*

* The amnesty Proclamation ran as follows:

'KABUL,
'12th November, 1879.

'To all whom it may concern. On the 12th October a Proclamation was issued in which I offered a reward for the surrender of any person who had fought against the British troops since the 3rd September, and had thereby become a rebel against the Amir Yakub Khan. I have now received information which tends to show that some, at least, of those who shared in the opposition encountered by the British troops during their advance on Kabul, were led to do so by the belief that the Amir was a prisoner in my camp, and had called upon the soldiery and people of Kabul to rise on his behalf. Such persons, although enemies to the British Government, were not rebels against their own Sovereign, and the great British Government does not seek for vengeance against enemies who no longer resist. It may be that few only of those who took up arms were thus led away by the statements of evil-minded men, but rather than punish the innocent with the guilty, I am willing to believe that all were alike deceived. On behalf of the British Government, therefore, I proclaim a free and complete amnesty to all persons to all persons not concerned, directly or indirectly, in the attack on the Residency, or who were not found hereafter in possession of property belonging to our countrymen or their escort, on the condition that they surrendered their arms and returned to their homes.

At Daud Shah's suggestion, I sent three influential Sirdars to the Logar, Kohistan, and Maidan valleys, to superintend the collection of the amount of forage which was to be levied from those districts; and in order to lessen the consumption at Kabul, I sent away all elephants,* spare bullocks, and sick transport animals. In furtherance of the same object, as soon as Macpherson returned, I sent Baker with a brigade into the Maidan district, about twenty miles from Kabul, on the Ghazni road, where the troops could more easily be fed, as it was the district from which a large proportion of our supplies was expected, and I also despatched to India all time-expired men and invalids who were no longer fit for service.†

Towards the end of November, Mr. Luke, the officer in charge of the telegraph department, who had done admirable work throughout the campaign, reported that communication was established with India. As, however, cutting the telegraph-wires was a favourite amusement of the tribesmen, a heliograph was arranged at suitable stations between Landi Kotal and Kabul, which was worked with fair success to the end of the war. Had we then possessed the more perfect heliographic apparatus which is now available, it would have

---

who have fought against the British troops since the 3rd September, provided that they now give up any arms in their possession and return to their homes. The offer of a reward for the surrender of such persons is now withdrawn, and they will not for the future be molested in any way on account of their opposition to the British advance; but it must be clearly understood that the benefits of this amnesty do not extend to anyone, whether soldier or civilian, who was concerned directly or indirectly in the attack upon the Residency, or who may hereafter be found in possession of any property belonging to members of the Embassy. To such persons no mercy will be shown. Further, I hold out no promise of pardon to those who, well knowing the Amir's position in the British camp, instigated the troops and people of Kabul to take up arms against the British troops. They have been guilty of wilful rebellion against the Amir's authority, and they will be considered and treated as rebels wherever found.'

* There was a slight fall of snow on the 11th November, followed by severe frost, and the elephants were beginning to suffer from the cold. Three of them succumbed on the Lataband Kotal, much to the annoyance of the olfactory nerves of all passers-by. It was impossible to bury the huge carcasses, as the ground was all rock, and there was not wood enough to burn them. So intense was the cold that the ink froze in my pen, and I was obliged to keep my inkstand under my pillow at night.

† This party marched towards India on the 14th November, followed by a second convoy of sickly men on the 27th idem. On this latter date the strength of the 1st and 2nd Divisions, Kabul Field Force, and the Reserve at Peshawar was as follows:

made us, in that land of bright sun, almost independent of the telegraph, so far as connexion with Landi Kotal was concerned.

Hearing that Baker was experiencing difficulty in collecting his supplies, I joined him at Maidan to satisfy myself how matters stood. The headmen in the neighbourhood refused to deliver the *khalsa* grain they had been ordered to furnish, and, assisted by a body of Ghilzais from Ghazni and Wardak, they attacked our Cavalry charged with collecting it, and murdered our agent, Sirdar Mahomed Hussein Khan. For these offences I destroyed the chief *malik's* fort and confiscated his store of grain, after which there was no more trouble, and supplies came in freely. I returned to Kabul, and Baker, with his brigade, followed me on the 1st December.

That same day Yakub Khan was despatched by double marches to India, careful precautions having been taken to prevent his being rescued on the way. When saying good-bye to him, he thanked me warmly for the kindness and consideration he had received, and assured me that he left his wives and children in my hands in the fullest confidence that they would be well treated and cared for.

A week later I sent off the two Sirdars, Yahia Khan and Zakariah Khan, as well as the Wazir, whose guilt had been clearly proved, and whose powerful influence, I had every reason to believe, was being used to stir up the country against us. The Mustaufi I allowed to remain; he had been less prominent than the others in opposing us, and, besides, I had an idea that he might prove useful to me in the administration of the country.

—	British Force.		Native Force.		Total.
	Officers.	Rank & File.	British Officers.	Troops.	
1st Division, at and around Kabul - - - - -	100	2,783	71	5,060	8,014
2nd Division, on the Khyber line - - - - - -	90	2,385	118	8,590	11,183
	190	5,168	189	13,650	19,197
Reserve at Peshawar - -	55	1,952	49	4,654	6,710
	245	7,120	238	18,304	25,907

Total :— 483 British officers.
7,120 British troops.
18.304 Native troops.

Grand total :— 25,907 with 60 guns, 24 with 1st Division, and 36 with 2nd Division and the Reserve.

CHAPTER LV.

The general political situation, as it developed itself in the early part of December, and the causes which appeared to me to have contributed to produce it, may be briefly summarized as follows. After the outbreak in the previous September and the massacre of our Envoy, the advance of the British force was too rapid to give the Afghans, as a nation, time to oppose us. At Charasia, the troops, aided by large numbers of the disaffected townspeople, were conspicuously beaten in the open field; their organization as an armed body was at an end, and their leaders all sought personal safety in flight.

It appears probable that at this period the general expectation amongst the Afghans was that the British Government would exact a heavy retribution from the nation and city, and that, after vengeance had been satisfied, the army would be withdrawn.

Thirty-seven years before, a British massacre had been followed by a temporary occupation of the city of Kabul, and just as the troops of Pollock and Nott, on that occasion, had sacked and destroyed the great bazaar and then retired, so in 1879 the people believed that some signal punishment would again be succeeded by the withdrawal of our troops. Thus a period of doubt and expectation ensued after the battle of Charasia; the Afghans were waiting on events, and the time had not arrived for a general movement.

This pause, however, was marked by certain occurrences which doubtless touched the national pride to the quick, and which were also susceptible of being used by the enemies of the British Government to excite into vivid fanaticism the religious sentiment, which has ever formed a prominent trait in the Afghan character.

The prolonged occupation by foreign troops of the fortified cantonment which had been prepared by the late Amir Sher Ali for his own army; the capture of the large park of Artillery, and of the vast munitions of war, which had raised the military strength of the Afghans to a standard unequalled among Asiatic nations; the destruction of their historic fortress, the residence of their Kings; and, lastly, the deportation to India of their Amir and his principal Ministers, were all circumstances which united to increase to a high pitch the antipathy naturally felt towards a foreign invader.

The temper of the people being in this inflammable condition, it was clear that only disunion and jealousy amongst their Chiefs prevented their combining against us, and that if any impetus could be given to their religious sentiment strong enough to unite the discordant elements in a common cause, a powerful movement would be initiated, having for its object our annihilation or expulsion from their country.

Such an impetus was supplied by the fervent preaching of the aged mulla Mushk-i-Alam,* who denounced the English in every mosque throughout the country. The people were further incited to rise by the appeals of the ladies of Yakub Khan's family to popular sympathy, and bribed to do so by the distribution of the concealed treasure at their command.

The mullas, in short, became masters of the situation, and, having once succeeded in subordinating private quarrels to hatred of the common foe, the movement rapidly assumed the aspect of a religious war. The Afghan successes of 1841-42 were cited as examples of what might happen again, and the people were assured that, if they would only act simultaneously, the small British army in Sherpur would be overwhelmed, and the plunder of our camp would be part of their reward.

From time to time reports reached me of what was going on, and, from the information supplied to me, I gathered that the Afghans intended to gain possession of the city, and, after occupying the numerous forts and villages in the neighbourhood of Sherpur, to surround the cantonment.

It was under the stimulating influences of religious enthusiasm, patriotic and military ardour, the prestige of former success, and the hope of remuneration and plunder, that the Afghans took the field against us early in December.

It was arranged that the forces from the south† should seize the range of hills extending from Charasia to the Shahr-i-Darwaza heights, including the fortifications of the upper Bala Hissar and the high conical peak called the Takht-i-Shah; that those from the north‡ should occupy the Asmai heights and hills to the north of Kabul; and those from the west§ should make direct for the city.

As it was evident to me that these several bodies, when once concentrated at Kabul, would be joined by the thousands in the city, and the inhabitants of the adjoining villages, I determined to try and deal with the advancing forces in detail, and disperse them, if possible, before the concentration could be effected. I had, however, but a very imperfect idea of the extent of the combination, or of the enormous numbers arrayed against us. My intelligence was most defective; neither the nature of the country nor the attitude of the people admitted of extended reconnaissances, and I was almost entirely dependent for information on Afghan sources. Some of the Afghan soldiers in our ranks aided me to the best of their ability, but by the Sirdars, notably Wali Mahomed Khan, I was, either wilfully or from

* Fragrance of the universe.

† Viz., Logar, Zurmat, the Mangal and Jadran districts, and the intervening Ghilzai country.

‡ Kohistan.

§ Maidan and Ghazni.

ignorance, grossly misinformed as to the formidable character of the rising. But that there was serious trouble ahead was plain enough when the conflicting reports had been carefully sifted, and I therefore thought it only prudent to telegraph to General Bright at Jalalabad to push on the Guide Corps, although I was very much averse to augmenting the Sherpur garrison, and thereby increasing the drain on our supplies.

In the meantime immediate action was necessary to carry out my idea of preventing the different sections of the enemy concentrating at Kabul. I accordingly prepared two columns: one under Macpherson, whose orders were to attack the tribesmen coming from the north before they could join those advancing from the west; the other under Baker, who was instructed to place himself across the line by which the enemy would have to retreat when beaten, as I hoped they would be, by Macpherson.

Macpherson* started on the 8th towards Kila Aushar, about three miles from Sherpur, *en route* to Arghandeh. And on the following morning Baker, with a small force,† proceeded to Chihal Dukhteran, giving out that his destination was the Logar valley, and that he would march by Charasia, as I had directed him to make a feint in that direction, and then to turn to the west, and place himself between Arghandeh and Maidan, on the Ghazni road.

To give Baker time to carry out this movement, I halted Macpherson at Kila Aushar on the 9th, whence he sent out two reconnoitring parties —one in the direction of Kohistan, the other, in charge of Lieutenant-Colonel Lockhart,‡ A.Q.M.G., towards Arghandeh.

The intelligence brought in induced me to change my orders to Macpherson. The first party reported that a very considerable force of Kohistanis had collected at Karez-i-Mir, about ten miles north of Kila Aushar, while Lockhart had discovered large numbers of the enemy moving from Arghandeh and Paghman towards Kohistan. Accordingly, I directed Macpherson to attack the Kohistanis, in the hope of being able to disperse them before the people from Ghazni could join them; and, as the part of the country through which he had to move was unsuited to Horse Artillery and Cavalry, I ordered him to leave the mounted portion of his column, except one squadron of Cavalry, at Kila Aushar.

Macpherson made a rapid advance on the morning of the 10th

* Macpherson had with him the following troops: 4 guns R.H.A.; 4 guns Mountain battery; 1 squadron 9th Lancers; 2 squadrons 14th Bengal Lancers; 401 rifles 67th Foot; 509 rifles 3rd Sikhs; 393 rifles 5th Ghurkas.

† Baker's column consisted of: 4 guns Mountain battery; 3 troops 5th Punjab Cavalry; 25 Sappers and Miners; 450 rifles 92nd Highlanders; 450 rifles 5th Punjab Infantry.

‡ Now Lieutenant-General Sir William Lockhart, K.C.B., K.C.S.I.

December, skirting the fringe of low hills which intervenes between Kohistan and the Chardeh valley. He reached the Surkh Kotal—which divides western Kohistan from the Arghandeh valley—without opposition. From this point, however, the Kohistanis were sighted, occupying a position about two miles to his right front, their centre on a steep, conical, isolated hill, at the base of which lay the village of Karez-i-Mir.

Macpherson was now able to obtain a good view of the Paghman and Chardeh valleys on his left and left rear, and the numerous standards planted on the different knolls near the villages of Paghman gave ample evidence of the presence of the enemy discovered by Lockhart the previous day, and showed him that, unless he could quickly succeed in scattering the Kohistanis, he would find himself attacked by an enemy in his rear, in fact, between two fires.

Macpherson made his disposition for an attack with skill and rapidity. Leaving Lieutenant-Colonel Money with one company of the 67th, five companies of the 3rd Sikhs, and two guns, to hold the ridge, he sent the remainder of the Sikhs to harass the enemy's left flank and support the Cavalry, who were ordered to hover about and threaten the line of retreat, while Macpherson himself went forward with the rest of the force.

The Kohistanis retreated rapidly before our skirmishers, and the attacking party, protected by a well-directed fire from Morgan's guns, advanced with such promptitude that the enemy made no attempt to rally until they reached the conical hill, where they made a stubborn resistance. The hill was carried by assault, its defenders were driven off, leaving seven standards on the field, and Morgan, bringing up his Artillery, inflicted severe loss on the flying Kohistanis. On this occasion Major Cook, V.C., of the 5th Gurkhas, was again noticed for his conspicuous gallantry, and Major Griffiths, of the 3rd Sikhs, greatly distinguished himself. Our casualties were one officer (Lieutenant-Colonel Fitz-Hugh) and six men wounded.

It was evident that the tribesmen from the directions of Arghandeh and Paghman intended to ascend the Surkh Kotal, but suddenly they appeared to change their minds, on discovering, probably, that our troops held all the commanding positions and that their allies were in full flight.

Soon after noon on the 10th I received the report of Macpherson's success and the enemy's retirement towards Arghandeh. I at once sent off Lieutenant-Colonel B. Gordon, R.H.A., with orders to intercept them with the Horse Artillery and Cavalry at Aushar; but when I rode over myself later in the day to that place, I was much disappointed to find that Gordon had not been able to give effect to my instructions, as the enemy, on perceiving his troops, dispersed and took shelter in the surrounding villages and on the slopes of the hills.

Macpherson encamped for the night between the Surkh Kotal and Karez-i-Mir, and Baker, who had steadily pursued his march along a very difficult road, halted a short distance west of Maidan and eight miles only from Arghandeh.

To Macpherson I sent orders to march very early the next morning —the 11th—through Paghman towards Arghandeh and in Baker's direction; at the same time I informed him that Massy, whom I had placed in command of the troops at Aushar, would, according to directions from me, leave that place at nine o'clock to co-operate with him, *viâ* the Arghandeh and Ghazni road. That evening Massy came to my room, and I carefully explained to him his part in the next day's proceedings; I told him that he was to advance cautiously and quietly by the road leading directly from the city of Kabul towards Arghandeh, feeling for the enemy; that he was to communicate with Macpherson and act in conformity with that officer's movements; and I impressed upon him that he was on no account to commit himself to an action until Macpherson had engaged the enemy.

Up to this time the combination of tribesmen, which later proved so formidable, had not been effected; Macpherson for the time being had dispersed the Kohistanis and checked the force advancing from Ghazni under the leadership of Mahomed Jan; the Logaris and Ghilzais were merely watching events, and waiting to see how it fared with the Kohistani and Ghazni factions, before committing themselves to hostilities; they had but recently witnessed our successful advance through their country; they knew that their homes and property would be at our mercy should we be victorious, and they were uncertain as to Baker's movements.

On the morning of the 11th December,* therefore, only one section was actually in opposition to us, that led by Mahomed Jan, who during the night of the 10th had taken up a position near the group of villages known as Kila Kazi.

Further, I felt that Mahomed Jan must be disheartened at our recent

* On the 11th December, the troops at and around Kabul amounted to 6,352 men and 20 guns, which were thus disposed:

	Men.		*Guns.*
Baker's column - - - -	1,325	-	4
Macpherson's column - - -	1,492	-	4
Massy's column - - - -	351	-	4
At Sherpur - - - - -	3,184	-	8
	6,352	-	20
There were besides at Butkhak and Lataband	1,343	-	2
And the Guides Corps, which reached Sherpur on the evening of the 11th December	679	-	
Total - - -	8,374	-	22

success, and at his failure to induce the Logaris to join him, and doubtless felt that a movement towards Kabul would expose his left flank to Macpherson, while his rear would be threatened by Baker.

The strength of Baker's and Macpherson's columns had been carefully considered, as well as the routes they were to take. I was thoroughly well acquainted with the ground comprised in the theatre of the proposed operations, having frequently ridden over it during the preceding two months; I was thus able to calculate to a nicety the difficulties each column would have to encounter and the distances they would have to cover, and arrange with the utmost precision the hour at which each Commander should move off to insure a timely junction. So that when I left Sherpur at ten o'clock on the 11th December to take command of Macpherson's and Massy's columns as soon as they should unite, I had no misgivings, and was sanguine that my carefully arranged programme would result in the discomfiture of Mahomed Jan; but the events which followed on that day afforded a striking exemplification of the uncertainty of war, and of how even a very slight divergence from a General's orders may upset plans made with the greatest care and thought, and lead to disastrous results.

Massy could not have clearly understood the part he was meant to take in co-operation with Macpherson, for instead of following the route I had directed him to take, he marched straight across country to the Ghazni road, which brought him face to face with the enemy before he could be joined by Macpherson. In his explanatory report Massy stated that he had been misled by a memorandum* which he received from the Assistant-Adjutant-General after his interview with me (although this memorandum contained nothing contradictory of the orders I had given him); that he understood from it that his business was to reach the Ghazni road at its nearest point in the direction of Arghandeh, and that he thought it better, with a thirty miles' march in prospect, to take the most direct line in order to save his horses, to economize time in a short December day, and to keep as near as he could to the column with which he was to co-operate; further, he stated that he was under the impression there was little likelihood of his meeting with any of the enemy nearer than Arghandeh.

On starting from Aushar Massy detached a troop of the 9th Lancers to communicate with Macpherson. This reduced his column to 247 British and 44 Native Cavalry, with 4 Horse Artillery guns.

As the party moved along the Chardeh valley, a loud beating of

* The memorandum was as follows:

'Brigadier-General Massy will start at eight a.m. to-morrow with a squadron of Cavalry, join the Cavalry and Horse Artillery now out under Colonel Gordon, taking command thereof, and operating towards Arghandeh in conjunction with Brigadier-General Macpherson. The troops to return in the evening.'

drums was heard, and Captain Bloomfield Gough, 9th Lancers, commanding the advance guard, perceived when he had moved to about a mile north of Kila Kazi, that the enemy were occupying hills on both sides of the Ghazni road, about two miles to his left front, and sent back word to that effect. Massy, not believing that the Afghans had collected in any considerable numbers, continued to advance; but he was soon undeceived by the crowds of men and waving standards which shortly came into view moving towards Kila Kazi. He then ordered Major Smith-Wyndham to open fire, but the range, 2,900 yards, being considered by Colonel Gordon, the senior Artillery officer, too far for his six-pounders, after a few rounds the guns were moved across the Ghazni road, and again brought into action at 2,500 yards; as this distance was still found to be too great, they were moved to 2,000 yards. The enemy now pressed forward on Massy's left flank, which was also his line of retreat, and the guns had to be retired about a mile, covered on the right and left by the 9th Lancers and the 14th Bengal Lancers respectively, and followed so closely by the Afghans that when fire was next opened they were only 1,700 yards distant. Four Horse Artillery guns could do nothing against such numbers attacking without any regular formation, and when the leading men came within carbine range, Massy tried to stop them by dismounting thirty of the 9th Lancers; but their fire 'had no appreciable effect.'

It was at this critical moment that I appeared on the scene. Warned by the firing that an engagement was taking place, I galloped across the Chardeh valley as fast as my horse could carry me, and on gaining the open ground beyond Bhagwana, an extraordinary spectacle was presented to my view. An unbroken line, extending for about two miles, and formed of not less than between 9,000 and 10,000 men, was moving rapidly towards me, all on foot save a small body of Cavalry on their left flank—in fact, the greater part of Mahomed Jan's army. To meet this formidable array, instead of Macpherson's and Massy's forces, which I hoped I should have found combined, there were but 4 guns, 198 of the 9th Lancers under Lieutenant-Colonel Cleland, 40 of the 14th Bengal Lancers under Captain Philip Neville, and at some little distance Gough's troop of the 9th Lancers, who were engaged in watching the enemy's Cavalry.

The inequality of the opposing forces was but too painfully apparent. The first glance at the situation showed me the hopelessness of continuing the struggle without Infantry. Up to that moment our casualties had not been many, as Afghans seldom play at long bowls, it being necessary for them to husband their ammunition, and when, as in the present instance, they outnumber their adversaries by forty to one, they universally try to come to close quarters and use their knives.

My first thought was how to secure the best and shortest line of retreat; it lay by Deh-i-Mazang, but in order to use it, the gorge close by that village had to be held; for if the enemy reached it first they would have no difficulty in gaining the heights above Kabul, which would practically place the city at their mercy.

I was very anxious also to prevent any panic or disturbance taking place in Kabul. I therefore told General Hills, who just then opportunely joined me, to gallop to Sherpur, explain to Brigadier-General Hugh Gough, who had been placed in temporary command of that place, how matters stood, and order 200 of the 72nd Highlanders to come to Deh-i-Mazang with the least possible delay. I directed Hills, after having delivered this message, to make for the city, shut the gates, and do all in his power to keep the people quiet, while warning the Kizilbashes* to be prepared to defend their quarter. I then despatched my nephew and A.D.C., Lieutenant John Sherston, to Macpherson to inform him of what had happened, and desire him to push on with the utmost speed.

Having taken these precautionary measures, I sent another A.D.C., Captain Pole Carew, to Brigadier-General Massy to direct him to try and find a way by which the guns could retire in case of a necessity, which appeared to me to be only too probable.

The engagement had now become a question of time. If Mahomed Jan could close with and overwhelm our small force, Kabul would be his; but if, by any possibility, his advance could be retarded until Macpherson should come up, we might hope to retain possession of the city. It was, therefore, to the Afghan leader's interest to press on, while it was to ours to delay him as long as we possibly could.

Pole Carew presently returned with a message from Massy that the enemy were close upon him, and that he could not keep them in check. I desired Pole Carew to go back, order Massy to retire the guns, and cover the movement by a charge of Cavalry.

The charge was led by Lieutenant-Colonel Cleland and Captain Neville, the former of whom fell dangerously wounded; but the ground, terraced for irrigation purposes and intersected by nullas, so impeded our Cavalry that the charge, heroic as it was, made little or no impression upon the overwhelming numbers of the enemy, now flushed with the triumph of having forced our guns to retire. The effort, however, was worthy of the best traditions of our British and Indian Cavalry, and that it failed in its object was no fault of our gallant soldiers. To assist them in their extremity, I ordered two of Smyth-Windham's four guns to halt and come into action while the other two continued to retire, but these had not gone far before they got into such difficult

* Kizilbashes are Persians by nationality and Shiah Mahomedans by religion. They formed the vanguard of Nadir Shah's invading army, and after his death a number of them settled in Kabul where they exercise considerable influence.

ground that one had to be spiked and abandoned in a water-cut, where Smyth-Windham found it when he came up after having fired a few rounds at the fast advancing foe. I now ordered Smyth-Windham to make for the village of Bhagwana with his three remaining guns, as the only chance left of saving them. This he did, and having reached the village, he again opened fire from behind a low wall which enclosed the houses; but the ammunition being nearly expended, and the enemy close at hand, there was nothing for it but to limber up again and continue the retirement through the village. At the further side, however, and forming part of its defences, was a formidable obstacle in the shape of a ditch fully twelve feet deep, narrowing towards the bottom; across this Smyth-Windham tried to take his guns, and the leading horses had just begun to scramble up the further bank, when one of the wheelers stumbled and fell, with the result that the shafts broke and the gun stuck fast, blocking the only point at which there was any possibility of getting the others across.

With a faint hope of saving the guns, I directed Captain Stewart-Mackenzie, who had assumed command of the 9th Lancers on Cleland being disabled, to make a second charge, which he executed with the utmost gallantry,* but to no purpose; and in the meanwhile Smyth-Windham had given the order to unhook and spike the guns.

By this time the enemy were within a few hundred yards of Bhagwana, and the inhabitants had begun to fire at us from the roofs of their houses. I was endeavouring to help some men out of the ditch, when the headman of the village rushed at me with his knife, seeing which, a Mahomedan† of the 1st Bengal Cavalry, who was following me on foot, having just had his horse shot under him, sprang at my assailant, and, seizing him round the waist, threw him to the bottom of the ditch, thereby saving my life.‡

* Stewart-Mackenzie's horse was shot, and fell on him, and he was extricated with the greatest difficulty.

† Mazr Ali was given the order of merit for his brave action, and is now a Native officer in the regiment.

‡ Our Chaplain (Adams), who had accompanied me throughout the day, behaved in this particular place with conspicuous gallantry. Seeing a wounded man of the 9th Lancers staggering towards him, Adams dismounted, and tried to lift the man on to his own charger. Unfortunately, the mare, a very valuable animal, broke loose, and was never seen again. Adams, however, managed to support the Lancer until he was able to make him over to some of his own comrades.

Adams rejoined me in time to assist two more of the 9th who were struggling under their horses at the bottom of the ditch. Without a moment's hesitation, Adams jumped into the ditch. He was an unusually powerful man, and by sheer strength dragged the Lancers clear of their horses. The Afghans meanwhile had reached Bhagwana, and were so close to the ditch that I thought my friend the padre could not possibly escape. I called out to him to look after himself, but he paid no attention to my warnings until

Suddenly the Afghans stayed their advance for a few minutes, thinking, as I afterwards learnt, that our Infantry were in the village —a pause which allowed many of our Cavalry who had lost their horses to escape.*

Directly we had got clear of the village the Cavalry reformed, and retired slowly by alternate squadrons, in a manner which excited my highest admiration, and reflected the greatest credit on the soldierly qualities of Stewart-Mackenzie and Neville. From Bhagwana, Deh-i-Mazang was three miles distant, and it was of vital importance to keep the enemy back in order to give the Highlanders from Sherpur time to reach the gorge.

For a time the Afghans continued to press on as before, but after a while their advance gradually became slower and their numbers somewhat decreased. This change in Mahomed Jan's tactics, it afterwards turned out, was caused by Macpherson's advance guard coming into collision with the rear portion of his army; it was of the greatest advantage to us, as it enabled the 72nd to arrive in time to bar the enemy's passage through the gorge. My relief was great when I beheld them, headed by their eager Commander, Brownlow, doubling through the gap and occupying the village of Deh-i-Mazang and the heights on either side. The Cavalry greeted them with hearty cheers, and the volleys delivered by the Highlanders from the roofs of the houses in the village soon checked the Afghans, some of whom turned back, while others made for Indiki and the slopes of the Takht-i-Shah. For a time, at any rate, their hopes of getting possession of Kabul had been frustrated.

It will be remembered that the orders I sent to Macpherson on the 10th were that he was to march very early the next morning, as Massy with the Horse Artillery and Cavalry would leave Aushar at 9 a.m.,

---

he had pulled the almost exhausted Lancers to the top of the slippery bank. Adams received the Victoria Cross for his conduct on this occasion.

* These men were much impeded by their long boots and their swords dangling between their legs; the sight, indeed, of Cavalry soldiers trying to defend themselves on foot without a firearm confirmed the opinion I had formed during the Mutiny, as to the desirability for the carbine being slung on the man's back when going into action. Lieutenant-Colonel Bushman (Colonel Cleland's successor) curiously enough had brought with him from England a sling which admitted of this being done, and also of the carbine being carried in the bucket on all ordinary occasions. This pattern was adopted, and during the remainder of the campaign the men of the 9th Lancers placed their carbines on their backs whenever the enemy were reported to be in sight. At the same time I authorized the adoption of an arrangement—also brought to my notice by Colonel Bushman—by which the sword was fastened to the saddle instead of round the man's body. This mode of wearing the sword was for some time strenuously opposed in this country, but its utility could not fail to be recognized, and in 1891 an order was issued sanctioning its adoption by all mounted troops.

and that he must join him on the Arghandeh road. Macpherson did not make so early a start as I had intended; from one cause or another, he said, he was not able to leave Karez-i-Mir before eight o'clock. On reaching the Surkh Kotal he observed dense bodies of the enemy hurrying from the Paghman and Arghandeh directions towards Kila Kazi, and he pushed on, hoping to be able to deal with them individually before they had time to concentrate. For the first three miles from the foot of the pass the view was obstructed by a range of hills, and nothing could be seen of the Horse Artillery and Cavalry; but soon after 10 a.m. the booming of guns warned Macpherson that fighting was going on, but he could not tell whether it was Baker's or Massy's troops which were engaged. He was, however, not left long in doubt, for Lieutenant Neville Chamberlain, attached to Macpherson as political officer, and who had gone on with his advance guard, sent back word that he could distinguish British Cavalry charging the Afghans, and as Baker had only Native Cavalry with him, Macpherson knew at once that the action was being fought by Massy. Suddenly the firing ceased, and he was informed that the enemy were advancing on Kabul, and that their vanguard had already reached the belt of orchards and enclosures, on the further fringe of which the smoke from our guns and the charge of our Cavalry had been seen.

Macpherson, feeling that something serious had occurred, called on his men to make a further effort. At 12.30 p.m., less than an hour after we had begun to retire, he reached the ground where the fight had taken place. The dead bodies of our officers and men, stripped and horribly mutilated, proved how fierce had been the struggle, and the dropping shots which came from the fortified villages in the neighbourhood and from the ravines, warned the Brigadier-General that some of the enemy were still in the neighbourhood. But these men, so bold in the confidence of overwhelming numbers when attacking Massy's Cavalry, were not prepared to withstand Macpherson's Infantry; after a brief resistance they broke and fled in confusion, some to Indiki, but the greater number to the shelter of the hills south of Kila Kazi, to which place Macpherson followed them, intending to halt there for the night. This I did not allow him to do, for, seeing the heavy odds we had opposed to us, and that the enemy were already in possession of the Takht-i-Shah, thus being in a position to threaten the Bala Hissar, I sent orders to him to fall back upon Deh-i-Mazang, where he arrived about 7 p.m.

Meanwhile, Macpherson's baggage, with a guard of the 5th Gurkhas, commanded by Major Cook, V.C., was attacked by some Afghans, who had remained concealed in the Paghman villages, and it would probably have fallen into their hands, as the Gurkhas were enormously outnumbered, but for the timely arrival of four companies of the 3rd Sikhs, under Major Griffiths, who had been left by Macpherson to see everything safely down the pass. Cook himself was knocked over and stunned by a blow, while his brother in the 3rd Sikhs received a severe bullet-wound close to his heart.

During the retirement from Bhagwana, Macgregor, my Chief of the Staff, Durand, Badcock, and one or two other staff officers, got separated from me and were presently overtaken by an officer (Captain Gerald Martin), sent by Macpherson to tell Massy he was coming to his assistance as fast as his Infantry could travel; Martin informed Macgregor that as he rode by Bhagwana he had come across our abandoned guns, and that there was no enemy anywhere near them. On hearing this, Macgregor retraced his steps, and, assisted by the staff officers with him and a few Horse Artillerymen and Lancers, and some Gurkhas of Macpherson's baggage guard picked up on the way, he managed to rescue the guns and bring them into Sherpur that night. They had been stripped of all their movable parts, and the ammunition-boxes had been emptied; otherwise they were intact, and were fit for use the next day.

I found assembled at Deh-i-Mazang Wali Mahomed and other Sirdars, who had been watching with considerable anxiety the issue of the fight, for they knew if the Afghans succeeded in their endeavours to enter Kabul, all property belonging to people supposed to be friendly to us would be plundered and their houses destroyed. I severely upbraided these men for having misled me as to the strength and movements of Mahomed Jan's army, and with having failed to fulfil their engagement to keep me in communication with Baker. They declared they had been misinformed themselves, and were powerless in the matter. It was difficult to believe that this was the case, and I was unwillingly forced to the conclusion that not a single Afghan could be trusted, however profuse he might be in his assurances of fidelity, and that we must depend entirely on our own resources for intelligence.

I waited at Deh-i-Mazang until Macpherson arrived, and thus did not get back to Sherpur till after dark. I was gratified on my arrival there to find that Hugh Gough had made every arrangement that could be desired for the defence of the cantonment, and that by his own cool and confident bearing he had kept the troops calm and steady, notwithstanding the untoward appearance of some fugitives from the field of battle, whose only too evident state of alarm might otherwise have caused a panic.

For the safety of Sherpur I never for one moment had the smallest apprehension during that eventful day. It was, I believe, thought by some that if Mahomed Jan, instead of trying for the city, had made for the cantonment, it would have fallen into his hands; but they were altogether wrong, for there were a sufficient number of men within the walls to have prevented such a catastrophe had Mahomed Jan been in a position to make an attack; but this, with Macpherson's brigade immediately in his rear, he could never have dreamt of attempting.

The city of Kabul remained perfectly quiet while all the excitement I have described was going on outside. Hills, with a few Sikhs, patrolled the principal streets, and even when the Afghan standard appeared on the Takht-i-Shah there was no sign of disturbance. Nevertheless, I thought it would be wise to withdraw from the city; I could not tell how long the people would remain well disposed, or whether they would assist us to keep the enemy out. I therefore directed Hills to come away and make over his charge to an influential Kizilbash named Futteh Khan. I also telegraphed to General Bright at Jalalabad to reinforce Gandamak by a sufficient number of troops to hold that post in case it should be necessary to order Brigadier-General Charles Gough, who was then occupying it, to move his brigade nearer to Kabul; for I felt sure that, unless I could succeed in driving Mahomed Jan out of the neighbourhood of Kabul, excitement would certainly spread along my line of communication. I concluded my message to Bright thus: 'If the wire should be cut, consider it a bad sign, and push on to Gandamak, sending Gough's Brigade towards Kabul.'

I could not help feeling somewhat depressed at the turn things had taken. I had no news from Baker, and we had undoubtedly suffered a reverse, which I knew only too well would give confidence to the Afghans, who, from the footing they had now gained on the heights above Kabul, threatened the Bala Hissar, which place, stored as it was with powder and other material of war, I had found it necessary to continue to occupy. Nevertheless, reviewing the incidents of the 11th December, as I have frequently done since, with all the concomitant circumstances deeply impressed on my memory, I have failed to discover that any disposition of my force different from that I made could have had better results, or that what did occur could have been averted by greater forethought or more careful calculation on my part. Two deviations from my programme (which probably at the time appeared unimportant to the Commanders in question) were the principal factors in bringing about the unfortunate occurrences of that day. Had Macpherson marched at 7 a.m. instead of 8, and had Massy followed the route I had arranged for him to take, Mahomed Jan must have fallen into the trap I had prepared for him.

Our casualties on the 11th were—killed, 4 British officers, 16 British and 9 Native rank and file; wounded, 4 British officers, 1 Native officer, 20 British and 10 Native rank and file.

CHAPTER LVI.

On the morning of the 12th I was cheered by hearing that the Guides had arrived during the night under the command of Colonel F. Jenkins —a most welcome reinforcement, for I knew how thoroughly to be depended upon was every man in that distinguished corps.

The first thing now to be done was to endeavour to drive the Afghans from the crest of the Takht-i-Shah; and I directed Macpherson, as soon as his men had breakfasted, to attack the position from Deh-i-Mazang. Just then my mind was considerably relieved by a heliogram from Baker informing me that he was on his way back to Kabul. The message was despatched from near Kila Kazi, within four miles of which place Baker had encamped on the afternoon of the previous day.

Macpherson deputed the task of trying to dislodge the enemy to Lieutenant-Colonel Money, of the 3rd Sikhs, with a detachment consisting of 2 Mountain guns and 560 British and Native Infantry.

It was a most formidable position to attack. The slopes leading up to it were covered with huge masses of jagged rock, intersected by perpendicular cliffs, and its natural great strength was increased by breastworks, and stockades thrown up at different points.

After a gallant and persistent attempt had been made, I ordered the assault to be deferred; for I perceived that the enemy were being reinforced from their rear, and to ensure success without great loss, it would be necessary to attack them in rear as well as in the front. The arrival of Baker's brigade made it possible to do this. I therefore ordered Macpherson to hold the ground of which he had gained possession until Baker could co-operate with him next morning from the Beni Hissar side.

During the night Mahomed Jan, who had been joined by several thousands from Logar and Wardak, occupied the villages situated between Beni Hissar and the Bala Hissar and along the *sang-i-nawishta* road. Baker, who started at 8 a.m. on the 13th,* had, therefore, in the first place, to gain the high ground above these villages, and, while holding the point over-looking Beni Hissar, to wheel to his right and move towards the Takht-i-Shah.

When he had proceeded some little distance, his advance guard reported that large bodies of the enemy were moving up the slope of the ridge from the villages near Beni Hissar. To check this movement, and prevent the already very difficult Afghan position being still further strengthened, Major White, who was in command of the leading

* His force consisted of 4 guns, Field Artillery; 4 Mountain guns; 1 squadron 9th Lancers; 5th Punjab Cavalry; 6 companies 92nd Highlanders; 7 companies Guides; and 300 3rd Sikhs; and subsequently it was strengthened by 150 of the 5th Punjab Infantry.

portion of the attacking party, turned and made for the nearest point on the ridge. It was now a race between the Highlanders and the Afghans as to who should gain the crest of the ridge first. The Artillery came into action at a range of 1,200 yards, and under cover of their fire the 92nd, supported by the Guides, rushed up the steep slopes. They were met by a furious onslaught, and a desperate conflict took place. The leading officer, Lieutenant Forbes, a lad of great promise, was killed, and Colour-Sergeant Drummond fell by his side. For a moment even the brave Highlanders were staggered by the numbers and fury of their antagonists, but only for a moment. Lieutenant Dick Cunyngham* sprang forward to cheer them on, and confidence was restored. With a wild shout the Highlanders threw themselves on the Afghans, and quickly succeeded in driving them down the further side of the ridge.

By this successful movement the enemy's line was cut in two, and while the Cavalry and a party of the 3rd Sikhs prevented their rallying in the direction of Beni Hissar, the 92nd and Guides, protected by the Mountain guns, which had been got on to the ridge, and the Field Artillery from below, advanced towards the Takht-i-Shah. The Afghans disputed every inch of the way, but by 11.30 a.m. White's men had reached the foot of the craggy eminence which formed the enemy's main position. They were here joined by some of the 72nd Highlanders, 3rd Sikhs, and 5th Gurkhas, under the command of Lieutenant-Colonel Money, who had fought their way from the upper Bala Hissar.

A brilliant charge by the combined troops now took place, the two Highlands corps vying with each other for the honour of reaching the summit first. It fell to the 72nd, Colour-Sergeant Yule† of that regiment being the foremost man on the top. The enemy made a most determined stand, and it was only after a severe struggle and heavy loss that they were driven off the heights.

From my position at Sherpur I had the satisfaction of witnessing this success. This satisfaction, however, was short-lived, for almost immediately I received a report from the city that the inhabitants had joined the tribesmen, and that the cantonment was being threatened; indeed, I could see large bodies of armed men emerging from the city and moving towards Siah Sang, whence the road between the Bala Hissar and Sherpur would be commanded.

Having only too evidently lost control over the city, the value of Deh-i-Mazang was gone, so I ordered Macpherson to abandon it and move to the Shahr-i-Darwaza heights, taking with him six companies of the 67th Foot for the protection of the Bala Hissar, to which it was

* Dick Cunyngham received the Victoria Cross for conspicuous gallantry and coolness on this occasion.

† This gallant non-commissioned officer was killed the following day.

desirable to hold on as long as possible. The remainder of his troops I ordered to be sent to Sherpur. To Baker I signalled to leave a party on the Takht-i-Shah under Lieutenant-Colonel Money, and to move himself towards the cantonment with the rest of his troops, driving the enemy off the Siah Sang on the way.

But from his point of vantage on the heights Baker could see, what I could not, that the Afghans had occupied two strongly fortified villages between Siah Sang and the Bala Hissar, from which it was necessary to dislodge them in the first instance, and for this service he detached the 5th Punjab Infantry and a battery of Artillery. It was carried out in a masterly manner by Major Pratt, who soon gained possession of one village. The other, however, was resolutely held, and the Artillery failing to effect a breach, the gates were set on fire; but even then a satisfactory opening was not made, and the place was eventually captured by means of scaling-ladders hastily made of poles tied together with the Native soldiers' turbans.

Baker was now able to turn his attention to Siah Sang, so I despatched the Cavalry under Massy, to act with him when a signal success was achieved. The enemy fought stubbornly, but were at last driven off. The 5th Punjab Cavalry, led by Lieutenant-Colonel Williams and Major Hammond, greatly distinguished themselves, and a grand charge was made by the Guides and 9th Lancers, in which Captain Butson, of the latter regiment, was killed, also the troop Sergeant-Major and 3 men; and Captain Chisholme,* Lieutenant Trower, and 8 men were wounded.

This ended the operations on the 13th. Our losses during the day were: killed, 2 British officers and 12 men; wounded, 2 British officers and 43 men, British and Native.

I was in great hopes that our successes and the heavy losses the enemy had sustained would result in the breaking up of the combination against us; but in case these hopes should not be realized, I decided to do away with some of the smaller posts on the line of communication, and order up more troops. Accordingly, I telegraphed to General Bright to send on Charles Gough's brigade, and I directed the detachment at Butkhak to return to Kabul, and that at Seh Baba to fall back on Lataband. Having great confidence in its Commander, Colonel Hudson, I determined to hold on to Lataband for a time, though by so doing the numbers I might otherwise have had at Sherpur were considerably diminished. Lataband was the most important link in the chain of communication between Kabul and Jalalabad; it was in direct heliographic connexion with Kabul; it had sufficient ammunition and supplies to last over the date on which Gough should arrive at Sherpur, and its being held would be a check

* Notwithstanding that his wound was most severe, Captain Chisholme remained in the saddle, and brought the regiment out of action.

on the Ghilzais, and prevent his encountering any serious opposition. At the same time, I could not disguise from myself that there was a certain amount of risk attached to leaving so small a garrison in this somewhat isolated position.

The night of the 13th passed quietly, but when day dawned on the 14th crowds of armed men, with numerous standards, could be seen occupying a hill on the Kohistan road; and as day advanced they proceeded in vast numbers to the Asmai heights, where they were joined by swarms from the city and the Chardeh valley. It thne became apparent that the combination was much more formidable than I had imagined, and that the numbers of the enemy now in opposition to us were far greater than I had dreamt was possible. Foiled in their attempt to close in upon us from the south and west, the tribesmen had concentrated to the north, and it was evident they were preparing to deliver an attack in great strength from that quarter. I quickly decided to drive the enemy off the Asmai heights, to cut their communication with Kohistan, and to operate towards the north, much as I had operated the previous day to the south of Sherpur.

At 9 a.m. I despatched Brigadier-General Baker to the eastern slope of the Asmai range with the following troops: 4 guns, Field Artillery; 4 guns, Mountain Artillery; 14th Bengal Lancers; 72nd Highlanders (192 rifles); 92nd Highlanders (100 rifles); Guides Infantry (460 rifles); and 5th Punjab Infantry (470 rifles).

Covered by the fire of his Artillery, Baker seized the conical hill which formed the northern boundary of the Aliabad Kotal, thus placing himself on the enemy's line of communication, and preventing them from being reinforced. He then proceeded to attack the Asmai heights, leaving 2 Mountain guns, 64 men of the 72nd, and 60 Guides, under the command of Lieutenant-Colonel W. H. Clarke, to hold the hill.

To aid Baker in his difficult task, I brought four guns into action near the north-west corner of the cantonment, and I signalled to Macpherson to give him every possible assistance. Macpherson at once sent the 67th across the Kabul river to threaten the enemy's left rear; while the marksmen of the regiment and the Mountain guns opened fire from the northern slope of the Bala Hissar heights.

The enemy fought with the greatest obstinacy, but eventually our troops reached the top of the hill, where, on the highest point, a number of *ghazis* had taken their stand, determined to sell their lives dearly.

All this I eagerly watched from my place of observation. There was a fierce struggle, and then, to my intense relief, I saw our men on the topmost pinnacle, and I knew the position was gained.*

* Lance-Corporal George Sellar, of the 72nd Highlanders, was given the Victoria Cross for gallantry on this occasion.

It was now a little past noon, and I was becoming anxious about the party left on the conical hill, as Macpherson had heliographed that very large bodies of Afghans were moving northwards from Indiki, with the intention, apparently, of effecting a junction with the tribesmen who were occupying the hills in the Kohistan direction. I therefore signalled to Baker to leave the 67th in charge of the Asmai heights, and himself return to the lower ridge, giving him my reasons.

Baker at once despatched a detachment of the 5th Punjab Infantry, under Captain Hall, to reinforce Clarke, who I could see might soon be hard pressed, and I sent 200 rifles of the 3rd Sikhs (the only troops available at the moment) to his assistance.

I watched what was taking place on the conical hill through my telescope, and was startled to perceive that the enemy were, unnoticed by him, creeping close up to Clarke's position. I could just see a long Afghan knife appear above the ridge, steadily mounting higher and higher, the bearer of which was being concealed by the contour of the hill, and I knew it was only one of the many weapons which were being carried by our enemies to the attack. The reinforcements were still some distance off, and my heart sank within me, for I felt convinced that after our recent victories the Afghans would never venture to cross the open and attack British soldiers unless an overwhelming superiority of numbers made success appear to them a certainty. Next I heard the boom of guns and the rattle of musketry, and a minute or two later (which, in my anxiety, seemed an eternity to me), I only too plainly saw our men retreating down the hill, closely followed by the enemy. The retirement was being conducted steadily and slowly, but from that moment I realized, what is hard for a British soldier, how much harder for a British commander, to realize, that we were over-matched, and that we could not hold our ground.

Clarke,* as well as every man with him, fought splendidly; the Afghans by force of numbers alone made themselves masters of the position and captured two guns.†

* Clarke never recovered the loss of this post. He and I had been cadets together at Sandhurst, and I often visited him while he was in hospital at Sherpur. He was apparently suffering from no disease, but gradually faded away, and died not long after he reached India.

† General Baker, in his despatch, stated that 'No blame for the loss of these guns is in any way to be attached to the officers and men of No. 2 Mountain Battery. . . . Every credit is due to Captain Swinley, the late Lieutenant Montanaro, and Lieutenant Liddell, and the several Native officers, non-commissioned officers and men composing the gun detachments, for the gallant manner in which they stood to their guns to the last, and it was only on the sudden rush of this overwhelming force of the enemy that they had to retire with the loss of two guns.'

Of the men composing the gun detachments, one was killed and six wounded, and Surgeon-Major Joshua Duke was specially mentioned for his attention to the wounded under heavy fire.

While all that I have described was going on, the enemy began to collect again on Siah Sang, and to make their way round the eastern flank of the cantonment towards Kohistan.

I had sent orders in the morning to Lieutenant-Colonel Williams, who was quartered with his regiment (the 5th Punjab Cavalry) in the King's Garden, between Sherpur and the city, to be on the look-out, and not to allow any of the enemy to pass in that direction. About 1 p.m. some 400 Afghans were observed moving along the left bank of the river: these were met by Captain Vousden of the same regiment, who with one troop was employed in reconnoitring; he most gallantly charged in amongst them with only twelve of his men, the remainder being effectually stopped by a heavy fire opened upon them from behind a low wall. Vousden succeeded in dispersing these heavy odds, and in inflicting severe loss upon them—a very brilliant service, for which he received the Victoria Cross.

My object throughout these operations had been, as I hope I have made clear, to break up the combination by dealing with the enemy in detail, and preventing them getting possession of the city and the Bala Hissar.

Up till noon on the 14th I had no idea of the extraordinary numbers they were able to bring together, and I had no reason to believe that it would be possible for them to cope with disciplined troops; but the manner in which the conical hill had been retaken gave me a more correct idea of their strength and determination, and shook my confidence in the ability of my comparatively small force to resist the ever-increasing hordes, on ground which gave every advantage to numerical superiority. It was a bitter thought that it might be my duty to retire for a time within the defences of Sherpur, a measure which would involve the abandonment of the city and the Bala Hissar, and which I knew, moreover, would give heart to the tribesmen.

I had to decide at once on the course I ought to pursue, for, if I continued to act on the defensive, food and ammunition must be sent before dark to Macpherson's brigade, occupying the hills above the city, and arrangements must be made for Baker's retention of the Asmai heights. I heliographed to Macpherson to inquire the direction in which the enemy were moving, and whether their numbers were still increasing. He replied that large masses were steadily advancing from north, south, and west, and that their numbers were momentarily becoming greater, to which the young officer in charge of the signalling station added, 'The crowds of Afghans in the Chardeh valley remind me of Epsom on the Derby day.'

This decided me; I determined to withdraw from all isolated positions, and concentrate my force at Sherpur, thereby securing the safety of the cantonment and avoiding what had now become a useless sacrifice of life. I only too thoroughly recognized the evils of the measure, but I considered that no other course would be justifiable, and that I must act for the present entirely on the defensive, and wait until the growing confidence of the enemy should afford me a favourable opportunity for attacking them, or until reinforcements could arrive.

The inevitable order reached the two Generals at 2 p.m., and the retirement was begun at once. The Afghans speedily discovered the retrograde movement, and no sooner had each post in its turn been evacuated than it was occupied by the enemy, who pressed our troops the whole way back to the cantonment. There was hand-to-hand fighting, and many splendid acts of courage were performed, Major Hammond, of the Guides, earning the Victoria Cross; but throughout there was no hurry or confusion, all was conducted with admirable coolness and skill, and shortly after dark the troops and baggage were safe inside Sherpur. That night the Afghans occupied the city and the Bala Hissar.

It is comparatively easy for a small body of well-trained soldiers, such as those of which the army in India is composed, to act on the offensive against Asiatics, however powerful they may be in point of numbers. There is something in the determined advance of a compact, disciplined body of troops which they can seldom resist. But a retirement is a different matter. They become full of confidence and valour the moment they see any signs of their opponents being unable to resist them, and if there is the smallest symptom of unsteadiness, wavering, or confusion, a disaster is certain to occur. It may be imagined, therefore, with what intense anxiety I watched for hours the withdrawal. The ground was all in favour of the Afghans, who, unimpeded by impedimenta of any kind, swarmed down upon the mere handful of men retreating before them, shouting cries of victory and brandishing their long knives; but our brave men, inspired by the undaunted bearing of their officers, were absolutely steady. They took up position after position with perfect coolness; every movement was carried out with as much precision as if they were manœuvring on an ordinary field-day; and the killed and wounded were brought away without the slightest hurry or confusion. In fact, the whole of the hazardous operation was most successfully and admirably carried out; and as each regiment and detachment filed through the Head-Quarters gateway I was able to offer my warm congratulations and heartfelt thanks to my gallant comrades.

Our losses during the day were: 19 killed, including Captain Spens and Lieutenant Gaisford, 72nd Highlanders, and 88 wounded, amongst whom were Captain Gordon, 92nd Highlanders, Lieutenant Egerton, 72nd Highlanders, and Captain Battye, of the Guides.*

* The same officer who so gallantly met his death during the recent Chitral campaign, while commanding the regiment of which he was so justly proud,

CHAPTER LVII.

THE moment the gates were closed I telegraphed the result of the day's operations to the Viceroy and Commander-in-Chief, for I knew that the enemy's first thought would be to stop communication with India by cutting the telegraph-wires. I reported that I had ordered Brigadier-General Charles Gough's brigade to push on from Gandamak as fast as possible; and I recommended that General Bright should have more troops sent up to him, to allow of his keeping open the route to Kabul, and of his reinforcing me should I find it impossible to clear the country with the force at my disposal. It was a satisfaction to be able to assure the authorities in these, to me, otherwise painful telegrams, that there was no cause for anxiety as to the safety of the troops; that sufficient supplies for men were stored in Sherpur for nearly four months, and for animals for six weeks; that there was abundance of firewood, medicines, and hospital comforts, and sufficient ammunition both for guns and rifles to admit of an active resistance being carried on for between three and four months.

It was fortunate there was no lack of provisions, for our numbers were considerably increased by the presence of Wali Mahomed Khan and many other Sirdars, who begged for shelter in Sherpur, on the plea that their lives would not be safe were they to return to the city. They were far from being welcome guests, for I could not trust them; ostensibly, however, they were our friends, and I could not refuse their petition. I therefore admitted them, on condition that each Sirdar should only be accompanied by a specified number of followers.

The stormy occurrences of the 14th were succeeded by a period of comparative calm, during which the entrenchments were strengthened, and the heavy guns found in the Kabul arsenal were prepared for service.

The great drawback to Sherpur, as I have already mentioned, was its extent and the impossibility of reducing the line of defences owing to the length of the Bimaru ridge. The cantonment was in the form of a parallelogram, with the Bimaru heights running along, and protecting, the northern side. Between this range and the hills, which form the southern boundary of Kohistan, lay a lake, or rather *jhil*, a barrier between which and the commanding Bimaru ridge no enemy would dare to advance.

The massive wall on the south and west faces was twenty feet high, covered at a distance of thirty feet by a lower wall fifteen feet high; the southern wall was pierced at intervals of about 700 yards by gate-

---

and in which two brave brothers had been killed before him—Quinton at Delhi, and Wigram during the first phase of the Afghan war.

ways, three in number, protected by lofty circular bastions, and between these and at the four corners were a series of low bastions which gave an admirable flanking fire. The wall on the western flank was of similar construction, but had been considerably damaged at the northern end, evidently by an explosion of gunpowder.

The weak part of our defence was on the eastern face, where the wall, which had never been completed, was only seven feet high, and did not extend for more than 700 yards from the south-east corner; the line then ran to the north-west, and, skirting the village of Bimaru, ended at the foot of the ridge.

From this description it will be seen that, though the perimeter* of Sherpur was rather too large for a force of 7,000 effective men to defend, its powers of resistance, both natural and artificial, were considerable. It was absolutely necessary to hold the Bimaru ridge for its entire length; to have given up any part of it would have been to repeat the mistake which proved so disastrous to Elphinstone's army in 1841. In fact, the Bimaru heights were at once the strength and the weakness of the position. So long as we could hold the heights we were safe from attack from the north; but if we had been forced, either from the weakness of our own garrison, or from any other cause, to relinquish the command of this natural barrier, the whole of the cantonment must have lain open to the enemy, and must forthwith have become untenable.

The question of how Sherpur could best be defended had been carefully considered by a committee,† assembled by my orders soon after our arrival in Kabul; and a scheme had been drawn up detailing the measures which should be adopted in case of attack.

On the recommendation of this committee six towers had been constructed on the Bimaru heights, and shelter trenches and gunpits made at the points where Infantry and Artillery fire could be used with the greatest advantage. These trenches were now deepened and prolonged, so as to form one continuous line of defence, protected by an abattis; and the defences in the depression between the heights were so arranged that fire could be brought to bear on an enemy advancing from the north. To strengthen the north-east corner, a battery was thrown up on the slope of the ridge, which was connected with the tower above and the village below. The village itself was loop-holed, the outlying buildings to the front made defensible, and the open space to the north-east secured by abattis and wire entanglements. The Native Field Hospital was strengthened in like manner, and sand-bag parapets were piled upon the roof, which was somewhat exposed.

* Four and a half miles.

† The committee consisted of Brigadier-General T. D. Baker, Lieutenant Colonel Æ. Perkins, commanding Royal Engineers, and Lieutenant-Colonel B. Gordon, commanding Royal Artillery.

The unfinished wall on the eastern face was raised by logs of wood, and abattis and wire entanglements were placed in front. In the open space lying between the Bimaru ridge and the north-west circular bastion, a defence on the *laager* system was constructed out of gun-carriages and limbers captured from the enemy; while the village of Ghulam Hasan Khan, which formed an excellent flanking defence along the northern and western faces, was held as an independent post.

I divided the whole of the defences into five sections, under the superintendence of five different commanders: Brigadier-General Macpherson, Colonel Jenkins, Brigadier-General Hugh Gough, Major-General Hills, and Colonel Brownlow. Brigadier-General Massy was given the centre of the cantonment, where were collected the forage and firewood; and Brigadier-General Baker commanded the reserve, which was formed up at the depression in the Bimaru heights mentioned above, that he might be able to move rapidly to either end of the ridge, the weakest points in our defences.

The several sections were connected with each other and with my Head-Quarters by a telegraph-wire, and visual signalling was established at all important points.

In my arrangements for the defence of Sherpur I relied to a great extent on the advice of my accomplished Chief Engineer, Colonel Æneas Perkins, and it was mainly owing to him, and to the exertions of his competent staff, that the work was carried on as rapidly and satisfactorily as it was.

During these days of preparation the enemy remained comparatively inactive, being chiefly employed in looting the city and emptying the Amir's arsenal. The gunpowder had been destroyed as far as possible; but a great deal still remained, and many tons of it were carried off by the army of Mahomed Jan, who had now become the practical leader of the Afghan combination, and had lately proclaimed Yakub Khan's eldest son, Musa Khan, Amir.

On the afternoon of the 16th I received the welcome news that Colonel Hudson had successfully resisted an attack on his position by the Ghilzais—welcome because I could now feel assured that Lataband could be depended upon to hold its own.

For the next five days nothing of much importance was done on either side. The enemy took up positions daily in the neighbouring forts and gardens, causing a few casualties, and some of our troops moved out to dislodge them from those places from which they could specially annoy us. I destroyed some of the forts, and removed other cover in the immediate vicinity of the walls; but I did not undertake any large sorties, for to have attempted to drive the enemy out of the outlying posts, which I could not then have held, would have been a useless waste of strength.

THE LAAGER AND ABATTIS NORTH-WEST CORNER, SHERPUR, DECEMBER 23, 1879.

From a photograph by J. Burke.

My chief trouble at this time was the presence of the Afghan Sirdars within the cantonment. I had good reason to believe that some of them, though full of protestations of friendship, had been in communication with Mahomed Jan, the high-priest Mushk-i-Alam and other Afghan leaders, so that I felt sure that neither they nor their followers were to be depended upon. I was also somewhat anxious about the Pathan soldiers in our ranks, a feeling which I was unwilling to acknowledge even to myself, for they had hitherto behaved with marked loyalty, and done splendid service; but they were now being exposed to a most severe trial, in that they were, as I knew, being constantly appealed to by their co-religionists to join in the *jahad* against us, and bitterly reproached for serving their infidel masters. Whether they would be strong enough to resist such appeals, it was impossible to tell; but it would have been most unwise, as well as most painful to me, to show the slightest suspicion of these fine soldiers. It happened that the Corps of Guides and 5th Punjab Infantry, which had of all regiments the largest number of Mahomedans amongst them, were located at the two extremities of the Bimaru range, the points most likely to be attacked; to have made any change in the disposition would have been to show that they were suspected, so I determined (after taking their commanding officers, Colonels Jenkins and McQueen, into my confidence) to leave them where they were, and merely to strengthen each post by a couple of companies of Highlanders.

I was also considerably exercised about the safety of the large stacks of firewood, grain, and forage, for if anything had happened to them we could not have continued to hold Sherpur. There were not enough British soldiers to furnish guards for these stacks, so I was obliged to have them watched for a time by officers; an opportune fall of snow, however, on the night of the 18th, rendered incendiarism impossible.

One other extremely unpleasant precaution I felt it my duty to take was the placing of Daud Shah, Yakub Khan's Commander-in-Chief, under arrest. I liked the man, and he had mixed freely with us all for more than two months. He was not, however, absolutely above suspicion: some of his near relatives were the most prominent amongst our enemies; and I had been struck by a change in his manner towards me of late. In trusting him to the extent I had done, I acted against the opinion of almost everyone about me, and now that I had a doubt myself, I felt I was not justified in leaving him at liberty, for if he were disposed to make use of his opportunities to our disadvantage, his unrestrained freedom of movement and observation would be certainly a source of great danger.

For three or four days cloudy weather prevented heliograph communication with Lataband, and messengers sent by Hudson had failed to reach Sherpur, so that we were without any news from the outer world; but on the afternoon of the 18th I received a letter from Brigadier-General Charles Gough, conveying the disappointing intelligence that he had only got as far as Jagdalak, twenty-one miles from Gandamak, and that he did not consider himself strong enough to advance on Kabul.

Gough no doubt felt himself in an awkward position. The line to his rear was weakly held, the telegraph-wire on both sides of him was cut, his rear guard had been attacked near Jagdalak, there was a considerable collection of men on the hills to his front, and, as he reported, 'the whole country was up.' Moreover, Major-General Bright, under whom Gough was immediately serving, shared his opinion that it would be wiser for him to wait until reinforcements came up from the rear.

Gough, however, had with him 4 Mountain guns and 125 Artillerymen, 73 Sappers and Miners, 222 Native Cavalry, 487 British Infantry, and 474 Gurkhas; in all, 1,381 men, besides 36 officers—not a very large force, but composed of excellent material, and large enough, I considered, augmented, as it would be, by the Lataband detachment, to move safely on Kabul. I had no hesitation, therefore, in sending Gough peremptory orders to advance without delay, thus relieving him of all responsibility in the event of anything unexpected occurring.

Hudson, at Lataband, as has already been recorded, was only victualled until the 23rd, before which date I had calculated that Gough would surely have relieved the garrison and brought the troops away. But now all was uncertain, and it was incumbent upon me to send them food. The difficulty as to how to get supplies to Lataband was solved by some Hazaras, who had been working in our camp for several weeks, volunteering to convey what was necessary, and it was arranged that the provisions should be sent with two parties, one on the 19th, the other on the 20th. The first got through safely, but the second almost entirely fell into the hands of the enemy.

On the 21st a heliogram from Hudson informed me that Gough's brigade was expected the next day; but as it had been found necessary to drop his Cavalry at the several posts he passed on the way for their better protection, I deemed it expedient to send him the 12th Bengal Cavalry, for he had to pass through some fairly open country near Butkhak, where they might possibly be of use to him. Accordingly, they started at 3 a.m. on the 22nd, with instructions to halt at Butkhak should that post be unoccupied, otherwise to push on to Lataband.

Finding the former place in possession of the Afghans, Major Green, who was in command of the regiment, made for the further post, where he arrived with the loss of only three men killed and three wounded.

It was not easy to get reliable information as to the movements or intentions of the enemy while we were surrounded in Sherpur; but from spies who managed to pass to and from the city under cover of night, I gathered that plans were being made to attack us.

It was not, however, until the 21st that there were any very great signs of activity. On that and the following day the several posts to the east of the cantonment were occupied preparatory to an attack from that quarter; and I was told that numbers of scaling-ladders were being constructed. This looked like business. Next, information was brought in that, in all the mosques, mullas were making frantic appeals to the people to unite in one final effort to exterminate the infidel; and that the aged Mushk-i-Alam was doing all in his power to fan the flame of fanaticism, promising to light with his own hand at dawn on the 23rd (the last day of the *Moharram*, when religious exaltation amongst Mahomedans is at its height) the beacon-fire which was to be the signal for assault.

The night of the 22nd was undisturbed, save by the songs and cries of the Afghans outside the walls, but just before day the flames of the signal-fire, shooting upwards from the topmost crag of the Asmai range, were painly to be seen, followed on the instant by a burst of firing.

Our troops were already under arms and at their posts, waiting for the assault, which commenced with heavy firing against the eastern and southern faces. The most determined attack was directed against the two sections commanded by Brigadier-General Hugh Gough and Colonel Jenkins, who by their able dispositions proved themselves worthy of the confidence I had reposed in them.

It was too dark at first to see anything in front of the walls, and orders were given to reserve fire until the advancing masses of the assailants could be clearly made out. Gough's Mountain guns, under Lieutenant Shirres, then fired star-shells, which disclosed the attacking force up to a thousand yards off. The 28th Punjab Infantry were the first to open fire; then the Guides, the 67th. and 92nd, each in their turn, greeted by their volleys the *ghazis* who approached close to the walls. Guns from every battery opened on the foe moving forward to the attack, and from 7 to 10 a.m. the fight was carried on. Repeated attempts were made to scale the south-eastern wall, and many times the enemy got up as far as the abattis, but were repulsed, heaps of dead marking the spots where these attempts had been most persistent.*

* A curious exemplification of the passive courage and indifference to danger of some Natives was the behaviour of an old Mahomedan servant of mine. At this juncture, just at the time when the fight was hottest, and I was receiving reports every few seconds from the officers commanding the several posts, Eli Bux (a brother of the man who had been with me throughout the Mutiny) whispered in my ear that my bath was ready. He was quite

Soon after 10 a.m. there was a slight lull in the fighting, leading us to believe that the Afghans were recoiling before the breechloaders. An hour later, however, the assault grew hot as ever, and finding we could not drive the enemy back by any fire which could be brought against them from the defences, I resolved to attack them in flank. Accordingly, I directed Major Craster, with four Field Artillery guns, and Lieutenant-Colonel Williams, with the 5th Punjab Cavalry, to move out over the hollow in the Bimaru range and open fire on a body of the enemy collected in and around the village of Kurja Kila. This fire had the desired effect; the Afghans wavered and broke.

From that moment the attacking force appeared to lose heart, the assault was no longer prosecuted with the same vigour, and by 1 p.m. it had ceased altogether, and the enemy were in full flight.

This was the Cavalry's opportunity. I ordered Massy to follow in pursuit with every available man, and before nightfall all the open ground in the neighbourhood of Sherpur was cleared of the enemy. Simultaneously with the movement of the Cavalry, a party was despatched to destroy some villages near the southern wall which had caused us much trouble, and whence it was necessary the enemy should be driven, to facilitate the entrance of Brigadier-General Charles Gough the next day, for that officer had arrived with his brigade within about six miles of Sherpur, where I could see his tents, and gathered from the fact of his pitching them that he meant to halt there for the night. The villages were found to be occupied by *ghazis*, who refused to surrender, preferring to remain and perish in the buildings, which were then blown up. Two gallant Engineer officers (Captain Dundas, V.C., and Lieutenant C. Nugent) were most unfortunately killed in carrying out this duty.

The relief I felt when I had gathered my force inside the walls of Sherpur on the evening of the 14th December was small compared to that which I experienced on the morning of the 24th, when I realized that not only had the assault been abandoned, but that the great tribal combination had dissolved, and that not a man of the many thousands who had been opposed to us the previous day remained in any of the villages, or on the surrounding hills. It was difficult to form an accurate estimate of the numbers opposed to us. As the Contingent from the more distant districts advanced, they received accessions from every place they passed, and as they neared Kabul they were joined by the inhabitants of the numerous villages, and by the disaffected in the city. It was calculated by those best able to judge that the combined forces exceeded 100,000, and I myself do not think that an excessive computation.

---

unmoved by the din and shots, and was carrying on his ordinary duties as if nothing at all unusual was occurring.

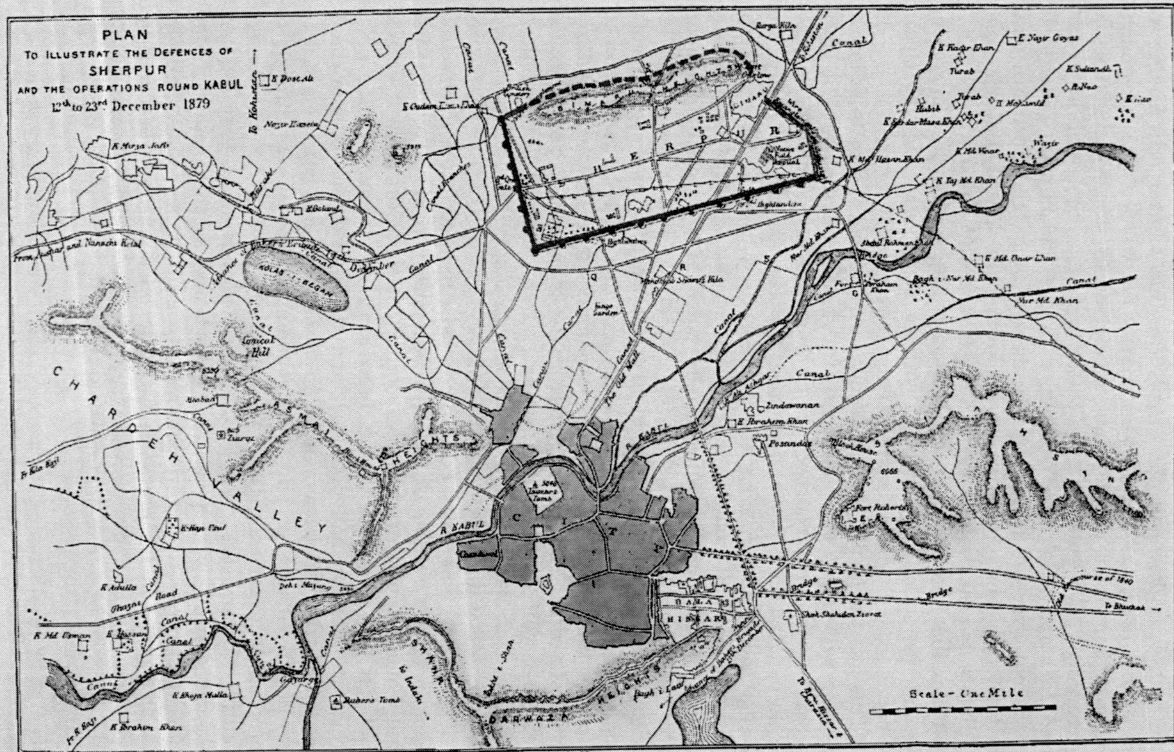
PLAN
TO ILLUSTRATE THE DEFENCES OF
SHERPUR
AND THE OPERATIONS ROUND KABUL
12th to 23rd December 1879
SHERPUR
CITY
BALA HISSAR
R. KABUL
CHARDEH VALLEY
ASMAI HEIGHTS
SHER DARWAZA HEIGHTS
KOLAS I BEGAM
Canal
Conical Hill
Siah Sang
Fort Roberts
Scale - One Mile
To Kohistan
To Bhutkak
Deh i Mazung
Ghazni Road
Babers Tomb
To Indaki
K. Md. Usman
K. Brahim Khan
K. Abdulla
Pusandas
Zindawanan
K. Ibrahim Khan
Bagh i Nur Md. Khan
K. Tej Md. Khan
K. Md. Hasan Khan
K. Nazir Gayas
K. Sultandil
Wazir
Bemaru
Kila

Our casualties between the 15th and 23rd were remarkably few: 2 officers, 9 men, and 7 followers killed, and 5 officers, 41 men, and 22 followers wounded; while the enemy lost not less than 3,000.

I think I had great reason to be proud of my force. All night and every night, the ground covered with snow and the thermometer marking sixteen degrees of frost, officers and men were at their posts, and each day every available man had to be hard at work strengthening the defences. Native and European soldiers alike bore the hardships and exposure with the utmost cheerfulness, and in perfect confidence that, when the assault should take place, victory would be ours.

Early on the 24th the fort of Mahomed Sharif was occupied, and a force moved out to escort Charles Gough's brigade into Sherpur, a precaution which, however, was hardly necessary, as there was no enemy to be seen.

I next set to work to re-open communication with India. Butkhak was re-occupied, and the relaying of the telegraph was taken in hand. General Hills resumed his position as military Governor of Kabul; the dispensary and hospital were re-established in the city under the energetic and intelligent guidance of Surgeon-Captain Owen;* and in the hope of reassuring the people, I issued the following Proclamation:

'At the instigation of some seditious men, the ignorant people, generally not considering the result, raised a rebellion. Now many of the insurgents have received their reward, and as subjects are a trust from God, the British Government, which is just and merciful, as well as strong, has forgiven their guilt. It is now proclaimed that all who come in without delay will be pardoned, excepting only Mahomed Jan of Wardak, Mir Bacha of Kohistan, Samandar Khan of Logar, Ghulam Hyder of Chardeh, and the murderers of Sirdar Mahomed Hassan Khan. Come and make your submission without fear, of whatsoever tribe you may be. You can then remain in your houses in comfort and safety, and no harm will befall you. The British Government has no enmity towards the people. Anyone who rebels again will, of course, be punished. This condition is necessary. But all who come in without delay need have no fear or suspicion. The British Government speaks only that which is in its heart.'

The effect of this Proclamation was most satisfactory: the city and the surrounding country quieted rapidly, shops were re-opened, and before the close of the year the bazaars were as densely thronged as ever. Most of the principal men of Logar and Kohistan came to pay their respects to me; they were treated with due consideration, and the political officers did all they could to find out what they really wanted,

* This hospital was admirably managed, and was attended by a large number of patients, half of whom were women. The disease most prevalent in Kabul was ophthalmia, caused by dust, dirt, and exposure, while cataract and other affections of the eye were very common. Dr. Owen, amongst his other many qualifications, excelled as an oculist, and his marvellous cures attracted sufferers from all parts of Afghanistan.

so that some basis of an arrangement for the peaceful administration of the country might be arrived at.

While taking these measures, which I thought would create confidence in our clemency and justice, I endeavoured in other ways to prevent a repetition of further serious troubles. Snow was still deep on the ground, but I did not let it prevent my sending General Baker to destroy a fort about twenty miles off, where dwelt an influential *malik*, who was one of the chief ringleaders in the revolt. All walled enclosures within 1,000 yards of the cantonment were razed to the ground, roads fit for guns were made all round the outside walls and towards the several gates of the city and Siah Sang, while two bridges, strong enough for Artillery to pass over, were thrown across the Kabul River.

The increased numbers to be accommodated on the arrival of Gough's brigade necessitated the re-occupation of the Bala Hissar, the defences of which were reconstructed so as to give a continuous line of fire, and admit of free circulation round the walls; roads were made through the lower Bala Hissar, and redoubts and towers were built on the Shahr-i-Darwaza range.

A strong fort—Fort Roberts—was constructed on the south-west point of Siah Sang, which commanded the Bala Hissar and the city; a smaller one was built at the crossing of the river; and as these two forts were not within sight of each other, a tower to connect them was constructed at the north-west extremity of Siah Sang.

Sherpur was thus made safe; but for the absolute protection of the city against an enemy operating from the Chardeh direction, a third fort was erected on the Asmai heights, which completed a formidable line of defences most skilfully carried out by Colonel Perkins and his staff.

CHAPTER LVIII.

THE outlook in Afghanistan on the 1st January, 1880, was fairly satisfactory; the tidings of the defeat and dispersion of the tribesmen had spread far and wide, and had apparently had the effect of tranquillizing the country even in remote Kandahar, where the people had been greatly excited by the news of our retiring from Sherpur, and by the exaggerated reports of their countrymen's success. No complications now existed anywhere, and preparations were commenced for Sir Donald Stewart's force in southern Afghanistan to move towards Ghazni, in anticipation of the carrying out of a complete and connected scheme* for the pacification of the country, and an early withdrawal

* In reply to a reference made to me on the subject, I represented that, before operations could be undertaken on so extensive a scale as was proposed,

from northern Afghanistan. No withdrawal, however, would be possible until durable foundations had been laid for the future safety of the Indian frontier, and reliable guarantees given for the continued good behaviour of India's Afghan neighbours.

The two questions, therefore, which chiefly exercised the minds of people in authority, both in England and in India, with regard to Afghan affairs were, What was to be done with Afghanistan now we had got it? and, Who could be set up as Ruler with any chance of being able to hold his own?

The second question depended a good deal on the decision which might be arrived at with regard to the first, for the selection of a Ruler could hardly be considered until it had been determined whether the several provinces of Afghanistan were to be again formed into one kingdom, or whether the political scheme for the future government of the country should be based on the separation of the several States.

I myself had come to the conclusion, after much deliberation and anxious thought, that the latter course was the least dangerous for us to adopt. Disintegration had been the normal condition of Afghanistan, except for a short period which ended as far back as 1818. Dost Mahomed was the first since that time to attempt its unification, and it took him (the strongest Amir of the century) eight years after his restoration to establish his supremacy over Afghan-Turkestan, fourteen years before Kandahar acknowledged his authority, and twenty-one years ere he got possession of Herat, a consummation which was achieved only just before his death. His successor, Sher Ali, was five years making himself master of Afghanistan, and he could never have attained that position but for the material assistance he received from us. I felt it would be in the future as it had been in the past, and that there would always be the danger of a Ruler, made supreme by the aid of our money and our arms, turning against us for some supposed griev-

---

it would be necessary to reinforce the Kabul garrison and the several posts on the Kyber line by:

One battery of Horse or Field Artillery.
One Heavy battery.
One Mountain battery.
A detachment of Garrison Artillery.
A brigade of Cavalry.
Three companies of Sappers and Miners.
Two regiments of British Infantry.
Six regiments of Native Infantry.
Drafts sufficient to raise each Infantry regiment at
Kabul to 800 men.

This was agreed to; the reinforcements were sent up by degrees, and a second division was formed at Kabul, to the command of which Major-General J. Ross,[1] C.B., was appointed.

[1] Now General Sir John Ross, G.C.B.

ance, or at the instigation of a foreign Power, as had happened with Sher Ali. A strong, united Afghanistan was very desirable, no doubt, could we be certain that its interests and ours would always remain identical; but, in addition to the chance of its strength and unity being used against us, there was the certainty that, even if the man we might choose as Amir were to remain perfectly loyal, at his death Afghan history would repeat itself; the succession to the throne would be disputed, and the unification would have to begin all over again. For these reasons I had no hesitation in giving it as my opinion that Afghanistan should be disintegrated, and that we should not again attempt to place the whole country under any one Sovereign.

My views must have commended themselves to the Government of India, for in their despatch to the Secretary of State, dated 7th January, 1880, they indicated them as the line of policy they proposed to adopt in pursuance of the object they had at heart, viz., the safety of the Indian Empire and the tranquillity of its northern frontier; and in the communication to myself, conveying their idea of the general principles upon which the permanent settlement of Afghanistan should be based, the Foreign Secretary wrote that all arrangements for the establishment of a durable Government at Kabul depended on the selection of a suitable Ruler for that province; and that, as it was essential to clear away any apprehension that the British Government contemplated territorial annexation, which might be caused by a prolonged interregnum, it would be very advantageous if one of the principal Sirdars, qualified by his family connexions, his local influence, and his personal following, could be selected as the Ruler of the Kabul State.

There was another very strong reason why the Government of India should wish to find some one to whom the administration of the country could safely be made over. The first warning notes of a General Election were heard in India early in January. Afghan affairs were being made a party question, and the policy of the Beaconsfield Government with regard to them was being severely and adversely criticized. Lord Lytton was, therefore, most anxious that a definite conclusion should be arrived at as to the administration of Afghanistan, and a period put to our occupation of the northern province before the meeting of Parliament should take place.

The difficulty was to find the right man. Abdur Rahman, who I had reason to believe would be acceptable to the army, was far away, I could not find out where, and I could think of no one else at all suitable. Under the circumstances, I deemed it advisable to open negotiations with the several leaders of the late combination against us, who were congregated at Ghazni, and had with them the young Heir-apparent, Musa Khan. In the middle of January I had received two communications from these people, one ostensibly written by

Musa Khan himself, the other signed by seventy of the most influential chiefs; the tenor of both was the same; they demanded Yakub Khan's restoration, and asserted his innocence as to the massacre of the Embassy. I replied that Yakub Khan's return was impossible, and that they must consider his abdication final, as he himself had declared that he wished it to be,* and a few days later I deputed the Mustaufi† to visit Ghazni, in the hope that he might be able to induce the leaders to make some more feasible suggestion for the government of the country.

The Mustaufi had scarcely started, before what seemed to be a reliable report reached me that Abdur Rahman was at Kanduz, on his way to Badakhshan, and I immediately communicated this news to Lord Lytton.

A fortnight later Abdur Rahman's mother, who resided at Kandahar, informed Sir Donald Stewart that Ayub Khan had received a letter from her son, in answer to an offer from Ayub to join him at Balkh and march with him against the British. In this letter Abdur Rahman had replied that he would have nothing to do with any of Sher Ali's family, who had deceived him and dealt with him in the same treacherous manner that characterized Sher Ali's dealings with the British; further, that he had no intention of opposing the British, knowing full well he was not strong enough to do so; that he could not leave Russian territory without the permission of the Russians, whose pensioner he was; and that, even if he got that permission, he could not come either into Turkestan or Kabul without an invitation

* As the deportation of Yakub Khan was believed to be one of the chief causes of recent disturbances, and as a powerful party in the country still looked forward to having him back as their Ruler, I was directed to make it clear to his adherents that the ex-Amir would never be allowed to return to Afghanistan, and that his abdication must be, as he himself at the time wished it to be, considered irrevocable. In support of this decision, I was informed that the unanimous verdict of guilty of murder, recorded against Yakub Khan by Colonel Macgregor's Commission, was substantially endorsed by the Chief Justice of Calcutta and the Advocate-General; and that, although other authorities who had considered the evidence did not quite go so far as these two high legal functionaries, the general conclusion come to was that, if the Amir did not connive at the massacre of the Mission, he made no attempt whatever to interpose on its behalf, and that his whole conduct on that occasion betrayed a culpable indifference to the fate of Sir Louis Cavagnari and his companions, and a total disregard of the solemn obligation which he had contracted with the British Government.

† I had released the Mustaufi from confinement when the general amnesty was published on the 26th December, and he had subsequently been usefully employed assisting the political officers in revenue matters. I did not suppose that he had any great love for the British, but he was anxious to see us out of the country, and was wise enough to know that no armed opposition could effect his purpose, and that it could only be accomplished by the establishment of a stable government, under a Ruler that we could accept.

from us, but that, if he received such an invitation, he would obey it as an order. He concluded by advising Ayub Khan to make his submission to the British, as opposition was useless. Sir Donald Stewart telegraphed the substance of this communication to the Foreign Secretary, adding that Abdur Rahman's family were well disposed towards us, and that there would be no difficulty in communicating with the Sirdar through them.

In the meantime, I had been careful to acquaint the Government of India with my failure to come to any conclusion with the Ghazni faction as to the future government of the country, and the hopelessness of finding anyone of sufficient strength of character to set up as Ruler of Kabul; and I had suggested, failing a really strong man, the alternative of letting the Afghans choose for themselves some Ruler, other than Yakub Khan, and thus leave us free to evacuate the country.

About this time Mr. Lyall, the Foreign Secretary, came to Kabul on a visit to me, and Captain West Ridgeway* took the place of my Political Secretary, Mr. Durand, who left me to join the Foreign Office at Simla, Mr. (now Sir) Lepel Griffin, Secretary to the Punjab Government, being appointed Chief of the political staff at Kabul.

Lyall told me that the Indian Government fully appreciated the difficulty I was in about finding a Ruler for the province, and that, unless Abdur Rahman could be brought within negotiable distance, the alternative I had suggested would have to be acted upon.

Lord Lytton, however, was very sanguine about Abdur Rahman, and he warned Mr. Griffin, before he started for Kabul, that the Sirdar's letter to Ayub Khan indicated possibilities that might have the most important bearing on the solution of the difficult problem to be dealt with in northern Afghanistan. It was lord Lytton's wish to place Abdur Rahman on the throne of Kabul, or, at least, to afford him the best opportunity of winning his own way to that position. The difficulty was to get at him, in the first instance, and, in the second, to convince him of our wish and power to help him; while a not unnatural hesitation on the Sirdar's part to enter Afghanistan without Russia's permission had to be considered.

Lord Lytton impressed upon Mr. Griffin the necessity for overcoming these difficulties in time to enable us to withdraw from northern Afghanistan in the early autumn at latest; and he desired Sir Oliver St. John (Sir Donald Stewart's political officer, who was at that time in Calcutta), immediately on his return to Kandahar, to communicate with Abdur Rahman, through his mother, the Viceroy's willingness to make him Ruler of Kabul and Turkestan, if he would accept the terms offered to him without delay.

* Now Colonel Sir West Ridgeway, K.C.B.

The Viceroy communicated his views to the Secretary of State in the following telegram:

'Necessary to find without delay some Native authority to which we can restore northern Afghanistan without risk of immediate anarchy on our evacuation of Kabul not later than next autumn, and if possible earlier. No prospect of finding in the country any man strong enough for this purpose. I therefore advocate early public recognition of Abdur Rahman as legitimate heir of Dost Mahomed, and open deputation of Sirdars with British concurrence to offer him throne of Afghanistan as sole means of saving the country from anarchy. Do you approve?'

Lord Cranbrook's reply was as follows:

'Assuming that Abdur Rahman is acceptable to the country, and that he would be content with northern Afghanistan, it is desirable to support him at Kabul; the more spontaneous any advances to him on the part of the Sirdars, and the less appearance of British influence, the better. But where is he? And how do you propose to learn his wishes and intentions? If invited by Chiefs, every inducement to bring him to Kabul should be then held out. Public recognition should not precede, but follow, his adoption by Sirdars, and his acceptance of the position.'

By the end of March authentic intelligence was received that Abdur Rahman had made himself master of Afghan-Turkestan, and was corresponding with the representative Sirdars at Kabul. It seemed, therefore, that the time had arrived when distinct overtures might be made to Abdur Rahman; accordingly, on the 1st April Mr. Griffin addressed to him the following letter:

'It has become known that you have entered Afghanistan, and consequently this letter is sent you by a confidential messenger, in order that you may submit to the British officers at Kabul any representations that you may desire to make to the British Government with regard to your object in entering Afghanistan.'

Abdur Rahman, in his friendly but guarded reply,* expressed in general terms his hope of being recognized as Amir. He greatly desired, he wrote, the friendship of the British, and their assistance in restoring peace and order to Afghanistan; but at the same time, he hinted that his obligations to the Russian Government for the hospitality they had extended to him placed him in some doubt as to the terms upon which our friendship might be accorded to him, and while he expressed a desire for the permanent establishment of Afghanistan, with our assistance and sympathy, he let it be understood that he wished to consider himself under the protection of Russia as well as of Great Britain.

In a verbal message, however, he added that he was ready to cross the Hindu Kush to discuss matters with our officers, and he begged that he might be furnished with information as to the 'nature of our friendship' and 'its conditions.'

* Abdur Rahman's letter is given in the Appendix.

In answer, Mr. Griffin was directed to inform Abdur Rahman that the relations of Afghanistan to the British and Russian Empires was a subject the Government of India must decline to discuss with him, and to explain that their declared determination had been the exclusion of foreign influence and interference from Afghanistan, a cardinal condition 'which had at all times and under all circumstances been deemed essential for the permanent security of Her Majesty's Indian Empire,' a condition, moreover, which had always been accepted by the Government of the Czar, which had repeatedly renewed those assurances, solemnly given to Her Majesty's Ministers, that 'Russia considered Afghanistan as entirely beyond the sphere of her influence.'*

Early in April the Mustaufi (whom, it will be remembered, I had sent to Ghazni to communicate with the Chiefs, and ascertain their ideas and desires as to the future government of Kabul) returned without having achieved much success. He had persuaded some of the leading men to accompany him as far as Maidan, whence a few representatives came on to Kabul as bearers of a document signed by Mahomed Jan, twelve other Sirdars, and 189 influential tribesmen, setting forth their views and wishes; but as these were all based upon the restoration of Yakub Khan, their proposals could not be entertained.

On the 13th April I held a durbar, at which I received this deputation; all the Sirdars, Chiefs, and *maliks* of Kabul and many Hazaras being present. Mr. Griffin, on the part of the Government, told them that Yakub Khan could not be allowed to return to Afghanistan, but that the names of any Sirdars, approved of by a large proportion of the people for the Amirship, would be laid before the Viceroy; that there was no intention of annexing Afghanistan, and that there would be no occupation of any places except such as were necessary for the safety of our Indian frontier. They were further informed that the British army would be withdrawn as soon as the country had settled down peacefully and an Amir, amicably disposed towards us, had been selected; but that Kandahar would not again be united to Kabul.

The effect produced was good. The deputation was greatly disappointed that Yakub Khan was not to be permitted to return, but all present felt that they had received a definite reply.

CHAPTER LIX.

SIR DONALD STEWART'S division, which, I have mentioned, it had been decided should be sent to Kabul to take part in the pacification of

* This letter from the Foreign Secretary to Mr. Griffin is given in full in the Appendix.

northern Afghanistan, left Kandahar* on the 30th March, and was expected to arrive at Ghazni about the 21st April. On the 16th I received a letter from Sir Donald, dated six days before, asking me to send supplies to meet him. I, therefore, that same day despatched a small column, under the command of Major-General Ross, C.B., with the articles of food required; and as I thought it likely that my object in sending this force might be misunderstood, the deputation which attended the durbar was told to explain matters to the Chiefs at Maidan, and assure them that the advance would be peaceful unless hostilities should be provoked by their own action. Notwithstanding this precaution, I thought it quite possible the column would be opposed, for the news concerning Abdur Rahman's advent was causing considerable excitement; and whilst the soldiers and a proportion of the tribesmen were disposed to welcome him as a deliverer, those from Wardak and Logar resented his appearance on the scene as putting an end to their hopes of having Yakub Khan reinstated.

With a view, therefore, to prevent the Logaris from joining any attack which might be made on General Ross, I sent a party, 1,200 strong, under Colonel Jenkins, in the direction of Charasia.

On the 22nd April Ross reached Sar-i-top, forty-one miles from Ghazni; Sir Donald Stewart having arrived that same day at the latter place, heliographic communication was at once opened with him, and the welcome news was signalled that Sir Donald had fought an engagement at Ahmedkhel on the 19th, and had been entirely successful. On receipt of this intelligence I ordered a Royal salute to be fired in honour of the victory, the announcement of which I hoped might have a quieting effect on the excitement which prevailed around Kabul.

In this I was disappointed. On the evening of the 24th, Jenkins, who was encamped at Charasia, heard that he was about to be attacked by the Logaris, under Mahomed Hasan Khan. At once striking his tents, and collecting his baggage in a sheltered spot, he ordered a party of Cavalry to reconnoitre up the Logar valley, strengthened his piquets, and sent off an express messenger to inform me of the situation.

I immediately despatched Brigadier-General Macpherson to Jenkins's assistance. By 9 a.m. he had started, with four Mountain guns and 962 Infantry, followed later by two more guns and a troop of the 3rd Punjab Cavalry; and as a support to Macpherson, Brigadier-General Hugh Gough, with the Cavalry brigade and four Horse Artillery guns, was ordered to take up a position half-way between Kabul and Charasia.

At 1 p.m. on the 25th Macpherson arrived on the high ground beyond the *sang-i-nawishta* gorge, whence he obtained a good view of Jenkins's position; and seeing that the enemy formed a complete semicircle round it, he pushed on. Jenkins had stood on the defensive

* Sir Donald Stewart's division was replaced at Kandahar by troops from Bombay.

from the early morning, and the Afghans, who had advanced to within a couple of hundred yards, were only kept at bay by the steadiness of his fire.

Macpherson first sent back the baggage to Sherpur, so as to free all hands for action, and then proceeded to attack the left horn of the semicircle. The enemy broke, fell back, and were completely scattered by a well-directed Artillery fire; the surrounding hills were speedily cleared, and the Cavalry and Horse Artillery pursued for four miles. By four o'clock not a single living Afghan was to be seen; more than 200 had been killed, while our casualties were only four killed and thirty-four wounded.

I came up just as the fight was over; and being sure from the decisive character of the defeat that a retirement could not be misunderstood, I ordered the troops to return to Kabul.

In anticipation of Sir Donald Stewart's arrival, and the consequent necessity for my making over to him, as my senior, the supreme command of the Kabul Field Force, I prepared a report* for his information, which explained the general military situation in northern Afghanistan, and contained a statement of economic details which I thought would be of use to the Government, and concerning which an experience of eighteen months in the field enabled me to give an opinion with some confidence.

The strength of the Kabul Field Force at the end of April amounted to nearly 14,000 men and thirty-eight guns, with 12,500 followers;† besides 15,000 men and thirty guns on the Khyber line, under the immediate command of Major-General Bright.

Sir Donald reached Kabul on the 5th May. On the same day we heard that the Beaconsfield Administration had come to an end; that a new Ministry had been formed under Mr. Gladstone; that Lord Lytton had resigned, and was to be succeeded by the Marquis of Ripon; and that the Marquis of Hartington had become Secretary of State for India.

Notwithstanding the pleasure of meeting an old friend in my new Commander, that 5th of May was altogether not a happy day for me. Lord Lytton's approaching departure was a source of real sorrow. Personally, I felt that I was deeply indebted to him for the confidence he had reposed in me, and for the warm support he had invariably accorded me. I had hoped that he would have had the gratification of seeing, while in office, the campaign in which he was so much

* The part of the report which deals with economic details is given in the Appendix; the military portion is omitted, as it was only intended for Sir Donald Stewart's information at the time.

† Of these, more than 3,000 were doolie-bearers, and nearly 8,000 were *saises* of Native Cavalry regiments, and men belonging to the Transport and other Departments.

interested satisfactorily concluded, and with the prospect of permanent results; and I dreaded that a change of Government might mean a reversal of the policy which I believed to be the best for the security of our position in India. Moreover, it was not in human nature to feel absolute satisfaction in yielding up the supreme command I had so greatly delighted in, into the hands of another, even though that other was one for whom I had so great a personal regard, and under whom I had already served in the field.

The amalgamated troops were now styled the Northern Afghanistan Field Force, and I retained the command of the two divisions at Kabul, with Major-General John Ross as second in command; while Major-General Hills was given the brigades from Kandahar, which now became the third division of the Force.

The idea in bringing Stewart away from Kandahar was that he should occupy Ghazni and Kabul; that my divisions should operate in Kohistan and in the direction of Bamian; that General Bright should move against the Ghilzais; and that a column from Kuram should march over the Shutargardan to Kabul. It was hoped that these operations would have the effect of quieting the country, and, by the time they had been carried out, it would be possible to evacuate northern Afghanistan.

With a view to having my divisions thoroughly efficient and mobile for the service they were expected to perform, I had largely replenished the numbers of my transport animals, which had suffered greatly from the strain put upon them in supplying the troops with food and other necessaries during the winter months; they had been continuously at work in the most inclement weather, numbers had died, and those that remained required to be carefully looked after and given complete rest to render them fit for the contemplated operations. Major Mark Heathcote, who had taken, at my particular request, the arduous charge of this department, wished to revert to regimental duty, so I applied for, and obtained, the services of Lieutenant-Colonel R. Low* as Director of Transport, under whose energetic and intelligent management the transport service was rendered as perfect as it was possible to make it. In the end, circumstances prevented the concerted movements for which these preparations were made being carried out, but I reaped the benefit of them when later in the year I was required to undertake a rapid march to Kandahar, which could not possibly have been successfully accomplished had my transport not been in such admirable condition.

In order to relieve the great pressure put upon the Commissariat Department by having to provide for the increased number of troops at Kabul, and with a view to opening up the roads upon which traffic

* Now Major-General Sir Robert Low, G.C.B.

had been more or less impeded for some months, it was considered desirable to send a strong brigade towards Maidan, which I accompanied, and remained away from Kabul for some weeks. On my return, I found a considerable change had taken place in the political situation. The Mustaufi had been deported to India; the correspondence between Abdur Rahman and Mr. Griffin had taken rather an unsatisfactory turn, and the Sirdar's dealings with the leading Chiefs and tribesmen had given cause to fear that, if he came to Kabul during our occupation, it might be as an enemy rather than a friend.

The Mustaufi was a firm adherent of the Sher Ali faction, and, finding there was no hope of Yakub Khan being reinstated, and that we were negotiating with Abdur Rahman, he had espoused the cause of Yakub's younger brother, Ayub Khan, and had been proved guilty of inciting the Sirdars and Chiefs to oppose us. For this he was very properly sent out of Afghanistan; nevertheless, I looked upon his removal as a misfortune, for it broke up the only party that could possibly be formed to counterbalance Abdur Rahman, who was astute enough to see that the weaker our position became, the more chance there was of his being able to get his own terms from us.

From the letters he had written to his friends and relations in northern Afghanistan (the majority of which had fallen into our hands), it was evident that he was doing all he could to strengthen himself, even at our expense, and that he greatly disliked the idea of Kandahar being separated from the kingdom of Kabul. Indeed, in one of his communications to Mr. Griffin he had made it clear that he expected the whole inheritance of his grandfather, Dost Mahomed Khan, to be made over to him.

The uncertainty as to the result of the correspondence with Abdur Rahman, the rumours in circulation regarding his real disposition and plans, and the general excitement throughout the country, suggested such grave doubts of the Sirdar's good faith that, in some quarters, the question was seriously discussed whether it might not be necessary to break off negotiations with him, and reinstate Yakub Khan, or else set up his brother, Ayub Khan, as Amir.

I myself was altogether opposed to Yakub Khan's restoration, and as to Ayub Khan, we were in total ignorance of his character and proclivities, even if he had been near enough to treat with. It appeared to me, moreover, that we had gone too far with Abdur Rahman to throw him over because, in conformity with Afghan character and tradition, he was not running quite straight. I, therefore, gave it as my opinion that we should not change our tactics unless it was found impossible to come to terms with him, or unless it was made evident on his nearer approach to Kabul that the majority of his countrymen were averse to have him as their Ruler.

Soon after this the situation began to improve, and early in July Mr. Griffin was able to inform the Government of India that 'the probabilities of a settlement with Abdur Rahman appear far more favourable than they did last week. . . .' 'Abdur Rahman has seen that we have been fully informed of the game he has been playing, that trickery and treachery would not be tolerated, and that, if he intends coming to a settlement with us at all, he must be prepared to accept our terms rather than dictate his own.'

A few days later a letter was received from Abdur Rahman, announcing his arrival in Kohistan. His near approach, and the report that he was willing to accept our terms, excited a keen and hopeful interest throughout the country, for the Afghans had at length become convinced that the only chance of getting rid of us was by agreeing to any form of settled government we might establish, and they had grown heartily tired of perpetual fighting and of having to maintain bands of *ghazis* to oppose us, who were eating them out of house and home. With the exception of the Sher Ali faction, therefore, whose interests were directly opposed to his, Abdur Rahman's advent was welcomed by the people, and several of the most influential amongst them went to meet him.

Towards the end of July Sir Donald Stewart was empowered to conclude all political and military arrangements preparatory to withdrawing from northern Afghanistan. Abdur Rahman was to be recognized as 'Amir of Kabul'; he was to be provided with a sufficient number of guns to strengthen effectively his occupation of the city, and he was to be given as much money (within a maximum of ten lakhs) as was thought necessary to meet his present wants. It was to be clearly explained to Abdur Rahman that the Government of India would not engage to give him a regular subsidy, or a continuous supply of arms or money, and that after he had taken possession of his capital he would have to rely upon his own resources for holding it. There was to be no treaty, and all questions of reciprocal engagements between the two Governments were to be postponed until some settled and responsible administration had been consolidated.

General Stewart was directed to make the best arrangements he could with Abdur Rahman for the protection of the tribes and individuals who had assisted us, and the Sirdar was to be informed that, if he desired our goodwill, he could give no better proof of his friendly disposition than by his behaviour towards those of his own nation in whom the British Government were interested.

Sir Donald Stewart considered that the best way of giving effect to these instructions was to publicly proclaim Abdur Rahman as Amir of Kabul; for this purpose he held a durbar on the 22nd July, at which the Sirdar's representatives were received. Sir Donald, in a few words, gave his reasons for summoning them to meet him, and Mr.

Griffin then explained more fully the motives by which the Government of India were actuated in acknowledging the claims of Abdur Rahman. Immediately after the durbar orders were issued for an early retirement.

I was to withdraw my column by the Kuram route; but being anxious to see something of the Khyber line while I had the opportunity, I started off the following day to ride through the Jagdalak Pass to Gandamak, where I was entertained by General Bright and his staff. The next day I went on to Jalalabad, and was greatly interested in wandering over the place where Sir Robert Sale in some measure redeemed the lamentable failures of the first Afghan war.

My intention, when I left Kabul, was to ride as far as the Khyber Pass, but suddenly a presentiment, which I have never been able to explain to myself, made me retrace my steps and hurry back towards Kabul—a presentiment of coming trouble which I can only characterize as instinctive.

The feeling was justified when, about half-way between Butkhak and Kabul, I was met by Sir Donald Stewart and my Chief of the Staff,* who brought me the astounding news of the total defeat by Ayub Khan of Brigadier-General Burrows's brigade at Maiwand, and of Lieutenant-General Primrose,† with the remainder of his force, being besieged at Kandahar.

CHAPTER LX.

For more than six months rumours had been afloat of Ayub Khan's determination to advance on Kandahar; but little attention was paid to them by the authorities at that place until towards the end of May, when a Sirdar, named Sher Ali,‡ who had been a few days before formally installed as Wali, or Ruler, of Kandahar, informed the political officer, Lieutenant-Colonel St. John, that the British occupation of Kabul had had the effect of bringing about a reconciliation between the various chiefs at Herat, who had placed themselves under the leadership of Ayub Khan and induced him to proclaim a *jahad*. Sher Ali, who evidently considered this news authentic, declared his belief that his own troops,§ who were then engaged in collecting revenue in

* Colonel Macgregor and Lieutenant-Colonel Chapman had changed places, the former joining Sir Donald Stewart as Chief of the Staff, and the latter taking up the same position with me.

† Lieutenant-General Primrose succeeded Sir Donald Stewart in command of the troops at Kandahar.

‡ Sirdar Sher Ali had been appointed Governor of Kandahar by the Amir Yakub Khan after the treaty of Gandamak, and had since assisted Sir Donald Stewart in the civil administration of the province.

§ Local Native levies.

Zamindawar, would desert to Ayub Khan as he approached Kandahar, and he begged that a brigade of British soldiers might be sent to Girishk to support him.

On General Primrose communicating this information to the Commander-in-Chief in India, he recommended to the Government that the Bombay reserve division, located at Jacobabad, Hyderabad, and Karachi, should be mobilized so soon as it became certain that Ayub Khan really contemplated this move, as in his opinion the garrison at Kandahar would be left dangerously weak after a brigade had been detached for Girishk.

Ayub Khan's movements, however, were not ascertained until the 27th June, when he had advanced halfway to the Helmand; it was too late then to mobilize troops so far off as Jacobabad, Hyderabad, and Karachi with any chance of their being in time to check his onward march. The news of his approach spread rapidly, and had the most disturbing effect in Kandahar and its neighbourhood. The Governor's authority daily diminished, and many of the inhabitants left the city.

Ayub Khan had with him, when he started from Herat on the 15th June, 7,500 men and ten guns as the nucleus of an army, which he calculated, as he moved forward, would be strongly reinforced by tribesmen, levies, and *ghazis*.

On the 4th July a brigade, under the command of Brigadier-General Burrows, started from Kandahar, and reached the Helmand on the 11th, encamping on the near bank of the river opposite Girishk. On the further bank Sirdar Sher Ali's troops were located, having with them six guns. Two days afterwards these troops deserted in a body to the enemy, but did not succeed in taking their Artillery with them, as Burrows, on perceiving their intention, crossed the river and captured the guns.

Brigadier-General Burrows's position had now entirely changed; instead of there being a loyal force under the Wali, with which to co-operate and prevent Ayub Khan crossing the Helmand, he found himself with an inadequate number of troops, the Wali's men gone over to the enemy, and the Wali himself a fugitive in the British camp. The Helmand was fordable everywhere at that season, making it easy for Ayub to cut off Burrows's retreat; the first twenty-five of the eighty miles by which he was separated from Kandahar was a desert, and no supplies were forthcoming owing to the hostile attitude of the people. Burrows therefore determined to retire to Khushk-i-Nakhud, an important position half-way to Kandahar, covering the road from Girishk, and where supplies and water were plentiful.

Burrows reached Khushk-i-Nakhud on the 16th July. On the 22nd the Commander-in-Chief in India, who had been inquiring from General Primrose whether there were 'any routes from the Helmand passing by the north to Ghazni, by which Ayub Khan might move with his guns,' telegraphed to Primrose: 'You will understand that you have full liberty to attack Ayub, if you consider you are strong enough to do so. Government consider it of the highest political importance that his force should be dispersed, and prevented by all possible means from passing on to Ghazni.'

On the afternoon of the 26th information was received by Brigadier-General Burrows that 2,000 of the enemy's Cavalry and a large body of *ghazis* had arrived at Maiwand, eleven miles off, and that Ayub Khan was about to follow with the main body of his army.

To prevent Ayub Khan getting to Ghazni, General Burrows had to do one of two things, either await him at Khushk-i-Nakhud, or intercept him at Maiwand. After consulting with Colonel St. John, he determined to adopt the latter course, as he hoped thus to be able to deal with the *ghazis* before they were joined by Ayub Khan.

The brigade started soon after 6 a.m. on the 27th. It was encumbered by a large number of baggage animals, which Burrows considered could not be left behind because of the hostile state of the country, and the impossibility of detaching any part of his already too small force for their protection.

At 10 a.m., when about half-way to Maiwand, a spy brought in information that Ayub Khan had arrived at that place, and was occupying it in force; General Burrows, however, considered it then too late to turn back, and decided to advance. At a quarter to twelve the forces came into collision, and the fight lasted until past three o'clock. The Afghans, who, Burrows reported, numbered 25,000, soon outflanked the British. Our Artillery expended their ammunition, and the Native portion of the brigade got out of hand, and pressed back on the few British Infantry, who were unable to hold their own against the overwhelming numbers of the enemy. Our troops were completely routed, and had to thank the apathy of the Afghans in not following them up for escaping total annihilation.

Of the 2,476 men engaged at Maiwand, 934 were killed and 175 were wounded and missing;* the remnant struggled on throughout the

	Killed.	*Wounded and Missing.*
* British officers	20	9
,, troops	290	48
Native ,, ...	624	118
	934	175
	Total,	1,109

Of the regimental followers 331 were killed and 7 were missing; 455 transport followers and drivers were reported as killed or missing, but a number of these, being Afghans, probably joined the enemy.

A large quantity of arms and ammunition was lost, including over 1,000 rifles and carbines, and 600 or 700 swords and bayonets.

night to Kandahar, where the first of the fugitives arrived early on the morning of the 28th. Brigadier-General Burrows, who had two horses shot under him during the engagement, was amongst the last to reach Kandahar.

This lamentable story imparted to me by Stewart almost took my breath away, and we eagerly discussed the situation as we rode back together to Sherpur. It was impossible to predict how the news would affect the recent arrangements entered into with Abdur Rahman, or what the attitude of the tribesmen would be; but we agreed that, whatever might happen in our immediate neighbourhood, the only means of affording speedy relief to the Kandahar garrison was by sending a force from Kabul.

It soon, however, became apparent, by telegrams received from Simla, that the Government were in doubt as to the best course to pursue, and looked to Quetta rather than Kabul as the place from which Kandahar could be most conveniently and rapidly succoured. This was not altogether surprising, for the authorities naturally hesitated to weaken Kabul until matters had been finally settled with Abdur Rahman, and it was only to be expected that, after what had occurred at Maiwand, they should be alarmed at the idea of a force being cut off from all communication with India during the four weeks, or thereabouts, it would take to reach Kandahar. But there was really no alternative, for, as Major-General Phayre* (commanding in Baluchistan) reported,† the troops available for Field Service were but few in number, it would require at least fifteen days to equip them, and there was no organized transport at hand, the animals having been sent to distant grazing grounds on account of the scarcity of water and forage.

I knew nothing as to the actual condition of the troops in Baluchistan, except that, as belonging to the Bombay Presidency, they could not be composed of the best fighting races, and I had a strong feeling that it would be extremely unwise to make use of any but the most proved Native soldiers against Ayub Khan's superior numbers, elated as his men must be with their victory at Maiwand.

The disaster to our arms caused, as was to be expected, considerable excitement all along the border; indeed, throughout India the announcement produced a certain feeling of uneasiness—a mere

---

201 horses were killed, and 1,676 camels, 355 ponies, 24 mules, 291 donkeys, and 79 bullocks, were not forthcoming.

* Afterwards General Sir Robert Phayre, G.C.B.

† General Phayre reported on the 28th July that there were only seven Native regiments in Baluchistan, three of which were required for the lines of communication, leaving only four available for Field Service; and that a battalion of British Infantry and a battery of Field Artillery required for his column were a long way off, being still in Sind.

surface ripple—but enough to make those who remembered the days of the Mutiny anxious for better news from the north.

To me it seemed of such supreme importance that Kandahar should be relieved without delay, and the reverse to our arms retrieved, that I made up my mind to communicate my views to the Viceroy through the Commander-in-Chief, in the hope that, when he realized that a thoroughly efficient force was ready and willing to start from Kabul, he would no longer hesitate as to what was best to do.

On the 30th July, I dined with Stewart, and, leaving his mess-tent at an early hour, I retired to my own quarters, and wrote out the following telegram in cipher, but, before despatching it, I showed it to Stewart, for, although I knew that his views were in accord with mine, I could not with propriety have sent it without his knowledge:

'To Major-General Greaves,* Adjutant-General in India, Simla.

'Kabul,

'*30th July*, 1880.

'Personal and secret. I strongly recommend that a force be sent from this to Kandahar. Stewart has organized a very complete one consisting of nine regiments of Infantry, three of Cavalry, and three Mountain batteries. This will suffice to overcome all opposition *en route;* it will have the best possible effect on the country, and will be ready to go anywhere on reaching Kandahar, being fully equipped in all respects. He proposes sending me in command.

'I am sure that but few Bombay regiments are able to cope with Afghans, and once the Kabul Field Force leaves this country, the chance of sending a thoroughly reliable and well-equipped column will be lost. The movement of the remainder of the Kabul troops towards India should be simultaneous with the advance of my division towards Kandahar, it being most desirable to limit the area of our responsibilities as soon as possible; at the same time, it is imperative that we should now show our strength throughout Afghanistan. The withdrawal, under existing circumstances, of the whole force from Kabul to India would certainly be misunderstood, both in Afghanistan and elsewhere. You need have no fears about my division. It can take care of itself, and will reach Kandahar under the month. I will answer for the loyalty and good feeling of the Native portion, and would propose to inform them that, as soon as matters have been satisfactorily settled at Kandahar, they will be sent straight back to India. Show this to Lyall.'

Exaggerated reports of the Maiwand affair being rife in the Kabul bazaars, which were daily becoming crowded with armed Afghans from Abdur Rahman's camp, and the prospect of troops having to leave at once for Kandahar, made it more than ever necessary to bring the negotiations with the new Amir to a speedy conclusion. It was accordingly arranged that Mr. Griffin should meet him at Zimma, about sixteen miles from Kabul. This interview had the happiest results, and must have been extremely gratifying to Mr. Griffin, whom we all heartily congratulated on the successful ending to the very

* Now General Sir George Greaves, G.C.B., G.C.M.G.

delicate and difficult negotiations which he had carried on with so much skill and patience.

In taking leave of His Highness, Mr. Griffin invited him to come to the British camp the following day to be received by Sir Donald Stewart. Abdur Rahman himself was quite willing to come, and some of his supporters were in favour of his doing so, but others vehemently opposed the idea, and 'swore by their faith they would leave him if he persisted.' After a stormy meeting with his Chiefs, the Amir wrote to Mr. Griffin as follows: 'If you really wish me to come to you, irrespective of the opinion of the people, I am quite ready to do so. Please write and let me know your wishes. I am in the hands of ignorant fools, who do not know their own interests, good or bad. What can I do? I am most anxious to meet you.'

Upon receipt of this note Stewart decided that it would be impolitic to press for an interview, for instead of strengthening the Amir, as had been the intention, it was evident it would have the opposite effect, so the meeting was given up.

On the morning of the 3rd August the telegram arrived from Lord Ripon, which I had been so anxiously expecting, authorizing the despatch of a force to Kandahar, and directing that I should be placed in command.

I heard afterwards that my message to the Adjutant-General was received at Simla at a most opportune moment. Lyall took it without delay to Lord Ripon, who from the first had been in favour of a force being sent from Kabul, but had refrained from ordering the movement in deference to the views held by some members of his Council, whose longer experience of India, His Excellency considered, entitled their opinions to be treated with respect.

I set to work at once to organize the column which I was to have the great honour of commanding. In this most congenial duty I received every possible assistance and encouragement from Stewart; he gave me carte-blanche, and I should only have had myself to blame if every unit had not been as efficiently equipped as circumstances would admit.

I wished that the force should be composed, as far as possible, of those who had served with me throughout the campaign; but as some of the regiments (more especially Native corps) had been away from their homes for two years, and had had more than their share of fighting, besides having suffered heavy losses in action and through sickness, I considered it right to consult their commanders before detailing the troops. With the exception of three, who thought that their regiments had been long enough away from India, all, to my great delight, eagerly responded to my call, and I took upon myself to promise the men that they should not be left to garrison Kandahar, but should be sent back to India as soon as the fighting ceased.

When the several regiments were decided upon, every man not likely to stand the strain of prolonged forced marches was weeded out, and the scale of baggage, tents, and impedimenta was reduced to a minimum.*

I had no fear as to the officers and men ably and cheerfully performing their part of the task; we had been long enough together to enable us thoroughly to understand and trust each other, and I felt that I could depend upon each and all to respond heartily to whatever call I might make upon them.

The question of supplies was my greatest anxiety, and I had many consultations with my experienced Commissariat officer, Major Badcock, before I could feel satisfied in this respect.

The transport, as I have already recorded, was in good order; it was fortunate that the soldiers had been practised in loading, leading, and tending the animals, for the Afghan drivers deserted to a man a march or two from Kabul, and the Hazaras followed their example on reaching their own country. Sir Donald Stewart's account of the troubles he had encountered during his march from Kandahar was not very encouraging, and I should have been glad if I could have taken a larger amount of supplies;† but on this point I had to be guided by

* Each British soldier was allowed for kit and camp-equipage, including great-coat and waterproof sheet - - - 30 lbs.

Each Native soldier	20 ,,
Each public and private follower	10 ,,
Each European officer	1 mule.
Every eight officers for mess	1 ,,
Each staff-officer for office purposes	80 lbs.
Each Native officer	30 ,,

† The amount of supplies taken with the force was as follows:

FOR BRITISH TROOPS.

Bread-stuff	5 days.
Preserved vegetables	15 ,,
Tea, sugar, salt, and rum	30 ,,

FOR NATIVE TROOPS AND FOLLOWERS.

Flour	5 days.
Dal and salt	30 ,,
Rum for spirit-drinking men	8 ,,

Sheep, ten days' supply for British troops and four issues for Native troops, with 20 per cent. spare. Nearly 5,000 sheep were purchased on the march. N.B.—There are no horned cattle in Afghanistan, except those used for the plough or transport.

In addition to the above, a small reserve of lime-juice, pea-soup, and tinned meat was taken; these proved most useful, and might have been increased with advantage had carriage been available.

I gave strict orders that the reserve of bread-stuff, flour, and sheep was never to be used without my sanction, and that wherever possible food for the number of animals that could be allotted to the column, which was necessarily limited, as carriage had to be provided simultaneously for the withdrawal of the rest of the army of occupation.

The strength of the force placed at my disposal consisted of 9,986 men of all ranks and eighteen guns, divided into three brigades of Infantry, one brigade of Cavalry, and three batteries of Mountain Artillery. There were, besides, over 8,000 followers* and 2,300 horses and gun-mules.

It was designated the Kabul-Kandahar Field Force.

Major-General J. Ross, C.B., was given the command of the Infantry division, his three Brigadier-Generals being Herbert Macpherson, T. D. Baker, and Charles Macgregor. Brigadier-General Hugh Gough commanded the Cavalry brigade; Colonel Alured Johnson the Artillery; while Colonel Æ. Perkins held the position of Commanding Royal Engineer; Deputy-Surgeon-General J. Hanbury that of Principal Medical Officer; and Lieutenant-Colonel E. F. Chapman, Chief of the Staff.

From the detail of the force given below,† it will be seen that there

---

the day's consumption was to be purchased. We had occasionally to trench upon the reserve, but we nearly made it up at other places, and we arrived at Kandahar with three days' supplies in hand.

* The followers consisted of:

Doolie-bearers	2,192
Transport and other departments	4,698
Private servants, and *saices* of Native Cavalry regiments	1,244
Total	8,134

† DETAIL OF FORCE.

1st Infantry Brigade.

	British.	*Native.*
92nd Highlanders	651	—
23rd Pioneers	—	701
24th Punjab Native Infantry	—	575
2nd Gurkhas	—	501
Total	651	1,777

2nd Infantry Brigade.

	British.	*Native.*
72nd Highlanders	787	—
2nd Sikh Infantry	—	612
3rd Sikh Infantry	—	570
5th Gurkhas	—	561
Total	787	1,743

was no wheeled Artillery, and that the number of guns was not in proportion to the strength of the other branches. This was my own doing; I was pressed to take more and heavier guns, but, after due consideration, I decided that I would only have Mountain batteries. We could not tell how long the Kandahar garrison would be able to hold out, so that our first object must be to reach that place with the

---

3RD INFANTRY BRIGADE.

	British.	*Native.*
60th Rifles, 2nd Battalion	616	—
15th Sikhs	—	650
25th Punjab Native Infantry	—	629
4th Gurkhas	—	637
Total	616	1,916

CAVALRY BRIGADE.

	British.	*Native.*
9th Queen's Royal Lancers	318	—
3rd Bengal Cavalry	—	394
3rd Punjab Cavalry	—	408
Central India Horse	—	495
Total	318	1,297

ARTILLERY DIVISION.

	British.	*Native.*	*Guns.*
6-8th Royal Artillery—screw guns	95	139	6
11-9th Royal Artillery	95	139	6
No. 2 Mountain Battery	—	140	6
Total	190	418	18

TOTAL OF FORCE.

British troops	2,562
Native ,,	7,151
British officers	273
Guns	18
Cavalry horses	1,779
Artillery mules	450

Two hundred rounds of ammunition were taken for each Infantry soldier: seventy rounds were carried by each man, thirty rounds were in reserve with the regiment, and a hundred rounds in the Field Park.

Each Mountain battery had:

Common shell	264
Double shell	60
Shrapnel shell	144
Star shell	24
Case shot	48
Total	540 rounds.

And thirty rounds per gun in the Field Park.

least possible delay, and wheeled Artillery would, in a country where there were practically no roads, have only prevented our moving as rapidly as we might otherwise have done.

For the equipment of the force, inclusive of carriage for footsore soldiers* and followers, and allowing ten per cent. spare, more than 8,000† animals were required.

Fortunately, it turned out that a fair amount of Indian corn in the ear was almost everywhere procurable, which was so nutritious that a large majority of the Cavalry horses and transport animals reached Kandahar in excellent condition.

Throughout the march great difficulties were experienced in procuring food, but they were always overcome, with the able assistance of Major Hastings and his political staff,‡ and by means of the admirable arrangements made by the Commissariat§ and Transport‖ officers, who were quite untiring, and after the longest march, and with the prospect of having to start again at an early hour the following morning, had often to work far into the night.

The want of fuel was our chief drawback. We had on many occasions to purchase houses and pull them to pieces for the sake of the wood to be got out of them, and frequently there was nothing to cook

* British troops were allowed ponies at the rate of 2 per cent. of strength. Native troops were allowed ponies at the rate of $2\frac{1}{2}$ per cent of strength. Followers were allowed ponies at the rate of $1\frac{1}{2}$ per cent. of strength.

	Yabus, or Afghan ponies.	Mules.	Indian ponies.	Donkeys.	Camels.
† Number of animals that left Kabul	1,589	4,510	1,244	912	6[1]
Purchased during the march[2]	35	1	—	208	171
Number of animals that reached Kandahar	1,179	4,293	1,138	1,078	177
Casualties during the march	445	218	106	42	

‡ Major E. Hastings, Captain West Ridgeway, Major Euan Smith, C.S.I., and Major M. Prothero.

§ Major A. Badcock, Captain A. Rind, and Lieutenants C. Fitzgerald, H. Hawkes, and H. Lyons Montgomery, all of the Bengal Staff Corps.

‖ Lieutenant-Colonel R. Low, Bengal Staff Corps; Captain W. Wynter, 33rd Foot; Captains G. H. Eliot and C. R. Macgregor, Bengal Staff Corps; Lieutenants L. Booth, 33rd Foot, H. Elverson, 2nd Foot, R. Fisher, 10th Hussars, R. Wilson, 10th Hussars, and C. Robertson, 8th Foot.

[1] With hospital equipment.

[2] Only twice had animals to be taken against the will of the owners, and on both occasions the matter was amicably settled in the end

with save tiny roots of southernwood, which had to be dug out and collected after a long day's march before the men could prepare their food and satisfy their hunger.

One day's corn was carried by each animal in addition to the ordinary load, and as far as Ghazni grain was tolerably plentiful; beyond that we had to depend for forage on the crops still standing. At the end of the day's march, certain fields were told off to the several brigades; from these all that was required was cut and carried away, the fields were then measured and assessed, and compensation was awarded by the political officers, who also adjusted all claims on account of wrecked houses, and fruit, vegetables, etc., brought in for the troops.

On Sunday, the 8th August, the force moved into camp by brigades, my Head-Quarters being with the first and third Infantry brigades at Beni Hissar, on the way to the Logar valley, which route I had chosen instead of the slightly shorter line by Maidan, on account of the greater facility it afforded for supplies.

Sir Donald Stewart paid us a farewell visit in the afternoon, and at 6 a.m. the following morning we began the march to Kandahar.

CHAPTER LXI.

Before daybreak on the 11th August, as I was starting from camp, I received my last communication from the outside world in the shape of a telegram from my wife, sent off from a little village in Somersetshire, congratulating me and the force, and wishing us all God's speed. She had taken our children to England a few months before, thinking that the war in Afghanistan was over, and that I would soon be able to follow.

Four days brought us to the end of the Logar valley, a distance of forty-six miles. So far the country was easy and supplies plentiful. I thought it wise, however, not to attempt long distances at first, that both men and animals might become gradually hardened before entering on the difficult and scantily cultivated ground between Ghazni and Kelat-i-Ghilzai, where I knew that forced marches were inevitable, and that their powers of endurance would be sorely taxed. Moreover, it was necessary to begin quietly, and organize some system by which confusion in the crowded camping-grounds might be avoided, and the physical strain upon everyone lightened as much as possible.

When it is remembered that the daily supply for over 18,000 men and 11 000 animals had to be drawn from the country after arrival in camp, that food had to be distributed to every individual, that the fuel with which it was cooked had often to be brought from long distances, and that a very limited time was available for the preparation of meals and for rest, it will readily be understood how essential it was that even the stupidest follower should be able to find his place in camp speedily, and that everyone should know exactly what to do and how to set about doing it.

On the march and in the formation of the camps the same principles were, as far as possible, applied each day. The 'rouse' sounded at 2.45 a.m., and by four o'clock tents had been struck, baggage loaded up, and everything was ready for a start.

As a general rule, the Cavalry covered the movement at a distance of about five miles, two of the four regiments being in front, with the other two on either flank. Two of the Infantry brigades came next, each accompanied by a Mountain battery; then followed the field hospitals, Ordnance and Engineer parks, treasure, and the baggage, massed according to the order in which the brigades were moving. The third Infantry brigade with its Mountain battery and one or two troops of Cavalry formed the rear guard.

A halt of ten minutes was made at the end of each hour, which at eight o'clock was prolonged to twenty minutes to give time for a hasty breakfast. Being able to sleep on the shortest notice, I usually took advantage of these intervals to get a nap, awaking greatly refreshed after a few minutes' sound sleep.

On arrival at the resting-place for the night, the front face of the camp was told off to the brigade on rear guard, and this became the leading brigade of the column on the next day's march. Thus every brigade had its turn of rear guard duty, which was very arduous, more particularly after leaving Ghazni, the troops so employed seldom reaching the halting-ground before six or seven o'clock in the evening, and sometimes even later.

One of the most troublesome duties of the rear guard was to prevent the followers from lagging behind, for it was certain death for anyone who strayed from the shelter of the column; numbers of Afghans always hovered about on the look-out for plunder, or in the hope of being able to send a Kaffir, or an almost equally-detested Hindu, to eternal perdition. Towards the end of the march particularly, this duty became most irksome, for the wretched followers were so weary and footsore that they hid themselves in ravines, making up their minds to die, and entreating, when discovered and urged to make an effort, to be left where they were. Every baggage animal that could possibly be spared was used to carry the worn-out followers; but notwithstanding this and the care taken by officers and men that none should be left behind, twenty of these poor creatures were lost, besides four Native soldiers.

The variation of temperature (at times as much as eighty degrees between day and night) was most trying to the troops, who had to carry the same clothes whether the thermometer was at freezing-point at dawn or at 110° Fahr. at mid-day. Scarcity of water, too, was a great trouble to them, while constant sand-storms, and the suffocating dust raised by the column in its progress, added greatly to their discomfort.

Daily reports regarding the health of the troops, followers, and transport animals were brought to me each evening, and I made it my business to ascertain how many men had fallen out during the day, and what had been the number of casualties amongst the animals.

On the 12th August the Head-Quarters and main body of the force halted to allow the Cavalry and the second Infantry brigade to push on and get clear over the Zamburak Kotal (8,100 feet high) before the rest of the column attempted its ascent. This kotal presented a serious obstacle to our rapid progress, the gradient being in many places one in four, and most difficult for the baggage animals; but by posting staff officers at intervals to control the flow of traffic, and by opening out fresh paths to relieve the pressure, we got over it much more quickly than I had expected.

On the 15th we reached Ghazni, ninety-eight miles from Kabul, a place of peculiar interest to me from the fact that it was for his share in its capture, forty-one years before, that my father was given the C.B.

I was met by the Governor, who handed me the keys of the fortress, and I placed my own guards and sentries in and around the city to prevent collisions between the inhabitants and our troops, and also to make sure that our demands for supplies were complied with. Up to this point we had been fairly well off for food, forage, and water.

Our next march was across a barren, inhospitable track for twenty miles to a place called Yarghati. On the way we passed Ahmedkhel, where Sir Donald Stewart won his victory; the name had been changed by the Natives to 'the Resting-place of Martyrs,' and the numerous freshly-covered-in graves testified to the *ghazis*' heavy losses. The remains of the few British soldiers, who had been buried where they had fallen, had been desecrated, and the bones were exposed to view and scattered about.

At Chardeh, our next halting-place, a communication from Colonel Tanner, Commanding at Kelat-i-Ghilzai, was brought to me by a Native messenger; it was dated the 12th August, and informed me that Kandahar was closely invested, but that the garrison had supplies for two months and forage for fifteen days.

On the 21st we arrived at a point thirty miles from Kelat-i-Ghilzai, whence we opened heliograph communication with that place, and were told of an unsuccessful sortie made from Kandahar five days

CROSSING THE ZAMBURAK KOTAL.

From a painting by the Chevalier Desanges.

before, in which General Brooke and eight other British officers had been killed.

On the 23rd Kelat-i-Ghilzai was reached. The garrison* had been well taken care of by Colonel Tanner,† and a large quantity of food for man and beast had been collected; but I thought it unadvisable at present to continue to hold the place, and have to keep open communication between it and Kandahar, and as I could see no compensating advantage in doing so, I determined to withdraw the troops and take them along with me.

Colonel Tanner's report satisfied me there was no immediate danger to be apprehended at Kandahar, so I decided to halt for one day; both men and animals greatly needed rest after a continuous march of 225 miles.

I had endeavoured to keep the Government of India informed of my progress by a message from Ghazni, and one from Oba Karez on the 18th August, but neither reached its destination. I now despatched a message which was more successful, and was delivered at Simla on the 30th August. It was as follows:

'KELAT-I-GHILZAI,
23rd August, 1880.

'The force under my command arrived here this morning. The authorities at Kandahar having stated on the 17th instant that they have abundant supplies and can make forage last until 1st September, I halt to-morrow to rest the troops, and more especially the transport animals and camp-followers. The force left Ghazni on the 16th, and has marched 136 miles during the last eight days; the troops are in good health and spirits. From this I purpose moving by regular stages, so that the men may arrive fresh at Kandahar. I hope to be in heliographic communication with Kandahar from Robat, distant twenty miles, on the 29th. If General Phayre reaches Takht-i-Pul, I should also hope to communicate with him and arrange a combined movement on Kandahar. I am taking the Kelat-i-Ghilzai garrison with me, making the Fort over to Mahomed Sadik Khan, a Toki Chief, who had charge of the place when we arrived in 1879; the present Governor, Sirdar Sherindil Khan, refuses to remain. We have met with no opposition during the march, and have been able to make satisfactory arrangements for supplies, especially forage, which at this season is plentiful. The Cavalry horses and Artillery mules are in excellent order; our casualties to date are, one soldier 72nd Highlanders, one sepoy 23rd Pioneers, one 2nd Sikhs, two sepoys 3rd Sikhs dead; one sepoy 4th Gurkhas, two sepoys 24th Punjab Native Infantry, one Duffadar 3rd Punjab Cavalry missing; six camp-followers dead, five missing. The missing men have, I fear, been murdered. I telegraphed from Ghazni on the 15th, and from Oba Karez on the 18th August.'

I wrote also to Major-General Phayre, telling him of the date on which I expected to reach Kandahar, and that if I heard of his being

* The garrison consisted of 2 guns of C/2, Royal Artillery, 145 rifles of the 66th Foot, 100 of the 3rd Sind Horse, and the 2nd Baluch Regiment, 639 strong.

† Now Lieutenant-General Sir Oriel Tanner, K.C.B.

anywhere near I would arrange my movements to suit his, in order that the two forces might make a combined attack on Ayub Khan's position.

As I was afraid the supplies at Kandahar would be insufficient for the additional troops about to be collected there, I sent General Phayre a memorandum* of the amount of food required daily by my force, and begged him to get pushed up from the rear such articles as were more particularly wanted. I pointed out that we were badly off for boots, and that the 92nd Highlanders had only one hundred great-coats fit for wear, which were used by the men on night duties.

On the 25th we marched to Jaldak, seventeen miles, and the same distance the next day to Tirandaz, where I received a letter from Lieutenant-General Primrose, informing me that Ayub Khan had raised the siege on the 23rd, and was entrenching himself at Mazra, beyond the Baba Wali Kotal, in the valley of the Arghandab.

I awoke on the morning of the 27th feeling very unwell, and soon found I was in for an attack of fever. The heat during the day was becoming more and more overpowering as we proceeded south, and I had lately been feeling somewhat knocked up by it and by exposure to the sun. I had now to give in for the time being, and was compelled to perform the march in a doolie, a most ignominious mode of conveyance for a General on service; but there was no help for it, for I could not sit a horse.

* Estimate of daily requirements for the Kabul-Kandahar Field Force and the Kelat-i-Ghilzai garrison:

Europeans	3,200
Native troops	8,000
Followers	8,500
Horses	2,300

Transport—yabus 1,592, mules and ponies 5,926, camels 400, donkeys 400.

Meat	4,000 lbs.
Bread-stuff	40 maunds.[1]
Vegetables	4,000 lbs.
Rice	800 ,,
Salt	133 ,,
Sugar	600 ,,
Tea	150 ,,
Rum, 25 per cent.	80 gallons.
Atta	320 maunds.
Dall	51½ ,,
Ghee	19¼ ,,
Salt	8½ ,,
Grain	700 ,,

A. R. BADCOCK, Major,
Deputy Commissary-General.

KELAT-I-GHILZAI,
24th August, 1880.

[1] A maund is equivalent to 80 lbs.

That day the 3rd Bengal and 3rd Punjab Cavalry marched thirty-four miles to Robat, in order to establish direct heliographic communication with Kandahar. The main body halted about half-way, when I again reported progress as follows:

'SHAHR-I-SAFA,
'27th August, 1880.

'My force arrived here to-day. I received a letter yesterday, dated 25th, from Colonel St. John. He writes: "The rumours of the approach of your force have been sufficient to relieve the city from investment. On Monday night the villages on the east and south were abandoned by their mixed garrisons of *ghazis* and regulars. Yesterday morning Ayub struck his camp, and marched to a position on the Arghandab, between Baba Wali and Sheikh Chela, due north of the city, and separated from it by a range of rocky hills. He has about 4,000 Infantry regulars, six 12-pounders and two 9-pounders rifled, four 6-pounder smooth-bore batteries, and one 4-pounder battery, 2,000 sowars, and perhaps twice that number of *ghazis*, of whom a third have firearms. The Kizilbashes and Kohistanis in his army, about 1,200 Infantry and 300 Cavalry, offered to desert and join us directly we made a show of attack. They are at last aware of Abdur Rahman's succession, but I think Ayub will remain unmolested until the arrival of the Kabul force, provided he waits, which is unlikely. He will, I expect, strike away north into Khakrez, on which line a vigorous pursuit will give us his guns. Maclaine, Royal Horse Artillery, is still a prisoner; I am making every effort to obtain his release, but I am not very hopeful of success. This morning, the 25th, I went to the field of the unlucky sortie of the 16th, and found the bodies of the poor fellows who fell there, some forty in number; they will be buried this afternoon. All the wounded are doing well. No signs or tidings of Phayre." General Gough, with two regiments of Cavalry, is at Robat; they are in heliographic communication with Kandahar. General Primrose heliographs that Ayub Khan has entrenched his camp at Baba Wali. The force marches for Robat to-morrow, seventeen miles distant from Kandahar.'

The following day the column joined the two Cavalry regiments at Robat, where I was met by Lieutenant-Colonel St. John, from whom I heard that Ayub Khan was likely to make a stand. I thought it prudent, therefore, to halt on Sunday, the 29th, and divide the last twenty miles into two short marches, in order that the men and animals might arrive as fresh as possible, and fit for any work which might be required of them; for should Ayub Khan retire towards Herat, he would have to be followed up, and his army attacked and defeated wherever we might overtake him.

Before leaving Robat, a letter arrived from General Phayre, which put an end to all hope of his force being able to co-operate with mine, for his leading brigade, he wrote, had only just got to the Kohjak Pass. This was to be regretted, but it was unavoidable. I was well aware of the strenuous efforts the gallant Commander had made to relieve the beleaguered garrison, and I knew if co-operation had been possible it would have been effected.

We encamped at Momund on the 30th, whence I sent the following telegram to Simla:

'My force arrived here to-day; we march to Kandahar to-morrow. General Primrose heliographs that a letter from Ayub's camp brings information that the mother of the late Heir-Apparent, Abdulla Jan, with other ladies, has been sent to Zamindawar. Arrival of the young Musa Jan in Ayub's camp is confirmed. Hashim Khan is also there. The position is being strengthened, especially on the Pir Paimal side, where two guns have been placed with two regiments. From further information, I learn that the Baba Wali Kotal is occupied by three regiments and two guns. The Kotal-i-Murcha is held by the Kabul regiments, and Ayub's own camp is at Mazra, where it is said that the majority of his guns are parked. I propose to encamp the Infantry to the west of Kandahar immediately under the walls, and the Cavalry under the walls to the south. Should I hear that Ayub contemplates flight, I shall attack without delay. If, on the contrary, he intends to resist, I shall take my own time. The country he is occupying is, from description and map, extremely difficult and easily defensible, and each separate advance will require careful study and reconnaissance to prevent unnecessary loss of life.'

On the morning of the 31st we marched into Kandahar, just over 313 miles from Kabul. The fever, which had attacked me rather sharply, had left me extremely weak, and I was unable to ride the whole way. I got on my horse, however, some distance from Kandahar to meet Generals Primrose, Burrows, and Nuttall, who came out to receive the column. As we approached the city, the whole garrison turned out and gave us a hearty welcome; officers and men, Native and British, crowded round us, loud in their expressions of gratitude for our having come so quickly to their assistance. We, on our side, were all anxiety to learn the particulars about Maiwand, how they had fared while invested, and all they could tell us of Ayub Khan, his position, strength of his army, etc.

I confess to being very greatly surprised, not to use a stronger expression, at the demoralized condition of the greater part of the garrison;* there were notable exceptions,† but the general bearing of the troops reminded me of the people at Agra in 1857. They seemed to consider themselves hopelessly defeated, and were utterly despondent; they never even hoisted the Union Jack until the relieving force was close at hand. The same excuses could not, however, be made for them, who were all soldiers by profession, as we had felt inclined to make for the residents at Agra, a great majority of whom were women, children, and civilians. The walls‡ which completely

* The effective garrison consisted of 1,000 British soldiers, 3,000 Native soldiers, and fifteen Field guns.

† One and all bore testimony to the unfailing good behaviour and creditable bearing of the Royal Artillery and the Bombay Sappers and Miners, not only during the investment, but in the very trying time of the retreat from Maiwand.

‡ The walls had an average height of 30 feet, and breadth of 15 feet on the north and east fronts.

surrounded Kandahar were so high and thick as to render the city absolutely impregnable to any army not equipped with a regular siege-train. Scaling-ladders had been prepared by the enemy, and there was an idea that an assault would be attempted; but for British soldiers to have contemplated the possibility of Kandahar being taken by an Afghan army showed what a miserable state of depression and demoralization they were in.

I halted the column for two hours outside the south wall of the city, where it was sheltered from the enemy's fire, Ayub Khan's position being within long range directly north of Kandahar. While the men rested and breakfasted, and the baggage animals were being unloaded, fed, and watered, I went into the citadel to talk matters over with General Primrose and Colonel St. John, and inquire whether there was sufficient accommodation for the sick men of my force, numbering 940, who needed to be taken into hospital. The thermometer now registered 105° Fahr. in tents during the day, but the nights were still bitterly cold, and the sudden changes of temperature were extremely trying to people in bad health.

On the advice of Lieutenant-Colonel Chapman, whose intimate acquaintance with the neighbourhood of Kandahar, gained while serving on Sir Donald Stewart's staff, was now most valuable to me, I determined to take up a position to the west of the city, with my right on the cantonment and my left touching Old Kandahar. This enabled me to cover the city, gave me command of a good supply of water, and placed me within striking distance of Ayub Khan's camp.

At 10 a.m. the first and third brigades moved off and occupied Piquet Hill, Karez Hill, and the north-east spur of the hill above Old Kandahar. A few shots were fired at the advance guard from distant orchards, and the ground proved to be within range of some of the enemy's Field-pieces on the Baba Wali Kotal, but it was a case of Hobson's choice, as water was not to be found anywhere else at a come-at-able distance.

Large numbers of men were to be seen crowning the Baba Wali Kotal, and constructing shelter-trenches along the crest of the low black ridge, which jutted out in a south-easterly direction from the more lofty range on which the kotal is situated. Piquets were immediately sent to occupy the northern spur of the Kohkeran Hill commanding the road to Gundigan, the village of Abbasabad, the Karez Hill, the village of Chihal Dukhtaran, the greater and lesser Piquet Hills, and the village of Kalachi, all of which were found to be deserted.

From a cursory examination of the ground, I satisfied myself that any attempt to carry the Baba Wali Kotal by direct attack must result in very severe loss, and I determined to turn it. But before I could decide how this could best be done, it was necessary to ascertain the strength and precise extent of the Afghan position. I therefore detailed a small party,* under the command of Brigadier-General Hugh Gough, to make as complete a reconnaissance as time would allow. In the meantime I despatched the following telegram to the authorities at Simla:

'KANDAHAR,
'31st August, 1880.

'The force under my command arrived here this morning without opposition. Enemy are said to be in considerable strength at Mazra, but the ridge of hills which divides Kandahar from the Arghandab completely covers their position, and at present I have only been able to ascertain that the Baba Wali Kotal and one or two other points on this ridge are held in great strength, and that the enemy are busily engaged in defensive works. Reconnaissances are now being conducted, and I shall soon, I hope, be sufficiently acquainted with affairs generally to enable me to arrange for an attack. The Kandahar garrison are in good health; the horses and transport animals appear to be in good condition. Major Vandeleur, 7th Fusiliers, has died of his wounds; the remainder of the wounded, both officers and men, are generally doing well. The troops from Kabul are in famous health and spirits. The assurance of the safety of this garrison enabled comparatively short marches to be made from Kelat-i-Ghilzai, which much benefited both men and animals. The Cavalry horses and Artillery mules are in excellent condition, and the transport animals are, as a rule, in very fair order. General Primrose has arranged for the sick of the force from Kabul being accommodated inside the city; many of the cases are sore feet; none are serious. To-morrow the telegraph line towards India will commence to be re-constructed, and as General Phayre is probably on this side of the Kohjak to-day, through communication should soon be restored.'

The reconnaissance, which started at 1 p.m., proceeded towards the high ground immediately above the villages of Gundigan and Murghan. Here the Infantry and guns were halted, while the Cavalry advanced between two or three miles, avoiding the numerous orchards and enclosures, and coming out in front of Pir Paimal, which was found to be strongly entrenched.

As soon as the enemy's fire along this line had been drawn, the 3rd Bengal Cavalry fell back, admirably handled by their Commandant, Lieutenant Colonel A. Mackenzie. In the meantime, two guns of No. 11 Battery 9th Brigade were brought into action, partly to test the range, and partly to check the enemy, who were passing rapidly into the gardens near Gundigan. The Infantry and Artillery then retired within the line of piquets, and the moment they began to fall back the Afghans came after them in great strength; they were so persistent that I ordered the whole of the 3rd Brigade and part of the 1st Brigade under arms. The enemy, however, were unable to come to close quarters owing to the bold front shown by the 15th Sikhs, under the

* Two Royal Artillery guns, 3rd Bengal Cavalry, and 15th Sikhs. Lieutenant-Colonel Chapman accompanied the party, and was of great assistance to Brigadier-General Gough.

command of Lieutenant-Colonel Hennessy, and before dark the troops were all back in camp, with a loss of five men killed and fifteen wounded.

From the information obtained by this reconnaissance, I found that it was quite practicable to turn the Afghan right, and thus place myself in rear of the Baba Wali range; I decided, therefore, to attack the position the following morning. It was too close to our camp to risk delay. Moreover, I knew that the retrograde movement of Gough's small body would be construed into a defeat by the enemy, who, if we did not move at once, would assuredly think that we were afraid to take the initiative, and would become correspondingly bold.

I accordingly issued orders for the troops to breakfast at 7 a.m., and for one day's cooked rations to be carried by the Infantry and two days by the Cavalry and Horse Artillery. Brigades were to be in position by eight o'clock, tents being previously struck and the baggage stored in a walled enclosure.

The night passed quietly except for occasional bursts of musketry along the line of piquets to the west, showing that the Afghans were holding the villages they had occupied the previous evening.

CHAPTER LXII.

The next morning, the 1st September, in accordance with instructions from Simla, I assumed command of the army in southern Afghanistan. There was no return to show the strength or composition of General Phayre's column, but the troops at Kandahar all told now amounted in round numbers to 3,800 British and 11,000 Native soldiers, with 36 guns.

An hour before daybreak the whole of the troops were under arms, and at 6 a.m. I explained to Generals Primrose and Ross and the officers commanding brigades the plan of operations. Briefly, it was to threaten the enemy's left (the Baba Wali Kotal), and to attack in force by the village of Pir Paimal.

The Infantry belonging to the Kabul column, upon whom devolved the duty of carrying the enemy's position, were formed up in rear of the low hills which covered the front of our camp, their right being at Piquet Hill and their left resting on Chitral Zina. The Cavalry of the Kabul column were drawn up in rear of the left, ready to operate by Gundigan towards the head of the Arghandab, so as to threaten the rear of Ayub Khan's camp and his line of retreat in the direction of Girishk. Four guns of E Battery Royal Horse Artillery, two companies of the 2—7th Fusiliers, and four companies of the 28th Bombay Infantry, were placed at the disposal of Brigadier-General Hugh Gough, whose orders were to occupy with these troops the position above Gundigan, which had been so useful during the previous day's reconnaissance, and to push his Cavalry on to the Arghandab.

Guards having been detailed for the protection of the city, the remainder of Lieutenant-General Primrose's troops were ordered to be disposed as follows: Brigadier-General Daubeny's brigade to occupy the ground between Piquet Hill and Chitral Zina as soon as the Infantry of the Kabul-Kandahar Field Force advanced to the attack. The remnant of Brigadier-General Burrows's brigade, with No. 5 Battery, 11th Brigade Royal Artillery, under Captain Hornsby, and the Cavalry under Brigadier-General Nuttall, to take up a position north of the cantonment, from which the 40-pounders could be brought to bear on the Baba Wali Kotal, while the Cavalry could watch the pass, called Kotal-i-Murcha, and cover the city.

From an early hour it was clear that the enemy contemplated an offensive movement; the villages of Gundigan and Gundi Mulla Sahibdab were being held in strength, and a desultory fire was brought to bear on the British front from the orchards connecting these two villages and from the Baba Wali Kotal.

The Bombay Cavalry moved out at 7.30 a.m., and Daubeny's brigade at eight o'clock. Burrows's troops followed, and shortly after 9 a.m., their disposition being completed, Captain Hornsby opened fire upon the kotal, which was one mass of *ghazis*.

This feint, made by General Primrose's troops, having had the effect I had hoped, of attracting the enemy's attention, I gave the order for Major-General Ross to make the real attack with the 1st and 2nd Brigades of his division. The 3rd Brigade, under Brigadier-General Macgregor, I placed in front of the village of Abbasabad, with the double object of being a reserve to the 1st and 2nd Brigades and of meeting a possible counter-attack from the Baba Wali Kotal.

Ross's orders were to advance against Gundi Mulla Sahibdad, capture the village, and then drive the enemy from the enclosures which lay between it and the low spur of Pir Paimal hill. This duty he entrusted to Brigadier-General Macpherson, and he directed Brigadier-General Baker to advance to the west, to keep touch with the 1st Brigade, and to clear the gardens and orchards in his immediate front.

Greig's 9-pounder and Robinson's 7-pounder (screw gun) batteries covered the attack on Gundi Mulla Sahibdad, which was made by the 2nd Gurkhas, under Lieutenant-Colonel Arthur Battye, and the 92nd Highlanders, under Lieutenant-Colonel G. Parker, supported by the 23rd Pioneers, under Lieutenant-Colonel H. Collett, and the 24th Punjab Infantry, under Colonel F. Norman. The village was carried with the utmost gallantry, Highlanders and Gurkhas, always friendly rivals in the race for glory, by turns outstripping each other in their efforts to be first within its walls. The enemy sullenly and slowly withdrew, a goodly number of *ghazis* remaining to the very last to receive a bayonet charge of the 92nd. Meanwhile, Baker's troops had been threading their way through the narrow lanes and loop-holed enclosures which lay in the line of their spirited attack; the resistance they encountered was most stubborn, and it was during this advance that the 72nd lost their dashing Commander, Lieutenant-Colonel F. Brownlow,* Captain Frome, and Lance-Sergeant Cameron, the latter a grand specimen of a Highland soldier.

In the 2nd Brigade, the 72nd Highlanders and the 2nd Sikhs bore the brunt of the fighting; they were the leading battalions, and frequently had to fix bayonets to carry different positions or to check the desperate rushes of the Afghans.

After continued and severe fighting, both leading brigades emerged at the point of the hill close to Pir Paimal, and, wheeling to their right, they pressed rapidly on, sweeping the enemy through the thickly-wooded gardens which covered the western slopes, until noon, when the whole of Pir Paimal was in our possession.†

During the early part of the advance the Afghans collected in great strength on the low hills beneath the Baba Wali Kotal, evidently preparing for a rush on our guns; their leaders could be seen urging them on, and a portion of them came down the hill, but the main body apparently refused to follow, and remained on the crest until the position was turned, when they at once retreated.

Having become assured of General Ross's complete success, and seeing that there was now no necessity for detaining Macgregor's (the 3rd) brigade to meet a counter-attack, I pushed on with it to join Ross, who, however, knowing how thoroughly he could depend upon his troops, without waiting to be reinforced, followed up the retreating

* Brownlow's death was a great loss, for throughout the war he had frequently distinguished himself as a leader—at the Peiwar Kotal, during the operations round Kabul, and notably on the 14th December, when he won the admiration of the whole force by his brilliant conduct in the attack on the Asmai heights.

† The following Native officers, British and Native non-commissioned officers, and Native soldiers were brought forward as having been very conspicuous during this part of the fight:

Colour-Sergeant G. Jacobs - - -	72nd Highlanders.
Colour-Sergeant R. Lauder - - -	" "
Lance-Corporal J. Gordon - - -	" "
Subadar-Major Gurbaj Sing - -	2nd Sikhs.
Jemadar Alla Sing - - - -	" "
Naick Dir Sing - - - -	" "
Sepoy Hakim - - - -	" "
Sepoy Taj Sing - - - -	" "
Sepoy Pertap Sing - - - -	" "
Sepoy Bir Sing - - - -	" "

foe, until he reached an entrenched position at the other side of the Baba Wali Kotal, where the Afghans made another most determined stand. *Ghazis* in large numbers flocked to this spot from the rear, while the guns on the kotal were turned round and brought to bear on our men, already exposed to a heavy Artillery fire from behind the entrenched camp.

It now became necessary to take this position by storm, and recognizing the fact with true soldierly instinct, Major White, who was leading the advanced companies of the 92nd, called upon the men for just one charge more 'to close the business.' The battery of screw guns had been shelling the position, and, under cover of its fire and supported by a portion of the 2nd Gurkhas and 23rd Pioneers, the Highlanders, responding with alacrity to their leader's call, dashed forward and drove the enemy from their entrenchments at the point of the bayonet.*

Major White was the first to reach the guns, being closely followed by Sepoy Inderbir Lama, who, placing his rifle upon one of them, exclaimed, 'Captured in the name of the 2nd (Prince of Wales' Own) Gurkhas!'

Whilst the 1st Brigade was advancing towards the last position, a half-battalion of the 3rd Sikhs (belonging to the 2nd Brigade), under Lieutenant-Colonel G. Money, charged a body of Afghans and captured three guns.

The enemy were now absolutely routed, but, owing to the nature of the ground, it was impossible for General Ross to realize how complete had been his victory, and he fully expected that the enemy would take up a fresh position further on; he therefore ordered the 1st and 2nd Brigades to halt while they replenished their ammunition, and then proceeded for about a mile, when they suddenly came in sight of Ayub Khan's enormous camp. It was entirely deserted, and apparently stood as it had been left in the morning when the Afghans moved out to the attack. With his camp was captured the whole of Ayub Khan's Artillery, thirty-two pieces, including our two Horse Artillery guns† which had been taken at Maiwand on the 27th July.

* During this engagement the following officers and men were specially remarked for their gallantry:

Major G. White - - -	92nd Highlanders.
Lieutenant C. Douglas - - -	,, ,,
Corporal William McGillvray - -	,, ,,
Private Peter Grieve - - -	,, ,,
Private D. Grey - - - -	,, ,,
Major Sullivan Becher - - -	2nd Gurkhas.
Havildar Gopal Borah - - -	,, ,,
Sepoy Inderbir Lama - - -	,, ,,
Sepoy Tikaram Kwas - - -	,, ,,

† These guns were presented to me by the Indian Government, and are now at the Royal Hospital Dublin.

Further pursuit by the Infantry being valueless, the 1st and 2nd Brigades halted on the far side of Mazra, where I with the 3rd Brigade shortly afterwards joined them.

Brigadier-General Hugh Gough, having satisfied himself as to the security of our left flank, scouted as far as Kohkeran, and then proceeded with the Cavalry of the Kabul-Kandahar Field Force to execute the extended movement entrusted to him. He crossed the Arghandab, and pushed round to get in front of the line of the enemy's retreat towards Khakrez. Some *ghazis* and Irregular Afghan troops were overtaken, but no Regular regiments were met with, the soldiers having, as is their custom, quickly divested themselves of their uniform and assumed the garb of harmless agriculturists.

Ayub Khan himself had fled early in the day with his principal Sirdars.

As I rode into the abandoned camp, I was horrified to hear that the body of Maclaine, the Horse Artillery officer who had been taken prisoner at Maiwand, was lying with the throat cut about forty yards from Ayub Khan's own tent. From what I could learn, the latter had not actually ordered the murder, but as a word from him would have prevented it, he must be held responsible for the assassination of an officer who had fallen into his hands as a prisoner of war.

Our losses during the day comprised: killed, 3 British officers,* 1 Native officer, and 36 men; wounded, 11 British officers, 4 Native officers, and 195 men, 18 of whom succumbed to their wounds. It was difficult to estimate the loss of the enemy, but it must have been heavy, as between Kandahar and the village of Pir Paimal alone 600 bodies were buried by us.

With the exception of the 1st Brigade, which remained at Mazra for the night to protect the captured guns and stores, the troops all returned to camp before 9 p.m.†

Utterly exhausted as I was from the hard day's work and the weakening effects of my late illness, the cheers with which I was

* The third British officer killed was Captain Straton, 22nd Foot, Superintendent of Army Signalling, a most accomplished officer, under whose direction signalling as applied to Field Service reached a wonderful pitch of perfection. His energy knew no difficulties, and his enthusiasm was beyond praise.

† The ammunition expended by the Kabul-Kandahar Field Force on the 31st August and 1st September was:

	Rounds.		
Gun - - -	102	Shrapnell shell	78
		Common ,,	24
Rifle - - -	57,705	Martini-Henry	15,129
		Snider	42,576

and in addition 313 rounds were fired by the Artillery and 4,971 rounds by the Infantry of the Kandahar Garrison.

greeted by the troops as I rode into Ayub Khan's camp and viewed the dead bodies of my gallant soldiers nearly unmanned me, and it was with a very big lump in my throat that I managed to say a few words of thanks to each corps in turn. When I returned to Kandahar, and threw myself on the bed in the little room prepared for me, I was dead-beat and quite unequal to the effort of reporting our success to the Queen or to the Viceroy. After an hour's rest, however, knowing how anxiously news from Kandahar was looked for both in England and India, I managed to pull myself together sufficiently to write out and despatch the following telegram:

'KANDAHAR,
'*1st September*, 1880 (6 p.m.).

'Ayub Khan's army was to-day defeated and completely dispersed with, I hope, comparatively slight loss on our side; his camp was captured, the two lost guns of E Battery, B Brigade Royal Horse Artillery were recovered, and several wheeled guns of various calibre fell to the splendid Infantry of this force; the Cavalry are still in pursuit. Our casualties are: 22nd Foot, Captain Straton, killed; 72nd Highlanders, Lieutenant-Colonel Brownlow, Captain Frome, killed, Captain Murray and Lieutenant Monro, wounded, 7 men killed, 18 wounded; 92nd Highlanders, Lieutenants Menzies and Donald Stewart wounded, 11 men killed and 39 wounded; 2nd Gurkhas, Lieutenant-Colonel Battye, and 2nd Sikhs, Major Slater wounded. It is at present impossible to ascertain the casualties amongst the Native troops, but I have no reason to believe they are excessive; full details will be telegraphed to-morrow. The quite recently murdered remains of Lieutenant Maclaine, Royal Horse Artillery, were found on the arrival of the British troops in Ayub Khan's camp. Ayub Khan is supposed to have fled towards Herat.'

It can easily be imagined with what an intense sense of relief I awoke on the morning of the 2nd September—the march had ended, Kandahar had been relieved, Ayub Khan's army had been beaten and dispersed, and there was an adequate force in southern Afghanistan to prevent further disturbances.

Amongst the innumerable questions of detail which now confronted me was the all-important one, and that which caused me greatest anxiety, of how the large body of troops hastily concentrated at Kandahar, and for which the produce of the country was quite inadequate, were to be fed.

No supplies and very little forage were procurable between Quetta and Kandahar, and in the neighbourhood of the latter place there was now hardly anything in the shape of food for man or beast to be had for love or money, the resources of this part of the country having been quite exhausted. Relief could only be obtained by reducing the number of mouths to be fed, and with this object I scattered the troops in different directions, to posts as far distant from each other as possible, consistent with safety; and in accordance with my promise to the Kabul-Kandahar Field Force, that they should not be required

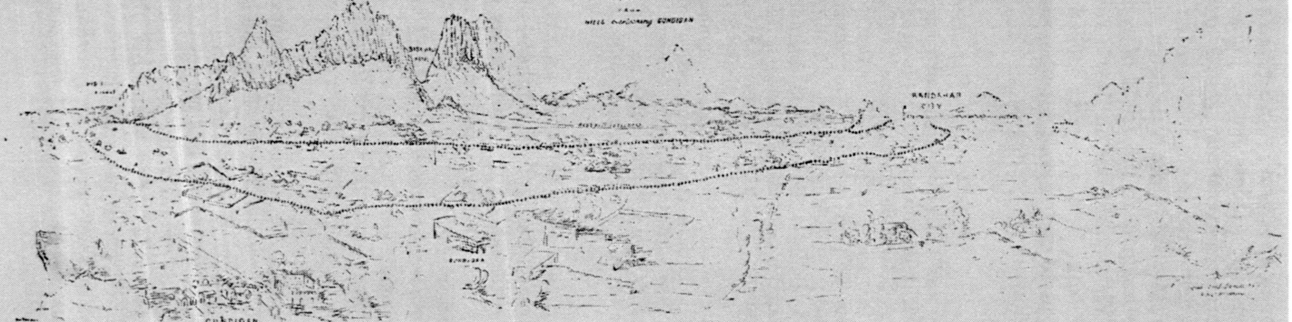
PEN AND INK SKETCH OF BATTLE-FIELD OF KANDAHAR
1st September 1880
FROM
HILLS overlooking GUNDIGAN
KANDAHAR CITY
GUNDIGAN

to garrison Kandahar when the fighting was at an end, I arranged to despatch without delay to India the corps which had come with me from northern Afghanistan.

One column proceeded to Maiwand to inter the bodies of our soldiers who fell on the 27th July. The Cavalry brigade moved with a number of sick men and transport animals to Kohkeran. Macgregor's brigade started for Quetta on the 8th, and was followed soon after by Baker's and Macpherson's brigades. I accompanied Macgregor in the hope that the change to Quetta (where I remained about a month) would pick me up, and enable me to meet Lord Ripon's wish that I should retain the command in southern Afghanistan until some satisfactory settlement could be arrived at.

Before leaving Kandahar I issued an order thanking all ranks of the Kabul-Kandahar Field Force for the work they had so nobly performed, and I had the gratification of acknowledging, on their behalf and my own, congratulatory messages from the Queen, the Duke of Cambridge, the Marquis of Ripon, and many others. On the way to Quetta I had the further gratification of being informed by the Viceroy that Her Majesty had been graciously pleased to make me a G.C.B., and to appoint me Commander-in-Chief of the Madras Army.

I now heard that Abdur Rahman had been finally nominated Amir of Kabul on the 10th August, and that immediately after the ceremony of installation Sir Donald Stewart had marched the whole British force of 6,678 men of all arms out of Kabul on their return to India. Sir Donald left Peshawar to take up his appointment of Military Member of Council at Simla on the 31st August, and by the 7th September the last of his troops had arrived at the former place, except one brigade left as a temporary measure in the Khyber Pass.

At Quetta I stayed with Sir Robert Sandeman, the capable Resident, who by his great personal influence had done much to allay excitement amongst the tribes, and to prevent serious trouble in Baluchistan and along the border. I had never before been to that part of the frontier, and I was greatly impressed by the hold Sandeman had obtained over the country; he was intimately acquainted with every leading man, and there was not a village, however out of the way, which he had not visited. 'Sinniman *sahib*,' as the Natives called him, had gained the confidence of the lawless Baluchis in a very remarkable manner, and it was mainly owing to his power over them that I was able to arrange with camel contractors to transport to Quetta and Kandahar the huge stocks of winter clothing, medical comforts, grain, and the various requirements of an army in the field, which had been brought by rail to Sibi, and had there remained for want of transport to take them further on.

As the change to Quetta did not benefit me, and as I found that, owing to indifferent health, I was unable to carry on my duty with satisfaction to myself, I applied to be relieved. My request was acceded to, and I started on the 12th October for India.

Riding through the Bolan Pass I overtook most of the regiments of the Kabul-Kandahar Field Force marching towards Sibi, thence to disperse to their respective destinations. As I parted with each corps in turn its band played 'Auld Lang Syne,' and I have never since heard that memory-stirring air without its bringing before my mind's eye the last view I had of the Kabul-Kandahar Field Force. I fancy myself crossing and re-crossing the river which winds through the pass; I hear the martial beat of drums and plaintive music of the pipes; and I see Riflemen and Gurkhas, Highlanders and Sikhs, guns and horses, camels and mules, with the endless following of an Indian army, winding through the narrow gorges, or over the interminable boulders which made the passage of the Bolan so difficult and wearisome to man and beast.

I shall never forget the feeling of sadness with which I said good-bye to the men who had done so much for me. I looked upon them all, Native as well as British, as my valued friends. And well I might, for never had a Commander been better served. From first to last a grand spirit of *camaraderie** pervaded all ranks. At the Peiwar Kotal, at Charasia, and during the fighting round Kabul, all were eager to close with the enemy, no matter how great the odds against them. Throughout the march from Kabul all seemed to be animated with but one desire, to effect, cost what it might in personal risk, fatigue, or discomfort, the speedy release of their beleaguered fellow-soldiers in Kandahar; and the unflagging energy and perseverance of my splendid troops seemed to reach their full height, when they realized they were about to put forth their strength against a hitherto successful enemy. Their exemplary conduct, too, under circumstances often of the most trying nature, cannot be praised in terms too strong or too full. Notwithstanding the provocation caused by the cruel murder of any stragglers who fell into the hands of the Afghans, not one act infringing the rules of civilized

* The 72nd Highlanders and 5th Gurkhas were brigaded together throughout the campaign, and at their return to India the latter regiment presented the former with a shield bearing the following inscription:

FROM THE

MEN OF THE 5TH GURKHAS

TO THE

MEN OF THE 72ND (DUKE OF ALBANY'S OWN) HIGHLANDERS

IN REMEMBRANCE OF

THE AFGHAN CAMPAIGN, 1878 TO 1880.

The gift was entirely spontaneous, and was subscribed for by the Native officers, non-commissioned officers, and men.

In return, the non-commissioned officers and men of the 72nd gave the 5th Gurkhas a very handsome ebony, silver-mounted Drum-Major's staff.

warfare was committed by my troops. The persons and property of the Natives were respected, and full compensation for supplies was everywhere given. In short, the inhabitants of the district through which we passed could not have been treated with greater consideration nor with a lighter hand, had they proved themselves friendly allies, and the conduct of the troops will ever be to me as pleasing a memory as are the results which they achieved.

CHAPTER LXIII.

On the 15th October I handed over my command to Major-General Phayre, and started for England, making, by the desire of the Viceroy, a diversion to Simla, where Lord Ripon received me most kindly, and, to my great pride and pleasure, delivered to me a letter from the Queen-Empress, written by Her Majesty's own hand, which conveyed in the most gracious terms the Queen's satisfaction at the manner in which the service entrusted to me had been performed, thanks to 'the brave officers and men under my command,' sorrow 'for those of her gallant soldiers who fell for Queen and country,' and anxiety for the wounded. Her Majesty also wrote of 'the thrill of horror' with which the news of the fate of Lieutenant Maclaine had been received, and concluded with words of hope that my own health and that of the troops would remain good, and that success might attend us 'till the blessings of peace are restored.'

A gracious letter, truly! And to me a deeply appreciated reward for what I had been able to do.

I landed at Dover on the 17th November. The reception I met with from my countrymen was as enthusiastic as it was unexpected and gratifying. After an absence of twelve years there must almost always be more or less of sadness mingled with the pleasure of the home-coming, and two vacant places in my family circle—those of my father and sister—cast a deep shadow upon what would otherwise have been a most joyous return, for my mother was alive to welcome me, and I found my children flourishing and my wife well, notwithstanding all the anxiety she had undergone.

I was fêted and feasted to almost an alarming extent, considering that for nearly two years I had been restricted to campaigning diet; but it surprised me very much to find that the kind people, by whom I was so greatly honoured, invariably appeared to think the march from Kabul to Kandahar was a much greater performance than the advance on Kabul the previous autumn, while, to my mind, the latter operation was in every particular more difficult, more dangerous, and placed upon me as the Commander infinitely more responsibility The force with which I started from Kuram to avenge the massacre of our fellow-countrymen was little more than half the strength of that with which I marched to Kandahar. Immediately on crossing the Shutargardan I found myself in the midst of a hostile and warlike people, entirely dependent on the country for supplies, heavily handicapped by want of transport, and practically as completely cut off from communication with India as I was a year later on the march to Kandahar. The Afghans' fanatical hatred of Europeans had been augmented by their defeats the year before, and by the occurrences at Kabul, and they looked upon my small column as a certain prey delivered into their hands by a sympathizing and all-powerful Allah.

Before me was Kabul, with its large and well-equipped arsenal, defended by an army better organized and more highly trained than that possessed by any former Ruler of Afghanistan. On all sides of me were tribesmen hurrying up to defend the approaches to their capital, and had there been on our part the smallest hesitation or delay, we should have found ourselves opposed by as formidable a combination as we had to deal with two months later at Sherpur. Nothing could then have saved the force, not one man of which I firmly believe would have ever returned to tell the tale in India. Worse than all, I had in my own camp a traitor, in the form of the Amir, posing as a friend to the British Government and a refugee seeking our protection, while he was at heart our bitterest enemy, and was doing everything in his power to make my task more difficult and ensure our defeat.

The march to Kandahar was certainly much longer, the country was equally unfriendly, and the feeding of so large a number of men and animals was a continual source of anxiety. But I had a force capable of holding its own against any Afghan army that could possibly be opposed to it, and good and sufficient transport to admit of its being kept together, with the definite object in view of rescuing our besieged countrymen and defeating Ayub Khan; instead of, as at Kabul, having to begin to unravel a difficult political problem after accomplishing the defeat of the tribesmen and the Afghan army.

I could only account to myself for the greater amount of interest displayed in the march to Kandahar, and the larger amount of credit given to me for that undertaking, by the glamour of romance thrown around an army of 10,000 men lost to view, as it were, for nearly a month, about the fate of which uninformed speculation was rife and pessimistic rumours were spread, until the tension became extreme, and the corresponding relief proportionably great when that army reappeared to dispose at once of Ayub and his hitherto victorious troops.

I did not return to India until the end of 1881, six weeks out of these precious months of leave having been spent in a wild-goose chase to the Cape of Good Hope and back, upon my being nominated by Mr. Gladstone's Government Governor of Natal and Commander of the Forces in South Africa, on the death of Sir George Colley and the receipt of the news of the disaster at Majuba Hill. While I was on my way out to take up my command, peace was made with the Boers in the most marvellously rapid and unexpected manner. A peace, alas! 'without honour,' to which may be attributed the recent regrettable state of affairs in the Transvaal—a state of affairs which was foreseen and predicted by many at the time. My stay at Cape Town was limited to twenty-four hours, the Government being apparently as anxious to get me away from Africa as they had been to hurry me out there.

In August I spent three very enjoyable and instructive weeks as the guest of His Imperial Majesty the Emperor of Germany, while the manœuvres at Hanover and Schleswig-Holstein were taking place.

Shortly before leaving England for Madras, I was asked by Mr. Childers, the then Secretary of State for War, whether I would accept the appointment of Quartermaster-General at the Horse Guards, in succession to Sir Garnet Wolseley. The offer, in some ways, was rather a temptation to me, for I had a great wish to take part in the administration of our army; and had it been made sooner, before my arrangements for going to Madras had been completed, I think I should have accepted it at once; as it was, I begged to be allowed to join my new command, and leave the question of the Quartermaster Generalship in abeyance until it was about to become vacant. This was agreed to, and I started for Madras, taking my wife and two little daughters with me, the boy being left at school in England.

On arriving in Madras, on the 27th November, I had the pleasure to find myself associated as a colleague in Council with Mr. Grant-Duff,* who had recently been appointed Governor of the Presidency. We spent a few pleasant days with him and Mrs. Grant-Duff at Government House, before proceeding to deposit our children at Ootacamund, that Queen of Indian Hill-stations, which was to be our home for four years. We spent Christmas there, and then went to Burma, visiting the Andaman Islands on the way. We had on board our ship some prisoners destined for that convict settlement, amongst whom cholera unfortunately broke out a few hours after we left Madras. They were accommodated just outside my wife's cabin, and their cries and groans were most distressing. Very little could be done for them on board, for the Native Doctor accompanying us possessed no remedy but castor oil! and as the disease was spreading rapidly, I took upon myself to have the party landed at Vizagapatam.

* Now Sir Mount-Stuart Grant-Duff, G.C.S.I.

The cholera patients were put into tents on the sea-shore, under the charge of a medical officer, and every arrangement possible for their comfort and relief was made before we proceeded on our journey.

During our stay at Port Blair, the Head-Quarters of the Andaman Administration, we were the guests of the hospitable Superintendent, Lieutenant-Colonel Protheroe, who had been one of the political officers on my staff in Afghanistan. The group of islands forming the settlement are extremely beautiful, but it is tropical beauty, and one pays the penalty for the luxuriant vegetation in the climate, which is very much like a Turkish bath, hot and damp. While going through the prisons, I came across some of the sepoys of the 29th Punjab Infantry who deserted during the advance on the Peiwar Kotal. I was told that they were behaving well, and might in time be allowed some remission of their sentences.

A voyage of thirty-six hours brought us to Rangoon, where we had the pleasure of meeting and being entertained by our old friends, Mr. Bernard,* the Chief Commissioner of Burma, and his wife.

In 1882 Thyetmyo and Tonghu were the two frontier stations of Burma, and I had been asked to consider the question of the defence of the proposed railway termini at these places. I accordingly visited them both, and as I thought I foresaw that the lines of railway could not end as then contemplated, I recommended that the absolutely necessary works only should be attempted, and that these should be as inexpensive as possible. Ere many years had passed, the line, as I anticipated, was completed to Mandalay.

The defences of Rangoon had also to be arranged for. An examination of the approaches, however, satisfied me that no elaborate system of fortification was necessary, and that Rangoon's best security lay in her winding, dangerous river; so I gave it as my opinion that, with two small batteries at Monkey Point and King's Point, and a couple of torpedo-boats, Rangoon would be reasonably safe against attack.

Before leaving Burma I received letters from H.R.H. the Duke of Cambridge and Mr. Childers, in which were repeated the offer of the Quartermaster-Generalship at the Horse Guards. But I had by this time begun to like my new work, and had no desire to leave Madras; I therefore definitely declined the appointment.

From Burma we returned to Ootacamund, *viâ* Calcutta, where we spent a few days with Lord and Lady Ripon and Sir Donald and Lady Stewart.

Life at 'Ooty' was very pleasant; such peace and repose I had never before experienced; I thoroughly enjoyed the rest after the turmoil of the preceding years, and I quite recovered my health, which had been somewhat shattered. Unlike other hill-stations,

* Now Sir Charles Bernard, K.C.S.I.

Ootacamund rests on an undulating tableland, 7,400 feet above the sea, with plenty of room in the neighbourhood for riding, driving, and hunting; and, although the scenery is nothing like as grand as in the Himalayas, there are exquisite views to be had, and it is more restful and homelike. We made many warm friends and agreeable acquaintances, who when our time in Madras came to an end presented my wife with a very beautiful clock 'as a token of esteem and affection'; we were very sorry to bid farewell to our friends and to our Nilgiri home.

Each cold season I made long tours in order to acquaint myself with the needs and capabilities of the men of the Madras Army. I tried hard to discover in them those fighting qualities which had distinguished their forefathers during the wars of the last and the beginning of the present century. But long years of peace, and the security and prosperity attending it, had evidently had upon them, as they always seem to have on Asiatics, a softening and deteriorating effect; and I was forced to the conclusion that the ancient military spirit had died in them, as it had died in the ordinary Hindustani of Bengal and the Mahratta of Bombay, and that they could no longer with safety be pitted against warlike races, or employed outside the limits of southern India.

It was with extreme reluctance that I formed this opinion with regard to the successors of the old Coast Army, for which I had always entertained a great admiration. For the sake of the British officers belonging to the Madras Army, too, I was very loath to be convinced of its inferiority, for many of them were devoted to their regiments, and were justly proud of their traditions.

However, there was the army, and it was my business as its Commander-in-Chief to do all that I possibly could towards rendering it an efficient part of the war establishment of India.

Madrassies, as a rule, are more intelligent and better educated than the fighting races of northern India, and I therefore thought it could not be difficult to teach them the value of musketry, and make them excel in it. To this end, I encouraged rifle meetings and endeavoured to get General Officers to take an interest in musketry inspections, and to make those inspections instructive and entertaining to the men. I took to rifle-shooting myself, as did the officers on my personal staff,* who were all good shots, and our team held its own in many exciting matches at the different rifle meetings.

At that time the importance of musketry training was not so generally recognized as it is now, especially by the senior officers, who

* Lieutenant-Colonel G. T. Pretyman, R.A., was Assistant Military Secretary until 1884, when he was succeeded by Lieutenant-Colonel R. Pole-Carew, Coldstream Guards. Lieutenant Neville Chamberlain, Central India Horse and Captain Ian Hamilton, the Gordon Highlanders, were Aides-de-camp.

had all entered the service in the days of 'Brown Bess.' Some of them had failed to note the remarkable alteration which the change from the musket to the rifle necessitated in the system of musketry instruction, or to study the very different conditions under which we could hope to win battles in the present day, compared with those under which some of our most celebrated victories had been won. It required time and patience to inspire officers with a belief in the wonderful shooting power of the Martini-Henry rifle, and it was even more difficult to make them realize that the better the weapon, the greater the necessity for its being intelligently used.

I had great faith in the value of Camps of Exercise, and notwithstanding the difficulty of obtaining an annual grant to defray their cost, I managed each year, by taking advantage of the movement of troops in course of relief, to form small camps at the more important stations, and on one occasion was able to collect 9,000 men together in the neighbourhood of Bangalore, where the Commanders-in-Chief in India and of Bombay (Sir Donald Stewart and the Hon. Arthur Hardinge) were present—the first and last time that the 'three Chiefs' in India met together at a Camp of Exercise. The Sappers and Miners were a brilliant exception to the rest of the Madras Army, being indeed a most useful, efficient body of men, but as no increase to that branch was considered necessary, I obtained permission to convert two Infantry regiments into Pioneers on the model of the Pioneer Corps of the Bengal Army, which had always proved themselves so useful on service. Promotion amongst the British officers was accelerated, recruits were not allowed to marry, or, if married, to have their wives with them, and many other minor changes were made which did much towards improving the efficiency of the Native portion of the Madras Army; and I hope I was able to increase the comfort and well-being of the British portion also by relaxing irksome and useless restrictions, and by impressing upon commanding officers the advisability of not punishing young soldiers with the extreme severity which had hitherto been considered necessary.

I had been unpleasantly struck by the frequent Courts-Martial on the younger soldiers, and by the disproportionate number of these lads to be met with in the military prisons. Even when the prisoners happened to be of some length of service, I usually found that they had undergone previous imprisonments, and had been severely punished within a short time of their enlistment. I urged that, in the first two or three years of a soldier's service, every allowance should be made for youth and inexperience, and that during that time faults should, whenever practicable, be dealt with summarily, and not visited with the heavier punishment which a Court-Martial sentence necessarily carries with it, and I pointed out that this procedure might receive a wider application, and become a guiding principle in the

THE THREE COMMANDERS-IN-CHIEF IN INDIA.

GENERAL SIR FREDERICK SLEIGH ROBERTS.

GENERAL SIR ARTHUR E. HARDINGE. GENERAL SIR DONALD MARTIN STEWART.

treatment of soldiers generally. I suggested that all men in possession of a good-conduct badge, or who had had no entry in their company defaulter sheets for one year, should be granted certain privileges, such as receiving the fullest indulgence in the grant of passes, consistent with the requirements of health, duty, and discipline, and being excused attendance at all roll-calls (including meals), except perhaps at tattoo. I had often remarked that those corps in which indulgences were most freely given contained the largest number of well-behaved men, and I had been assured that such indulgences were seldom abused, and that, while they were greatly appreciated by those who received them, they acted as an incentive to less well conducted men to try and redeem their characters.

The reports of commanding officers, on the results of these small ameliorations, after a six months' trial, were so favourable that I was able to authorize still further concessions as a premium on good behaviour.

The Madras Presidency abounds in places of interest connected with our earlier struggles in India, and it was possible to combine pleasure with duty in a very delightful manner while travelling about the country. My wife frequently accompanied me in my tours, and enjoyed as much as I did our visits to many famous and beautiful places. Madras itself recalled the struggles for supremacy between the English and French in the middle of the eighteenth century. Arcot reminded one that it was in the brilliant capture and still more brilliant defence of the fort at that place that Clive's soldierly genius first became conspicuous. Trichinopoly and Wandewash made one think of Stringer Lawrence's and Eyre Coote's splendid services, and while standing on the breach at Seringapatam, one was reminded of Wellington's early life in India, and marvelled how heavily-armed men could have ventured to cross the single plank which alone spanned the deep, broad ditch of the inner defences.

I should like to dwell on the architectural wonders of Tanjore and the Caves of Ellora; the magnificent entertainments and Princely hospitality accorded to us by the Nizam of Hyderabad, the late Maharajas of Mysore and Travancore, the Maharaja of Vizianagram, the Raja of Cochin, and many other Rulers of Native States; the delights of a trip along the west coast by the beautiful 'back-water,' and the return journey through the glorious forests of Cannara and Mysore; the pleasure of visiting the lovely 'White Lady'* and the wonderful Kaveri falls; but to give my readers any idea of their marvels would be to put too great a strain upon their patience, which I fear has already been severely taxed.

The late Maharaja of Travancore was an unusually enlightened

* The finest of the Gassapa falls.

Native. He spoke and wrote English fluently; his appearance was distinguished, and his manners those of a well-bred, courteous English gentleman of the old school. His speech on proposing the Queen's health was a model of fine feeling and fine expression, and yet this man was steeped in superstition. His Highness sat, slightly retired from the table, between my wife and myself while dinner was going on; he partook of no food or wine, but his close contact with us (he led my wife in to dinner and took her out on his arm) necessitated his undergoing a severe course of purification at the hands of the Brahmins as soon as the entertainment was over; he dared not do anything without the sanction of the priests, and he spent enormous sums in propitiating them.

Notwithstanding the high civilization, luxury, and refinement to be found in these Native States, my visits to them strengthened my opinion that, however capable and enlightened the Ruler, he could have no chance of holding his country if deprived of the guiding hand of the British Government as embodied in the Resident. It is just that control, so light in ordinary times as to be hardly perceptible, but firm enough when occasion demands, which saves the State from being rent by factions and internal intrigue, or swallowed up by a more powerful neighbour, for, owing to the influence of the Brahmins and the practical seclusion which caste prejudices entail, involving ignorance of what is taking place immediately outside their own palaces, the Native Princes of the less warlike peoples would have no chance amidst the anarchy and confusion that would follow the withdrawal of British influence.

A remark made to me by the late Sir Madhava Rao, ex-Minister of the Baroda State, which exemplifies my meaning, comes back to me at this moment. Sir Madhava was one of the most astute Hindu gentlemen in India, and when discussing with him the excitement produced by the 'Ilbert Bill,' he said: 'Why do you English raise these unnecessary questions? It is your doing, not ours. We have heard of the cry, "India for the Indians," which some of your philanthropists have raised in England; but you have only to go to the Zoological Gardens and open the doors of the cages, and you will very soon see what would be the result of putting that theory into practice. There would be a terrific fight amongst the animals, which would end in the tiger walking proudly over the dead bodies of the rest.' 'Whom,' I inquired, 'do you consider to be the tiger?' 'The Mahomedan from the North,' was his reply.

THE MARQUIS OF DUFFERIN, K.P., G.C.B., G.C.M.G., G.M.S.I., G.M.I.E.
VICEROY OF INDIA.

From
an engraving by the Fine Art Society of a portrait by the late Frank Holl, R.A.

CHAPTER LXIV.

In March, 1885, we again visited Calcutta. The Marquis of Ripon had departed, and the Earl of Dufferin reigned in his stead.

Affairs on our north-west and south-east frontiers were at this time in a very unsettled state. Indeed, the political outlook altogether had assumed rather a gloomy aspect. Our relations with the French had become somewhat strained in consequence of their interference with Upper Burma and our occupation of Egypt; while Russia's activity in the valley of the Oxus necessitated our looking after our interests in Afghanistan. These considerations rendered it advisable to increase the army in India by 11,000 British and 12,000 Native troops, bringing the strength of the former up to nearly 70,000, with 414 guns, and that of the latter to 128,636.

Russia's movements could not be regarded with indifference, for, while we had retreated from our dominating position at Kandahar, she had approached considerably nearer to Afghanistan, and in a direction infinitely more advantageous than before for a further onward move. Up to 1881 a Russian army advancing on Afghanistan would have had to solve the difficult problem of the formidable Hindu Kush barrier, or if it took the Herat line it must have faced the deserts of Khiva and Bokhara. But all this was changed by Skobeloff's victories over the Tekke Turkomans, which gave Merv and Sarakhs to Russia, and enabled her to transfer her base from Orenburg to the Caspian—by far the most important step ever made by Russia in her advance towards India. I had some years before pointed out to the Government of India how immeasurably Russia would gain, if by the conquest of Merv—a conquest which I then looked upon as certain to be accomplished in the near future—she should be able to make this transfer. My words were unheeded or ridiculed at the time, and I, like others who thought as I did, was supposed to be suffering from a disease diagnosed by a distinguished politician as 'Mervousness.' But a little later those words were verified. Merv had become a Russian possession, and Turkestan was in direct communication by rail and steamer with St. Petersburg. And can it be denied that this fact, which would have enabled the army in the Caucasus to be rapidly transported to the scene of operations, made it possible for General Komaroff practically to dictate terms to the Boundary Commission which was sent to define the northern limits of Afghanistan, and to forcibly eject an Afghan garrison from Panjdeh under the eyes of British officers?

Lord Dufferin took up the reins of the Government of India at a time when things had come to such a pass that a personal conference with the Amir was considered necessary to arrange for the defence and demarcation of His Highness's frontier, the strengthening of

Herat, the extension of the Sakkur-Sibi railway to Quetta, and the discussion of the general situation. Abdur Rahman was therefore invited to meet the Viceroy at Rawal Pindi, where a large standing camp was prepared, and my wife and I were bidden amongst a numerous company, including Their Royal Highnesses the Duke and Duchess of Connaught, the Ruling Punjab Chiefs, and the high officers of Government from various parts of India, to be the guests of His Excellency and Lady Dufferin on the interesting occasion.

The meeting was fixed for the end of March, and as there was scarcely time for us to return to Madras and get back again before then, we proceeded leisurely up country, visiting different places and one or two old friends on the way.

At Multan I received a cipher telegram from Sir Donald Stewart informing me that it had been decided to mobilize two Army Corps, and that I was to have command of the first. This was exciting news, and we lost no time in making our way to Rawal Pindi, where we should be in direct communication with Head-Quarters, and hoped to hear what had taken place since we left Calcutta to make it necessary to prepare for war.

I soon found out that this action on the part of the Government was forced on them by the representatives of Russia on the Boundary Commission, who were persistent in their attempts to encroach on Afghan territory, in order that they might be in a position to control the approaches to Herat, a Russian occupation of which fortress we could not permit.

Abdur Rahman arrived at Rawal Pindi on the last day of March; he was about forty-five years of age, and although he required a stick to walk with, being a martyr to rheumatism, and very stout, his appearance was decidedly dignified and imposing. He had a manly, clever, and rather handsome face, marred only by the cruel expression of the mouth, and his manner was sufficiently courteous though somewhat abrupt.

Several semi-private meetings took place between the Viceroy and the Amir, at the first of which His Highness, after expressing his appreciation of the flattering and cordial reception he had met with, reminded Lord Dufferin that he had consistently warned the British Government of the approach of the Russians towards Afghanistan and of the unsettling effect their advance was producing on the minds of his countrymen; and he advocated the necessity for timely action. No attention, he said, had been paid to his warnings, owing, probably, to the strife of parties in England, and to the excessive caution of the British Government.

Lord Dufferin, in reply, pointed out that the Amir had been advised to strengthen northern Afghanistan, and that the services of Engineer officers had been offered to him for the purpose of putting Herat into

HIS HIGHNESS
ABDUR RAHMAN, AMIR OF AFGHANISTAN.

a satisfactory state of defence. His Excellency declared that England was resolved that a Russian advance on Herat should be met by a declaration of war; that preparations were then being made to give effect to that resolve; and that it was now absolutely necessary for His Highness to make up his mind which of his two powerful neighbours he would elect to choose as his ally.

Abdur Rahman thanked the Viceroy for his offer of help, but showed plainly that he had no intention of availing himself of the services of our Engineers. He vowed that his own personal wishes were entirely in favour of a close and practical alliance with the British, but that his subjects did not share his feelings towards us. They were 'rude, uneducated, and suspicious.' He hoped that in time they might become more disposed to be friendly, but at present he could not pretend to rely upon them. He then disclosed the real reason for his ready response to the Viceroy's invitation by saying that he would gratefully receive the assistance of the British Government in the shape of money, arms, and munitions of war.

At a later visit the conversation turned upon the difficulty of the position in which the British members of the Boundary Commission were placed, and the impossibility of the Afghan posts being able to hold their own in the face of a Russian advance was explained to the Amir. A map was produced, on which the country to the north of Herat was carefully examined, and Russia's claims were made known to him. Abdur Rahman's ideas of topography were not very accurate, but he displayed considerable intelligence in his questions and perception of the meaning of the answers, and eventually expressed his willingness to leave the question of the delimitation of his northern frontier in the hands of the British Government.

On the 6th April there was a parade of the troops, 17,000 in number, and that evening the Amir was present at a state banquet, at which, after the usual loyal toasts, the Viceroy proposed the Amir's health. His Highness, in reply, expressed a fervent hope that the prosperity of the British Empire might long endure, as with it the welfare of Afghanistan was bound up. He had watched, he said, the progress of India under British rule, and he hoped that Afghanistan might flourish in like manner; and he ended with a prayer that the Almighty would preserve Her Majesty's troops in safety, honour, and efficiency.

Two days later the Amir was publicly received in durbar by the Viceroy, on whose right hand he was placed, while the Duke of Connaught occupied the seat on his left. After a few words had been exchanged, Abdur Rahman rose, and spoke as follows: 'I am deeply sensible of the kindness which I have received from His Excellency the Viceroy, and of the favour shown me by Her Majesty the Queen-Empress. In return for this kindness and favour, I am ready with my army and people to render any services that may be required of me or of the Afghan nation. As the British Government has declared that it will assist me in repelling any foreign enemy, so it is right and proper that Afghanistan should unite in the firmest manner, and side by side by the British Government.'

On being presented, amongst other gifts, with a sword of honour, he said in a loud and determined voice: 'With this sword I hope to smite any enemy of the British Government.'

That same evening the Viceroy received news of the Russian attack on Panjdeh, and communicated it to the Amir, who heard it with extraordinary equanimity, not appearing to attach any great importance to the matter, and attributing the defeat of his troops to the inferiority of their weapons. He observed that the excuse given by the Russians, that the Afghans intended to attack them, was a frivolous pretext, and declared all that his men had done was very properly to make preparations to defend themselves.

Abdur Rahman had expressed a desire for a British decoration, so shortly before his departure from India he was invested, informally, with the G.C.S.I. As the train was moving off, he said to the British officers assembled on the platform: 'I wish you all farewell, and commend you to the care of God. May your Government endure and your honour increase. I have been greatly pleased and gratified by the sight of the British Army. I hope and am certain that the friendship now existing between us will last for ever.'

Abdur Rahman had, indeed, every reason to be satisfied with the result of his visit, for not only was Lord Ripon's promise that England would defend his kingdom against foreign aggression ratified by Lord Dufferin, but the Amir was given, in addition to the large sums of money and the considerable amount of munitions of war already received by him, ten lakhs of rupees, 20,000 breech-loading rifles, a Heavy battery of four guns and two howitzers, a Mountain battery, and a liberal supply of ammunition for both guns and rifles.

On the Amir's departure the great camp was broken up, and the troops returned to their respective stations, all prepared to move towards the Quetta frontier at a moment's notice. The Native Chiefs, in taking their leave of the Viceroy, were profuse in their offers and promises of help should a recourse to arms be found necessary; and Lord and Lady Dufferin's numerous guests, who, like my wife and myself, had for more than a fortnight been recipients of the most profuse hospitality, wished their generous host and hostess a hearty good-bye.

Interesting as the whole proceeding had been, by far the most gratifying result of the gathering was the unmistakable loyalty displayed by the Native Rulers who were present, as well as by those in distant parts of India, on hearing of the unprovoked attack made by the Russians on the Afghan troops at Panjdeh, and our consequent

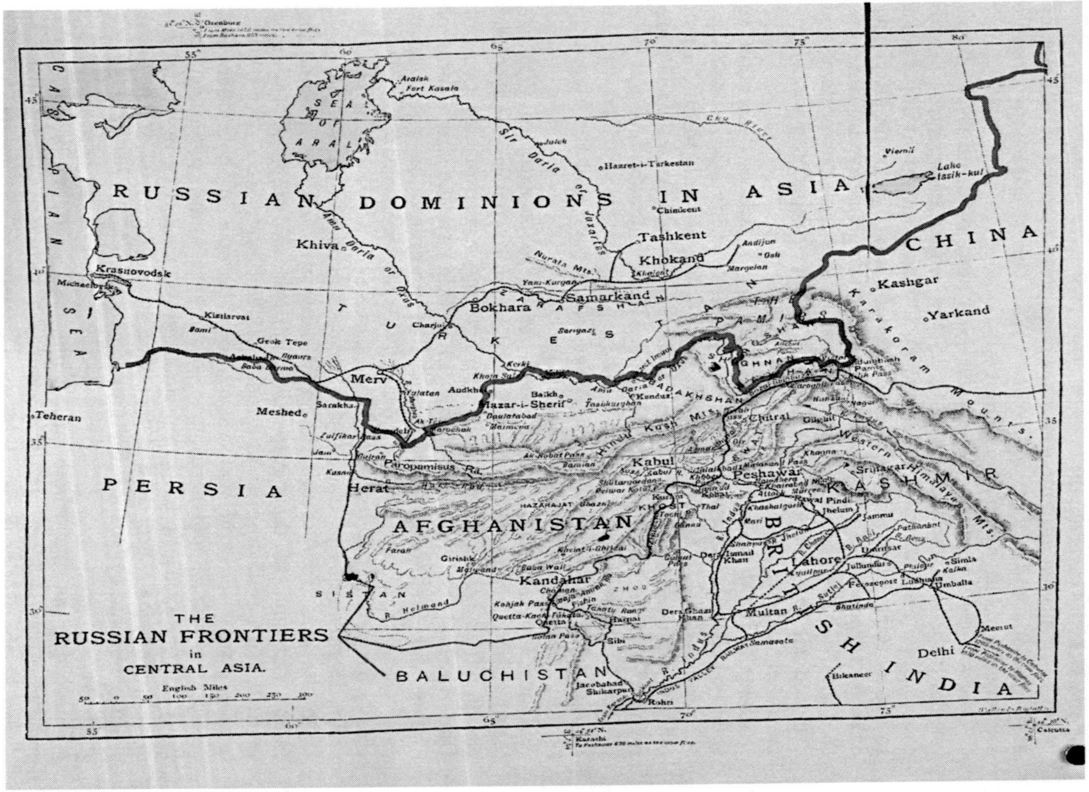

THE RUSSIAN FRONTIERS in CENTRAL ASIA.

preparations for war. The greatest enthusiasm prevailed, and the various military camps at Rawal Pindi were crowded with men desirous of joining the ranks of our army. I was literally besieged by old soldiers, begging that they might be allowed to return to the colours and fight once more for the *Sirkar;* and one Native officer, who had been with me in Afghanistan, came to me and said: 'I am afraid, *sahib*, I am too old and infirm to do more work myself; but you must take my two sons with you—they are ready to die for the *Angrese*.'*

We hastened back to Madras, and reached Ootacamund after seven consecutive nights in the train, with a thermometer at 104° in the daytime, the only pause in our journey being at Poona, where we spent a few hours with our friend General Sir John Ross.

I left my horses at Lahore, and for some weeks lived in daily expectation of being ordered back to the Punjab to take command of the 1st Army Corps. A change of Government, however, took place just in time to prevent the war. Lord Salisbury's determined attitude convinced Russia that no further encroachments on the Afghan frontier would be permitted; she ceased the 'game of brag' she had been allowed to play, and the Boundary Commission were enabled to proceed with the work of delimitation.

CHAPTER LXV.

We only remained three months at 'Ooty,' for on the 8th July a telegram arrived from Lord Dufferin announcing the Queen's approval of my being appointed to succeed Sir Donald Stewart as Commander-in-Chief in India, and granting me leave to visit England before taking up the appointment.

At the end of a fortnight all our preparations for departure had been made, and on the 18th August we left Bombay, in the teeth of the monsoon.

Our boy, whose holidays had just commenced, met us at Venice, and we loitered in Italy and Switzerland on our way home. I spent but six weeks in England, returning to the East at the end of November, to join my new command. I met Lord Dufferin at Agra, and accompanied him to Gwalior, whither his Excellency went for the purpose of formally restoring to the Maharaja Sindhia the much coveted fortress of Gwalior, which had been occupied by us since 1858—an act of sound policy, enabling us to withdraw a brigade which could be far more usefully employed elsewhere.

At Gwalior we received the news of the capture of Mandalay, and I

* A Native corruption of the word 'English.'

sent a telegram to Lieutenant-General Prendergast,* to congratulate him on the successful conduct of the Burma Expedition.

Affairs in Burma had been going from bad to worse from the time King Thebaw came to the throne in 1878. Wholesale murders were of constant occurrence within the precincts of the palace; dacoity was rife throughout the country, and British officers were insulted to such an extent that the Resident had to be withdrawn. In 1883 a special Mission was sent by the King of Burma to Paris, with a view to making such a treaty with the French Government as would enable him to appeal to France for assistance, in the event of his being involved in difficulties with England. The Mission remained eighteen months in Paris, and succeeded in ratifying what the French called a 'Commercial Convention,' under the terms of which a French Consul was located at Mandalay, who soon gained sufficient ascendancy over King Thebaw to enable him to arrange for the construction of a railway between Mandalay and Tonghu, and the establishment of a French bank at Mandalay, by means of which France would speedily have gained full control over the principal sources of Burmese revenue, and power to exclude British trade from the valley of the Irrawaddy. In furtherance of these designs, the King picked a quarrel with a British trading company, threatened to cancel their leases for cutting timber, and demanded a fine of ten lakhs of rupees.

The Chief Commissioner proposed arbitration, but this was declined, and the King refusing to modify his action with regard to the trading company, the Viceroy proposed to the Secretary of State for India that an ultimatum† should be sent to King Thebaw.

In approving of the ultimatum, Lord Randolph Churchill expressed his opinion that its despatch should be concurrent with the movement of troops and ships to Rangoon, that an answer should be demanded within a specified time, and that if the ultimatum were rejected, an immediate advance on Mandalay should be made.

A force‡ of nearly 10,000 men and 77 guns, under the command of Lieutenant-General Prendergast, was accordingly ordered to be in readiness at Thyetmyo by the 14th November, and as the reply of the

* Now General Sir Harry Prendergast, V.C., K.C.B.

† The ultimatum informed King Thebaw that the British Government insisted upon an Envoy being received at Mandalay, with free access to the King, without having to submit to any humiliating ceremony; that proceedings against the trading company would not be permitted; that a British Agent, with a suitable guard of honour and steamer for his personal protection, must be permanently stationed at the Burmese capital; that the Burmese Government must regulate their external relations in accordance with British advice; and that proper facilities must be granted for the opening up of British trade with China viâ Bhamo.

‡ The force consisted of 861 seamen and 69 Marines formed into a Naval Brigade, with 49 guns, including 27 machine guns, and 3,029 British and 6,005 Native soldiers, with 28 guns.

Burmese Government was tantamount to a refusal, Prendergast was instructed to advance on Mandalay, with the result which it was my pleasant duty to congratulate him upon in my capacity of Commander-in-Chief of the Army in India.

From Gwalior I went to Delhi to prepare for a Camp of Exercise on a much larger scale than had ever before been held. Many weak points in the Commissariat and Transport Department having become only too apparent when the mobilization of the two Army Corps had been imminent the previous spring, it was considered necessary to test our readiness for war, and orders for the strength and composition of the force to be manœuvred had been issued before Sir Donald Stewart left India.

The troops were divided into two Army Corps. The northern assembled at Umballa, and the southern at Gurgaon, 25 miles from Delhi, the points of concentration being 150 miles apart.

After a fortnight passed in brigade and divisional movements, the opposing forces advanced, and on the 7th January they came into contact on the historic battlefield of Panipat.*

Lord Dufferin, whose interest in the efficiency of the army induced him to come all the way from Calcutta to witness the last two days' manœuvres, was present—with the twelve 'foreign officers'† from the principal armies of Europe and America, who had been invited to attend the camp—at a march-past of the whole force of 35,000 men on the 18th. It was a fine sight, though marred by a heavy thunderstorm and a perfect deluge of rain, and was really a greater test of what the troops could do than if we had had the perfect weather we had hoped for. The 'foreign officers' were, apparently, somewhat surprised at the fine physique and efficiency of our Native soldiers, but they all remarked on the paucity of British officers with the Indian regiments, which I could not but acknowledge was, as it still is, a weak point in our military organization.

When the camp was broken up, I accompanied the Viceroy to Burma, where we arrived early in February, 1886. Lord Dufferin must, I think, have been pleased at the reception he met with at Rangoon. The people generally tried in every possible way to show

* Panipat is famous for three great battles fought in its immediate neighbourhood: one in 1526, by the Emperor Baber against Sultan Ibrahim, which resulted in the establishment of the Mogul dynasty; the second in 1556, when the Emperor Akbar beat the Hindu General of the Afghan usurper, and re-established the Moguls in power: and the third in 1761, when Ahmed Shah Durani defeated the Mahrattas.

† I was much gratified at receiving subsequently from His Imperial Majesty the Emperor William I. and from the Crown Princess of Prussia autograph letters of acknowledgment of, and thanks for, the reception accorded and the attention paid to Majors von Huene and von Hagenau, the two representatives of the German army who attended these manœuvres.

their gratitude to the Viceroy, under whose auspices the annexation of Upper Burma had been carried out, and each nationality had erected a triumphal arch in its own particular quarter of the town.

From Rangoon we went to Mandalay, where Lord Dufferin formally announced the annexation by England of all that part of Upper Burma over which King Thebaw had held sway. We then proceeded to Madras, where I parted from the Viceregal party and travelled to Bombay to meet my wife. Leaving her at Simla to arrange our house, which had been considerably altered and added to, I proceeded to the North-West Frontier, for the question of its defence was one which interested me very deeply, and I hoped that, from the position I now held as a member of the Government of India, I should be able to get my ideas on this, to India, all-important subject listened to, if not altogether carried out.

The defence of the frontier had been considered under the orders of my predecessor by a Committee, the members of which had recorded their several opinions as to the means which should be adopted to make India secure. But Sir Donald Stewart relinquished his command before anything could be done to give effect to the measures they advised.

The matter had therefore to be taken up afresh by me, and I carefully studied the recommendations of the 'Defence Committee' before visiting the frontier to refresh my memory by personal inspection as to the points to be defended.

It seemed to me that none of the members, with the exception of Sir Charles Macgregor and the secretary, Major W. G. Nicholson, at all appreciated the great change which had taken place in our position since the near approach of Russia, and our consequent promise to the Amir to preserve the integrity of his kingdom, had widened the limit of our responsibilities from the southern to the northern boundary of Afghanistan.

Less than a year before we had been on the point of declaring war with Russia because of her active interference with 'the authority of a sovereign—our protected ally—who had committed no offence*;' and even now it was not certain that peace could be preserved, by reason of the outrageous demands made by the Russian members of the Boundary Commission as to the direction which the line of delimitation between Russian and Afghan territory should take.

It was this widening of our responsibilities which prevented me from agreeing with the recommendations of the Defence Committee, for the majority of the members laid greater stress on the necessity for constructing numerous fortifications, than upon lines of communication, which I conceived to be of infinitely greater importance,

* Words used by Mr. Gladstone when asking for a vote of credit for £6,500,000 for special preparations in connection with the Afghan difficulty.

as affording the means of bringing all the strategical points on the frontier into direct communication with the railway system of India, and enabling us to mass our troops rapidly, should we be called upon to aid Afghanistan in repelling attack from a foreign Power.

Fortifications, of the nature of entrenched positions, were no doubt, to some extent, necessary, not to guard against our immediate neighbours, for experience had taught us that without outside assistance they are incapable of a combined movement, but for the protection of such depots and storehouses as would have to be constructed, and as a support to the army in the field.

The line chosen at that time for an advance was by Quetta and Kandahar. In the first instance, therefore, I wended my way to Baluchistan, where I met and consulted with the Governor-General's Agent, Sir Robert Sandeman, and the Chief Engineer of the Sind-Pishin Railway, Brigadier-General Browne.*

We together inspected the Kwaja-Amran range, through which the Kohjak tunnel now runs, and I decided that the best position for an entrenched camp was to the rear of that range, in the space between the Takatu and Mashalik mountains. This open ground was less than four miles broad; nature had made its flanks perfectly secure, and in front was a network of ravines capable of being made quite impassable by simply flooding them. It was unfortunate that the railway had been marked out in front instead of in rear of the Takatu range, and that its construction was too far advanced before the question of defence came to be considered to admit of its being altered, otherwise this position would have been a complete protection for the line of rail also.

Having come to a definite conclusion as to the measures to be taken for meeting the offensive and defensive requirements of Quetta and the Bolan Pass, I turned my attention to Peshawar and the Khyber Pass, which were infinitely more difficult to deal with, because of the political considerations involved.

Over the whole of Baluchistan we had entire control, so that in the event of an army moving in that direction we could depend upon the resources of the country being at our disposal, and the people remaining, at least, neutral. But on the Peshawar side the circumstances were altogether different: the tribes were hostile to a degree, and no European's life was safe across the frontier. Except in the Khyber itself (where the policy of establishing friendly relations with the Afridis, and utilizing them to keep open the pass, had been most successfully practised by the political officer, Lieutenant-Colonel Warburton), we could not depend on the tribesmen remaining passive,

* The late Major-General Sir James Browne, K.C.S.I., C.B., who, like Sir Robert Sandeman, died while holding the important and responsible position of Governor-General's Agent in Baluchistan.

much less helping us if we advanced into Afghanistan. While, should an army attempt to invade India from that direction, we should to a certainty have every man of the 200,000 warlike people who inhabit the mountainous district from Chitral to Baluchistan combining against us, and pouring into India from every outlet.

For these reasons I recorded a strong opinion in opposition to the proposals of the Defence Committee, which were in favour of the construction of a large magazine at Peshawar and extensive entrenched works at the mouth of the Khyber. I pointed out the extreme danger of a position communication with which could be cut off, and which could be more or less easily turned, for it was clear to me that until we had succeeded in inducing the border tribes to be on friendly terms with us, and to believe that their interests were identical with ours, the Peshawar valley would become untenable should any general disturbance take place; and that, instead of entrenchments close to the Khyber Pass, we required a position upon which the garrisons of Peshawar and Nowshera could fall back and await the arrival of reinforcements.

For this position I selected a spot on the right bank of the Kabul river, between Khairabad and the Indus; it commanded the passage of the latter river, and could easily be strengthened by defensive works outside the old fort of Attock.

It will be readily understood by those of my readers who have any knowledge of our North-West Frontier, or are interested in the question of the defence of India, that other routes exist between the Bolan and the Khyber Passes which might be made use of either by an army invading India, or by a force sent from India to the assistance of Afghanistan; and by such it will probably be asked, as was the case when my recommendations were being discussed, why I did not advise these lines to be similarly guarded. My reply was, and is, that there are no arsenals or depots near these passes to be protected, as at Quetta and Rawul Pindi; that we should not be likely to use them for an army moving into Afghanistan; that, although small parties of the enemy might come by them, the main body of a force operating towards India is bound to advance by the Khyber, for the reason that it would debouch directly on highly cultivated country and good roads leading to all the great cities of the Punjab; and finally that, even if our finances would admit of the construction of such a long line of forts, it would be impossible for our limited army to supply the garrisons for them.

Having completed my inspection of the frontier, I returned to Simla and drew up a memorandum declaring the conviction I had arrived at after careful deliberation, that the improvement of our communications was of far greater importance than the immediate construction of forts and entrenchments, and that, while I would not spare money in strengthening well-defined positions, the strategical value of which was unmistakable, I would not trouble about those places the primary importance of fortifying which was open to argument, and which might never be required to be defended; these, I contended, might be left alone, except so far as to make a careful study of their localities and determine how they could best be taken advantage of should occasion require. My note ended with the following words: 'Meanwhile I would push on our communications with all possible speed; we must have roads, and we must have railways; they cannot be made on short notice, and every rupee spent upon them now will repay us tenfold hereafter. Nothing will tend to secure the safety of the frontier so much as the power of rapidly concentrating troops on any threatened point, and nothing will strengthen our military position more than to open out the country and improve our relations with the frontier tribes. There are no better civilizers than roads and railways; and although some of those recommended to be made may never be required for military purposes, they will be of the greatest assistance to the civil power in the administration of the country.'

Accompanying this paper was a statement of the defensive works which, in my opinion, should be taken in hand without delay; also of the positions which required careful study, and the roads and railways which should be constructed, to make the scheme of defence complete.

Seven years later, when I gave up my command of the Army in India, I had the supreme satisfaction of knowing that I left our North-West Frontier secure, so far as it was possible to make it so, hampered as we were by want of money. The necessary fortifications had been completed, schemes for the defence of the various less important positions had been prepared, and the roads and railways, in my estimation of such vast importance, had either been finished or were well advanced.

Moreover, our position with regard to the border tribes had gradually come to be better understood, and it had been realized that they would be a powerful support to whichever side might be able to count upon their aid; the policy of keeping them at arm's length had been abandoned, and the advantages of reciprocal communication were becoming more appreciated by them and by us.

It was not to be expected that these results could be achieved without a considerable amount of opposition, owing partly to the majority of our countrymen (even amongst those who had spent the greater part of their lives in India) failing to recognize the change that had taken place in the relative positions of Great Britain and Russia in Asia, and to their disbelief in the steady advance of Russia towards Afghanistan being in any way connected with India, or in Russia's wish or power to threaten our Eastern Empire.* The idea was very common, too, amongst people who had not deeply considered the subject, that all proposals for gaining control over our troublesome neighbours on the border, or for facilitating the massing of troops, meant an aggressive policy, and were made with the idea of annexing more territory, instead of for the purpose of securing the safety of India, and enabling us to fulfil our engagements.

Happily, the Viceroys who governed India while I was Commander-in-Chief were not amongst those who held these opinions; and while they had no expectation of India being invaded in the near future, they realized that we could not unconcernedly look on while a great Power was, step by step, creeping closer to our possessions. It was a fortunate circumstance, too, that, for the first five years I was at the head of the Army in India, I had as my military colleague in Council the late General Sir George Chesney, a man of unquestionable talent and sound judgment, to whose cordial support, not only in frontier affairs, but in all my efforts to promote the efficiency and welfare of the soldier, I was very greatly indebted.

CHAPTER LXVI.

Many interesting and important questions had to be dealt with during this my first year as a member of the Viceroy's Council, and it was pleasant to me to be able to bring before the Government of India a scheme which my wife had had very much at heart for many years—for supplying skilled nursing to the military hospitals in India. That our sick soldiers (officers and men) should be entirely dependent for nursing, even in times of the most dangerous illness, on the tender mercies of 'the orderly on duty,' who, whether kind-hearted or the reverse, was necessarily utterly untrained and ignorant of the requirements of sickness, was a source of unhappiness to her, and had been felt as a cruel want by many; but whenever she had discussed the subject with those who might have helped her, she was told that proposals for supplying this want had already been made, that the Government could not, nor would they ever be able to, act on such proposals, on account of the prohibitory expense, so she felt there was no use in making any appeal until I might be in a position to see that any suggestions made by her would be certain to receive the careful

* A Statesman of high reputation in England was so strong in his disbelief of the necessity for making any preparations in India, that he publicly stated that if the only barrier between Russia in Asia and Britain in Asia were a mountain ridge, or a stream, or a fence, there would be no difficulty in preserving peace between Russia and the United Kingdom.—Speech delivered by the Right Hon. John Bright, M.P., at Birmingham on the 16th April, 1879.

LADY ROBERTS OF KANDAHAR.

From
a photograph by Messrs. Johnson and Hoffmann.

consideration of Government. This time had now arrived, and almost directly Lady Roberts returned to India in 1886 she drew up a scheme for supplying lady nurses to the military hospitals throughout India, and set to work to try and get the support of some of the principal Medical officers. To her great joy, her recommendations were accepted by Lord Dufferin and his Council, and her note upon the subject was sent home to the Secretary of State, strongly backed up by the Government of India. Lord Cross happily viewed the matter in a favourable light, and consented, not only to a certain number of nurses being sent out the following year as an experiment, but to the whole of the cost of the movement being borne by the State, with the exception of the provision of 'Homes in the Hills' for the nursing sisters as health resorts, and to prevent the expense to Government of their having to be sent home on sick-leave when worn out by their trying work in the plains. The Secretary of State, however, declared these 'Homes' to be 'an important part' of the nursing scheme, 'and indispensable to its practical working,' but considered that they should be provided by private subscription, a condition my wife undertook to carry out. She appealed to the Army in India to help her, and with scarcely an exception every regiment and battery generously responded—even the private soldiers subscribed largely in proportion to their small means—so that by the beginning of the following year my wife was able to set about purchasing and building suitable houses.

'Homes' were established at Murree, Kasauli and Quetta, in Bengal, and at Wellington* in Madras, and by making a further appeal to the officers of the army, and with the assistance of kind and liberal friends in England and India, and the proceeds of various entertainments, Lady Roberts was able to supply, in connexion with the 'Homes' at Murree and Kasauli, wards for the reception of sick officers, with a staff of nurses† in attendance, whose salaries, passages, etc., are all paid out of 'Lady Roberts's Fund.' My wife was induced to do this from having known many young officers succumb owing to want of care and improper food at hotels or clubs on being sent to the Hills after a hard fight for life in the plains, if they were not fortunate enough to have personal friends to look after them. Although it is anticipating events, I may as well say here that the nursing experiment proved a complete success, and now every large military hospital in India has its staff of nurses, and there are altogether 4 superintendents,

* The homes at Quetta and Wellington were eventually taken over by Government, and Lady Roberts' nurses, who worked in the military hospitals at these stations, were replaced by Government nurses when the increase to the Army Nursing Service admitted of this being done.

† When the 'Homes in the Hills' are closed during the cold months, these nurses attend sick officers in their own houses in the plains, free of charge except travelling expenses.

9 deputy superintendents, and 39 nursing sisters, in India. There are many more wanted in the smaller stations, where there is often great loss of life from lack of proper nursing, and surely, as my wife pointed out in her first appeal, 'when one considers what an expensive article the British soldier is, costing, as he does, £100 before landing in India, it seems certain that on the score of economy alone, altogether setting aside the humane aspect of the question, it is well worth the State's while to provide him with the skilled nursing care' which has up to now saved so many lives.

That officers as well as men might benefit by the devotion of the 'nursing sister,' I was able to arrange in all the large hospitals for some room, or rooms, used until then for other purposes, to be appropriated for an officers' ward or wards, and these have proved a great boon to the younger officers whose income does not admit of their obtaining the expensive care of a nurse from one of the large civil hospitals in the Presidency towns.

The next most interesting question, and also the most pressing, which had to be considered by the Viceroy's Council during the summer of 1886, was the pacification of Upper Burma. People in England had expressed surprise at this being so long delayed. It is extremely easy, however, to sit at home and talk of what should be done, but very difficult to say how to do it, and more difficult still to carry it out. To establish law and order in a country nearly as large as France, in which dacoity is looked upon as an honourable profession, would be no light task even in Europe: but when the country to be settled has a deadly climate for several months in the year, is covered to a great extent with jungle, and is without a vestige of a road, the task assumes gigantic proportions. In Upper Burma the garrison was only sufficient to keep open communication along the line of the Irrawaddy, and, to add to the embarrassment of the situation, disaffection had spread to Lower Burma, and disturbances had broken out in the almost unknown district between Upper Burma and Assam.

It was arranged to send strong reinforcements to Burma so soon as the unhealthy season should be over and it would be safe for the troops to go there, and Lieutenant-General Sir Herbert Macpherson (who had succeeded me as Commander-in-Chief in Madras) was directed to proceed thither.

In October my wife and I, with some of my staff, started from Simla on a trip across the Hills, with the object of inspecting the stations of Dhurmsala and Dalhousie before it was cool enough to begin my winter tour in the plains. We crossed the Jalauric Pass, between 11,000 and 12,000 feet high, and travelling through the beautiful Kulu valley and over the Bubbu mountain, we finally arrived at Palampur, the centre of the tea industry in the Kangra valley. Having been cut off from telegraphic communication for some time, we went straight to the telegraph-office for news, and found at the moment a message being deciphered which brought me the terribly sad information that General Macpherson had died of fever in Burma. In him the country had lost a good soldier, and I a friend and comrade for whom I had a great regard and admiration. We were discussing his untimely end, and I was considering who should replace him, when a second message arrived. This was from Lord Dufferin, telling me that he wished me to transfer my Head-Quarters to Burma, and arrange to remain there until 'the neck of the business was broken.'

I hurried to Calcutta, embarked in the first mail-steamer, and landed at Rangoon on the 9th November.

Sir Charles Bernard (the Chief Commissioner) and General White had done well under very difficult circumstances; but owing partly to large districts being impassable from months of heavy rain, and partly to the change in Commanders, unavoidable inaction had been forced upon our troops, and the dacoits had in consequence made head against us.

Having been in constant correspondence with General White, I had been kept informed of his plans, and, as his responsible Chief, I had approved of them; I therefore had the somewhat complicated military situation at my fingers' ends, and did not need to lose a single day in arranging for a series of combined movements being carried on all over the country.

It was hoped that the recently arrived reinforcements would be sufficient for all requirements, but it soon became apparent that the difficulties connected with the pacification of Burma had been underrated, and that, in addition to more troops, an efficient civil administration would have to be provided, to take the place of military authority so soon as anything like organized resistance had been crushed; for to deal with ordinary robbers I conceived to be work more suited to police than to soldiers. Upwards of thirty years' experience had proved that the Burmese could not be relied upon for this kind of service; I therefore recommended that a large body of police should be raised in India without delay, and given a semi-military organization, and in the meantime I asked for, and was given, five additional regiments.

I felt very confident of success, for I had taken great care in the selection of the brigade commanders and staff officers, and I knew the troops could be depended upon in any emergency that was likely to arise. Nevertheless, as the work they would have to perform was of rather an unusual character, irksome as well as difficult, I thought it advisable to issue some general instructions for the guidance of the officers in command of the different columns.* These instructions were carried out so intelligently, and the troops did such good service,

* These instructions are given in the Appendix.

especially a very fine body of Mounted Infantry raised and organized by Major Symons, of the South Wales Borderers, that before I returned to India in February, 1887, I was able to report that the country was gradually becoming quiet and the Burmese reconciled to our rule. Most of the principal dacoit leaders had been killed or captured. and villages which had been in their hands for months were being re-occupied by their legitimate inhabitants; caravans were coming into Mandalay almost daily from districts on the Chinese borders; contracts for making roads were readily taken up, and there was no difficulty in obtaining labour for the railway then being constructed between Lower Burma and Mandalay, the first sod of which was turned within a month of my arrival at that place.

In achieving these satisfactory results I was materially aided by the hearty co-operation of Sir Charles Bernard and the civil officers serving under him; while the entire absence of fanaticism amongst the Burmese, and their cheerful, happy natures, facilitated our intercourse with them. I received, besides, most valuable assistance from the Buddhist *Poonghies*, or monks, with many of whom I made friends. From the fact that education, secular and religious, is imparted by these monks, and that every male, from the King to the humblest peasant, was obliged to enter a monastery and wear the saffron garb of a monk for a certain period, the priesthood had enormous influence with the Burmese. There are no hereditary Chiefs or Nobles in Burma, the *Poonghies* being the advisers of the people and the centre round which Native society revolves.

Our occupation of Upper Burma was necessarily a great blow to the Buddhist priesthood, for many of the monasteries* were kept up entirely by the King, Queen, and Ministers of State; and, as it was most advisable to have the influence of the monks in our favour, I recommended that a monthly stipend should be paid to the Archbishop and two senior Bishops of Mandalay. They showed their gratitude by doing all they could to help me, and when I was leaving the country the old *Thathanabain* (Archbishop) accompanied me as far as Rangoon. We corresponded till his death, and I still hear occasionally from one or other of my *Poonghie* friends.

I remained only a short time in Calcutta on my return to India, and then started off again for the North-West Frontier, in company with General Chesney, who had previously expressed his general concurrence in my defence proposals, but was anxious to see the several positions and judge for himself, from an Engineer's point of view, of their suitability to be treated as I suggested. It was a great source of contentment to me to find that the sites chosen and the style of entrench-

* Monasteries in Burma are not merely dwelling-places for the monks, but are the schools where all education is carried on.

ments I had advocated commended themselves to my expert companion.

Simla was more than usually gay during the summer of 1887, in consequence of the numerous entertainments given in celebration of Her Majesty's Jubilee. We had just added a ballroom to 'Snowdon,' and we inaugurated its opening by a fancy ball on the 21st June, in honour of the auspicious anniversary.

My name appeared in the Jubilee *Gazette* as having been given the Grand Cross of the Indian Empire, but what I valued still more was the acceptance by the Government of India of my strong recommendation for the establishment of a Club or Institute in every British regiment and battery in India. In urging that this measure should be favourably considered, I had said that the British Army in India could have no better or more generally beneficial memorial of the Queen's Jubilee than the abolition of that relic of barbarism, the canteen, and its supersession by an Institute, in which the soldier would have under the same roof a reading-room, recreation room, and a decently-managed refreshment-room.

Lord Dufferin's Government met my views in the most liberal spirit, and with the sanction of Lord Cross 'The Regimental Institute' became a recognized establishment, a fact which my colleagues in Council referred to as a second Jubilee honour for me!

At a time when nearly every soldier could read and write, and when we hoped to attract to the army men of a better stamp and more respectable antecedents than those of which it was composed in 'the good old days,' it appeared to me a humiliating anachronism that the degrading system of the canteen should still prevail, and that it was impossible for any man to retain his self-respect if he were driven to take his glass of beer under the rules by which regimental canteens were governed. I believed, too, that the more the status of the rank and file could be raised, and the greater the efforts made to provide them with rational recreation and occupation in their leisure hours, the less there would be of drunkenness, and consequently of crime, the less immorality and the greater the number of efficient soldiers in the army.

Funds having been granted, a scheme was drawn up for the erection of buildings and for the management of the Institutes. Canteens were reduced in size, and such attractions as musical instruments were removed to the recreation-rooms; the name 'liquor bar' was substituted for that of 'canteen,' and, that there should be no excuse for frequenting the 'liquor bar,' I authorized a moderate and limited amount of beer to be served, if required, with the men's suppers in the refreshment-room—an arrangement which has been followed by the happiest results.

At first it was thought that these changes would cause a great falling off in regimental funds, but experience has proved the reverse. With good management, the profits from the coffee-shop and the soda-water manufactory far exceed those to be derived from the canteen, and this without permitting anyone outside the regiment to purchase from the coffee-shop and without interfering at all with local tradesmen.

Another measure which I succeeded in carrying through the same year was the amalgamation of the various sectarian societies that existed in India for the prevention of drunkenness in the army into one undenominational society, under the name of the Army Temperance Association, which I hoped would admit of more united action and a more advantageous use of funds, besides making it easier for the Government to assist the movement. The different religious and 'total abstinence' associations had no doubt done much towards the object they had in view, but their work was necessarily spasmodic, and being carried on independently of regimental authority, it was not always looked upon with favour by officers.

There was of necessity at first a good deal of opposition on the part of the promoters of the older societies, but those who were loudest in denouncing my proposals soon came to understand that there was nothing in the constitution of the Army Temperance Association which could in any way interfere with total abstinence, and that the only difference between their systems and mine consisted in mine being regimental in its character, and including men for whom it was not necessary or expedient to forego stimulants altogether, but who earnestly desired to lead temperate lives, and to be strengthened in their resolve by being allowed to share in the advantages of the new Institution.

To make the movement a complete success, it was above all things important to secure the active co-operation of the ministers of the various religions. To this end I addressed the heads of the different churches, explaining my reasons and the results I hoped to attain in establishing the amalgamated association, and I invited them to testify their approval of the scheme by becoming patrons of it. With two exceptions, the dignitaries to whom I appealed accepted my invitation, and expressed sympathy with my aims and efforts, an encouragement I had hardly dared to hope for, and a proof of liberal-mindedness on the part of the prelates which was extremely refreshing.

The Government of India were good enough to sanction the allotment of a separate room in each soldiers' Institute for the exclusive use of the Association, where alcohol in any shape was not admitted, and to the grant of this room I attribute, in a great measure, the success of the undertaking. The success was proved by the fact that, when I left India, nearly one third of the 70,000 British soldiers in that country were members or honorary members of the Army Temperance Association.

CHAPTER LXVII.

In December I made a prolonged tour along the North-West Frontier, accompanied by my wife, who was greatly delighted at being able at last to see many places and meet many people of whom she had often heard me speak. Part of this trip was made in company with the Viceroy and Lady Dufferin, who visited all the principal stations on the frontier, including Quetta. I rode with Lord Dufferin through the Khyber Pass, and to the top of the Kwaja Amran range, our visit to this latter point resulting, as I earnestly hoped it would, in His Excellency being convinced by personal inspection of the advantage to be gained by making the Kohjak tunnel, and of the necessity for our endeavouring to cultivate more friendly relations with the border tribes. We ended this very enjoyable tour at Rawal Pindi in order to be present at the winding-up of a Cavalry Camp of Exercise in the neighbourhood. There were assembled together under the direction of Major-General Luck one regiment of British and eight regiments of Native Cavalry, with two batteries of Royal Horse Artillery, and it was a pretty sight, their advance at full gallop, and the halt, as of one man, of that long line of Cavalry within a few yards of the Viceroy, for the Royal salute. The spectators were much impressed with Lord Dufferin's nerve in being able to remain perfectly calm and still on his horse in the face of such an onslaught, and it certainly did seem rather close quarters; but General Luck knew his regiments, and had confidence in his men, and we knew General Luck.

In the early part of 1888 I visited all the chief military stations in the Bengal Presidency, and attended Camps of Exercise for all arms, held at Rawal Pindi, Umballa, Meerut, and Lucknow, before going to Calcutta for the usual discussion on the Budget; after which the Government generally breaks up for the hot weather, and assembles in Simla two or three weeks later.

During 1887 and 1888 much useful work was got through by the Defence Committee, and by another Committee which was assembled for the consideration of all questions bearing upon the mobilization of the army. As Commander-in-Chief I presided over both, and was fortunate in being able to secure as my secretaries two officers of exceptional ability, Lieutenant-Colonel W. Nicholson, R.E., for defence, and Lieutenant-Colonel E. Elles, R.A., for mobilization. It was in a great measure due to Colonel Nicholson's clear-sighted judgment on the many knotty questions which came before us, and to his technical knowledge, that the schemes for the defence of the frontier, and for the ports of Bombay, Karachi, Calcutta, Rangoon and Madras, were carried out so rapidly, thoroughly and economically as they were;*

* The total cost of the coast and frontier defences amounted to the very moderate sum of five crores of rupees, or about three and a half millions sterling.

and with regard to measures for rendering the army mobile, Colonel Elles proved himself equally capable and practical. The Secretary to Government in the Military Department, Major-General Edwin Collen, was a particularly helpful member of the Committees* from his intimate acquaintance with the various subjects which had to be discussed.

If my readers have had the patience to follow in detail the several campaigns in which I took part, they will have grasped the fact that our greatest difficulties on all occasions arose from the want of a properly organized Transport Department, and they will understand that I was able to make this very apparent when the necessity for mobilizing rapidly only one Army Corps came to be seriously considered. We were able to demonstrate conclusively the impossibility of putting a force into the field, sufficiently strong to cope with a European enemy, without a considerable increase to the existing number of transport animals, and without some description of light cart strong enough to stand the rough work of a campaign in a country without roads; for it is no exaggeration to say that in the autumn of 1880, when I left Kandahar, it would have been possible to have picked out the road thence to Quetta, and onward to Sibi, a distance of 250 miles, with no other guide than that of the line of dead animals and broken-down carts left behind by the several columns and convoys that had marched into Afghanistan by that route.

Soon after I took over the command of the Army in India, while voyaging to Burma, I had brought this most pressing question of transport to the notice of Lord Dufferin, who, with his usual quick appreciation of a situation, at once fully recognized its urgency, and promised to give me all possible help in my endeavour to render the army mobile—a promise which he amply fulfilled by taking a keen personal interest in the proceedings of the Committee, and giving his hearty support to our various recommendations.†

Our labours resulted in several thousand good pack animals (chiefly mules) being purchased, and information collected and recorded as to the districts where others could be rapidly procured in case of emergency. A transport service was established, for which officers had to go through

* The Committees consisted, besides the Military Member of Council and myself, of the heads of Departments with the Government of India and at Army Head-Quarters.

† When the report of the Mobilization Committee was submitted to the Viceroy, he recorded a minute expressing his 'warm admiration of the manner in which the arduous duty had been conducted,' and 'his belief that no scheme of a similar description had ever been worked out with greater thoroughness, in more detail, and with clearer apprehension of the ends to be accomplished.' He concluded by conveying to the members an expression of his great satisfaction at what had been done, and recording that 'the result of the Committee's labours is a magnificent monument of industry and professional ability.'

a regular course of instruction, and pass an examination in the loading and general management of the animals. A prize was offered for a strong, useful light cart; and when the most suitable had been selected, large numbers were made up of the same pattern.* The constitution of two Army Corps, to be in readiness for taking the field on short notice, was decided upon, and the units to form the several divisions and brigades were told off and provided with the necessary equipment. A railway time-table was prepared, giving the hours at which the troops should leave their stations so as to avoid any block *en route*. Special platforms were constructed for training and detraining Cavalry and Artillery, and storehouses were erected and stocked at those stations where road marching would probably commence. Finally, the conclusions we had arrived at were embodied in a manual entitled 'General Regulations for Mobilization.' It was extremely gratifying to me to learn from India that this manual, with such additions and alterations as our subsequent experience in Burma and various frontier expeditions proved would be advantageous, was the guide by which the Chitral relieving force was last year so expeditiously and completely equipped and despatched.

Of the many subjects discussed and measures adopted during this, the last year of Lord Dufferin's Viceroyalty, I think the scheme for utilizing the armies of Native States, as an auxiliary force for the service of the Empire, was the most important both from a political and military point of view.

The idea was, in the first instance, propounded by Lord Lytton, who appointed a committee to consider the pros and cons of the question. I was a member of that committee, but at that time I, in common with many others, was doubtful as to the wisdom of encouraging a high state of efficiency amongst the troops of independent States; the excellent work, however, done by the Native Contingent I had with me in Kuram, and the genuine desire of all ranks to be allowed to serve side by side with our own soldiers, together with the unmistakable spirit of

* Statement of transport carriage maintained in India in the years 1878 and 1893 for military purposes, exclusive of animals registered by the civil authorities on the latter date, and liable to be requisitioned in time of war:

Date.	Elephants.	Camels.	Mules.	Ponies.	Bullocks.	Donkeys.	Army Transport Carts.	Field Ambulance Carts.
September, 1878	733	6,353	1,536	...	1,424	...	...	...
April, 1893	359	3,175	16,825	782	7,211	31	5,316	799

loyalty displayed by Native Rulers when war with Russia was imminent in 1885, convinced me that the time had arrived for us to prove to the people of India that we had faith in their loyalty, and in their recognition of the fact that their concern in the defence of the Empire was at least as great as ours, and that we looked to them to take their part in strengthening our rule and in keeping out all intruders. I believed, too, that we had now little to fear from internal trouble so long as our Government continued just and sympathetic, but that, on the other hand, we could not expect to remain free from outside interference, and that it would be wise to prepare ourselves for a struggle which, as my readers must be aware, I consider to be inevitable in the end. We have done much, and may still do more, to delay it, but when that struggle comes it will be incumbent upon us, both for political and military reasons, to make use of all the troops and war material that the Native States can place at our disposal, and it is therefore to our advantage to render both as efficient and useful as possible.

The subject was, of course, most delicate and complex, and had to be treated with the greatest caution, for not only was the measure adapted to materially strengthen our military position in India, but I was convinced it was politically sound, and likely to be generally acceptable to the Native Rulers, provided we studied their wishes, and were careful not to offend their prejudices and susceptibilities by unnecessary interference.

It was very satisfactory to find how cordially the Chiefs responded to Lord Dufferin's proposals, and extremely interesting to watch the steady improvement in their armies under the guidance of carefully selected British officers. Substantial results have been already obtained, valuable help having been afforded to the Chitral expedition by the transport trains organized by the Maharajas of Gwalior and Jaipur, and by the gallantry of the Imperial Service Troops belonging to His Highness the Maharaja of Kashmir at Hunza-Naga and during the siege and relief of Chitral.

Two minor expeditions took place this year: one against the Thibetans in retaliation for their having invaded the territory of our ally, the Raja of Sikim; the other to punish the Black Mountain tribes for the murder of two British officers. Both were a success from a military point of view, but in the Black Mountain the determination of the Punjab Government to limit the sphere of action of the troops, and to hurry out of the country, prevented our reaping any political advantage. We lost a grand opportunity for gaining control over this lawless and troublesome district; no survey was made, no roads opened out, the tribesmen were not made to feel our power, and, consequently, very soon another costly expedition had to be undertaken.

In November, 1888, Lord Dufferin left India amidst a storm of regret from all classes of Her Majesty's subjects. He was succeeded

THE MARQUESS OF LANSDOWNE, K.G., G.C.M.G., G.M.S.I., G.M.I.E.,
VICEROY OF INDIA.

From
a photograph by Cowell, Simla.

by Lord Lansdowne, one of whose earliest communications to me rejoiced my heart, for in it His Excellency inquired whether anything could be done towards improving our relations with the frontier tribes. This augured well for the abandonment of the traditional, selfish, and, to my mind, short-sighted policy of keeping aloof. and I hoped that endeavours would at last be made to turn the tribesmen into friendly neighbours, to their advantage and ours, instead of being obliged to have recourse to useless blockades or constant and expensive expeditions for their punishment, or else to induce them to refrain from troubling us by the payment of a heavy blackmail.

After a visit to the frontier in the autumn to see how the defences were advancing, I attended a Cavalry Camp of Exercise at Delhi, and an Artillery Practice Camp at Gurgaon, and then went to Meerut to be present at the first meeting of the Bengal Presidency Rifle Association, which was most interesting and successful. We spent Christmas in camp—the first Christmas we had all been together for ten years. Our boy, having left Eton, came out in the early part of the year with a tutor, to be with us for eighteen months before entering Sandhurst.

At the end of December I proceeded to Calcutta rather earlier than usual, to pay my respects to the new Viceroy, and in January of the following year, accompanied by my wife and daughter, I started off on a long tour to inspect the local regiments in Central India and Rajputana, and to ascertain what progress had been made in organizing the Imperial Service Troops in that part of India.

Did space permit, I should like to tell my readers of the beauties of Udaipur and the magnificent hospitality accorded to us there, as well as at Bhopal, Jodhpur, Jaipur, and Ulwar, but, if I once began, it would be difficult to stop, and I feel I have already made an unconscionably heavy demand on the interest of the public in things Indian, and must soon cease my 'labour of love.' I must therefore confine myself to those subjects which I am desirous should be better understood in England than they generally are.

Upon seeing the troops of the Begum of Bhopal and the Maharana of Udaipur, I recommended that Their Highnesses should be invited to allow their share of Imperial defence to take the form of paying for the services of an increased number of officers with their respective local corps,* for I did not think it would be possible to make any useful addition to our strength out of the material of which their small

* According to treaty, the Bhopal State pays nearly two lakhs of rupees a year towards the cost of the local battalion maintained by the British Government for the purpose of keeping order within the State itself. The battalion, however, has only four, instead of eight, British officers, and it appeared to me only reasonable that the Begum should be invited to pay the additional amount necessary to make the battalion as efficient as the rest of the Native army, as a 'premium of insurance' for the peace and prosperity which Her Highness's State enjoys under our protection, and as her quota towards the general scheme for the defence of the Empire.

armies were composed. The men were relics of a past age, fit only for police purposes, and it would have been a waste of time and money to give them any special training. My recommendation, however, was not accepted, and neither of these States takes any part in the defence scheme.

At Jodhpur, on the contrary, there was splendid material, and a most useful force was being organized by the Maharaja's brother, Lieutenant-Colonel Sir Pertap Sing, himself a Rajput, and of the bluest blood of India. The Cavalry were specially fine. The gallant Rajput horsemen of Jodhpur had always been famous for their chivalrous bravery, unswerving fidelity, and fearless self-devotion in their wars with the Mahrattas and the armies of the Mogul Emperors, and I felt, as the superbly mounted squadrons passed before me, that they had lost none of their characteristics, and that blood and breeding must tell, and would, if put to the test, achieve the same results now as of old. There could be but one opinion as to the value of the 'Sirdar Rissala,'* so named after the Maharaja's son and heir, Sirdar Sing, a lad of only nine years old, who led the little army past the saluting flag mounted on a beautiful thorough-bred Arab.

The Jaipur troops were much on a par with those of Bhopal and Udaipur. I was glad, therefore, that in lieu of troops, the Maharaja had agreed to organize, as his contribution to the Imperial service, a transport corps of 1,000 fully-equipped animals.

At Ulwar I found the 600 Cavalry and 1,000 Infantry (all Rajputs) well advanced in their drill and training; this was evidently owing to the personal interest taken in them by the Maharaja, who seldom allowed a day to pass without visiting the parade grounds.

By the end of March I had finished my tour in Central India and Rajputana, and as the heat was every day becoming more intense, I was not sorry to turn my steps northwards towards Kashmir, the army of which State still remained to be inspected, and the measures most suitable for its re-organization determined upon.

Our whole family party re-assembled at Murree early in April, and we all went into the 'Happy Valley' together, where between business and pleasure we spent a most delightful six weeks. The Maharaja personally superintended the arrangements for our comfort. Our travelling was made easy—indeed luxurious—and everything that the greatest care and forethought and the most lavish hospitality could accomplish to make our visit happy was done by the Maharaja and by the popular Resident, Colonel Nisbet.

The Kashmir army was much larger than any of those belonging to the Native States I had lately visited; it consisted of 18,000 men and 66 guns—more than was needed, even with the Gilgit frontier to guard.

* Rissala is a body of Cavalry.

Some of the regiments were composed of excellent material, chiefly Dogras; but as the cost of such a force was a heavy drain upon the State, and as many of the men were old and decrepit, I recommended that the Maharaja should be invited to get rid of all who were physically unfit, and to reduce his army to a total of 10,000 thoroughly reliable men and 30 guns. I knew this would be a very difficult, and perhaps distasteful, task for the Commander-in-Chief (who was also the Maharaja's brother), Raja Ram Sing, to perform, so I recommended that a British officer should be appointed military adviser to the Kashmir Government, under whose supervision the work of reformation should be carried out.

At that time we had none of our own troops in the neighbourhood of Gilgit, and as I thought it advisable, in case of disturbance, that the Kashmir troops should be speedily put into such a state of efficiency as would enable us to depend upon them to hold the passes until help could arrive from India, I urged that the military adviser should be given three British officers to assist him in carrying out his difficult and troublesome duty; and at the same time I pointed out that it was absolutely essential to construct at an early date a serviceable road between Kashmir and Gilgit, as the sole approach to that strategic position was not only difficult, but very dangerous.

All these proposals commended themselves to, and were acted upon by, the Viceroy.

Lieutenant-Colonel Neville Chamberlain—a *persona grata* to the Kashmir authorities—was appointed Military Secretary to the Kashmir State, and by his ability, tact, and happy way of dealing with Natives, quickly overcame all obstacles. The Maharaja and his two brothers, Rajas Ram Sing and Amar Sing, entered heartily into the scheme; the army was remodelled and rendered fit for service; and an excellent road was made to Gilgit.

During the summer of 1889 I was able to introduce several much needed reforms in the annual course of musketry for the Native Army. The necessity for these reforms had not been overlooked by my distinguished predecessors, nor by the able officers who served under them in the Musketry Department, but it had not been possible to do much with a system which dated from a period when fire discipline was not thought of, and when the whole object of the course was to make soldiers individually good shots. After the Delhi Camp of Exercise in 1885-86, when the want of fire control was almost the only point unfavourably criticized by the foreign officers, the Army in India made a great advance in this important branch of musketry training; nevertheless, I felt that further progress was possible, and that the course of instruction was not altogether as practical as it might be. I therefore gave over the work of improvement in this respect to an enthusiast in the matter of rifle-shooting and an officer of exceptional energy and intelligence, Lieutenant-Colonel Ian Hamilton, and directed him, as Assistant Adjutant-General of Musketry, to arrange a course of instruction, in which the conditions should resemble as nearly as possible those of field service, and in which fire discipline should be developed to the utmost extent. He was most successful in carrying out my wishes, and the results from the first year's trial of the new system were infinitely better than even I had anticipated.

Simultaneously with the improvement in musketry, a great advance was made in gunnery. Artillery, like Infantry officers, had failed to realize the value of the new weapon, and it required the teaching of a man who himself thoroughly believed in and understood the breech-loading gun to arouse Artillerymen to a sense of the tremendous power placed in their hands, and to the importance of devoting much more care and attention to practice than had hitherto been thought necessary. Such a man was Major-General Nairne, and I was happily able to induce the Government to revive in him the appointment of Inspector-General of Artillery.

Under the unwearying supervision of this officer, there was quite as remarkable an improvement in Artillery shooting as Colonel Hamilton had effected in musketry. Practice camps were annually formed at convenient localities, and all ranks began to take as much pride in belonging to the 'best shooting battery' as they had hitherto taken in belonging to the 'smartest,' the 'best-horsed,' or the 'best-turned-out' battery. I impressed upon officers and men that the two things were quite compatible; that, according to my experience, the smartest and best-turned-out men made the best soldiers; and while I urged every detail being most carefully attended to which could enable them to become proficient gunners and take their proper place on a field of battle, I expressed my earnest hope that the Royal Artillery would always maintain its hitherto high reputation for turn-out and smartness.

The improvement in the Cavalry was equally apparent. For this arm of the service also the Government consented to an Inspector-General being appointed, and I was fortunate enough to be able to secure for the post the services of Major-General Luck, an officer as eminently fitted for this position as was General Nairne for his.

Just at first the British officers belonging to Native Cavalry were apprehensive that their sowars would be turned into dragoons, but they soon found that there was no intention of changing any of their traditional characteristics, and that the only object of giving them an Inspector-General was to make them even better in their own way than they had been before, the finest Irregular Cavalry in the world, as I have not the slightest doubt they will always prove themselves to be.

Towards the end of the Simla season of 1889, Lord Lansdowne, to my great satisfaction, announced his intention of visiting the frontier, and asked me to accompany him.

We rode through the Khyber and Gomal Passes, visited Peshawar, Kohat, Bannu, Dera Ismail Khan, and Quetta, looked into the Kohjak tunnel, and attended some interesting manœuvres, carried out with a view of testing, in as practical a manner as possible, the defensive power of the recently-finished Takatu-Mashalik entrenchment. The principal works were fired upon by Artillery and Infantry, and, notwithstanding the excellent practice made, infinitesimal damage was done, which proved the suitability of the particular design adopted for the defences.

Lord Lansdowne expressed himself greatly interested, and much impressed by all he saw of the frontier; and he was confirmed in his opinion as to the desirability of establishing British influence amongst the border tribes. With this object in view, His Excellency authorized Sir Robert Sandeman (the Governor-General's Agent at Quetta) to establish a series of police posts in the Gomal Pass, and encourage intercourse between the people of the Zhob district and ourselves.

It was high time that something should be done in this direction, for the Amir's attitude towards us was becoming day by day more unaccountably antagonistic. He was gradually encroaching on territory and occupying places altogether outside the limits of Afghan control; and every movement of ours—made quite as much in His Highness's interest as in our own—for strengthening the frontier and improving the communications, evidently aroused in him distrust and suspicion as to our motives.

CHAPTER LXVIII.

New Year's Day, 1890, found me in Calcutta, where I went to meet Prince Albert Victor on his arrival in India. On my way thither I received a letter from Mr. Edward Stanhope, Secretary of State for War, telling me that he had heard from Lord Cross, the Secretary of State for India, that there was a proposal to ask me to retain my appointment of Commander-in-Chief in India for some time after the expiration of the usual term of office; but that, while such an arrangement would have his hearty approval, he thought the question should be considered from another point of view, and that it would be extremely agreeable to himself, and he felt to the Duke of Cambridge also, if he could secure me for the post of Adjutant-General in succession to Lord Wolseley. Mr. Stanhope went on to say he would like to know whether I would be willing to accept the appointment, or whatever position Lord Wolseley's successor would fill, should the report of Lord Hartington's Commission cause a change to be made in the staff at the Horse Guards.

I was pleased, though somewhat surprised, at this communication, and I replied to the Right Honourable gentleman that I would gladly accept the offer, and that I could arrange to join on the 1st October, when the appointment would become vacant, but that, as Lord Lansdowne had expressed a wish that I should remain in India over the next cold season, I hoped, if it were possible, some arrangement might be made to admit of my doing so. The idea of employment in England, now that I allowed myself to dwell upon it, was very attractive, for dearly as I loved my Indian command, and bitterly as I knew I should grieve at leaving the country, the peoples, and the grand army, which were all sources of such intense interest to me, I felt that the evil day at longest could only be postponed for a few years, and that there is a limit to the time that even the strongest European can with impunity live in an eastern climate, while I was glad to think I should still be in a position to work for my country and for the benefit of the army.

From Calcutta I travelled north to Muridki, where a large force of Horse Artillery and Cavalry was assembled for practice, and where we had a standing camp, at which Prince Albert Victor did us the honour of being our guest for the final manœuvres. I think His Royal Highness enjoyed the novelty of camp life, and was greatly attracted by the picturesque and soldier-like appearance of the Native troops. The Native officers were very proud at being presented to the grandson of their Empress, and at His Royal Highness being appointed Honorary Colonel of the 1st Punjab Cavalry.

Towards the end of April I returned to Simla for what I thought was to be our last season in that place; and shortly after I got up there, a telegram from Mr. Stanhope informed me that my appointment had been accepted by the Cabinet, and that my presence in England was strongly desired in the autumn. It was therefore with very great surprise that I received a second telegram three weeks later from the Secretary of State, telling me that, as it was then found to be impossible to choose my successor, and as the exigencies of the public service urgently required my presence in India, the Cabinet, with the approval of Her Majesty and the concurrence of the Duke of Cambridge, had decided to ask me to retain my command for two more years.

I felt it my duty to obey the wishes of the Queen, Her Majesty's Government, and the Commander-in-Chief; but I fully realized that in doing so I was forfeiting my chance of employment in England, and that a long and irksome term of enforced idleness would in all probability follow on my return home, and I did not attempt to conceal from Mr. Stanhope that I was disappointed.

At the latter end of this year, and in the early part of 1891, it was found necessary to undertake three small expeditions: one to Zhob, under the leadership of Sir George White, for the protection of our

FIELD-MARSHAL LORD ROBERTS ON HIS ARAB CHARGER 'VONOLEL.'

From an oil-painting by Charles Furse.

newly-acquired subjects in that valley; one on the Kohat border, commanded by Sir William Lockhart, to punish the people of the Miranzai valley for repeated acts of hostility; and the third, under Major-General Elles,* against the Black Mountain tribes, who, quite unsubdued by the fruitless expedition of 1888, had given trouble almost immediately afterwards. All these were as completely successful in their political results as in their military conduct. The columns were not withdrawn until the tribesmen had become convinced that they were powerless to sustain a hostile attitude towards us, and that it was their interest, as it was our wish, that they should henceforth be on amicable terms with us.

While a considerable number of troops were thus employed, a fourth expedition had to be hurriedly equipped and despatched in quite the opposite direction to punish the Raja of Manipur, a petty State on the confines of Assam, for the treacherous murder of Mr. Quinton, the Chief Commissioner of Assam, and four other British officers.

Notwithstanding its inaccessibility, two columns, one from Burma, the other from Cachar, quickly and simultaneously reached Manipur, our countrymen were avenged, and the administration of the State was taken over for a time by the Government of India.†

Towards the end of January the Cesarewitch came to Calcutta, where I had the honour of being introduced to our august visitor, who expressed himself as pleased with what he had seen of the country and the arrangements made for His Imperial Highness's somewhat hurried journey through India.

In April my military colleague in the Viceroy's Council for five years, and my personal friend, General Sir George Chesney, left India, to my great regret. We had worked together most harmoniously, and, as he wrote in his farewell letter, there was scarcely a point in regard to the Army in India about which he and I did not agree.

Sir George was succeeded by Lieutenant-General Brackenbury, who had been Director of Military Intelligence at the War Office. I was relieved to find that, although in some particulars my new coadjutor's views differed from mine, we were in accord upon all essential points, particularly as to the value of the Indian Army and the necessity for its being maintained in a state of preparedness for war.

From the time I became Commander-in-Chief in Madras until I left India the question of how to render the army in that country as perfect a fighting machine as it was possible to make it, was the one which caused me the most anxious thought, and to its solution my most earnest efforts had been at all times directed.

The first step to be taken towards this end was, it seemed to me, to

* The late Lieutenant-General Sir W. K. Elles, K.C.B.

† A detachment of the Calcutta Volunteer Rifles, at the particular request of the regiment, took part in the expedition, and did good service.

substitute men of the more warlike and hardy races for the Hindustani sepoys of Bengal, the Tamils and Telagus of Madras, and the so-called Mahrattas of Bombay; but I found it difficult to get my views accepted, because of the theory which prevailed that it was necessary to maintain an equilibrium between the armies of the three Presidencies, and because of the ignorance that was only too universal with respect to the characteristics of the different races, which encouraged the erroneous belief that one Native was as good as another for purposes of war.

In former days, when the Native Army in India was so much stronger in point of numbers than the British Army, and there existed no means of rapid communication, it was only prudent to guard against a predominance of soldiers of any one creed or nationality; but with British troops nearly doubled and the Native Army reduced by more than one-third, with all the forts and arsenals protected, and nearly the whole of the Artillery manned by British soldiers, with railway and telegraph communication from one end of India to the other, with the risk of internal trouble greatly diminished, and the possibility of external complications becoming daily more apparent, circumstances and our requirements were completely altered, and it had become essential to have in the ranks of our Native Army men who might confidently be trusted to take their share of fighting against a European foe.

In the British Army the superiority of one regiment over another is mainly a matter of training; the same courage and military instinct are inherent in English, Scotch, and Irish alike, but no comparison can be made between the martial value of a regiment recruited amongst the Gurkhas of Nepal or the warlike races of northern India, and of one recruited from the effeminate peoples of the south.

How little this was understood, even by those who had spent a great part of their service in India, was a marvel to me; but, then, I had had peculiar opportunities of judging of the relative fighting qualities of Natives, and I was in despair at not being able to get people to see the matter with my eyes, for I knew that nothing was more sure to lead to disaster than to imagine that the whole Indian Army, as it was then constituted, could be relied on in time of war.

General Chesney fortunately shared my opinions, and as Lords Dufferin and Lansdowne trusted us, we were able to do a great deal towards increasing the efficiency of the Native Army and improving the status and prospects of the Native soldier. Several companies and regiments composed of doubtful material were disbanded, and men of well-known fighting castes entertained instead. Class regiments were formed, as being more congenial to the men and more conducive to *esprit de corps;* recruiting was made the business of carefully selected officers who understood Native character, and whose duty it was to become acquainted with the various tribes inhabiting the districts from which the recruits for their own regiments were drawn; and special arrangements were made with the Nepalese Government by which a sufficient number of the best class of men could be obtained for our thirteen Gurkha regiments.

The pay of Cavalry soldiers was improved, and it was pointed out to the Government that an increase to the Infantry soldiers' pay could not be long deferred;* the issue of good-conduct pay was accelerated; *jagirs*† were sanctioned annually for a limited number of specially distinguished Native officers; full pay was authorized for recruits from date of enlistment instead of from the date of joining their regiments; field *batta*‡ was sanctioned whenever troops should be employed beyond sea or on service; pensions were granted after a shorter period of service than heretofore; medals for meritorious service and good conduct were given in commemoration of Her Majesty's Jubilee; bronze war medals were sanctioned for all authorized Government followers; a reserve, which it was arranged should undergo an annual course of training, was formed for the Artillery and Infantry; and a system of linked battalions was organized, three battalions being grouped together, and the men being interchangeable during war-time.

While the tendency of these alterations and concessions was to make all ranks happy and contented, their training was carefully attended to, and, as I have before mentioned, musketry particularly reached a very high standard.

The one thing left undone, and which I should like to have been able to accomplish before leaving India, was to induce the Government to arrange for more British officers to be given to the Native regiments in time of war. Nine to a Cavalry and eight to an Infantry corps may be sufficient in time of peace, but that number is quite too small to stand the strain of war. Indian soldiers, like soldiers of every nationality, require to be led; and history and experience teach us that eastern races (fortunately for us), however brave and accustomed to war, do not possess the qualities that go to make leaders of men, and that Native officers in this respect can never take the place of British officers. I have known many Natives whose gallantry and devotion could not be surpassed, but I have never known one who would not have looked to the youngest British officer for support in time of difficulty and danger. It is therefore most unwise to allow Native regiments to enter upon a war with so much smaller a

* The pay of the Native Infantry has been suitably increased since I left India.

† *Jagirs* are grants of land.

‡ *Batta*, extra allowances given to Native soldiers when proceeding on field service.

proportion of British officers than is considered necessary for European regiments. I have no doubt whatever of the fighting powers of our best Indian troops; I have a thorough belief in, and admiration for, Gurkhas, Sikhs, Dogras, Rajputs, Jats, and selected Mahomedans; I thoroughly appreciate their soldierly qualities; brigaded with British troops, I would be proud to lead them against any European enemy; but we cannot expect them to do with less leading than our own soldiers require, and it is, I maintain, trying them too highly to send them into action with the present establishment of British officers.*

In the late autumn of 1891 our latest acquisition, the Zhob Valley, was included in my frontier tour, which I had the pleasure of making, for the greater part of the way, in the company of General Brackenbury. He was prevented from getting as far as Quetta by an accident which laid him up for some time, but not, as he told me, before he had seen enough of the frontier to satisfy him that the tribes were a factor in our system of defence which could not be ignored, and that I had not exaggerated the importance of having them on our side.

During this winter the brilliant little Hunza-Naga campaign took

* During the Mutiny the casualties amongst the British officers with the six Punjab regiments which saw the most fighting amounted to 60 per cent.! Luckily, these were able to be replaced by officers belonging to corps which had mutinied. This supply, however, has long since been used up, and it behoves the Government either to provide an adequate reserve of officers, or to arrange for a sufficient number being sent out from England whenever India is likely to be engaged in a serious war.

Corps.	Number of Officers who did Duty with each Corps.	Casualties.				
		Killed in Action.	Died of Wounds.	Died of Disease.	Wounded.	Invalided.
1st Punjab Cavalry (1 squadron)	12	1	...	...	6	7
2nd Punjab Cavalry -	20	1	...	...	5	4
5th Punjab Cavalry (1 squadron)	7	1	1	...	...	...
1st Punjab Infantry -	15	3	...	...	6	...
2nd Punjab Infantry -	22	3	...	...	4	3
4th Punjab Infantry -	24	2	3	2	8	...
Total -	100	11	4	2	29	14

place, which has been so graphically described in Mr. Knight's 'Where Three Empires Meet.' It was brought about by Russia's intrigues with the Rulers of the petty States on the northern boundary of Kashmir; and our attention was first roused to the necessity for action by two British officers, who were journeying to India by way of the Pamirs and Gilgit, being forced by Russian soldiers to leave what the leader of the party called 'newly-acquired Russian territory'*—territory to which Russia had not the shadow of a claim.

In addition to this unjustifiable treatment of Captain Younghusband and Lieutenant Davison, Colonel Yanoff crossed the Hindu Kush with his Cossacks by the Korabhut Pass, and, after reconnoitring the country on the borders of Kashmir, re-crossed the range by the Baroghil Pass. As this was a distinct breach of the promises made by the Russian Government, and an infringement of the boundary line as agreed to between England and Russia in 1873, it was necessary to take steps to prevent any recurrence of such interference, and a small force was accordingly sent against the Chief of Hunza, who had openly declared himself in favour of Russia. He made a desperate stand, but was eventually driven from his almost inaccessible position by the determined gallantry of our Indian troops, assisted by a Contingent from Kashmir. Three Victoria Crosses were given for this business, and many more were earned, but of necessity there must be a limit to the disposal of decorations; and in an affair of this kind, in which all proved themselves heroes, each individual must have felt himself honoured by the small force being awarded such a large number of the coveted reward, in proportion to its size.

We reaped the benefit of having taken this district under our own control when Chitral required to be relieved, and the Hunza-Naga people afforded Colonel Kelly such valuable help.

On the 1st January, 1892, I received an intimation that Her Majesty had been graciously pleased to bestow a peerage upon me, and the same day the Secretary of State for India offered me a further extension of my appointment as Commander-in-Chief—an offer I would gladly have accepted, as I knew it had been made with the concurrence of the Viceroy, if I could have taken even a few months' leave to England. But during a quarter of a century I had only been able to spend eighteen months out of India, and I felt the need of change of climate and a little rest after so many years of continued hard work. Under the existing regulations a Commander-in-Chief could have no leave. Lord Cross had tried to remedy this hard rule by bringing in the 'Officers' Leave Bill'; but as he informed Lord Lansdowne it was impossible to get it through the House of Commons that session, I was

* Captain Younghusband was at Bozai-Gumbaz, and Lieutenant Davison on the Alichur Pamirs, both places being south of the Aksu branch of the Oxus, flowing from the Little Pamir Lake.

obliged very reluctantly to beg to be allowed to resign my command in the spring of 1893.

Before returning to Simla for really the last time, my wife and I made another trip to Burma as far as Mandalay, and after this was over we paid a most interesting visit to Nepal, having received the very unusual honour of an invitation to Khatmandu from Maharaja Bir Shumsher Jung Rana Bahadur.

Khatmandu is about a hundred miles from our frontier station of Segowli, by a very rough road over a succession of steep, high hills and along deep, narrow valleys, which would have been quite impossible for a lady to travel by but for the excellent arrangements made by the Nepalese officials; the last descent was the worst of all; we literally dropped from one rock to the next in some places. But on reaching the base of the mountain all was changed. A beautifully cultivated valley spread itself out before us; comfortable tents were prepared for our reception, where we were met by some of the State officials; and a perfectly appointed carriage-and-four was waiting to carry us on to Khatmandu, where we were received by the Resident, Lieutenant-Colonel Wylie, and his wife, old friends of ours. That afternoon the Maharaja paid me a private visit.

The next morning the official call was made, which I returned soon afterwards; and in the evening the Maharaja, accompanied by his eldest son and eight of his brothers, all high officers of state, were present at Mrs. Wylie's reception, wearing military frock-coats and forage-caps. They all spoke English fluently; their manners were those of well-bred gentlemen, easy and quiet, as free from awkwardness as from forwardness; each, coming up in turn, talked very pleasantly to Lady Roberts for a time, and then made way for someone else. The Maharaja is extremely musical, and has several well-trained bands, taught by an English bandmaster; three of them were in attendance, and were directed to play selections from our favourite operas, and then a number of the beautiful plaintive Nepalese airs. Altogether, we passed a most agreeable evening.

The following day a review of all the troops (18,000 men and 78 guns)* was held on a ground one mile in length by half a mile in breadth, perfectly level and well turfed. It would be considered a fine parade-ground for the plains of India, and must have entailed a considerable expenditure of time, labour, and money to make in such a hilly place as Khatmandu.

On reaching the ground, I was received by the Maharaja and Deb

* The Infantry comprised twenty-four battalions drawn up in line of quarter columns. The Artillery consisted of one battery (six 7-pounders) carried on elephants, six batteries (six guns each, 5-pounders and 7-pounders) dragged by soldiers, and six batteries (six guns each, 3-pounders and 5-pounders) carried by Bhutia coolies.

Shamsher Jung, the eldest of his many brothers, and the nominal Commander-in-Chief of the army; we rode along the line together, and the march-past then began. Everything was done with the utmost precision; there was no fuss or talking, and from first to last not a single bugle sound was heard, showing how carefully officers and men had been drilled. I was told that the executive Commander-in-Chief, the third brother, by name Chandra Shamsher, had almost lived on the parade-ground for weeks before my arrival. The Maharaja's sons and brothers, who all knew their work, and were evidently fond of soldiering, commanded the several divisions and brigades.

The troops were not, perhaps, turned out quite so smartly as those in our service, and several of the officers were old and feeble; but these were the only faults perceptible, and I came to the conclusion that the great majority of the 18,000 men were quite as good as the Gurkhas we enlist; and I could not help thinking that they would be a valuable addition to our strength in the event of war.

General Chandra Shamsher is a very red-hot soldier. He said to my wife: 'Lady Roberts, when are the Russians coming? I wish they would make haste. We have 40,000 soldiers in Nepal ready for war, and there is no one to fight!'

The next day a grand durbar was held, at which the King (the Maharaja Dhiraj, as he is called) presided; he was an unusually handsome lad of about eighteen years of age, fairer than most Nepalese, and very refined looking. As on all previous occasions, everyone wore uniform except the King, who had on a perfectly plain dress of spotless white. Great deference is outwardly paid to the Dhiraj, but he has no power, and is never consulted in matters of State, being considered too sacred to be troubled with mundane affairs. Although a mere boy, he had four wives, two of them daughters of the Maharaja Bir Shamsher Jung.

After the durbar, I was shown over the principal school and hospital; both appeared to be well conducted, and evidently no expense was spared upon them. I was then taken to a magazine, in which were a number of guns of various calibre and any amount of ammunition. I was told there were several other magazines, which I had not time to see, and a few miles from Khatmandu extensive workshops, where all kinds of munitions of war were manufactured.

That evening, accompanied by Colonel and Mrs. Wylie, we attended a reception at the Maharaja's palace. The durbar hall, which was filled with men in uniform, was of beautiful proportions, and very handsomely decorated and furnished. After the usual introductions and some conversation with the chief officers, we were invited to visit the Maharani in her own apartments, and having ascended a flight of steps and passed through numerous corridors and luxuriously furnished rooms, we were shown into a spacious apartment, the prevailing colour of which was rose, lighted by lamps of the same colour. The Maharani was sitting on a sofa at the further end of the room, gorgeously apparelled in rose-coloured gauze dotted over with golden spangles; her skirts were very voluminous, and she wore magnificent jewels on her head and about her person. Two Maids of Honour stood behind her, holding fans, and dressed in the same colour as their mistress, but without jewels. On each side of her, forming a semicircle, were grouped the ladies of the Court, all arrayed in artistically contrasting colours; they were more or less pretty and refined looking, and the Maharani herself was extremely handsome. My wife was placed by her side on the sofa, and carried on a long conversation with her through one of the ladies who spoke Hindustani and acted as Interpreter. The Maharani presented Lady Roberts with a beautiful little Chinese pug-dog, and the Maharaja gave me a gold-mounted *kookri* (Gurkha knife). After this little ceremony there was a grand display of fireworks, and we took our leave.

Nothing could exceed the kindness we met with during our stay in Nepal. The Maharaja endeavoured in every way to make our visit enjoyable, and his brothers vied with each other in their efforts to do us honour. It was impressed upon me that the Nepalese army was at the disposal of the Queen-Empress, and hopes were repeatedly expressed that we would make use of it in the event of war.

Notwithstanding the occasional differences which have occurred between our Government and the Nepal Durbar, I believe that, ever since 1817, when the Nepal war was brought to a successful conclusion by Sir David Ochterlony, the Gurkhas have had a great respect and liking for us: but they are in perpetual dread of our taking their country, and they think the only way to prevent this is not to allow anyone to enter it except by invitation, and to insist upon the few thus favoured travelling by the difficult route that we traversed. Nepal can never be required by us for defensive purposes, and as we get our best class of Native soldiers thence, everything should, I think, be done to show our confidence in the Nepalese alliance, and convince them that we have no ulterior designs on the independence of their kingdom.

On leaving Nepal we made a short tour in the Punjab, and then went to Simla for the season.

One of the subjects which chiefly occupied the attention of the Government at this time was the unfriendly attitude of the Ruler of Afghanistan towards us. Abdur Rahman Khan appeared to have entirely forgotten that he owed everything to us, and that, but for our support and lavish aid in money and munitions of war, he could neither have gained nor held the throne of Kabul. We refused to Sher Ali much that we could have gracefully granted and that would have made him a firm friend, but in our dealings with Abdur Rahman we rushed into the other extreme, and showered favours upon him; in fact, we made too much of him, and allowed him to get out of hand. The result was that he mistook the patience and forbearance with which we bore his fits of temper for weakness, and was encouraged in an overweening and altogether unjustifiable idea of his own importance; he considered that he ought to be treated as the equal of the Shah of Persia, and keenly resented not being allowed to communicate direct with Her Majesty's Ministers.

In the hope of being able to establish more satisfactory relations with the Amir, Lord Lansdowne invited him to come to India, and, on His Highness pleading that his country was in too disturbed a condition to admit of his leaving it, the Viceroy expressed his willingness to meet him on the frontier, but Abdur Rahman evaded this arrangement also under one pretext or another. It was at last proposed to send me with a Mission as far as Jalalabad, a proposal I gladly accepted, for I was sanguine enough to hope that, by personal explanation, I should be able to remove the suspicions which the Amir evidently entertained as to the motives for our action on the frontier, and to convince him that our help in the time of his need must depend upon our mutually agreeing in what manner that help should be given, and on arrangements being completed beforehand to enable our troops to be rapidly transported to the threatened points.

Abdur Rahman agreed to receive me in the autumn, and expressed pleasure at the prospect of meeting me, but eventually he apparently became alarmed at the size of the escort by which the Government thought it necessary that I, as Commander-in-Chief, should be accompanied; and, as the time approached for the Mission to start, he informed Lord Lansdowne that his health would not permit of his undertaking the journey to Jalalabad.

Thus the opportunity was lost to which I had looked forward as a chance for settling many vexed questions, and I am afraid that there has been very little improvement in our relations with Abdur Rahman since then, and that we are no nearer the completion of our plans for the defence of his kingdom than we were four years ago*—a defence which (and this cannot be too strongly impressed upon the Amir) it would be impossible for us to aid him to carry through unless Kabul and Kandahar are brought into connexion with the railway system of India.

In the autumn, just before we left Simla, our friends bestowed upon my wife a farewell gift in the shape of a very beautiful diamond bracelet and a sum of money for her fund for 'Homes in the Hills, and Officers' Hospitals,' made doubly acceptable by the kind words with which Lord Lansdowne, on behalf of the donors, presented it. Shortly

* I am not unmindful of the visit which Sir Mortimer Durand paid to Kabul after I had left India, but on that occasion. I believe, the question of the defence of Afghanistan was not discussed.

afterwards we bade a regretful adieu to our happy home of so many years, and made our way to the Punjab for a final visit.

We spent a few days at Peshawar, and then went to Rawal Pindi to be present at a Camp of Exercise, and see how the works under construction for the protection of the arsenal were progressing. These works had been put in hand in 1890, when, according to my recommendation, it had been decided not to fortify Multan. No place in the Punjab appeared to my mind to possess the same military value as Rawal Pindi, its strategical importance with regard to the right flank of the frontier line being hardly inferior to that of Quetta in relation to the left flank; but of late the advisability of completing the works had been questioned by my colleagues in Council, greatly to my concern, for I felt that it would be unwise to leave the elaboration of the defences of such a position until war should be imminent.*

In January, 1893, a series of farewell entertainments were organized for me at Lahore by the people of the Punjab, as touching as they were highly appreciated, and intensely gratifying. Amongst the crowds assembled in the Town Hall to bid me good-bye, I was greatly pleased to see, besides the Maharaja of Kashmir, Chiefs and men from beyond our frontier, from Kuram, from the confines of Baluchistan, even from the wilds of Waziristan; for their presence on this occasion I felt to be, not only a proof of their kindly feeling towards me personally, and of their approval of the measures for their safety and welfare that I had always advocated, but a very distinct sign of the much to be desired change that was taking place in the sentiments of the border tribes towards us as a nation.

Four addresses were presented to me, from the Sikh, Hindu, Mahomedan, and European communities of the Punjab, respectively, which I will venture to give in the Appendix, as I feel sure that the

* The works were stopped after I left India, but not, I was glad to think, before the redoubts had been finished, with the communications thereto. The reasons given were that a change of plans was necessary for economy's sake, and that the construction of fortifications might induce the Natives to think we were doubtful of the continuance of our supremacy. As regarded the first, I explained that the total outlay for works and armaments was estimated at only £332,274—considerably less than one half the cost of a British line-of-battle ship; and as to the second, I urged that an argument of this sort against frontier defences would hardly bear examination; that the possibility of external attack was freely discussed in every newspaper; that Russian movements and frontier difficulties were known and commented on in every bazaar; that the construction of fortifications in support of the Ruling Power had been an Oriental practice from time immemorial; that our action in this respect was at least as likely to instil the idea that we meant to retain our eastern possessions at any cost, as to give an impression of weakness; that the progressive re-organization and mobilization of our army were well known to have reference to service beyond the frontier; and that we had extended our confidence in this respect to Native Princes by encouraging them to train their own troops and fit them to take their place in line with ours.

spirit of loyalty which pervades them will be a revelation to many, and a source of satisfaction to all who are interested in the country to which we owe so much of our present greatness, and which I conceive to be the brightest jewel in England's crown.

It was a wonderful and moving scene upon which we looked from the platform of the Town Hall on this memorable occasion, made up as it was of such different elements, each race and creed easily recognizable from their different costumes and characteristics, but all united by the same kindly desire to do honour to their departing friend, or comrade, for there were a great number of old soldiers present.

At each place that we visited on our way to Calcutta there was the same display of kindly regret at our departure; friends assembled to see us off at the railway-stations, bands played 'Auld lang syne,' and hearty cheers speeded us on our way.

In February we went to Lucknow for a few days, when the Talukdars of Oudh gave my wife and me an entertainment on a very splendid scale in the Wingfield Park, and presented me with an address* and a sword of honour.

On our return to Calcutta, just before we left for England, the European community entertained me at a dinner, at which more than two hundred were present, presided over by Sir James Mackay, K.C.I.E., Chairman of the Calcutta Chamber of Commerce. Sir James was far too kind and eulogistic in speaking of my services, but for his appreciative allusion to my wife I could only feel deeply gratified and thankful. After dinner a reception was given to Lady Roberts and myself, at which the Viceroy and Lady Lansdowne and all the principal Native and European residents of Calcutta were assembled. An address† was presented to me on this never-to be-forgotten occasion, in which, to my supreme satisfaction, the Native noblemen and gentlemen expressed their hearty approval of what had been done during my tenure of office as Commander-in-Chief to strengthen the defences of the frontier and render the army in India efficient, and declared that 'we cheerfully bear our share of the cost, as in possession of these protections against aggressions from without we believe all who dwell within the borders of the land will find their best guarantee for peace, and in peace the best safeguard they and their children can possess to enable them to pass their lives in happiness and prosperity, and escape the misery and ruin which follow war and invasion.'

We travelled to Bombay *viâ* Jeypur and Jodhpur. At both places we were royally entertained by the Rulers of those states, and my staff and I were given excellent sport amongst the wild boar, which was much enjoyed by all, particularly by my son, who, having joined the King's Royal Rifles at Rawal Pindi, was attached to me as A.D.C.

* Given in the Appendix † *Ibid*

during my last six months in India, and had not before had an opportunity of tasting the joys of pig-sticking.

At Jodhpur my friend the Maharaja Sir Pertap Sing gave us a signal proof that the ancient valour of the Rajputs had not deteriorated in the present day. I had wounded a fine boar, and on his making for some rocky ground, where I could hardly have followed him on horseback, I shouted to Sir Pertap to get between him and the rocks, and turn him in my direction. The Maharaja promptly responded, but just as he came face-to-face with the boar, his horse put his foot into a hole and fell; the infuriated animal rushed on the fallen rider, and, before the latter could extricate himself, gave him a severe wound in the leg with his formidable tushes. On going to his assistance, I found Sir Pertap bleeding profusely, but standing erect, facing the boar and holding the creature (who was upright on his hind-legs) at arms' length by his mouth. The spear without the impetus given by the horse at full speed is not a very effective weapon against the tough hide of a boar's back, and on realizing that mine did not make much impression, Pertap Sing, letting go his hold of the boar's mouth, quickly seized his hind-legs, and turned him over on his back, crying: '*Maro, sahib, maro!*' ('Strike, sir, strike!') which I instantly did, and killed him. Anyone who is able to realize the strength and weight of a wild boar will appreciate the pluck and presence of mind of Sir Pertap Sing in this performance. Fortunately, my wife and daughter, who had been following the pig-stickers in a light cart, were close at hand, and we were able to drive my friend home at once. The wound was found to be rather a bad one, but it did not prevent Sir Pertap from attending some tent-pegging and other amusements in the afternoon, though he had to be carried to the scene.

A few months after my return to England the boar's head arrived, set up, and with a silver plate attached to it, on which was an inscription commemorating the adventure.

At Ahmedabad, where the train stopped while we lunched, I was presented with an address by the President and members of the Municipality, who, 'with loyal devotion to Her Imperial Majesty the Queen and Empress of India, to whose glorious reign we sincerely wish a continuance of brilliant prosperity,' expressed their hope that Lady Roberts and I would have 'a happy voyage home and enjoyment of perfect health and prosperity in future.'

The day before we left Bombay for England, the members of the Byculla Club gave me a parting dinner. It was with great difficulty I could get through my speech in response to the toast of my health on that occasion, for, pleased and grateful as I was at this last mark of friendship and approval from my countrymen, I could not help feeling inexpressibly sad and deeply depressed at the thought uppermost in my mind, that the time had come to separate myself from India and my gallant comrades and friends, British and Native.

In dwelling on the long list of farewell addresses and entertainments with which I was honoured on leaving India, I feel that I may be laying myself open to the charge of egotism; but in writing of one's own experiences it is difficult to avoid being egotistical, and distasteful as it is to me to think that I may be considered so, I would rather that, than that those who treated me so kindly and generously should deem me unmindful or ungrateful.

Thus ended forty-one years in India. No one can, I think, wonder that I left the country with heartfelt regret. The greater number of my most valued friendships had been formed there; from almost everyone with whom I had been associated, whether European or Native, civilian or soldier, I had experienced unfailing kindness, sympathy, and support; and to the discipline, bravery, and devotion to duty of the Army in India, in peace and war, I felt that I owed whatever success it was my good fortune to achieve.

APPENDICES

APPENDIX I.

(See p. 97.)

THE 9th Native Infantry, to which Captain Donald Stewart belonged, was divided between Aligarh, Mainpuri, Bulandshahr, and Etawa, Stewart being with the Head-Quarters of the regiment at Aligarh.

The news from Meerut and Delhi had caused a certain amount of alarm amongst the residents at Aligarh, and arrangements had been made for sending away the ladies and children, but, owing to the confidence placed in the men of the 9th, none of them had left the station. Happen what might in other regiments, the officers were certain that the 9th could never be faithless to their salt! The Native officers and men were profuse in their expressions of loyalty, and as a proof of their sincerity they arrested and disarmed several rebel sepoys, who were making for their homes in Oudh and the adjoining districts. As a further proof, they gave up the regimental pandit for endeavouring to persuade them to mutiny. He was tried by a Court-Martial composed of European and Native officers, found guilty, and sentenced to be hanged. The sentence was carried out that same afternoon. It was intended that the regiment should witness the execution, but it did not reach the gaol in time; the men were therefore marched back to their lines, and Stewart, in his capacity of Interpreter, was ordered to explain to them the purpose for which they had been paraded. While he was speaking a man of his own company shouted out something. Stewart did not hear the words, and no one would repeat them. The parade was then dismissed, when the same man, tearing off his uniform, called upon his comrades not to serve a Government which had hanged a Brahmin. A general uproar ensued. The Commanding Officer ordered the few Sikhs in the regiment to seize the ring-leader; they did so, but not being supported by the rest they released him. The Subadar Major was then told to arrest the mutineer, but he took no notice whatever of the order. This Native officer had been upwards of forty years in the regiment and was entitled to his full pension. He had been a member of the Court-Martial which tried the pandit, and, though a Brahmin himself, had given his vote in favour of the prisoner being hanged; moreover he was a personal friend of all the officers. Stewart, who had been for many years Adjutant, knew him intimately, and believed implicitly in his loyalty. The man had constantly discussed the situation with Stewart and others, and had been mainly instrumental in disarming the sepoys who had passed through Aligarh: and yet when the hour of trial came he failed as completely as the last-joined recruit.

The British officers went amongst their men and tried to keep order, but the excitement rapidly spread; some of the young soldiers began to load, and the older ones warned the officers that it was time for them to be off. The sepoys then plundered the treasury, broke open the gaol doors, released the prisoners, and marched in a body towards Delhi.*

Stewart, being thus left without a regiment, attached himself to the magistrate of the district, and took command of a small body of volunteers sent from Agra by the Lieutenant-Governor of the North-West Provinces, to aid the civil authorities in restoring order. Not caring for this work, and thinking he might be more usefully employed, Stewart made up his mind to find his way to Delhi; his idea was to try and get there *viâ* Meerut, but before deciding on the route, he went to Agra, where he had been invited by the Lieutenant-Governor. At the interview, Mr. Colvin advised Stewart to travel *viâ* Muttra, as the safer of the two routes, and told him that despatches had been received from the Government in Calcutta for the Commander-in-Chief, then understood to be with the army before Delhi. At the same time the Lieutenant-Governor impressed upon Stewart that he was not giving him any order to go, and that if he undertook to carry the despatches it must be a voluntary act on his part, entailing no responsibility on the Government of the North-West Provinces.

Stewart accepted the duty, and took his leave of Mr. Colvin as the sun was setting on the 18th June, delighted at the chance of being able to join the army before Delhi. He reached Muttra, thirty-five miles distant, without mishap. The streets of this city were crowded with men, all carrying arms of some sort; they showed no signs of hostility, however, and even pointed out to Stewart the house of which he was in search. The owner of this house, to whose care he had been commended by the Agra authorities, was a Brahmin holding an official position in the town. This Native gentleman behaved with civility, but did not attempt to conceal his embarrassment at the presence of a British officer, or his relief when Stewart announced his intention of resuming his journey an hour or so before daybreak.

The Brahmin provided him with two sowars belonging to the Raja of Bhartpur with orders to accompany him as far as Kosi. They were cut-throat-looking individuals, and Stewart felt rather inclined to dispense with their services, but, thinking it unwise to show any signs of distrust, he accepted them with the best grace he could.

After riding fifteen or sixteen miles, Stewart's horse fell from exhaustion, on which his so-called escort laughed uproariously, and galloped off, leaving our poor traveller to his own devices.

Believing the horse could not recover, Stewart took off the saddle and bridle and tramped to the nearest village, where he hoped to be able to buy or hire an animal of some kind on which to continue his journey. No one, however, would help him, and he was forced to seize a donkey which he found grazing in a field hard by. About sunset he reached Kosi, thirty-seven miles from Muttra. The *tehsildar*† received him courteously, and gave him some bread and milk, but would not hear of his staying for the night. He told him that his appearance in the town was causing considerable excitement, and that he could not be responsible for his safety. Stewart was much exhausted after his hot ride, but as the *tehsildar* stood firm there was nothing for him to do but to continue his journey, and he consented to start if he were provided with a horse. The *tehsildar* promptly offered his own pony, and as soon as it

* While the regiment was in the act of mutinying one of the sepoys left the parade-ground, and running round to all the civilians' houses, told the occupants what had happened, and warned them to make their escape. He asked for no reward, and was never seen again.

† Native magistrate.

was dark Stewart set out for the Jaipur camp. His progress during the night was slow, and it was not until eight o'clock the next morning that he reached his destination, where he was hospitably received by the Political Agent, Major Eden, who introduced him to the Maharaja's Wazir. This official at first promised to give Stewart a small escort as far as Delhi, but on various pretexts he put him off from day to day. At the end of a week Stewart saw that the Wazir either could not or would not give him an escort, and thinking it useless to delay any longer, he made up his mind to start without one.

There were several refugees in the camp, and one of them, Mr. Ford, collector and magistrate of Gurgaon, offered to join Stewart in his venture.

Stewart and his companion left the Jaipur camp on the afternoon of the 27th June, and reached Palwal soon after dark. Ford sent for the *kotwal*,* who was one of his own district officials, and asked him for food. This was produced, but the *kotwal* besought the *sahibs* to move on without delay, telling them that their lives were in imminent danger, as there was a rebel regiment in the town, and he was quite unable to protect them. So they continued their journey, and, escaping from one or two threatened attacks by robbers, reached Badshahpur in the morning. Here they rested during the heat of the day, being kindly treated by the villagers, who were mostly Hindus.

The travellers were now not far from Delhi, but could hardly proceed further without a guide, and the people of Badshahpur declined to provide one. They pleaded that they were men of peace, and could not possibly leave their village in such evil times. Suddenly a man from the crowd offered his services. His appearance was against him, and the villagers declared that he was a notorious cattle-lifter, who was strongly suspected of having set fire to the collector's (Mr. Ford's) office at Gurgaon, in order that the evidences of his offences might be destroyed. Not a pleasant *compagnon de voyage*, but there was nothing for it but to accept his offer.

As soon as it was dark a start was made, and at daybreak on the 29th the minarets of Delhi rose out of the morning mist, while an occasional shell might be seen bursting near the city.

On reaching the Hansi road, the guide, by name Jumna Das, who, in spite of appearances, had proved true to his word, stopped and said he could go no further. He would not take any reward that it was then in the power of Stewart or Ford to offer him, but he expressed a hope that, when the country became settled, the slight service he had performed would not be forgotten. They gratefully assured him on this point, and thanked him cordially, giving him at the same time a letter testifying to his valuable service. Stewart then went to the nearest village, and for a small reward found a man who undertook to conduct them safely to one of our piquets.

One curious circumstance remarked by Stewart throughout the ride was that the peasants and villagers, though not generally hostile to him, had evidently made up their minds that the British *raj* was at an end, and were busily engaged in rendering their villages defensible, to meet the troubles and disturbances which they considered would surely follow on the resumption of Native rule.

It is difficult to over-estimate the pluck and enterprise displayed by Stewart during this most adventurous ride. It was a marvel that he ever reached Delhi. His coming there turned out to be the best thing that ever happened to him, for the qualities which prompted him to undertake and carried him through his dangerous journey, marked him as a man worthy of advancement and likely to do well.

* City magistrate.

APPENDIX II.

(These two memoranda are referred to in the note on page 196.)

Memorandum by Lieutenant McLeod Innes.

'1. Sir H. Lawrence joined at Lucknow about the end of March, 1857, succeeding Mr. Coverley Jackson in the Chief Commissionership.

'2. On his arrival he found himself in the midst of troubles, of which the most important were these:

I. A general agitation of the empire, from the discontent of the soldiery.

II. A weak European force at Oudh, with all the military arrangements defective.

III. Grievous discontent among several classes of the population of Oudh, viz., the nobility of Lucknow and the members and retainers of the Royal Family, the official classes, the old soldiery and the entire country population, noble and peasant alike.

'3. This third was due to disobedience of, or departure from, the instructions laid down by Government at the annexation, as very clearly shown in Lord Stanley's letter of October 13, 1858. The promised pensions had either been entirely withheld or very sparingly doled out; the old officials were entirely without employment; three-quarters of the army the same; while the country Barons had, by forced interpretation of rules, been deprived of the mass of their estates, which had been parcelled out among their followers, who, for clannish reasons, were more indignant at the spoliation and loss of power and place of their Chiefs than they were glad for their own individual acquisitions.

'4. The weakness of the European force could not be helped; it was deemed politic to show the country that the annexation did not require force.

'5. But the inefficiency of the military arrangements arose from mere want of skill, and was serious, under the threatening aspect of the political horizon.

'6. The discontent of the province, and the coming general storm, had already found vent in the brigandage of Fuzl Ali, and the seditions of the Fyzabad Moulvie.

'7. And with all these Sir H. Lawrence had to grapple immediately on his arrival.

'8. But I may safely say that ten days saw the mass of them disappear. The Fyzabad Moulvie had been seized and imprisoned. Fuzl Ali had been surrounded and slain. The promised pensions had been paid, by Sir H. Lawrence's peremptory orders, to the members and retainers of the Royal Family. A recognition had been published of the fair rights of the old Oudh officials to employment in preference to immigrants from our old provinces, and instructions had been issued for giving it effect. The disbanded soldiers of the Royal Army of Oudh were promised preference in enlistment in the local corps and the police, and a reorganization and increase to the latter, which were almost immediately sanctioned, gave instant opportunities for the fulfilment of the first instalment of these promises. While last, but not least, durbars were held, in which Sir Henry Lawrence was able to proclaim his views and policy, by which the landholders should be reinstated in the possessions which they held at the annexation, the basis on which the instructions had been originally issued, which had been hitherto practically ignored, but to which he pledged himself to give effect.

'9. To strengthen his military position, he placed Artillery with the European Infantry; he distributed his Irregular Cavalry; he examined the city, decided on taking possession of the Muchee Bawn and garrisoning it as a fort; and summoned in Colonel Fisher and Captain George Hardinge; and with them, Brigadier Handscombe and Major Anderson, consulted and arranged for future plans against the storms which he saw to be impending.

'10. Much of this, and his policy for remaining in Oudh, and the conduct of the defence of Lucknow, I know from recollections of what he occasionally let drop to me in his confidential conversations while inspecting the Muchee Bawn. He told me that nearly the whole army would go; that he did not think the Sikhs would go; that in every regiment there were men that, with proper management, would remain entirely on our side; and that, therefore, he meant to segregate from the rest of the troops the Sikhs and selected men, and to do his best to keep them faithful allies when the rest should go; that, if Cawnpore should hold out, we would not be attacked; but that if it should fall, we would be invested, and more or less closely besieged; that no troops could come to our relief before the middle of August; that the besieging forces would, he thought, be confined to the sepoys, for the people of the country had always liked our European officers, whom they had frequently had to bless for the safety of their lives and the honour of their families; and the whole Hindu population had a lively recollection of our friendly line of conduct in the late quarrel with the Mussulmans regarding the Hunnooman Gurhee; that to hold out where we were was necessary, for the slightest appearance of yielding, or of not showing a bold front, would result in annihilation; that to hold out we must get provisions; that to get provisions and prepare for an efficient defence we must keep open our communication with the country, and keep the city quiet; that to the former end the retention of the cantonment was necessary, and of the Muchee Bawn to the latter, while the site of the permanent defences, in case of the need of concentration, should be the Residency.

'11. All this I know, as before said, from Sir Henry Lawrence's own casual and hurried remarks to me. Whether they are officially recorded anywhere I do not know; but they must have been written in letters to various persons, and repeated to others of his subordinates at Lucknow. I mention these matters thus early, as although the facts on which they bear did not immediately occur, still, Sir Henry Lawrence had prescience of them, and had decided on his line of policy.

'12. I understand, further, but not on authentic grounds, that Sir Henry wrote at a very early stage to Sir H. Wheeler, urging him to construct entrenchments at the magazine at Cawnpore, and to ensure his command of the boats, whatever might happen: that he wrote early to the Government, entreating them to divert one of the European regiments in the course of relief, and divide it between Cawnpore and Allahabad; and that subsequently he urged on Government to employ the troops of the Persian expedition in Bengal, and to stop the Chinese force for the same end, and to subsidize some of the Nepal troops for the protection of our older provinces east of Oudh.

'13. To revert to the narrative, the measures already mentioned so entirely pacified the province, that, in spite of the previous discontent, the previous troubles, the proverbial turbulence of its inhabitants, and the increasing agitation throughout the empire, there was no difficulty experienced in collecting the revenue by the close of April. And the subsequent disturbances were, as will be shown, entirely due to the soldiery, and, till long after Sir Henry's death, participated in only by them, by the city ruffians, and by a few of the Mussulman families of the country population. The mass of the city people and the entire Hindu population held aloof, and would have nothing to say to the outbreak; and, with one single exception, every Talookdar to whom the chance offered itself aided, more or less actively, in the protection of European fugitives. This phase in the character of the disturbances in Oudh is not generally known; but it is nevertheless true, and is due emphatically and solely, under Divine Providence, to the benignant personal character and the popular policy of Sir Henry Lawrence.

'14. The 1st of May saw our disturbances commence with the mutiny of the 7th Oudh Irregular Infantry. This, its suppression, and the durbar in which he distributed rewards and delivered a speech on the aspect of affairs, have been fully described elsewhere, and need not be repeated by me.

'15. The durbar was held on the twelfth. I am not aware whether he had any intelligence at that time of the Meerut outbreak. The telegrams, when they did arrive, were vague; but he indubitably kept on his guard immediately on receiving them. The Cavalry were piqueted between the cantonments and the Residency, and the Infantry and Artillery were kept prepared for movement. His plans were evidently already decided; but they were to be effected simultaneously and not successively, and the movements of the Europeans were somewhat dependent on the arrangements of the Quartermaster-General's Department. It was not until the sixteenth that the tents required for the 32nd were ready; and the morning of the 17th May saw an entirely new and effective disposition of the troops. Half the Europeans were at the Residency, commanding the Iron Bridge; half, with the Artillery, were at the south end of the cantonments; the bridge of boats was moved and under control, while the Muchee Bawn, not yet sufficiently cleansed from its old conglomeration of filth, was garrisoned by a selected body of Native troops. The whole of these dispositions could not have been effected at an earlier date, and Sir Henry would not do them piecemeal or successively. Simultaneous, they were effective, and tended to paralyze any seditious plots that may have been hatching. Successive and piecemeal, they would have incited the sepoys to mutiny and the turbulent to insurrection.'

Memorandum, 18th May, inserted in Sir Henry's own hand in his ledger-book.

'Time is everything just now. Time, firmness, promptness, conciliation, and prudence; every officer, each individual European, high and low, may at this crisis prove most useful, or even dangerous. A firm and cheerful aspect must be maintained—there must be no bustle, no appearance of alarm, still less of panic; but, at the same time, there must be the utmost watchfulness and promptness; everywhere the first germ of insurrection must be put down instantly. Ten men may in an hour quell a row which, after a day's delay, may take weeks to put down. I wish this point to be well understood. In preserving internal tranquillity, the Chiefs and people of substance may be most usefully employed at this juncture; many of them have as much to lose as we have. Their property, at least, is at stake. Many of them have armed retainers—some few are good shots and have double-barrelled guns. For instance [name illegible], can hit a bottle at 100 yards. He is with the ordinary soldiers. I want a dozen such men, European or Native, to arm their own people and to make *thannahs* of their own houses, or some near position, and preserve tranquillity within a circuit around them.'

APPENDIX III.

(Referred to at p. 351.)

THE column was composed as follows:	*Men.*	*Guns.*
F Battery, A Brigade, R.H.A., commanded by Colonel W. Sterling...	135	6
One squadron 10th Hussars, commanded by Major Bulkeley	102	
G Battery, 3rd Brigade, R.A., commanded by Major Sydney Parry	83	3
2nd Battalion 8th Foot, commanded by Colonel Barry Drew	620	
Wing 72nd Highlanders, commanded by Lieutenant-Colonel F. Brownlow	405	
Total British troops	1,345	9
12th Bengal Cavalry, commanded by Colonel Hugh Gough, V.C.	337	
No. 1 Mountain Battery, commanded by Captain Kelso ...	136	4
7th Company Bengal Sappers and Miners	113	
2nd (Punjab Frontier Force) Infantry, commanded by Lieutenant-Colonel Tyndall	647	
5th (Punjab Frontier Force) Infantry, commanded by Major McQueen	502	
5th (Punjab Frontier Force) Gurkhas, commanded by Major Fitz-Hugh	438	
21st Punjab Infantry, commanded by Major Collis ...	496	
23rd Pioneers, commanded by Colonel Currie	650	
29th Punjab Infantry, commanded by Colonel J. J. Gordon	671	
Total Natives	3,990	4
Grand total	5,335	13

Lieutenant-Colonel Alexander Lindsay commanded the Artillery, Colonel Æneas Perkins was Commanding Royal Engineer. Colonel Hugh Gough commanded the Cavalry, Brigadier-Generals Cobbe (17th Foot) and Thelwall (21st Punjab Infantry) the two Infantry brigades. Major W. Galbraith (85th Foot) was Assistant-Adjutant-General; Major H. Collett, Assistant, and Captains 'Dick' Kennedy and F. Carr, Deputy-Assistant-Quartermasters-General. Captains G. de C. Morton and A. Scott, V.C., Brigade-Majors. Captain A. Badcock, Chief Commissariat officer; Captain J. Colquhoun, R.A., Commissary of Ordnance; Major Moriarty, Captain Goad, and Lieutenant F. Maisey, Transport officers; Captain A. Wynne (51st Foot), Superintendent o Field Telegraphs; Captain R. Woodthorpe, R.E., Superintendent of Surveys; Deputy-Surgeon-General F. Allen, Principal Medical officer; Rev. J. W. Adams, Chaplain.

APPENDIX IV.

(Referred to at p. 391.)

Translation of a letter from MAJOR-GENERAL SIR FREDERICK ROBERTS *to His Highness* THE AMIR OF KABUL.

ALIKHEL, 18*th September*, 1879.

(AFTER the usual compliments.) Your Highness's letter of the 28th Ramazan, with the enclosures from Herat and Turkestan, reached me last night. I have acquainted myself with the contents. I am glad to find your Highness is in good health, but sorry to hear of the unfortunate disturbances in your Highness's dominions. Your Highness's letter, in original, has been sent with enclosures to His Excellency the Viceroy. I have already informed your Highness of the wishes of His Excellency the Viceroy, and the reasons for the movements of the British troops, and I have requested your Highness to send a confidential representative to my camp. I am awaiting a reply to that letter, and the arrival of your Highness's confidential representative.

In the meantime I have sent a Proclamation to the tribes, and letters to some of the Logar *maliks*, your Highness's subjects, to assure those not concerned in the hateful massacre, and asking them for assistance in carriage and supplies on payment. As it appears to me proper I should inform your Highness of what I have done, I enclose copies of the Proclamation to the tribes and of my letter to the Logar *maliks*, and hope that your Highness may also issue necessary orders for the furtherance of our plans. Rest assured of the support of the Government of India.

APPENDIX V.

(Referred to at p. 391.)

Notes of an interview between GENERAL SIR FREDERICK ROBERTS *and the* AMIR'S AGENTS, MUSTAUFI HABIBULLA KHAN *and* WAZIR SHAH MAHOMED KHAN. *Dated* ALIKHEL, 23*rd September*, 1879.

AFTER compliments, General Roberts intimated to the Agents that at their desire he had granted them a second interview. He now requested them to be good enough to speak freely all that they wished him to know.

The MUSTAUFI then spoke in the following sense: The interests of England and Afghanistan are the same, and the Amir and his officials are deeply grieved at the late occurrences in Kabul. Moreover, the Amir is anxious to do whatever the British Government wishes, and most desirous that the dignity of the British Government should be maintained by any means which may seem proper to the Viceroy. But His Highness cannot conceal from himself that the mutinous troops and his people in general, ryots as well as soldiers, are in fear of an indiscriminate revenge, which will fall alike upon innocent and guilty. He hopes, therefore, that measures will be taken to guard against the possibility of a general rising consequent on fear.

The Mustaufi was here reminded of the tenor of General Roberts's Proclamation on 15th September. He answered that the people were too ignorant to be acted upon by a Proclamation, and then went on as follows:

Of course, it is possible that no such combination may take place. The

Afghans are selfish, and divided against themselves. Still, lest he should be blamed if it should occur, the Amir thinks it right to express his opinion, and give the British Government all the information in his power. On the whole, his advice, as an earnest friend, is that the advance of a British force on Kabul should be delayed for a short time (*'Panjroz'*). In the interval he will endeavour to disarm the Regular troops, raise new levies, and, by the aid of the latter, punish all concerned in the late abominable outrage. His idea is to get rid of Sher Ali's soldiery--always a source of danger—and keep only 15,000 men for the future. It would be very desirable to delay the advance until he could establish his power. The Amir does not mean to imply that any Afghan army, were it 50,000 strong, could resist the British. The mutinous troops have neither organization nor leaders. But the mutinous troops are of all tribes; and if the British army destroys them, as it would undoubtedly do in case of resistance, the whole country may combine against the British and the Amir. It is for this reason that he advises delay, and that the punishment of the guilty be left to him. The Viceroy may rest assured that he will show no mercy. He will make an example which will be conspicuous in the eyes of the world as the sun at noonday. Already everyone in Kabul regards the Amir as an infidel, because of the way in which he and his have thrown in their lot with the British Government.

Notwithstanding all that has been said, however, things might go right if the mutinous troops would keep together and attempt a stand. But the Amir fears they will not do so. They are more likely to scatter here and there, and raise the country. In that case there will be constant attacks on the communications of the force, and the gathering of supplies will be difficult. They would come chiefly from the direction of Ghazni, partly also from Logar. If the tribes rise it would be hard to collect them. Only one month remains before the setting in of winter. Of course, it is impossible to say what may happen. There may be no opposition, and the Amir is in any case ready to do what the British Government desires. But he feels it is his duty to express his strong opinion that the present season is unsuited for a forward movement.

General Roberts replied that on behalf of the Viceroy he thanked the Amir for his kind advice, which he was confident was the advice of a friend. He said the matter was important, and required careful consideration, and asked whether the Agents had anything more to bring forward.

The Mustaufi then spoke as follows: The Amir's advice to delay the advance is that of a sincere friend, and it is the best he can give. But if the British Army is to march on Kabul, there is one thing more which I am desired to say: let it march in such strength as to crush all hopes of mischief, and put down all rebellion throughout the country. You cannot wait for reinforcements. If you come, you must come in full strength—in sufficient strength to put down all opposition. There may be no opposition, but you cannot count on this.

General Roberts replied: The Amir's advice is of great importance, and must be carefully considered. When His Highness first wrote, announcing the outbreak at Kabul and asking for help, the first desire of the Viceroy was to send British forces without delay. I was ordered to Kuram at once to lead the force here. Simultaneously the Kandahar force was ordered by telegram to return to Kandahar, which it was then leaving, and to advance towards Kelat-i-Ghilzai, and instructions were issued to collect a third force at Peshawar; all this was to help the Amir. The Viceroy from the first contemplated the possibility of such a general rising as the Amir now fears, and the several armies were, therefore, by His Excellency's order, made up to such strength that all Afghanistan combined could not stand against them for a moment. The Kandahar troops were ready in a very short time, and are now beyond Kandahar, on the road to Kabul.* The Peshawar force was rapidly collected and pushed on; and the Amir may rest assured that the British army is advancing in ample strength. I will think over the Amir's advice, nevertheless, for it is important. But His Highness must remember that the late occurrences at Kabul do not affect only the English officers and the fifty or sixty men who were treacherously killed—the honour of the English Government is concerned; and so long as the bodies of these officers and men remain unburied or uncared for in Kabul, I do not believe the English people will ever be satisfied. They will require the advance of a British force, and the adequate punishment of the crime. Still, the Amir's advice, which I am convinced is that of a friend, must be carefully considered, and I will think over it and give an answer later.

The MUSTAUFI then said: We quite understand what has been said about the strength of the British army. Doubtless it is sufficient, and all Afghanistan could not stand against it. But the Amir asked us to mention, what I have hitherto forgotten, that there are in Turkestan 24 regiments of Infantry, 6 of Cavalry, and 56 guns. These troops were the first to show a disaffected spirit at Mazar-i-Sharif; and putting aside external enemies, there are Abdur Rahman and the sons of Azim Khan waiting their chance. Herat again is doubtful; when the troops there hear what has occurred at Kabul, there is no saying what they may do. If Abdur Rahman ingratiates himself with these people, Herat and Turkestan will be permanently severed from the Afghan dominions. This is another reason why the advance of the British force should be delayed, in order that the Amir may have time to gain over the Herat and Turkestan troops.

GENERAL ROBERTS replied: All these reasons will have full consideration. The Viceroy's first order was to push on at once to help the Amir; but I am sure His Highness's advice is friendly, and that in any case he will do his utmost to co-operate with the British Government. Therefore every consideration will be given to what His Highness has desired you to say.

The MUSTAUFI: The Viceroy may be sure the Amir will do what he pleases.

The WAZIR: When the Amir learnt from General Roberts's letter that the Viceroy had given General Roberts power to deal with the whole matter, he was very pleased, knowing General Roberts's character as a soldier and his kindness of heart.

GENERAL ROBERTS replied that he would carefully consider the proposals brought forward, and give an answer later on. Meanwhile, he must request the Agents to stay a day or two in camp until he should have thoroughly weighed the Amir's advice, which was of the utmost importance to both the British and Afghan Governments.

The interview then came to an end.

(Signed) H. M. DURAND,
Political Secretary to General Roberts, K.C.B., V.C.,
Commanding Kabul Field Force.

---

* The Agents here seemed surprised and anxious.—H. M. D.

APPENDIX VI.

(Referred to at p. 421.)

From LIEUTENANT-GENERAL SIR F. ROBERTS, K.C.B., V.C., *Commanding Kabul Field Force, to* A. C. LYALL, ESQ., C.B., *Secretary to the Government of India, Foreign Department.*

KABUL, 22*nd November*, 1879.

1. I HAVE the honour to submit a brief account of an interview which took place between the Amir Yakub Khan and myself on the 22nd October. The interview was a private and informal one; but recent events have lent some interest to what passed on the occasion, and I have, therefore, thought it desirable that a report should be prepared for the information of the Governor-General in Council.

2. After some conversation upon matters of no special importance, the Amir introduced his father's name, and thus gave me the opportunity I had often wished to have of leading him on to speak naturally and unconstrainedly about Sher Ali Khan's feelings and policy during the last ten years. I was most careful to avoid any expression of my own views upon the subject in order that I might, if possible, obtain from the Amir a perfectly spontaneous and truthful account of the circumstances which led, in his opinion, to Sher Ali's estrangement from ourselves and *rapprochement* to Russia. In this I think I succeeded. Yakub Khan spoke readily and freely of all that had passed, and needed no question or suggestion from me to declare his conviction regarding the cause of his father's unfriendly attitude towards us during the past few years.

3. The substance of the Amir's statement was as follows:

'In 1869 my father was fully prepared to throw in his lot with you. He had suffered many reverses before making himself secure on the throne of Afghanistan; and he had come to the conclusion that his best chance of holding what he had won lay in an alliance with the British Government. He did not receive from Lord Mayo as large a supply of arms and ammunition as he had hoped, but, nevertheless, he returned to Kabul fairly satisfied, and so he remained until the visit of Saiyad Nur Muhammud to India in 1873. This visit brought matters to a head. The diaries received from Saiyad Nur Mahomed during his stay in India, and the report which he brought back on his return, convinced my father that he could no longer hope to obtain from the British Government all the aid that he wanted; and from that time he began to turn his attention to the thoughts of a Russian alliance. You know how this ended.

'When my father received from the Government of India the letter informing him that a British Mission was about to proceed to Kabul, he read it out in durbar. The members of the Russian Embassy were present. After the reading was finished, Colonel Stolietoff rose, saluted the Amir and asked permission to leave Kabul. If permitted, he would, he said, travel without delay to Tashkent, and report the state of affairs to General Kauffmann, who would inform the Czar, and thus bring pressure to bear on England. He promised to return in six weeks or two months, and urged the Amir to do everything in his power meanwhile to prevent the British Mission from reaching Kabul.

'Colonel Stolietoff never returned to Kabul. He lost no time in reaching Tashkent, where he remained for a few weeks, and he then started for Russia.

'The Afghan official, Mirza Mahomed Hassan Khan, generally known as the "Dabir-ul-Mulk," who had travelled with Colonel Stolietoff from the Oxus to Kabul, accompanied him on his return journey to Tashkent. Here the Mirza was detained under pretence that orders would shortly be received from the Emperor, until the news of my father's flight from Kabul reached General Kauffmann. He was then permitted to leave. Two Aides-de-Camp were sent with him, one a European, the other a Native of Bokhara.

'My father was strongly urged by General Kauffmann not to leave Kabul. At the same time the members of the Embassy were ordered to return to Tashkent, the Doctor being permitted to remain with my father if his services were required.

'Throughout, the Russian Embassy was treated with great honour,' and at all stations between Mazar-i-Shariff and Kabul, orders were given for the troops to turn out, and for a salute to be fired on their arrival and departure.'

4. I cannot, of course, vouch for the exact words used by Yakub Khan, but I am confident that the foregoing paragraph, which is written from notes taken at the time, contains a substantially accurate record of the conversation.

5. It would be superfluous for me to advance any proof of the fact that for one reason or another, Sher Ali did during the latter part of his reign fall away from us and incline towards an alliance with Russia. But I think the closeness of the connection between Russia and Kabul, and the extent of the Amir's hostility towards ourselves, has not hitherto been fully recognized. Yakub Khan's statements throw some light upon this question, and they are confirmed by various circumstances which have lately come to my knowledge. The prevalence of Russian coin and wares in Kabul, and the extensive military preparations made by Sher Ali of late years, appear to me to afford an instructive comment upon Yakub Khan's assertions. Our recent rupture with Sher Ali has, in fact, been the means of unmasking and checking a very serious conspiracy against the peace and security of our Indian Empire.

6. The magnitude of Sher Ali's military preparations is, in my opinion, a fact of peculiar significance. I have already touched upon this point in a former letter, but I shall perhaps be excused for noticing it again. Before the outbreak of hostilities last year the Amir had raised and equipped with arms of precision 68 regiments of Infantry and 16 of Cavalry. The Afghan Artillery amounted to nearly 300 guns. Numbers of skilled artizans were constantly employed in the manufacture of rifled cannon and breach-loading small arms. More than a million pounds of powder, and I believe several million rounds of home-made Snider ammunition, were in the Bala Hissar at the time of the late explosion. Swords, helmets, uniforms, and other articles of military equipment were stored in proportionate quantities. Finally, Sher Ali had expended upon the construction of the Sherpur cantonments an astonishing amount of labour and money. The extent and cost of this work may be judged of from the fact that the whole of the troops under my command will find cover during the winter within the cantonment, and the bulk of them in the main line of rampart itself, which extends to a length of nearly two miles under the southern and western slopes of the Bimaru hills. Sher Ali's original design was apparently to carry the wall entirely round the hills, a distance of nearly five miles, and the foundations were already laid for a considerable portion of this length. All these military preparations were quite unnecessary except as a provision for contemplated hostilities with ourselves, and it is difficult to understand how their entire cost could have been met from the Afghan treasury, the gross revenue of the country amounting only to about eighty lakhs of rupees per annum.

7. I have referred to the prevalence of Russian coin and wares in Kabul as evidence of the growing connexion between Russia and Afghanistan. I am unable to find proof that the Czar's coin was introduced in any other way

than by the usual channels of trade. It is quite possible that the bulk of it, if not the whole, came in gradually by this means, the accumulation of foreign gold in particular being considerable in this country, where little gold is coined. Nevertheless, it seems to me a curious fact that the amount of Russian money in circulation should be so large. No less than 13,000 gold pieces were found among the Amir's treasure alone; similar coins are exceedingly common in the city bazaar; and great numbers of them are known to be in possession of the Sirdars. Of course English goods of all kinds are plentiful here—that is inevitable, particularly with a considerable body of Hindu merchants settled in the city, but Russian goods also abound. Glass, crockery, silks, tea, and many other things which would seem to be far more easily procurable from India than from Russian territory, are to be found in great quantities. A habit, too, seems to have been growing up among the Sirdars and others of wearing uniforms of Russian cut, Russian buttons, Russian boots, and the like. Russian goods and Russian ways seem, in fact, to have become the fashion in Afghanistan.

APPENDIX VII.

(Referred to at p. 421.)

Translations of letters from General-Adjutant Von Kauffmann, *Governor-General of Turkestan, to the address of the* Amir of Afghanistan, *received on 10th Shaban,* 1295, *through* General Stolietoff, *9th August,* 1878.

Be it known to you that in these days the relations between the British Government and ours with regard to your kingdom require deep consideration. As I am unable to communicate my opinion verbally to you, I have deputed my agent, Major-General Stolietoff. This gentleman is a near friend of mine, and performed excellent services in the Russo-Turkish war, by which he earned favour of the Emperor. The Emperor has always had a regard for him. He will inform you of all that is hidden in my mind. I hope you will pay great attention to what he says, and believe him as you would myself, and, after due consideration, you will give him your reply. Meanwhile, be it known to you that your union and friendship with the Russian Government will be beneficial to the latter, and still more so to you. The advantages of a close alliance with the Russian Government will be permanently evident.

This friendly letter is written by the Governor-General of Turkestan and Adjutant-General to the Emperor, Von Kauffmann, Tashkent, Jamadial Akbar, 1295 (=June, 1878).

To the Amir *of the whole of Afghanistan,* Sher Ali Khan.

(After compliments.) Be it known to you that our relations with the British Government are of great importance to Afghanistan and its dependencies. As I am unable to see you, I have deputed my trustworthy (official) General Stolietoff to you. The General is an old friend of mine, and during the late Russo-Turkish war earned the favour of the Emperor by his spirit and bravery. He has become well known to the Emperor. This trustworthy person will communicate to you what he thinks best. I hope you will pay attention to what he says, and repose as much confidence in his words as if they were my own; and that you will give your answer in this matter through him. In the meantime, be it known to you that if a friendly treaty will be of benefit to us, it will be of far greater benefit to yourself.

GENERAL STOLIETOFF *sent the following letter, on his return to Tashkent from Kabul, to the address of the Foreign Minister,* WAZIR SHAH MAHOMED KHAN, *dated* 23*rd of the holy month of Ramazan,* 1295 (=21*st September,* 1878).

Thank God, I reached Tashkent safely, and at an auspicious moment paid my respects to the Viceroy (Yaroui Padishah means 'half king'). I am trying day and night to gain our objects, and hope I shall be successful. I am starting to see the Emperor to-day, in order to inform His Majesty personally of our affairs. If God pleases, everything that is necessary will be done and affirmed. *I hope that those who want to enter the gate of Kabul from the east will see that the door is closed; then, please God, they will tremble.* I hope you will give my respects to His Highness the Amir. May God make his life long and increase his wealth! May you remain in good health, and know that the protection of God will arrange our affairs!

(Signed) GENERAL STOLIETOFF.

From GENERAL KAUFFMANN *to the* AMIR, *dated Tashkent,* 8*th Zekada,* 1295 (=22*nd October,* 1878).

(After compliments.) Be it known to you that your letter, dated 12th Shawal, reached me at Tashkent on the 16th October, *i.e.*, 3rd Zekada, and I understood its contents. I have telegraphed an abstract of your letter to the address of the Emperor, and have sent the letter itself, as also that addressed to General Stolietoff, by post to Livadia, where the Emperor now is. I am informed on good authority that the English want to come to terms with you; and, as a friend, I advise you to make peace with them if they offer it.

From GENERAL STOLIETOFF *to* WAZIR SHAH MAHOMED KHAN, *dated* 8*th October,* 1878.

First of all, I hope you will be kind enough to give my respects to the Amir. May God make his life long and increase his wealth! I shall always remember his royal hospitality. I am busy day and night in his affairs, and, thank God, my labours have not been without result. The great Emperor is a true friend of the Amir's and of Afghanistan, and His Majesty will do whatever he may think necessary. Of course, you have not forgotten what I told you, that the affairs of kingdoms are like a country which has many mountains, valleys, and rivers. One who sits on a high mountain can see things well. By the power and order of God, there is no empire equal to that of our great Emperor. May God make his life long! Therefore, whatever our Government advises you, you should give ear to it. I tell you the truth that our Government is wise as a serpent and harmless as a dove. There are many things which you cannot understand, but our Government understands them well. It often happens that a thing which is unpleasant at first is regarded as a blessing afterwards. Now, my kind friend, I inform you that the enemy of your famous religion wants to make peace with you through the Kaisar (Sultan) of Turkey. Therefore you should look to your brothers who live on the other side of the river. If God stirs them up, and gives the sword of fight into their hands, then go on, in the name of God (Bismilla), otherwise you should be as a serpent; make peace openly, and in secret prepare for war, and when God reveals His order to you, declare yourself. It will be well, when the Envoy of your enemy wants to enter the country, if you send an able emissary, possessing the tongue of a serpent and full of deceit, to the enemy's country, so that he may with sweet words perplex the enemy's mind, and induce him to give up the intention of fighting with you.

My kind friend, I entrust you to the protection of God. May God be the protector of the Amir's kingdom, and may trembling fall upon the limbs of your enemies! Amen.

Write to me soon, and send the letter to the capital. Please write in Arabic characters, so that I may be able to read your letter.

From GENERAL KAUFFMANN *to the* AMIR OF AFGHANISTAN, *dated 30th Zekada* (=*26th November*, 1878).

(After compliments.) I was much pleased to receive your letter, dated 24th Zekada, 1295 (=18th November, 1878), and to hear of your good health. I have also received a copy of the letter which you sent to the Governor-General. May God be pleased with you. The British Ministers have given a pledge to our Ambassador in London that they will not interfere with the independence of Afghanistan. I am directed by His Majesty the Emperor to communicate this news to you, and then, after forming friendship, to go to His Majesty. I intend to go to the Russian capital after I have arranged the affairs of this country (Turkestan). As I do not consider it advisable to keep your trusted officials, whom you are in want of, here any more, I send Mahomed Hassan Khan, Kamuah (Deputy-Governor), and Gholam Haidar Khan, with two officers, back to you. I hope you will consider me a well-wisher of your kingdom, and write to me now and then. I have given instructions that, until my return, every letter of yours which they receive at Turkestan should be forwarded to the capital. Your good fortune is a cause of happiness to me, and if any troubles come upon you, I also shall be grieved. Some presents have been sent by me through Mirza Mahomed Hassan, Kamuah; perhaps they may be accepted.

Translation of a letter from GENERAL KAUFFMANN *to* GENERAL VOZGONOFF, *dated Zel Hijja*, 1295 (=*December*, 1878).

The Amir knows perfectly well that it is impossible for me to assist him with troops in winter. Therefore it is necessary that war should not be commenced at this unseasonable time. If the English, in spite of the Amir's exertions to avoid the war, commence it, you must then take leave of the Amir and start for Tashkent, because your presence in Afghanistan in winter is useless. Moreover, at such a juncture as the commencement of war in Afghanistan, you ought to come here and explain the whole thing to me, so that I may communicate it to the Emperor. This will be of great benefit to Afghanistan and to Russia.

From GENERAL KAUFFMANN *to the* AMIR OF AFGHANISTAN, dated *25th December*, 1878 (*Russian*, *13th Muharram*, 1296).

Your letter, dated 27th Zel Hijja (=20th November), 1878, has reached me. I was pleased to hear tidings of your good health. The Emperor has caused the British Government to agree to the continuance of Afghan independence. The English Ministers have promised this. I earnestly request you not to leave your kingdom. As far as possible, consider your own interests, and do not lose your independence. For the present come to terms with the British Government. If you do not want to go back to Kabul for this purpose, you can write to your son, Mahomed Yakub Khan, to make peace with the English as you may direct him. Do not leave the soil of Afghanistan at this time, because it will be of benefit to you. My words are not without truth, because your arrival in Russian territory will make things worse.

From GENERAL KAUFFMANN *to the* AMIR OF AFGHANISTAN, *received at Mazir-i-Sharif on the 17th January*, 1879.

I have received your friendly letter, dated 13th Zel Hijja (=8th December, 1878). In that letter you asked me to send you as many troops as could be got ready. I have written to you a letter to the effect that the Emperor, on account of your troubles, had communicated with the British Government, and that the Russian Ambassador at London had obtained a promise from the British Ministers to the effect that they would not injure the independence of Afghanistan. Perhaps you sent your letter before you got mine. Now, I have heard that you have appointed your son, Mahomed Yakub, as your Regent, and have come out of Kabul with some troops. I have received an order from the Emperor to the effect that it is impossible to assist you with troops now. I hope you will be fortunate. It all depends on the decree of God. Believe me, that the friendship which I made with you will be perpetual. It is necessary to send back General Vozgonoff and his companions. You can keep Dr. Yuralski with you if you please. No doubt the doctor will be of use to you and to your dependents. I hope our friendship will continue to be strengthened, and that intercourse will be carried on between us.

From GENERAL KAUFFMANN *to the* AMIR SHER ALI, *dated 29th December*, 1878 (=*17th Muharram*, 1296).

(After compliments.) The Foreign Minister, General Gortchakoff, has informed me by telegraph that the Emperor has directed me to trouble you to come to Tashkent for the present. I therefore communicate this news to you with great pleasure; at the same time, I may mention that I have received no instructions about your journey to St. Petersburg. My personal interview with you will increase our friendship greatly.

Translation of a letter from MAJOR-GENERAL IVANOFF, *Governor of Zarafshan, to the Heir-Apparent*, MAHOMED MUSA KHAN, *and others.*

On the 26th of Rabi-ul-Awul, at an auspicious moment, I received your letter which you sent me, and understood its contents. I was very much pleased, and at once communicated it to General Kauffmann, the Governor-General. With regard to what you wrote about the friendly relations between the Russian and Afghan Governments, and your own desire for friendship, I have the honour to state that we are also desirous of being friends. The friendship between the two Governments existed in the time of the late Amir, and I hope that it will be increased and strengthened by Amir Mahomed Yakub Khan.

May God change the wars in your country to happiness; may peace reign in it; and may your Government be strengthened! I have been forwarding all your letters to the Governor-General, General Kauffmann. May God keep you safe!

The Zarafshan Province Governor,
MAJOR-GENERAL IVANOFF.

Written and sealed by the General.
Written on 29th Mart (March), 1879 (=5th Rabi-ul-Sani, 1296).

Treaty between the RUSSIAN GOVERNMENT *and* AMIR SHER ALI KHAN; *written from memory by* MIRZA MAHOMED NABBI.

1. The Russian Government engages that the friendship of the Russian Government with the Government of Amir Sher Ali Khan, Amir of all Afghanistan, will be a permanent and perpetual one.

2. The Russian Government engages that, as Sirdar Abdulla Khan, son of

the Amir, is dead, the friendship of the Russian Government with any person whom the Amir may appoint Heir-Apparent to the throne of Afghanistan, and with the heir of the Heir-Apparent, will remain firm and perpetual.

3. The Russian Government engages that if any foreign enemy attacks Afghanistan, and the Amir is unable to drive him out, and asks the assistance of the Russian Government, the Russian Government will repel the enemy, either by means of advice, or by such other means as it may consider proper.

4. The Amir of Afghanistan will not wage war with any foreign power without consulting the Russian Government, and without its permission.

5. The Amir of Afghanistan engages that he will always report in a friendly manner to the Russian Government what goes on in his kingdom.

6. The Amir of Afghanistan will communicate every wish and important affair of his to General Kauffmann, Governor-General of Turkestan, and the Governor-General will be authorized by the Russian Government to fulfil the wishes of the Amir.

7. The Russian Government engages that the Afghan merchants who may trade and sojourn in Russian territory will be safe from wrong, and that they will be allowed to carry away their profits.

8. The Amir of Afghanistan will have the power to send his servants to Russia to learn arts and trades, and the Russian officers will treat them with consideration and respect as men of rank.

9. (Does not remember.)

10. I, Major-General Stolietoff Nicholas, being a trusted Agent of the Russian Government, have made the above-mentioned Articles between the Russian Government and the Government of Amir Sher Ali Khan, and have put my seal to them.

APPENDIX VIII.

(Referred to at p. 461.)

Letter from SIRDAR ABDUR RAHMAN KHAN *to* LEPEL GRIFFIN, ESQ., *dated* 15*th April*, 1880.

WHEREAS at this happy time I have received your kind letter. In a spirit of justice and friendship you wrote to inquire what I wished in Afghanistan. My honoured friend, the servants of the great [British] Government know well that, throughout these twelve years of exile in the territories of the Emperor of Russia, night and day I have cherished the hope of revisiting my native land. When the late Amir Sher Ali Khan died, and there was no one to rule our tribes, I proposed to return to Afghanistan, but it was not fated [that I should do so]; then I went to Tashkent. Consequently, Amir Mahomed Yakub Khan, having come to terms and made peace with the British Government, was appointed Amir of Afghanistan; but since, after he had left you, he listened to the advice of every interested [dishonest] person, and raised fools to power, until the ignorant men directed the affairs of Afghanistan, which during the reign of my grandfather, who had eighteen able sons, was so managed that night was bright like day, Afghanistan was, in consequence, disgraced before all States, and ruined. Now, therefore, that you seek to learn my hopes and wishes, they are these: that as long as your Empire and that of Russia exist, my countrymen, the tribes of Afghanistan, should live quietly in ease and peace; that these two States should find us true and faithful, and that we should rest at peace between them [England and

37

Russia], for my tribesmen are unable to struggle with Empires, and are ruined by want of commerce; and we hope of your friendship that, sympathizing with and assisting the people of Afghanistan, you will place them under the honourable protection of the two Powers. This would redound to the credit of both, would give peace to Afghanistan, and quiet and comfort to God's people.

This is my wish; for the rest, it is yours to decide.

APPENDIX IX.

(Referred to at p. 462.)

Letter from A. C. LYALL, ESQ., C.B., *Secretary to the Government of India, Foreign Department, to* LEPEL H. GRIFFIN, ESQ., C.S.I., *Chief Political Officer, Kabul, dated Simla, April,* 1880.

I HAVE the honour to inform you that the Governor-General has received and considered in council your telegrams of the 22nd and 23rd instant, forwarding the translation of a letter received by you from Sirdar Abdur Rahman on the 21st instant, together with a summary of certain oral explanations which accompanied that letter, and a statement of the recommendations suggested by it to Lieutenant-General Sir Frederick Roberts and yourself.

In conveying to you its instructions on the subject of this important communication, the Government of India considers it expedient to recapitulate the principles on which it has hitherto been acting in northern Afghanistan, and clearly to define the point of view from which it contemplates the present situation of affairs in that country. The single object to which, as you are well aware, the Afghan policy of this Government has at all times been directed and limited, is the security of the North-West frontier of India. The Government of India has, however, no less invariably held and acted on the conviction that the security of this frontier is incompatible with the intrusion of any foreign influence into the great border State of Afghanistan. To exclude or eject such influence the Government of India has frequently subsidized and otherwise assisted the Amirs of Kabul. It has also, more than once, taken up arms against them. But it has never interfered, for any other purpose, in the affairs of their kingdom. Regulating on this principle and limiting to this object the conduct of our relations with the rulers of Kabul, it was our long-continued endeavour to find in their friendship and their strength the requisite guarantees for the security of our own frontier. Failing in that endeavour, we were compelled to seek the attainment of the object to which our Afghan policy was, and is still, exclusively directed, by rendering the permanent security of our frontier as much as possible independent of such conditions.

This obligation was not accepted without reluctance. Not even when forced into hostilities by the late Amir Sher Ali Khan's espousal of a Russian alliance, proposed by Russia in contemplation of a rupture with the British Government, did we relinquish our desire for the renewal of relations with a strong and friendly Afghan Power, and, when the son of Sher Ali subsequently sought our alliance and protection, they were at once accorded to him, on conditions of which His Highness professed to appreciate the generosity. The crime, however, which dissolved the Treaty of Gandamak, and the disclosures which followed that event, finally convinced the Government of India that the interests committed to its care could not but be gravely imperilled by further adhesion to a policy dependent for its fruition on the gratitude, the good faith, the assumed self-interest, or the personal character of any Afghan Prince.

When, therefore, Her Majesty's troops re-entered Afghanistan in September last, it was with two well-defined and plainly-avowed objects. The first was to avenge the treacherous massacre of the British Mission at Kabul; the second was to maintain the safeguards sought through the Treaty of Gandamak, by providing for their maintenance guarantees of a more substantial and less precarious character.

These two objects have been maintained: the first by the capture of Kabul and the punishment of the crime committed there, the second by the severance of Kandahar from the Kabul power.

Satisfied with their attainment, the Government of India has no longer any motive or desire to enter into fresh treaty engagements with the Rulers of Kabul. The arrangements and exchange of friendly assurances with the Amir Sher Ali, though supplemented on the part of the Government of India by subsidies and favours of various kinds, wholly failed to secure the object of them, which was, nevertheless, a thoroughly friendly one, and no less conducive to the security and advantage of the Afghan than to those of the British Power. The treaty with Yakub Khan, which secured to him our friendship and material support, was equally ineffectual. Moreover, recent events and arrangements have fundamentally changed the situation to which our correspondence and engagements with the Amir of Afghanistan formally applied. Our advance frontier positions at Kandahar and Kuram have materially diminished the political importance of Kabul in relation to India, and although we shall always appreciate the friendship of its Ruler, our relations with him are now of so little importance to the paramount objects of our policy that we no longer require to maintain British agents in any part of his dominions.

Our only reasons, therefore, for not immediately withdrawing our forces from northern Afghanistan have hitherto been—*first*, the excited and unsettled condition of the country round Kabul, with the attitude of hostility assumed by some leaders of armed gatherings near Ghazni; and, *secondly*, the inability of the Kabul Sirdars to agree among themselves on the selection of a Ruler strong enough to maintain order after our evacuation of the country.

The first-named of these reasons has now ceased to exist. In a minute dated the 30th ultimo the Viceroy and Governor-General stated that 'the Government is anxious to withdraw as soon as possible the troops from Kabul and from all points beyond those to be occupied under the Treaty of Gandamak, except Kandahar. In order that this may be done, it is desirable to find a Ruler for Kabul, which will be separated from Kandahar. Steps,' continued His Excellency, 'are being taken for this purpose. Meanwhile, it is essential that we should make such a display of strength in Afghanistan as will show that we are masters of the situation, and will overawe disaffection.' . . . 'All that is necessary, from a political point of view, is for General Stewart to march to Ghazni, break up any opposition he may find there or in the neighbourhood, and open up direct communication with General Sir Frederick Roberts at Kabul.' The military operations thus defined have been accomplished by General Stewart's successful action before Ghazni.

With regard to the second reason mentioned for the retention of our troops in northern Afghanistan, the appearance of Abdur Rahman as a candidate for the throne of Kabul, whose claims the Government of India has no cause to oppose, and who seems to be approved, and likely to be supported, by at least a majority of the population, affords fair ground for anticipating that our wishes in regard to the restoration, before our departure, of order in that part of the country will now be fulfilled.

The Governor-General in Council has consequently decided that the evacuation of Kabul shall be effected not later than October next, and it is with special reference to this decision that the letter and message addressed to you by Sirdar Abdur Rahman have been carefully considered by His Excellency in Council.

What first claims notice in the consideration of that letter is the desire that it expresses for the permanent establishment of Afghanistan with our assistance and sympathy under the joint protection of the British and Russian Empires. This suggestion, which is more fully developed in the Sirdar's unwritten message, cannot be entertained or discussed.

As already stated, the primary object and declared determination of the Government of India have been the exclusion of foreign influence or interference from Afghanistan. This cardinal condition of amicable relations with Afghanistan has, at all times and in all circumstances, been deemed essential for the permanent security of Her Majesty's Indian Empire. As such, it has hitherto been firmly maintained by successive Governors-General of India under the explicit instructions of Her Majesty's Government. Nor has it ever been ignored, or officially contested, by the Russian Government. That Government, on the contrary, has repeatedly, and under every recent change of circumstances in Afghanistan, renewed the assurances solemnly given to the British Government that 'Russia considers Afghanistan as entirely beyond the sphere of her influence.'

It is true that negotiations at one time passed between the two Governments with a view to the mutual recognition of certain territories as constituting a neutral zone between their respective spheres of legitimate influence and action, and that at one time it was proposed by Russia to treat Afghanistan itself as a neutral territory. Those negotiations, however, having proved fruitless, the northern frontier of Afghanistan was finally determined by mutual agreement, and in 1876 the Russian Government formally reiterated its adherence to the conclusion that, 'while maintaining on either side the arrangement come to as regards the limits of Afghanistan, which is to remain outside the sphere of Russian action, the two Cabinets should regard as terminated the discussions relative to the intermediate zone, which promised no practical result.'

The position of Afghanistan as defined and settled by these engagements was again distinctly affirmed on behalf of the Queen's Government by the Marquis of Salisbury in 1879, and the Government of India unreservedly maintains it in the fullest conviction of its essential necessity for the peaceable protection of Her Majesty's Indian dominions. It is therefore desirable that you should take occasion to inform Abdur Rahman that the relations of Afghanistan to the British and Russian Empires are matters which the Government of India must decline to bring into discussion with the Sirdar. The Afghan states and tribes are too contiguous with India, whose North-Western frontier they surround, for the Government of India ever willingly to accept partnership with any other Power in the exercise of its legitimate and recognized influence over those tribes and States.

The Governor-General in Council is, nevertheless, most anxious that the Sirdar should not misunderstand the light in which his personal sentiments and obligations towards Russia are regarded by the Government of India. So long as the Rulers of Kabul were amenable to its advice, this Government has never ceased to impress on them the international duty of scrupulously respecting all the recognized rights and interests of their Russian neighbour, refraining from every act calculated to afford the Russian authorities in

Central Asia any just cause of umbrage or complaint. The intelligence and good sense which are conspicuous in the Sirdar's letter and messages to you will enable him to appreciate the difference between conduct regulated on these principles and that which cost Sher Ali the loss of his throne. This Government does not desire, nor has it ever desired, to impose on any Ruler of Kabul conditions incompatible with that behaviour which Russia, as a powerful and neighbouring Empire, is entitled to expect from him; least of all can we desire to impose such conditions on a Prince who has received hospitality and protection in Russian territory. I am therefore to observe that, in the natural repugnance expressed by Abdur Rahman to conditions which 'might make him appear ungrateful' to those 'whose salt he has eaten,' the Governor-General in Council recognizes a sentiment altogether honourable to the Sirdar, and perfectly consistent with the sincerity of his professed goodwill towards ourselves.

These observations will furnish you with a sufficient answer to the question asked by Abdur Rahman as to the 'nature of our friendship' and 'its conditions.'

The frankness with which he has explained his position entitles him to receive from us a no less unreserved statement of our own. The Government of India cordially shares the wish expressed by Abdur Rahman that, between the British and Russian Empires, his 'tribes and countrymen may live quietly in ease and peace.' We do not desire to place them in a position of unfriendliness towards a Power which is pledged to us to regard their country as 'entirely beyond the sphere of its action.' The injury to Afghan commerce caused by the present condition of Afghanistan, to which the Sirdar has alluded, is fully appreciated by the Government of India, and on the restoration of peace between the two countries the revival and development of trade intercourse need present no difficulty. As regards our own friendship, it will, if sincerely sought, be freely given, and fully continued so long as it is loyally reciprocated. But we attach to it no other condition. We have no concessions to ask or make, and the Sirdar will therefore perceive that there is really no matter for negotiation or bargain between him and us.

On this point your reply to Abdur Rahman cannot be too explicit. Previous to the Sirdar's arrival in Turkestan, the hostility and treachery of those whose misconduct he admits and deplores had compelled the Government of India to make territorial arrangements of a material and permanent character for the better protection of our frontier. The maintenance of these arrangements is in no wise dependent on the assent or dissent, on the good-will or ill-will, of any Chief at Kabul. The character of them has been so fully explained by you to all the other Kabul Sirdars that it is probably well known to Abdur Rahman. But in order that our present intercourse and future relations with the Sirdar may be perfectly clear of doubt on a point affecting the position he aspires to fill, the Governor-General in Council authorizes you, if necessary, to make him plainly understand that neither the district assigned to us by the Treaty of Gandamak, nor any part of the province of Kandahar, will ever be restored to the Kabul Power.

As regards this last-mentioned province, the Government of India has been authorized by that of Her Majesty to give to Sher Ali Khan, the present Wali of Kandahar, a distinct assurance that he will be not only recognized, but maintained, by the British Government as the Ruler of that province. Sher Ali Khan is one of the Native nobles of Kandahar. He is administering the province with ability, good sense, and complete loyalty to the British Government, which has promised him the support of a British garrison so long as he requires such support. The Governor-General in Council cannot doubt that Sirdar Abdur Rahman will readily recognize the obligation incumbent on the honour of the British Government to keep faith with all who, whether at Kandahar or elsewhere, have proved themselves true and loyal adherents. Yakub Khan forfeited our alliance, and with it his throne, by mistrusting the assurances we gave him, and falsifying those which he had given to us. If, misled by his example, Yakub Khan's successor attempts to injure or oppress the friends of the British Government, its power will again be put forth to protect or avenge them. Similarly, if the next Kabul Ruler reintroduces into his Court or country foreign influences adverse to our own, the Government of India will again take such steps as it may deem expedient to deal with such a case. These contingencies, however, cannot occur if the sentiments of Abdur Rahman are such as he represents them to be. Meanwhile, the territorial and administrative arrangements already completed by us for the permanent protection of our own interests are not susceptible of negotiation or discussion with Abdur Rahman or any other claimant to the throne of Kabul.

To the settlement of Herat, which is not included in these completed arrangements, the Governor-General in Council cannot authorize you to make or invite any reference in your reply to Abdur Rahman. The settlement of the future administration of Herat has been undertaken by Her Majesty's Government; with those present views in regard to this important question, the Government of India is not yet acquainted.

Nor can our evacuation of Kabul constitute any subject for proposals in your correspondence with the Sirdar. This measure was determined on by the Government of India long before the appearance of Abdur Rahman as a candidate for the government of the country we are about to evacuate. It has not been caused by the hostility, and is not, therefore, conditional on the goodwill, of any Afghan Power.

The Government of India is, however, very willing to carry out the evacuation of Kabul in the manner most conducive to the personal advantage of Abdur Rahman, whose interests we believe to be, more than those of any other Sirdar, in accordance with the general interests of the Afghan people. For this reason it is desirable that you should inform Abdur Rahman of our intention to evacuate Kabul, and our desire to take that opportunity of unconditionally transferring to his authority the whole of the country from which our troops will be withdrawn. You are authorized to add that our military and political officers at Kabul will be empowered to facilitate any practical arrangement suggested by the Sirdar for promptly and peaceably effecting, in co-operation with him, the transfer thus contemplated on his behalf. Such arrangement must, however, be consistent with our obligations towards those who have served and aided the British Government during our occupation of those territories.

For this purpose, it appears to the Governor-General in Council desirable that the Sirdar should lose no time in proceeding to Kabul, and there settling, in conference with General Stewart and yourself, such preliminary arrangements as may best promote the undisturbed establishment of his future government.

The Governor-General in Council has, however, no desire to press this suggestion, should it appear to the Sirdar that his presence at Kabul, previous to the withdrawal of our troops for the purpose of personal conference with the British authorities, might have the effect of weakening his popularity, or compromising his position in the eyes of his future subjects.

The point is one which must be left entirely to the Sirdar's own judgment and inclination.

But Abdur Rahman is doubtless aware that there are at present, in and around Kabul, personages not destitute of influence, who themselves aspire to the sovereignty he seeks, and that the family of Yakub has still numerous personal adherents, who may possibly take advantage of the withdrawal of our troops to oppose the Sirdar's authority if he is not personally present to assert it.

It should on both sides be remembered and understood that it is not the policy of this Government to impose upon the Afghan people an unpopular Ruler or to interfere uninvited in the administration of a friendly one. If Abdur Rahman proves able and disposed to conciliate the confidence of his countrymen, without forfeiting the good understanding which he seeks with us, he will assuredly find his best support in our political appreciation of that fact. Our reason for unconditionally transferring to him the government of the country, from which our forces will in any case be withdrawn a few months hence, is that, on the whole, he appears to be the Chief best able to restore order in that country, and also best entitled to undertake such a task. In his performance of it he will receive, if he requires it, our assistance. But we neither need nor wish to hamper, by preliminary stipulations or provisoes, his independent exercise of a sovereignty which he declares himself anxious to maintain on a footing of peace and friendship with the British Government.

The present statement of the views and intentions of His Excellency the Governor-General in Council respecting Abdur Rahman will enable you to represent them with adequate accuracy in your reply to the Sirdar's friendly overtures, and it will now be your duty to convey to Abdur Rahman, without any avoidable delay, the answer of the Government of India to the letter and message received from him. His Excellency feels assured that you will give full expression to the spirit of candour and goodwill in which these communications have been received and are reciprocated.

But I am to impress on your attention the importance of avoiding any expression which might appear to suggest or admit matter for negotiation or discussion in reference to the relative positions of the Sirdar and the Government of India.

In conclusion, I am to request that on receipt of this letter you will be so good as to lose no time in submitting its contents to General Sir Donald Stewart, should he then have reached Kabul. In any case, you will, of course, communicate them to General Roberts, and act upon them in consultation with the chief military authority on the spot.

APPENDIX X.

(Referred to at p. 464.)

Extract from a Report by LIEUTENANT-GENERAL SIR FREDERICK ROBERTS, V.C., K.C.B., *to the* QUARTERMASTER-GENERAL IN INDIA, *dated Kabul, 17th April*, 1880.

25. I THINK I have now dealt with all the points of military importance connected with the military position in northern Afghanistan, but there are a few questions of more general interest which I desire to bring to the notice of His Excellency the Commander-in-Chief and the Government of India.

26. First with regard to rations. The daily scale of issue to Native troops is given in the margin. It has been found throughout the campaign, even when the men were employed upon hard work, that '12 chittacks' of 'atta' daily are amply sufficient for the Native troops, supplemented, as of late, through the liberality of Government, by a bi-weekly issue of 1 lb. of meat. In a climate like Afghanistan, where the inhabitants are all meat-eaters, this liberality has been most wise. Every endeavour was made, before this sanction was granted, to supply the Native portion of the force with meat on payment, and I attribute to this in great measure the sound health and excellent stamina which they now exhibit.

Daily ration of Native soldiers:

Atta*	12 chittacks†
Dall‡	2 ,,
Ghi§	1 chittack
Salt	⅛ ,,
Meat	1 lb. bi-weekly
Rum	1 dram ,,

With regard to the issue of rum, I would suggest that it should not be issued free to Native troops, except under exceptional circumstances of fatigue and weather, but that the Commissariat Department should be authorized to have in store a sufficiency of rum to admit of a bi-weekly issue to such troops as drink the spirit, *on payment*, and then only on the recommendation of the Medical Officer, and under the sanction of the General Officer commanding. On all occasions when rum is sanctioned, either free or on payment, those who do not partake of spirits should be allowed a ration of tea and sugar under similar conditions.

27. The scale of rations for Native followers requires no alteration.

28. The European rations now under issue in Kabul are as per margin, and with reference to them I would make the following remarks: The increase of ¼ lb. in bread and meat is, in my opinion, very desirable, for not only is the meat, as a rule, on service inferior to that served in cantonments, but the extras which can be procured from the coffee-shop are not here forthcoming. When the vegetable ration consists of potatoes, 1 lb. is sufficient, but when it is made of mixed vegetables 1¼ lb. is necessary. The substitution of *dall* for any portion of the vegetable ration I consider undesirable.

Daily ration of European soldiers:

Meat	1¼ lb.
Bread	1¼ ,,
Vegetables	1¼ ,,
Rice	4 oz.
Salt	⅔ ,,
Tea	⅞ ,,
Sugar	3 ,,
Rum	1 dr.

Tinned soups and meats and biscuits are most valuable, and should be liberally supplied to every force in the field. They are portable and liked by the men, to whom they furnish a very welcome change of diet. I would very strongly recommend that a much larger issue of these articles than has hitherto been sanctioned should be provided.

29. A question which has arisen during this campaign, and which may crop up again, has been the provision of firewood for cooking to Native troops and followers. Throughout the winter firewood could not be purchased at Kabul, and it was absolutely necessary to issue it to these men. This was done at the rate of one *seer*‖ per man, but this amount is not arbitrary, and might, under certain circumstances, be diminished. Since roads were re-opened and markets re-established the issue of wood has been discontinued. In framing any future rules for the guidance of a force in the field, the question of providing firewood through the Commissariat Department for Native troops and followers, free or on payment, should be vested in the General Officers commanding.

Firewood.

---

* Flour. † A chittack = 2 ounces.
‡ A kind of pea. § Clarified butter.
‖ A seer = 2 lb.

30. The scale of clothing authorized by Government for Native troops and followers was found, even in the rigorous climate of Afghanistan, to be most liberal, except that during the very coldest weather a second blanket was required. This want I was able to meet from stock in hand, and as the weather became milder these extra blankets were withdrawn and returned into store. Warm stockings, too, are very necessary in a climate where frost-bite is not uncommon; fortunately, some thousands were procured locally and issued to followers. The ordinary Native shoe of India, as provided by the Commissariat Department, is utterly unfitted for a country such as Afghanistan. Major Badcock will send to Peshawar (where they can easily be made up) a pattern Kabali shoe, which I am convinced would be found admirably suited for Native troops and followers crossing the frontier. We are now almost entirely dependent on the local market for our shoes.

Shoes.

A large supply of English-made ammunition boots should always accompany a force in the field, in order to allow those Natives who use them, and who are often crippled by wearing other descriptions of shoe, to obtain them on payment at the moderate rate now fixed, viz., Rs. 4 per pair.

Ammunition boots.

The country-made waterproof sheets, though slightly heavier, have proved themselves quite as serviceable, if not more so, than the English-made ones.

Waterproof sheets.

At the close of the campaign, I would very strongly recommend that an intelligent committee should be required to go thoroughly into these questions of clothing for troops, British and Native, and for followers. I would also suggest that when a decision is arrived at, sealed patterns of every article approved should be deposited at all manufacturing centres and in all the large jails, so that when certain articles are required they need only be called for, and precious time (often wasted in reference and correspondence) saved.

31. The number of doolie-bearers with the two divisions of the Kabul Field Force now at Kabul is 3,536, with the very moderate sick report of 35, or 1 per cent. of strength.

Doolie-bearers.

Doolies and dandies are distributed as follows:

British troops { doolies, 3 per cent.
dandies, 2 per cent.

Native troops { doolies, 2 per cent.
dandies, 3 per cent.

—a percentage which I consider sufficient for field-service, as, in the event of any unusual number of casualties, transport animals could and would be made use of, and it is most undesirable to increase the number of followers.

The Lushai dandy for this sort of warfare is much preferable to the carpet or dhurrie dandy, as it can be made into a bed, and men are not so liable to fall out of it.

The Lushai dandy.

Bourke's doolie is very good, but liable to get out of order, and difficult to repair when broken; the ordinary kind is fairly good and serviceable.

Bourke's doolie.

32. I would urge that in future all field-service tents should be made after the pattern of the Mountain Battery tent, single fly for Natives, double for Europeans, and that the poles should be constructed on the telescopic principle: that is, that no thinning of the wood where it enters the socket should be allowed either on uprights or ridge-pole, and that the old system of paring away should be abandoned. Instead, the upper section should sit flat on the lower. Doubtless the sockets will have to be longer and stronger than those now in use,

Field-service tents.

but this is the only means by which tents can be adapted to mule and pony carriage, which will no doubt in future wars be our chief means of transport.

Waler horses.

33. The Waler horses of the Cavalry and Artillery have stood the strain remarkably well, considering the hard work and great exposure they have had to bear, and also that for a considerable time they were entirely deprived of green food. I feel sure this information will be most satisfactory, seeing that, for the future, the Artillery and Cavalry in India must mainly depend upon the Australian market for their remounts.

Committee to record suggestions on equipment.

34. As there are some minor points of detail which might advantageously be considered by those who have had the experience of recent service, I have convened a committee, with Colonel MacGregor, C.B., as President, which will take suggestions and record opinions regarding packing transport animals, equipment, kit, dress, etc., of both officers and men of the several branches of the service. From the constitution of the committee, I feel certain that their recommendations cannot but be valuable, and I hope to have the honour of submitting them shortly for the consideration of His Excellency the Commander-in-Chief.

APPENDIX XI.

(Referred to at p. 517.)

Instructions for the Guidance of General and other Officers commanding Columns in Burma.

Mandalay,
20th November, 1886.

The following general instructions for the guidance of Brigadier-Generals and Officers in command of columns are published by order of His Excellency the Commander-in-Chief in India:

1*st*.—Columns sent out for the pacification of a district, or in pursuit of a particular gang of dacoits, must be amply provided and able to keep the field for ten days at least. To enable this to be done without employing an undue number of transport animals, it is necessary that every endeavour be made to obtain grain for Cavalry horses and Transport ponies from the villages passed through; careful inquiry must be made as to where supplies can be obtained locally, and the line of advance determined accordingly. Arrangements must be made for replenishing the supply when necessary from depots which must be formed at convenient centres when the nature of the operations may necessitate it. These depots should be pushed forward from time to time as the troops advance. The work of a column obliged to return to its base of supply before it has had an opportunity of completing the object of the expedition must be more harmful than beneficial, as its failure emboldens the enemy and weakens the confidence of the people in our power to protect them and to reach the offenders.

2*nd*.—Where two or more columns are acting in concert, the details of time and place of movement should be settled beforehand with the greatest nicety, and the commanding officers of all such columns should be provided with the same maps, or tracings from them, so that subsequent changes of plan, rendered necessary by later information, may be understood and conformed to by all. Officers commanding columns must do their utmost to get into, and keep up, communication with one another. This can be effected by:

Visual signalling,
Spies and scouts,
Patrolling.

3rd.—Movements to be executed in concert with the troops in other brigades or commands, or likely to tell directly or indirectly on the districts commanded by other officers, will be fully communicated to those officers, both beforehand and when in progress.

4th.—Brigadier-Generals are empowered to give very liberal remuneration for the effective service of guides and for information involving danger to those who give it. They may delegate this power to selected officers in detached commands, but a close watch must be kept on expenditure under this head. Opportunities should be afforded to timid informers who are afraid to compromise themselves by entering camp to interview officers at some distance out and in secrecy.

5th.—Cavalry horses and Mounted Infantry ponies must be saved as much as is compatible with occasional forced and rapid marches. On ordinary occasions the riders should dismount, from time to time, and march alongside of their horses or ponies.

6th.—The special attention of all officers is called to the careful treatment of pack-animals, and officers in command of columns and parties will be held strictly responsible that the animals are properly loaded for the march, saved as much as possible during it, and carefully attended to and fed after it. Officers in command will ascertain by daily personal supervision and inspection that these orders are carried out.

7th.—It must be remembered that the chief object of traversing the country with columns is to cultivate friendly relations with the inhabitants, and at the same time to put before them evidences of our power, thus gaining their good-will and their confidence. It is therefore the bounden duty of commanding officers to ascertain that the troops under their command are not permitted to injure the property of the people or to wound their susceptibilities.

8th.—The most injurious accounts of our intentions have been circulated amongst, and believed by, the people, and too much pains cannot be taken to eradicate this impression, and to assure the people both by act and word of our good-will towards the law-abiding. Chief men of districts should be treated with consideration and distinction. The success of the present operations will much depend on the tact with which the inhabitants are treated.

9th.—When there is an enemy in arms against British rule, all arrangements must be made not only to drive him from his position, but also to surround the position so as to inflict the heaviest loss possible. Resistance overcome without inflicting punishment on the enemy only emboldens him to repeat the game, and thus, by protracting operations, costs more lives than a severe lesson promptly administered, even though that lesson may cause some casualties on our side. Arrangements should be made to surround villages and jungle retreats with Cavalry, and afterwards to hunt them closely with Infantry. In the pursuit the broadest margin possible will be drawn between leaders of rebellion and the professional dacoit on the one part, and the villagers who have been forced into combinations against us. *Bohs* and leaders will generally be found heading the column of fugitives, and a portion of the Cavalry should be directed to pursue them without wasting time over the rank and file of the enemy.

10*th*.—Unless otherwise ordered, columns of occupation should move in short marches, halting at the principal towns and villages. This will give civil officers opportunities for becoming thoroughly acquainted with their districts, and give military officers time to reconnoitre and sketch the country.

11*th*.—Where troops are likely to be quartered for some time, bamboo platforms should be erected to keep the men off the ground. Tents, if afterwards provided, can be pitched on the platforms.

12*th*.—The greatest latitude will be allowed to Brigadier-Generals and officers in local command in ordering and carrying out movements for the pacification of their districts. They will, however, report as fully as possible all movements intended and in progress, through the regular channel, for the information of His Excellency the Commander-in-Chief.

13*th*.—Civil officers will be detailed under the orders of the Chief Commissioner to accompany columns. As they are in a position to reward loyalty and good service, they will be able to obtain more reliable guides and intelligence than the military officers can hope to get. The Chief Commissioner has authorized selected Burmans, men of position who may look for official appointments, being employed as scouts by the civil officers of districts and being attached to columns. These scouts should wear some distinguishing and conspicuous mark or badge to prevent them being fired on by the troops. They should not be called upon to take the front when approaching an unbroken enemy, or where ambuscades may be expected, but their services will be most valuable in gaining information, and later in hunting down the individuals of a broken-up gang.

14*th*.—Absolute secrecy must be maintained regarding movements against the enemy and every device resorted to to mislead him.

15*th*.—When civil officers accompany columns, all prisoners will be handed over to them for disposal. When no civil officer is present, the officer commanding the column will, *ex officio*, have magisterial powers to inflict punishment up to two years' imprisonment, or 30 lashes. Offenders deserving heavier punishment must be reserved for disposal by the civil officers.

16*th*.—Officers commanding columns will be held responsible that the troops are not kept in unhealthy districts, and that, when a locality has proved itself unhealthy, the troops are removed at the earliest possible opportunity. Military officers are responsible for the location of the troops. The requisitions of civil officers will be complied with, whenever practicable, but military officers are to judge in all matters involving the military or sanitary suitability of a position.

17*th*.—In the class of warfare in which we are now engaged, where night surprises and ambuscades are the only formidable tactics of the enemy, the greatest care must be taken to ensure the safety of the camp at night. To meet ambuscades, which usually take the form of a volley followed by flight, and which, in very dense jungle, it may be impossible to discover or guard against by means of flankers, His Excellency the Commander-in-Chief would wish the following plan to be tried: Supposing, for instance, the fire of the enemy to be delivered from the right, a portion of the force in front should be ready to dash along the road for 100 yards, or so, or until some opening in the jungle offers itself. The party should then turn to the right and sweep round with a view to intercepting the enemy in his flight. A party in rear should similarly enter the jungle to their right with the same object. The centre of the column would hold the ground and protect the baggage or any wounded men. The different parties must be previously told off, put under the command of selected leaders, and must act with promptitude and dash. Each party must be kept in compact order, and individual firing must be prohibited, except when there is a clear prospect. Past experience suggests the adoption of some such plan as the above, but in guerilla warfare officers must suit their tactics to the peculiar and ever-varying circumstances in which they may find themselves engaged.

18*th*.—The Government have ordered a general disarmament of the country, as soon as the large bands of rebels and dacoits are dispersed. The orders for this disarmament direct that all firearms are to be taken from the people, but that a moderate number may be returned to responsible villagers who are loyal and are able to defend themselves. No firearms will be returned save under registered licenses; and licenses will be given only for villages which can produce a certain number (5 to 10) guns, and are either stockaded or fenced against sudden attack. The duty of disarming lies on civil officers and the police; but as it is desirable that the disarmament should be effected as quickly as possible, officers commanding posts and columns will give such assistance as may be in their power in carrying it out.

APPENDIX XII.

(Referred to at p. 540.)

To His Excellency the Right Honourable Frederick Baron Roberts of Kandahar and Waterford, Bart., V.C., G.C.B., G.C.I.E., R.A., *Commander-in-Chief of Her Majesty's Forces in India.*

May it please Your Excellency,

We, the undersigned, representing the Sikhs of the Punjab, most respectfully beg to approach Your Excellency with this humble address of farewell on Your Lordship's approaching departure from this country. We cannot give adequate expression to the various ideas which are agitating our minds at this juncture, relating as they do to the past, present, and future, making us feel, at one and the same time, grateful, happy, and sorrowful. The success which Your Excellency has achieved in Asia is such as makes India and England proud of it. The history of the British Empire in India has not, at least for the last thirty years, produced a hero like Your Lordship, whose soldier-like qualities are fully known to the world. The country which had been the cradle of Indian invasions came to realize the extent of your power and recognized your generalship. The victories gained by Sale, Nott, and Pollock in the plains of Afghanistan have been shadowed by those gained by Your Excellency. The occupation of Kabul and the glorious battle of Kandahar are among the brightest jewels in the diadem of Your Lordship's Baronage. Your Excellency's achievements checked the aggressive advance of the Great Northern Bear, whose ambitious progress received a check from the roar of a lion in the person of Your Lordship; and a zone of neutral ground has now been fixed, and a line of peace marked by the Boundary Commission. The strong defences which Your Excellency has provided on the frontier add another bright stone to the building of your fame, and constitute in themselves a lasting memorial of Your Excellency's martial skill. Never had any British General to face more arduous tasks, and none has proved more completely successful in overcoming them than Your Lordship. The result is that India has been rendered safe from the fear of invasion from without. Your Excellency is not only adorned with heroic qualifications, but the love and affection with which the people of India regard Your Lordship show what admirable qualities are exhibited in the person of Your Excellency. Terrible in war and merciful in peace, Your Excellency's name has become a dread to the enemies of England and lovely to your friends. The interest which Your Lordship has always taken in the welfare of those with whom you have worked in India is well known to everybody. The Sikhs in particular are, more than any other community in India, indebted to Your Lordship. We find in Your Excellency a true friend of the Sikh community —a community which is always devoted heart and soul to the service of Her Most Gracious Majesty the Empress of India. No one understands better than Your Excellency the value of a Sikh soldier, and we feel very grateful that the military authorities recognize the necessity of requiring every Sikh recruit to be baptized according to the Sikh religion before admission to the Army—a practice which makes the Sikhs more true and faithful, and which preserves the existence of a very useful community. The Sikhs are said to be born soldiers, but they undoubtedly make very good citizens in time of peace also. Unfortunately, however, they have had no opportunity of fully developing their mental powers, so as to enable them to advance with the spirit of the age. We thank God that Your Excellency was among those who most desired to see the Sikhs refined and educated by establishing a Central College in the Punjab for the use of the Sikh people, and we confidently hope that the Sikhs, of whom a large portion is under Your Excellency's command, will give their mite in support of this national seminary. The subscriptions given by Your Lordship, His Excellency the Viceroy, and His Honour the late Lieutenant-Governor, were very valuable to the Institution, and the Sikhs are highly gratified by the honour Your Excellency has lately given to the Khalsa Diwan by becoming its honorary patron. In conclusion, we beg only to repeat that it is quite beyond our power to state how much we are indebted to Your Excellency, and how much we are affected by the news that Your Lordship will shortly leave this land. The very idea of our separation from the direct contact of so strong and affectionate a leader, as Your Excellency undoubtedly is, makes us feel very sorrowful; but as our hearts and prayers will always be with you and Lady Roberts, we shall be consoled if Your Excellency would only keep us in your memory, and on arrival in England assure Her Most Gracious Majesty, the Mother-Empress, that all Sikhs, whether high or low, strong or weak, old or young, are heartily devoted to her Crown and her representatives in this country. Before retiring, we thank Your Excellency for the very great honour that has been done to the people of Lahore by Your Lordship's visit to this city.

APPENDIX XIII.

(Referred to at p. 540.)

To HIS EXCELLENCY GENERAL THE RIGHT HONOURABLE FREDERICK BARON ROBERTS OF KANDAHAR AND WATERFORD, BART., V.C., G.C.B., G.C.I.E., R.A., *Commander-in-Chief of Her Majesty's Forces in India.*

MAY IT PLEASE YOUR EXCELLENCY,

We are proud to stand in Your Lordship's presence to-day on behalf of the Hindus of the Punjab, the loyal subjects of the Queen-Empress, who appreciate the countless blessings which British Rule has conferred upon this country, to give expression to the feelings of gratitude which are uppermost in their hearts. We feel it really an honour that we are able to show our appreciation of British Rule in the presence of the eminent soldier and statesman who has taken an important part in making the India of to-day what it is—contented within and strengthened against aggression from abroad. The Punjab is the province where the military strength of the Empire is being concentrated, and the bravery of the warlike races inhabiting it, which furnish the flower of Her Gracious Majesty's forces of the Army in India, has been conspicuously displayed on several occasions during the last thirty years. We Hindus have availed ourselves the most of the facilities which British Rule has provided for the progress of the people in commercial enterprise, educational advance, and political progress. We are, therefore, all the more proud that we have been allowed to-day to greet in person the mighty soldier, the sympathetic Commander, and the sagacious Statesman, the record of whose distinguished career in the East is virtually the history of nearly half a century of glorious victories—victories both of peace and war—achieved by the British Power in Asia, to show how intense is our gratitude towards the Queen-Empress and one of her eminent representatives in India, who have striven to do their duty by the people of this country, and done it to the satisfaction of the people and of their Gracious Sovereign. The interests of India and England are identical, and the Hindus of the Punjab regard British Rule as a Providential gift to this country—an agency sent to raise the people in the scale of civilization. Anything that is done to guarantee the continuance of the present profoundly peaceful condition of the country is highly appreciated by us, and we are, therefore, all the more grateful to Your Lordship for all that your courage, foresight, sagacity, and high statesmanship have been able to achieve. At a time when all the races and communities inhabiting this frontier province, which has been truly described as the sword-hand in India, are vying with each other in showing their high appreciation of the good work done by Your Excellency, of which not the least significant proof lies in the arrangement for the defence of the country at all vulnerable points of the frontier, the Hindus are anxious to show that they yield to none in the enthusiasm which marks the demonstrations held in your honour. But Your Excellency commands our esteem and regard on other grounds also. The deep interest that you have throughout your career felt in the welfare of the sepoy, and the closest ties of genuine friendship which you have established with many a notable of our community, have laid us under deep obligations to Your Excellency. The encouragement that you have given to the organization of the Imperial Service Troops of the Native States is also gratefully appreciated by us; and only the other day we were gratified to learn the high opinion Your Excellency entertained of the appearance and military equipment of the Imperial Service Troops of Jammu and Kashmir, the most important Hindu State in this part of India. We should be wanting in duty, we feel, did we not on this occasion give expression to the great regret which the news of your approaching departure from India has caused among the Hindus of the Punjab, who feel that they are parting from a kind friend and a sympathetic Ruler. At the same time, we feel that the country will not lose the benefit of your mature experience and wise counsel for long; for we are hopeful that you may some day be called upon to guide the helm of the State in India, a work for which you are so specially fitted. In conclusion, we have only to pray to the Father of All Good that He may shower His choicest blessings upon you and your consort—that noble lady who has, in addition to cheering you in your hard and onerous work in India, herself done a great deal for the comfort of the soldier and the sepoy, and that He may grant you many years of happy life—a life which has done so much for the Queen-Empress's dominions, and which may yet do much more.

APPENDIX XIV.

(Referred to at p. 540.)

To HIS EXCELLENCY GENERAL THE RIGHT HONOURABLE FREDERICK BARON ROBERTS OF KANDAHAR AND WATERFORD, BART., V.C., G.C.B., G.C.I.E., R.A., *Commander-in-Chief of Her Majesty's Forces in India.*

MAY IT PLEASE YOUR EXCELLENCY,

We, the Mahomedans of the Punjab, have dared to approach Your Excellency with this address with eyes tear-bedimmed, but a face smiling. The departure of a noble and well-beloved General like yourself from our country is in itself a fact that naturally fills our eyes with tears. What could be more sorrowful than this, our farewell to an old officer and patron of ours, who has passed the prominent portion of his life in our country, developed our young progeny to bravery and regular soldiery, decorated them with honours, and created them to high titles? Your Excellency's separation is the harder to bear for the men of the Punjab because it is our Punjab that is proud of the fact that about forty years ago the foundation stone of all your famous and noble achievements, which not only India, but England, rightly boasts of, was laid down in one of its frontier cities, and that the greater part of your indomitable energies was spent in the Punjab frontier defence. If, therefore, we are sad at separating from Your Excellency, it will not in any way be looked upon as strange. But these feelings of sorrow are mixed with joy when we see that the useful officer whom in 1852 we had welcomed at Peshawar, when the star of his merits was beginning to rise, departs from us in splendour and glory in the capacity of the Commander-in-Chief of the Armies of a vast Empire like India, and is an example of the highest type to all soldiers. This address is too brief for a detail of all the meritorious services rendered by your Excellency in the Punjab, India and other foreign countries from that early epoch to this date. Your zeal in the Mutiny of 1857, your heroic achievements in the Abyssinian and Afghan wars, your repeated victories of Kandahar, and your statesmanlike conduct of the Burma wars—all these are facts which deserve to be written in golden characters in the annals of Indian history. Your appointment as legislative and executive member of the Supreme Council of the Government of India for a considerable period has proved a source of blessings to the whole of India, and Your Excellency deserves an ample share of the credit due to the Council for all its useful regulations and reforms. The great liking that men of noble birth in India have been showing for some time towards military service is a clear demonstration of the excellent treatment received at your hands by military officers, as in the reforms made by you in the military pay and pension and other regulations. Another boon for which the Natives of India will always remember your name with gratitude, is that you have fully relied upon, and placed your confidence in, the Natives, thus uniting them the more firmly to the British Crown, making them more loyal, and establishing the good relations between the Rulers and the ruled on a firmer footing to their mutual good. Especially as Mussalmans of the Punjab are we proud that before Your Excellency's departure you have had the opportunity of reviewing the Imperial Service Troops of the Mahomedan State of Bhawalpur, one of the leading Native States of the Punjab, whose Ruler's efforts to make his troops worthy to take their place by the side of British troops for the defence of India is only one instance of the spirit of active loyalty which we are glad to say animates the entire Mussalman community of the Punjab. Disturbances arising from foreign intrusions are not unknown to us, and we have not sufficient words to thank your Lordship for the admirable management of the frontier defence work carried on to protect our country from all possible encroachments. The greatest pleasure and satisfaction, however, that we Mahomedans feel in presenting this address to Your Lordship emanates from the idea that you go on your way home to your native country with a high and favourable opinion of the Mahomedans of India, true and loyal subjects to Her Majesty the Queen-Empress, whose number exceeds six crores, and who are rapidly growing. During the Mutiny of 1857 the Chieftains and soldiers of our nation spared neither money nor arms in the reduction and submission of the rebels. Your Lordship is also aware what loyalty was displayed by the Mahomedans of India during the Afghan and Egyptian wars, waged against their own co-religionists, and the cheerfulness shown by them in following your Lordship in all your victories. Frontier services, such as the Kabul Embassy and the Delimitation Commission, rendered by the officers of our creed are also well known to you. We are therefore sanguine that Your Lordship's own observation will enable all the members of the Ruling race in India to form an opinion of the relations that exist between us and the British Crown. The Mahomedans of India and the Punjab are proud of being the devoted subjects of the Queen-Empress. In so acting we perform our religious duties, for our sacred religion enjoins upon us faithfulness and obedience towards our Ruling monarch, and teaches us to regard the Christians as our own brethren. The regard and esteem which we should have, therefore, for a Christian Government, as that of our kind mother the Queen-Empress, needs no demonstration. Although, for certain reasons which we need not detail here, our nation has been deficient in education, and we have been left much behind in obtaining civil employment, we hope that your long experience of our service will prove a good testimonial in favour of the warlike spirit, military genius, and loyalty of our nation, and if the circle of civil employment has become too straitened for us, the military line will be generously opened to us. We do not want to encroach upon Your Lordship's valuable time any further. We therefore finish our address, offering our heartfelt thanks to your Lordship for all those kindnesses you have been wont to show during your time towards India and Indians in general, and the Punjab and Punjabis in particular, and take leave of Your Lordship with the following prayer: 'May God bless thee wherever thou mayest be, and may thy generosities continue to prevail upon us for a long time.' While actuated by these feelings, we are not the less aware that our country owes a great deal to Lady Roberts, to whom we beg that Your Excellency will convey our heartfelt thanks for her lively interest in the welfare of Indian soldiers in particular and the people generally. In conclusion, we wish Your Excellencies God-speed and a pleasant and safe voyage. That Your Excellencies may have long, happy, and prosperous lives, and achieve ever so many more distinctions and honours, and return to us very shortly in a still higher position, to confer upon the Empire the blessings of a beneficent Rule, is our heartfelt and most sincere prayer.

APPENDIX XV.

(Referred to at p. 540.)

To HIS EXCELLENCY GENERAL THE RIGHT HONOURABLE FREDERICK BARON ROBERTS OF KANDAHAR AND WATERFORD, BART., V.C., G.C.B., G.C.I.E., R.A., *Commander-in-Chief of Her Majesty's Forces in India.*

MAY IT PLEASE YOUR EXCELLENCY,

We, the representatives of the European community in the Punjab, are the prouder to-day of our British blood, in that it links us in close kinship to one who has so bravely maintained the honour of the British Empire alike in the years of peace and storm that India has seen during the last three decades. During the Mutiny Your Excellency performed feats of gallantry that are historic. Since then your career has been one of brilliant success and growing military renown. Whenever, in the histories of war, men speak of famous marches, that from Kabul to Kandahar comes straightway to the lips. When our mind turns to military administration, we remember the unqualified success of Your Excellency's career as Quartermaster-General and as Commander-in-Chief of Her Majesty's Forces in India, in both of which high offices you have added honour and glory to your great name, which will never be forgotten in India. When the private soldier, rightly or wrongly, thinks he has a grievance, his desire is only that somehow it may be brought to the notice of Your Excellency, from whom, through experience, he expects full justice and generous sympathy. When we look towards our frontier and see the strategic railways and roads, and the strong places of arms that threaten the invader, we know that for those safeguards the Empire is in no small degree indebted to the resolute wisdom of Your Excellency as military adviser to the Government of India. Last, but not least, as a Statesman, Your Excellency ranks second to none in the Empire in the opinion of your countrymen in this North-West frontier province; and we should gladly welcome the day, if it might ever arrive, when Your Excellency returned to India. It is here that we see most clearly the passage of events beyond our borders and mark the signs of brooding trouble; and our hope has always been that, when that trouble should break forth, yours might be the hand to guide England's flag to victory again. The Punjab is the sword of India, and Your Excellency has had the courage to lean most strongly upon that sword. It is here that the pulse of the army beats in India; it is hence that the enemies of our country shall feel the downright blow; and it is here that the greatest grief is felt in parting from so true a soldier and so far seeing a Statesman as Your Excellency. It is meet, therefore, that here we should assemble upon this occasion of farewell to express the great sorrow which we, the representatives of the Europeans in the Punjab, feel at the prospect of losing so soon the clear brain and strong hand that Your Excellency has always brought to the control of the Army in India and to the solution of all questions of political or military moment. In doing so, we mourn for the loss of one of the best statesmen, the best general, and the best friend to the soldier in India. We say nothing of the kindly relations Your Excellency has always been able to establish with the other races in India; our fellow-subjects here will doubtless do so in their turn. We say nothing of Your Excellency's and Lady Roberts' charming social qualities, nor Her Ladyship's philanthropic work in India. We are here only to express our grief at parting with one whom we value so highly for the sake of our common country, and our hope that as your past has been full of glory to the Empire and honour to yourself, so may your future be; and that you may be spared for many years to wield the sword and guide the counsels of our country.

APPENDIX XVI.

(Referred to at p. 541.)

To His Excellency General the Right Honourable Frederick Baron Roberts of Kandahar and Waterford, Bart., V.C., G.C.B., G.C.I.E., R.A., *Commander-in-Chief of Her Imperial Majesty's Army in India.*

May it please Your Excellency,

We, the Talukdars of Oudh, as loyal and faithful subjects of the Empress of India, avail ourselves of the present opportunity of offering Your Excellency a most cordial and respectful welcome to the Capital of Oudh.

The long and valuable services rendered by Your Excellency to the Crown and the country are well known to, and are deeply appreciated by, us. Your Excellency's wise and vigorous administration of Her Majesty's Army in India has won for you our respectful admiration; while your prowess in the battle-field, and your wisdom in Council during the eventful period of your supreme command of Her Majesty's Indian Forces, have inspired us with confidence in your great military talents and your single-minded and earnest devotion to duty. In many a battle you have led the British Army to victory, and the brilliant success which has invariably attended the British Arms under Your Excellency's command has added to the glory of the British Empire.

But the pride and pleasure we feel at being honoured by Your Excellency's presence in our capital town give place to sorrow and regret at the approaching retirement of Your Excellency from the great service of which you are an ornament.

In grateful acknowledgment of the most important services rendered by Your Excellency to our Empress and our country, we beg to be allowed the privilege of presenting you with a Sword of Indian manufacture, which will, we hope, from time to time, remind you of us and of Oudh.

Wishing Your Lordship a safe and pleasant voyage home, and a long and happy life,

We subscribe ourselves,
Your Lordship's most humble
and obedient servants
The Talukdars of Oudh.

APPENDIX XVII.

(Referred to at p. 541.)

To HIS EXCELLENCY GENERAL THE RIGHT HONOURABLE SIR FREDERICK SLEIGH, BARON ROBERTS OF KANDAHAR AND WATERFORD, BART., V.C., G.C.B., G.C.I.E., D.C.L., LL.D., R.A., *Commander-in-Chief in India.*

YOUR EXCELLENCY,

Viewing with concern and regret your approaching departure from India, we beg—in bidding you farewell—to express our admiration of your life and work as Commander-in-Chief of the Imperial Forces in India, and to request you to permit your portrait to be placed in the Town Hall of Calcutta, in token for the present generation of their high appreciation of your eminent services, and in witness to a future generation of the esteem in which you were held by your contemporaries.

With foresight denoting wise statesmanship, Governments which you have served have initiated and maintained a policy of Frontier Defence, and encouraged the increased efficiency of the Forces.

In the furtherance of these objects we recognize the salient points of your career and character whilst holding the high rank of Commander-in-Chief.

In your continued efforts to ameliorate the condition of the private soldier we recognize broad humanity. In the increasing efficiency of the Army, which, in our belief, characterizes your tenure of command, we recognize high soldierly qualities. In the state of strength which the Frontier Defences have attained, mainly due, we believe, to you, we recognize practical sagacity, conspicuous ability in discernment of requirements, and in pursuit of your aims an unwearying industry, a resolute persistence, and a determination that no difficulty can turn, in which a noble example for all true workers may be found.

In a word, your life and work are to us identified with Frontier Defence and Efficient Forces. We cheerfully bear our share of the cost, as in possession of these protections against aggression from without, we believe all who dwell within the borders of the land will find their best guarantee for peace, and in peace the best safeguard they and their children can possess to enable them to pass their lives in happiness and prosperity, and escape the misery and ruin which follow war and invasion. For all that you have done to give them such security, we feel you deserve, and we freely give, our heartfelt thanks.

Within the limitations of a farewell address, we hardly feel justified in personal allusions trenching on your private life, but we cannot refrain from noticing with responsive sympathy the feeling of personal attachment to yourself which is widespread throughout India, and assuring you that we share in it to the fullest extent that private feeling can be affected by public services. We endorse our assurance with an expression of the wish that, in whatever part of the British Empire your future life may be spent, it may be attended, as in the past, with honour, and, by the blessing of God, with health and happiness for yourself and all those you hold dear.

It is the prerogative of the Crown alone to bestow honours on those who have served their country well, and none have been better merited than those which you enjoy, and to which, we trust, additions may be made. It is the privilege of a community to make public profession of merit in a fellow-citizen where they consider it is due, and in availing ourselves of the privilege to make this public recognition of the great services which, in our opinion, you have rendered to India, we beg with all sincerity to add a hearty God-speed and a regretful Farewell.

We have the honour to be,
Your Excellency,
Your obedient servants.

CALCUTTA,
11th March, 1893.

NOTE

(*to Chapter XVIII., page* 183, *footnote*).

Such is the story which has been generally believed. The church exists at the present day, but it is only right to state that Skinner's children deny that their father erected a temple and a mosque. Whether Skinner did or did not build a temple will probably always remain open to question, but as regards the mosque, the date inscribed on it shows it was built at the beginning of the eighteenth century, or long before he was born.

INDEX.

PERSONS.

CHIEF PUBLIC EVENTS.

THE END.

Works on Military Art and History

THE LIFE OF JOHN CHURCHILL, FIRST DUKE OF MARLBOROUGH. Vols. I. and II., to the Accession of Queen Anne. With Portraits of the Duke and Duchess of Marlborough, James II., William III., the Duke of Monmouth, Duchess of Cleveland, and other Illustrations or Plans. 8vo. 32*s*.

SOME ACCOUNT OF THE MILITARY, POLITICAL, AND SOCIAL LIFE OF THE RIGHT HON. JOHN MANNERS, MARQUIS OF GRANBY, P.C., M.P., D.C.L. By WALTER EVELYN MANNERS. 8vo. With Portrait and Plans. 18 . net.

ADMIRALTY AND HORSE GUARDS GAZETTE.—"The story is well told because the author allows his characters to tell their own tale, and his style is neither stilted nor didactic. The personages who move through these pages are made to live and refresh our knowledge of English history without that strain on the attention which the prosaic historian inflicts upon his readers by a multiplicity of footnotes and addenda."

A HISTORY OF THE BRITISH ARMY. By the Hon. J. W. FORTESCUE. First Part.—To the Close of the Seven Years' War. Two Volumes. 8vo. 36*s*. net.

DAILY CHRONICLE.—"Fills a gap in our historical literature. Judging by this first instalment, it promises to fill it in a very satisfactory way. . . . We have only touched upon a few of the points of interest in Mr. Fortescue's splendid volumes, but before closing this review we must say a word in praise of the excellent maps that illustrate them, and the well-arranged index that will make the book a most useful work of reference."

HISTORY OF THE 17th LANCERS. By the Hon. J. W. FORTESCUE. Royal 8vo. 25*s*. net.

THE HISTORY OF THE SECOND QUEEN'S (ROYAL WEST SURREY) REGIMENT. By Lieut.-Colonel JOHN DAVIS, F.S.A. Royal 8vo. With numerous Illustrations. Vol. I., 1661-1684; Vol. II., 1684-1714; Vol. III., 1715-1799. 8vo. 24*s*. each.

RECORDS OF THE 91st HIGHLANDERS, now the 1st Battalion of the Princess Louise's Argyll and Sutherland Highlanders, 1794 to 1881. Arranged by Captain GERALD LIONEL GOFF. With Coloured Plates and numerous other Illustrations. 8vo. 30*s*.

RECORDS OF THE 93rd HIGHLANDERS, now the 2nd Battalion Princess Louise's Argyll and Sutherland Highlanders. By Captain RODERICK HAMILTON BURGOYNE, late 93rd Highlanders. A history of the Regiment from its formation to the present time. With numerous illustrations of dress, etc. 8vo. 30*s*.

A HISTORY OF THE 57th REGIMENT, from 1755 to 1881. Including a Record of the Services of the (West Middlesex) 'Die Hards,' in the American War of Independence, Flanders, the West Indies, the Peninsula, France, the Crimea, New Zealand, Zululand, etc. By Captain HENRY H. WOOLLRIGHT, Middlesex Regiment. With Coloured Plates, Maps, and other Illustrations. 8vo. 30*s*.

LONDON: MACMILLAN AND CO., LTD.

SKETCH

SHOWING THE OPERATIONS

IN

THE CHARDEH VALLEY

ON

December 10th and 11th, 1879.

DISTANCES.

Sherpur to Aushar ...	5½	miles
Deh-i-Mazang to Sherpur ...	2½	,,
Deh-i-Mazang to Aushar ...	3	,,
Deh-i-Mazang to Surkh Kotal (by Bagkousa) ...	18	,,
Surkh Kotal to Karez-i-Mir	12	,,
Karez-i-Mir to Aushar (by Kiza Khana Kotal) ...	11	,,

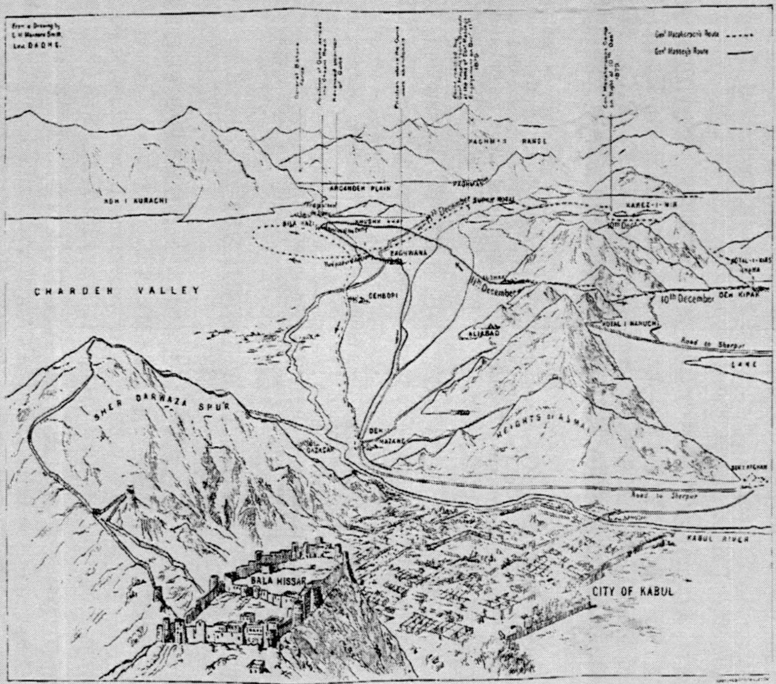

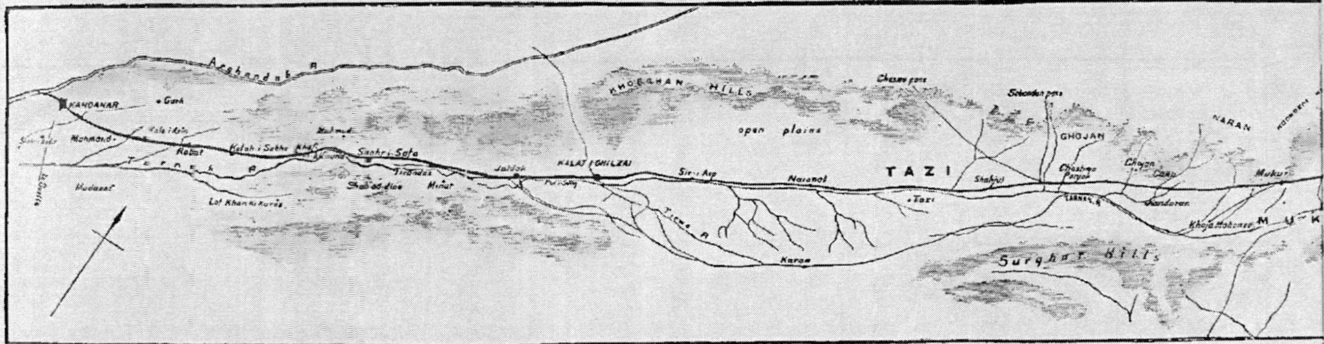

KANDAHAR
Arghandab R
Tarnak R
Kalah i Sathe Khaf
Shahr-i-Safa
KALAT I GHILZAI
Siri Asp
Nauroz
TAZI
open plains
GHOJAN
NARAN
Karez
Surghar Hills

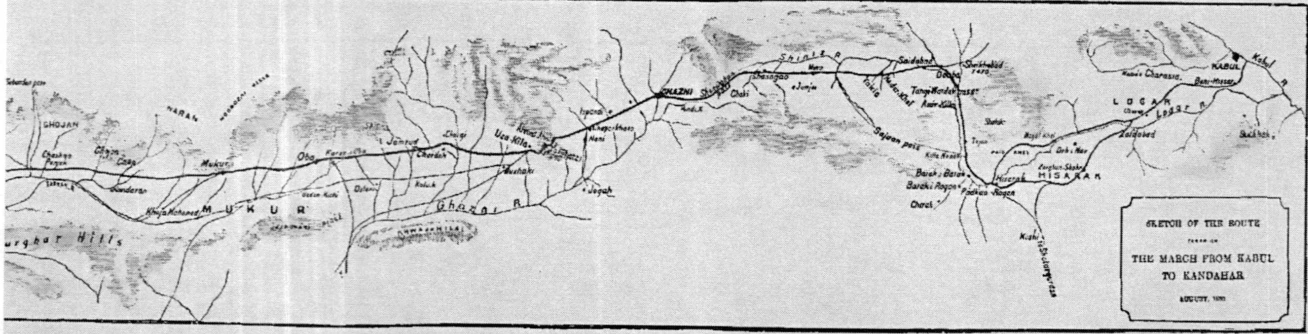
SKETCH OF THE ROUTE
THE MARCH FROM KABUL
TO KANDAHAR
AUGUST, 1880
KABUL
Kabul R.
Beni-Hissar
LOGAR
Logar R.
Zaidabad
HISARAK
Shinız R.
Saidabad
Sajaan pass
GHAZNI
Shasgao
Chahi
Uza Kila
Jamrud
Chardeh
Oba
Mukur
MUKUR
Ghazni R.
Jegah
Khoja Mahomed
Sanderan
GHOJAN
NARAH
Surghar Hills